Earth Science
The Challenge of Discovery

ROBERT E. SNYDER
Earth and Space Science Teacher
Brookline High School
Brookline, MA

BARBARA L. MANN
Earth Science Teacher, Triton
Regional Junior / Senior High School
Byfield, MA

FRANCES A. LUDWIG
Science Consultant, Lexington Public
Schools, Lexington, MA
Staff Member, Massachusetts
Audubon Society

WILLIAM A. BRECHT
Earth Science Teacher
Jefferson Middle School
St. Charles, MO

JOHN H. STASIK
Earth Science Teacher
Weston Middle School
Weston, MA

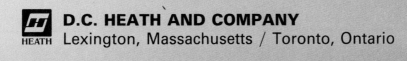
D.C. HEATH AND COMPANY
Lexington, Massachusetts / Toronto, Ontario

Earth Science: The Challenge of Discovery Program

Pupil's Edition
Teacher's Edition
Laboratory Manual
Study Guide
Teacher's Answer Book
Teacher's Resource File
Overhead Transparencies
Computer Test Bank
Computer Test Bank Teacher's Guide

Executive Editor: Ellen M. Lappa
Editorial Development: Marianne P. Knowles, Andrew L. Amster, Joel Gendler, Mary Ashman, Anne Jones
Marketing Manager: Richard G. Ravich
Project Design: Angela Sciaraffa
Design Development: Leslie Hartwell
Production Coordinator: Bryan Quible
Editorial Services: Marianna Frew Palmer, Anne Edmondson
Writing Assistance: Concept Mapping—'Laine Gurley-Dilger. Science, Technology, and Society; Science in Action—Laurel G. Sherman
Readability Testing: J & F Readability Service
Cover Design/Photography: Martucci Studio

Other Programs in This Series: *Life Science: The Challenge of Discovery*
Physical Science: The Challenge of Discovery

Content Reviewers

Thomas E. Eastler, Ph.D.
Professor of Environmental Geology
University of Maine at Farmington
Farmington, ME

Jack K. Fletcher, Ed.D.
Director, Hummel Planetarium
Assistant Professor of Astronomy
Eastern Kentucky University
Richmond, KY

Wayne R. Geyer, Ph.D.
Physical Oceanographer
Woods Hole Oceanographic Institution
Woods Hole, MA

Margaret A. LeMone, Ph.D.
Scientist
National Center for Atmospheric Research
Boulder, CO

Jack L. Mason, Ed.D.
Director of Secondary Education
Emory and Henry College
Emory, VA

Christopher M. Palmer
Senior Geologist
Geostrategies, Inc.
Hayward, CA

Jay Young, Ph.D.
Chemical Safety and Health
Consultant
Silver Spring, MD

Published simultaneously in Canada
Printed in the United States of America
International Standard Book Number: 0-669-18048-3

3 4 5 6 7 8 9 0

CONTENTS

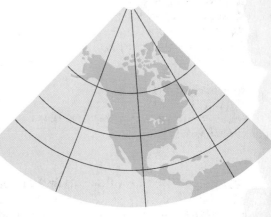

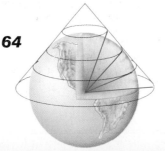

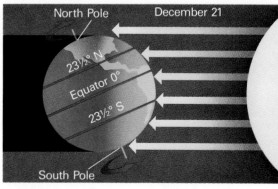

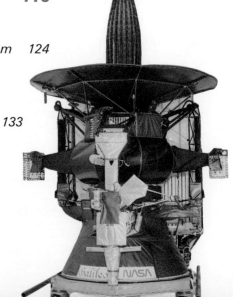

UNIT 3   Composition of Earth   172

Earth's Chemistry   174

v

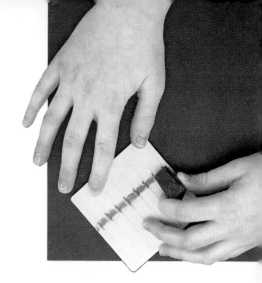

UNIT 4 Changes in Earth's Crust 252

UNIT 6   The Atmosphere   440

UNIT 7 Earth's Water 542

Waves and Currents 592

Appendices

SPECIAL FEATURES

Science, Technology, and Society Issues

Science in Action

Environmental Awareness

A Study Strategy for Success

How do you study? Do you reread a chapter over and over the night before a test, hoping you will remember all the information the next day? Do you take notes and try to memorize them? Perhaps you make flash cards of the information and quiz yourself. If your study method is one of the methods described here, you are learning by rote memorization. When you learn by rote memorization, information is stored in your short-term memory. Very often this kind of learning only lasts a short time.

Learning information so that you can remember it longer and use it to solve problems involves getting that information into your long-term memory. Does your method of studying help you transfer information from short-term memory to long-term memory? Does your method of studying help you find relationships between ideas you are learning? Most methods do not. Making a concept map or idea map does.

Processing Information

Making a concept map is based on how you process or remember information. Quickly read the sentences below. Then cover up the sentences and take the mini-quiz that immediately follows.

1. Nick walked on the roof.
2. George chopped down the tree.
3. Chris sailed the boat.
4. Ben flew the kite.

(Cover it up!)

Mini-Quiz:

1. Who chopped down the tree?
2. Who walked on the roof?
3. Who flew the kite?
4. Who sailed the boat?

You probably did fairly well on the quiz because deep in your long-term memory you know about Santa "St. Nick" Claus, George Washington, Christopher Columbus, and Benjamin Franklin. Now look at this list of words. Read it over slowly for about 20 seconds, and then cover up the words. Recall as many as you can.

black	sweater	brown	shirt
cinnamon	dove	gloves	green
canary	garlic	parrot	pepper

Look at this second list of words and again memorize as many as you can in 20 seconds:

vanilla	horse	yellow	desk
chocolate	camel	red	table
strawberry	elephant	green	chair

Which list was easier to remember? The second list was easier to remember because the words are grouped.

The grouping or categories linked the words together and helped you remember them. For example, the category *flavors* helped you remember vanilla, chocolate, and strawberry. Grouping words also reduces how much information you must memorize. For example, by using what's in your long-term memory and recognizing four groups in the list, you could more easily memorize twelve concepts.

You can also look at groups of terms and give them a name that represents their main idea. For example: math, science, English, history, art are all *school subjects*. The main idea for that group of items is *school subjects*. Try to find the main idea for these terms:

Canada, Germany, Mexico, USA,
    France = _____

banjo, guitar, violin, piano,
    drum = _____

Concept Mapping

Concept mapping helps you figure out the main ideas in a piece of reading material. The main ideas are the categories into which new concepts will be placed. A concept map can also help you understand that ideas have meanings because they are connected to other ideas. For example, when you define a pencil as a writing utensil, you have linked the idea or concept of a *pencil* to the ideas of *writing* and *utensil*. Look at the following words:

| car | raining | tree | thundering |
| dog | playing | cloud | thinking |

Words are labels for ideas, or concepts. All of these words are concepts because they cause a picture to form in your mind. Are the following words concept words?

| are | when | where | then |
| the | with | is | to |

No. These are linkage words. They connect, or link, concept words together. In a concept map, words that are concepts go in circles or boxes, and words that are linking the concepts go on a line connecting the circles or boxes.

How is a concept map different from note-taking or making an outline? If you outlined pages 222–225 it might look like this:

Outline

I. Rocks
    A. A rock is a natural solid that is usually a mixture of different minerals.
    B. Rocks are grouped by the way they formed.

II. Rock Types
    A. Igneous rocks form when molten rock cools into a solid.
    B. Sedimentary rocks form when pieces of rock are cemented together.
    C. Metamorphic rocks form when existing rocks are changed.

III. Rock Characteristics
    A. The minerals in some rocks are visible.
    B. Some rocks have grains.
        1. Grains can be sand.
        2. Grains can be pieces of crystals, rocks, or shells.
    C. Some rocks have crystals.
    D. Texture is the pattern of sizes, shapes, and arrangements of crystals or grains.
        1. Sandstone has a coarse texture.
        2. Slate has a fine texture.
        3. Obsidian has a glassy texture.

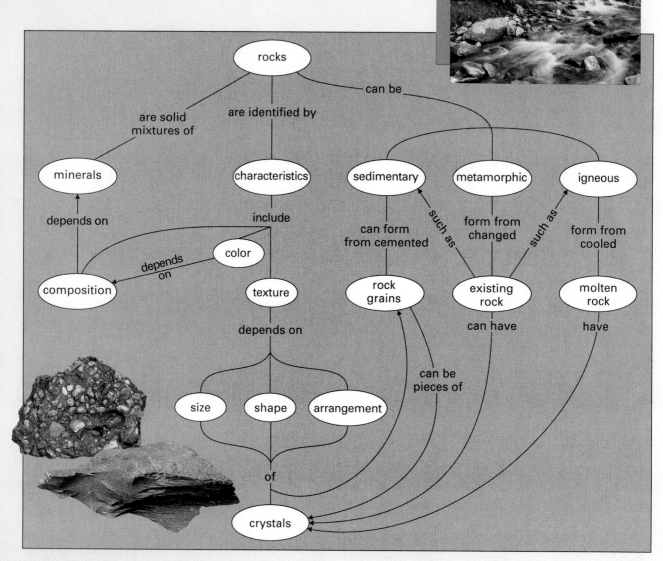

The concept map above shows the relationships between rocks and their characteristics:

- **rocks** — are solid mixtures of **minerals**
- **rocks** — are identified by **characteristics**
- **rocks** — can be **sedimentary**, **metamorphic**, **igneous**
- **minerals** — depends on **composition**
- **composition** — depends on **color**
- **characteristics** — include **color**, **texture**
- **texture** — depends on **size**, **shape**, **arrangement** — of **crystals**
- **sedimentary** — can form from cemented **rock grains**
- **metamorphic** — form from changed **existing rock**
- **igneous** — form from cooled **molten rock**
- **sedimentary** — such as **existing rock**
- **igneous** — such as **existing rock**
- **rock grains** — can be pieces of **crystals**
- **existing rock** — can have **crystals**
- **molten rock** — have **crystals**

Now look back at pages 222–225. Would you want to reread those pages over and over again, trying to learn all of that information for a test? Would you prefer the slightly shorter outline? Or would you rather study a concept map like the one above, especially if you had made it yourself? If you made the map, your long-term memory would already *know* parts of that map. You would have learned the main ideas well while you constructed the relationships among the terms.

How to Make a Concept Map

A feature of concept maps is that main ideas are placed at the top of the map. Smaller, more specific concepts and examples go below the main ideas. It might help you to write the main concept in capital letters and write the specific concepts in lowercase letters. Your map should show a pattern, from top to bottom, of most general ideas to most specific.

Turn to pages 410–411 and read the beginning of Lesson 16.1, *Fossil Fuels*, stopping at *Coal*. Then try to make a concept map. **First, identify the main concepts by writing them in a list. Then put each separate concept from your list on a small piece of paper.** You will not have to use this paper technique once you make a few maps, but it is helpful at first. Remember, your list shows how the concepts appeared in the reading, but this may not necessarily represent how you link the concepts to each other in your mind.

The next step is to put the concepts in order of most general to most specific. Examples are most specific and will go at the bottom.

Now begin to rearrange the concepts you have written on the pieces of paper on a table or desktop. Start with the most general main idea. If that main idea can be broken down into two or more equal concepts, place those concepts on the same line. Continue to do this until all the concepts have been laid out.

Now the connections between the concepts need to be made. **Use lines to connect the concepts. Write a statement on the line that tells why concepts are connected.** Do this for all the lines connecting the concepts.

Do not expect your map to be exactly like anyone else's map. Everyone thinks a little differently and will see different relationships between certain concepts. Practice is the key to good concept mapping. Here are some points to remember as you get started:

1. A concept map does not have to be symmetrical. It can be lopsided or have more concepts on the right side than on the left.

2. Remember that a concept map is a short-cut for representing information. Do not add anything but concepts and links.

3. There is no perfect or single correct concept map for a set of concepts, only maps that come closer to representing the map-maker's understanding of concepts. Errors in a concept map occur only if the links between concepts are incorrect.

Getting Started

Even by concept mapping old and familiar material, you can recognize new relationships and meanings. The best thing you can do is to choose a topic you know a lot about—stereos, baseball cards, music, or sports, for example. Use one of these or some other topic as your main idea at the top of a concept map and branch out into subtopics. Begin to break it down from more general to more specific ideas. You'll probably be quite successful with this, and it will give you encouragement and confidence to concept map new material in your text.

Introduction to Earth Science

You Know More Than You Think

You may be surprised at how much you already know about earth science. To find out, try to answer the following questions.

- *What shape is Earth?*
- *During the year, what weather patterns occur where you live?*
- *How could you measure air temperature and rainfall?*
- *Which way does a magnetic compass needle point?*
- *What kinds of information do maps give you?*

When you finish this unit, answer these questions again to see how much you have learned.

Earth can be observed up close and from a distance. This person is studying a volcano.

Chapter 1   Introducing Earth Science
Chapter 2   Mapping the Earth

Introducing Earth Science

Chapter Preview

*H*ave You Ever
WONDERED?

What Earth patterns could you see from space?

The photo at left shows a view you might see if you could ride a spaceship around Earth. Look at the patterns in the photo. Some clouds swirl in a spiral pattern. Other clouds make long streaks or patterns of dots. There are patterns in the land as well as in the clouds. The eastern coast of northern Africa follows a pattern similar to the western coast of the Arabian Peninsula.

You would see other patterns as you traveled around Earth on a spaceship. About half the time you would be in sunlight. About half the time you would be in Earth's shadow. On the ground, you call Earth's shadow nighttime.

You can see many other Earth patterns from right here on the ground. Have you ever been curious about what you have seen happening in the sky, in oceans, in rivers, or on Earth itself? In this course, you will study patterns in, on, and around Earth. Your understanding of those patterns will help you describe the world and the universe in which you live.

1.1 The Earth Sciences

Lesson Objectives

▸ **Name** and **describe** the four branches of earth science.

▸ **Give examples** of patterns and events that occur in each branch of earth science.

▸ **Demonstrate** that the earth science branches are related to each other.

▸ **Activity** **Observe** and **describe** the contents of a box without opening it.

New Terms

pattern	meteorology
astronomy	oceanography
geology	

Imagine that you are your school's new basketball coach. You would teach your team as much as you could about some basic skills in basketball: dribbling, passing, rebounding, and shooting. Your players need to know something about each of these skills in order to play basketball well.

Like basketball, earth science involves many skills. Earth science is the study of Earth, its atmosphere, oceans, and the universe of which it is a part. Objects and events in earth science often form patterns. A **pattern** is a set of events that occurs repeatedly. For example, light follows darkness in a pattern you call days. Spring, summer, autumn, and winter form a pattern called seasons. Patterns in each branch of earth science affect each other.

Astronomy

Astronomy is the scientific study of objects beyond Earth's atmosphere. Astronomy includes the study of the sun, the moon, and other solar-system neighbors. It also includes the study of other stars and of groups of stars called galaxies. The science of astronomy has existed for centuries. Ancient astronomers observed patterns in the apparent motions of the sun, moon, and stars. They used these patterns to design calendars and to find their way when they traveled. Modern astronomers continue the search for information about the universe. The information they gather about other planets and stars helps you to better understand your own planet, Earth.

Figure 1-1 Astronomy includes looking for patterns in space. Where in the sky do stars appear closest together?

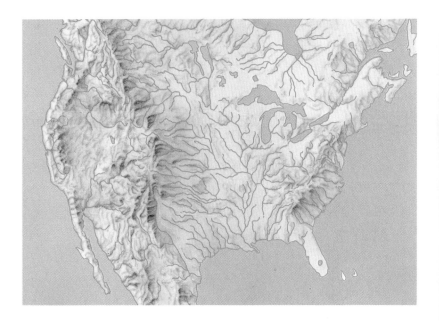

Geology

Geology is the study of the materials that make up Earth, as well as the patterns and changes in those materials. Some geologic changes occur quickly. For example, volcanoes and earthquakes can cause changes in a matter of minutes. Other changes take longer. The soil in your backyard or playground probably took thousands of years to form.

A large part of geology is searching for patterns in Earth's materials. Patterns can occur over any size area. For example, look at the area shown in Figure 1-2 *(left)*. Notice that the rivers flow into each other, forming a tree-shaped pattern. Now look at the rocks in Figure 1-2 *(right)*. What patterns do you observe in these rocks?

Some patterns in earth materials provide clues about the planet's history. There are fossils of sea animals and plants on the top of Mt. Everest. The remains of tropical plants and animals have been found in Antarctica. As you study earth science this year, you will collect information that will help you explain those, and other, geologic mysteries.

Figure 1-2 Geology patterns occur in many sizes. *Left:* Many river systems form a treelike pattern. *Right:* Rocks and other earth materials also have patterns.

Meteorology

When was the last time you talked about the weather? The weather changes because of patterns in the movement of the atmosphere, the thin layer of gases that surround Earth. The study of the patterns of change that take place in the atmosphere is called **meteorology.** Knowing about these patterns will help you understand weather and other changes in the atmosphere.

Figure 1-3 You probably recognize weather patterns. What kind of weather do you expect when you see this kind of scene?

You have probably noticed many meteorology patterns. Have you ever seen a certain kind of cloud and guessed that it was going to rain? Maybe you have noticed that some kinds of storms happen in the same season each year. Which gets hotter in the summer, pavement or grassy areas? All of these observations are examples of meteorology patterns.

People have been interested in weather and climate for thousands of years. The kind of apartment or house you live in depends in part on the kind of weather in your area. Weather affects your travel plans, whether you are going to another state or just going to the store. Weather helps determine how much food there is because weather affects crop growth. If you understand meteorology, you will be able to make some of your own weather predictions.

Oceanography

Photographs of Earth taken from outer space show why Earth is often called the blue planet. More than two thirds of Earth's surface is covered by oceans. **Oceanography** is the study of oceans, including ocean water, its movements, and the ocean floor. Oceans are important to everyone, even to people who live thousands of miles inland. Many businesses use ocean going ships to carry goods for sale overseas. Many foods and animal feeds contain products from the oceans. There are also valuable minerals on the ocean floor which could be worth mining.

Patterns occur in oceanography, just as they do in other branches of earth science. Huge currents flow in circular patterns in each ocean. The surface of the oceans tends to be warmer than the depths. Fish live in some places in the ocean, but not in others. The ocean floor has patterns that have helped solve geologic mysteries. In some parts of the ocean floor new rocks are forming, while in other parts, rock is entering Earth's interior.

The branches of earth science are connected to each other. The movement of Earth around the sun causes seasons (astronomy and meteorology). The weather in each season can be affected by warm or cold ocean currents (meteorology and oceanography). The movement of the oceans can shape the rocky land (oceanography and geology). Large mountains affect the weather around them (geology and meteorology). No matter which part of Earth you study, you will find that it is connected to all the other parts.

In your study of earth science, you will discover many new ideas and theories about Earth, its land, water, air, and its place in the universe. These ideas will help you to develop a more complete understanding of the planet you call home.

Figure 1-4 You need to know something about each branch of earth science to study the area around this beach.

Lesson Review 1.1

1. Name the four branches of earth science. Give examples of what is studied in each branch.

2. Define the term *pattern* and give three examples of patterns that are observed in earth science.

3. List two earth science events that show that the branches of earth science are related to each other.

Interpret and Apply

4. For each event described below (a–d), name the branch or branches of earth science to which it belongs. Explain your reason for each answer.
   a. A river cuts a valley into hard rock as it flows toward the ocean.
   b. As the temperature rises, a huge piece breaks off an Arctic ice sheet and floats out to sea.
   c. A volcano erupts clouds of ash into the atmosphere.
   d. A meteorite streaks through the atmosphere and lands in a desert.

EXPANDING YOUR POWERS OF OBSERVATION

Purpose To observe and describe the contents of a box without opening it.

Materials

sealed box with objects inside
probes (coffee stirrers)
plain paper (for sketch)
lined paper (for notes)

Procedure

1. Read all instructions for this activity before you begin your work.

2. The box contains from 2 to 4 objects. At least 1 object can move. At least 1 object will not move. Gently move and turn the box and observe the results. You may not open the box or peek inside. Write down your observations.

3. From your observations, estimate how many objects are inside the box. Record your estimate and the observations you used for your estimate.

4. There are several small holes in each side of your box. Observe the box by pushing 1 probe through the holes, as shown in the figure. Do not push the probe so far into the box that you lose it. Record your observations.

5. Do you want to change your estimate based on your new observations? If so, record your new estimate and your reason for it.

6. Now you will observe an object in the box. Use as many probes as you like to observe the object. Where is the object? About how large is it? What is its shape? Write down all the observations.

7. Repeat step 6 for the other objects in the box. Record observations.

8. Before leaving the laboratory, clean up all materials.

Collecting and Analyzing Data

1. On the plain paper, trace an outline of one side of your box.

2. Reread your observations from steps 4, 6, and 7. Estimate the place, size, and shape of each object you observed. On your box outline, draw the objects in the box, based on your observations.

Drawing Conclusions

3. Your teacher has a collection of objects like the ones in the boxes. Ask to look at the collection. Compare the collection with your observations. Estimate the number of objects in your box. Where do you think they are? What are they? Which of those objects can move? Which are held still? Write down your final guesses.

4. What other tools would have helped you gather even more information about the box?

5. How could you improve the probes-and-holes method to make more precise observations of the box?

1.2 Earth Science Measurements

Imagine that each person in your class needs to measure the length of a desk, but no one has a ruler. You might use the length of this book as your unit of length. But what happens when you need to tell someone else how long your desk is? You may be the only person in the class who measures distance in a unit called book lengths.

Fortunately, a standard system of measurement has been established. With this system, everyone can compare information that is collected as measurements. The system of measurement used in science is called the International System of Units, or SI. You will be using SI units for time, distance, and mass in your earth science studies. You will use some units for volume, time, and temperature that are not SI, but that can be used with the SI system.

Time

The standard SI unit of time is the **second,** abbreviated s. Years ago the second was based on the motion of Earth. Earth spins once each day. Each day is divided into 24 hours. Each hour is divided into 60 minutes. Each minute is then divided into 60 seconds. Later, people found that the time it takes Earth to spin can vary by a second or so. The original definition of the second is not precise enough for some measurements. Today the duration of a second is based on regular changes in a kind of atom.

You can use a clock or watch to measure how much time it takes for the sun to move across the sky, or how much time it takes a storm to travel from one state to another. Events like these are measured using a combination of the SI unit, seconds, and the units hours and minutes.

Lesson Objectives

▸ *Identify* and *use* units and measuring devices for time, distance, volume, temperature, and mass.

▸ *Give an example* of how a standard unit was established.

▸ *Compare* direct and indirect measurements and *identify* values that would be indirect measurements.

▸ *Activity   Measure* the number of objects in a box, using indirect measurements.

New Terms

second
meter
volume
liter
cubic centimeter
Celsius degree
mass
gram
direct measurement
indirect measurement

Figure 1-5 The time this lava flow lasts would be measured in the units *hours* or *days*. What time unit would you use to measure a lightning flash?

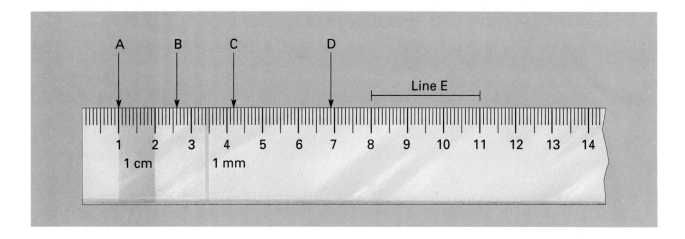

Figure 1-6 On this meterstick, point B is at 2.6 cm. Where are points A, C, and D? Where does line E begin and end?

Length

The **meter** (m) is the standard SI unit of length. A meter is about the height of a doorknob. The distance between the goalposts of a football field is about 100 meters. The meter is the standard unit of length for Olympic events.

A meterstick is divided into 100 equal parts called centimeters (cm). Figure 1-6 shows part of a meterstick. Each centimeter is divided into 10 equal parts called millimeters (mm). The millimeter and the centimeter can be used to measure small distances. The width of your small finger is about 1 centimeter. What is the width of your small finger in millimeters?

Notice that both centimeters and millimeters are made by dividing the meter by a multiple of 10. This makes it easy to figure out how the units are related. Larger length units are made by multiplying the meter by a multiple of 10. For example, a kilometer (km) equals 1000 meters (10 × 10 × 10 meters). The length of a river and the distance around Earth are measured in kilometers.

Notice also that the names of the larger and smaller units are made by adding a prefix to the base unit *meter*. In SI, each prefix has a meaning. The prefix *kilo-* always means 1000. The prefix *centi-* always means one one-hundredth (1/100). Table 1-1 lists the SI prefixes and their meanings.

Table 1-1 Prefixes for Units			
Prefix	**Symbol**	**Meaning**	**Example**
kilo	k	1000	kilogram (kg)
(no prefix)		1	meter (m)
centi	c	1/100	centimeter (cm)
milli	m	1/1000	milliliter (mL)
micro	μ	1/1 000 000	micrometer (μm)

Volume

Volume is a measurement of how much space something takes up. A unit of volume that you will use in science is the **liter,** abbreviated L. You may have noticed that some gasoline pumps show how many liters of gasoline you are buying. Can you think of other common uses of the liter?

Another common unit of volume is the milliliter (mL). There are 1000 milliliters in a liter. A small cube with a length, width, and depth of just one centimeter has a volume of one milliliter. This means that a milliliter can also be called a **cubic centimeter** (cm^3). Milliliters and cubic centimeters are useful units for measuring the volumes of laboratory materials, such as water and loose sand.

A science instrument often used for measuring volume is a graduated cylinder. When you use a graduated cylinder, read the volume of liquid from the bottom of the curved surface that the liquid makes. Figure 1-7 *(left)* shows a graduated cylinder holding 58 milliliters (58 mL) of colored water. Figure 1-7 *(right)* shows the same graduated cylinder with a rock sample in it. The height of the water in the graduated cylinder equals the volume of the water plus the volume of the rock. How can you figure out the volume of the rock?

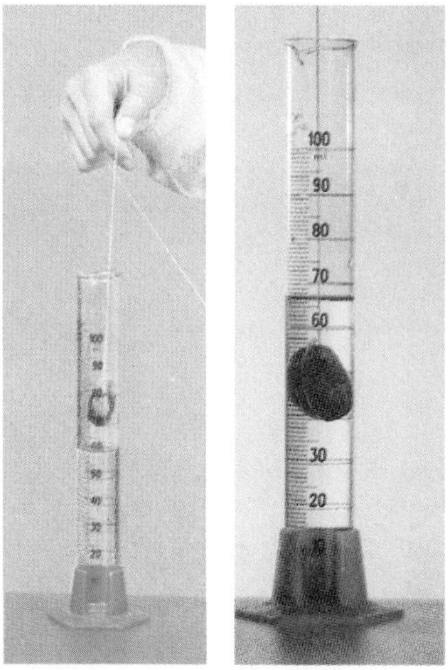

Figure 1-7 You can use a graduated cylinder to measure the volume of liquids and small solids.

Temperature

The unit of temperature you will use in earth science is the **Celsius degree.** Your normal body temperature is about 37 degrees Celsius (37°C). Average room temperature ranges from 18 to 24 degrees Celsius. You can use a Celsius thermometer to measure many temperatures. If you place a Celsius thermometer in ice water, you will find the water has a temperature of about 0 degrees Celsius. The temperature of boiling water at sea level is 100 degrees Celsius. The freezing point and boiling point of water were used to set the standards for the Celsius temperature scale.

Figure 1-8 Some examples of mass

Mass

The **mass** of an object is a measure of how much material is in it. The unit of mass that you will use most often in science is the **gram** (g). The mass of one large potato chip is about one gram. You may have noticed that many food packages show the mass of food in grams. More massive objects are measured in kilograms (kg). One kilogram is equal to 1000 grams. Figure 1-8 shows several objects that would be measured using grams and kilograms.

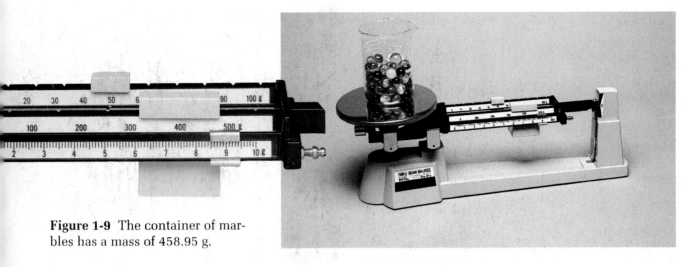

Figure 1-9 The container of marbles has a mass of 458.95 g.

In science, you will use a balance to measure mass. Many laboratories have triple-beam balances like the one shown in Figure 1-9. To use a triple-beam balance, first make sure that all the riders are at the left. Then make sure that the balance points to zero. If the balance does not point to zero, move the smallest rider until it does. (Remember to subtract this "zero" amount from your final reading.) Next, place the object on the pan. Move the riders along the beams until the pointer is at zero again. The mass of the object equals the sum of the values on the three riders. If the object is in a container, remember to subtract the mass of the container from your final measurement.

Direct and Indirect Measurements

Many of the measurements you will make will be direct measurements. When you make a **direct measurement,** you compare the quantity to be measured with a standard unit. For example, you can make a direct measurement of the mass of the marbles in Figure 1-9 using a balance.

In earth science, there are many cases when you must make an indirect measurement. An **indirect measurement** is usually made by using direct measurements and calculations. Figure 1-10 illustrates the difference between a direct and an indirect measurement. You can use a graduated cylinder to directly measure the volume of water in the container. But there is too much water in a lake to measure it using a graduated cylinder. To measure the water in the lake, you would make an indirect measurement. To do this, you would make direct measurements of the area and depth of the lake. With these data and some mathematics, you could make an indirect measurement of the volume of water in the lake.

Figure 1-10 How is measuring the water in the pitcher different from measuring the water in the lake?

Earth science includes many measurement challenges. You can make a direct measurement of the length of a soccer field with a meterstick, but the distance to the moon is an indirect measurement. Indirect measurements are used to find the age of rocks, the size of the sun, and the height of some layers in the atmosphere. In earth science, you will make and use many indirect measurements.

Lesson Review 1.2

5. Name the units and instruments you will use in science to measure each of the following quantities:
   a. time
   b. distance
   c. volume
   d. temperature
   e. mass

6. Describe how the standard unit of time was originally established. Explain why the definition of the standard was changed.

7. What is the difference between a direct and an indirect measurement?

8. Give one example each of a direct and an indirect distance measurement.

Interpret and Apply

9. How could you make an indirect measurement of the number of students in your school? In your answer, identify the direct measurements you would make and use.

A C T I V I T Y 1.2

MAKING AN INDIRECT MEASUREMENT

Purpose   To measure indirectly the number of items in a container.

Materials _____

small box of identical objects such as
  packing chips or dry beans
metric ruler

Procedure

1. Read all directions for this activity before you begin your work.

2. Remove one object from the container. Measure the length, width, and height of the object. Record measurements.

3. Find the average thickness of the object and record your answer.

4. On your paper, copy the data table.

5. Measure the height of your box from the bottom of the box up to the surface of the objects, as shown in the figure. Record the height in your data table.

6. Count the number of objects that you can see when you look straight down into the box. Record the number of objects that you see in your data table.

7. Before leaving the laboratory, clean up all materials.

Collecting and Analyzing Data

Data Table	
Value	**Measurement**
Height of objects	
Number of objects in top layer	
Number of layers in box = (depth of box) ÷ (average thickness of object)	
Number of objects in box = (number of layers) × (number of objects in top layer)	

1. Calculate the number of layers of objects in the box, using the formula in the data table. Record the number of layers in your data table.

2. Find the number of objects in the box, using the formula in the data table. Record your indirect measurement in your data table.

3. Look at all of the measurements that you made in this activity. Which are direct measurements? Which are indirect measurements? Explain the reason for your answers.

Drawing Conclusions

4. If your teacher approves, make a direct measurement of the objects in your box by counting them. How close was your indirect measurement to the direct measurement?

5. Imagine that your box of objects is one small part of a roomful of objects. How could you make an indirect measurement of the objects in the room?

1.3 Science Investigations

When people have trouble with locks, like the person in Figure 1-11, they try different experiments. The experiments are usually based on their knowledge of how a lock works. Most people know that something in the lock must move before the lock will open. They try to think of actions that will help the gadgets inside the lock move. Sometimes there is a logic behind what they try. Sometimes it is a trial-and-error process.

The Scientific Method

The scientific method is a process that you can use to investigate a science problem, object, or event. Steps in the scientific method include stating a problem, gathering information, forming a hypothesis, testing the hypothesis, drawing conclusions, and reporting results.

Stating a Problem One of nature's most dramatic events is a tornado. Each year hundreds of tornadoes occur in the United States. Earth science events such as this raise a lot of questions—for example, "Why do tornadoes happen?" When you ask a question about an earth science event, you are stating a problem that you can investigate.

Gathering Information Once you have stated a problem you need to gather more information about it. You could find out where and when tornadoes happen. You could find out the weather conditions just before a tornado.

Figure 1-11 The scientific method begins when you state a problem, such as "How can I open my locker?"

| Table 1-2 |
The Scientific Method
1. Stating a problem
2. Gathering information
3. Forming a hypothesis
4. Testing the hypothesis
5. Drawing conclusions
6. Reporting results

Finding information involves making observations. The people in Figure 1-12 *(left)* are placing weather instruments in the path a tornado might take. Such instruments provide them with observations of this dramatic event.

Forming a Hypothesis A **hypothesis** [hī päth′ə sis] is a possible explanation of an event or a possible solution to a problem. A hypothesis is usually based on the information you have gathered. It can also be based on your understanding of similar events. For example, a meteorologist may compare tornadoes with other storms.

Suppose you observe that tornadoes occur mostly in late spring, in the central and southern United States. Your weather instruments show that, in late spring, large amounts of cold air and warm air collide over the central United States. You might form this hypothesis: If cold air and warm air collide, then a tornado will occur.

Testing the Hypothesis To test a hypothesis, look for a connection between the event and the variable you are testing. A **variable** [var′ ē ə bəl] is something that may cause or change an event. The above hypothesis refers to this variable: air of two different temperatures colliding. You would test to see if the collision of air at different temperatures leads to tornados. You would collect information from many tornado events and near-tornado events.

All of the information gathered during an experiment is called **data.** Data must be collected carefully. The data collected near a tornado can include air temperature, wind speed, wind direction, cloud type, air moisture, and air pressure. You want to know whether air temperature affects tornadoes. To do this, you must make sure that other things, such as air moisture and air pressure, are kept the same.

Figure 1-12 *Left:* Gathering information about tornadoes; *Right:* Using a computer model to analyze data

Something that is kept the same while you are testing a hypothesis is called a **control.** Of course, scientists cannot keep events in nature the same. To make sure that the experiment does have controls, earth scientists compare data from many different events. The more events they study, the more likely they will find a pattern that may exist between a variable and an event.

Another way to test a hypothesis is by designing and testing a scientific model. A **scientific model** is a picture, object, or demonstration that tries to show or explain what is observed in nature. A globe is a common model of Earth. A cutaway picture of a volcano is another model. Models can be used to help analyze data. For example, you could program a computer model to study tornadoes.

Drawing Conclusions Once you have formed and tested a hypothesis, you need to ask a very important question. Do the data support the original hypothesis? A **conclusion** is an opinion about the original hypothesis, based on data you have collected. Suppose your data show that tornadoes happen only when warm air and cold air collide. These data support your hypothesis. You could conclude that tornadoes occur when warm and cold air collide.

It is more likely that your data would show that tornadoes are more complicated. Your data might only partly support your hypothesis. It may not support your hypothesis at all. In that case, you have some choices. One choice is to try a different way to test the hypothesis. Another choice is to change the hypothesis. Ask a different question, such as, Do tornadoes happen only in moist air? Many of the greatest experiments bring up more questions than they answer. You may make a totally unexpected discovery.

If repeated tests do support a hypothesis, it may develop into a theory. A **theory** [thiər′ ē] is a hypothesis that is supported by many careful experiments. A theory is usually tested by many scientists. It may go through several changes before it is accepted as an explanation of an event.

Reporting Results When people work together, they can find out about earth science events sooner and more completely than if they work alone. Perhaps someone has data that would help you test your hypothesis. Maybe you have an idea that could help someone else's conclusion. One way that earth scientists work together is by reporting the results of their experiments. Scientists report results at meetings and in special magazines. In this way, all the scientists who are working on the problem can compare their results. You report your results when you write activity reports and give spoken reports in class.

Figure 1-13 A globe is a model of Earth.

Each chapter in this book has activities that will help you practice skills in the scientific method. When you do an activity, you will make observations about an object or event. Often, you will use a model to study an event. Your observations, data, and models will help you draw conclusions. Finally, you will share your results in your lab reports.

Laboratory Safety

Data about many earth science events, like tornadoes, are collected outdoors. Other earth science data are gathered in a laboratory. A **laboratory,** or lab, is a room that is used for collecting data. The equipment in scientists' laboratories varies, depending on the problem being investigated. School laboratories also vary. Your earth science laboratory may be in the back of your science classroom. It may be in a separate room. Maybe you do your lab work on the same desks at which you take notes and review for tests.

As you do the activities in this text, you will notice small pictures in front of some of the steps. These pictures and their meanings are shown in Table 1-3. The pictures call attention to cautions in specific activities. Statements within the activities tell you what to watch out for. Be familiar with all cautions in an activity before you begin your lab work. You must also read and be familiar with general safety rules, listed in Appendix A near the back of this book.

Table 1-3 Laboratory Safety Symbols			
Symbol	**Meaning**	**Symbol**	**Meaning**
	Wear safety goggles and lab aprons. Activity uses chemicals, hot materials, lab burners, or the possibility of broken glass.		Activity involves heating or handling equipment that could burn you. Use heat-resistant gloves, a clamp, or tongs to handle hot equipment.
	Danger of cuts exists. Activity involves scissors, wire cutters, pins, or other sharp instruments.		Activity involves the use of electric equipment, such as electric lamps and hot plates.
	Extreme care is needed. Activity involves hot plates, lab burners, or lighted matches.		The arrow alerts you to additional, specific safety procedures in an Activity. Always discuss safety cautions with your teacher before you begin work.
	Extreme care is needed. Activity involves chemicals that may be irritating, corrosive, flammable, or poisonous. Avoid spills. Avoid touching the chemicals.		

Figure 1-14 You can make many earth science observations in a laboratory.

No matter where you do your lab work, it is important to remember that you are working in a laboratory. Approach all laboratory work with a mature attitude. The most important words to remember in a lab are **BE CAREFUL.** The substances and equipment used in labs can be dangerous if you do not use them correctly. Careless laboratory work can lead to accidents. Even when your experiments use safe and simple equipment, you must still work carefully so your data will be collected safely and accurately.

Lesson Review 1.3

10. List and describe the steps of the scientific method.
11. What is the purpose of a variable in an experiment? What is the purpose of a control?
12. How is a hypothesis like a theory? How is it different?
13. Design a poster to illustrate one of the safety rules listed in Appendix A. In your poster, tell why it is important to follow that rule.

Interpret and Apply

14. How could you use the scientific method to find the quickest route from home to school or other location? Use the terms *hypothesis, variable, control,* and *conclusion* in your description.
15. An oceanographer does an experiment to determine if cold water is saltier than warm water. What would be the variable in this experiment?

ACTIVITY 1.3   General Supplies

MAKING AND TESTING A PREDICTION

Purpose   To predict a water temperature change based on observations.

Materials

2 water containers (400 mL or larger)	lab apron
	safety goggles
graduated cylinder	room temperature water
thermometer	
stirring rod	cold water

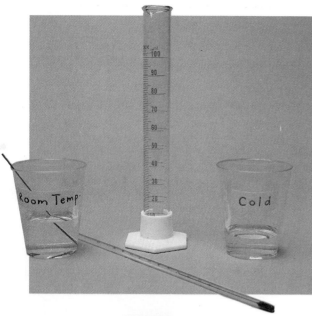

Procedure

1. Read all directions for this activity before you begin your work.

2. Copy the data table onto your paper. Put on your lab apron and safety goggles.

3. Use a graduated cylinder to measure 100 mL of room temperature water. Pour the water into one of the containers.

4. Measure the temperature (in °C) of the room temperature water. Record the temperature in your data table for Part A.

5. Measure 100 mL of cold water and pour it into the other container.

6. Measure and record the temperature of the cold water.

7. Pour the cold water into the room temperature water. Gently stir the mixture with the stirring rod. (Do not stir with the thermometer.)

8. Measure the temperature of the water mixture after you are finished stirring. Record the temperature in your data table for Part A.

9. Pour out the water mixture after you have measured its temperature. Dry both water containers.

10. For Part B, repeat steps 3 through 9 using 100 mL of room temperature water and 75 mL of cold water. Record all measurements.

11. For Part C, repeat steps 3 through 9 using 100 mL of room temperature water and 50 mL of cold water.

12. Look at your data table. Compare the temperature after mixing for parts A, B, and C. Then copy and complete this prediction:

    If I mix 25 mL of cold water with 100 mL of room temperature water, then the temperature of the mixture will be _____°C.

13. For Part D, repeat steps 3 through 9 for 100 mL of room temperature water and 25 mL of cold water. Record your measurements in your data table for Part D.

14. Before leaving the laboratory, clean up all materials.

Collecting and Analyzing Data

Data Table		Volume (mL)	Temperature (°C)	Temperature after Mixing (°C)
A	Room temperature	100		
	Cold	100		
B	Room temperature	100		
	Cold	75		
C	Room temperature	100		
	Cold	50		
D	Room temperature	100		
	Cold	25		

1. Look at the volumes for each part (A through D). Explain why the room temperature water can be called a control.

2. Review the definitions of control and variable on pages 22 and 23. Explain why the cold water can be called a variable.

3. Describe the pattern of temperature change as you added less cold water to 100 mL of room temperature water.

4. What would you expect the temperature to be if you added 12 mL cold water to 100 mL room temperature water?

Drawing Conclusions

5. What observations did you use to make your prediction about Part D? Describe the pattern you used to make your prediction.

6. How closely were you able to predict the temperature of Part D?

7. In any experiment, there are sources of error—things that make the measurements less precise than they could be. Review the procedure. List all the sources of error you can think of.

Earth Science in the News

What will be the front-page earth science news items this year? How much of the news will be good? How much of the news will cause concern? During the next year, you will hear news items about earthquakes, floods, and severe storms. Other news will be about the effect people have on the environment. You will also hear reports on earth science research. For example, there are plans to construct a space station. Scientists are testing the hypothesis that Earth's climates are changing. Ocean research turns up new surprises all the time. Newspapers, radio, and television carry reports that focus on these events.

What role do earth scientists play in news-making events? If you listen to the news or read the paper, you will find that scientists have many roles. Three of their roles are in the areas of technology, natural events, and in planning for the future.

The Impact of Technology

Science is the study of events in the natural world. For thousands of years, people have used knowledge about the natural world to invent useful tools and materials. **Technology** [tek näl′ə jē] is the use of science knowledge for practical purposes. The science knowledge gained through years of research has led to the invention of automobiles, airplanes, life saving medicines, plastics, refrigerators, computers, and countless other developments.

Not all results of technology have been helpful. Scientists have learned that the use of technology is placing a tremendous burden on our environment. All raw materials and

Figure 1-15 *Left:* Drilling for oil; *Right:* Gasoline, car wax, tires, plastics, dyes, asphalt, and many other products all come from oil.

Figure 1-16 Workers in Alaska clean rocks after the *Exxon Valdez* oil spill in 1989; Earth scientists help determine the impact such disasters have on the environment.

most energy sources come from the earth. The demand for these materials continues to increase. Wastes from factories and power plants must be put somewhere. These wastes could be harmful to the environment. Accidents can cause even greater harm to the environment, as Figure 1-16 shows. Earth scientists help determine the impact technology can have on the air, land, fresh water, and oceans. An important role of earth scientists is to report and predict the effects technology has on the earth. Scientists' reports help people make informed decisions about using technology.

ENVIRONMENTAL AWARENESS

Making a Difference

A student in Massachusetts convinces her town to recycle school lunch trays. Students in Washington help clean up a local stream and see fish return to live there. Countless Scout and school groups organize recycling drives. In Chicago, students and teachers from around the world meet to discuss their role as caretakers of Earth's resources.

What do these people have in common? They are all aware of how their actions affect Earth. Earth includes the environment, which is the area that you and other living things depend on to stay alive. Earth is the source for everything you use, from food and air to clothes and amusements. If you are aware of how your actions affect the environment, you can make wiser decisions about using Earth's resources.

In each chapter, you will find a feature called Environmental Awareness. This feature serves three main purposes: to help you understand Earth and your environment; to show how people and the environment affect each other; and, in many cases, to let you know how you can help conserve Earth's environment and resources. ■

Natural Events

Earth scientists must understand the environment to help determine technology's impact on it. Earth scientists use technology to collect and analyze data about the natural world. They use the data to discover patterns in natural events. Earth scientists play an important role in providing information about storms, earthquakes, volcanoes, coastline erosion, and other natural events. They are learning how to predict some of these events. Prediction helps save thousands of lives and billions of dollars in property damage.

Every year new technology is developed to collect and analyze data about Earth. Satellites are placed into orbit around Earth to collect information. Powerful computers help analyze the information in far less time than was possible a few years ago. Robots carry cameras to ocean depths that are difficult for people to endure. Special rockets gather data on the upper atmosphere. All these devices increase the data available about Earth.

Figure 1-17 Natural events can affect people's lives. *Left:* Distributing water after Hurricane Hugo in 1989; *Top:* People start to clean up after the 1989 Bay Area earthquake. *Bottom:* A wave crashes over a street during a hurricane.

AN EARTH SCIENCE SPECIAL NEWS REPORT

Purpose   To collect news information about an earth science topic and share that information on a regular basis.

Materials

a note-keeping system (notebook, index cards, folder, or other method of collecting and organizing written information)

Procedure

1. Read all instructions for this activity before you begin your work.

2. Review Lesson 1.1 and choose one branch of earth science (astronomy, geology, meteorology, or oceanography).

3. Decide on a note-keeping system to use. You can choose one of the systems listed above or think of one on your own. Your note-keeping system must:
   - be easy for you to use;
   - have places for you to write in it;
   - organize materials so they are easy to find and do not get crumpled;
   - be large enough to hold information gathered over many months;
   - be sturdy enough to protect the materials in it.

Collecting and Analyzing Data

1. Read the list of questions in the data table at right. Find a newspaper or magazine article that relates to the branch of earth science you chose. This article can be from any newspaper or magazine from the past year. Read the article and write a short summary of it (about six to ten sentences). In your summary, answer as many of the questions listed in the data table as you can.

Reporting Results

2. Put the summary in your note-keeping system. Your teacher will let you know how and when to share your summary.

3. All this year, watch for news about your earth science branch. You can read articles or listen to the news. Write a summary of each news story, just as you did in step 1. If you can, keep clippings or copies of pictures that go with the news story. Place all the materials in your note-keeping system. Share your summaries as directed by your teacher.

Data Table

Ask yourself these questions when you read or hear a science news story.

1. Which branches of earth science does this article relate to?

2. Is the article about an earth science event, about research, or about both?

3. How are people affected by the event or research described in the article?

4. Are any scientists mentioned? What role do they have in the event? Where do they work?

5. Does the article mention any measurements? Are the measurements direct or indirect?

6. Does the article mention any patterns in earth science objects or events?

7. If the article describes research, is there a hypothesis the scientists are testing? Have the scientists made any conclusions? Are they planning to do more research on this problem? What do other scientists think about their research?

Figure 1-18 *Left:* The robot *Jason Jr.* explores the ocean floor. *Right:* The United States and Italy are working together to build this satellite. The satellite will study Earth's upper atmosphere.

Planning the Future

People have always been explorers. Some people travel because of a natural curiosity about places they have never seen. Other people explore because of the chance to make a better life for themselves. Pioneers take tremendous risks to start new lives. The wagon trains that headed west across North America in the 1800's had no guarantee of a safe arrival. Many people who move to a new country today have no guarantee of a job when they get there. People are willing to take these risks because of the chance for a better life. In the modern world, a better life often means a greater demand for resources.

Today people are searching for resources in a number of ways. New technology helps earth scientists explore deeper into Earth and its oceans. These are places that may hold undiscovered resources. Earth is not the only place to look for resources. Space exploration shows that the moon and other planets may someday be a source of materials. The first people to live on the moon or Mars will probably be miners.

The search for new resources will not be risk-free. Pioneers in the future will face challenges and dangers, just as pioneers have always done. Progress will require the cooperative effort of many countries. While the United States has been developing the Space Shuttle, the Soviet Union has been working on long-term space travel. The adventure of setting up colonies on the moon or Mars can be a chance for cooperation among countries.

Lesson Review 1.4

16. Compare and contrast science and technology.

17. Describe the role that earth scientists play in the use of technology.

18. What role do earth scientists play in natural events?

19. How has technology helped provide information for the study of earth materials and events?

Interpret and Apply

20. Suppose you are on a committee to select a team of people to explore a newly discovered planet. Write a paragraph explaining the roles an earth scientist would play on the exploration team.

Chapter Summary

Read this summary of the main ideas in this chapter. If any are not clear to you, go back and review that lesson.

1.1 The Earth Sciences

■ Earth science is the study of objects and events that occur in Earth, the atmosphere, the oceans, and in the universe.

■ Looking for patterns is an important part of making observations in each branch of earth science.

■ Earth science includes astronomy, geology, meteorology, and oceanography.

1.2 Earth Science Measurements

■ Standard units of measurement allow people to compare the results of experiments and observations.

■ In earth science, you need to know and use standard units for time, length, volume, temperature, and mass.

■ Observations in earth science often require indirect measurements.

1.3 Science Investigations

■ The scientific method can be described as stating a problem, gathering information, forming a hypothesis, testing it, drawing conclusions, and reporting results.

■ Testing a hypothesis includes collecting data about the variable. Controls help make sure that you are testing the variable.

■ A scientific model is another way to test or illustrate a hypothesis. When tests support a hypothesis, it may become a theory.

■ Work carefully in the laboratory for safety and precise results.

1.4 Earth Science in the News

■ Technology has both affected the environment and increased understanding of it.

■ Roles of earth scientists include studying technology and the environment, understanding and predicting natural events, and helping to plan for future resource needs.

Chapter Review

■ Vocabulary

astronomy
Celsius degree
conclusion
control
cubic centimeter
data
direct measurement
geology
gram
hypothesis
indirect measurement
laboratory

liter
mass
meteorology
meter
oceanography
pattern
scientific model
second
technology
theory
variable
volume

■ Concept Mapping

Using the method of concept mapping described on pages 3–5, complete a concept map for measurement. Copy the incomplete map below. Then fill in the missing terms.

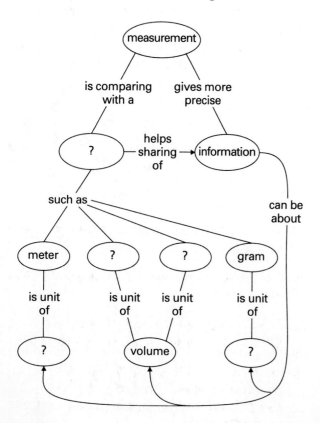

■ Review

Number your paper from 1 to 22. Match each term in List **A** to a phrase in List **B**.

List A

a. data
b. technology
c. gathering information
d. pattern
e. control
f. oceanography
g. geology
h. variable
i. meter (m)
j. volume
k. hypothesis

l. astronomy
m. indirect measurement
n. theory
o. gram (g)
p. scientific method
q. direct measurement
r. second (s)
s. meteorology
t. scientific model
u. laboratory
v. mass

List B

1. the study of the atmosphere
2. a set of events that repeats
3. a factor that may affect an event
4. an explanation of an event that is supported by experiments
5. includes the study of meteors and comets
6. a picture, object, or demonstration that shows an object or event
7. a unit of measurement originally based on Earth's motion
8. a factor that is kept the same during an experiment
9. a possible explanation of an event
10. study of patterns in Earth materials
11. an activity that comes before forming a hypothesis
12. measuring the mass of this book is an example of this
13. measuring the mass of Earth is an example of this
14. amount of material in an object

15. information collected during the test of a hypothesis

16. room used for collecting data

17. use of science knowledge for practical purposes

18. measurement of the space that an object occupies

19. a unit of measurement for length

20. study of the largest part of Earth's surface

21. a process for science investigations

22. a unit of measurement used for mass

■ Interpret and Apply

On your paper, answer each question.

23. Think about activities that you like to do throughout the year. Describe at least one pattern of events in nature that affects whether you do any of these activities.

24. Look at Figure 1-4 on page 13. List the branches of earth science that relate to the photo. Then describe how the photo illustrates that the branches of earth science are connected.

25. How could you make an indirect measurement of the thickness of one page of this book?

26. Identify each activity listed below as safe or unsafe.
  a. Jane hangs up her jacket before beginning a lab activity.
  b. Anton removes his safety goggles to read a thermometer.
  c. Dana eats a snack while waiting for a beaker of water to boil.

27. Paula notices that the moon appears to be larger when it is near the horizon than when it is overhead. Describe how Paula could investigate this problem using the scientific method.

■ Writing in Science

28. Suppose you have a time machine and can travel back in time. You can choose two inventions of modern technology to take with you. The purpose of your trip is to demonstrate the usefulness of technology. Assume that the time machine can provide electric energy. Write a paragraph explaining which two inventions you would take with you and why you chose them. Before you write, you need to give careful thought to choosing the time period you would like to visit and the two inventions you would take. Why would it be difficult to take only two inventions?

■ Critical Thinking

Jamal is visiting the ocean for the first time. In the morning, he notices that the water level is very low. In the afternoon, he sees that the level is much higher. He decides to keep track of the water level three times a day for three days. His results are in the table below.

Ocean Water Level			
Day	7:30 A.M.	1:30 P.M.	7:30 P.M.
Tuesday	low	high	low
Wednesday	low	high	low
Thursday	low	high	low

29. What step of the scientific method is Jamal doing?

30. Has Jamal made any measurements? Explain your answer.

31. Predict the water level at 1:30 A.M. on Wednesday, based on these observations.

32. In the library, Jamal finds out that these events are caused partly by the moon. To which branches of earth science do these events belong?

Mapping the Earth

Chapter Preview

Have You Ever WONDERED?

Why do so many states have straight lines for borders?

Out of the 50 United States, only 2, Hawaii and New Jersey, do not have any straight north-south or east-west lines as borders. The straight-line borders of Colorado, Utah, New Mexico, and Arizona meet at a place called the Four Corners, shown in the photo at left. At the Four Corners, you can stand in one place and be in four different states at the same time.

People who came to the colonies a few hundred years ago made the first known maps of the continent of North America. They were able to measure straight lines in geographic directions using the sun, stars, and simple instruments. The borders of territories were often determined before towns and roads were built. These territory borders later became state borders. The system of straight lines used to decide borders is still used today. In this chapter, you will learn how to use this system and other symbols to read maps.

2.1 *Finding Direction*

Often, you give or follow directions. For example, you may direct a visitor to take a right at the end of the hallway to find your school's auditorium. Familiar hallways, buildings, and crossroads work well as landmarks when you are near familiar places. However, hikers, hunters, pilots, sailors, and others who travel in unfamiliar settings need to know how to find and follow geographic directions. You can find geographic directions by using the sun, the North Star, or a magnetic compass and map.

Geographic North

In the northern hemisphere, the easiest direction to find is geographic north. **Geographic north** is the direction of the geographic North Pole. Maps usually show geographic north, along with other information, in the map's legend. A map **legend** is a list at the edge of a map that explains symbols, colors, and other information about the map.

If you live north of the tropics, you can use your changing shadow to find geographic north. Your shortest shadow is at midday, which is usually within an hour of noon. Your shortest shadow of the day points toward geographic north. Figure 2-1 *(left)* shows how you can use this shadow to find other geographic directions.

At night, you can use the North Star to find geographic north. Figure 2-1 *(right)* shows how to use the Big Dipper to find the North Star. Once you have found the North Star, point to it. Then slowly move your arm down until you are pointing to geographic north on the horizon. At home, try finding north using these two methods. Do you get the same results using your shadow and using the North Star?

Figure 2-1 In most of the United States, you can find north using these methods. *Left:* Point in the direction of your shortest shadow of the day. *Right:* Find the North Star and point to the horizon beneath it.

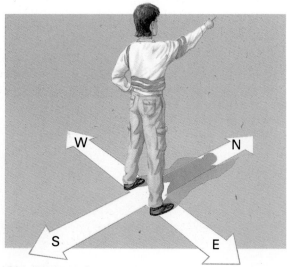

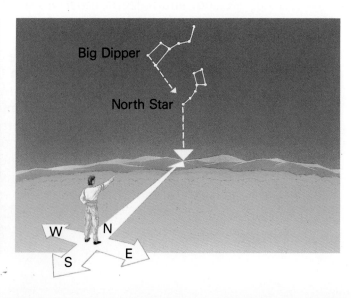

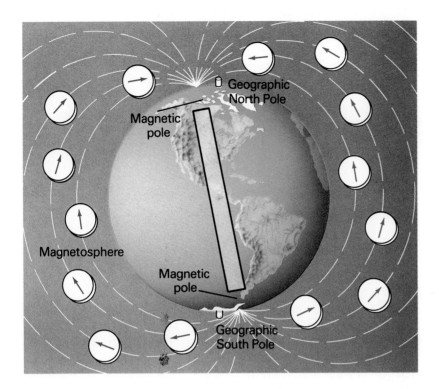

Magnetic North

Earth acts like a giant magnet. Like any magnet, Earth has a magnetic field, called its **magnetosphere** [mag nēt′ ə sfir]. Earth's magnetosphere has two magnetic poles, one at each end. In Figure 2-2, notice that one of Earth's magnetic poles lies near Bathurst Island in northern Canada. **Magnetic north** is the direction from where you are on Earth to the magnetic pole in northern Canada. Earth's other magnetic pole is near the coast of Wilkes Land in Antarctica. Earth's magnetic poles are not in the same places as Earth's geographic poles. However, Earth's magnetic poles are close enough to its geographic poles that you can use the magnetic poles to find direction.

When a magnet is allowed to swing freely, it turns until it points toward one of Earth's magnetic poles. A magnetic compass is simply a small magnet that is able to turn in any direction. Figure 2-3 shows a magnetic compass. The end of the compass needle that points toward magnetic north is marked *north* or *N*, or it is colored.

In most places, magnetic north and geographic north are not the same direction. However, you can use a magnetic compass to find geographic north if you know the difference between the two directions. **Magnetic declination** is an angle that measures the difference between geographic north and magnetic north.

Figure 2-3 Why is it important to adjust a compass for your local magnetic declination?

Figure 2-4 Each line on this map connects places that have the same angle of magnetic declination.

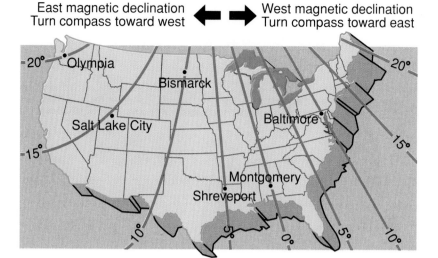

East magnetic declination
Turn compass toward west ← → West magnetic declination
Turn compass toward east

The lines in Figure 2-4 indicate angles of magnetic declination for different places in the United States. Suppose you are near Shreveport, Louisiana. Your compass is pointing toward magnetic north, and you are facing in that direction. From the map in Figure 2-4, you know that the magnetic declination near Shreveport is 5° east of geographic north. To find geographic north, you need to turn 5° toward the west until your compass needle points to 5° east and you are facing geographic north. Use Figure 2-4 to find the magnetic declination where you live. How would you use a compass to find geographic north in your area?

Maps that are used during boating and hiking usually show magnetic declination. Even if the difference between magnetic and geographic north is small, you should still adjust for it. Otherwise, you can become seriously lost.

Lesson Review 2.1

Figure 2-5 Finding north

1. How can you use your shadow to find direction? How can you use the North Star?

2. What is magnetic declination? Draw a diagram as part of your answer.

Interpret and Apply

3. To impress a friend, you use the North Star to find north. Your friend insists that you are wrong because a compass needle is pointing in a different direction. Write a short, polite conversation in which you explain to your friend why you are correct.

USING A MAGNETIC COMPASS

Purpose To state a conclusion about geographic north and magnetic north.

Materials

drawing compass	metric ruler
magnetic compass	map of magnetic
plain paper	declinations
protractor	(Figure 2-4)

Procedure

1. Read all instructions for this activity before you begin your work.

2. Make a dot in the middle of the paper. Use the drawing compass to draw the largest circle you can, using the dot as the center point.

3. Use the ruler to draw a diameter line through the center of the circle. Put an arrow at one end of the line.

4. Estimate the magnetic declination where you live, using the map in Figure 2-4. (Refer to the map on page 47 for the names of states and cities.)

5. To draw the angle of magnetic declination, place the protractor so its center is on the dot and its 0° line lies along the arrow. Measure and mark the degrees of magnetic declination that you estimated. Draw an arrow from the dot through the mark.

6. If your area has west magnetic declination, the arrow on the right points to geographic north. If your area has east magnetic declination, the arrow on the left points to geographic north. Label your arrows.

7. Put a magnetic compass on the dot. Make sure that the *N* on the base of the compass lines up with geographic north on your drawing.

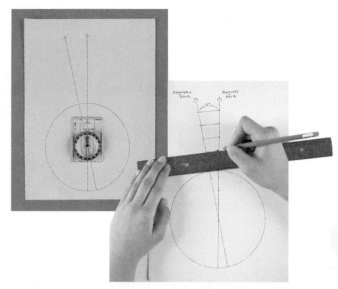

8. Slowly turn the paper until the compass needle lines up with magnetic north on your drawing. Your geographic north arrow now points toward geographic north. Ask your teacher to check your results.

Collecting and Analyzing Data

1. Mark each arrow every 2 cm, beginning at the center of the circle. Use a ruler to draw a line between each pair of 2-cm marks, as shown.

2. Measure the distance between the two arrows along each line you just drew. Write the distances next to each line on your drawing.

3. What happens to the distance between the two arrows as you move farther away from the compass?

Drawing Conclusions

4. Why does the difference between magnetic north and geographic north mean more the farther you travel?

5. Why is it important to check your compass every so often while you are traveling?

Latitude and Longitude

Figure 2-6 Labeled rows and seats help you find your place at an event. Latitude and longitude help you find your place on Earth.

A football or soccer game is difficult to play or referee if there are no lines on the field. A baseball or softball game is just as difficult with no bases. Checkers is almost impossible if there are no squares on the board. Lines, bases, and squares provide a frame of reference. A **frame of reference** is a set of points or lines that acts as a guide.

Lines in a frame of reference often are drawn in one direction but mark off distance in another direction. For example, the seats in the theater in Figure 2-6 are lined up in rows from side to side. When you say you are sitting in the tenth row, you are measuring your distance from the stage. The side-to-side rows of seats mark off the front-to-back distance in the theater.

Cartographers, or mapmakers, use reference lines to locate places on Earth's surface. Unlike the flat floor of a theater, Earth is a sphere that is slightly flattened at the poles. The frame of reference used to locate places on Earth's surface is called latitude and longitude.

Latitude

Halfway between Earth's geographic North and South poles lies Earth's **equator,** an imaginary east-west line that runs all the way around Earth. The equator is the reference line for latitude. **Latitude** is a measurement of how far a place is from the equator. Latitude is measured in degrees, rather than in kilometers or miles. Figure 2-7 (left) shows an imaginary line from the center of Earth to Denver, Colorado. Another imaginary line goes from the center of Earth to a point on the equator directly south of Denver. These two imaginary lines create an angle of about 40 degrees. Thus Denver has a latitude of about 40 degrees north, which is abbreviated as 40° N. Indianapolis, Indiana, also has a latitude of about 40° N. One of the first highways across the United States was U.S. Route 40. It is an east-west highway which roughly follows a line of latitude at 40° N.

You can compare latitude lines with rows of seats in a theater. Although latitude lines go east to west, they mark off distances north and south of the equator. Figure 2-7 (left) shows that the longest latitude line on Earth is the equator. The equator divides Earth into two halves, called the Northern and Southern hemispheres. The United States is in the Northern Hemisphere.

Latitude measurements always include a north or south label. The geographic North Pole has a latitude of exactly 90° N. The geographic South Pole has a latitude of exactly

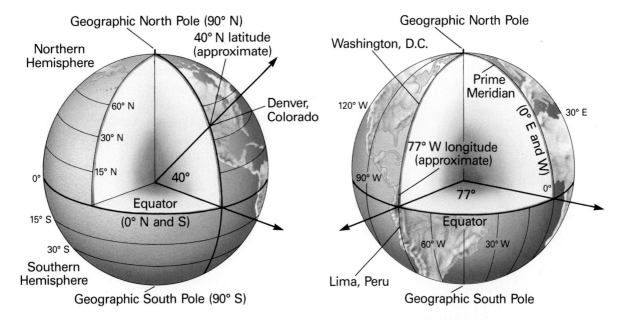

90° S. Any place on the equator has a latitude of 0° N and S. On the globe in Figure 2-7 *(left)*, can you find the 15° S latitude line? In which hemisphere is this latitude line?

Latitude lines are also called parallels because they do not cross each other. Because latitude lines are parallel, a degree of latitude is always the same distance on Earth's surface—about 112 kilometers.

Figure 2-7 *Left:* Earth's equator is the reference line for latitude measurements. *Right:* The prime meridian is the reference line for longitude measurements.

Longitude

Have you ever "done a 180"? If you spin halfway around, you have turned through 180 degrees. You end up facing in the opposite direction. Distances east and west on Earth can also be described in terms of degrees. **Longitude** is a measure of distance in degrees east or west of a reference line called the prime meridian. The **prime meridian** is an imaginary line that passes from the geographic North Pole through Greenwich, England, and on to the geographic South Pole. The prime meridian has a value of 0 degrees east and west longitude (0° E and W). On the opposite side of Earth is a line of longitude with a value of 180° east and west. Other lines of longitude, which are also called meridians, have values between 0° and 180° and are labeled E or W.

Figure 2-7 *(right)* illustrates the longitude of Washington, D.C. One imaginary line is drawn from Earth's center to the prime meridian. Another line is drawn from Earth's center to a longitude line that passes through Washington, D.C. The two lines form an angle of 77°. Washington, D.C. has a longitude of about 77° W. Lima, Peru, also has a longitude of about 77° W.

Unlike degrees of latitude, degrees of longitude do not equal the same distance in kilometers everywhere on Earth. This is because lines of longitude are not parallel. In Figure 2-7 (right), notice that lines of longitude come together at the geographic poles. At the equator, a degree of longitude equals about 112 kilometers. As you approach the geographic North or South Poles, the distance covered by a degree of longitude gets smaller. At the North and South Poles, a degree of longitude is equal to 0 kilometers.

Using Latitude and Longitude

There are thousands of towns and cities with the same latitude. Knowing only a place's distance north or south of the equator is not enough information. Just knowing a place's longitude is not enough, either, since many places have the same longitude. However, each place on Earth has its own unique combination of latitude and longitude that can be used to describe its location. For example, on the map in Figure 2-9, point A has a latitude of 10° S and a longitude of 15° E. Point B in Figure 2-9 is New York City, which is at 41° N, 74° W. Use the map in Figure 2-9 to determine the latitudes at points C and D. Then compare your answers with the positions of features listed in Table 2-1. Which feature is at point C? Which are at points D, E, F, G, H, and I? You can get more practice using latitude and longitude in Activity 2.2.

You can use an astrolabe like the one shown in Figure 2-8 to measure your latitude. The angle of the North Star above the horizon is the same as your latitude north of the equator. In most of the United States, the angle of the North Star is between 25° and 50°. Where on Earth would the angle of the North Star equal 0°? Where would it equal 90°?

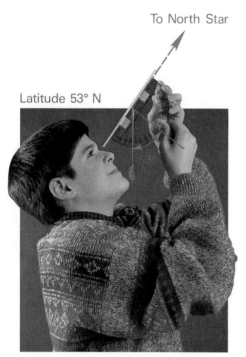

To North Star

Latitude 53° N

Figure 2-8 You can find your latitude using a simple astrolabe. Look through the straw at the North Star. The angle shown equals your latitude.

Table 2-1 Latitude and Longitude of Some Locations*		
Location	**Latitude**	**Longitude**
Caribbean Sea	15° N	75° W
New Guinea	5° S	140° E
Japan	35° N	140° E
Persian Gulf	25° N	54° W
Hawaii	20° N	156° W
Tierra del Fuego	55° S	67° W
Strait of Gibraltar	36° N	6° W

*Values are approximate.

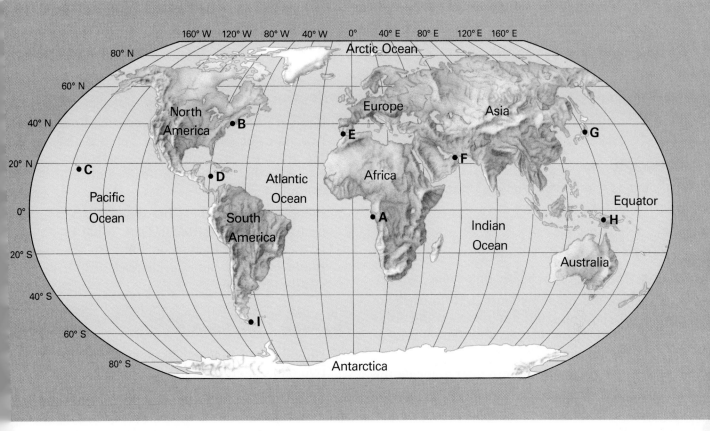

Figure 2-9 Map of Earth, showing physical features

Lesson Review 2.2

4. Compare and contrast an angle of longitude and an angle of latitude.

5. What is the reference line for latitude? For longitude?

6. Which lines run east to west around Earth? Do these lines measure distances east to west? Explain.

7. Which lines run from the North Pole to the South Pole? Do these lines measure distances north to south? Explain.

Interpret and Apply

8. Use the map in Figure 2-9 to find the continent or ocean at each latitude and longitude listed.
   a. 80° S, 20° W
   b. 36° N, 140° E
   c. 34° S, 140° E
   d. 0° S, 70° W

USING LATITUDE AND LONGITUDE

Purpose   To interpret data about the latitude and longitude of cities in the United States.

Materials _____
map of the United States (Figure 2-10)
metric ruler

Procedure

1. Copy the data tables onto your paper.

2. Use the map in Figure 2-10 to estimate the latitudes and longitudes of the cities listed in the first part of Data Table A. Record your estimates.

3. Use the map in Figure 2-10 to locate the cities at the latitudes and longitudes in the second part of Data Table A.

4. Use the ruler to measure the distance on the map in millimeters between the pairs of cities listed in Data Table B. Record these two measurements.

5. Now estimate and record the degrees of latitude or longitude between the pairs of cities in Data Table B.

Collecting and Analyzing Data

1. Compare the distances between the first two pairs of cities in Data Table B. Is the distance in mm on the map the same? Is the distance in degrees of latitude the same?

2. Compare the distances between the second two pairs of cities in Data Table B. Is the distance in mm on the map the same? Is the distance in degrees of longitude the same?

Drawing Conclusions

3. How do your measurements for the first two pairs of cities help demonstrate that lines of latitude are parallel?

4. Which pair of cities is closer to Earth's geographic North Pole, New Orleans and Houston or New York and Pittsburgh? How does nearness to Earth's poles affect the map distance between degrees of longitude?

5. A map is a flat model of part of Earth's surface. What are you assuming about the map in Figure 2-10 when you measure map distance?

Data Table A		
City	**Latitude**	**Longitude**
Honolulu		
Houston		
Los Angeles		
Miami		
St. Louis		
Seattle		
	40° N	80° W
	39° N	120° W
	40° N	105° W
	39° N	95° W
	58° N	134° W
	45° N	93° W

Data Table B		
Pair of Cities	**Distance Between Cities**	
	On Map	**In Degrees**
Los Angeles and Reno	____ mm	____ ° of latitude
Charleston and Miami	____ mm	____ ° of latitude
New Orleans and Houston	____ mm	____ ° of longitude
New York and Pittsburgh	____ mm	____ ° of longitude

Figure 2-10 Map of the United States, showing physical features

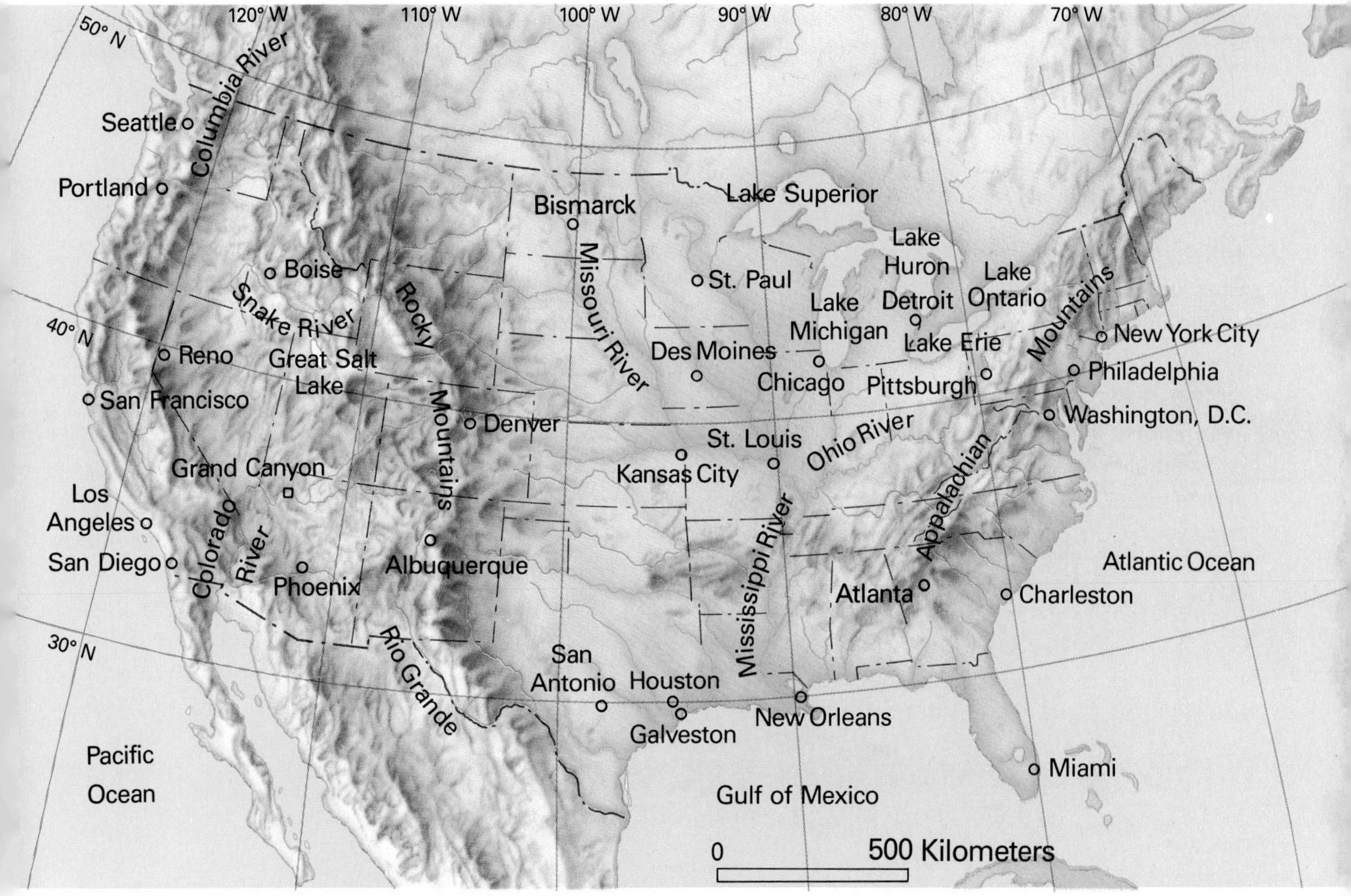

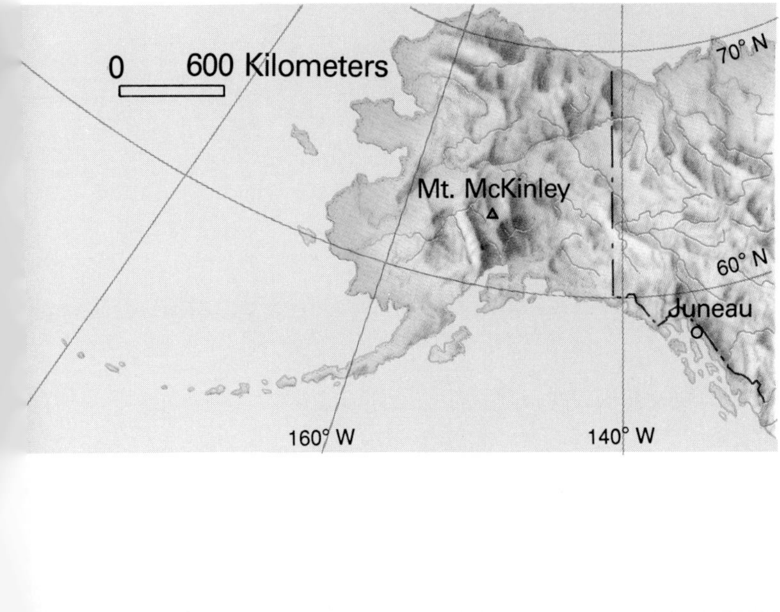

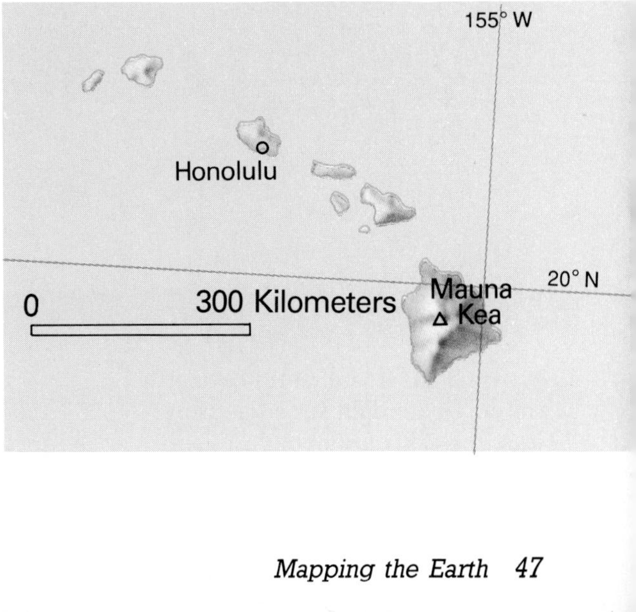

2.3 Models of Earth

The idea that Earth is a sphere was accepted thousands of years ago. A museum in Italy has an ancient statue of the mythical character Atlas carrying a globe on his shoulders. Because Earth is nearly spherical, a globe is the best model to show Earth's surface. Globes, however, are not always convenient. Often, you need other models of Earth.

Earth's Interior

The layers of Earth are illustrated in the model in Figure 2-11. At Earth's center is its **inner core,** which is made of the metal elements iron and nickel. The temperature of the inner core is at least 6000° Celsius. The pressure at Earth's center keeps the inner core solid, even though it is hot enough to boil the metals. The distance from the center of Earth to the edge of the inner core is about 1400 kilometers. Surrounding the inner core is the **outer core,** which is also made of iron and nickel; but the metals in the outer core are liquid. How thick is the outer core, according to Figure 2-11? Earth's **mantle** is a hot, solid layer about 2800 kilometers thick. It is rich in the elements iron, magnesium, and silicon. The uppermost part of the mantle behaves like both a liquid and a solid. Finally, you walk on a layer of cooled, solid rock called the **crust.** In some places, the crust is 65 kilometers thick, while in other places, it may only be a few kilometers thick.

Lesson Objectives

▸ **Diagram** a model of the interior regions of Earth.

▸ **Compare** the distortion of direction, size, and shape on different map projections.

▸ **Describe** the meaning and use of scales in maps.

▸ **Activity** **Predict** the shape of an Earth circumference on a Mercator projection map.

New Terms

inner core	Mercator
outer core	gnomonic
mantle	polyconic
crust	map scale

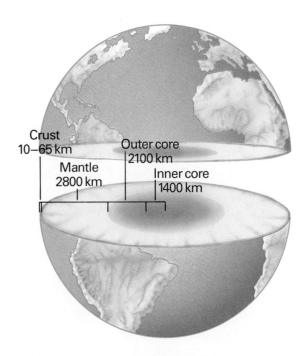

Figure 2-11 If you could cut Earth in two, you might see something like this. The model of Earth's interior is based on indirect evidence from earthquake waves.

Crust
10–65 km

Outer core
2100 km

Mantle
2800 km

Inner core
1400 km

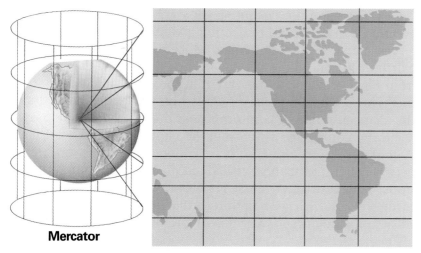

Mercator

Map Projections

Maps are another kind of Earth model. Often, a flat map is a more useful model than a globe, but making a flat map can be difficult. Have you ever tried to fold a tent? While the tent is in use, its walls and floor are smooth. As you take down the tent, you need to fold it to make it lie flat. Cartographers have a similar problem. They draw flat maps of an object that is nearly a sphere—Earth.

Cartographers use several kinds of models, called map projections, to draw Earth on a flat map. The perfect map projection would show correctly the shapes and sizes of continents and oceans. It would show accurately the distance and direction from one place on Earth to another. Unfortunately, there are no map projections that can do all of these things. Instead, different map projections are used for different tasks.

A **Mercator** [mər kāt′ ər] projection, like the one labeled in Figure 2-12, is drawn as if a piece of paper were wrapped around Earth at the equator. Imaginary lines from the center of Earth pass through the surface and on toward the paper, where the map is drawn. As you can see in Figure 2-12, some of the lines spread far apart before they reach the paper. This distorts landforms, that is, it makes landforms appear a different size than they really are. The most distortion is near Earth's North and South Poles. For example, a globe shows that Greenland is about one fifth of the width of South America. On a Mercator projection, those widths appear to be equal. The width of Greenland has been distorted by the Mercator projection.

Mercator projections do have an advantage. A straight line on a Mercator projection is the same as a geographic direction. Thus, Mercator projections are useful for finding out which direction you are traveling.

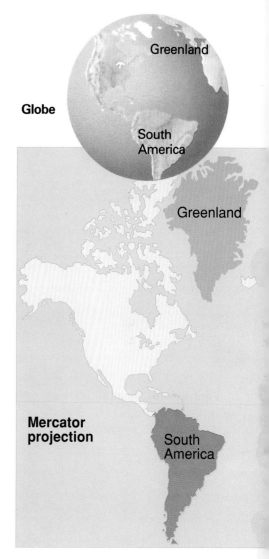

Figure 2-12 *Left:* A Mercator projection map; *Right:* Mercator projection maps make lands near the poles, like Greenland, appear larger than they really are.

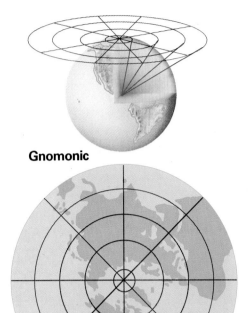

Gnomonic

Figure 2-13 A gnomonic map projection

Distances are more accurate on a gnomonic projection. A **gnomonic** [nō män′ ik] projection is drawn by placing a sheet of flat paper on a point on a globe, often the geographic North or South Pole. Once again, imaginary lines are drawn from Earth's center to the paper. In the gnomonic projection in Figure 2-13, the paper is placed on the North Pole, thus the shape and size of landforms near the North Pole are most accurate. Landforms away from the North Pole are distorted. A gnomonic projection correctly shows the shortest distance between two points on Earth. This makes gnomonic projections useful for navigators. However, directions are harder to figure out with a gnomonic projection because the lines of latitude are curved. Nor does a gnomonic projection show all of Earth.

To demonstrate a **polyconic** [päl′ i kän′ ik] projection, roll the paper into a shape like an ice cream cone and place it on a globe as shown in Figure 2-13. The paper touches all the way around the globe at a middle latitude. For small areas, a polyconic projection is close to a perfect map projection. The lines of latitude and longitude have only a slight curve, so directions are easy to determine. The paper is close to the surface of the globe, so shapes and sizes of landforms are accurate. Many maps of the United States are polyconic projections, including the map in Figure 2-10. You can see the slight curve of a latitude line along the border between the United States and Canada.

Polyconic projections are commonly used to map small areas of Earth. In a polyconic projection, small land areas are hardly distorted at all. In Lesson 2.4, you will learn more about these maps which are used to describe the surface features of Earth in detail.

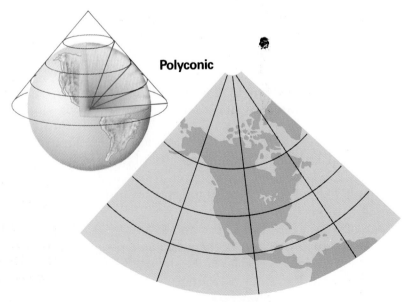

Polyconic

Figure 2-14 A polyconic map projection; Polyconic projections are very accurate for small areas of land.

A C T I V I T Y   2 . 3

GLOBES AND MAPS

Purpose   To predict the mapped shape of an Earth circumference on a Mercator projection map.

Materials

small globe	colored pencils
string	protractor
scissors	Mercator projection
metric ruler	outline map (copy)

Procedure

1. Read all instructions for this activity before you begin your work.

2. Cut a length of string that is 20 cm longer than the circumference of the globe. Mark the string every 2 cm along its length. Wrap the string around the equator of the globe. Tie it snugly.

3. Adjust the position of the string until a mark on the string lies where the equator and the prime meridian cross (latitude 0°, longitude 0°). Mark that same location on your Mercator projection map.

4. Determine the latitude and longitude of a place on the globe that is beneath a mark on the string. Mark that same location on your map. Repeat this step for every mark on your string.

5. Use a colored pencil to connect all of the points on the map.

6. Move the string so that it wraps around the globe along lines of longitude. Write a prediction about the shape of the line you will get when you plot the string marks on the Mercator projection map.

7. Determine the location of the marks on the string as you did in step 4. Mark these locations on your map and connect the points.

8. Move the string so that it crosses the equator at an angle of 45° on two sides of the globe. Write a prediction about the shape of this line on the map. Plot the locations of the string marks on your map as you did in step 4.

Collecting and Analyzing Data

1. Describe the shape of the line on your map that follows Earth's equator. How does the shape of this line on your map compare with the shape of the string around the globe?

2. Compare your predictions with the shapes you drew for the second and third map lines. Were your predictions correct?

3. Each mark on the string is at a specific latitude and longitude when it is on the globe. What must be true about the same positions on the Mercator projection map?

Drawing Conclusions

4. In which case is the shape of the line on the Mercator projection least like the shape of the string on the globe?

5. In which direction(s) must you travel on Earth for your path to be a straight line on a Mercator projection? Support your answer using data from this activity.

ENVIRONMENTAL AWARENESS

Maps—Tools for Exploring the Environment

What tools do you use to explore your environment? Maybe you have used a hand lens, ruler, or thermometer to collect data about the environment. You use tools such as tables and drawings to look for patterns in your data. Maps are also important tools.

The map at the right shows how clouds affected the temperature of Earth on one day. Tools on board a satellite collected the data, and another tool, a computer program, helped analyze the data and draw this map. The map makes it easy to see where clouds caused cooler temperatures. Scientists are using this map and others like it as they try to predict how additional clouds that result from human activity will affect Earth's temperature in the future. ■

Map Scales

For a model to be useful, it needs to be made to scale. A scale model is a small version of an object that shows details of the object in the correct proportion to each other. For example, a model car might be $\frac{1}{1000}$ scale. That means that the model is $\frac{1}{1000}$ the size of the actual car.

A **map scale** is a statement, number, or graph that indicates the relationship between distance on a map and the actual distance on Earth. Map scales are included in map legends. Figure 2-15 shows three ways to express map scale. A simple way is to state the relationship in words, for example, "One centimeter equals one kilometer," or "1 cm = 1 km." This statement means that one centimeter of map distance equals 1 kilometer of actual distance. Another way to show map scale is with a small line that is marked off in distances.

You will often see a map scale shown as a fraction or ratio, such as $\frac{1}{100}$ or 1:100. This kind of scale also tells you the relationship between map distance and actual distance.

Figure 2-15 Map scales can be given as a math statement, as a marked line, or as a ratio. Are these three scales from the same map? How can you tell?

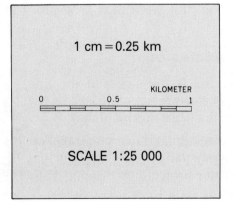

$$map\ scale = \frac{map\ distance}{actual\ distance}$$

When map scales are given as fractions, they do not need measurement units. For example, suppose you are measuring the size of your room using a shoe. You find that your room is 40 shoe lengths long. You draw a map of your room that is only 4 shoe lengths long. You can calculate your map scale as shown.

$$map\ scale = \frac{4\ shoe\ lengths}{40\ shoe\ lengths}$$

$$map\ scale = \frac{1}{10}$$

One shoe length on your map equals 10 shoe lengths in your room. When you simplify the fraction of your map scale, the shoe length units cancel out. If you then measured 1 centimeter on your map, you would find that it equaled 10 centimeters in your room. Your map scale, $\frac{1}{10}$, would work for any unit.

Reading maps is an important part of your study of Earth and the universe. Maps can show the relationship between Earth features like land, water, and the atmosphere far better than written words. In Lesson 2.4, you will learn how to use detailed maps of the landforms on Earth's surface.

Fact or Fiction?

Was Christopher Columbus trying to prove that Earth is a sphere? Many people think that his voyage in 1492 was to prove the shape of the Earth. His real interest, however, was in finding a new trade route to the Far East. Columbus was confident that he could reach Asia from Europe by sailing west. When he reached the land later called America, he thought he had reached Asia. He never learned his mistake. His efforts did, however, lead to future expeditions from Europe to the Americas.

Lesson Review 2.3

9. Draw and label a model of Earth's interior layers. Briefly describe the properties of each layer.

10. Copy the table on map projections below. Complete the table by filling in the missing information.

Projection	How Drawn	Advantages	Disadvantages
Mercator			
Gnomonic			
Polyconic			

11. A legend gives a map scale as $\frac{1}{100\ 000}$.
    a. What does the 1 in the numerator represent?
    b. What does the 100 000 in the denominator represent?
    c. Why are there no units on this kind of scale?

Interpret and Apply

12. Before you move, you draw a map of your new room. You draw the walls using a scale of 1:10, but you do not bother using a scale to draw your furniture. What problems could you have when you try to move furniture into your room based on this map?

2.4 *Topographic Maps*

The participants race through woods and over hills with a good pair of hiking shoes, a set of directions, and a map and compass. The sport of orienteering combines finding directions with a natural obstacle course. The course can include steep hills, swamps, dense vegetation, and rivers. The topographic maps used in orienteering help the participants choose the best path from one checkpoint to another. A **topographic map** illustrates the height and depth of the land and the locations of natural and artificial features, such as woods, marshes, bridges, and roads. The height and depth of land is called **relief.** A topographic map shows relief using lines. Figure 2-10 shows a map that uses color to show relief.

Contour Lines

On a topographic map, a landscape is described with lines that look like fingerprints. Unlike fingerprints, the lines on a topographic map are a flat model of a surface that changes elevation. Elevation is the distance of land above sea level. On a topographic map, **contour lines** connect points on land that have the same elevation. In Figure 2-16, the land surface is hilly. A road runs around the lake. Notice that the road crosses a contour line. There the road goes uphill. Contour lines connect points of equal elevations around the hill. Contour lines never cross each other, and they always close in a loop. Often, however, the whole loop of a contour line does not show on one map.

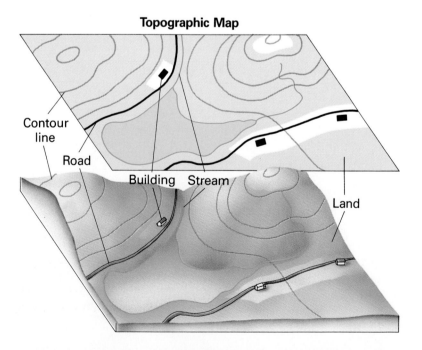

Topographic Map

Contour line

Road

Building   Stream

Land

Figure 2-16 Contour lines show three-dimensional landforms on a flat map.

The **contour interval** is the vertical difference in elevation between one contour line and the next on a map. The contour interval for the map in Figure 2-17 is 10 feet. That means that the land rises 10 feet between each contour line on the map. You can find the contour interval of a topographic map in its legend.

In Figure 2-17, notice that every fifth contour line is darker than the other lines, and is labeled with its elevation. Use the contour interval, 10 feet, to figure out the elevation of the contour lines that are not labeled. For example, point *A* is at the 320-foot contour line, which is the second contour line uphill from the one labeled 300 feet. What is the elevation of point *B*?

You can estimate the elevation of points between contour lines. In Figure 2-17, find Dumplingtown Hill. You know that the peak of the hill is greater than 620 feet, because the 620-foot contour line circles the hill. You know that the hill is less than 630 feet because there is no 630-foot contour line. You can estimate that the elevation of the hill is greater than 620 feet, but less than 630 feet. What are the elevations of points *C* and *D* in Figure 2-17?

Figure 2-17 A portion of a topographic map

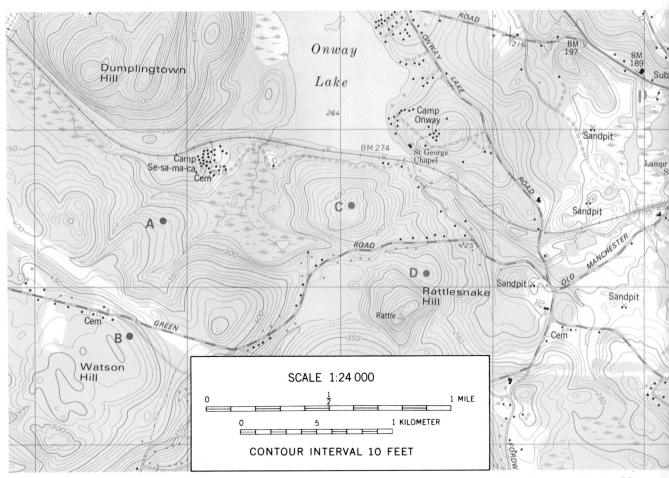

SCALE 1:24 000

CONTOUR INTERVAL 10 FEET

Figure 2-18 A topographic map helps this person choose the quickest path in his orienteering contest.

You can identify landforms using contours even without reading the elevations. A large number of contour lines close together shows a steep area such as a cliff. In Figure 2-17, which hill has a cliff? River valleys form V-shapes that point uphill. A cluster of contour lines that form smaller and smaller circles shows a hill. A cluster of circles on a map can also show a bowl-shaped area, called a depression. A sinkhole is a common depression feature. Topographic maps show depressions with short marks on the inside of the contour line. Find a depression in Figure 2-17.

Slope

Hikers, skiers, and building developers are especially interested in judging the steepness of the land. The closer the contour lines on a topographic map, the steeper the land.

The steepness of an area of land can be expressed as average slope. **Average slope** indicates how much the elevation of an area of land changes as you travel across it. You can calculate average slope using this formula.

$$average\ slope = \frac{change\ in\ elevation}{distance\ traveled}$$

For example, suppose the contour interval on a map is 20 feet. There are 6 contour lines between two points on the map. Thus, the elevation changes by a total of 120 feet as you move from one point to the other. You use the map scale and find that the distance between the two points is 1.2 miles. Use these values to find the average slope as shown below.

Figure 2-19 The average slope of this area is 200 ft/mile. If the person climbed 10 feet in a distance of 0.1 mile, would that slope be more or less steep than the one shown here?

$$average\ slope = \frac{120\ feet}{1.2\ miles}$$

$$average\ slope = 100\ feet/mile$$

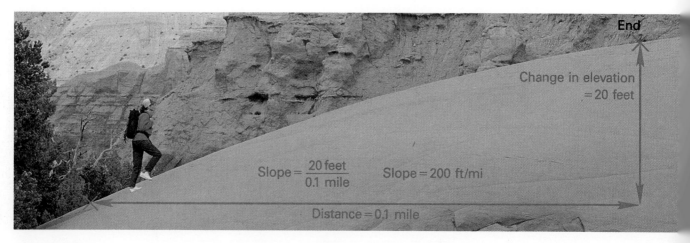

End

Change in elevation = 20 feet

Slope = $\frac{20\ feet}{0.1\ mile}$ Slope = 200 ft/mi

Distance = 0.1 mile

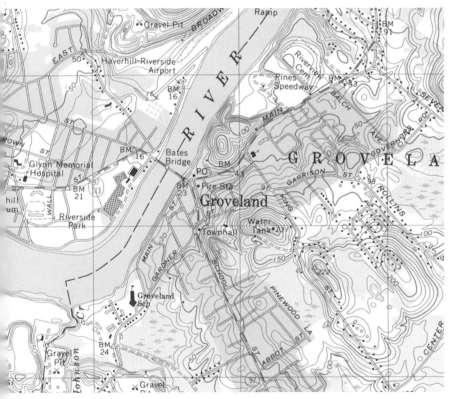

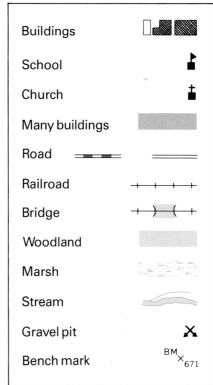

Buildings	
School	
Church	
Many buildings	
Road	
Railroad	
Bridge	
Woodland	
Marsh	
Stream	
Gravel pit	
Bench mark	

Map Symbols

The United States Geological Survey, or USGS, publishes many topographic maps. Figures 2-17 and 2-20 show portions of USGS maps. The latitude and longitude of the area is printed at each corner of the map. The map scale appears at the bottom of the map, along with arrows showing the magnetic declination. This information allows you to determine the location shown on the map, the size of the land area on the map, and your direction as you travel across the area shown on the map. The contour lines allow you to judge changes in elevation.

Figure 2-20 (right) illustrates some symbols that appear on USGS topographic maps. These symbols are published on separate sheets of paper. Notice the colors used to show different features. On a USGS map, wooded areas are green, while open areas are white. Built-up areas such as cities are shaded in pink. Buildings, bridges, and other constructed features each have special symbols, usually in black. Contour lines are brown. Water is shown in blue.

Find a benchmark symbol on Figure 2-20. A benchmark symbol shows a location where the elevation has been carefully measured, and sometimes the latitude and longitude. If you travel to that place, you will find a small metal plate set in concrete or stone. Figure 2-21 shows a bench mark.

Figure 2-20 *Left:* A portion of a USGS topographic map; *Right:* Some symbols used on topographic maps.

Figure 2-21 Bench marks show exact elevations for specific places.

ACTIVITY 2.4

General Supplies

LANDFORMS AND CONTOUR LINES

Purpose   To form a model of a landform from information on a contour map.

Materials

2 copies of Figure 2-22	straws
thin cardboard	glue or paste
scissors	metric ruler

Procedure

1. Read all instructions for this activity before you begin your work.

2. ![] Cut one of your copies of the map along the longest contour line. **CAUTION: Scissors are sharp. Handle them with care.**

3. Trace the outline of the largest contour line onto the cardboard. Cut the cardboard along that line.

4. Now trim the same copy of the map along the next longest contour line. Place the map on another piece of cardboard. Trace around the paper and cut the cardboard as you did before.

5. Cut three lengths of straw that are shorter than the second piece of cardboard. Glue the straw pieces onto the first cardboard piece in a triangle shape, as shown in the figure. Then glue the smaller cardboard piece on top of the straws. Make sure the smaller cardboard piece is in about the same place as the second contour line on your uncut map.

6. To complete your landform, repeat steps 4 and 5 for all the contour lines.

7. Locate points A, B, and C on the uncut map. Mark those locations in the correct position on your landform.

8. Keep your landform and the metric ruler to answer questions 1–6, but clean up all other materials and dispose of scraps.

Collecting and Analyzing Data

1. Each layer in your model is a contour line. Measure and record your contour interval in mm.

2. How much does the elevation change as you move from point A to point B? From point B to C?

3. On the uncut map, measure the distance in mm between points A and B. Then measure the distance between points B and C. Record this information.

4. Calculate the average slope of your model between points A and B, using the formula in the text. Then calculate the average slope between points B and C.

Drawing Conclusions

5. If your landform were a real hill, what would be the most challenging route you could follow to the top? How does the flat map show that this is a challenging route?

6. On your model, what would be the longest path you could follow in a straight line without moving up or down hill? What does this route look like on the map?

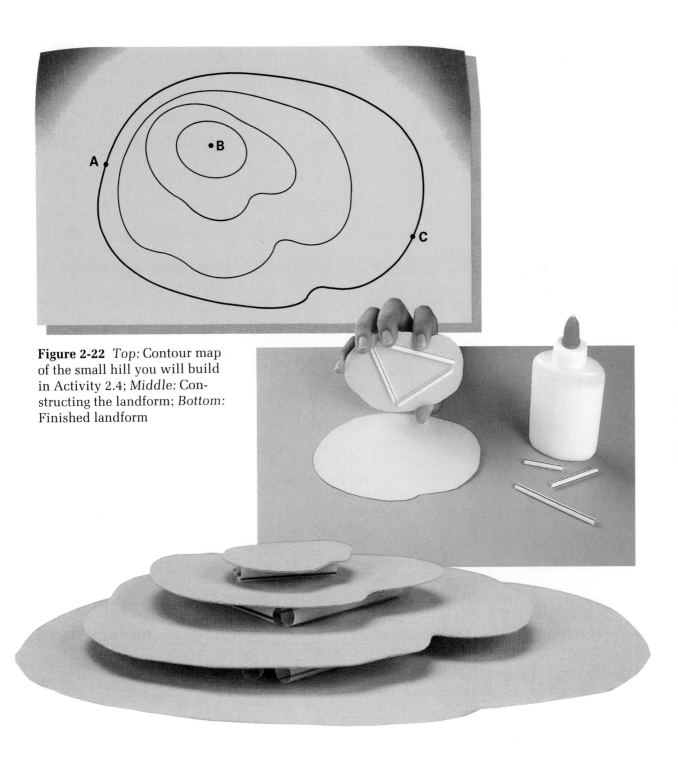

Figure 2-22 *Top:* Contour map of the small hill you will build in Activity 2.4; *Middle:* Constructing the landform; *Bottom:* Finished landform

Figure 2-23 *Clockwise from left:* Geologic map, soil types map, aerial photo, weather map, navigation map

Map Uses and Technology

Topographic maps are just one kind of map. Astronomers use maps that show the locations of stars. Maps used for agriculture may show soil types, water resources, or other features of an area. You have seen weather maps that show conditions in the atmosphere. Maps of the ocean show water movement, temperature, ocean life, or other features. Figure 2-23 shows a few of the many kinds of special purpose maps used in earth science.

Advances in technology provide more map information every year. Satellites and computers have dramatically improved the ability to map Earth's surface. The *Landsat* satellite program has provided views of Earth from space since 1972. *Landsat* satellites carry special cameras that produce images like the one in Figure 2-24. The satellite's cameras receive different kinds of energy from different locations on the surface. A computer on board the satellite converts this energy into a coded radio signal, which it sends to computers on Earth. The computers on Earth decode the signal to form an image of Earth's surface. The colors in a *Landsat* image are not the actual colors of the objects. The computers assign colors that make certain features, such as trees or crops, show up more clearly.

Weather satellites produce the weather images you see on the evening news. Some satellites measure the changing land surface by detecting reflected laser beams. This kind of measurement can help predict volcanic eruptions and detect the slow movement of the continents. Satellite images also show how land is being used, and have helped people take care of Earth's resources.

Figure 2-24 In this *Landsat* image of Vancouver, Canada, plants are red, water is black, city areas are blue, and snow is white.

Lesson Review 2.4

13. Define the terms *contour line* and *contour interval*.

14. On your paper, copy Figure 2-25. On your copy, label these features: hill, swamp, depression, bridge, road.

15. On your copy of Figure 2-25, label the steepest side of the hill. How did you recognize the steepest side?

16. Give some examples of special-purpose maps used in earth science. Why are satellites important to the study of Earth?

Interpret and Apply

17. Explain why it is impossible for contour lines to cross.

18. A student begins a hike at an elevation of 550 feet. After hiking 1.8 miles, the student is at 680 feet. What is the average slope of the land the student hiked?

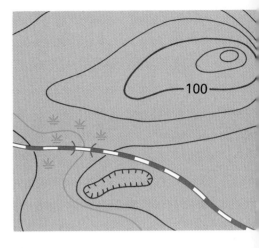

Figure 2-25 Contour map

Chapter Summary

Read this summary of the main ideas in the chapter. If any are not clear to you, go back and review that lesson.

2.1 Finding Direction

■ Geographic north is the direction of the geographic North Pole. In most of the Northern Hemisphere, you can find geographic north by using a midday shadow or the North Star.

■ Magnetic north is the direction of the magnetic pole in Canada. Magnetic declination is the angular difference between magnetic and geographic direction.

2.2 Latitude and Longitude

■ The system of latitude and longitude uses two sets of lines to locate places.

■ Latitude lines measure distances north and south of the equator. Longitude lines measure distances east and west of the prime meridian.

2.3 Models of Earth

■ The model of Earth's interior, based on indirect evidence, shows layers: the inner core, outer core, mantle, and crust.

■ Flat models of Earth, called maps, cannot show distances, directions, and shapes as accurately as a globe. Mercator, gnomonic, and polyconic map projections are used for different purposes.

■ Map scales can be expressed in words, in a line, or in a fraction.

2.4 Topographic Maps

■ A topographic map includes contour lines showing land elevation, as well as symbols showing natural and constructed features.

■ Contour lines connect points of equal elevation. Contour interval tells the distance in elevation between two contour lines.

■ Average slope is the change in elevation divided by the distance traveled.

Chapter Review

■ Vocabulary

average slope
cartographer
contour interval
contour line
crust
equator
frame of reference
geographic north
gnomonic
inner core
latitude
legend

longitude
magnetic declination
magnetic north
magnetosphere
mantle
map scale
Mercator
outer core
polyconic
prime meridian
relief
topographic map

■ Concept Mapping

Use the method of concept mapping described on pages 3–5 to complete a concept map for geographic location. Copy the incomplete map shown. Then fill in the missing terms.

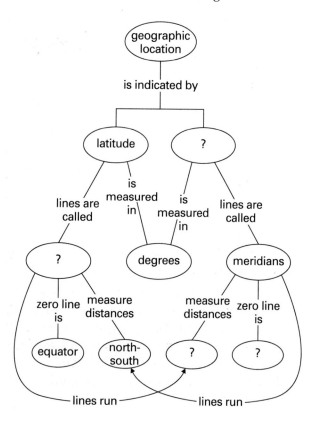

■ Review

On your paper, write the word or words that best complete each sentence.

1. _____ expresses the difference between magnetic and geographic north.

2. _____ is a line that connects points of the same elevation.

3. An Earth layer that is made of melted iron and nickel is the _____ .

4. A(n) _____ indicates the relationship between map distance and actual distance.

5. A(n) _____ constructs maps.

6. The direction to Earth's geographic north pole is _____ .

7. The _____ divides Earth into a Northern and a Southern Hemisphere.

8. You live on the thinnest layer of Earth, called the _____ .

9. _____ is distance from the equator, measured as an angle.

10. A(n) _____ map projection distorts land near the geographic poles.

11. A(n) _____ map uses contour lines to show elevation of land.

12. _____ is a calculation of the steepness of land over a distance.

13. A satellite system that has helped expand knowledge of Earth's surface is called _____ .

14. Longitude lines measure distances in a(n) _____ direction.

15. A set of lines or points that acts as a guide is a(n) _____ .

16. The difference in elevation between two neighboring contour lines is the _____ .

17. You can find information about symbols in a map by using the map's _____ .

18. _____ is a place's angular distance from the prime meridian.

19. A(n) _____ projection is the closest to an ideal projection because it accurately shows distance, direction, and shape.

■ *Interpret and Apply*

On your paper, answer each question.

20. Which way would a magnetic compass needle point if you were standing on the geographic North Pole?

21. Choose one of the following and describe how it works as a frame of reference: athletic field, numbered streets, parking lot, swimming pool. What are the reference lines for the frame of reference?

22. A football field with its end zones is about 100 meters long. A small television screen is 0.10 meter across. What is the map scale of this television screen?

23. On the map in Figure 2-10 on page 47, find the features at these locations.
   a. 28° N, 90° W
   b. 33° N, 112° W
   c. 63° N, 150° W

24. Use the map below to find the following information:
   a. elevation of point *A*
   b. kind of feature at *C*
   c. elevation at benchmark
   d. average slope between points *A* and *B*

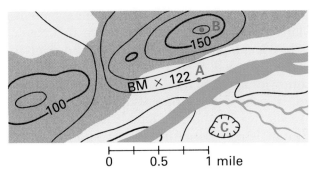

■ *Writing in Science*

25. Good science fiction, while telling an imaginary story, includes some accurate scientific information to make the story seem believable. Imagine that you are part of an expedition that is traveling to the center of Earth. Write a story about what happens on the expedition. Use information that you have learned in this chapter to describe the conditions that you would find. Also name the layers of Earth and the depths at which you find them. The rest of the story is up to your imagination.

■ *Critical Thinking*

The table below describes a journey taken by a student traveler. Copy and complete the table. Then answer questions 26–27. Hint: What is the distance traveled for 1° of latitude?

Part	Starting Location	Direction Traveled	Distance Traveled	Final Location
1	0° N 0° W	east	1120 km	
2	same as end of 1	north		30° N 10° E
3	same as end of 2		3360 km	0° N 10° E
4	same as end of 3	west		0° N 0° W

26. Would you need a boat or airplane for any part of this journey? Explain how you found your answer.

27. What assumption is made in phrases like "down south" and "up north"? How do most maps contribute to this assumption? Think about Earth in space and explain why it would be equally correct and equally incorrect to say "up south" and "down north."

FIRES RAGE IN RAIN FORESTS—GLOBAL WARMING PREDICTED

Issue: *How can the world preserve tropical rain forests?*

Each year as the dry season starts, the skies over Brazil's Rondônia region turn dark. Clouds of smoke rise from fires that destroy 80 000 square kilometers of tropical rain forest each year. The fires are started by settlers who clear the land for farming or herding. The destruction of the world's tropical rain forests endangers millions of species of plants and animals, and it may affect the climate everywhere on Earth.

Tropical rain forests are dense, wet forests in hot climates near the equator. The tropical rain forest has many layers. The highest trees form a canopy that protects the lower layers from the tropical sun. Tropical rain forests cover less than 10 percent of Earth's surface. However, they contain more than half of the world's plant and animal species. If the tropical rain forests disappear, so will all of the species adapted to living there.

Human activities have destroyed about half of the world's tropical rain forests in the last 40 years. Government dams built to supply electricity flood large areas of the rain forest. Loggers cut down trees that never grow back. Cattle ranchers clear trees to make pastures for their herds, and miners use the trees as fuel in furnaces. In the 1970's, Brazil built a new road into the rain forest that attracted thousands of settlers. These settlers hoped that farming would be better than the poverty of large cities. Unfortunately, tropical rain-forest soil has very few nutrients. Every few years, farmers must clear new land when the nutrients are used up.

Developing countries need rain-forest resources for development.

Scientists think that destroying tropical rain forests could cause global warming through the "greenhouse effect." Carbon dioxide in the atmosphere acts like the glass in a greenhouse to help keep Earth's surface warm. But too much carbon dioxide may lead to global warming. Burning trees in the rain forest adds carbon dioxide to the atmosphere, which contributes to the greenhouse effect. Scientists predict that the greenhouse effect could cause major changes in Earth's climate.

Most tropical rain forests are in developing countries that have little money or resources. Many of these poor countries are in debt to rich, developed countries like the United States. In "debt-for-nature swaps," developed countries agree to reduce the debt in exchange for increased government protection of rain forests. Rock concerts have raised money to support debt-for-nature swaps sponsored by environmental groups. These concerts also let people know how important rain forests are.

Some countries are trying to use their tropical rain forests productively without destroying them. People can harvest nuts, fruit, and rubber from the rain forest without harming trees. In Peru, some lumber companies are trying a new method of logging that cuts down narrow strips of forest 25 meters wide. This does not destroy the forest canopy, and the rain forest soon grows back in the shaded clearings. Many countries have used their national parks to preserve tropical rain forests. Costa Rica's national park system, one of the best in the world, protects about one quarter of their tropical rain forests.

It costs money to save the tropical rain forests. But in many cases, developing nations do not have enough money to keep intruders out of their national parks. In Costa Rica, there are not enough rangers to keep loggers from removing trees in the middle of the night. Logging companies can easily bribe the rangers, who are paid very little by the government.

If countries do not work together, the rain forests will be destroyed.

Many countries are pressuring developing nations to stop clearing the tropical rain forests. But developing nations resent being told how to manage their land, especially by countries that pollute their own environments. Many developing nations see the tropical rain forests as their only resource for paying off their large debts. Large-scale projects, such as dams and mines, offer short-term profits that can repay debts. However, these large-scale projects upset the delicate balance of the tropical rain forests. In the future, countries will have to work together to save the tropical rain forests.

Act on the Issue

Gather the Facts

1. Use library articles and books listed in the *Readers' Guide to Periodical Literature* to find out which countries have tropical rain forests. Use an almanac to find out the per person, or per capita income of each country. Then make a table that compares per capita income to the rain-forest area in each country.

2. The rubber industry uses rain forests without destroying them. Look in library books and an encyclopedia to find out how rubber is harvested. Write a one-paragraph report that explains why harvesting rubber does not harm trees.

Take Action

3. Organize an event to raise public awareness about the destruction of tropical rain forests—a school assembly, for example. Write to the Rainforest Action Network (RAN), an international organization that works to preserve rain forests. Ask them for suggestions about organizing your event. You might want the event to coincide with World Rain Forest Week, which takes place each fall. RAN will be able to tell you where and when it will be held this year.

4. One reason that developing nations ignore United States conservation demands is that the United States continues to destroy its forests in the Pacific Northwest and in the Tongass National Forest in Alaska. Find out about logging in national forests by writing to the U.S. Forest Service (U.S.D.A., Public Affairs, P.O. Box 96090, Washington, DC 20090-6090). Then write to your senators or representatives in Congress and ask them what their position is on this issue.

Science in Action

CAREER: Marine Entomologist

Lanna Cheng works at the Scripps Institute of Oceanography, where she studies insects that live in the open ocean. Scripps is located in La Jolla, California.

How did you get interested in such a specialized area of insects?

When I was in school, I was told that there were insects everywhere on Earth except in the ocean. In fact, there are many insects that live out on the open sea. I like working in such a little-known area of study.

Is there a particular insect that you study?

I'm most interested in the water skater. There are at least five species of water skater that live on the sea. But you can find skaters—some people call these insects water striders—in freshwater streams and lakes, and in the intertidal zone between the areas of fresh and salt water.

How would we recognize a water skater?

They're easy to spot because of the way they scoot along the water surface. They rest on four legs. Even before you see the insect, you can see the tiny depressions that each leg makes in the water. The surface tension of the water holds the insect up. When they move, they almost look as though they're rowing along. If there's a strong wind, or if there is a current, then they move in droves along with the surface water.

How did you become an entomologist?

I received a B.S. and an M.S. degree from the University of Singapore, and a Ph.D. from Oxford University in England, where I studied insect ecology. Today I am one of only a couple of dozen people who study this unusual insect habitat.

CAREER: Survey Technician

Sharon Randall is a survey technician for a state department of transportation. She works in a team, setting markers for road and bridge construction.

How did you become a survey technician?

In high school, I spent two years at a vocational school studying technical drafting. When I finished, I had a drafting certificate. When I came to the State Department of Transportation, they needed a person to work on a survey team. With my drafting background, I got the job.

How did you learn about surveying?

They taught me on the job. Running the theodolite is the most interesting part of the job. The theodolite measures angles and directions. It also stores points of information, which I later download into my computer back at the office.

Your work sounds very technical.

It is. We frequently check the grading or cutting needed to build a road. We see if the road will drain properly once it is finished. Sometimes we set marks along a highway that is going to be resurfaced. Then the inspector can figure out how many tons of asphalt will be needed to complete the job.

You seem to enjoy your work.

I really do. I'm also the only woman who has ever been in the surveying department in this state.

HOBBY: Environmental Action

Ivor Kiwi is one of four founding members of Cleveland Youth for the Environment in Cleveland, Ohio.

When did you first become interested in the environment?

I started to take classes at the Cleveland Museum of Natural History when I was in the eighth grade. For the past three years, I've volunteered at the museum's Wildlife Resource Center. That's where people bring injured and orphaned animals. One summer I raised eight baby opossums, all at one time.

I had to get up every three hours to feed them! That's when I began to be concerned about the environment. If we can't take better care of the world, the animals won't survive.

How did your group get started?

I was involved in an environmental awareness group at the museum. One year they organized a conference in Cleveland and raised money to preserve a park in Costa Rica. After that conference, four of us decided to start a group of our own. We're an organization of high school students. Our goal is to increase awareness of environmental issues among young people.

How many students are in the organization?

We have a core group of 10 and about 40 additional members. One of our projects is to try to get schools and churches to start environmental groups of their own. Even though we've only been working on this for a few months, five schools have already started environmental groups.

Astronomy

You Know More Than You Think

You may be surprised at how much you already know about astronomy. To find out, try to answer the following questions.

- *How often do you see a full moon?*
- *What are telescopes used for?*
- *How many planets can you name?*
- *Why does the sun rise and set?*
- *Which star is closest to Earth?*

When you finish this unit, answer these questions again to see how much you have learned.

Telescopes and photographs help you see faint objects, like the cloud of dust and gas shown at the far right.

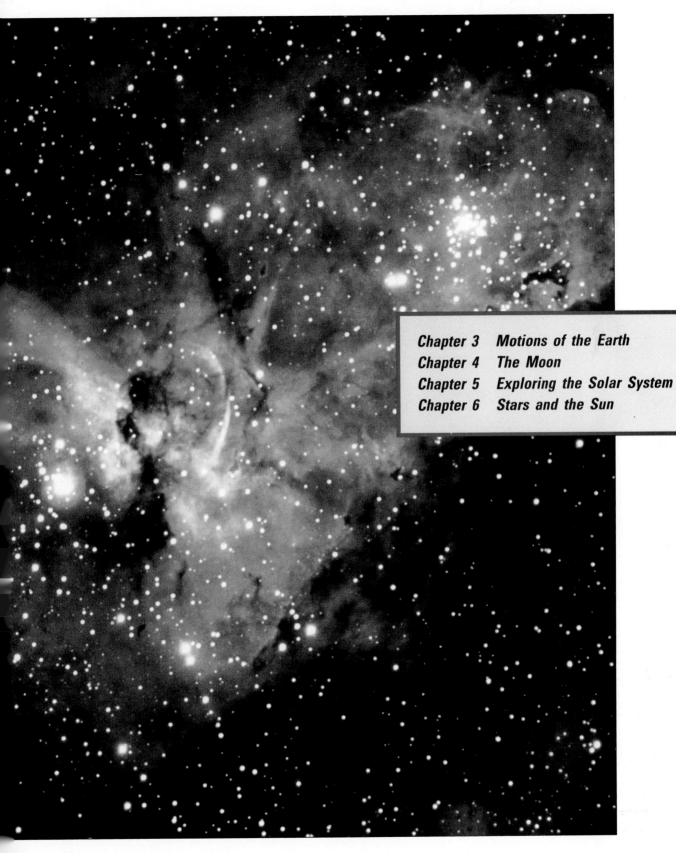

B

Motions of the Earth

Chapter Preview

Have You Ever WONDERED?

Why does summer have to end?

It happens every year. The sun sets earlier each evening as summer passes by. As the nights become longer, the weather becomes cooler. Calendars show that summer ends and autumn begins on or near September 23.

You are familiar with the patterns of change from season to season. The clothes you wear, the sports you play, and the holidays you celebrate change from season to season. The sun's position in the sky is a clue to recognizing the first day of each season. Ancient astronomers noticed the pattern of change in the position of the sun through the year. They designed clocks and calendars based on their observations. Modern astronomers can design very precise clocks and calendars that indicate the exact moment summer ends.

In this chapter, you will observe the position of the sun in the sky. You will also find out how such observations led people to discover how Earth moves during the day and during the year.

3.1 Earth's Rotation

Lesson Objectives

▸ **Demonstrate** a way to locate objects in the sky.

▸ **Use a model** to explain why the sun appears to rise and set.

▸ **List** some of the effects of Earth's rotation.

▸ **Activity** **Measure** the position of the sun using a shadow.

New Terms

altitude	rotation
gnomon	axis

Have you ever asked for help to find an item in a store? Many stores use a frame of reference to help customers find items. One set of lines in a store's frame of reference is the aisles. Each aisle guides you to groups of items. Another set of lines is the shelves in each aisle. You may be told that an item is on the top shelf, about halfway down the fourth aisle. The aisle number, the shelf, and the distance are equally important for finding an item.

You learned about one frame of reference in Chapter 2. Longitude and latitude are used to find places on Earth. You can also use a frame of reference to find an object in the sky, such as the sun, the moon, or a star. To find an object in the sky, you need to know how high in the sky to look. You also need to know in what direction to look. Direction and height are the two sets of lines in a frame of reference for the sky.

The Sun in the Sky

The word *altitude* has a number of meanings. For example, to a mountain climber or mapmaker, *altitude* refers to the height of land above sea level. In astronomy, **altitude** refers to the height of an object in the sky above the horizon. The altitude of an object in the sky is measured by an angle instead of by meters or miles. Figure 3-1 shows how you can demonstrate the sun's altitude. With one arm, point to the sun. Hold your other arm level and point to the horizon directly under the sun. The angle between your arms is the altitude of the sun. The level arm provides a frame of reference for measuring the sun's altitude above the horizon.

Figure 3-1 The sun's altitude is its height above the horizon, measured as an angle.

Ancient astronomers used instruments called gnomons to measure the sun's altitude. A **gnomon** [no′ mən] casts a shadow that can be used to find the sun's position. Sundials, like the one in Figure 3-2, are one kind of gnomon. The simplest kind of gnomon is an object that points straight to the center of Earth. Buildings, towers, and sticks can all be simple gnomons.

Figure 3-3 shows how to use a gnomon. Place the gnomon on a level surface outdoors in the sunlight. Check that the gnomon and the level surface form a right angle. (A right angle is a 90° angle.) The shadow of the gnomon is the level reference line for measuring altitude. Now imagine a line between the end of the shadow and the top of the gnomon. In Figure 3-3, this line is drawn in and is labeled *Line A*. Line A points to the sun. The angle between the shadow and Line A is the sun's altitude.

Because you cannot really see Line A, you need an extra tool to measure altitude. Your extra tool is a scale drawing. You learned about map scales in Chapter 2. A scale drawing is similar to a map scale. In Figure 3-3 *(left)*, the actual gnomon is 66 centimeters tall, including the base. The gnomon's shadow is 94 centimeters long. In Figure 3-3 *(right)*, the scale is 1 centimeter = 11 centimeters. In Figure 3-3 *(right)*, the drawing of the gnomon is 6 centimeters tall. The drawing of the shadow is 8.5 centimeters long. Use a protractor to measure the sun's altitude angle, which is between the shadow and Line A. The altitude angle in both Figure 3-3 *(left)* and *(right)* equals about 35°. Ninety degrees (90°) is the highest altitude an object can have in the sky.

Figure 3-2 A sundial casts a shadow that can be used to find the sun's position. What is another name for the stick on the sundial?

Figure 3-3 Using the shadow of a gnomon to find the sun's altitude; *Left:* the gnomon; *Right:* a scale model of the gnomon

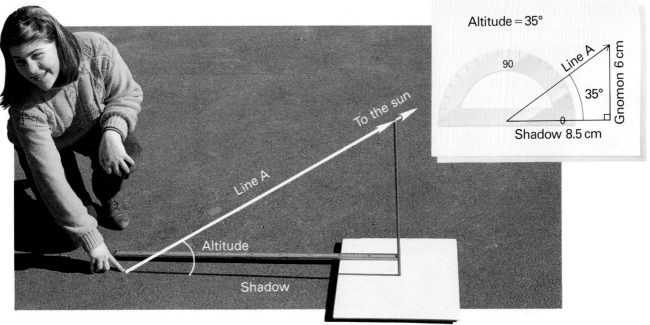

MEASURING THE SUN'S POSITION

Purpose To measure the altitude of the sun.

Materials

index card	protractor
paper clip	large sheet of paper
tape	(about 60 cm × 60 cm)
straw	standard size plain paper
metric ruler	watch or clock
meterstick	

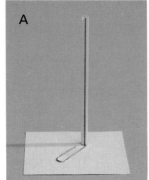
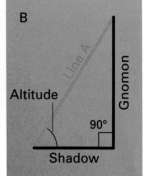

Procedure

1. Read all instructions for this activity before you begin your work. Copy the data table onto your paper.

2. To make a gnomon, bend a paper clip so it forms a right angle (90°), as shown in Figure A. Tape the paper clip to the index card. Push one end of the straw over the standing loop of the paper clip.

3. Measure and record the height of your gnomon.

4. Draw a line across the large sheet of paper. Label one end of the line *geographic north*. Make a dot in the middle of the line. Push your pencil through the dot to punch a hole in the paper.

5. Push your gnomon up through the center hole on the paper. Put the sheet of paper and the gnomon on a sunny, level surface. DO NOT MOVE THE PAPER UNTIL YOU ARE FINISHED.

6. Use a ruler and pencil to trace the shadow of the gnomon on the paper. Write the time next to the shadow tracing and in your data table.

7. If your teacher says to, wait a few minutes and then repeat step 6. Then take your materials and return to your desk.

Collecting and Analyzing Data

Data Table			
Time	**Height of Gnomon (cm)**	**Length of Shadow (cm)**	**Altitude Angle (°)**

1. Measure the length of the shadow tracing. Record the length in your data table.

2. Make a drawing of the gnomon and its shadow, similar to Figure B. Make the line lengths the same as the length of your real gnomon and its shadow.

3. Draw Line A to connect the gnomon and its shadow in your drawing. Measure the angle between the shadow line and Line A. Record this as the altitude.

Drawing Conclusions

4. If you made two shadow tracings, describe any differences between them.

5. Why would the length of the gnomon's shadow change during the day?

6. If you made this measurement later today, would there be much change? Explain.

Models of Earth's Spin

Albert Einstein supposedly asked some students this question: "How would the sun appear to move across the sky if the sun moved around Earth?" Earth is not to be moving in this situation. Think about the question. The answer may seem too simple! If the sun moved around Earth, then the sun would appear to move across the sky.

Many ancient astronomers thought that all objects in the sky moved around Earth. Dr. Einstein wanted his students to respect this hypothesis of the ancient astronomers. You learned in Chapter 1 that a hypothesis is a possible solution or explanation for an event. A model, you recall, is a picture or demonstration that explains what is observed in nature. Early astronomers based their model of the universe on their observations of Earth and the sky.

You probably have made the same observations as those early astronomers. You have seen that the sun rises in the morning. You have seen shadows change their length and direction as the sun changes position. Different windows are sunny at different times of day.

Early astronomers made other observations about the sky. Objects such as the moon and stars appear to rise in the east, move across the sky, and set in the west. Stars also appear to move around the star Polaris, which is the North Star. Figure 3-4 *(top)* is a photo of the night sky. At night, the lens of a camera must be held open to get enough light for a photograph. If something moves while a photo is being taken, a streak is left on the film. The streaks of light in Figure 3-4 *(top)* were made by stars. Compare these star streaks to the streaks of light made by the headlights of moving cars in Figure 3-4 *(bottom)*. Both photos show that something moved while the photo was being taken.

Some early astronomers found it hard to accept that the sun and other objects moved around Earth. One reason was the incredible speed those objects would need to make it around Earth once a day. Another reason was that the sun did not look like a moving object. Astronomers compared the sun to shooting stars, which are also called meteors. Meteors move across the sky in any direction. They do not always move from east to west, like the sun. The sun appears to be a round ball of fire. It does not leave a streak of light, like a moving meteor does.

The astronomers who questioned the earth-centered model needed a new model. What if the sun is not moving? Perhaps Earth is rotating. **Rotation** is the spinning of an object around an axis. An **axis** is a real or imaginary straight line that goes through the center of a rotating object.

Figure 3-4 *Top:* Which moved during this photo: the stars in the sky or the camera on Earth's surface? *Bottom:* These headlight trails show that the cars moved.

ENVIRONMENTAL AWARENESS

Saving Energy with the Sun

Summer or winter months can bring long spells of hot or cold weather. As people use electric energy to cool or heat homes and businesses, electric companies may be unable to keep up with the extra demand, and an energy shortage results. You can conserve electric energy by using the sun.

In summer, keep your home cool by lowering window blinds. Lower the blinds on the east side of your home in the morning; in the evening, lower blinds on the west. If your home has awnings, check to make sure they shade the windows from mid-morning until mid-afternoon when sunlight is most direct. On sunny winter days, raise blinds on windows that face the sun. Lower all blinds at night to help hold in thermal energy.

In any season, remember that sunlight is free. By using natural light to read, play games, and do outdoor work, you are saving energy. ■

The wheels of a car rotate around a real axis. A basketball spinning on the end of your finger rotates around an imaginary axis. Earth's spinning around an axis would make objects in the sky appear to move around you.

Eventually, astronomers found out that their model of Earth rotating is correct. The observations of the sun and stars can be explained by the new model. Imagine that you are standing at point X in Figure 3-5. As Earth rotates, the sun comes into view in the eastern sky. As Earth continues to rotate, the sun appears to move across the sky. It then disappears from view in the west. This happens every day.

Figure 3-5 To the person at Point X, it looks as though the sun moves across the sky while Earth turns.

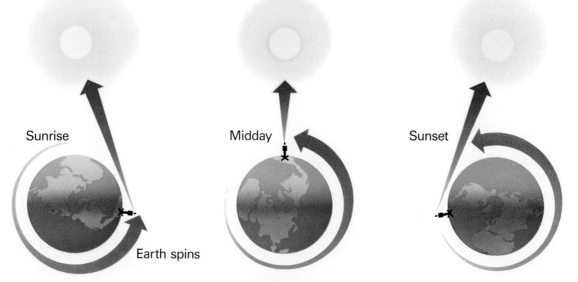

Sunrise — Earth spins

Midday

Sunset

Effects of Earth's Spin

Some effects of Earth's rotation are not as obvious as day and night. Earth's rotation also causes the streaks of light left by the stars in Figure 3-4. There are always two places on a spinning object that do not move in a circle. These places are at each end of the axis. On Earth, the ends of the axis are the geographic North and South Poles. A star directly over one end of Earth's axis would not appear to move. The star directly over Earth's North Pole is called Polaris. Other stars appear to move around Polaris because you are riding on Earth. The other stars in the photo made streaks because the camera was also riding on Earth.

You learned in Chapter 2 that Earth is not a perfect sphere. Earth's shape is affected by its rotation. Think about pizza dough stretching out as it spins in the air. Like the spinning pizza, Earth bulges out at the equator as it spins. Compared with the bulging equator, Earth's North and South Poles are slightly flattened.

Figuring out that Earth spins was a major turning point for early astronomers. The new model explained the sun's changing position during the day. Early astronomers made other observations as well. For example, why does the sun's position in the sky change from season to season? In Lesson 3.2, you will learn about these observations and how to explain them using a model of Earth's motions.

Lesson Review 3.1

1. Define the term *altitude*.

2. Describe how you could use your arms to show a friend the altitude of the sun.

3. Draw and label a diagram that shows how Earth's rotation causes day and night. Write a short explanation of your diagram.

4. List and describe two results of Earth's rotation.

Interpret and Apply

5. Copy Figure 3-6 of a gnomon, shown at right. On your copy, use the gnomon's shadow to draw and label the sun's altitude.

6. In Figure 3-6, is it morning or afternoon? Explain.

7. Predict what would happen to Earth's shape if Earth rotated more quickly.

Figure 3-6 A gnomon

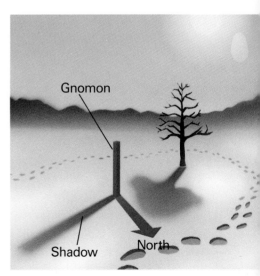

Gnomon

Shadow   North

3.2 Earth's Revolution

New Terms

revolution	fall equinox
orbit	winter solstice
ellipse	spring equinox
summer solstice	

Have you ever noticed that during the summer, the daytime is long and nights are short? As summer passes, there are fewer hours of daylight. The shadows at midday become longer. The weather turns cooler. These and other familiar changes happen every year.

In Lesson 3.1, you learned how the sun's apparent movement across the sky can be explained by Earth's rotation. Early astronomers made other observations they also wanted to explain. The changing times of daylight and darkness during the year was one observation. The fact that shadows are generally longer in winter than in summer was another. Some astronomers already thought that the sun was not moving around Earth. They wondered whether Earth might be moving around the sun. The movement of one object around another object is called **revolution.**

A Model of Earth's Orbit

In the early 1600's, astronomers developed an accurate model of Earth's orbit. An **orbit** is the path an object follows as it revolves around another object. In the sun-centered model, Earth spins (rotates) on its axis as it revolves around the sun. The sun-centered model best explains observations of objects in the sky. Modern astronomers have been able to prove that this model is correct.

One part of the sun-centered model that may surprise you is that Earth's orbit is not a perfect circle. Orbits of planets, including Earth, are ellipses. An **ellipse** is an oval shape with two focal points. Figure 3-7 shows how to draw an ellipse using a pencil, string, and two tacks. In the picture, the two tacks are the two focal points of the ellipse.

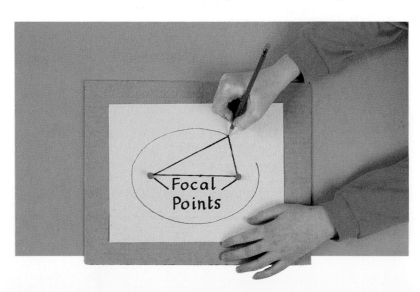

Figure 3-7 You can draw an ellipse using these simple materials. Earth's orbit is an ellipse, but it is more circular than this ellipse is.

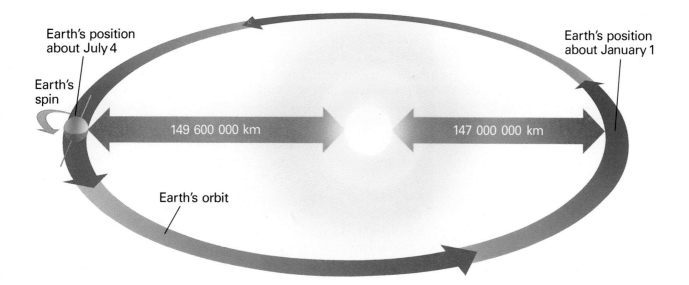

Earth's position
about July 4

Earth's
spin

149 600 000 km

147 000 000 km

Earth's position
about January 1

Earth's orbit

Figure 3-8 illustrates the sun-centered model of Earth's orbit. Earth takes one year to go all the way around its orbit once. Notice that the sun is at one of the focal points of Earth's ellipse-shaped orbit. The sun's location means that Earth is not always the same distance from the sun. Earth is closest to the sun on about January 3 of each year. On that date, the distance between the sun and Earth is about 147 000 000 kilometers. Earth is farthest from the sun, 149 600 000 kilometers, about July 4 of each year. Thus, Earth's distance to the sun changes by 2 600 000 kilometers from January to July. Although this difference may seem great, it is not important when compared with the size of Earth's orbit. The difference in Earth's distance from the sun is not enough to cause seasons. Think about it this way: If you live in Los Angeles, you are farther from New York City than from Philadelphia, but the difference is not important. You are about as far away from both cities.

Recall from Lesson 3.1 that shadows change length as the sun changes altitude, from sunrise to midday to sunset. Midday is defined as the time when the sun reaches its highest altitude for the day. Midday occurs at a time near noon each day (near 1:00 P.M. daylight saving time). Early astronomers who measured the sun noticed that the sun's midday altitude changes every day of the year. Table 3-1 lists examples of the sun's midday altitude on different days of the year, measured at 40 degrees north latitude. In Table 3-1, notice that the sun's greatest midday altitude is on June 21. The values for the sun's midday altitude decrease during the summer and autumn months. The values increase during the winter and spring months. When is the sun's midday altitude the smallest?

Figure 3-8 Earth moves around the sun in an ellipse-shaped path called an orbit.

Table 3-1
Sun's Midday Altitude at 40° N Latitude

Date	Altitude*
January 21	30°
February 21	39°
March 21	50°
April 21	62°
May 21	70°
June 21	74°
July 21	71°
August 21	62°
September 21	50°
October 21	40°
November 21	30°
December 21	27°

*values rounded to the nearest degree

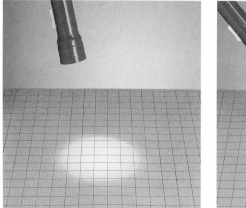
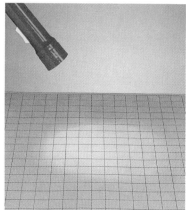

Figure 3-9 In which case does the light energy from the flashlight hit the paper more directly?

Seasons

The sun's changing altitude is the main reason temperatures are different each season. Figure 3-9 shows how you can demonstrate the reason that the sun's altitude affects temperature. In the photo, the flashlight represents the sun. On the left, the flashlight is at a high altitude. Light from the flashlight strikes the surface more directly. On the right, the flashlight is at a low altitude. The same amount of light spreads out over a larger part of the surface. In winter, when the sun is at lower altitudes, the spreading out of the sun's energy causes lower temperatures.

The model of Earth's revolution in Figure 3-10 includes an explanation for the changes in the sun's position. Figure 3-10 shows that Earth's orbit lies in an imaginary flat surface called a plane. Compare the position of Earth's axis with the plane of Earth's orbit. You might expect Earth's axis to be

Figure 3-10 As Earth revolves around the sun during the year, its axis always points in the same direction.

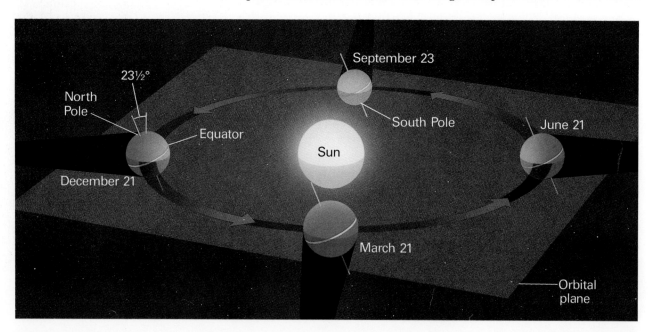

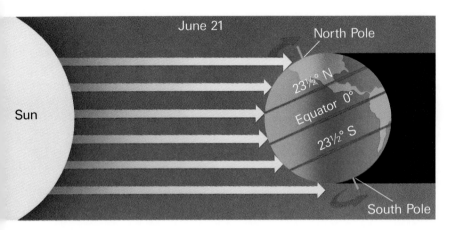

June 21

North Pole

23½° N

Equator 0°

23½° S

Sun

South Pole

Figure 3-11 About June 21, the Northern Hemisphere is facing the sun more directly than any other day of the year. What is this day called?

straight up and down at an angle of 90° when compared with Earth's orbital plane, but it is not. Figure 3-10 shows that Earth's axis is tilted at an angle of 23½° when you compare the axis with a line that makes a 90° angle with Earth's orbit. Earth's axis keeps this same tilt as Earth moves through its orbit during the year.

The tilt of Earth's axis explains several observations about the sun's position in the sky during the year. On Figure 3-10, place your finger on Earth on June 21. As you read, follow Earth's path through the year. About June 21, the sun shines most directly on Earth's Northern Hemisphere, because the Northern Hemisphere is tilted toward the sun. Remember from Table 3-1 that the day when the sun is highest in the sky at midday is near June 21. The day when the sun's midday altitude is greatest is called the **summer solstice,** or the first day of summer. In the summer, you need to look high in the sky to see the sun. People living at latitude 23½ degrees north see the midday sun directly overhead on the summer solstice.

The day of the summer solstice has the most hours of daylight. In Figure 3-11, imagine Earth spinning once on June 21. Places north of the equator spin through sunlight for more hours than they spin through Earth's shadow. The sun rises earlier and sets later than at other times of the year. Because of the more direct angle of the sun and the longer hours of sunlight, temperatures are warmer in summer than at other times of year.

Now move your finger around Earth's orbit toward the September position in Figure 3-10. As summer passes, the sun rises later and sets earlier. About September 23, the hours of daylight equal the hours of night. Earth's axis is still tilted, but the tilt does not make Earth point toward or away from the sun. This day, halfway between summer and winter, when daylight and night are equal, is called the **fall equinox.** The word *equinox* means "equal night."

Figure 3-12 *Top:* You can tell seasons are changing by observing changes in nature. *Bottom:* The length of day and night are equal on the fall equinox.

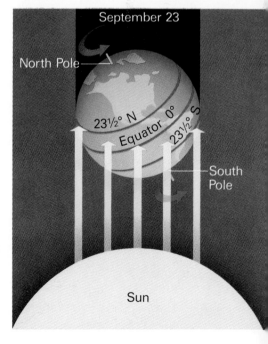

September 23

North Pole

23½° N

Equator 0°

23½° S

South Pole

Sun

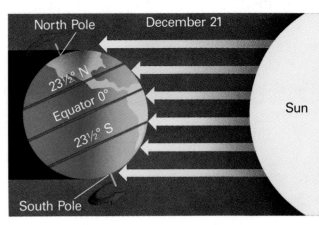

North Pole

December 21

23½° N

Equator 0°

23½° S

Sun

South Pole

Figure 3-13 *Left:* These students are enjoying winter weather. *Right:* Does the North Pole face the sun at any time on the winter solstice?

You may have noticed that winter nights are much longer than winter days. In Figure 3-10, follow Earth's orbit to December. The **winter solstice** happens when the Northern Hemisphere spends the fewest hours facing the sun. Because of the tilt of Earth's axis, the Northern Hemisphere is tilted away from the sun in the winter. The winter solstice happens near December 21. On the winter solstice, the midday altitude of the sun is the smallest. This means you need to look lower in the sky to see the sun. It also means that the sunlight is less direct and temperatures are lower.

The tradition of the Yule log began in northern European countries. As winter approaches, the nights become longer and the midday altitude of the sun decreases. People would find a fireplace log so large that it would burn until daytime was getting longer again.

From December 21 until June 21, the hours of daylight increase again as Earth continues in its orbit. As you trace Earth's orbit in Figure 3-10, pause at March 21. The spring equinox occurs about this time. On the **spring equinox,** the hours of daylight equal the hours of nighttime. The fall and spring equinoxes are halfway between the summer and winter solstices. On both equinoxes, the sun is directly overhead at midday for people who live near the equator. People who live at middle latitudes know the spring equinox as a time of renewed plant growth.

Figure 3-14 In areas with four seasons, the time near the spring equinox means renewed plant growth.

All of the solstice and equinox dates you have just learned are opposite for people living south of the equator. Find a place south of the equator on Figure 3-10 and follow it through a year's orbit. In places south of the equator, such as Australia and Chile, the sun has its highest altitude about December 21. Remember that the sun's highest altitude means the first day of summer. Thus, December 21 is the first day of summer in the Southern Hemisphere! Which dates would be the first day of fall, winter, and spring in the Southern Hemisphere?

ACTIVITY 3.2

A MODEL OF EARTH'S ORBIT

Purpose To build a model that shows Earth's position at the beginning of each season.

Materials
4 foam balls	heavy cardboard
4 round toothpicks	drawing compass
2 thumbtacks	scissors
string loop	dark crayon or paint
lightweight cardboard	

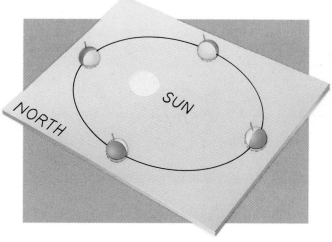

Procedure

1. Read all instructions for this activity before you begin your work.

2. Push a toothpick through the middle of each foam ball. **CAUTION: The toothpicks are sharp.** Each toothpick should stick out on two sides of its ball.

3. Place the lightweight cardboard over the heavy cardboard. Use the thumbtacks and string loop to draw a large ellipse on the cardboard, using the method shown in Figure 3-7. **CAUTION: Thumbtacks are sharp.**

4. The ellipse you drew represents Earth's orbit. Draw and label the sun at one focus of the ellipse. Label this side of the cardboard *North*.

5. Draw four circles on the ellipse, one near each edge of the cardboard. Each circle should be about the size of one of the foam balls. Use the scissors to carefully cut out the inside of each circle to make four holes. DO NOT CUT OUT THE SHAPE OF THE ELLIPSE.

6. Find the hole nearest the sun. Push one ball into the hole. Adjust the ball so the toothpick points slightly away from the sun, to show that Earth's axis is tilted.

7. Now push the other balls into the holes. Make sure that the toothpicks in each ball point in the same direction, as shown in the figure.

8. Use the paints or crayon to color the night side of each foam ball.

Collecting and Analyzing Data

1. Refer to Figure 3-10. Label the cardboard near each of your Earth models with the closest date—March 21, June 21, September 23, or December 21.

2. Look at your model. On which dates is sunlight falling evenly on both the Northern and Southern Hemispheres?

3. What does your model show about the North Pole on December 21? June 21?

Drawing Conclusions

4. On which of the four dates shown in your model does the Northern Hemisphere have the most direct sunlight?

5. On which of the four dates shown is Earth closest to the sun? What is this date called in the Northern Hemisphere?

6. Explain how your model shows that Earth's distance from the sun is not the cause of seasons on Earth.

January—
Orion visible

Orion

July—
Sunlight makes
Orion invisible, but
Lyra is visible.

Lyra

Figure 3-15 Earth's revolution makes the constellation Orion visible in winter months but not in summer months. The constellation Lyra is visible in summer months but not in winter months.

Stars and Seasons

Have you ever noticed the group of bright stars in Figure 3-15 *(left)*? This group of stars forms a constellation named Orion, the hunter. For many people in the Northern Hemisphere, Orion is visible in early evenings in winter. It is not visible in the summer.

The changes in the stars you see can also be explained by the sun-centered model. There are thousands of stars visible in the sky. As Earth moves through its orbit during the year, you face different stars at different times of day or night. Figure 3-15 *(middle)* helps illustrate the reason. During winter days, your part of Earth faces the sun. Any stars that you are facing during the daytime are invisible because of the bright sun lighting up Earth's atmosphere. During winter nights, your part of Earth faces away from the sun. You can see stars like the ones that make up Orion.

Lesson Review 3.2

8. Explain why Earth is not always the same distance from the sun.

9. Describe the changes in the midday altitude of the sun between June and December. Explain why these changes occur, according to the model of Earth's orbit.

10. Why do the stars you see at night change during the year?

Interpret and Apply

11. How much would the midday altitude of the sun change during a year if Earth's axis were not tilted?

3.3 Clocks and Calendars

Early people, such as ancient Egyptians, noticed that the length of nighttime increases and decreases during a year. They noticed that during times of the year when the sun's altitude was large, the seasons were warm. During times of the year when the altitudes were small, the seasons were cooler. These observations of patterns led to the designs of clocks and calendars.

Recall that on an equinox, the length of daylight is equal to the length of night. Early people divided the period of daylight on an equinox into 12 equal parts called hours. On an equinox, night also lasts 12 hours. An entire day, which is one rotation of Earth, was thus divided into 24 hours of time. Each new day starts at 12:00 midnight. For convenience, people decided to make the length of an hour the same throughout the day, even when the period of daylight and night are unequal.

Time Zones

Suppose you set a clock to 12:00 noon when you see the sun at its highest altitude. A friend who lives several kilometers east or west of you does the same. When you call your friend on the phone, you find out that your watches are not set to the same time. Because Earth rotates, you and your friend saw the sun at its highest altitude at different times. Thus, you have different times on your clocks. If you wanted to meet your friend at 3:00 P.M., you would not know whose clock setting to go by.

To avoid problems created by different local times, Earth was divided into standard time zones. A **standard time zone** is a wide area in which all clocks are set to the same time. There are 24 time zones worldwide, one for each hour in the day. Each time zone is about 15 degrees of longitude wide. The borders of time zones vary. Generally, highly populated places are not divided by time zone borders. As you travel west, you go back to an earlier hour each time you cross a time zone border. As you travel east, you move ahead to a later hour at each time zone border.

You can cross all 24 time zone borders if you travel all the way around Earth. With 24 time zones, one for each hour, a change in the date has to occur somewhere. The **international date line** is an imaginary north-south line in the Pacific Ocean. As you travel west across the date line, you travel to a later day. If it is 8:00 A.M. Wednesday east of the line, it is 8:00 A.M. Thursday west of the line. What happens if you travel from west to east across the date line?

Lesson Objectives

▶ **Relate** the measurement of time to the motions of Earth.

▶ **Demonstrate** the use of time zones and the international date line.

▶ **Explain** the need for leap years and leap seconds.

▶ **Activity** *Interpret data* in a map of time zones.

New Terms

standard time zone
international date line
leap year

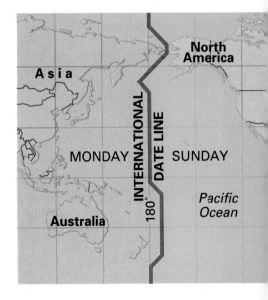

Figure 3-16 The international date line generally follows 180° east and west longitude, except where it would cause one country to have two different days.

There are other changes that affect how you set your clock. Like most of the United States, you may have daylight saving time. If you do, you set your clock one hour ahead of standard time in the spring. In daylight saving time, the sun's highest altitude occurs around 1:00 P.M. instead of around 12:00 noon. Daylight saving time is a clock change that gives you more daylight in the evening. In the fall, you set your clock back one hour to standard time to get more daylight in the morning again. You can remember how to set your clock by saying, "Spring forward, fall back."

Figure 3-17 The United States has six time zones. Which time zone do you live in?

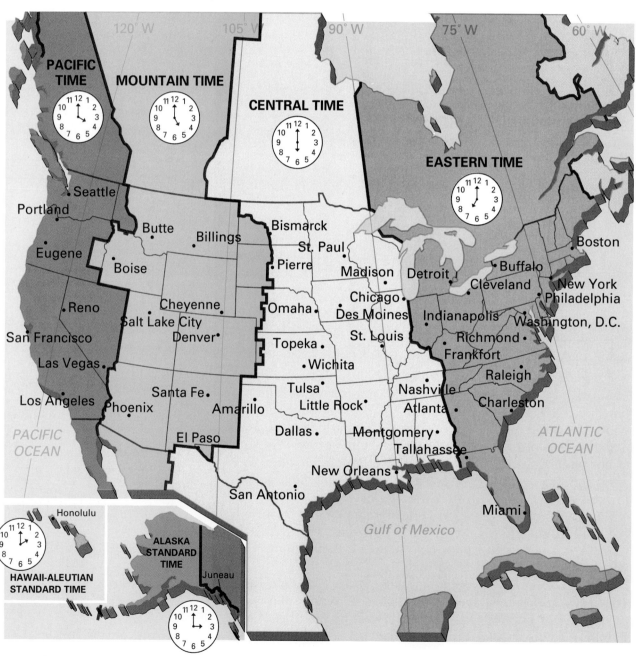

ACTIVITY 3.3

Paper & Pencil

READING A TIME ZONE MAP

Purpose To interpret a time zone map of the United States.

Materials

United States	paper
time zone map	pencil
(Figure 3-17)	

Procedure

1. Read all instructions for this activity before you begin your work.

2. Copy the data table onto your paper.

3. On the map in Figure 3-17, different time zones are shown with different colors. Small clocks show the time in each zone when it is 7:00 P.M. in the Eastern time zone. To use the map for other times of the day, count the number of hours difference between the zones. For example, if it is 1:00 P.M. Mountain time, it is 3:00 P.M. Eastern time, because Eastern time is 2 hours later than Mountain time. Refer to the map in Figure 3-17 to complete your data table. Then answer Questions 1–6 under Collecting and Analyzing Data and Drawing Conclusions.

Collecting and Analyzing Data

Data Table			
City	Time A	Time B	Time C
Atlanta	12 noon		
Boise			
Chicago			1:00 A.M.
Juneau			
Honolulu			
Los Angeles		6:30 P.M.	
New York			
San Antonio			
Seattle			

1. How many different time zones are represented by the cities in your data table?

2. List pairs of cities from your data table that are in the same time zone.

3. For which time (Time A, Time B, or Time C) do some cities have different dates as well as different times? Explain how you know.

4. Clocks in Detroit and Boston are both set to Eastern time. In which of these two cities would the sun rise later by clock time? Explain your answer.

5. The state of Arizona and many counties in the state of Indiana stay on standard time while other areas change to daylight saving time. If it is 9:00 P.M. daylight saving time in San Francisco, California, then what time is it in the following areas:
   a. Phoenix, Arizona
   b. Santa Fe, New Mexico
   c. Dallas, Texas

Drawing Conclusions

6. Notice that the distance from Bismarck, North Dakota, to Dallas, Texas, is about the same as the distance from Bismarck to Seattle, Washington.
   a. What is the difference in time between Bismarck and Dallas? Between Bismarck and Seattle?
   b. Does the distance between two cities help you predict whether they are in the same time zone? Explain your answer.

Motions of the Earth 87

Figure 3-18 This structure may have served as a calendar for the ancestors of the Pueblo Indians.

Calendars

As you learned in Lesson 3.2, people know the first day of each season by the position of the sun. The first days of each season are the days that calendars are based on. A calendar measures the passing of time during a year.

The ancestors of the Pueblo Indians built a city in Chaco Canyon, New Mexico, about 1000 years ago. Figure 3-18 shows one of their buildings, which seems to work like a giant calendar. The building uses the sun to tell time. On the first day of summer, sunlight passes through a window and hits a special shelf in the wall. That does not happen on any other day of the year. There are structures like the one in Chaco Canyon all over the world. Stonehenge, in England, may also have been built to mark the first day of each season.

Today's calendar was first designed thousands of years ago. Since then, it has been changed several times to make sure it keeps up with Earth. Earth needs about 365¼ days to make a complete revolution around the sun. After four years, Earth is a whole day behind in its orbit compared with the same calendar day four years before. Every four years, your calendar has an extra day, February 29. The extra day, called leap day, gives Earth a chance to catch up to the starting point in its orbit. Years that have an extra day are called **leap years.**

Have you ever heard of a leap second being added to December 31? Every few years, a leap second is needed because Earth does not quite make a complete rotation each day. Some work that is done in astronomy and with satellites requires this level of precision. For everyday life, however, keeping track of leap year is precise enough.

Lesson Review 3.3

12. Which Earth motion determines the length of a day? Of a year?

13. How many rotations of Earth take place during the time Earth completes one revolution of the sun?

14. Explain why leap day is added to the calendar every four years.

Interpret and Apply

15. If it is 2:00 P.M. where you are, what time is it for a friend who lives two time zones to the west of you?

Chapter Summary

Read this summary of the main ideas in this chapter. If any are not clear to you, go back and review that lesson.

3.1 Earth's Rotation

■ The length of a shadow can be used to measure the altitude of the sun in the sky.

■ The sun appears to move in a path across the sky. The sun's apparent movement was originally explained by an Earth-centered model, but is now known to be a result of Earth's rotation.

■ Earth rotates on an imaginary axis. Earth's rotation causes day and night.

3.2 Earth's Revolution

■ Earth has an elliptical orbit and thus is not always the same distance from the sun.

■ The sun's midday altitude changes from season to season in a regular pattern.

■ Earth's axis is tilted at an angle of 23½° when compared with a line that makes a 90° angle with Earth's orbit. This tilt is the reason Earth has changing seasons. Distance from the sun does not cause seasons.

■ The position of the sun in the sky at midday determines the beginning of each season.

■ Earth's revolution also causes a change in the stars that are visible during each season.

3.3 Clocks and Calendars

■ The length of a day is based on the time it takes Earth to rotate once on its axis.

■ Earth is divided into 24 time zones. Time changes by one hour at each time zone boundary. The date changes at the international date line.

■ The length of a year is based on the time it takes Earth to revolve once around the sun.

■ Leap years and leap seconds provide time for Earth's rotation to catch up with its revolution.

Chapter Review

Vocabulary

altitude	orbit
axis	revolution
ellipse	rotation
fall equinox	spring equinox
gnomon	standard time zone
international date line	summer solstice
leap year	winter solstice

Concept Mapping

Using the method of concept mapping described on pages 3–5, complete a concept map for Earth's motions. Copy the map below. Then fill in the missing terms.

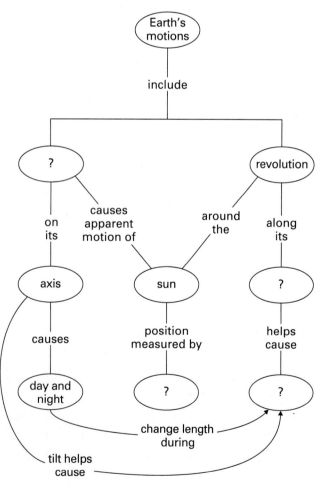

Review

Number your paper from 1–14. Match each term in List **A** with a phrase in list **B**.

List A

a. altitude	**h.** orbit
b. axis	**i.** revolution
c. day	**j.** rotation
d. ellipse	**k.** standard time zone
e. equinox	**l.** summer solstice
f. gnomon	**m.** winter solstice
g. leap year	**n.** year

List B

1. an object that casts a shadow used to measure the sun's position in the sky
2. the shape of Earth's orbit
3. Earth's spin on its axis
4. an imaginary line around which an object rotates
5. movement of Earth in its orbit
6. the angle between a level line and a line pointing to an object in the sky
7. a day when daylight and night are equal lengths
8. path of an object as it moves around another object
9. occurs every four years
10. area in which all clocks are set the same
11. period of time determined by Earth's revolution
12. period of time determined by Earth's rotation
13. day when the sun reaches its highest midday altitude of the year
14. day when the sun has its lowest midday altitude of the year

■ Interpret and Apply

On your paper, answer each question in complete sentences.

15. An athletic field has one end facing east and another facing west. Why would it be equally fair for teams if the games were played at midday?

16. What adjustments would have to be made to the calendar if Earth moved more slowly along its orbit?

17. When you use a gnomon, why is it important to set it up on a level surface?

18. Explain why the roof overhang shown below allows more sunlight through the windows during winter months but less during summer months.

19. Imagine a planet whose axis is at a 90° angle when compared with the plane of its orbit. (In other words, the axis is not tilted.) Explain why this planet would not have changing seasons.

20. On the planet in question 19, would you see the same stars every night of the year? Explain your answer.

21. Many objects are used to provide shade. Some of these objects can be adjusted so they keep providing shade during the day.
   a. Name at least three everyday objects that are used to provide shade.
   b. Why is it important for these objects to be adjustable?

■ Writing in Science

22. A topic sentence is a sentence in a paragraph that expresses the paragraph's main idea. Write a paragraph explaining why it is impossible to design a calendar in which every year has exactly the same number of days. Choose the best of the following choices for your topic sentence.
   a. Every fourth year has an extra day added to the month of February.
   b. A year is the exact time it takes Earth to make one complete revolution around the sun.
   c. The calendar that we use today is considerably different from the one that was used in ancient times.

■ Critical Thinking

The table below lists information about six imaginary planets near an imaginary sun. Use the information in the table to answer questions 23–26. Explain and support your answers, using drawings when necessary.

Planet	Is Axis Tilted?	Does Planet Rotate?	Does Planet Revolve?
A	yes	yes	yes
B	yes	yes	no
C	yes	no	no
D	no	no	no
E	no	no	yes
F	no	yes	yes .

23. Which planet(s) would have changing seasons? Which planet(s) would not?

24. On which planet(s) would the sun rise and set just once each year?

25. On which planet(s) would the sun reach the same midday altitude every day?

26. Which planet(s) would not need time zones?

4 The Moon

Chapter Preview

Have You Ever WONDERED?

Why can't you see a full moon every night?

The full moon on the opposite page has dark patches on its surface. To some people, these patches look like an outline of a face or a rabbit. Once a month, you can see the full moon rising at sunset. The full moon stays up all night, and sets around the time the sun rises. In the nights that follow a full moon, the moon rises later each night, and less and less of the moon's surface is lighted. Eventually, you see only a thin crescent moon rising at dawn. After that, the moon disappears for a few days. The moon then reappears in the evening as a thin crescent. With each passing night, more of the moon's surface is lighted, until the moon is full once again.

Have you ever heard someone say that things are so crazy that it must be a full moon? Some people think that lunacy is more common around the time of the full moon. Perhaps people are more likely to notice the full moon when something unusual occurs, but they may fail to notice when things are normal around the time of the full moon. In this chapter, you will discover the effects of the moon's motions. You will also learn about its features and about space vehicles that travel around Earth, to the moon, and beyond.

4.1 *The Motions of the Moon*

Lesson Objectives

▶ **Compare** the rotation and revolution of the moon.

▶ **Describe** the phases of the moon.

▶ **Distinguish** between solar and lunar eclipses.

▶ **Determine** the effects of the gravitational attraction between the moon and Earth.

▶ **Activity** **Form a model** that explains the phases of the moon.

New Terms

phases	lunar eclipse
umbra	tides
penumbra	universal law of
solar eclipse	gravitation

Have you ever noticed that the moon's shape and position in the sky changes night by night? In Chapter 3, you learned that our modern clocks and calendars are based on Earth's motions. Many ancient calendars were based instead on the regular, repeating patterns of the moon's motions.

The moon, like Earth, rotates on its imaginary axis. It revolves in an orbit around Earth. These motions result in the phases of the moon, eclipses of the sun and moon, and ocean tides on Earth. In this lesson, you will find out how the moon's motions explain these events.

Rotation and Revolution

As you read in Lesson 3.2, Earth's orbit is an ellipse. The moon's orbit also is an ellipse. On average, the distance from Earth to the moon is 382 000 kilometers, or about 30 times Earth's diameter. The moon takes 27.3 days to complete one revolution around Earth. This is the same period of time the moon takes to complete one rotation on its imaginary axis. Because the moon's rotation period equals its revolution period, you always see the same side of the moon from Earth.

The side of the moon that always faces Earth is called the near side. Figure 4-1 illustrates why you see only the near side of the moon from Earth. The person sitting in the chair represents Earth. Imagine that you are the person representing the moon. To keep facing the person in the chair, you must slowly rotate as you revolve. In the time it takes to complete one revolution, you must rotate once. The moon also rotates once on its axis as it makes one complete revolution.

Figure 4-1 Because the moon rotates once per revolution, its near side always faces Earth.

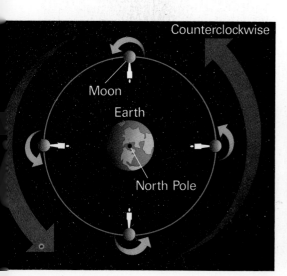

The photograph in Figure 4-2 shows the side of the moon that you cannot see from Earth. Where could this photograph be taken from? The side of the moon you never see is called the far side of the moon. You may hear it called the dark side, but that name is incorrect. Every part of the moon receives sunlight at some time of the month.

Phases of the Moon

If the moon produced its own light, as the sun does, you would see a full moon every day. But the moon shines by reflected light from the sun. As a result, the moon changes its appearance during a month. These monthly changes in the appearance of the moon are called **phases.**

The phases of the moon are shown in Figure 4-3. In this figure, you are looking down on Earth and the moon from above Earth's North Pole. The moon orbits Earth counter-clockwise, as shown by the curved arrows. Sunlight shines on Earth, creating daytime on one half of Earth, and night-time on the other half. Sunlight also causes day and night on the moon. Notice that the daytime side of the moon does not always face Earth. As the moon orbits Earth, your changing view of its lighted side causes the phases.

What does the new moon look like? In Figure 4-3, imagine yourself on the side of Earth facing the new moon. Turn your book to do this. What do you see? You cannot see the new moon because the lighted side faces away from you.

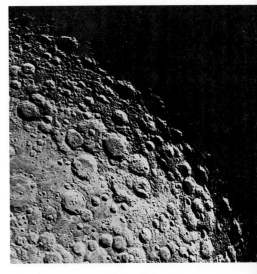

Figure 4-2 How does the moon's far side look different from its near side?

Figure 4-3 The phases of the moon depend on the angle between the sun, the moon, and Earth. Which side of the moon is always lighted?

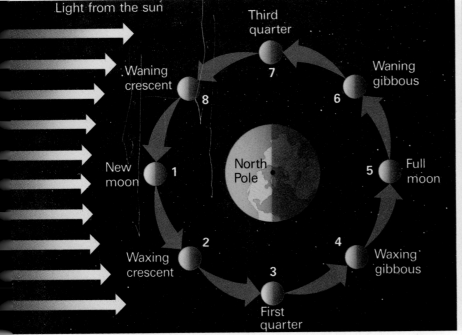

Phases of the moon as seen from Earth

1 New moon
2 Waxing crescent
3 First quarter
4 Waxing gibbous
5 Full moon
6 Waning gibbous
7 Third quarter
8 Waning crescent

The Moon 95

After the new moon, the percentage of the near side that is lighted slowly increases. As the moon grows fuller, it is said to be waxing. A few days after the new moon, you see the waxing crescent phase. The crescent phase is curved, or crescent-shaped. About one week after the new moon, you see the first quarter phase. At this phase, the moon has completed one quarter of its orbit. From your viewpoint on Earth, which side of the first quarter moon is shining?[1]

As you can see in Figure 4-3, the waxing gibbous phase follows the first quarter phase. In the gibbous phase, more than half of the near side of the moon is lighted. About two weeks after the new moon, the moon is full. At the full moon phase, the entire near side is lighted. After the full moon, the percentage of the near side that is lighted slowly decreases. Between the full moon and the new moon, the moon is said to be waning. The waning gibbous phase is followed by the third quarter and waning crescent phases.

The complete cycle from new moon to new moon or from full moon to full moon takes about 29.5 days. Figure 4-4 shows why this period is longer than the revolution period of the moon. The new moon occurs at position A, when the moon is between Earth and the sun. After 27.3 days, the moon is at position B, having completed one orbit. However, the moon is not yet between Earth and the sun because Earth has moved. The new moon occurs two days later, when the moon "catches up" to Earth.

You may want to observe the phases of the moon yourself. Look for the waxing moon in the afternoon or evening sky. If you look for it at the same time each night, you can watch the moon move eastward as it grows fuller. By the night the moon is full, it rises in the east at sunset and stays up all night. In the waning phases, look for the moon rising later at night or setting during the day.

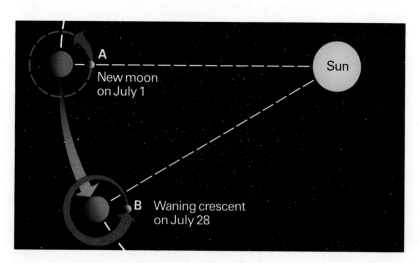

Figure 4-4 The cycle of lunar phases takes longer than the orbital period of the moon.

ACTIVITY 4.1   General Supplies

PHASES OF THE MOON

Purpose   To make a model of the moon's phases.

Materials

clear light bulb   plastic foam ball
lamp   pencil

Procedure

1. Read all instructions for this activity before you begin your work. Copy the data table onto your paper.

2. Attach the plastic foam ball to the pencil by gently pushing the pencil point into the ball. The ball is a model of the moon.

3. Put the lamp on a table where several student groups can use it as a light source. **CAUTION: Make sure electrical cords do not dangle from worktables.** Turn on the lamp. Darken the room as much as possible.

4. Hold the moon model at arm's length directly between you and the source of light. This represents position 1 in the figure, with your head as Earth and the lamp as the sun.

5. Make a sketch showing the light and dark areas on the model moon. Record the name of the phase and a description of the side of the moon facing you.

6. Move the moon model to position 2. To do this, rotate to your left through an angle of 45° (⅛ of a full circle). Then repeat step 5 for this position.

7. Repeat step 5 as you move the moon model to the remaining positions of the lunar cycle. IMPORTANT: In position 5, you must hold the moon higher than your head.

8. Before leaving the laboratory, clean up all materials.

Collecting and Analyzing Data

Data Table			
Position	Phase	Sketch	Description
1			
2			

1. Compare your observations at positions 1 and 5.

2. In which phase(s) is the left side of the moon lighted and the right side dark?

3. Compare your observations at positions 3 and 7. How does the angle between the sun, moon, and Earth compare for these positions?

Drawing Conclusions

4. What causes the phases of the moon? (Hint: From where in space would you always see a full moon?)

5. How could you demonstrate that the rotation of the moon on its axis does not affect the phases of the moon?

Solar Eclipses

The moon and Earth have shadows that always point away from the sun. As you can see in Figure 4-5, shadows caused by large light sources such as the sun have two parts. The darkest part of the shadow is called the **umbra.** The umbras of the moon and Earth are shaped somewhat like cones. From within the umbra, no part of the sun can be seen. The lighter parts of the shadow are called the **penumbra.** From within the penumbra, you could see part, but not all, of the sun.

The shadows of Earth and the moon cause eclipses of the moon and sun. A **solar eclipse** occurs when the moon's shadow hits Earth. As seen from Earth, the moon passes in front of the sun, blocking its light. **CAUTION: Never view a solar eclipse directly! Do not trust filters or film negatives to protect your eyes!**

A total solar eclipse occurs when the moon's umbra strikes Earth. During a total eclipse, the moon blocks the sun's light completely. The sky darkens, and stars become visible. Because Earth rotates, the sun is totally eclipsed for only a few minutes at any one location on Earth. A partial solar eclipse occurs where the moon's penumbra strikes Earth's surface. During a partial solar eclipse, the moon partially blocks the sun's light, and the sky darkens slightly. All total eclipses start with a partial eclipse because the penumbra hits Earth before the umbra does.

Solar eclipses can occur only at the new moon, when the sun, moon, and Earth are lined up. Why doesn't a solar eclipse occur at every new moon? The new moon's shadow usually misses Earth because the moon's orbit is tilted at an angle of 5° compared to Earth's orbit. Sometimes the new moon is north of the line between the sun and Earth, as shown in Figure 4-6. Then the shadow of the moon falls to

Figure 4-5 *Top:* All solar eclipses begin with a partial eclipse. *Bottom:* During a total solar eclipse, which lasts only a few minutes at any given location on Earth, the sun's corona becomes visible. *Right:* Solar eclipses can occur only at the new moon. Notice that only a small area of Earth sees a total solar eclipse.

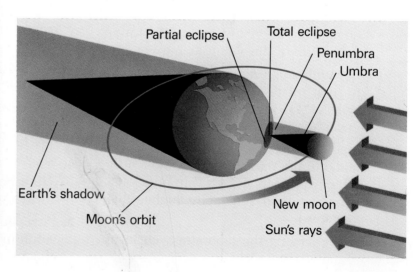

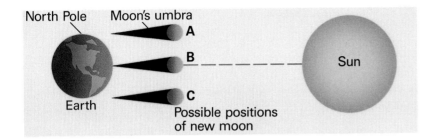

North Pole — Moon's umbra

A

B — — — — — Sun

C

Earth

Possible positions of new moon

Figure 4-6 Because the moon's orbit is tilted, the new moon's umbra usually falls north or south of Earth. In which position of the moon, A, B, or C, does an eclipse occur?

the north of Earth. At other times, the new moon is south of the sun-Earth line. Then the moon's shadow is south of Earth. A solar eclipse occurs only when the new moon is in a direct line with the sun and Earth. This happens about twice each year.

Lunar Eclipses

A **lunar eclipse** occurs when the moon passes through Earth's shadow. A lunar eclipse can occur only at the full moon phase, as shown in Figure 4-7. During a total lunar eclipse, the full moon completely enters Earth's umbra. Although most of the sun's light is blocked by Earth, Earth's atmosphere bends some red light toward the moon. The red light gives the eclipsed moon a reddish glow. In a partial lunar eclipse, part of the moon remains in Earth's penumbra. Only some of the sun's light is blocked.

Lunar eclipses, like solar eclipses, do not occur every month. When the full moon is north or south of the line between Earth and the sun, Earth's shadow misses the moon. As a result, lunar eclipses occur about as often as solar eclipses. But you are more likely to see a lunar eclipse because anyone on the night side of Earth can see it. Solar eclipses are visible only from a small area of Earth.

Figure 4-7 *Left:* Lunar eclipses can occur only at the full moon. Notice that anyone on Earth's night side can see a lunar eclipse. *Top:* All lunar eclipses begin with a partial lunar eclipse. *Bottom:* By what light do you see a total lunar eclipse?

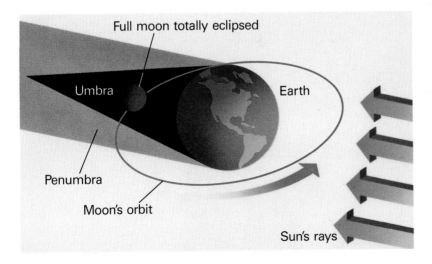

Full moon totally eclipsed

Umbra

Earth

Penumbra

Moon's orbit

Sun's rays

Figure 4-8 The Bay of Fundy, in Nova Scotia, Canada, has extreme low tides and extreme high tides.

Gravity and Tides

The moon affects you with more than its light and shadow. The gravity of the moon and the sun combine to produce the tides on Earth. **Tides** are the daily rise and fall of sea level in oceans, seas, and other large bodies of water. High tide occurs when the sea level is highest. Low tide occurs when the sea level is lowest. In most coastal areas, there are two high tides and two low tides each day.

The tides were first explained by Sir Isaac Newton as he studied the force of gravity. Newton realized that Earth's gravity keeps the moon in its orbit. If you tie a ball to a string, you can spin it in a circle. You must pull on the string to keep the ball moving in a circle. If you let go of the string, the ball will fly off in a straight line. If Earth did not pull on the moon, the moon would fly off into space.

Newton developed a **universal law of gravitation,** which states that *each object in the universe has a gravitational attraction for every other object.* The attraction between two objects depends on their masses and on the distance between them. The greater the mass of an object, the greater its gravitational pull on other objects. The closer two objects are to each other, the greater the attraction between them. According to this law, the moon must exert a gravitational pull on Earth. Newton realized that this force causes the tides.

Figure 4-9 illustrates the gravitational pull of the moon at three points on Earth. The moon's gravity pulls on Earth's near side more than it pulls on Earth's far side, because gravity depends on distance. These forces tend to create two bulges in Earth's oceans. One bulge is on the near side of Earth; the other bulge is on the far side. As Earth rotates, a coastline approaching a bulge has a high tide. Between the bulges, coastlines have low tides.

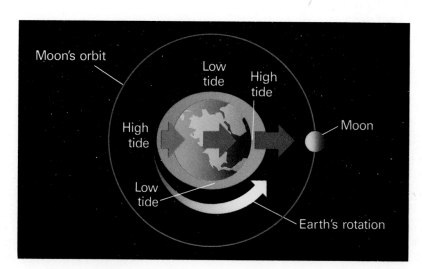

Figure 4-9 The moon's gravity causes tides on Earth by stretching the oceans into an oval shape.

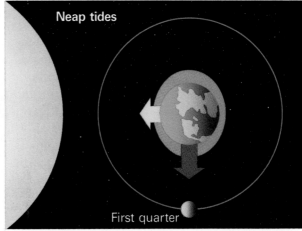

The sun's gravity also contributes to the tides. Twice each month, at new moon and full moon, the sun and moon combine their gravity to produce very high tides and very low tides. These tides, shown in Figure 4-10, are called spring tides. At the first quarter and the third quarter phases, the sun and moon are not working together, and there is a smaller difference from low to high tide. These smaller-than-average changes are called neap tides.

Newton's study of the tides led to a better understanding of gravity. The force of gravity that holds the moon in its orbit pulls on all objects on Earth. In the next lesson, you will learn how spacecraft overcome Earth's gravity to orbit Earth or travel to the moon.

Figure 4-10 *Left:* Spring tides occur at new moon and full moon. *Right:* Neap tides occur at the first quarter and third quarter phases. How do these diagrams show that the moon's gravity affects the tides more than the sun's gravity?

Lesson Review 4.1

1. How are the rotation and revolution of the moon similar? How are they different?

2. Sketch and label the moon's waxing phases. Then draw the waning phases. How do the waxing phases compare with the waning phases?

3. Sketch and label the sun, Earth, and moon in a solar eclipse. Include the shadows of both the moon and Earth. Then sketch a lunar eclipse.

4. Spring tides occur at what phase(s) of the moon? When do neap tides occur?

Interpret and Apply

5. How much of the moon's surface could you see from Earth if the moon did not rotate as it revolves?

4.2 Exploring Space

In the early 1900's, Dr. Robert Goddard dreamed that rockets could go into space and even to the moon. Goddard launched his first liquid-fuel rocket in 1926. Over many years, he did experiments to develop larger and more powerful rockets. Although Goddard's rockets never reached space, other scientists built on his work. In 1957, Goddard's dreams were realized when the Soviet Union launched *Sputnik I* into orbit. Since then, thousands of satellites and other spacecraft have been launched into space.

Rocket Launches

The muscles in your legs can exert a lot of force. You use those muscles to move forward or jump up. As your legs push against Earth, the rest of your body goes in the opposite direction. If you could push hard enough, you would launch yourself into space. But you wouldn't get far, would you? As soon as your feet leave the ground, you are no longer pushing against Earth. Gravity brings you back to Earth.

The speed, or velocity, needed to escape the gravity of a planet or moon is called the **escape velocity.** The escape velocity at the surface of Earth is 11.2 kilometers per second. At that speed, you could travel across the United States in just over seven minutes! Spacecraft and satellites are launched by rockets. To escape Earth's gravity, rocket engines must provide a steady and powerful push, or thrust. The heavier the satellite or spacecraft being launched, the greater the thrust needed to send it into orbit.

How do the engines continue to push the rocket upward after it has left the surface of Earth? Look at Figure 4-11. The burning fuel in a rocket produces a steady supply of hot, expanding gases. The gases rush out of an opening in the rear of the rocket. The rocket moves forward. Many people think that the gases push on the air behind the rocket, sending the rocket forward. But if that were true, then how could a rocket work in the vacuum of space, where there is no air?

Imagine that you throw a ball to someone while you are on roller skates. You move backward when the ball leaves your hand. According to the principle of action and reaction, when object A exerts a force on object B, object B reacts by exerting an equal but opposite force on object A. When you throw the ball, you exert a force on it. In turn, the ball exerts a force on you. In the same way, a rocket pushes on the exhaust gases, sending them out the rear of the engine. The gases in turn push on the rocket, sending it forward.

Lesson Objectives

▶ **Explain** how rockets overcome the pull of gravity.

▶ **Describe** the relationship between a satellite's speed and its distance from Earth.

▶ **Describe** the environment inside a spacecraft.

▶ **Activity** **Perform an experiment** showing how a spacecraft could simulate gravity.

New Terms

escape velocity
orbital speed
orbital period
geosynchronous satellite

Figure 4-11 As the space shuttle blasts off, the rocket boosters push down on the exhaust gases, and the exhaust gases push up on the rocket boosters.

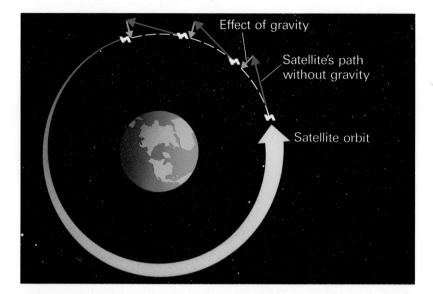

Effect of gravity

Satellite's path
without gravity

Satellite orbit

Figure 4-12 A satellite is constantly falling at just the right rate to stay in orbit. If Earth's gravity suddenly disappeared, what would happen to the satellite?

Satellites

What keeps a satellite in orbit? A satellite is constantly falling toward Earth, as you can see in Figure 4-12. However, it is also moving forward. Because the surface of Earth is curved, the forward motion of the satellite tends to move the satellite away from Earth. If a satellite moves forward at just the right speed, it stays at the same height above Earth in a perfectly circular orbit. However, most satellite orbits are actually ellipses.

The speed of a satellite is called its **orbital speed.** Each satellite at a particular distance from Earth moves at the same orbital speed, regardless of the mass of the satellite. Satellites at different distances from Earth have different orbital speeds. Satellites closer to Earth move faster than satellites farther from Earth because gravity is stronger closer to Earth's surface.

The time required for a satellite to complete one revolution around Earth is called its **orbital period.** Satellites in smaller orbits have shorter orbital periods than satellites in larger orbits. The data in Table 4-1 show the distance from Earth, the orbital speed, and the orbital period for three satellite orbits.

Table 4-1 Satellite Orbits			
Satellite	Distance from Earth's Surface	Orbital Speed	Orbital Period
Space shuttle	500–1000 km	28 000 km/h	85–105 minutes
Communication satellite	35 900 km	11 000 km/h	24 hours
Moon	384 000 km	3680 km/h	27.3 days

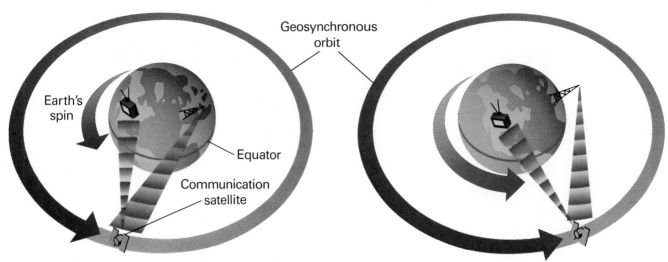

Figure 4-13 *Left:* This communication satellite orbits above the equator. *Right:* Because the satellite is in geosynchronous orbit, it always stays above one point on Earth.

The communication satellite in Figure 4-13 moves in an equatorial orbit, parallel to Earth's equator. Because this satellite has an orbital period of 24 hours, it keeps pace with Earth's rotation and stays above one point on Earth's surface. This kind of satellite is called a geosynchronous satellite. **Geosynchronous** [jē′ ō sin krə nəs] **satellites** move in equatorial orbits at a distance of 35 900 kilometers from Earth's surface. Many communication satellites are geosynchronous satellites. You use them to send and receive television and telephone signals.

ENVIRONMENTAL AWARENESS

A Junkyard in Space

Since 1957, more than 15 000 artificial satellites have been launched into orbit. About two thirds of these have reentered Earth's atmosphere and burned up. Of the 5000 remaining satellites, only 300 still function. The rest are "space junk."

Space junk now includes more than 40 000 fragments larger than golf balls and billions of smaller fragments. Many fragments come from military tests and accidental explosions of rocket boosters. While small fragments pose no direct threat to people on Earth, there is a growing danger to

satellites and spacecraft. A small chip of paint cracked the windshield of the space shuttle *Challenger* in June of 1983. A similar collision could destroy the Hubble Space Telescope during its 17-year life span.

What can be done about space junk? New "garbage-disposal" satellites have been proposed to clean up space. However, it is cheaper and easier to reduce space junk at its source. Many countries have agreed to ban military explosions in space, while scientists are finding ways to prevent accidental explosions. ■

Getting to the Moon

In 1961, President John F. Kennedy set a goal: to land people on the moon by the end of the decade. This goal was realized when the lunar module from the *Apollo 11* mission landed on the moon on July 20, 1969. Ten previous *Apollo* missions and thousands of people had prepared for this event, and no one was disappointed. Five more successful *Apollo* missions followed, landing astronauts on several other locations on the moon.

Figure 4-15 shows the path taken to the moon by the *Apollo 11* spacecraft. The first stage and second stage of the *Saturn 5* rocket fired the spacecraft into Earth orbit. Then the third stage of the rocket propelled *Apollo 11* toward the moon. Because the moon is a moving target, the spacecraft was not pointed at the moon. Instead, it was pointed toward the place where the moon would be three days later when the spacecraft arrived.

Once in orbit around the moon, a smaller spacecraft, the lunar module, separated and landed. The lunar module carried two astronauts, Neil Armstrong and Edwin "Buzz" Aldrin. The third astronaut, Michael Collins, remained behind to pilot the command module. The astronauts explored the lunar surface for just over two and a half hours, collecting 22 kilograms of surface material. After they completed their mission, part of the lunar module separated and blasted off to return to lunar orbit. Small rockets provided enough power for lift-off because the moon's gravity is much weaker than Earth's gravity. Once in lunar orbit again, the lunar module docked with the command module, which returned the astronauts to Earth orbit. The spacecraft then entered Earth's atmosphere, using air friction as a brake to slow its speed and safely descend.

Figure 4-14 An *Apollo* lunar module prepares to land.

Figure 4-15 The *Saturn 5* rocket used three sections, called stages, to send *Apollo* to the moon.

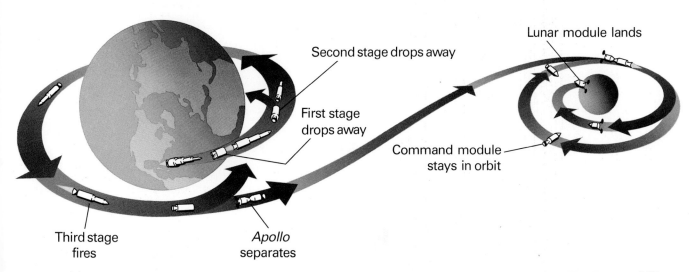

Second stage drops away

Lunar module lands

First stage drops away

Command module stays in orbit

Third stage fires

Apollo separates

Figure 4-16 Large spacecraft of the future will have their own farms and rivers. The spacecraft will spin slowly to create artificial gravity.

Future Space Missions

What will the future of space exploration be like? Plans include space stations in Earth orbit as a base for travel to other planets such as Mars. The space shuttle has paved the way for future construction projects in space. Constructing a spacecraft in orbit has many advantages. Spacecraft constructed in orbit could be large because they would not have to support their own weight or survive a launch from Earth. Also, with no atmosphere or wind resistance, the spacecraft could be any shape.

The ability to construct large spacecraft is important to future space travel. The trips to the other parts of the solar system will take a long time. Ships cannot carry all of the water, food, and air needed for the voyages. The spacecraft like the one shown in Figure 4-16 will have life-support systems that recycle water, oxygen, carbon dioxide, and waste products. Astronauts will grow their own food from the materials on board.

Plants, animals, and people need some form of gravitational force to function normally. In a weightless environment, muscles and bones become weaker. The spacecraft that travel to Mars and beyond will have to provide some sort of artificial gravity. Notice that the spacecraft in Figure 4-16 is shaped like a cylinder. The spacecraft would slowly spin on its axis to simulate gravity. The spinning motion creates a force that tends to push things outward from the axis. You feel this same force when you ride on a merry-go-round. By designing the space station with the "ground" on the inner surface of the spinning cylinder, the force would keep your feet on the ground and thus simulate gravity.

Lesson Review 4.2

6. Describe how a rocket works.
7. Compare the orbits of a space shuttle and a geosynchronous satellite.
8. Why must large spacecraft be constructed in Earth orbit rather than on Earth's surface?

Interpret and Apply

9. Design an experiment using a balloon to demonstrate that a rocket engine works in a vacuum. Check with your teacher before performing the experiment.
10. How does a satellite stay in orbit?

ACTIVITY 4.2 General Supplies

ARTIFICIAL GRAVITY

Purpose To perform an experiment showing how a spacecraft could simulate gravity.

Materials

thin cardboard	tape
compass	2 pencils
ruler	2 large paper clips
scissors	

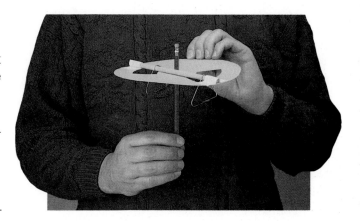

Procedure

1. Read all instructions for this activity before you begin your work.

2. On a piece of cardboard, draw a large copy of the shape shown below. Use the compass and ruler to make the three circles 6 cm, 14 cm, and 20 cm in diameter.

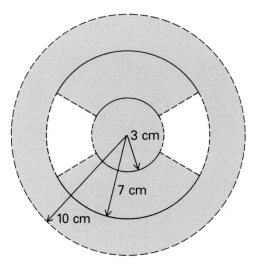

3 cm

7 cm

10 cm

3. ✂ Cut out the 20-cm disk with the scissors. **CAUTION: Use scissors with care. The points and edges are sharp.** Carefully cut out the slots in the disk along the dotted lines. Poke a hole at the disk's center with the scissors. Push a pencil through the hole so the model spins freely on the pencil without wobbling.

4. Tape a pencil to the disk as shown in the figure. Bend two paper clips into triangle shapes. Attach each paper clip to the pencil as shown.

5. Insert a second pencil through the hole in the disk's center. Hold the disk horizontally as shown, and push the paper clips toward the center. Spin the disk. Record your observations.

6. Try holding the disk vertically. Repeat step 5 and record your observations.

Collecting and Analyzing Data

1. Before you spin the disk, where do the paper clips rest?

2. While the disk is spinning, what happens to the paper clips?

3. How does holding the disk vertically affect your results?

Drawing Conclusions

4. When you spin the disk, a force pushes on the paper clips. Is this force stronger or weaker than the force of gravity?

5. Draw a circle to represent a cross section of the spacecraft in Figure 4-16. Indicate which way you think the spacecraft should spin. Then sketch people to show the directions up and down at four points inside the cylinder.

4.3 The Moon's Features

Lesson Objectives

▶ **Describe** the basic characteristics of the moon.

▶ **Describe** the features of the moon's surface.

▶ **Compare** hypotheses about the formation of the moon.

▶ **Activity** *Form a hypothesis* about factors that affect the size of craters.

New Terms

crater	maria
meteorite	rilles
rays	

Many spacecraft have gone to the moon to get a better look at its features. Astronauts and robotic equipment tested the lunar soil and rocks and brought back samples to Earth. Scientists analyzed the data to better understand the moon's surface and its interior. In this lesson, you will learn about the moon's features and theories about how the moon formed.

The Moon Compared to Earth

Even though the moon is one of the largest natural satellites in the solar system, it is much smaller than Earth. With a diameter only ¼ of Earth's diameter, you could fit about 50 moons inside of Earth. But the mass of the moon is only ¹⁄₈₁ the mass of Earth.

Because of its size and mass, the moon's gravity is about ⅙ as strong as Earth's gravity. If a scale measures your weight as 600 newtons (134.7 pounds) on Earth, the same scale would measure your weight as 100 newtons (22.5 pounds) on the moon. Your weight is different on other planets and moons because the gravitational attraction between two objects depends on their masses and on the distance between them. On the moon, you would have to learn to control your movements. If you jumped up, you could easily hit the ceiling! On the other hand, you would be able to lift massive objects easily because they would weigh very little.

The surface of the moon, like space, is a vacuum with no air. Astronauts must bring their own supply of air to survive on the lunar surface. The moon has no atmosphere because of its weak gravity. The particles that make up atmospheric gases are in motion all of the time. Most of the particles do not move fast enough to reach the escape velocity on Earth. But on the moon, where the escape velocity is about ⅕ of Earth's escape velocity, the gas particles escape into space.

On Earth, the atmosphere absorbs a lot of harmful radiation from the sun. Because the moon has no protective atmosphere, intense solar radiation heats its surface. Temperatures on the sunlit side of the moon are hot enough to boil water, about 100°C. On Earth, the atmosphere acts like a blanket that insulates the surface, keeping it warm at night. On the moon, the surface temperature drops below −170°C after the sun sets. Even oil is frozen at this temperature.

Without an atmosphere, water cannot exist on the moon's surface. With no water or air, there is little weathering on the moon's surface. Most features you see on the moon today have been there for billions of years.

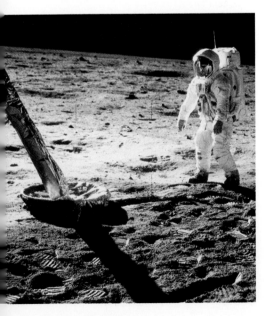

Figure 4-17 Space suits protect astronauts from the vacuum and radiation at the moon's surface.

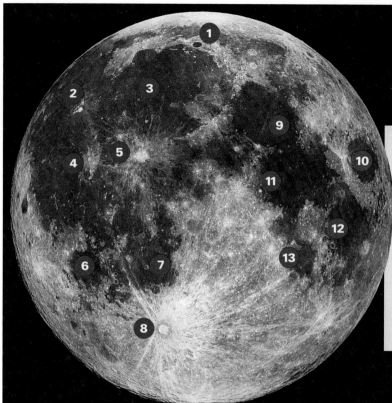

Figure 4-18 This map shows some of the moon's larger features. See if you can find these features with binoculars.

1 Plato
2 Aristarchus
3 Mare Imbrium
4 Kepler
5 Copernicus
6 Mare Humorum
7 Mare Nubium
8 Tycho
9 Mare Serenitatis
10 Mare Crisium
11 Mare Tranquillitatis
12 Mare Foecunditatis
13 Mare Nectaris

Craters and Rays

The moon is covered with hundreds of thousands of craters. A **crater** is a circular depression, or hole, on the surface of a moon or a planet. There are two types of craters, volcanic craters and impact craters. Volcanic craters are caused by volcanic activity beneath the surface of a planet or moon. Most of Earth's craters are volcanic craters. Almost all of the moon's craters are impact craters, caused by the impact of meteorites. A **meteorite** is a piece of debris that strikes the surface of a moon or planet. Most lunar craters formed between 3 and 4 billion years ago, when the moon was bombarded by meteorites left over from the formation of the solar system. Every planet and moon was bombarded at this time. Why do you think so few impact craters are left on Earth?

One goal of the *Apollo 12* mission was to explore the streaks, called **rays,** that lead away from craters on the moon's surface. Astronomers observing photographs like the one in Figure 4-19 hypothesized that the rays are made of fragments that were scattered when the crater was formed. Their hypothesis was confirmed when the *Apollo 12* mission collected material ejected 250 kilometers from the edge of the crater Copernicus.

Figure 4-19 The crater Copernicus is 90 kilometers in diameter. Its massive walls rise as high as 5 kilometers.

A C T I V I T Y   4 . 3   *General Supplies*

FORMATION OF CRATERS

Purpose   To form a hypothesis about factors that affect the size of craters.

Materials

shallow pan	thread
sand	tape
meterstick	newspaper
metric ruler	piece of cardboard
marbles of	
different sizes	

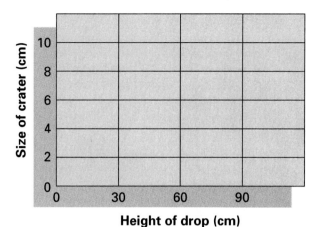

Height of drop (cm)

Procedure

1. Read all instructions for this activity before you begin your work. Copy the data table and the graph onto your paper.

2. Lay newspaper on your worktable. Put the pan on the newspaper. Put sand in the pan to a depth of 3 cm. Smooth the sand with the cardboard.

3. Measure and record the diameters of the marbles.

4. Complete the following hypotheses:

    If I increase the height from which I drop a marble, then the diameter of the crater will _____.

    If I increase the size of the marble I drop, then the diameter of the crater will _____.

5. Tape 100 cm of thread to one of the marbles. Holding the loose end of the thread with one hand, drop the marble into the sand from a height of 30 cm. Then use the thread to gently lift the marble from the sand. Record the crater's diameter.

6. Smooth the sand. Drop the marble again from heights of 60 cm and 90 cm. Record the diameters of the craters.

7. Repeat steps 5 and 6 for each marble. Record your results.

Collecting and Analyzing Data

Data Table		
Marble size (cm)	**Height of Drop (cm)**	**Crater Size (cm)**

1. For each marble, graph the size of the crater versus the height of the drop, using your copy of the sample graph.

2. How does the height of the drop affect the size of the crater? How does the marble size affect the size of the crater?

3. For each marble, predict the crater size for a drop from 120 cm. Predict the size of a crater formed by a marble twice as big as your largest marble.

Drawing Conclusions

4. Which do you think would have a greater effect on lunar crater size, the size of the meteorite or its speed?

5. Did the experiment confirm either of your hypotheses? Can you think of possible explanations for any unexpected results?

Maria and Highlands

When you observe the full moon, you see dark and light areas. When Galileo viewed the moon through a telescope more than 350 years ago, he noticed that the dark areas, called maria, have few craters. The **maria** [mär′ ē ə] are smooth areas of darker rock that formed when lava spread across the surface of the moon billions of years ago. The lava resulted either from volcanic activity or from impacts of large meteorites. As the lava flowed, it filled in the lowest areas of the moon, which are huge circular basins left behind by the largest meteorite impacts. The *Apollo* astronauts collected rock samples from several maria and brought them back to Earth. Geologists used special dating methods to determine that the maria formed between 3 and 3.5 billion years ago.

The maria are not completely smooth. The moon's **rilles** are long, narrow valleys found mostly in the lunar maria. Rilles like the one shown in Figure 4-20 are several hundred kilometers in length. Some are straight, while others twist and wind through the landscape. Scientists are still trying to understand how rilles formed.

The final three *Apollo* missions explored the lunar highlands, which are heavily cratered hills and mountains on the moon's surface. The jagged peaks of the lunar highlands reach as high as 8 kilometers. When you look at the moon, you see the light-colored rock of the highlands as bright areas that contrast sharply with the maria. Rocks collected from the highlands are older than those from the maria. Most highland rocks are about 4 billion years old, with the oldest rocks over 4.5 billion years old. How do you think lunar mountains compare with mountains on Earth, which have been weathered for millions of years?

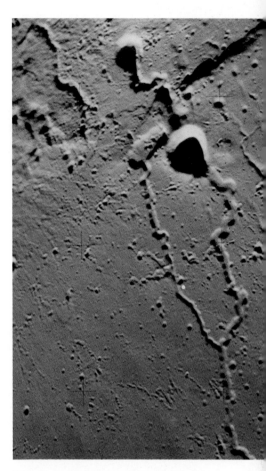

Figure 4-20 The maria are ancient lava flows that covered any craters that were already there. Can you find the rille in this photograph?

Figure 4-21 You can see lunar highlands in the background of this photograph taken during the *Apollo 15* mission.

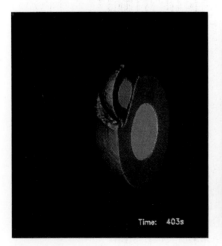

Maria on near side

Crust

Partly molten zone

Inner core

Mantle

Figure 4-22 The moon probably has a small iron core. Notice that the moon is unbalanced, with most of the maria facing Earth.

Figure 4-23 In this computer simulation, a Mars-sized planet struck Earth soon after it formed. Notice that the core of the Mars-sized planet sinks into Earth. The moon then formed from material thrown out by the impact.

Formation of the Moon

In the past, several hypotheses were developed to explain how the moon formed. One hypothesis, called the daughter hypothesis, is that a part of Earth pulled away to become the moon. This would have happened when Earth was just forming and was still very hot. Another hypothesis, the sister hypothesis, is that Earth and the moon formed at the same time from the same materials. The third hypothesis, called the capture hypothesis, is that the gravitational pull of Earth captured the moon when it came near to Earth. Unfortunately, the data collected from the lunar missions did not verify any of these hypotheses. But one problem, related to lunar magnetism, led to a new hypothesis.

Satellites orbiting the moon discovered that it has a very weak magnetic field, or magnetosphere. The moon's weak magnetosphere suggests that the moon probably has a small iron core, as shown in Figure 4-22. Geologists know that when molten rock cools and hardens, the rock preserves a record, or magnetic code, of the magnetism around it at the time it cooled. When geologists tested the lunar rocks, they were surprised to find that some of the samples have a strong magnetic code. They wondered how some moon rocks could have a strong magnetic code even though the moon has a weak magnetosphere.

A new hypothesis was proposed to explain these new facts. The hypothesis suggests that Earth was struck early in its history by a small planet about the size of Mars. This small planet had a large iron core and a strong magnetosphere. The collision is shown in Figure 4-23. As the Mars-sized planet struck Earth, most of its iron core sank into Earth's core. A small part of the iron core and some of the surface rock of the two planets were sent into orbit around Earth. Gravity gradually pulled together this material to form

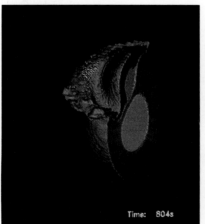

Time: 804s

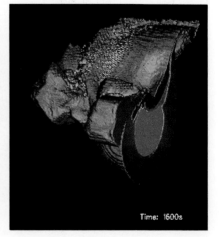

Time: 1600s

the moon. This hypothesis explains why the moon has a small iron core. It also explains how some of the lunar rock could have a strong magnetic code, because the rock formed near a strong magnetosphere. Perhaps future missions to the moon will collect more data that support this hypothesis or lead to a better one.

Lesson Review 4.3

11. Compare the lunar highlands with the maria.

12. Describe the origin of lunar craters.

13. Why was a new hypothesis about the formation of the moon needed after the *Apollo* missions?

Interpret and Apply

14. Why does the moon have more impact craters than Earth?

15. If two craters on the moon overlap, how could you tell which crater formed first?

Chapter Summary

Read this chapter summary. If any ideas are not clear to you, review that lesson.

4.1 The Motions of the Moon

■ The moon rotates on its axis and revolves in an orbit around Earth. The moon's rotation period equals its revolution period.

■ The moon has phases because the sunlit side of the moon does not always face Earth.

■ Eclipses occur when the moon passes through Earth's shadow (lunar) or the moon's shadow falls on Earth (solar).

■ Gravity keeps the moon in its orbit and creates tides in Earth's oceans.

4.2 Exploring Space

■ The expanding gases leaving the rear of a rocket push the rocket forward by the principle of action and reaction.

■ The orbital speed and period of a satellite depend on its distance from Earth.

■ The *Apollo* missions collected data that have changed our understanding of the moon.

4.3 The Moon's Features

■ The moon has weak gravity, no atmosphere, and extreme temperature changes.

■ Most of the craters on the moon formed from meteorite collisions that occurred more than 3.5 billion years ago.

■ Lava flows covered the moon's largest basins between 3 and 3.5 billion years ago to form the lunar maria. The lunar highlands formed about 4 billion years ago.

■ The moon probably formed when Earth collided with a small Mars-sized planet.

Chapter Review

■ Vocabulary

crater
escape velocity
geosynchronous
  satellite
lunar eclipse
maria
meteorite
orbital period
orbital speed

penumbra
phase
ray
rille
solar eclipse
tide
umbra
universal law of
  gravitation

■ Concept Mapping

Using the method of concept mapping described on pages 3–5, complete a concept map for the moon's motions. Copy the incomplete concept map shown below. Then fill in the missing terms.

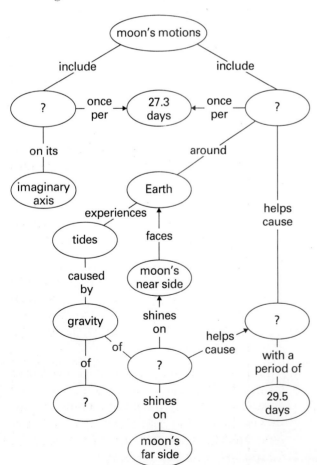

■ Review

On your paper, write the word or words that best complete each statement.

1. Changes in sea level due to the moon's gravitational pull are called _____ .

2. Objects striking the moon's surface are called _____ .

3. _____ are the smooth, dark areas of the moon's surface.

4. A(n) _____ occurs when the shadow of the moon falls on Earth.

5. The _____ is the darkest part of the moon's or Earth's shadow.

6. A(n) _____ will stay above one point on Earth.

7. A(n) _____ occurs when the moon passes through Earth's shadow.

8. The scattering of shattered rock from a crater sometimes forms _____ .

9. _____ are long narrow, valleys found mostly in the maria.

10. Some rocks on the moon have a strong magnetic code even though the moon does not have a strong _____ .

11. Most of the lunar _____ were filled in between 3 and 3.5 billion years ago.

12. A(n) _____ is a depression in the moon's surface created by a meteorite.

13. The _____ is the lighter part of the moon's or Earth's shadow.

14. The speed required to escape the gravity of a planet or moon is called the _____ .

15. The principle of action and reaction explains how _____ work.

16. The hypothesis in which the moon broke off from Earth early in Earth's history is called _____ .

17. The _____ states that each object in the universe is attracted to all other objects.

■ Interpret and Apply

On your paper, answer each question.

18. When is the near side of the moon also the dark side?

19. Compare and contrast the two different quarter moon phases that you see during each lunar month.

20. How do the shadows on the moon's surface change as the moon moves from a crescent moon to a full moon?

21. How would a change in the speed of the moon's rotation affect which surface features that you see on the moon?

22. Describe the two kinds of eclipses that you could see from the moon. For each kind of eclipse, give the phase of the moon and state whether the eclipse would be total or partial.

23. Compare the tides when the moon is closer to Earth in its orbit with tides when the moon is farther from Earth.

24. Because of tidal forces, the moon is actually moving away from Earth at a rate of 4 centimeters per year. How does this affect the orbital period of the moon?

25. How can collecting more data about the surface rocks on the moon support or disprove the newest theory of the moon's formation?

■ Writing in Science

26. Many of your daily activities are affected by your weight or the weight of other objects. Imagine that you are on a space voyage where gravity is very weak. Write an explanation of some problems that a lack of gravity would cause and suggest ways that these problems might be solved. (Your writing will be most effective if you choose two or three problems and develop them in detail.)

■ Critical Thinking

In the diagram, Circle S represents the sun, Circle M represents the moon, and Point E represents a point on Earth. Circle M hides Circle S from a person at point E. This represents a total eclipse of Circle S as seen from point E. Circle M, with a diameter of 1 centimeter, is 4 centimeters from point E. Circle S, with a diameter of 2 centimeters, is 8 centimeters from point E. Refer to this diagram as you answer the following questions.

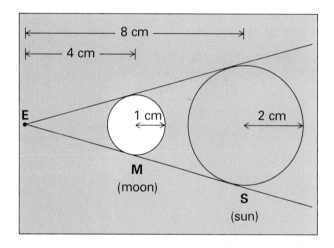

27. Suppose Circle S were 12 centimeters from point E. How large could Circle S be and still be totally eclipsed as seen by an observer at point E?

28. Suppose Circle S were 16 centimeters from point E. How large could it be and still be totally eclipsed?

29. How would you calculate the maximum possible size of Circle S if you are given the distance of Circle S from point E, distance of Circle M from point E, and the size of Circle M?

30. In fact, the sun is an average of 397 times farther from Earth than the moon is. The moon is 3476 kilometers in diameter. Calculate the diameter of the sun in kilometers. NOTE: The sun can just barely be totally eclipsed by the moon.

5 Exploring the Solar System

Chapter Preview

Have You Ever WONDERED?

Is there another planet like Earth in the universe?

Is there only one sun? Is there only one solar system? Is there life anywhere else in the universe?

Scientists have found no evidence of life anywhere in the universe except on Earth. But astronomers have observed several stars that have some kind of material near them. Astronomers do not know what the material around these stars looks like. The material may be all gas, dust, large chunks of rock and ice, or even planets and moons. As telescopes improve, astronomers may be able to confirm the discovery of another solar system. Within one of these solar systems, there just might be another planet similar to Earth.

A Model of the Solar System

▶ **Compare** the planets' sizes and distances from the sun.

▶ **Explain** why it is difficult to make a scale model of the solar system.

▶ **List** and **explain** Kepler's laws.

▶ **Describe** some recent planetary space probes.

▶ **Activity** **Form models** for planet size and distance and use the models to compare these values.

New Terms

planet	astronomical
inner planet	unit
outer planet	space probe

On a clear night, look up at the stars. Do they all look alike or can you see differences among them? Watch the way they move from night to night. Can you pick out a special star that moves differently from the others?

The photographs in Figure 5-1 show the same part of the sky at the same time of night. The photograph on the right was taken two weeks after the one on the left. Find the arrowed image in both photographs. Notice that this object's position changed. How does that object's shift in position compare to the shift in position for the other stars?

The object that moved in Figure 5-1 is not a star. The object is a planet. A **planet** is a large object that orbits the sun, just as Earth does. A planet's orbital motion makes it appear to shift against the background stars when you observe it from night to night. Planets differ from stars in another important way. Planets shine by reflected sunlight, while stars produce their own light. Figure 5-2 shows how the light reflected by a planet travels from the sun to your eyes.

Planet Distances and Sizes

Exploring the solar system may be the most exciting real adventure story of the next century. Explorers will have to be experts on the planets they plan to visit. They will have to know the distance to the planet and the time the trip will take. The mission planners will need to know where the planet is located compared to other planets.

Look at the approximate distances to the planets listed in the second column of Table 5-1. These numbers show that there is a pattern to the arrangement of the planets. The first four planets are all within two times Earth's distance from

Figure 5-1 These photos were taken two weeks apart. Notice how the planet moved slightly when compared to the two stars.

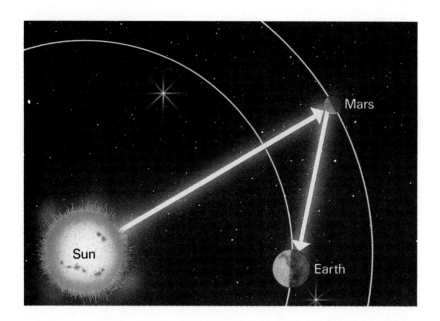

Figure 5-2 The planets shine by reflected light. The light you see from the planets originally came from the sun.

the sun. These four planets—Mercury, Venus, Earth, and Mars—are called the **inner planets.** Two planets are in the middle, and three are somewhat evenly spaced to the outer edges of the solar system. These five planets—Jupiter, Saturn, Uranus, Neptune, and Pluto—are called the **outer planets.** To make distances in the solar system easier to picture, astronomers call the distance between Earth and the sun one **astronomical unit,** or A.U. A distance expressed in astronomical units tells how many times farther from the sun a planet is than Earth. For example, Jupiter's average distance from the sun is 5.2 astronomical units. This means that Jupiter is 5.2 times as far from the sun as Earth is.

Table 5-1 Sizes and Motions of the Planets

Planet	Average Distance from Sun (A.U.)	Diameter Compared to Earth	Period of Rotation (Earth Days)	Period of Revolution (Earth Years)	Number of Orbits in One Year
Mercury	0.38	0.38	59	0.24	4.2
Venus	0.72	0.95	243	0.62	1.6
Earth	1.0	1.0	1.0	1.0	1.0
Mars	1.5	0.53	1.0	1.9	0.53
Jupiter	5.2	11.0	0.41	12	0.083
Saturn	9.6	9.4	0.43	29	0.034
Uranus	19	4.1	0.65	84	0.012
Neptune	30	3.9	0.67	165	0.0061
Pluto	39	0.18	6.3	249	0.0040

It is very hard for you to grasp the enormous distances and sizes in the solar system. A scale model makes the distances and sizes of the planets much easier to picture. However, it is difficult to design an accurate scale model for the entire solar system. If the outer planets are spaced a reasonable distance apart from one another on the model, the inner planets are usually too close together. If the inner planets are spaced a reasonable distance apart on the model, the outer planets often do not fit onto the same sheet of paper. Figure 5-3 shows a chart that uses different scales for the inner and outer planets.

Now look at the diameter comparisons in the third column of Table 5-1. Pluto, the smallest planet, is about one sixth the size of Earth. Venus and Earth are about the same diameter. Saturn and Jupiter are roughly ten times Earth's diameter.

The scaled diagrams and tables of distance and diameter suggest an interesting pattern to the solar system. There are two groupings of planets. The small planets, which are Earth's size or smaller, are clustered comparatively close to the sun. The large planets are far from the sun. The exception to this grouping is Pluto, which is both the smallest planet and usually the farthest planet from the sun.

Figure 5-3 Two separate scales for distance make a scale model of the solar system easier to picture.

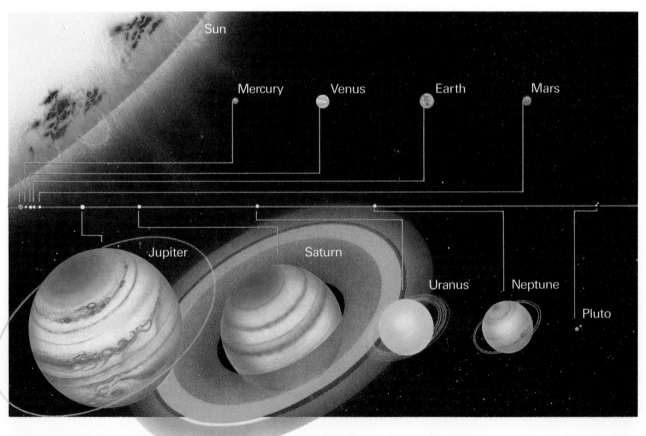

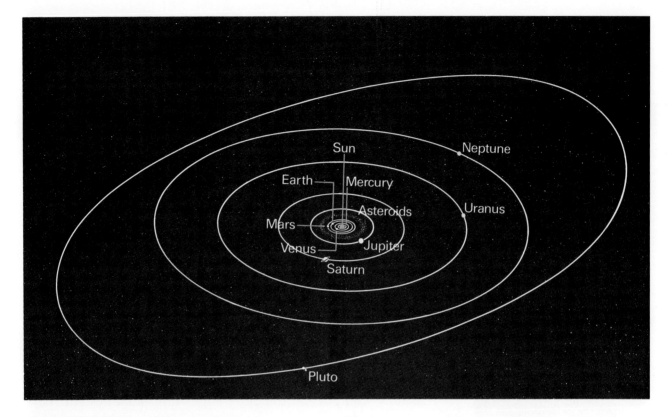

Interplanetary Space Travel

Who is your favorite explorer? Would you travel to another planet if you had the chance? Curiosity leads people to learn about places that no one has explored before, like the planets. For thousands of years, people could only imagine what the planets were like. People measured changes in the planets' positions with only their eyes and simple tools. In 1610, an Italian astronomer named Galileo turned his telescope on the planets. This instrument offered a new look at the known universe.

In this century, rocket scientists have launched spacecraft that fly past the planets. An example is *Voyager 2*, which flew past Neptune in August of 1989. **Space probes** like *Voyager 2* beam images to Earth that reveal new and exciting worlds for future space exploration and discovery. Recent probes to Venus and Mars, and close flybys of Jupiter, Saturn, Uranus, and Neptune have given scientists a wealth of new information about the solar system. In fact, most of scientists' knowledge about the planets comes from space probes launched within the past 20 years. Cooperation among space scientists from many countries is becoming more common. For example, scientists from France, Japan, the Soviet Union, and the United States hope to begin planning in the 1990's for an astronaut trip to Mars.

Figure 5-4 This is what the solar system would look like if you could view it from beyond the orbit of Pluto.

Figure 5-5 *Top left: Voyager 2*, the space probe that flew by the outer planets; *Top right:* The space probe *Magellan*, sent to explore Venus; *Bottom:* The probe *Galileo* will explore the moons and atmosphere of Jupiter.

Voyagers 1 and *2* are probably the best-known space probes launched so far. Launched in 1977, they traveled over 4.5 billion miles in 12 years. During that time, the *Voyagers* sent back to Earth much new information about Jupiter, Saturn, Uranus, and Neptune. *Voyager 1* was launched from Earth two weeks after *Voyager 2. Voyager 1*'s path allowed it to reach Jupiter and Saturn before *Voyager 2. Voyager 1* is now well beyond the outer edge of the solar system. *Voyager 2*, however, took advantage of a unique arrangement of the outer planets in their orbits, traveling from one to the next. As *Voyager 2* approached a planet, it sent back to Earth hundreds of thousands of computer bits of information. On Earth, scientists put together the bits of information into images. You will learn more about the *Voyagers'* discoveries in the next lesson.

The *Voyagers* completed their successful tours of duty in the solar system at the end of 1989. But new probes are already underway or are being planned. *Voyager* and two of the new probes are shown in Figure 5-5. The *Magellan* spacecraft should provide a detailed look at the atmosphere and surface of Venus. The *Galileo* space probe will launch sensing equipment into the atmosphere of Jupiter.

The *Magellan* mission to Venus was launched on May 4, 1989, aboard the space shuttle *Atlantis*. Mission planners had to launch *Magellan* between April 28 and May 23, 1989, in order for the space probe to orbit Venus correctly. Scientists knew that if they missed this time interval, they would have to wait until 1991. Once in orbit around Venus in August 1990, *Magellan* will use a new radar system to map 70 percent of the planet's surface. Earlier spacecraft, such as *Pioneer*, also mapped Venus's surface using radar. The images *Magellan* sends back to Earth, however, should be much sharper than *Pioneer*'s images.

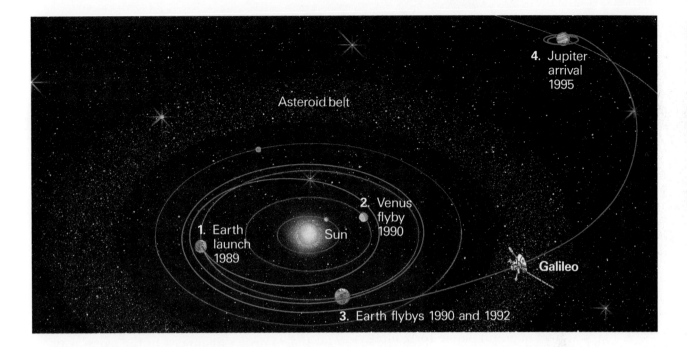

The *Galileo* probe consists of an orbiter and a sensor. *Galileo* was launched on October 12, 1989. The space probe will use the gravity of both Venus and Earth to help propel it to Jupiter. Mission scientists had to choose a time when Venus and Earth would be properly aligned with Jupiter. *Galileo* should finally arrive at Jupiter in 1995. Figure 5-6 summarizes the six-year journey.

Magellan and *Galileo* are only two members of an exciting new group of space projects planned for the end of the twentieth century. As you can see in Table 5-2, these probes will travel to the region of space around the sun as well as to the planets. Scientists are planning one space probe to study the climate and surface of Mars. Another probe will travel to Saturn. These probes will use the planets' gravity as much as possible to set their courses and increase their speeds.

Figure 5-6 *Galileo*'s long journey will take it inward to Venus before it heads outward to Jupiter.

Table 5-2 New Space Probes		
Name of Probe	**Launch Date**	**Purpose**
Magellan	May 4, 1989	Use radar to map the surface of Venus
Galileo	October 12, 1989	Study Jupiter's atmosphere and moons
Ulysses	October 1990	Study region of space near the sun
Mars Observer	September 1992	Study atmosphere and surface of Mars
Comet Rendezvous/ Asteroid Flyby	1996 (?)	Study matter in comets
Cassini	1998 (?)	Study Saturn

SCALE MODELS OF THE SOLAR SYSTEM

Purpose To form models for the planets' distances and diameters and use the models to make comparisons.

Materials

graph paper   drawing compass
ruler

Procedure

Part A

1. Read all instructions for this activity before you begin your work.

2. Place a sheet of graph paper horizontally in front of you.

3. Draw a horizontal line through the middle grid line on your sheet of graph paper. You will place all planets on this line to show their distances.

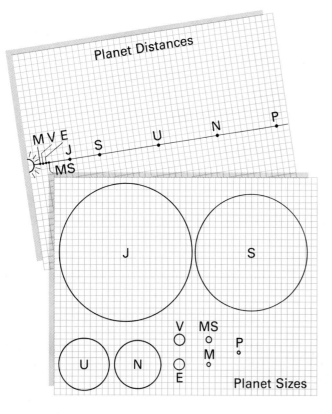

4. Use the compass to draw an arc representing the sun at the left end of the line. The arc should be 2 blocks in diameter.

5. Each block represents 1 A.U. Place a dot for Earth one block to the right of the sun. Label that dot with the letter *E*.

6. Place Mercury one half block from the sun and Venus three fourths of a block from the sun. Label them *M* and *V*. Place Mars one half block to the right of Earth. Label Mars *MS*.

7. Place the outer planets on the line at their correct distances in the same way. Label the planets *J, S, U, N,* and *P*.

Part B

8. Turn your paper over and draw a circle with a 2-block diameter in the center of the paper. This will represent the size of Earth.

9. Use your compass to draw circles for the other eight planets. Draw the circles in order from largest to smallest. Draw the small ones by hand. Label each planet.

Collecting and Analyzing Data

1. List the planets in order of distance, starting with Mercury, on the distance side of your paper.

2. List the planets in order of size from largest to smallest on the size side of your paper.

Drawing Conclusions

3. What is the relationship between the sizes of the planets and their distances from the sun?

4. Does any planet appear to be an exception to the relationship you described in question 3? If so, which one?

Planetary Positions

In order to plan successfully the mission for an interplanetary space probe, space scientists must first be able to predict the positions of planets. Planets constantly move in at least two different ways. Like Earth, all planets rotate or spin on an imaginary axis and revolve around the sun. The spinning of a planet causes its day-night cycle. Table 5-1 on page 119 lists the rotation periods of the planets. One rotation of a planet on its axis is one day for that planet.

Most planets spin counterclockwise as viewed from their North Poles. As shown in Figure 5-7, an exception is Venus, which turns clockwise. If you were on Venus and could see through the clouds, you would see the sun rise in the west. For reasons astronomers do not understand, both Uranus and Pluto are tipped over on their sides. Their spins are unlike those of the other planets.

Revolution is the movement of a planet in its orbit around the sun. You learned in Chapter 3 that Earth takes one year to revolve once around the sun. Likewise, a planet's year is the time the planet takes to revolve around the sun once. Table 5-1 lists the revolution periods for all the planets. Notice that each planet requires a different time to revolve around the sun. Those planets closer to the sun than Earth require less than one Earth year to revolve around the sun once. Those planets farther away require more than one Earth year to revolve around the sun. Yet all planets revolve around the sun in the same direction, counterclockwise, when viewed from above their North Poles.

Trying to get to a planet from Earth is like trying to hit a flying mosquito at 50 meters with a BB gun. A planet is a distant, constantly moving target. To plan the path of a space probe to a planet, scientists must know the planet's position in its orbit on the probe's arrival date. You can find the planet's position from its period of revolution. Table 5-1 lists the number of orbits each planet makes in one Earth orbit, or one year. Mercury requires 0.24 year to orbit the sun once. How many times does Mercury revolve around the sun while Earth revolves around the sun once? To find out, divide Earth's period of revolution by Mercury's period of revolution:

$$\frac{1 \text{ year}}{0.24 \text{ year}} = 4.1 \text{ orbits for Mercury}$$

Planets farther from the sun than Earth make less than one orbit around the sun in one Earth year. By predicting the position of a planet in its orbit, space scientists can plan a mission to that planet.

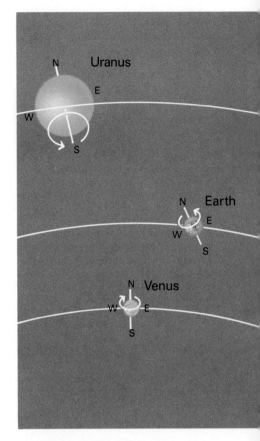

Figure 5-7 Most of the planets spin counterclockwise as viewed from their North Poles. Uranus and Venus, however, have spins unlike the other planets.

People have not always understood the movements of the planets. People once feared that planet wandering would bring war, famine, and disease. In the 1600's, a mathematician named Johannes Kepler worked out three simple laws for the motions of the planets. Because of his work and that of others, it is possible today to predict the planets' positions in the sky far in advance.

Law of Orbits Kepler's first law describes the shape of planet orbits. You learned in Chapter 3 that Earth's orbit is an ellipse, not a circle. Kepler showed that the planets' orbits around the sun are elliptical, like the diagram in Figure 5-8. Each planet's orbit has points where the planet is closest to and farthest from the sun. Mercury and Pluto have the most elliptical orbits. The other planets revolve in orbits that are nearly circular. In a nearly circular orbit, the difference between the smallest and largest distances from the sun is very small.

Law of Areas Imagine a planet connected to the sun as in Figure 5-8 by an imaginary elastic band. As the planet revolves around the sun, the elastic band passes over an area in space. Kepler's Law of Areas states that the areas crossed by the elastic band are equal during equal units of time. When the planet is far from the sun, the area is long and thin. When the planet is close to the sun, the area is short and thick.

The Law of Areas means that the speed at which a planet travels around the sun is not constant. Planets travel more rapidly when they are close to the sun.

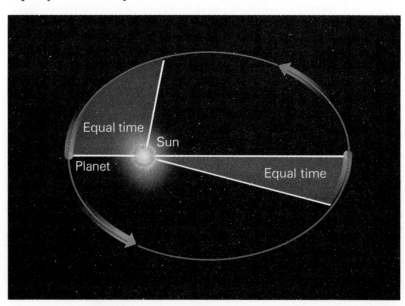

Figure 5-8 Planets revolve around the sun in elliptical orbits. A line joining the planet and the sun covers the shaded areas within equal periods of time.

Harmonic Law Imagine a whirlpool of water carrying particles of silt as the water goes down a drain. The particles in Figure 5-9 revolve slowly at the outer edge of the whirlpool. As the particles get closer to the drain, they move faster and faster. The farther away a particle is from the drain, the longer it takes to revolve once around the drain. Planets move in their orbits like the silt particles in the whirlpool, except that planets do not spiral inward toward the sun.

Kepler's Harmonic Law states that the farther a planet is from the sun, the more time the planet takes to revolve once around the sun. One reason is that its orbit is larger. Another is that it moves more slowly than nearer planets. The average speed of Earth in orbit is about 30 kilometers per second. Mercury, nearest to the sun, moves at about 49 kilometers per second. Pluto, usually farthest out, travels at 5 kilometers per second.

Kepler's three laws made it possible to predict the positions of planets for any date. But it was another 350 years until people launched actual space missions to the planets. Students of space science today will make up the team of engineers, mission specialists, and astronauts for tomorrow's space probes. Would you like to join the team?

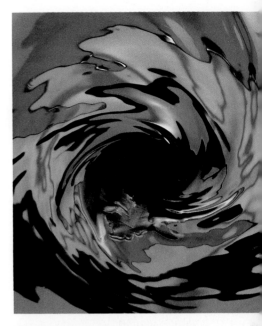

Figure 5-9 As the debris in the water gets closer to the drain, the time the debris needs to revolve once around the drain decreases.

Lesson Review 5.1

1. List the planets according to increasing distance from the sun.

2. List the planets in order of size, beginning with the smallest planet.

3. Why is it difficult to design a scale model for the distances and diameters of the planets that fits on one standard sheet of paper?

4. Explain Kepler's three laws of planetary motion.

5. Make a table comparing the space probes *Voyager*, *Magellan*, and *Galileo*. Include these headings in your chart: *Purpose*, *Type of Probe*, and *Planets Visited*.

Interpret and Apply

6. Imagine a planet that was knocked out of its orbit by a large passing object. The planet would begin to spiral inward toward the sun. Use Kepler's laws to predict how the planet's speed would change as it came closer to the sun.

5.2 A Tour of the Planets

Lesson Objectives

▸ **Compare and contrast** the planets' physical features.

▸ **Relate** each planet's surface type to its distance from the sun.

▸ **Describe** some important discoveries by space probes.

▸ **Activity** **Form a model** to show how a planet's gravity can assist space probes in flight.

New Terms

terrestrial planet
gaseous planet

Unlike the space probes of the 1970's and 1980's, you can visit all nine planets in a single imaginary trip. Mercury, Venus, Earth, and Mars are called the **terrestrial** (tə res′ trē əl) **planets.** These planets all have rocky surfaces. You begin at Mercury and fly past each of the other terrestrial planets as you head for the edge of the solar system.

The Inner Planets

Mercury's surface is covered with craters. In fact, Mercury reminds you of Earth's moon. Mercury is a planet of extremes. It is small, battered, airless, moonless, and very heavy for its size. The sun constantly bombards the surface of Mercury with fast-moving, charged particles. There is no atmosphere to slow down rocks from outer space, which crash into Mercury's surface, forming craters.

Mercury has the most extreme daily temperature change of any planet. With so little atmosphere, most of the sun's heat is lost into space during the night. The result is a temperature change from over 400°C during the day to about −200°C at night. The 600°C change in temperature causes the rocks to expand and contract. The rocky surface cracks, producing cliffs, crevices, and canyons. However, the *Mariner* space probe found no evidence of volcanic activity on Mercury. This lack of activity suggests that the inner core of Mercury is cooling faster than Earth's core.

Figure 5-10 *Left:* Mercury, which has no atmosphere, is covered with craters. *Right:* Venus has an atmosphere full of thick clouds.

Venus is often called the morning star or evening star because the planet is sometimes the brightest starlike object in the sky. But Venus is not a star. Venus reflects the sun's light, rather than making its own light. Venus is very different from its appearance at a distance. The United States *Pioneer* spacecraft in 1978 and the USSR's *Venera* in 1978 and 1982 revealed a hot and stormy environment. Winds moving at 450 kilometers per hour in violent thunderstorms stir acid clouds, dust, and gases. Bolts of lightning create faintly glowing blue patches of light. The atmosphere of Venus is mostly carbon dioxide. The atmosphere acts as a blanket, holding in much of the thermal energy the planet absorbs during an extremely long day. Venus's long day and its thick atmosphere cause its surface temperature to remain very high. At the present time, the average temperature at the surface is 460°C.

The *Pioneer* spacecraft in 1979 used radar to map the surface of Venus. *Pioneer* found that the surface has plateaus, high mountains, and gently rolling hills. Craters on the surface may have been caused by volcanoes or by rock impacts.

Earth is already familiar to you as the only planet with liquid water and living things on its surface. For many years, scientists hoped that Mars might also have life. Simple forms of life might be able to survive in the Martian soil if Mars has water. The *Viking 1* and *Viking 2* spacecrafts arrived at Mars in 1976. The landers sent to the surface by *Viking* did not find any water. But evidence that water once flowed on Mars's surface still exists. The channels visible in photographs taken of the Martian surface may be old riverbeds. The white polar ice caps contain frozen carbon dioxide and a small amount of water. However, the atmosphere of Mars is thin. Any surface water that once existed probably evaporated into the thin air a long time ago. *Viking's* landers found that Mars is red because the rocky surface is covered with rust-colored rocks. The Martian landscape also boasts the highest mountain peak in the solar system.

Figure 5-11 *Left:* The *Viking 2* lander sent back this image of frost on Mars's surface. *Right:* You can see one of Mars's extinct volcanoes and its central canyon in this image from *Viking 2*.

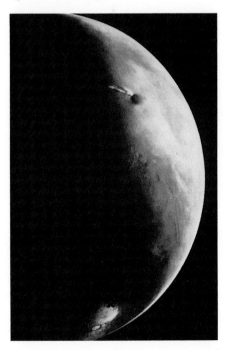

Figure 5-12 *Left: Voyager 1* sent this image of Jupiter. *Right:* In this composite photo of Saturn, the moons are not shown at their actual relative size.

The Outer Planets

After you leave Mars on your trip, you cross a large gap of space. Landing a space probe on the **gaseous planets**—Jupiter, Saturn, Uranus, and Neptune—would be more difficult than landing on the inner planets because the outer planets lack a solid surface. Instead, their thick atmospheres gradually change into liquid oceans deep inside the planets.

Jupiter is the most massive planet in the solar system. Figure 5-12 *(left)* shows that bands of gases and swirling storms cover the planet. The gigantic Great Red Spot is a huge storm, big enough to hold two Earths. The Great Red Spot has been churning for at least three hundred years. Beneath Jupiter's atmosphere is an ocean of liquid hydrogen and helium. Next is a solid core of ice and rock.

Jupiter gives off more thermal energy than it receives from the sun. If Jupiter had contained a little more matter than it does, it might have become a star. *Voyager 1* discovered a narrow ring around the planet. The ring contains dust and small rock particles. Beyond the ring, both *Voyagers* observed Jupiter's cluster of moons.

Jupiter has 16 moons, but the four largest moons are of special interest. Jupiter's most unusual moon is Io. Jupiter's powerful gravity churns and heats Io, causing Io's volcanoes to erupt sulfur. Jupiter's three other large moons—Europa, Ganymede, and Callisto—have icy surfaces covering a rocky core.

Saturn is similar to Jupiter. Both are gas planets consisting of a thick outer atmosphere, a liquid hydrogen ocean, and a core of rock and ice. Saturn's density is even lower than Jupiter's, so low that Saturn would actually float if you could put it in water.

Saturn's most distinctive feature is its enormous set of rings. The rings are less than 1 kilometer thick, but they extend 113 000 kilometers across on each side of Saturn. Both *Voyagers'* close-up views of the rings showed that they consist of hundreds of thin ringlets. Saturn has more moons than any other planet. The *Voyagers* discovered many new moons during their 1980 and 1981 visits.

Uranus is a blue-green, icy planet. Uranus is so far from the sun that the gases in its lower atmosphere are frozen. Uranus is now moving through a section of its orbit where its pole points toward the sun. Some astronomers think that the planet may have been knocked over on its side by a collision with a passing object.

Astronomers discovered Uranus's ring system from Earth in 1977. There are five major moons around Uranus. Like the four large moons of Jupiter, they are made of ice and rock. *Voyager 2* discovered ten smaller moons in 1986. *Voyager 2's* close-up images of Uranus' five major moons revealed some of the most unusual surface features yet found in the solar system.

Figure 5-13 *Voyager 2's* image of Uranus shows this planet as an almost featureless blue ball.

ENVIRONMENTAL AWARENESS

Earth's Temperature Range

Earth is exactly the right distance from the sun. The right distance, that is, for liquid water to exist. If Earth were any closer to the sun, it would be too hot for water vapor to condense into rain. If Earth were any farther away from the sun, it would be too cold for ice to melt. Without liquid water, there would be no rain, rivers, lakes, and oceans. There would be no life.

Remember that the required temperature range for liquid water is only 0°C to 100°C. A temperature range of 100° may seem like a lot to you. For life, it is a wide extreme. But in astronomical terms, 100°C is an extremely small range. For example, the temperature range on Mercury is 700°C. The sun's surface has a temperature of about 6000°C, and its core has a temperature of 15 000 000°C.

Earth's narrow temperature range is a result of its atmosphere. The atmosphere traps some thermal energy so that Earth does not cool off too much at night. The atmosphere also prevents liquid water in oceans and lakes from evaporating and being lost into space. Earth's temperature range and water supply remain roughly the same over time. As a result, Earth continues to be the only planet in the solar system with conditions that can support life. ■

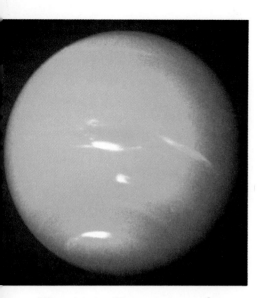

Figure 5-14 Neptune is another plant covered by thick clouds.

Because Pluto's elliptical orbit dips inside Neptune's orbit, Neptune is the farthest planet from the sun from 1979 until 1999. Neptune appears blue-green in color, similar to Uranus. The blue-green color on both planets is caused by the gas methane. *Voyager 2's* image in Figure 5-14 revealed a dark-colored storm on Neptune similar to the Great Red Spot on Jupiter. The methane gas deep within the atmosphere of Neptune freezes on the surface, as it does on Uranus's surface. But Neptune is not identical to Uranus. Although Neptune is smaller than Uranus in size, it has more mass than Uranus. Possibly Neptune's core is larger and is made of different materials than the core of Uranus. Four rings and eight moons circle the planet. One moon, Triton, is covered with frozen methane and nitrogen.

No spacecraft has yet visited Pluto. The little information astronomers have about Pluto comes from telescopes on Earth. Pluto is probably the strangest planet in the solar system. Pluto is small and mostly made of rock, like the inner planets. But Pluto orbits the sun at the edge of the solar system with the gaseous planets. Pluto's orbit is very elliptical. Pluto's orbit is also tilted compared to the rest of the planets' orbits. Pluto has a moon named Charon that is fully half as large as Pluto itself. Charon also revolves in an orbit very close to Pluto. Because Pluto and Charon are so close together and similar in size, astronomers often refer to Pluto as a double planet.

The tilt of Uranus's axis and Pluto's odd characteristics suggest that a major collision may have occurred in the outer solar system sometime in the past. Astronomers need further observations from space in order to solve this mystery.

Lesson Review 5.2

7. List four space probes that have visited the planets. Give the planet(s) visited by each and the most important discoveries of each probe.

8. Classify planets according to their surface type. Name those planets found in each classification.

9. List three moons in the solar system and the planets around which they revolve.

10. Describe one unusual feature of each planet.

Interpret and Apply

11. Discuss a possible origin for the rings of Uranus.

A C T I V I T Y 5.2

General Supplies

GRAVITY-ASSISTED SPACE TRAVEL

Purpose To form a model demonstrating how a planet's gravity can assist space probes in flight.

Materials

3 strong slab magnets
2 plastic rulers with center grooves
2 steel ball bearings
block of wood, 1 cm thick
spool of thread or string
newsprint sheets

Procedure

1. Read all instructions for this activity before you begin your work. Copy the data table onto your paper.

2. Arrange the equipment as shown in the figure. Make sure that the newsprint sheets extend well beyond your equipment.

3. Roll the larger ball bearing down the ramp so that the ball curves around the magnet. If the bearing sticks to the magnet or if the ball rolls straight ahead, move the magnet and try again.

4. Sketch the path of the ball from the end of the ramp on the newsprint. Lay a piece of thread along the path. Mark the positions of the end of the second ruler and the end of the ball's path on the thread. Measure the length of thread between the two marks. This thread length is the length of the ball's path beyond the end of the ruler.

5. Repeat using 2 and 3 magnets. Try to roll the ball so that it makes a U-turn by placing the magnets inside the curved path. Use a sketch and the thread to measure the ball's path length as in step 4. Record your results in the Data Table.

Collecting and Analyzing Data

Data Table		
Trial	Distance with 2 Magnets (cm)	Distance with 3 Magnets (cm)
1		
2		
3		
4		
Average		

1. Calculate averages for each set of trials you did.

2. What effect did the magnet have on the ball's roll distance?

3. Describe the most curved path you produced with the magnets.

Drawing Conclusions

4. The ball bearing represents a space probe. What does the magnet represent?

5. What effect does a planet have on an approaching space probe?

6. How can space probes use a planet's gravity to visit more than one planet on a single mission?

Exploring the Solar System **133**

5.3 Comets, Asteroids, and Meteors

New Terms

protoplanet	asteroid
comet	meteor
solar wind	meteor shower

People once thought comets brought floods, war, disease, and famine. Now people understand comets much better. Comet orbits obey Kepler's laws, as do the planets' orbital motions.

Scientists can calculate orbits of comets after only a few observations. In addition, astronomers have learned much about the composition of comets from recent spacecraft fly-bys. The materials in a comet are probably the same today as they were when they formed billions of years ago. Information about comets and other solar system debris will tell astronomers more about the young solar system.

How the Solar System Formed

Figure 5-16 illustrates a well-known theory describing the origin of the solar system. According to the theory, the solar system formed from a cloud of gas and dust. A nearby star exploded, pushing particles in the cloud closer together. A large lump that eventually became the sun formed in the center of the cloud. Smaller lumps called **protoplanets** that eventually formed the planets began to revolve around the early sun. At this stage, the young solar system would have looked like Figure 5-16 *(left)*. The dense material, including rock and metal, gathered close to the cloud's central lump.

Figure 5-15 A comet

The less dense gases were flung out to the edges of the cloud, which flattened into a rotating disk. Gases too far from the heat of the central lump condensed into ice. Over millions of years, the protoplanets shrank further to form the planets, as shown in Figure 5-16 (middle and right). The gravity of the planets, like a giant vacuum cleaner, cleared most space of loose rock and ice crystals. Since the larger planets had stronger gravity, they attracted more loose pieces of rock and ice. Their loose pieces eventually formed moons and rings. However, astronomers have found several areas of space that still contain leftover pieces of rock and ice. One such area might lie beyond the orbit of Pluto. Another area lies between the orbits of Mars and Jupiter.

Figure 5-16 *Left:* In the young solar system, lumps of material pulled together within a cloud of gas and dust. *Middle:* As the protoplanets shrank, the sun ignited. *Right:* Further shrinking of the protoplanets formed planets.

Comets and Asteroids

Comets are made of dust and rock pieces mixed with ices of water, methane, and carbon dioxide. According to theory, a large swarm of these "dirty snowballs" orbits the sun beyond the orbit of Pluto. Scientists think that a passing star or perhaps an unknown planet throws comets out of the swarm and into elliptical orbits around the sun. Once a comet is in orbit, it follows a predictable path around the sun. As the comet approaches the sun, the comet's ices heat up. The ices boil away, forming a bright cloud of gases around the head of the comet. Radiation and fast-moving particles streaming away from the sun, called the **solar wind**, blow the comet's gases into a tail. The length of the comet's tail depends on the comet's composition and the strength of the solar wind. Some comets have tails millions of kilometers long, while others have no tails. A comet's tail always points away from the sun. After hundreds of trips around the sun, the solar wind completely vaporizes a comet's ices. The rocks that were in the ice are released. These rocks stay in orbit around the sun and spread out.

Figure 5-17 A series of positions for a single comet

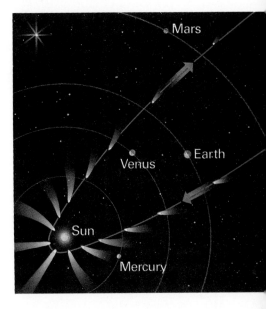

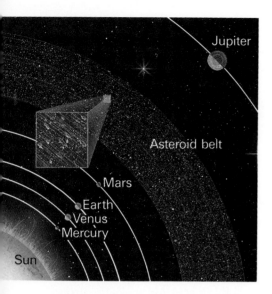

Figure 5-18 Most asteroids are located in a belt between Mars and Jupiter.

On June 30, 1908, a huge fireball exploded over the Russian province of Siberia. The fireball flattened 4000 square kilometers of forests. (Fortunately, no one was close enough to the site to be injured.) The explosion had the power of a 12-megaton atomic bomb. Yet the explosion left no crater. Some scientists claim that a comet entered the atmosphere and then exploded before striking Earth's surface.

According to one theory, a tug-of-war was going on between the sun and Jupiter as the protoplanets shrank. The opposing pulls of the two large objects kept loose material in one location from collecting together to form a planet. It is also possible that a rocky planet already there broke apart into many pieces. Figure 5-18 shows that these loose pieces, called **asteroids,** still orbit the sun between the orbits of Mars and Jupiter. The orbits of most asteroids are nearly circular, like the planets' orbits. Astronomers think that today's asteroids are a fraction of what was there two billion years ago. Most of the asteroids were pulled out of the belt between Mars and Jupiter by the gravity of the planets and the sun. These astronomers point out that several moons in the solar system have the irregular, rocky appearance of asteroids. The moons may be asteroids that were captured by a planet's gravity. In addition, many asteroids have been discovered far from the belt between Mars and Jupiter. Astronomers have concluded that asteroids are scattered throughout the solar system.

Meteors

Pieces of rock from asteroids or from old comets sometimes enter the earth's atmosphere. As they fall through the atmosphere, these **meteors** leave a glowing trail in the night sky. Sometimes they are called shooting stars. Entering Earth's atmosphere at speeds of around 70 000 kilometers per hour, most meteors burn up. Those that hit Earth's surface are called meteorites. People have discovered about 2000 meteorites on Earth. Figure 5-19 shows examples of meteorites. Meteorite fragments, like observations of comets and asteroids, give scientists information about the beginning of the solar system.

On certain dates each year, Earth's motion along its orbit carries it through rock fragments left behind by comets. These fragments fall into Earth's atmosphere, causing a **meteor shower.** Most meteor showers are named for the constellation in the sky from which they appear to come. Most meteor showers consist of only five or six meteors per hour. Shower meteors usually burn up completely in the atmosphere.

Figure 5-19 Three meteorites; the one at bottom left is a piece cut from a larger meteorite.

Table 5-3 Some Yearly Meteor Showers			
Name of Shower	**Dates**	**Constellation**	**Comet**
Lyrids	April 19–23	Hercules	1861 I
Eta Aquarids	May 1–6	Aquarids	Halley
Perseids	August 10–14	Cassiopeia	1862 III
Orionids	October 18–23	Orion	Halley
Andromedids	November 14	Andromeda	Biela
Leonids	November 14–18	Leo	1866 I

Most of the impact craters on the planets and moons of the solar system were made by debris that came from asteroids. These impacts occurred during the first billion years of the solar system. Now large impacts occur at a rate of about one every million years. Figure 5-20 (right) shows a large meteor that passed into and out of the atmosphere over Wyoming in 1972. The meteor was bright enough to be visible in full daylight. There was another narrow escape on March 22, 1989. The asteroid 1989FC passed Earth at less than twice the distance of the moon. 1989FC will return in the year 2015, but will pass Earth at a safer distance. Figure 5-20 (left) shows the Barringer Crater in Arizona, which is the best-preserved crater caused by a meteorite impact. The meteorite that formed the crater struck the Arizona desert about 40 000 years ago.

Figure 5-20 *Left:* Barringer Crater in Arizona; *Right:* This meteor passed over Grand Teton National Park in 1972.

ACTIVITY 5.3

Paper & Pencil

SOLAR-SYSTEM MODEL

Purpose To form a model to summarize the features of solar system objects.

Materials

light cardboard
ruler
pencil

drawing compass
colored pencils

Procedure

1. Read all instructions for this activity before you begin your work.

2. Place the cardboard in front of you so that the long side faces you.

3. In the lower left corner of the cardboard, draw a 2-cm-wide arc to represent the sun.

4. Use your compass to draw circles to represent the planets. Group the planets by size and surface type:

   1-cm circles for Mercury, Mars, and Pluto
   2-cm circles for Earth and Venus
   5-cm circles for Uranus and Neptune
   8-cm circles for Jupiter and Saturn

5. Draw rings and moons for the planets that have them, making their sizes as realistic as you can.

6. Add the asteroid belt between the sun and the two planet-groups. The exact location of the belt is not important.

7. Use your colored pencils to color the planets, moons, and rings realistically. Label all planets and major moons.

Collecting and Analyzing Data

1. List the planets that have no moons.

2. List the planets that have rings.

Drawing Conclusions

3. Explain how the two planetary groupings you have learned about—inner and outer, terrestrial and gaseous—differ from one another.

4. Why do the largest planets have so many moons and rings?

5. In general, what determines the colors of the planets?

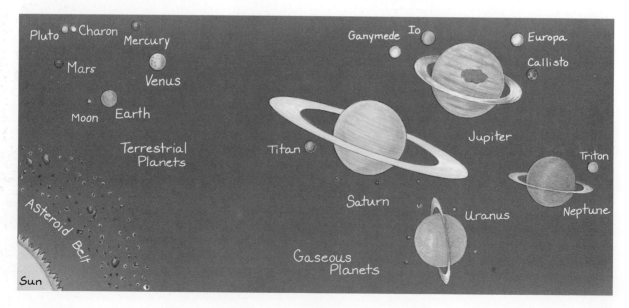

Lesson Review 5.3

12. List and describe the three groups of objects that are left over from the origin of the solar system.

13. Describe one theory for the origin of the solar system.

14. How did the asteroids most likely form?

15. What role have impacts by comet or asteroid pieces played in changing Earth's surface?

Interpret and Apply

16. How can you tell the direction a comet is moving?

17. Halley's Comet has been observed for at least 2000 years. During this time, it has made about 30 trips around the sun. Predict what will happen to the size of the head of Halley's Comet in the future.

Chapter Summary

Read this summary of the main ideas in this chapter. If any are not clear to you, go back and review that lesson.

5.1 A Model of the Solar System

■ The planets revolve around the sun and shine by reflected sunlight.

■ The inner planets are smaller than the outer planets. The exception is Pluto, which is both the smallest and the farthest planet.

■ All planets revolve around the sun in elliptical orbits. A line joining a planet and the sun passes over equal areas of space in equal time intervals. The farther a planet is from the sun, the longer is the planet's period of revolution.

■ Some recent and planned space probes include the *Voyagers*, *Magellan*, and *Galileo*.

5.2 A Tour of the Planets

■ The terrestrial planets have rocky surfaces. The gaseous planets have thick atmospheres over oceans and rock-ice cores.

■ The inner planets are all terrestrial in surface type. The outer planets are gaseous. The exception is probably Pluto, which appears to be an outer, rocky planet.

■ Spacecraft have observed all of the planets except Pluto.

5.3 Comets, Asteroids, and Meteors

■ The solar system may have formed from a cloud of gas and dust 4.6 billion years ago. Asteroids and comets may be leftovers from the origin of the solar system.

■ Comets are balls of rock and frozen gas that come from beyond Pluto and revolve around the sun in elliptical orbits.

■ Most asteroids revolve around the sun between the orbits of Mars and Jupiter.

■ Meteors are pieces of old asteroids or comets that burn up as they fall through Earth's atmosphere.

■ Pieces of asteroids and old comets have struck Earth in the past.

Chapter Review

■ Vocabulary

asteroid
astronomical unit
comet
gaseous planet
inner planet
meteor
meteor shower

outer planet
planet
protoplanet
solar wind
space probe
terrestrial planet

■ Concept Mapping

Construct a concept map for the origin of the solar system. Include the following terms: *gas and dust, protoplanets, closer to sun, farther from sun, rock, asteroids, terrestrial planets, gaseous planets, comets, Venus, Earth, Jupiter, Uranus.*

■ Review

Number your paper from 1 to 20. Match each term in List **A** with a phrase in List **B.**

List A

a. Barringer Crater
b. Mars
c. exploding star
d. meteor shower
e. *Magellan*
f. Law of Areas
g. Venus
h. asteroids
i. Uranus
j. Pluto

k. sun
l. Mercury
m. *Voyager 2*
n. protoplanet
o. Earth
p. Jupiter
q. meteors
r. Neptune
s. Comet West
t. Saturn

List B

1. planet that would float if you could put it in water
2. pieces of rock that burn up as they fall through the atmosphere
3. lumps that shrank to form the planets
4. space probe that observed all of the outer planets except Pluto
5. planet that has no atmosphere
6. created by a meteorite in Arizona
7. dirty snowball that passed Earth on its way around the sun in 1976
8. most are located between Mars and Jupiter
9. largest object in the solar system
10. is tipped over with its pole now facing the sun
11. has liquid water on its surface
12. the largest planet
13. observed by *Voyager 2* in August 1989
14. a double planet
15. caused by leftover rock pieces from an old comet
16. caused the collapse of a cloud of gas and dust that formed the solar system
17. describes the motions of solar-system objects in their orbits
18. has polar ice caps made of carbon dioxide and water
19. scheduled to map the surface of Venus
20. planet with highest average temperature

■ Interpret and Apply

On your paper, answer each question.

21. Explain why drawing a single diagram of planet distances and sizes using the scale "1 cm = 1 A.U." would not work well.
22. Pluto is an exceptional planet in many ways. Explain how it may have become the way it is. Refer to the origin of the solar system and objects other than planets in your explanation.
23. Use Kepler's laws to explain how a planet's average orbital speed relates to its distance from the sun.

24. Explain why you can never see Mercury and Venus at midnight. Hint: Draw a sketch of the inner planets in their orbits.

25. Use Table 5-1 to calculate how many days an imaginary resident of Jupiter would experience in one of Jupiter's years.

26. Use the theory for the origin of the solar system to explain why the terrestrial and gaseous planets are nearly the same groups as the inner and outer planets.

27. Chiron (kī run) is a strange object that follows a highly elliptical orbit between Jupiter and Uranus. Chiron is the size of an average asteroid. Chiron has no visible tail. Explain why astronomers have had difficulty classifying Chiron as a comet or an asteroid.

28. The Orionid meteors appear to come from the constellation Orion in mid-October every year. Explain why the part of the sky from which the Orionids come is the same every year.

29. Why would it be difficult to include Pluto in any space probe mission to the outer planets? Explain your answer.

30. How should the number of impact craters on Venus compare with the number on Mercury? Explain your answer.

■ Writing in Science

31. Kepler and Galileo were alive at the same time, and had heard of each other's work. Imagine that you are Johannes Kepler. You have received a letter from Galileo. Galileo has heard that you think a planet travels faster when it is nearest the sun than when it is farthest away. He wants you to explain this idea. Write a letter to Galileo in which you use the Law of Areas to explain why a planet's orbital speed is not always the same.

■ Critical Thinking

The table below compares the volumes and masses of other planets to Earth's volume and mass. Use the information to answer the questions.

Planet	Volume	Mass
Mercury	0.056	0.056
Venus	0.855	0.815
Earth	1.000	1.000
Mars	0.15	0.11
Jupiter	1430	318
Saturn	841	95
Uranus	69	15
Neptune	58	17

32. How many Mercury volumes would be required to fill one Earth volume?

33. How many Mercury masses would be required to balance the mass of one Earth?

34. How many Earth volumes would be needed to fill one Jupiter volume?

35. How many Mars masses would be needed to balance the mass of one Saturn?

36. According to the data, Uranus is larger but less massive than Neptune. That is, Uranus takes up more space than Neptune but is less massive than Neptune. Write a hypothesis to explain this fact.

37. Use Table 5-1 on page 119 to calculate the number of Earth-sized planets that you could place side by side through the center of Jupiter.

Stars and the Sun

Chapter Preview

Have You Ever WONDERED?

Where did the names of the constellations come from?

Constellations are fixed patterns of stars in the sky. Throughout history, different societies gave different names to the constellations. People told stories to remember the constellations and their place in the sky. In one Greek myth, Orion the Hunter was slain by the Scorpion. Zeus put these constellations at opposite ends of the sky to keep them apart. It is still true today that Orion sets in the west when Scorpio rises in the east.

Most of the constellation names used today come from ancient Babylonian, Greek, and Roman myths. The constellations were inherited from these cultures along with much of our language, science, and mathematics. The constellations you see now look about the same as they did thousands of years ago. In this chapter, you will learn about the stars—what they are made of, how they shine, and what their fates will be.

Observing Stars

If you study the stars, you will see that some stars are much brighter than others. Some stars are red; others are yellow or blue. With practice, you can find **constellations,** which are groups of stars in fixed patterns. In this lesson, you will learn how to find several constellations.

Star Motions

Do stars move through space? If they do, then why do constellations always look the same? In fact, stars move through space at speeds hundreds of times faster than a jet plane. When you see a plane from a distance, it seems to cross the sky very slowly. The farther away the plane is, the slower it seems to move. But the nearest star is more than 40 trillion kilometers from Earth! At that distance, a star's motion is too small to see without telescopes.

Of course, stars appear to move because Earth is moving. The stars move in a full circle once every 24 hours because Earth is rotating on its axis. Stars also circle the sky once each year as Earth orbits the sun. Finding constellations is easy once you understand the motions of the stars.

Looking south, the daily motion of stars is different from what you observe toward the north. Figure 6-1 *(left)* shows the star trails you get by taking a long-exposure photograph facing south. Compare this with the star trails in the north shown in Figure 6-1 *(right)*. In the south, stars move in large arcs, rising in the east and setting in the west. In the north, stars circle around Polaris. Stars close to Polaris move in such small circles that they never rise or set. These stars are called circumpolar stars. Circumpolar stars are visible all year, weather permitting.

Lesson Objectives

▸ **Name and identify** several constellations.

▸ **Illustrate** the daily and yearly movements of seasonal and circumpolar constellations.

▸ **Explain** what a light-year is.

▸ **Contrast** a star's absolute magnitude with its apparent magnitude.

▸ **Activity** *Observe and describe* how the stars change position throughout the night.

New Terms

constellation
light-year
parallax
apparent magnitude
absolute magnitude

Figure 6-1 *Left:* Facing south, stars seem to move from east to west. *Right:* Facing north, stars seem to move in counterclockwise circles around Polaris.

You can observe the daily motion of the stars in the south in a period of an hour or two. Go out at 8 P.M. on a clear night and face south. Look up and choose a bright star. Sketch the position of your star compared to a landmark on the horizon. Then observe the same star again at 9 P.M. and 10 P.M. Which way did the star move?

The yearly motion of the stars is too small to notice in one night, but you can observe this motion over longer periods of time. Go out at 8 P.M. on a clear night two weeks after your first observations. Find the same star in the south and record its position on your sketch. Compared to the star's position at 8 P.M. two weeks earlier, how has the star moved? As Earth orbits the sun, stars in the south move slightly westward each day. As the months pass, some stars disappear below the western horizon, while other stars appear above the eastern horizon. After one full year, the stars return to their original positions.

What happens to the circumpolar stars in the north throughout the year? Observe the Big Dipper for several weeks at 8 P.M. In about a month, you will notice its counterclockwise motion about Polaris.

Constellations

Astronomers worldwide have agreed to divide the sky into 88 constellations. Dividing the night sky into pieces is like dividing the United States into states. Each star has a location in its constellation, like a city has a location in its state. Once you know a few constellations, you can use them as landmarks to find other stars and constellations.

The Big Dipper is one of the easiest constellations to find because it has seven bright stars. The Big Dipper is part of a larger constellation called Ursa Major. You used the Big Dipper in Chapter 2 to find Polaris, the North Star. Polaris is the last star in the handle of the Little Dipper, also called Ursa Minor. You need a clear night to see the Little Dipper because its stars are dim. An easier constellation to find is Cassiopeia [kas ē ə pē′ yə]. Look for five bright stars that make a big "W" or big "M" in the north. Cassiopeia is sometimes upside down, depending on the time of year.

Figure 6-2 shows the position of the circumpolar constellations as they appear in the autumn. The Big Dipper, the Little Dipper, and Cassiopeia are circumpolar constellations for most latitudes in the United States. You can see these constellations looking north on every night of the year. Constellations in the southern part of your sky are visible only at a particular season. The star charts on the next two pages show the constellations of each season.

Figure 6-2 The circumpolar constellations can be seen all year. They are shown here in their position during the autumn evenings.

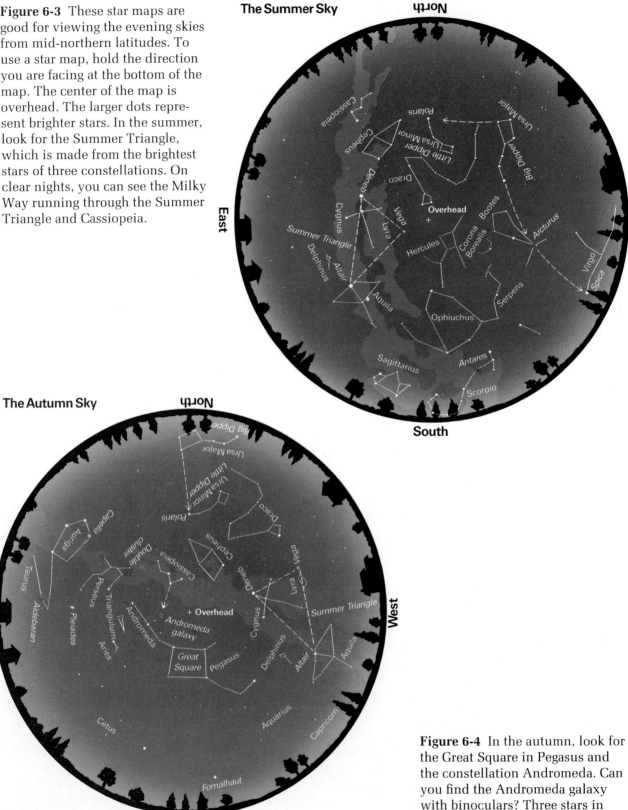

Figure 6-3 These star maps are good for viewing the evening skies from mid-northern latitudes. To use a star map, hold the direction you are facing at the bottom of the map. The center of the map is overhead. The larger dots represent brighter stars. In the summer, look for the Summer Triangle, which is made from the brightest stars of three constellations. On clear nights, you can see the Milky Way running through the Summer Triangle and Cassiopeia.

Figure 6-4 In the autumn, look for the Great Square in Pegasus and the constellation Andromeda. Can you find the Andromeda galaxy with binoculars? Three stars in Cassiopeia point the way.

Figure 6-5 In the winter, look for Orion, one of the brightest constellations. The three stars in Orion's belt point to Sirius, the brightest star in the sky. Can you find the Orion Nebula and the Pleiades with binoculars?

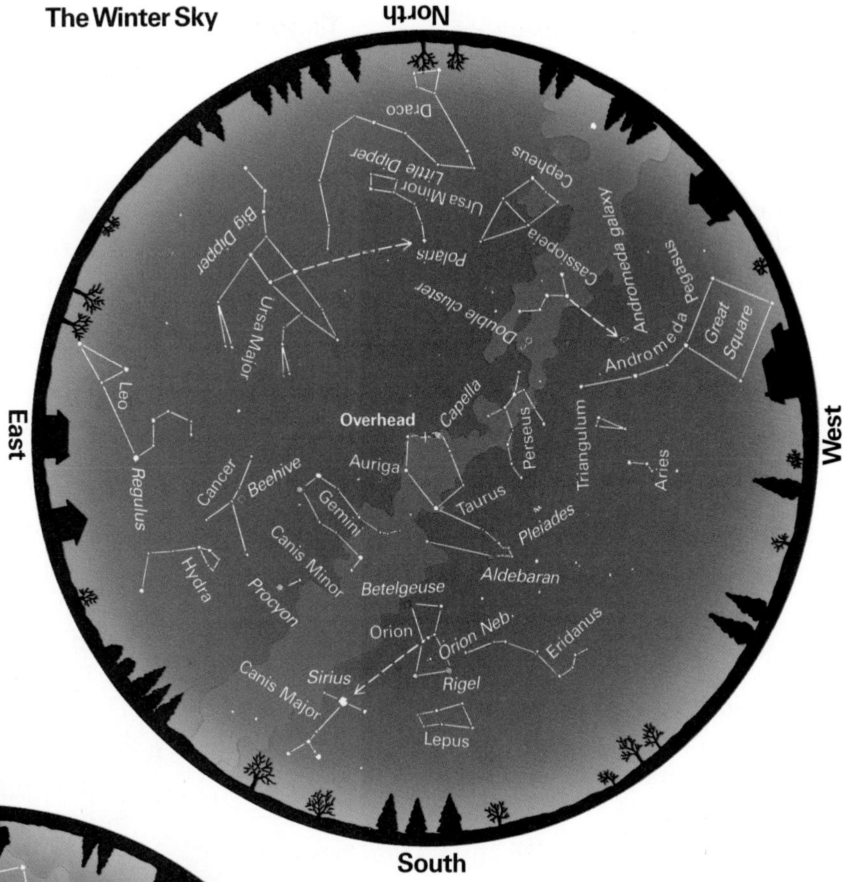

The Winter Sky

North

East

West

South

Draco
Cepheus
Little Dipper
Ursa Minor
Cassiopeia
Andromeda galaxy
Pegasus
Big Dipper
Polaris
Double cluster
Andromeda
Great Square
Ursa Major
Capella
Perseus
Triangulum
Aries
Leo
Overhead
Auriga
Taurus
Pleiades
Regulus
Cancer
Beehive
Gemini
Aldebaran
Hydra
Canis Minor
Betelgeuse
Procyon
Orion
Orion Neb.
Eridanus
Canis Major
Sirius
Rigel
Lepus

The Spring Sky

North

East

West

South

Deneb
Cassiopeia
Cepheus
Vega
Little Dipper
Draco
Ursa Minor
Capella
Hercules
Polaris
Auriga
Bootes
Big Dipper
Serpens
Ursa Major
Gemini
Betelgeuse
Corona Borealis
Overhead
Beehive
Canis Minor
Arcturus
Cancer
Procyon
Denebola
Leo
Regulus
Virgo
Hydra
Spica
Corvus

Figure 6-6 You can use the Big Dipper's handle to find two of the brightest stars of the spring sky. Just "arc to Arcturus and spike to Spica." Compare the red color of Arcturus to the blue color of Spica.

A C T I V I T Y   6 . 1

MAKING A STAR DOME MAP

Purpose   To observe and describe how the stars change position throughout the night.

Materials _____

tape	protractor
pushpin	copy of star dome
pencil with eraser	(Figure 6-7)
scissors	

Procedure

1. Read all instructions for this activity before you begin your work.

2. Cut out the large pentagon on the copy of the star dome and then cut along the dashed lines. **CAUTION: Use scissors with care. The points and edges are sharp.**

3. Fold at each solid line. Then tape each shaded triangle to the back of the next pentagon. The star dome should look like the one in the figure.

4. Push the pushpin through Polaris and firmly into the eraser on the end of the pencil, as shown in the photograph. **CAUTION: Be careful with the pushpin. The point is sharp.** You should be able to turn the star dome by turning the pencil.

5. Hold the star dome above your head, pointing the pencil up at a 45° angle as shown in the photograph. Imagine that the pencil points at the real Polaris. Spin the star dome counterclockwise by turning the pencil. Does Polaris move? Record your observations of the motions of the constellations Cassiopeia, the Big Dipper, and the Little Dipper.

6. Turn the star dome around so that the pencil points up at a 45° angle behind your head. You are now looking south. Find Orion. Spin the pencil so that Orion rises in the east (your left) and sets in the west (your right). Can you always see Orion? Record your observations of Orion's motion.

Collecting and Analyzing Data

1. Do the circumpolar constellations move in circles as you turn the star dome? Describe the size of the circle compared to the distance from Polaris.

2. How is the motion of Orion similar to the motions of circumpolar constellations? How is it different?

Drawing Conclusions

3. Explain why the circumpolar stars never set. Why do the constellations in the south rise and set?

4. If the circumpolar constellations never set, why do you think you cannot see them during the day?

Figure 6-7 This Star Dome shows the winter
sky from mid-northern latitudes.

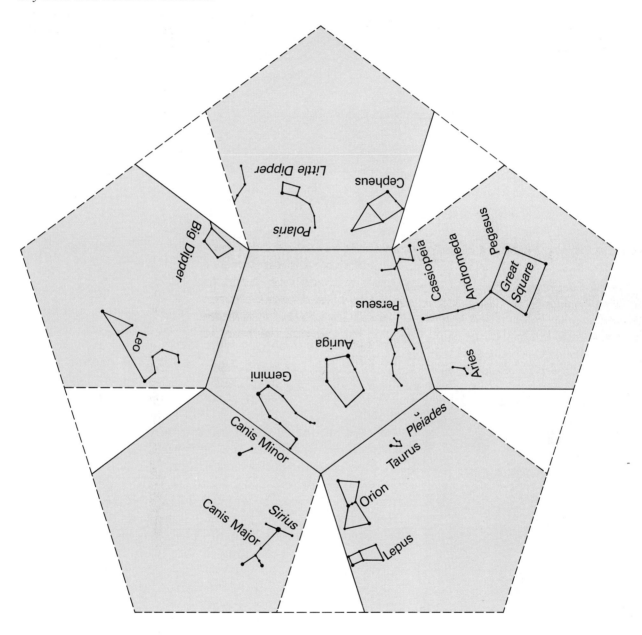

Figure 6-8 The stars in the Big Dipper appear to be the same brightness. Does this mean that all of these stars are the same distance from Earth?

Figure 6-9 In January, the close star appears to be at point *A*. Six months later, when Earth is at the opposite end of its orbit, the close star seems to be at point *B*. This apparent shift is called parallax.

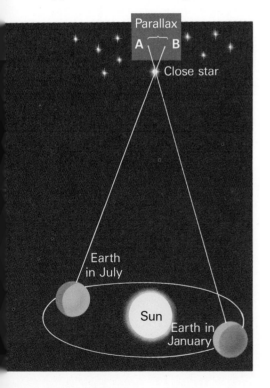

Star Distances

All of the stars that you see at night are part of the Milky Way galaxy. The Milky Way contains about 200 billion stars. On a clear night, you might think that you can see millions of stars. Actually, you see only about 3000 stars with your unaided eye. To understand why so few stars are visible, think about how you see a flashlight from a distance. At 1 meter, the flashlight is bright. At 50 meters, it appears dimmer. If the flashlight were far enough away, it would be too faint to see. For the same reason, you cannot see most of the stars in the Milky Way because they are too far away.

Astronomers measure distances to stars using the speed of light. Light travels at 300 000 kilometers per second. At this rate, sunlight takes 8 minutes to reach your eyes. Thus, the distance to the sun is 8 light-minutes. Distances to stars are measured in light-years. A **light-year** is the distance that light travels in one year, about 9.5 trillion kilometers. The nearest star, Proxima Centauri, is 4.2 light-years from Earth. The distance to Polaris is 680 light-years. When you look into space, you look into the past. The light you see from Polaris left the star long before Columbus set sail for America.

Figure 6-9 shows how to measure distance to a star by measuring its parallax. **Parallax** is the apparent shift in an object's position that is caused by the motion of the observer. You can see the parallax of your finger if you look at it only with your left eye and then only with your right eye. Your finger seems to move compared to the background. Try observing the parallax again with your finger closer to your eyes. How does the parallax change? You can observe the parallax of nearby stars with a telescope. The closer a star is, the greater is its parallax.

Table 6-1 Distance of Several Bright Stars

Star	Constellation	Apparent Magnitude	Absolute Magnitude	Distance (light-years)
Sun		−26	5	0.00002
Alpha Centauri	Centaurus	0	4	4.3
Sirius	Canis Major	−1	1	8.7
Arcturus	Bootes	0	0	36
Spica	Virgo	1	−3	270
Polaris	Ursa Minor	2	−5	680
Rigel	Orion	0	−7	815

How could you measure the distance to stars that are far-ther away? If all stars gave off the same amount of light, then the stars that appear brighter would be closer to you. However, stars differ in the amount of light they give off. Table 6-1 compares the brightness and distance of several stars. The **apparent magnitude** tells you how bright a star appears as seen from Earth. Stars that appear bright have a low magnitude, while dim stars have a high magnitude. For example, a first-magnitude star (magnitude = 1) appears brighter than a sixth-magnitude star (magnitude = 6). The **absolute magnitude** tells you how much light a star gives off. Astronomers have agreed to measure the absolute mag-nitude of stars as how bright they would appear from a distance of 32.6 light-years. The apparent magnitude of a star depends on both its distance from Earth and the amount of light it gives off. If you know a star's apparent magnitude and absolute magnitude, you can calculate its distance.

Lesson Review 6.1

1. Sketch one seasonal and one circumpolar constellation.
2. Using the constellations in question 1, sketch how each constellation moves in one night.
3. What is a light-year?
4. Compare two stars in Table 6-1 to explain the difference between absolute and apparent magnitude.

Interpret and Apply

5. Explain why stars change position during the year.
6. Explain why you cannot always see a particular planet. (Hint: Planets are never near Polaris.)

6.2 Telescopes

The most important purpose of a telescope is to gather light. You can think of a telescope as catching light the same way a bucket in the rain catches water. The larger the diameter of the bucket, the more rain it will catch. A telescope gathers more light than your eyes because it has a larger diameter. With a telescope, you see stars too dim to see with your unaided eye. A telescope also magnifies images, which makes it easier to study distant objects in the sky. In this lesson, you will find out how telescopes work.

Electromagnetic Spectrum

What is light? Light is an energy wave that moves through space. Light is one kind of electromagnetic wave. All electromagnetic waves have no mass, can travel through empty space, move through empty space at 300 000 kilometers per second, and travel in straight lines.

You probably have seen waves in the ocean. Ocean waves rise and fall as they move through the water. The distance between the peak of one wave and the peak of the next wave is called the **wavelength**. Ocean waves can have many different wavelengths. Electromagnetic waves also have many different wavelengths. You can use a prism to separate white light into the colors of the spectrum. Each color of light has a different wavelength. Red light has a longer wavelength than blue light.

Figure 6-10 shows the entire **electromagnetic spectrum**, which includes electromagnetic waves of all different wavelengths. The short wavelength radiation includes ultraviolet radiation, gamma rays, and X rays. These are high-energy

Figure 6-10 The electromagnetic spectrum is made up of electromagnetic waves with many different wavelengths.

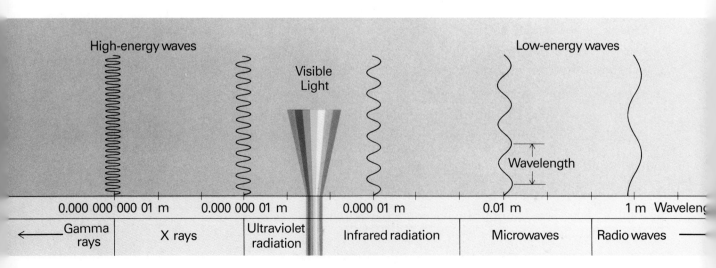

High-energy waves

Low-energy waves

Visible Light

Wavelength

| 0.000 000 000 01 m | 0.000 000 01 m | 0.000 01 m | 0.01 m | 1 m Wavelength |

| Gamma rays | X rays | Ultraviolet radiation | Infrared radiation | Microwaves | Radio waves |

waves. The long wavelength radiation includes infrared radiation, microwaves, and radio waves. These are low-energy waves. In fact, radio waves are hitting your body right now, but they are not dangerous because they do not carry much energy.

Optical Telescopes

There are two kinds of optical (visible-light) telescopes, the refracting telescope and the reflecting telescope, shown in Figure 6-11. A **refracting telescope** is made of a series of lenses that collect light and focus it to form a magnified image. The large glass lens gathers light. The purpose of the smaller lens, which is called an eyepiece, is to focus the light and magnify the image. In 1609, Galileo used a refracting telescope to discover craters on the moon and the moons of Jupiter. Astronomers soon built larger refracting telescopes that led to more discoveries. The largest refracting telescope in use today is at the Yerkes Observatory in Wisconsin. The lens of the Yerkes telescope is 1 meter in diameter. If the lens of the Yerkes telescope were any larger, it would bend from its own weight.

Reflecting telescopes use a dish-shaped, or concave, mirror instead of a lens. The mirror gathers light and bounces it off a second mirror. A glass eyepiece then focuses the light and magnifies the image. A mirror can be much larger than a lens because it can be supported from behind. For many years, the largest reflecting telescope was the Hale telescope on Mount Palomar in California, shown in Figure 6-12. The mirror is 5 meters in diameter and weighs 5500 kilograms! Because a heavier mirror would bend, many people thought the Hale telescope was the largest possible telescope.

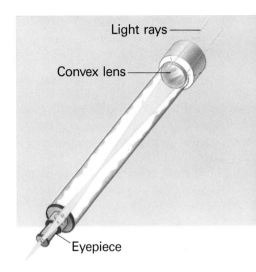

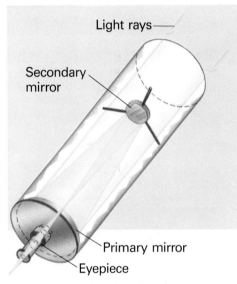

Figure 6-11 *Top:* A refracting telescope uses a convex glass lens to gather and focus light. *Bottom:* In a reflecting telescope, the concave primary mirror gathers light. The secondary mirror then reflects the light to the eyepiece. Why is there a hole in the primary mirror?

Figure 6-12 The Hale telescope, at the Mount Palomar Observatory in California, is used by astronomers from all over the world.

Figure 6-13 Why does the Keck telescope, with 36 mirrors, collect more light than a telescope would with just one of these mirrors?

In the 1980's, astronomers designed several new types of reflecting telescopes. One exciting new design is the Multiple Mirror telescope, which uses several small mirrors instead of one large one. The first Multiple Mirror telescope was a 4.5-meter telescope at Mount Hopkins Observatory in Arizona. In the early 1990's, the Keck telescope is due to begin working on Mauna Kea, an extinct volcano in Hawaii. The Keck telescope uses 36 hexagon-shaped mirrors, shown in Figure 6-13. Together, these mirrors equal a single mirror 10 meters across.

Another type of reflecting telescope uses a new, lighter mirror. In the past, mirrors were made by pouring hot liquid glass into a mold and cooling the glass slowly. The new method, called spin casting, spins the mirror slowly while it cools. The result is a much larger, but lighter, mirror. One of these new mirrors, 6.5 meters in diameter, is due to start working in 1992 on Mount Hopkins.

Yet another type of telescope is a reflecting telescope launched into orbit. The Hubble Space Telescope was launched in 1990. Although the 2.5-meter Space Telescope is smaller than many telescopes, its view is not affected by Earth's atmosphere. You see the effect of the atmosphere when you watch a star twinkle. The Space Telescope, at a height of 600 kilometers above Earth's surface, avoids all of the problems of the atmosphere.

ENVIRONMENTAL AWARENESS

Light Pollution

Have you ever noticed how many more stars you see when you are far away from city lights? The glow of the sky above cities or towns, called light pollution, washes out the light from dim stars. Light pollution is a serious problem for observatories built near cities that have grown larger. To avoid light pollution, new observatories are built far away from cities. For example, the Cerro Tololo Observatory is on a remote mountain in Chile, South America. This observatory will be safe from light pollution for years to come.

There is some hope for observatories near cities. Tucson is a fast-growing city only 80 kilometers from the observatory at Kitt Peak, Arizona. To protect the Kitt Peak telescopes, Tucson replaced its streetlights with special lights that reduce light pollution. The new lights shine in a narrow range of wavelengths that can be filtered out at the telescopes. As it turns out, the new lights also use less electricity. In the future, cooperation between scientists and local communities may save other observatories. ∎

Invisible Astronomy

Some telescopes gather invisible electromagnetic radiation. Radio waves are produced by the sun, planets, stars, and clouds of gas and dust in the galaxy. The largest single radio telescope, shown in Figure 6-14, is at Arecibo, Puerto Rico. The 305-meter metallic dish is like the mirror of a reflecting telescope. The dish reflects radio waves to the receiver above it. The receiver responds to the strength of the radio waves by producing an electric signal that goes to a computer for processing. The receiver in a radio telescope works like the one inside a radio that you listen to. In fact, some of the noise you hear between radio stations is caused by radio waves from the sun.

Radio telescopes work day and night. They are not affected by the weather because clouds and rain do not block radio waves. Astronomers use radio waves to map the center of our galaxy, which is hidden from optical telescopes by large clouds of gas and dust in space.

Telescopes on Earth are limited mostly to visible light and radio waves because these wavelengths can travel through Earth's atmosphere. To observe other wavelengths, such as infrared radiation, gamma rays, and X rays, many telescopes have been sent into orbit.

Telescopes can analyze electromagnetic radiation with a special device called a spectroscope. A **spectroscope** acts like a prism to separate electromagnetic waves into a spectrum. The spectrum of each star is different. The spectrum reveals what a star is made of, its temperature, age, size, and brightness. You will learn more about this information in Lesson 6.4.

Figure 6-14 The Arecibo radio telescope in Puerto Rico is built into a large depression in the ground.

Lesson Review 6.2

7. List four properties of electromagnetic waves.

8. List the different kinds of energy in the electromagnetic spectrum, in order from short to long wavelength.

9. What is the main purpose of a telescope?

10. Give one example of each type of telescope discussed in this lesson.

Interpret and Apply

11. What are the advantages of putting a telescope in orbit?

12. Why do you think radio telescopes have to be larger than optical telescopes?

USING A SPECTROSCOPE

Purpose   To observe and describe different light sources with a spectroscope.

Materials

diffraction grating	masking tape
cardboard tube	scissors
incandescent light	blue cellophane
fluorescent light	red cellophane
index card	

Procedure

1. Read all instructions for this activity before you begin your work. Copy the data table onto your paper.

2. Using scissors, cut the index card in half. **CAUTION: Use scissors with care. The points and edges are sharp.** Cut a thin slit in one half of the index card. In the other half, poke a hole about 0.5 cm in diameter.

3. Cover each end of the cardboard tube with one piece of the index card. Center the slit and the hole in the tube. Tape the index cards to the tube, sealing it all the way around so that light can enter the tube only through the hole or slit.

4. Cover the hole with a piece of diffraction grating. Tape the grating to the tube by its edges.

5. Plug in the two lights and place them on tables where several students can view them. **CAUTION: Make sure electric cords do not dangle from tables.**

6. Aim the narrow slit at the incandescent light and look at the light through the spectroscope. **CAUTION: Never look at the sun.** Slowly move the spectroscope up and down or sideways. Record your observations.

7. Observe the light with the blue cellophane in front of the slit. Then observe the light with the red cellophane in front of the slit. Record your observations.

8. Repeat steps 6–7 with the fluorescent light.

9. Before leaving the laboratory, clean up all materials.

Collecting and Analyzing Data

Data Table

Light Source	Observations		
	No Filter	Red	Blue
Incandescent			
Fluorescent			

1. Describe your observations without the filters. What does the spectroscope do to visible light?

2. What similarities and differences are there between your observation of the incandescent and fluorescent lights?

3. How did the colored cellophane affect your observations? Was the change the same for both lights?

Drawing Conclusions

4. Predict what you would observe if you looked at a red incandescent light with a spectroscope? A red fluorescent light?

5. Does the spectrum of a light source give you information about the source? Explain.

6.3 The Sun

The sun is the nearest star, 250 000 times closer to Earth than any other star. In comparison to the planets, the sun is gigantic. The sun has 1000 times the volume of Jupiter and 1 000 000 (1 million) times the volume of Earth. In fact, the sun contains 99 percent of the mass in the solar system. But compared to other stars, the sun is just average.

The Sun's Structure

The sun radiates energy in all parts of the electromagnetic spectrum. Observing the sun at many wavelengths has led to a new understanding of the sun's structure. The current model of the sun has several layers: the core, the radiation zone, the convection zone, the photosphere, the chromosphere, and the corona. The boundaries between these layers are not sharp because the sun is always changing. Different activities occur in each layer.

Energy moves outward from the core through a radiation zone. Energy radiates in only one direction through this layer, toward the convection zone. The energy heats the convection zone, causing solar material to rise the same way that a hot air balloon rises in Earth's atmosphere. As the material rises, it cools and then sinks. The rising and falling of solar material in the convection zone gives the sun's surface a granular appearance.

Lesson Objectives

▸ **Explain** how the sun produces energy.

▸ **Relate** the layers of the sun to specific solar events.

▸ **Activity**   *Observe and describe* the motion of sunspots.

New Terms

photosphere	sunspot
chromosphere	solar flare
corona	prominence

Figure 6-15 The sun has many layers in which different activities take place. What is the hottest part of the sun?

Corona
(2 000 000°C)

Chromosphere
(15 000°C)

Photosphere
(5800°C)

Convection zone

Radiation zone

Core
(15 000 000°C)

Sunspots
(4000°C)

The visible surface of the sun is called the **photosphere.** The yellow color of the photosphere tells you that the temperature there is about 6000°C. To understand why color relates to temperature, think about a metal knife that is heated in a flame. The knife changes color as it gets hotter, starting off red, then turning yellow-orange, and finally changing to blue-white. At higher temperatures, the knife radiates higher-energy wavelengths of light. By the same logic, the color of the photosphere tells you its temperature.

The photosphere releases hot, electrically-charged particles into the **chromosphere,** the thin layer just above the photosphere. In the chromosphere, which is only 2000 kilometers thick, all the charged particles move outward. Judging from the red color of the chromosphere, would you say it is hotter or colder than the photosphere?

Above the chromosphere is the main part of the sun's atmosphere, the **corona,** which extends millions of kilometers into space. Temperatures in the corona rise to more than 2 000 000°C. Radiation and hot, charged particles that escape from the corona are called the solar wind. You learned in Chapter 5 that the position of a comet's tail demonstrates the effect of the solar wind. No one knows how far the solar wind extends. *Voyager I* and *Voyager II*, now beyond the solar system, may find out.

Solar Activity

Have you ever wondered what makes the sun shine? In the sun's core, where temperatures reach 15 000 000°C, hydrogen changes into helium in a process called fusion. During fusion, a small percentage of hydrogen's mass changes into energy, according to Einstein's famous equation, $E = mc^2$, where E is *energy*, m is *mass*, and c is the *speed of light*. Remember that the speed of light is a very large number. According to this equation, the fusion of a small amount of matter produces a lot of energy. In the sun's core, about 3500 kilograms of matter changes into energy every second. At this rate, the sun loses 300 000 000 kilograms of mass each day. But because the sun's total mass is so great, the sun will shine for billions of years before it uses up the hydrogen in its core.

Although the sun always looks the same, it is the most dynamic object in the solar system. Galileo realized that the sun changes when he observed sunspots crossing the sun's surface. **Sunspots** are the small dark spots on the photosphere shown in Figure 6-16. Sunspots are caused by the sun's strong magnetosphere, which is thousands of times stronger than Earth's magnetosphere. The sun's magnetism

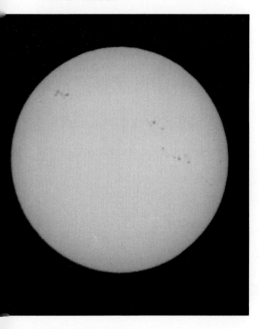

Figure 6-16 Sunspots are cooler and darker than the rest of the sun's surface.

pulls up cool material from the convection zone to the sun's surface. Sunspots appear dark because they are cooler than the surrounding photosphere. A sunspot by itself would appear very bright, just as a streetlight appears brighter at night than it does in daylight. Activity 6.3 shows you how to safely observe a projection of the sun's image. **NEVER LOOK DIRECTLY AT THE SUN.** The sun's ultraviolet radiation can burn your eyes before you realize it.

Sunspots can last for hours or for months. They move across the sun's surface in the same direction as the sun rotates on its imaginary axis. Sunspots take only 25 days to circle the sun near its equator. Sunspot activity follows an 11-year cycle. At sunspot maximum, sunspots are larger and more numerous. At sunspot minimum, the sun has fewer sunspots, and they are smaller. The last sunspot maximum started in 1990. When do you think the next sunspot maximum will start?

At sunspot maximum, the number of solar flares increases. **Solar flares,** shown in Figure 6-17, are outbursts of energy that last only a few hours. Radio waves given off by solar flares can disrupt radio transmissions on Earth. Solar flares also add charged particles to the solar wind. A few days after a solar flare, charged particles reach Earth and get trapped in Earth's magnetosphere. The charged particles excite the atmosphere near Earth's magnetic poles and cause beautiful light displays called auroras. Auroras are difficult to predict, but they are more likely to occur after energetic solar flares. Auroras are most common near Earth's magnetic poles, but they are sometimes seen from the tropics.

Prominences are another event related to sunspot activity. A **prominence** is a loop of solar material that can extend more than a million kilometers above the photosphere. Although a prominence looks like an eruption moving away from the sun's surface, it actually is material from the corona that is falling back toward the sun.

Figure 6-17 *Top:* Solar flares are violent eruptions associated with sunspot activity. *Bottom:* A few days after a solar flare, auroras are more likely to occur on Earth.

Lesson Review 6.3

13. Describe the process that makes the sun shine.

14. List the layers of the sun and describe the activities that occur in each layer.

Interpret and Apply

15. Why do you think that radio broadcasts on Earth are affected by solar flares?

OBSERVING SUNSPOTS

Purpose
To observe and describe the motion of sunspots.

Materials

simple telescope	white paper
masking tape	pencil
piece of cardboard	tripod or stand
clipboard	scissors

Procedure

1. Read all instructions for this activity before you begin your work.

2. Use the scissors to cut a hole in the piece of cardboard. **CAUTION: Use scissors with care. The points and edges are sharp.** The hole should just fit the telescope, as shown in the figure. Use masking tape to attach the cardboard to the telescope. (Binoculars can also be used.)

3. On a sunny day, mount the telescope, clipboard, and white paper as shown. **CAUTION: Never look at the sun directly. Filters or photographic negatives do not protect your eyes.** Move the white paper until the sun's image is focused on it.

4. Outline the sun on the white paper using a sharp pencil. Sketch in any sunspots you observe. Record the date and time on the paper.

5. Store the materials in a safe place. On the next sunny day, set up the materials again. On a new sheet of paper, make another observation. Record the date and time for each observation.

Collecting and Analyzing Data

1. How many different sunspots did you observe?

2. How could you tell if a sunspot on one day was the same as a sunspot on another day?

3. How long did it take for sunspots to move off the edge of the sun?

Drawing Conclusions

4. What does sunspot movement suggest to you about the sun?

5. Can you tell from this activity if the sun and sunspots rotate at the same rate? Why or why not?

6.4 Stars and Galaxies

Compared to the rest of the universe, Earth is anything but average. The universe is mostly hydrogen and helium, at temperatures much colder or hotter than Earth's surface. In this lesson, you will learn about stars, galaxies, and the big bang theory of how the universe began.

Comparing Stars

If you make a graph that compares star color to the light given off by a star (absolute magnitude), you get the graph shown in Figure 6-18. The graph is called a Hertzsprung-Russell (or H-R) diagram. To understand this graph, suppose you made a similar graph that compares height to weight for the students in your class. The graph would show that taller people weigh more, on average. In the same way, the H-R diagram shows a pattern between star brightness and star color. For example, only a few stars are both red and bright. Few stars are both blue and dim. About 90 percent of the stars fall in a line on the graph called the **main sequence.** The main sequence includes dim red stars and bright blue stars, with average yellow, orange, and blue-white stars in between.

Why are blue stars on the main sequence bright? Remember that short wavelengths of light correspond to high energy. A blue star has a higher surface temperature than a red star. So, if other properties such as size are the same, a blue star is brighter than a red star because it is hotter.

Lesson Objectives

▶ **Describe** differences and similarities among stars.

▶ **Describe** the origin and stages of a star.

▶ **List** the three common types of galaxies.

▶ **Explain** the evidence for the big bang theory.

▶ **Activity** *Form a model* of the expanding universe.

New Terms

main sequence	black hole
red giant	galaxy
white dwarf	quasar
nebula	big bang
supernova	theory
neutron star	

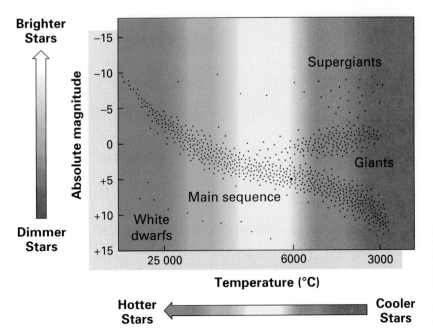

Figure 6-18 Each point on the Hertzsprung-Russell diagram is plotted from the values for a star's temperature (color) and its absolute magnitude (the amount of light it gives off).

What about stars that are off the main sequence? If two stars are the same color but different sizes, the larger star is brighter because it has more surface area. Thus, the brightness and color of a star tells you the star's size. By this logic, the bright red stars in the upper right of the H-R diagram are called **red giants.** The dim white stars in the lower left are called **white dwarfs.**

Stages of Stars

Figure 6-19 shows how a star develops. Most stars form from the collapse of a large cloud of gas and dust called a **nebula.** You learned in Chapter 5 that the sun formed this way. As a nebula collapses, the pressure and temperature increase over millions of years. When temperatures reach 10 000 000°C, hydrogen fusion begins, and a star forms.

A star will shine for millions or even billions of years until it uses up the hydrogen in its core. At this stage, the star is on the main sequence of the H-R diagram. The starting mass of a star determines what happens next. Stars with more mass than the sun build up higher temperatures in their cores because of the greater force of gravity pulling the star together. These high-mass stars are hot blue stars that use up the hydrogen in their cores in just 50 million years. Low-mass stars are cool red stars that last for billions of years before using up the hydrogen in their cores. High-mass stars are like racing cars that travel fast but get poor gas mileage. Low-mass stars are like economy cars that cannot go fast but have good fuel economy.

Figure 6-19 *Top:* The bright stars at the center of the Orion Nebula are young stars that formed only a few million years ago. *Bottom:* The changes that a star goes through depend on the starting mass of the star.

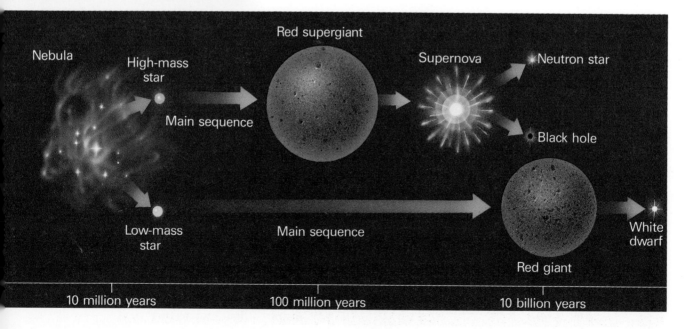

What happens when the hydrogen in a star's core is gone? First the star collapses, causing the core to heat up. This in turn causes the outer layers of the star to expand and cool off. If the star has about the same mass as the sun, it becomes a red giant, more than 100 times the diameter of the original star. In the core of a red giant, energy is produced by the fusion of helium into heavier elements such as carbon. Millions of years later, when the core runs out of helium, the star expands violently and loses its outer layers. This leaves behind the dense, hot core, called a white dwarf.

For stars that are more than eight times the sun's mass, the end is far more spectacular. When the hydrogen in the core is used up, the core collapses and heats up. Then the outer layers expand to form a red supergiant. A red supergiant is 1000 times the original diameter of the star. The core of the supergiant collapses further and explodes violently. This explosion, called a **supernova,** is millions of times brighter than a star. The supernova leaves behind a small hot core, no larger than Earth, called a **neutron star.** Some neutron stars spin very fast and give off strong radio waves. Fast-spinning neutron stars are called pulsars.

For stars more than 30 times the mass of the sun, the final stage of the star is a black hole. A **black hole** is a star so massive that nothing can escape its gravity, not even light. Black holes are like vacuum cleaners that pull everything nearby into them. As material falls into the black hole, it gets very hot and gives off X rays. Figure 6-21 is an artist's view of what a black hole might look like.

Figure 6-20 In A.D. 1054, Chinese astronomers recorded the position of a supernova that was visible in the daytime. Today the Crab Nebula is found at this same position in the sky. The Crab Nebula formed from the outer layers of the star that exploded.

Figure 6-21 This is an artist's view of a black hole pulling in matter from another star. How would you observe a black hole?

Figure 6-22 This is what the Milky Way galaxy would look like if you were outside of it. The Milky Way is 100 000 light-years across. The solar system takes 200 million years to complete one orbit around the galactic center.

Figure 6-23 Galaxies look like nebulas, but they contain billions of stars. *Left:* The Andromeda galaxy is a typical spiral galaxy. *Middle:* An elliptical galaxy. *Right:* The Large Magellanic Cloud is an irregular galaxy.

Galaxies

Groups of hundreds of billions of stars held together by gravity are called **galaxies.** The sun and all the stars that you can see belong to the Milky Way galaxy. The Milky Way is a spiral galaxy that slowly rotates. The spiral arms of the galaxy contain gas and dust where star formation takes place. You cannot see the spiral of the Milky Way because you are inside the galaxy. Instead, you see the Milky Way as a band of stars that makes a complete circle in the sky. The nearest spiral galaxy to your own is the Andromeda galaxy, about 2.2 million light-years from Earth. While that might seem far, you could fit only 15 galaxies between the Milky Way and the Andromeda galaxy. Figure 6-23 *(left)* shows the spiral structure of the Andromeda galaxy.

There are two other kinds of galaxies—elliptical and irregular galaxies. Elliptical galaxies, like the one shown in Figure 6-23 *(middle),* have a round globular shape, with most of their stars in the center. Elliptical galaxies do not rotate. These galaxies mostly contain old stars because they do not have much gas and dust. The Large Magellanic Cloud, shown in Figure 6-23 *(right),* is a good example of an irregular galaxy. The Magellanic Clouds are best seen from the Southern Hemisphere. They are satellites of the Milky Way galaxy, at a distance of only 170 000 light-years.

The force of gravity holds groups of galaxies together in clusters. The Milky Way, the Magellanic Clouds, and the Andromeda galaxy all belong to the Local Cluster. Most galaxies are far away and appear as dim smudges of light on photographs. Beyond the most distant galaxies are **quasars,** which are the most energetic objects known. A quasar gives off more energy in one hour than the sun has given off in its entire history! What are quasars and how do they generate so much energy? This question may help astronomers understand how the universe formed.

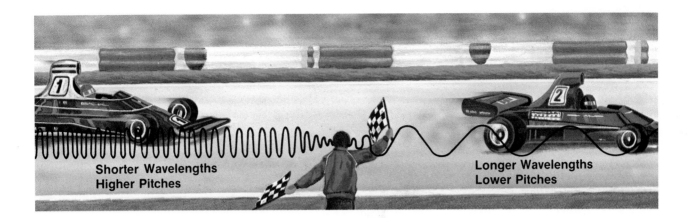

Shorter Wavelengths
Higher Pitches

Longer Wavelengths
Lower Pitches

Big Bang Theory

Light from moving objects appears to change its wavelength. This is called a Doppler shift. You have heard the Doppler shift of a race car as it passes you. Look at Figure 6-24. As the car approaches, engine noise has a higher pitch. As the car moves away from you, the pitch sounds lower. In the same way, the wavelength of light decreases when an object approaches you. The wavelength increases when the object moves away from you. The increase in wavelength is called a redshift because the wavelength shifts toward longer wavelengths.

Scientists know that the universe is expanding because the light of most galaxies is redshifted. It turns out that the farther away a galaxy is, the faster it is moving away from Earth. Thus, redshifts give the distances to galaxies. Quasars, the most distant objects known, have redshifts that indicate they are moving away from Earth at speeds greater than one quarter of the speed of light! What could have thrown the galaxies and quasars apart with such great speed?

The theory that the entire universe started from a single enormous explosion between 10 and 20 billion years ago is called the **big bang theory.** At that time, all of the matter in the universe was packed into a small volume. The big bang would have sent everything flying apart at speeds near the speed of light.

Will the universe keep on expanding forever? If there is enough matter in the universe, gravity could slow down the explosion. Eventually the expansion would stop, and the universe would pull together again. Most astronomers think the universe will expand forever because there doesn't seem to be enough visible mass around to stop the expansion. Other astronomers think there is enough hidden mass to stop the expansion, perhaps in the form of black holes. This is a question you will hear more about in the years to come.

Figure 6-24 The sound of the approaching car has a higher pitch because the sound waves have a shorter wavelength. The sound of the car moving away from you has a lower pitch because the sound waves have a longer wavelength.

Figure 6-25 Most galaxies are moving away from each other. The farther away a galaxy is from Earth, the faster it is moving.

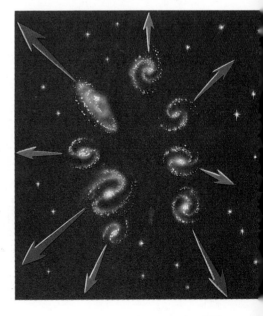

ACTIVITY 6.4

THE EXPANDING UNIVERSE

Purpose To form a model of the expanding universe.

Materials

large round balloon	string
black marker	metric ruler
red marker	

Procedure

1. Read all instructions for this activity before you begin your work. Copy the data table onto your paper.

2. Partially inflate the balloon. Cover one area of the balloon with 16 small black dots, 4 rows of 4. These dots represent galaxies. Number the dots as shown in the figure. The dots should be evenly spaced at 1 cm apart. Measure the distances using a string and a ruler.

3. Draw a red circle around one of the black dots near the middle of the grid. The circled dot represents the Milky Way.

4. Inflate the balloon until the dots nearest to the Milky Way are 2 cm away. Measure the distances from the other galaxies to the Milky Way. Record the distances in your data table in the column marked Stage 1.

5. Inflate the balloon so that the nearest galaxies are 3 cm from the Milky Way. Measure the distances to the other galaxies. Record the data in the column marked Stage 2.

6. Before leaving the laboratory, clean up all materials.

Collecting and Analyzing Data

Data Table		
	Distance from Milky Way	
Number of Galaxy	Stage 1	Stage 2
1.		
2.		

1. In Stage 1, which galaxies moved the least distance from the Milky Way? Which galaxies moved the greatest distance from the Milky Way?

2. After Stage 2, are the galaxies moving away from the Milky Way faster than in Stage 1?

3. Predict the distance to each galaxy if the balloon were inflated until the closest galaxies were 4 cm from the Milky Way.

Drawing Conclusions

4. Is the Milky Way the center of your model balloon universe? Explain.

5. Predict how your observations would have changed if you had put the Milky Way at one edge of the grid. Explain.

Lesson Review 6.4

16. Describe where you would plot the sun on the H-R diagram.

17. Illustrate the possible stages of a star. Explain why a star's end depends upon the mass the star began with.

18. What kind of galaxy is the Milky Way? Describe two other galaxies in the Local Group.

19. What evidence supports the big bang theory?

Interpret and Apply

20. If the spiral galaxies in Figure 6-26 are the same actual size, which would be closest to Earth? If the galaxies were all the same distance from Earth, which would be the largest galaxy? Explain your answers.

Figure 6-26 A cluster of galaxies in the constellation Virgo.

Chapter Summary

Read the chapter summary. If any ideas are not clear to you, review that lesson.

6.1 Observing Stars

■ Earth's rotation and revolution make the stars appear to move in a westerly direction.

■ There are two kinds of constellations: circumpolar constellations that are visible every night, and seasonal constellations that change with the seasons.

■ Brightness of stars from Earth (apparent magnitude) depends on their distance and the light they give off (absolute magnitude).

6.2 Telescopes

■ The main purposes of a telescope are to gather light and magnify an image.

■ The electromagnetic spectrum consists of electromagnetic waves of different wavelengths.

■ Specific types of telescopes collect and analyze different ranges of wavelengths.

6.3 The Sun

■ The sun produces energy in its core by fusion of hydrogen into helium.

■ The layers of the sun include the core, radiation zone, convection zone, photosphere, chromosphere, and corona.

■ Features of the sun include sunspots, solar flares, and prominences.

6.4 Stars and Galaxies

■ The Hertzsprung-Russell diagram compares the absolute magnitude of stars to the color (or temperature) of stars.

■ Stars change over millions or billions of years. The changes a star goes through depend upon the original mass of the star.

■ Galaxies are groups of billions of stars that are bound together by gravity. Clusters of galaxies are held together by gravity.

■ According to the big bang theory, the universe began with an explosion 10 to 20 billion years ago.

Chapter Review

■ Vocabulary

absolute magnitude
apparent magnitude
big bang theory
black hole
chromosphere
constellation
corona
electromagnetic
  spectrum
galaxy
light-year
main sequence
nebula
neutron star

parallax
photosphere
prominence
quasar
red giant
reflecting telescope
refracting telescope
solar flare
spectroscope
sunspot
supernova
wavelength
white dwarf

■ Concept Mapping

Using the method of concept mapping described on pages 3–5, make a concept map for the *electromagnetic spectrum*. Include at least five terms from the vocabulary list.

■ Review

On your paper, write the word or words that best complete each statement.

1. Each night, the stars you see facing toward the south (rise in the east and set in the west, rise in the west and set in the east, do not rise or set).

2. Polaris is (the brightest star, the North Star, in the Big Dipper).

3. The constellation that you could probably see every night of the year is (Orion, Cassiopeia, Polaris).

4. Every star you see in the night sky is (in the Milky Way, a main-sequence star, within 32.6 light-years of Earth).

5. The property of a main-sequence star that determines the star's absolute magnitude is (its color, its temperature, the mass it started with).

6. Which telescope collects invisible radiation from a star? (reflecting telescopes, refracting telescopes, radio telescopes)

7. All blue stars (have a higher temperature, are larger, are smaller) than all red stars.

8. The color of a star is determined by its (brightness, temperature, distance from Earth).

9. The atmosphere blocks (visible light, radio waves, X rays) from stars.

10. (A radio telescope, A reflecting telescope, The Hubble Space Telescope) can see through clouds.

11. The energy that keeps a star shining comes from (burning its fuel, changing hydrogen into helium, giving off electromagnetic radiation).

12. Billions of stars occur together in galaxies because of (gravity, fusion, electromagnetic radiation).

13. The expanding universe started with an explosion called (a supernova, the big bang, the Doppler shift).

14. A star that does not allow light to escape from its surface is a (red giant, black hole, white dwarf).

15. A star that explodes is called (fusion, a supernova, a galaxy).

16. (Supernovas, Redshifts, Black holes) are evidence of the big bang.

17. The sun is the (closest, largest, most massive) star.

18. The sun is (bigger than, smaller than, about the same size as) most other stars.

19. Looking at the sun directly is dangerous because the (ultraviolet radiation, radio waves, microwave radiation) will harm your eyes.

20. The sun will end as a (red giant, black hole, white dwarf).

◼ Interpret and Apply

On your paper, answer each question.

21. If you saw Rigel, a bright star in Orion, rising on the eastern horizon at 9 P.M. one night, where would you expect to find Rigel one month later at the same time of night?

22. Which of the following has the most energy: microwaves, infrared radiation, visible light, or radio waves?

23. Explain two ways that telescopes help you to see objects that are invisible to your unaided eye.

24. Name two types of solar radiation that reach Earth's surface. How does this energy affect Earth?

25. How do stars on the main sequence differ from each other in color, temperature, and mass?

26. If a quasar were discovered at a distance of 24 billion light-years from Earth, how would this change the estimated age of the universe?

◼ Writing in Science

27. Writers often need to revise their first drafts. Revise the following paragraph, which explains the fate of a star with a mass about eight times greater than the mass of the sun. Concentrate on whether the information is accurate and arranged in the correct order.

When the oxygen in the star's core has been used up by fusion, the core collapses and becomes very cold. This causes the star's outer layers to expand, and the star becomes a red giant. The inner core then collapses further, and the star becomes a small hot neutron star. Finally, the neutron star explodes into an extremely bright supernova.

◼ Critical Thinking

Below is a table of some of the brighter stars. Study the list carefully. Compare the absolute magnitude, apparent magnitude, and distance from Earth among the various stars. Then answer the questions that follow the table.

Star	Apparent Magnitude	Absolute Magnitude	Distance in Light-years
Sun	−26	4.8	0.00002
Sirius	−1.5	1.4	8.7
Alpha Centauri	0.1	4.4	4.3
Rigel	0.1	−7.0	815
Betelgeuse	0.4	−5.9	520
Capella	1.0	−0.6	45

28. Which star would appear brightest from a distance of 10 light-years? Which star would appear dimmest from this distance?

29. Which star appears the brightest from Earth? Which star appears dimmest from Earth?

30. Is the brightest star seen from Earth the same as the brightest star as seen from 10 light-years? Explain.

31. Rigel is blue and Alpha Centauri is yellow. Both stars appear to be about the same brightness from Earth. A friend says these stars cannot be the same size. Do you agree? Explain your reasoning.

32. Betelgeuse is the brightest star in the constellation Orion. But Betelgeuse is far from Earth, and it is a cool red star. If Betelgeuse is far away and has a cool surface, how can it appear so bright?

SPACE STATION DELAYED AGAIN DUE TO BUDGET CUTS

Issue: *Should the United States continue the space program while other programs go unfunded?*

Seven lives and two billion dollars is a lot to lose all at once. But that's exactly what happened when the Space Shuttle *Challenger* exploded tragically in 1986. To prevent such a loss in future missions, the National Aeronautics and Space Agency (NASA) spent $400 million more to redesign the Space Shuttle. Many people feel that the United States should spend this money to help people more directly. They argue that domestic programs that provide food, shelter, and education will always be more important than space exploration.

Ever since 1957, when the Soviet Union launched the first artificial satellite, *Sputnik*, the United States and the Soviet Union have competed in a "space race." Although the United States landed the first people on the moon, the Soviet Union is ahead in setting up

Astronauts rescuing a satellite

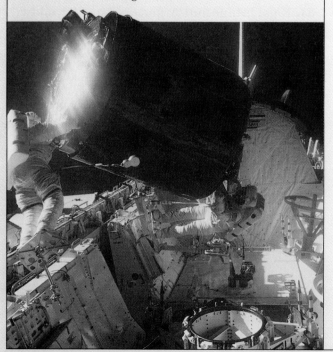

a permanent space station. Soviet cosmonauts hold the world record for the longest stay in space—366 days, aboard *Soyuz 4*. In comparison, the United States' longest stay is only 84 days, set in 1973 aboard the space station *Skylab*. Some people think the United States must spend more on the space program to catch up in the race for space.

In the next century, people may colonize space much as the Americas were colonized 500 years ago.

What are the benefits of space exploration? In the past, many people thought the only benefits were spin-offs, or advances in technology that were by-products of exploring space. For example, hand-held calculators developed from the need to make smaller computers for spacecraft. Many new plastic and graphite materials, which are now used in tennis rackets, telephones, and even lunch boxes, were first used in spacecraft. Weather satellites save lives by giving early hurricane warnings, and communication satellites send signals around the world. It is hard to imagine life without these things.

Some people think that the greatest benefit of space exploration will come from making things in space that are expensive or difficult to make on Earth. Robot factories could make computer chips cheaply in the vacuum and low temperature of space. Some new medicines can be made only in space, where gravity is very weak. Medicines to treat diabetes, hemophilia, and cancer were developed on Space Shuttle flights in the 1980's. The first step in using space for manufacturing is to build a space station in Earth orbit. Eventually, people may colonize space much as the Americas were colonized 500 years ago.

NASA is planning to build a permanent space station where people will live and work. By the time it is completed in the 1990's, the space station will have cost more than $15 billion to build. Are the benefits of the space station and other space programs worth the tremendous cost? It may help to compare the cost of space programs to the cost of other government programs. Each year, the federal government spends about $10 billion on NASA space exploration and research. In comparison, the federal government spends only about $15 billion each year on cleaning up the environment. About $40 billion goes to education and social services, and $50 billion to health. If the government stopped spending money on space exploration, more money could be spent on human services such as food, housing, and schools. Many people feel that if the government is forced to cut back programs, the space program should be cut before human service programs.

Each year, the United States space program costs taxpayers more than $11 billion.

Some businesspeople think that more money, not less, must be spent on space programs like the space station. They argue that the space station could earn $40 billion per year by renting space to industries. This money could pay for the space station and help the government to expand the space program. Other people point out that the Space Shuttle was supposed to pay for itself by launching commercial satellites, but this did not work out. Many people feel that the government should develop a long-range plan before spending large amounts of money on the space station.

Act on the Issue

Gather the Facts

1. Use library resources such as the *Readers' Guide to Periodical Literature* to learn more about the following projects that NASA is considering: the space station, a mission to Mars, a telescope on the moon, and a mission to a comet. Be sure to find out the yearly and total costs of each project. You may want to write to NASA in Washington, D.C. and ask for information about these projects. Then make a chart of the pros and cons of each project.

2. Find a recent almanac in the library and look up "Budget—United States Government." The budget is listed by government agency. Record the budget totals for each agency for this year and next year. Which budget will change the most in the coming year? How does this change compare to the total NASA budget?

Take Action

3. Imagine that you are a United States senator voting on a bill to fund the four projects in question 1. If only two projects could be funded, which would you vote for? Be sure to consider both the short-term and long-term costs and benefits. Write to your senator in Congress and explain your position.

4. Write a short questionnaire (about five questions) to give to at least a dozen students and teachers. Your questions should ask people how they feel about spending tax dollars on space research. Do they think it is important to keep up with or to get ahead of other countries in the space race? What are their opinions about specific NASA projects? Share the results of the survey with the rest of your class.

Composition of Earth

You Know More Than You Think

You may be surprised at how much you already know about Earth's composition. To find out, try to answer the following questions.

- Which is harder, chalk or the chalkboard?
- Where does water go when it evaporates?
- What happens to lava as it cools?
- Are there any rocks where you live? What do they look like?
- Can you name any gemstones or other minerals?

When you finish this unit, answer these questions again to see how much you have learned.

These crystals, salt formations, and mountains are all made of minerals.

Earth's Chemistry

Chapter Preview

Have You Ever WONDERED?

How does the stage crew make clouds appear on stage at rock concerts and plays?

An amazing substance called carbon dioxide is used to create many special effects like clouds, fog, and smoke. It helps turn an ordinary stage into a magical world.

Carbon dioxide is normally an invisible gas that makes up a tiny percentage of air. However, under the right conditions, pure carbon dioxide can be compressed and cooled into a solid form. Solid carbon dioxide is called dry ice. On stage, chunks of dry ice are dropped into a bucket of water and carbon dioxide gas is released. The cold gas changes water vapor in the air into clouds of tiny water droplets. These artificial clouds then swirl across the stage.

In this chapter, you will learn more about common substances, such as carbon dioxide. You will study how solids, liquids, and gases behave and how they change from one state to another. None of this is magic—it is just basic chemistry.

Properties of Matter

As a small child, you began to study your surroundings. You probably learned to classify objects by color or by shape. You quickly realized that milk splashed in many directions when it hit the floor, while toys kept their shape. You learned to use characteristics to classify objects and substances. A characteristic of an object is called a **property.** Chemistry is the study of the properties of matter.

Lesson Objectives

▸ *Identify* the basic properties of matter.

▸ *Describe* the effects of energy on matter.

▸ *Compare* and *contrast* the three states of matter.

▸ *Explain* the processes of evaporation and condensation.

▸ *Activity*   *Observe* and *describe* changes in the state of matter.

New Terms

property	solid
volume	liquid
mass	gas
matter	evaporation
density	condensation
energy	

Matter and Energy

All of the materials around you have two properties in common. First, each material takes up a certain amount of space. Rocks, water, and even air takes up space. The space that a material takes up is called its **volume.** The second property refers to the amount of material found in any object or substance. The amount of material in an object is called its **mass.** Anything that has volume and mass is called **matter.**

You can use volume and mass to calculate density. **Density** is the mass of an object per unit volume. Density is calculated as follows:

$$density = \frac{mass}{volume} \quad \text{or} \quad D = \frac{m}{V}$$

For example, the density of an object that has a mass of 50 grams and a volume of 25 cubic centimeters is:

$$D = \frac{m}{v}$$

$$D = \frac{50 \text{ g}}{25 \text{ cm}^3}$$

$$D = 2 \text{ g/cm}^3$$

Observations of volume, mass, and density are used to study rocks and soil, the atmosphere, the oceans, and other earth and space materials.

Energy is needed to move matter from one place to another or to cause matter to change from one form to another. Several forms of energy help to shape Earth's surface. Thermal energy from the sun warms Earth, producing winds and weather changes. Powerful river currents transport rock and soil grains for hundreds of kilometers. Coastlines can be changed dramatically by the energy of hurricane winds and waves. Each of these examples shows the importance of energy in Earth's environment.

Table 7-1
Densities of Some Common Substances

Substance	Density (g/cm³)
cork	0.24
fresh water	1.00
carbon	1.9 to 2.3
granite	2.6 to 2.8
diamond	3.2 to 3.5
iron	7.9
lead	11.3

States of Matter

Matter on Earth exists in three states: solid, liquid, and gas. You tend to think of matter in its state at room temperature. For example, you think of rock as a solid, water as a liquid, and helium as a gas. Each of these substances has very different properties. The properties of all types of matter can be described using particle models.

The particle models in Figure 7-1 show the different structures of solids, liquids, and gases. A **solid** has a definite shape and volume. For example, this book has a definite shape and always takes up the same amount of space in your book bag. As the diagram shows, the particles of a solid vibrate as they stay in the same positions.

A **liquid** has a definite volume, but its shape can vary. In Figure 7-1 (*middle*), note that the particles stay close together as they move around one another. Their positions change, but the amount of space they occupy remains the same. Therefore, a liquid will take the shape of its container. For example, a soft drink will take the shape of your glass when you pour it from a can. But you still have the same volume of liquid whether it is in the can or in the glass.

A **gas** has no definite volume or shape. As you can see in Figure 7-1 (*right*), the particles are far apart from one another and move in any direction. A gas will fill the entire volume of its container. This explains how some food odors travel from your kitchen to other parts of your house.

Figure 7-1 Particle models help explain the behavior of matter in its different states. *Left:* Model for solids, *Middle:* Model for liquids, *Right:* Model for gases

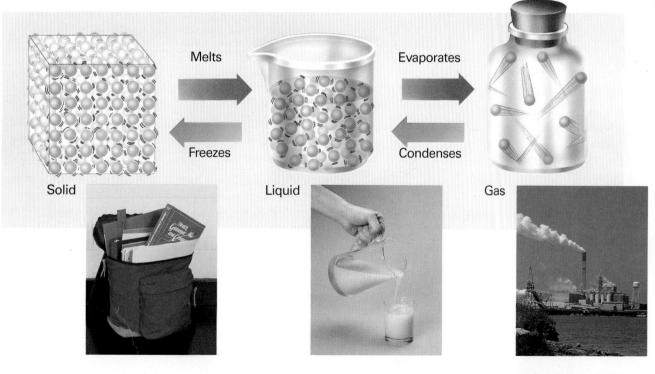

Solid   Melts →   Liquid   Evaporates →   Gas

← Freezes   ← Condenses

Figure 7-2 At cool temperatures, water vapor in your breath and in the atmosphere may change from the gas state to the liquid state, forming clouds. What is the process called?

Changing States of Matter

Matter changes state if its particles gain or lose enough energy. For example, water becomes a solid if you place it in a freezer. If you leave an ice cube out on the counter it melts. If you leave the water on the counter for a few hours, it disappears as the liquid becomes water vapor.

Different types of matter melt or boil within different temperature ranges. Butter melts at a low temperature. Other solids, such as iron, melt at much higher temperatures. Oil refineries use the principle of different boiling points to separate petroleum into many useful products like jet fuel, heating oil, gasoline, and kerosene. Each product boils and changes to a gas at a different temperature.

Changes in the state of water can often be observed in nature. When heated by the sun, some of Earth's water is changed into water vapor. The process by which a liquid changes to a gas is called **evaporation.** After a rainstorm, as the sun heats the street, the puddles evaporate.

When water vapor is cooled to a low enough temperature, it returns to its liquid state. The change from a gas to a liquid is called **condensation.** Two examples of condensation are shown in Figure 7-2. You can easily demonstrate condensation by breathing on a cold glass or mirror. The water vapor in your breath cools and condenses on the glass as tiny droplets of water. A similar process causes clouds of water droplets to form in the sky.

Lesson Review 7.1

1. What are the two properties all matter has in common?
2. List two natural energy sources that have an effect on Earth's environment.
3. Describe the characteristics of solids, liquids, and gases using the particle model.
4. Explain the difference between the processes of evaporation and condensation.

Interpret and Apply

5. A small rock has a mass of 27 grams and a volume of 9 cubic centimeters. What is the density of the rock?
6. The quantity of liquid inside a thermometer is always the same. How does the density of the liquid change when the temperature rises? Explain your reasoning.

ACTIVITY 7.1

CHANGES OF STATE

Purpose To observe and describe how water changes as it is heated and cooled.

Materials

safety goggles	glass elbow
lab apron	hot plate
flask	wire mesh
single-hole stopper	beaker
shallow pan	pot holders
clear plastic tubing	paper towels
food coloring	ice water

Procedure

1. Read all the directions for this activity before you begin your work.

2. Put on your safety goggles and your lab apron.

3. Place 15 mL of water and 1 drop of food coloring in the flask. Fit the stopper with its glass elbow and plastic tubing into the flask.

4. Place the wire mesh on the hot plate. Plug in and turn on the hot plate to medium high. Wipe the bottom of the flask dry with a paper towel. Place the flask on top of the hot plate. **CAUTION: Never reach over a heat source; you may get burned accidentally.**

5. Put the beaker into the pan of ice water and place the end of the plastic tubing in the beaker as shown in the figure.

6. Heat the flask and observe what happens in the tubing and the beaker. Record your observations.

7. Turn off the hot plate before all of the water in the flask is gone. **CAUTION: Do not allow all of the water to boil away from the flask.**

8. Clean up all materials.

Collecting and Analyzing Data

1. In what part of the process did water change from a liquid to a gas?

2. In what part of the process did water change from a gas to a liquid?

3. Compare the color of water in the beaker to the color of water that was originally in the flask.

4. What was left in the flask when most of the water was gone?

Drawing Conclusions

5. When were the water particles gaining energy? Losing energy?

6. The type of procedure used in this experiment is called distillation. Why is distillation an effective way to purify water?

7. Write a short procedure to describe a method for purifying salt water. Do not try your procedure without written permission from your teacher.

7.2 Building Blocks of Matter

Lesson Objectives

▶ **Describe** atoms and elements and list several examples of each.

▶ **Describe** the atomic model.

▶ **Explain** why elements have different properties.

▶ **Examine** how elements are represented on the periodic table.

▶ **Activity** **Observe** and **describe** the results of chemical flame tests of several substances.

New Terms

atoms	nucleus
protons	elements
neutrons	atomic number
electrons	

The variety of matter on Earth is amazing. Solids range from the hardness of a rock to the softness of a flower petal. Water is a colorless liquid, while copper is a reddish-brown solid. Despite this variety, most matter is made of tiny particles called atoms. An **atom** is the smallest unit of matter that cannot be broken down by ordinary means.

The Atomic Model

Until recently, no one had ever produced a photographic image from an atom. However, for some time, scientists have used a widely accepted model that describes the structure of atoms. In general, atoms are made up of three types of particles: **protons, neutrons,** and **electrons.** Protons and neutrons are found in a region at the center of an atom called the **nucleus,** shown in Figure 7-3 (right). A proton has a positive electric charge. Neutrons have no charge. Electrons have a negative charge, and their motion creates a cloud of negative charge around the nucleus, shown in Figure 7-3 (left). Under certain conditions, an atom has the same number of electrons as protons. Because the number of negative charges equals the number of positive charges, the atom is electrically neutral.

Most of the mass of an atom is located in the nucleus. Look again at the atomic model in Figure 7-3. Each proton has about two thousand times the mass of an electron. An atom's size, however, depends on the size of its electron cloud. The electron cloud is much larger than the nucleus. If the cloud were the size of two football fields placed end to end, the nucleus would be a small dot on the boundary between two fields.

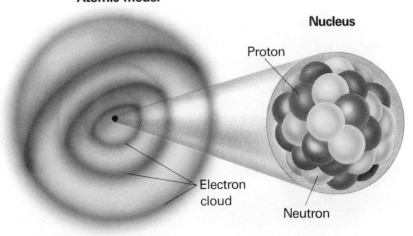

Atomic model

Nucleus

Proton

Electron cloud

Neutron

Figure 7-3 A model of an atom and its nucleus; In which part of the atom is most of the mass?

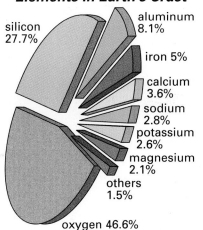

Elements in Earth's Crust

silicon 27.7%
aluminum 8.1%
iron 5%
calcium 3.6%
sodium 2.8%
potassium 2.6%
magnesium 2.1%
others 1.5%
oxygen 46.6%

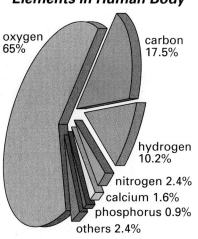

Elements in Human Body

oxygen 65%
carbon 17.5%
hydrogen 10.2%
nitrogen 2.4%
calcium 1.6%
phosphorus 0.9%
others 2.4%

Figure 7-4 Compare the elements in Earth's crust to the elements in your body. How many elements are the same?

Elements

Substances called **elements** are composed of a single type of atom. Elements are the building blocks of matter. Scientists have identified over 100 different elements. Several elements occur only in a laboratory. However, 89 elements are natural and occur on Earth or in its atmosphere. Gold and sulfur are examples of natural elements. It may surprise you to learn that many of the elements that make up rocks and soil are also in your body. For example, iron is mined in several parts of the United States. Iron is also important in hemoglobin, the oxygen-carrying substance in human blood. Oxygen, an element in air, is also in rocks.

Elements are basic materials. The atoms of each element are unique. For example, a gold atom is different from a silver atom. However, each gold atom is similar to every other gold atom. No matter how you bend, melt, or even vaporize a piece of gold, you will find that it is still gold.

What is the difference between a copper penny and a silver dime? Although they contain different elements, their basic matter is the same. They both contain protons, neutrons and electrons. Then why are the elements copper and silver different? Amazingly enough, it is the number of protons in the atom that distinguishes one atom from another and gives an element its special properties.

All of the known elements are listed on a chart called the periodic table. Take a moment to look at the periodic table on pages 182–183. Notice the number that appears at the top of each block. This is the atomic number for each element. The **atomic number** represents the number of protons in an atom of that element. For example, hydrogen has one proton in its nucleus, and therefore it is number 1 on the chart. How many protons does oxygen have?

Fact or Fiction?

Did early chemists transform lead into gold? Craftworkers in the area around the Mediterranean Sea developed a practice called alchemy around the year 300. Alchemy was based on an earlier Greek idea that all matter was composed of four primary elements: earth, air, fire, and water. One kind of matter could be changed into another kind of matter by adding fire or water. The alchemists failed to make gold from other metals, but they did develop many tools still used by modern chemists.

Table 7-2

Periodic Table of the Elements

					Atomic number → 14					
					Symbol → Si					
					Name → Silicon					
					Atomic mass → 28.1					

METALS

GROUP 1	2	3	4	5	6	7	8	9
PERIOD 1 1 **H** Hydrogen 1.0								
3 **Li** Lithium 6.9	4 **Be** Beryllium 9.0							
2								
11 **Na** Sodium 23.0	12 **Mg** Magnesium 24.3							
3								
19 **K** Potassium 39.1	20 **Ca** Calcium 40.1	21 **Sc** Scandium 45.0	22 **Ti** Titanium 47.9	23 **V** Vanadium 50.9	24 **Cr** Chromium 52.0	25 **Mn** Manganese 54.9	26 **Fe** Iron 55.8	27 **Co** Cobalt 58.9
4								
37 **Rb** Rubidium 85.5	38 **Sr** Strontium 87.6	39 **Y** Yttrium 88.9	40 **Zr** Zirconium 91.2	41 **Nb** Niobium 92.9	42 **Mo** Molybdenum 95.9	43 **Tc** Technetium 98.9	44 **Ru** Ruthenium 101.1	45 **Rh** Rhodium 102.9
5								
55 **Cs** Cesium 132.9	56 **Ba** Barium 137.3	57 **La** Lanthanum 138.9	72 **Hf** Hafnium 178.5	73 **Ta** Tantalum 180.9	74 **W** Tungsten 183.9	75 **Re** Rhenium 186.2	76 **Os** Osmium 190.2	77 **Ir** Iridium 192.2
6								
87 **Fr** Francium 223.0	88 **Ra** Radium 226.0	89 **Ac** Actinium 227.0	104* 261.1	105* 262.1	106* 263.1	107* 262.1	108*	109*
7								

Lanthanide Series

58 **Ce** Cerium 140.1	59 **Pr** Praseodymium 140.9	60 **Nd** Neodymium 144.2	61 **Pm** Promethium 146.9	62 **Sm** Samarium 150.4
90 **Th** Thorium 232.0	91 **Pa** Protactinium 231.0	92 **U** Uranium 238.0	93 **Np** Neptunium 237.0	94 **Pu** Plutonium 244.1

Actinide Series

* The use of 3-letter symbols for these elements is the subject of debate. They are not used in the literature by practicing scientists, so they are not introduced here.

																	18
																	2 **He** Helium 4.0

13	14	15	16	17	
5 **B** Boron 10.8	6 **C** Carbon 12.0	7 **N** Nitrogen 14.0	8 **O** Oxygen 16.0	9 **F** Fluorine 19.0	10 **Ne** Neon 20.2

10	11	12	13	14	15	16	17	18
			13 **Al** Aluminum 27.0	14 **Si** Silicon 28.1	15 **P** Phosphorus 31.0	16 **S** Sulfur 32.1	17 **Cl** Chlorine 35.4	18 **Ar** Argon 39.9
28 **Ni** Nickel 58.7	29 **Cu** Copper 63.6	30 **Zn** Zinc 65.4	31 **Ga** Gallium 69.7	32 **Ge** Germanium 72.6	33 **As** Arsenic 74.9	34 **Se** Selenium 79.0	35 **Br** Bromine 79.9	36 **Kr** Krypton 83.8
46 **Pd** Palladium 106.4	47 **Ag** Silver 107.9	48 **Cd** Cadmium 112.4	49 **In** Indium 114.8	50 **Sn** Tin 118.7	51 **Sb** Antimony 121.8	52 **Te** Tellurium 127.6	53 **I** Iodine 126.9	54 **Xe** Xenon 131.3
78 **Pt** Platinum 195.1	79 **Au** Gold 197.0	80 **Hg** Mercury 200.6	81 **Tl** Thallium 204.4	82 **Pb** Lead 207.2	83 **Bi** Bismuth 209.0	84 **Po** Polonium 209.0	85 **At** Astatine 210.0	86 **Rn** Radon 222.0

Metals | **Nonmetals**

* Group 18, called the Noble gases, are a special group of nonmetals.

63 **Eu** Europium 152.0	64 **Gd** Gadolinium 157.2	65 **Tb** Terbium 158.9	66 **Dy** Dysprosium 162.5	67 **Ho** Holmium 164.9	68 **Er** Erbium 167.3	69 **Tm** Thulium 168.9	70 **Yb** Ytterbium 173.0	71 **Lu** Lutetium 175.0
95 **Am** Americium 243.1	96 **Cm** Curium 247.1	97 **Bk** Berkelium 247.1	98 **Cf** Californium 251.1	99 **Es** Einsteinium 252.1	100 **Fm** Fermium 257.1	101 **Md** Mendelevium 258.1	102 **No** Nobelium 259.1	103 **Lr** Lawrencium 260.1

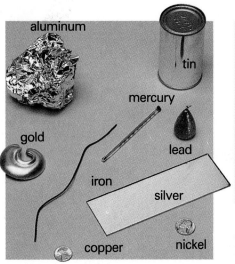

aluminum

tin

mercury

gold

lead

iron

silver

copper

nickel

Figure 7-5 *Left:* Metal elements are shiny, bendable, and conduct heat and electricity well. The metal mercury is liquid at room temperature. *Right:* Except for bromine, nonmetal elements are solids or gases at room temperature.

chlorine

sulfur

red phosphorus

bromine

In addition to their atomic numbers, the elements in the periodic table are grouped according to similarities in their properties. For example, the yellow-shaded elements are metals and the orange-shaded ones are nonmetals. Figure 7-5 shows some examples of metals and nonmetals. Locate copper and silver in the yellow-shaded portion of the table. Notice that the atomic number for copper is 29, while the atomic number for silver is 47. In other words, a silver atom has 18 more protons than a copper atom. Because these two metals have different numbers of protons, they have some differences in their properties.

Each element has an abbreviation called a symbol. A symbol may be one single capital letter or a capital letter followed by a lowercase letter. Some of the symbols are what you would expect. For example, H stands for hydrogen and Si stands for silicon. Other symbols are from Latin names of elements. The symbol for iron (Fe) comes from *ferrum* and gold (Au) from *aurum*. In later chapters, these symbols will be used to describe the composition of Earth.

Lesson Review 7.2

7. How is one element different from any other element?

8. Name the three different particles of an atom and describe each particle's electrical charge.

9. Which particle determines the size of an atom?

10. According to what two factors are elements arranged on the periodic table?

11. Name four elements people use in their everyday lives.

Interpret and Apply

12. Use the periodic table to compare and contrast the atoms and properties of the elements uranium and lead.

IDENTIFYING MATTER

Purpose To observe and describe the results of chemical flame tests of some substances.

Materials

safety goggles	spoons
lab apron	watch glass
small dish	wood splints
samples 1–5	clay
candle	

Procedure

1. Read all directions for this activity before you begin your work.

2. Put on your safety goggles and your lab apron. Tie back long hair and confine loose clothing.

3. Copy the data table onto your paper.

Data Table

Sample number	Name of substance	Element tested	Color seen
1			
2			
3			
4			
5			

4. Place a ball of clay on the dish and stand the candle in the clay. Light the candle. **CAUTION: Keep hair and clothing away from the flame.**

5. Spoon a small amount of Sample 1 (sodium chloride) onto the watch glass.

6. Dab one end of a presoaked wood splint into the sample, making sure that some of the sample clings to the splint.

7. Place the end of the splint in the lower part of the candle flame. Record your observations in the data table.

8. Repeat steps 4–7 for each of the remaining samples. Be sure to keep each set of spoons and splints at its own station, so that it is used for only one type of sample. Record your observations.

9. Before leaving the laboratory, clean up all materials and wash your hands.

Collecting and Analyzing Data

1. What happened when you inserted the splint into the flame?

2. Look at your observations. Which samples gave the most colorful flame?

3. Which samples, if any, produced a barely noticeable color change?

4. What flame color indicates copper?

Drawing Conclusions

5. Identify the mystery sample and explain your reasoning.

6. How do you think this test could be helpful in identifying minerals?

7. From your observations, why do you think fireworks explode in different colors?

7.3 Behavior of Matter

Lesson Objectives

▸ **Contrast** physical and chemical changes and properties.

▸ **Define** compound and molecule and **list** several examples of compounds.

▸ **Explain** how compounds form.

▸ **Compare** and **contrast** compounds and mixtures.

▸ **Activity** **Perform an experiment** to separate a mixture.

New Terms

physical property	molecule
chemical property	ions
physical change	chemical
chemical change	formula
compound	mixture
chemical bond	solution

How often are you asked to write a composition? Sometimes your mind goes blank. You may end up doodling or crumpling the paper into a ball shape. The paper's shape, color, and texture are examples of its physical properties. A characteristic of an object that you can observe without changing the object into a chemically different substance is called a **physical property.**

Suppose you toss the paper into the fireplace. The ability of paper to burn into ash, a new substance, is an example of a chemical property. A **chemical property** of a substance describes how that substance will react chemically.

Physical Change versus Chemical Change

When you wrinkled up your composition paper, you changed one of its physical properties. A change in a substance's physical properties that does not produce a new substance is a **physical change.** Figure 7-6 *(left)* shows an example of a physical change. Bumping around in moving water gives the rocks a rounded shape, but the rocks still contain the same type of matter. The rocks have simply undergone a physical change. A change in the state of matter is also a physical change. The melting of ice to form liquid water is one example. Whether water exists in its frozen state or liquid state, it is still the same matter.

A change that affects the chemical properties of matter is a **chemical change.** A chemical change produces a totally new substance. Have you ever seen a rusty piece of iron like that in Figure 7-6 *(right)*? The rust formed when iron combined chemically with oxygen in the air. Rust has different chemical properties than iron.

Figure 7-6 *Left:* An example of a physical change, *Right:* An example of a chemical change; How are the changes different?

Compounds, Molecules, and Ions

Perhaps you noticed that many familiar forms of matter were omitted from the periodic table. There is no listing for substances such as water, sand, or sugar. These substances are not listed because they are not pure elements. They are made up of a combination of elements. If two or more elements combine chemically, a new substance, which is called a **compound**, is formed.

Compounds are different from the elements that form them. Elements give up their own properties when they form compounds, as illustrated in Figure 7-7. Sodium is a soft metallic solid that explodes and burns when exposed to water. (The sodium in the photo is in kerosene.) Chlorine is a deadly green gas. Neither element seems safe for people to handle. Yet, when joined together, these two elements become the compound sodium chloride—table salt.

Figure 7-7 How are the properties of the elements sodium and chlorine different from the properties of the compound sodium chloride?

ENVIRONMENTAL AWARENESS

Radon—A Dangerous Element

You have probably heard reports on radon gas in the news. Radon is colorless, odorless, tasteless gas that forms from the breakdown of the element *uranium*. Radon occurs in some soil and in some rocks such as granite and shale. If radon builds up in an enclosed area, like your basement, it can cause cancer and other health problems.

High levels of radon gas have been found in some homes across the United States. The gas enters the homes through cracks in the floors and drains. Radon in well water circulates through heating pipes, showers, and washing machines.

Today homes can be tested for radon gas using kits like the one shown. If the amount of radon is too high, steps can be taken to lower it. Repair cracks in basements. Install fans to move the gas outside. The Environmental Protection Agency (EPA) offers more information about radon gas. ■

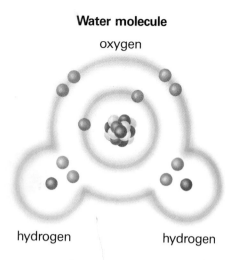

Water molecule

oxygen

hydrogen   hydrogen

Figure 7-8 In a molecule, two or more atoms share electrons. This is a model of a water molecule.

Compounds are made of combinations of two or more atoms joined together in a **chemical bond.** There are two types of chemical bonds. One type of bond forms when atoms share electrons. As you can see in Figure 7-8, the bonds in a water molecule result from the sharing of electrons. The two hydrogen atoms of a water molecule share electrons with the oxygen atom.

Two or more atoms bonded together by the sharing of electrons form a **molecule.** In most substances, molecules are made of atoms of different elements. For example, the molecules of table sugar contain atoms of carbon, hydrogen, and oxygen. However, some substances consist of molecules containing atoms of only one element. The molecules of oxygen in our atmosphere, for example, contain two atoms joined together.

Another type of chemical bond forms as a result of a gain or loss of electrons. As you recall from Lesson 7.2, atoms are electrically neutral. They have the same number of protons and electrons. However, if an atom should gain or lose electrons, it becomes electrically charged. Atoms that gain electrons have a negative charge. Atoms that lose electrons have a positive charge. Atoms that have become charged are called **ions.** Since opposite electrical charges attract one another, ions can form chemical bonds. Figure 7-9 shows this type of bond. Notice how a positively charged sodium ion is attracted to a negatively charged chloride ion. These two ions form a strong chemical bond.

Just as symbols are used to represent elements, they are also used to represent compounds. The composition of a compound is written out as a series of symbols and numbers called a **chemical formula.** A formula is like a list of ingredients in a recipe. It gives the relative number of atoms of each element in a compound.

Figure 7-9 When atoms lose or gain electrons, ions form. This model shows a sodium atom losing an electron to a chlorine atom. What compound is made of sodium and chloride ions?

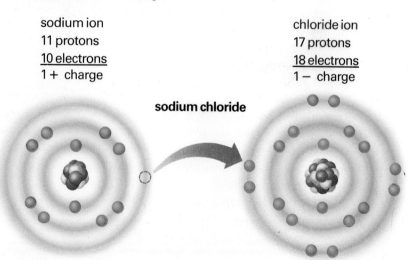

sodium ion
11 protons
10 electrons
1 + charge

chloride ion
17 protons
18 electrons
1 − charge

sodium chloride

Table 7-3 Some Compounds and Their Chemical Formulas

Common Name	Chemical Name	Chemical Formula
water	dihydrogen oxide	H_2O
salt	sodium chloride	$NaCl$
baking soda	sodium hydrogen carbonate	$NaHCO_3$
chalk	calcium carbonate	$CaCO_3$
quartz	silicon dioxide	SiO_2
sugar	sucrose	$C_{12}H_{22}O_{11}$
rust	iron(III) oxide	Fe_2O_3

For example, the mineral *calcite* has the chemical formula $CaCO_3$. For every atom of calcium, there are three atoms of oxygen and one atom of carbon. Table 7-3 lists several chemical compounds. Notice that some elements are found in many different compounds.

Mixtures

Sometimes elements or compounds are mixed together physically, with no change in the chemical composition. Two or more substances that are physically combined form a **mixture.** Each part of a mixture keeps its own physical properties. Soil, for example, is a mixture of small rock fragments and decaying organic material. Since the particles are not combined chemically, there is no chemical formula for soil. In Figure 7-10 (*top*), you can see particles of different sizes, shapes, and colors. As you see in Figure 7-10 (*bottom*), separating large particles from soil is a fairly simple process. Other mixtures require more complex separation methods. Whatever the method, the substances in a mixture can be separated physically.

In some mixtures, the different ingredients may be invisible. Some solids, like salt crystals, seem to disappear when mixed with water. The sodium ions and chloride ions separate from one another and spread out evenly among the water molecules. If the particles are too small to be visible even with the most powerful microscopes, and they are uniformly spread out, the mixture is called a **solution.** Sea water is a solution because salt is dissolved evenly throughout the water. If you let all of the water evaporate from a bucket of sea water, what would be left behind? You'll have a chance to test your hypothesis in Activity 7.3.

Figure 7-10 *Top:* Soil is a natural mixture that contains elements and compounds. *Bottom:* Which parts of the soil mixture stay on the grate?

SEPARATING A MIXTURE

Purpose   To perform an experiment to separate a mixture into its original parts.

Materials

safety goggles	magnet
lab apron	filter paper
hot plate	sandwich bag
test tube with cork	water
beaker	sand
funnel	salt
pot holders	iron filings

Procedure

1. Read all directions before beginning your work. Put on your safety goggles and lab apron.

2. Place 15–20 mL of water and a pinch each of salt, sand, and iron filings into the test tube. Stopper and shake the test tube.

3. Carefully fold the filter paper as shown in the figure and place it in the funnel. Set the funnel on top of the beaker.

3 thicknesses —
1 thickness —
Fold in quarters, then open as shown

4. Shake the mixture one more time and pour the mixture carefully into the funnel. Wait for all the liquid to filter through into the beaker.

5. Carefully remove the filter paper. Unfold the paper so that it lies flat and the mixture can dry.

6. Remove the funnel from the beaker. Dry the bottom of the beaker with a paper towel and place the beaker on a hot plate.

7. Turn on the hot plate and gently heat the liquid until it has almost completely evaporated. Note what is left inside the beaker. **CAUTION: Use pot holders to handle the hot beaker.**

8. While the liquid is heating, wrap the magnet in the sandwich bag. Pick up the iron filings from the dry filter paper with the magnet. Brush the filings off into a container labeled *iron*. Brush the sand into a container marked *sand*.

9. Before leaving the laboratory, clean up all materials and wash your hands.

Collecting and Analyzing Data

1. What materials were separated by filtering? By evaporation?

Drawing Conclusions

2. What property of salt allowed you to separate it from the sand and iron?

3. What property of iron allowed you to separate it from the sand?

4. Explain how your results show that the material in the test tube was a mixture and not a compound.

Lesson Review 7.3

13. What is a compound? Give one example.
14. Describe two ways atoms can bond together to form compounds.
15. How is a compound different from a mixture?
16. What is the difference between a physical property and a chemical property? Give one example of each.

Interpret and Apply

17. A tree branch is put through a tree chipper and turned into mulch. Is this a physical or a chemical change?
18. Certain metal products, like copper and silver, can be tarnished over time. Is this a physical change or a chemical change? Explain your answer.

Chapter Summary

Read this chapter summary. If any ideas are not clear to you, review that lesson.

7.1 Properties of Matter

■ Matter is anything that has volume and mass. The density of a substance is its mass per unit volume.

■ Energy is needed to move matter from one place to another or to change matter from one form to another.

■ Matter on Earth usually exists in one of three states: solid, liquid, or gas. Matter can change from one state to another.

7.2 Building Blocks of Matter

■ Most matter is made of tiny particles called atoms. Atoms consist of protons, neutrons, and electrons.

■ A substance containing atoms of a single type is called an element. There are over 100 elements which are arranged on a chart called the periodic table.

■ The atomic number of an element refers to the number of protons in its nucleus, which determines the element.

7.3 Behavior of Matter

■ A physical property can be observed without changing the substance chemically. A chemical property describes how the substance reacts chemically.

■ A change that does not produce a new substance is a physical change. A chemical change forms a new substance.

■ A chemical combination of two or more elements is called a compound.

■ Two or more atoms chemically bonded by the sharing of electrons make up a molecule.

■ Ions are formed when atoms become charged due to the loss or gain of electrons.

■ Mixtures are physical combinations of materials. The chemical composition of a mixture can vary.

Chapter Review

Vocabulary

atom
atomic number
chemical bond
chemical change
chemical formula
chemical property
compound
condensation
density
electron
element
energy
evaporation
gas
ion

liquid
mass
matter
mixture
molecule
neutron
nucleus
physical change
physical property
property
proton
solid
solution
volume

Concept Mapping

Using the method of concept mapping described on pages 3–5, complete a concept map for elements. Copy the incomplete concept map below. Then fill in the missing terms.

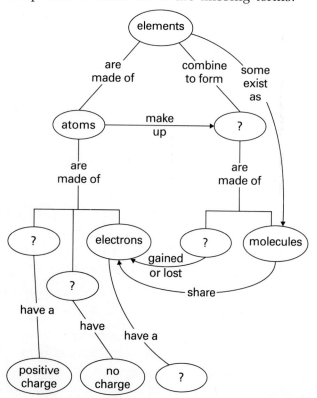

Review

Number your paper from 1 through 15. Write the word that best completes each statement.

1. Particles are closest together and move least in a (solid, liquid, gas).

2. (Water, Gas, Energy) must be added to or taken away from matter in order for it to change state.

3. Particles are far apart and move freely in a (solid, liquid, gas).

4. The amount of matter in an object is called its (mass, volume, density).

5. (Evaporation, Condensation, Freezing) occurs when a gas is cooled and changed into a liquid.

6. The names of the elements are abbreviated with (symbols, formulas, numbers).

7. Gold, hydrogen, and copper are examples of (elements, compounds, mixtures).

8. The atom is generally made up of (one, two, three) different types of particles.

9. (Protons, Neutrons, Electrons) are the particles generally located outside the nucleus of an atom.

10. The atomic number of an element is determined by the number of (protons, electrons, neutrons).

11. Two or more atoms bonded together by the sharing of electrons form a(n) (proton, molecule, ion).

12. Ice melting and becoming water is a (chemical property, chemical change, physical change).

13. Elements combine chemically to form a(n) (element, compound, mixture).

14. (Elements, Compounds, Mixtures) are substances that can be separated into simpler parts by physical means.

15. A solution is a type of (compound, mixture, element).

■ *Interpret and Apply*

On your paper, answer each question.

16. Classify each example listed as a physical change, physical property, chemical change, and/or chemical property.
    a. A piece of gold has a brilliant luster.
    b. Gold does not tarnish because it does not react easily with other substances.
    c. You have lighted a match by striking it against the side of the match box.
    d. The wax in the candles is melting all over your birthday cake.

17. Suggest methods for separating the components of each of these mixtures:
    a. sugar and soil
    b. 1-mm aluminum spheres and 3-mm zinc spheres
    c. small grains of iron, copper, and baking soda

18. An ancient Greek named Democritus believed all matter was made of tiny particles. He named these particles *atomoi*, which means "indivisible" in Greek. Explain how Democritus's idea differs from the modern atomic model. How is his idea similar to the model?

19. Look carefully at the close-up photograph of granite below. Is granite a mixture, a compound, or an element? Justify your answer.

20. A certain type of rock has a density of 2 grams per cubic centimeter. If a piece of this rock has a volume of 30 cubic centimeters, what is its mass?

21. Different types of rock have different densities. List three ways in which this fact is useful to geologists.

22. Do you think there are more compounds or more elements on Earth? Explain your answer.

■ *Writing in Science*

23. If you hang wet clothes on a clothesline on a sunny day, the clothes will become dry after a while. Write an explanation of why this happens. When you have written your explanation, reread it to make sure that your ideas are expressed clearly.

■ *Critical Thinking*

Imagine that one day you turn on the kitchen tap and discover there is no water. You are lucky enough to find a small, murky pond near your home. You scoop out a bucketful of water and return home.

24. How would you remove any plants or other solid matter from the water?

25. How could you find out whether any salt or other chemicals are dissolved in the water?

26. What method could you use to make the pond water cleaner and safer to drink?

27. Can you think of a safer source for clean drinking water? (**Caution:** do not drink any water that you obtain using these methods.)

Minerals

Chapter Preview

Have You Ever WONDERED?

Why do materials glow in the dark?

You have seen white clothing glow under special lights at a dance, in a theater, or at a museum. Cloth may look this way because it is fluorescent or has fluorescent materials added to it.

Unlike toys that glow on their own in the dark, fluorescent materials glow when exposed to a special kind of light. Fluorescent materials have the ability to absorb invisible ultraviolet light and change it into light you can see. Artificial black lights are used as a strong source of ultraviolet light. These purplish lights may cause your clothing to glow when used at a dance or in a science museum.

Some materials found in Earth's crust are naturally fluorescent. Certain minerals glow under a black light and are used to make fluorescent paints and pigments. Did you know that nonmineral fluorescent dyes are added to laundry detergent to brighten white fabrics? That is why some white clothing may glow under a black light.

Not all minerals are fluorescent, but all minerals do have their own special properties. In this chapter, you will learn more about minerals, their interesting properties, where minerals occur, and the many uses that make minerals important in your life.

Minerals and Crystals

Lesson Objectives

▶ **Define** mineral *and* **discuss** *the five characteristics of a mineral.*

▶ **Relate** *crystal structure to mineral properties.*

▶ **Compare** *the two ways crystals can form.*

▶ **Activity** **Perform an experiment** *to see if crystal size depends on the rate of evaporation.*

New Terms _____

mineral
crystal
magma

You may not realize it, but many important times in your life are associated with minerals. When you were only a few hours old, you were probably introduced to your first mineral, talc. Talc is in the talcum powder used to keep babies comfortable and dry. Now that you are older, you enjoy minerals in other ways. For instance, without an artificial form of the mineral quartz, you would not be able to enjoy video games, quartz watches, home computers, radios, or television. Birthstones, such as those shown in Figure 8-1, are minerals too. In a few years, you may fall in love and give or receive a diamond engagement ring. Diamond is a mineral with great beauty and value. After you marry, perhaps you will one day celebrate your silver or golden wedding anniversary. Gold and silver are minerals too.

Talc, quartz, diamond, and gold are four very different substances. What makes them all minerals?

Defining a Mineral

A **mineral** can be defined as a naturally occurring, inorganic, solid substance with a definite chemical composition and structure. What does this definition mean? Let's break it apart and examine the five basic characteristics it says all minerals share.

First, a mineral must be natural, meaning it is not made by humans; therefore materials like concrete, steel, and plastic are not minerals. Second, a mineral must be inorganic. *Inorganic* means a mineral cannot be made from living tissue or the remains of something that was once living. Coal is not a mineral because it is formed from the remains of plants. Third, a mineral must be a solid, not a liquid or gas.

Figure 8-1 Everyone has a mineral birthstone. Which one is yours?

	Month	Birthstone
1	January	garnet
2	February	amethyst
3	March	aquamarine
4	April	diamond
5	May	emerald
6	June	alexandrite
7	July	ruby
8	August	peridot
9	September	sapphire
10	October	opal
11	November	topaz
12	December	turquoise

Fourth, all minerals must have a definite chemical makeup. Some minerals, like gold, silver, and diamond are made of atoms of a single element. Most of the 2500 known minerals are compounds. You recall from Chapter 7 that a compound contains atoms or ions of two or more different elements. For example, halite, the mineral name for salt, is a compound made of the elements sodium and chlorine. Quartz, a very common mineral, is a compound made up of silicon and oxygen.

The fifth characteristic of all minerals is their crystal structure. In a **crystal,** the atoms or ions in a substance are arranged in an orderly pattern that repeats over and over again. Quartz, for example, always forms six-sided crystals. However, a crystal is not always large enough to be easily seen. Not seeing a mineral's crystal structure does not mean it isn't there.

A material must possess all five of these characteristics to be classified as a mineral. If even one characteristic is missing, the material is not a mineral. Can the water flowing in a stream be considered a mineral? Water is a natural substance. Water is also inorganic and has a definite chemical makeup. However, the water flowing in a stream is a liquid, not a solid. It does not have a crystal structure. Therefore, liquid water is not a mineral.

Figure 8-2 Native minerals, like silver, are made of a single element.

Crystal Structure

Have you ever watched an apartment building, like the one in Figure 8-3 *(right)*, being built? Without the walls, you can easily see that all the apartments will be the same shape and very much alike. The steel skeleton forms a pattern that is repeated over and over again. Like the building, minerals also have a repeating internal structure. The atoms or ions in a mineral are arranged in a definite pattern that is repeated over and over again. This is called a crystal.

Figure 8-3 *Left:* A mineral crystal has a repeating pattern of atoms or ions. *Right:* A building has a repeating pattern of steel girders.

Cubic crystal
pattern

Cubic crystal

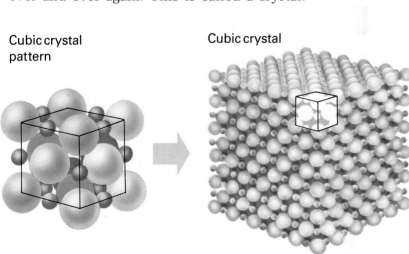

Table 8-1 The Six Crystal Systems

	System					
	cubic	tetragonal	hexagonal	orthorhombic	monoclinic	triclinic
Shape						
Example						
	halite	rutile	corundum	topaz	gypsum	feldspar

As more atoms or ions attach themselves to the crystal, it grows larger and larger. The repeated pattern of atoms forms smooth, flat sides on the surface of the crystal. These flat sides are called crystal faces.

Each mineral has a characteristic crystal shape. A mineral's crystal shape is determined by the number of crystal faces and the angles formed when two adjacent faces meet. In the mineral halite, sodium and chloride ions always join together to form cube-shaped crystals. The smooth crystal faces meeting at 90-degree angles are signs of an orderly arrangement of atoms. Table 8-1 shows examples of several different crystal shapes. How many crystal faces are in a hexagonal crystal? How do the angles formed in a cubic crystal compare with the angles in an orthorhombic crystal? The crystal pattern is a clue about the atoms or ions present in the mineral.

Atoms can join together in more than one arrangement. Therefore, the same element or compound can form different minerals depending on the arrangement of the same type of atoms. For example, the lead in your pencil is made from the mineral graphite. Graphite is black, slippery to the touch, and very soft. Diamond, on the other hand, is clear, shiny, and extremely hard. Look at Figure 8-4. You may not believe it, but graphite and diamond are both made of the same element, carbon. The two minerals, graphite and diamond, have different properties because of the different arrangement of their identical carbon atoms.

Figure 8-4 Graphite and diamond have different properties because their identical carbon atoms are arranged in different crystal structures.

Crystal Formation

The size of mineral crystals depends on the conditions under which they are formed. Generally, the longer it takes for a mineral to form, the larger the crystals in the mineral will be. Some mineral samples in your classroom may not have visible crystals. The crystals may be present, but may be too small to see.

There are two ways that crystals may form. Some crystals form when melted or partially melted rock cools on or beneath Earth's surface. Melted rock beneath Earth's surface is called **magma**. As magma cools, atoms have plenty of time to become arranged. The atoms or ions add on to the basic crystal shape. Crystals formed this way can become large and have well-developed crystal faces. If left undisturbed, the crystals will grow as large as space allows. In most cases, the crystals are kept fairly small by other crystals crowding around them.

Crystals also can form when minerals dissolved in water are left behind. For example, as salt water evaporates, sodium and chloride ions are arranged into crystals of halite. The size of the salt crystals depends on how slowly evaporation takes place. Sometimes mineral-rich water fills a hole or cavity in a rock, and the dissolved minerals are deposited inside the hole as the water evaporates. These beautiful, crystal-lined rocks are called geodes.

No matter how or where mineral crystals form, their crystal structure is one way you can tell minerals apart. What other properties do minerals have that can be used as identification tools?

Figure 8-5 Solutions rich in dissolved quartz once filled this hollow geode. Geodes are called water stones because water sometimes comes out when geodes are broken open. Can you explain why?

Lesson Review 8.1

1. What is a mineral?
2. How are the atoms arranged in a mineral that makes it different from other materials?
3. Describe the two processes by which crystals are formed.

Interpret and Apply

4. Is ice a mineral? Refer to Figure 8-6 to support your answer.
5. You are given two samples of quartz. Both samples have crystals. In one sample, the crystals are too small to be seen easily. Give two reasons why the two samples might have different size crystals.

Figure 8-6

MAKING CRYSTALS

Purpose   To compare the rate of evaporation with the size of crystals formed.

Materials

hot plate	lab apron
beaker	hand lens
watch glass	solution to be tested
safety goggles	water

Procedure

1. Read all instructions for this activity before beginning your work. Copy the data table onto a clean sheet of paper.

2. Put on your safety goggles and lab apron.

3. Select a clean, dry watch glass. This will be called watch glass A.

4. Put a small amount of a solution in watch glass A. **CAUTION: Solutions used may be poisonous. Wash off spills and splashes immediately with plenty of water.**

5. Fill the beaker halfway with water and set it on the hot plate.

6. Carefully place watch glass A on top of the beaker. **CAUTION: Be careful—hot water can cause burns.**

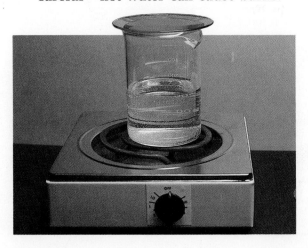

7. Turn the hot plate to a medium setting. Observe the solution as it is heated, being careful not to get too close. Time how long it takes for the liquid to evaporate.

8. When all liquid has evaporated, shut off the hot plate. **CAUTION: The setup is still hot. Do not touch anything until it has cooled for 10 minutes.**

9. After it has cooled, remove watch glass A from the beaker. Go get watch glass B from your teacher. Use a hand lens to compare the crystals in both glasses. Sketch the crystals and complete the data table.

10. Clean and return all materials and wash your hands thoroughly.

Collecting and Analyzing Data

Data Table		
Watch Glass	**A**	**B**
Amount of Time to Evaporate		24 h
Sketch of Crystals	–	
Describe Crystals		

1. Which watch glass had large crystals?

2. Were all the crystals in your two watch glasses basically the same shape?

Drawing Conclusions

3. Could atoms or ions move once the liquid evaporated? Explain.

4. Did the time allowed for evaporation affect the size of the crystals? Explain.

8.2 Identifying Minerals

Everyone in your science class is different in some way. Each student has his or her own unique combination of weight, height, and hair coloring. Some students may act shy; others are outgoing. Everyone looks and behaves a little differently. If strangers were asked to pick you out of your class, they would have to know a little about you, and then try to match the person they see to the description of your personal characteristics.

Similarly, every mineral has a combination of characteristics unique only to that mineral. These are called a mineral's properties. Some properties of minerals, such as color, are physical and can be observed directly. Minerals also have chemical properties that can be discovered only if the mineral is chemically broken apart or changed into a new product. In this lesson, you will learn how to use these mineral properties to identify the minerals themselves.

Mineral Properties

Color Color is the first property you will notice when you look at a mineral. Some minerals have unusual colors that make them easy to identify. Malachite [mal′ ə kīt], a mineral rich in the element copper, is green.

Color, however, is not always a dependable property to use when identifying minerals. One problem is that the same mineral can be different colors. Sometimes elements not normally part of the mineral are present in small amounts. These are called impurities. The type and amount of an impurity can change a mineral's natural color. For example, quartz is usually colorless or white. Small amounts of the element iron can make quartz purple. Purple quartz, shown in Figure 8-7 *(right)*, is called amethyst [am′ ə thəst]. Small amounts of titanium make up the pink variety called rose quartz.

Lesson Objectives

▶ *List* and *describe* observable mineral properties, such as color, luster, fracture, and cleavage.

▶ *Explain* how to test a mineral's streak, hardness, and heft.

▶ *Describe* chemical and special properties that aid mineral identification.

▶ **Activity** *Observe and describe* mineral properties used in mineral identification.

New Terms

streak	fracture
luster	specific gravity
hardness	heft
cleavage	

Figure 8-7 Color is one property of minerals. *Left:* Malachite is easy to recognize because of its green color. *Right:* Quartz occurs in different colors. Why?

Figure 8-8 Some minerals have the same color. *Left:* Gold is a valuable mineral. *Right:* Pyrite, or fool's gold, looks like gold, but has little value.

Color is also undependable because many minerals share the same color. Look at Figure 8-8. The mineral pyrite [pī′ rīt] has a color similar to gold. Because so many people have mistaken pyrite for gold, it is often called fool's gold. Do you see why?

Sometimes the original color of a mineral changes when the mineral is exposed to air, rain, heat, or pollution. For example, the brownish color of bornite turns purple when exposed to the air. This change of color also happens when silver starts to tarnish, or turn black. This hides the mineral's true color. To find the true color, you must find an unchanged mineral surface. This is possible by breaking the sample or by doing a streak test.

Streak The **streak** is the color you see when a sample of a mineral is powdered. You make a streak of a mineral by rubbing the sample across an unglazed piece of ceramic tile, called a streak plate. The back of an ordinary bathroom tile can be used as a streak plate. Although the color of a mineral may vary, its streak is always the same. This makes streak a good test to help identify a mineral. Hematite [hē′ mə tīt], for example, can appear brown, red, or silver, but its streak will always be a reddish-brown color. Gold has a gold streak, but fool's gold leaves a black streak. This is one way to tell the two minerals apart.

Some minerals have dark-colored streaks. Graphite has a black streak. You see the streak of graphite whenever you write on a piece of paper. Other minerals, like feldspar, talc, and calcite have clear or white streaks. There are minerals so hard that they will not turn to powder when rubbed across a streak plate. These minerals are said to have no streak. Topaz is an example of a mineral with no streak.

Luster **Luster** is the way a mineral reflects light from its surface. A mineral's luster can be classified as metallic or nonmetallic. A mineral has a metallic luster if it shines like the polished surface of metal. Look around the room for objects with a metallic luster. Look back at Figure 8-8. Gold and pyrite both have a metallic luster.

Figure 8-9 Hematite always has a reddish-brown streak even though the color of a piece of hematite can be brown, silver, or red.

The minerals in Figure 8-10 do not have a metallic luster. A mineral that does not shine like a metal has a nonmetallic luster. Minerals with nonmetallic lusters are said to be glassy like quartz, brilliant like diamond, or waxy like talc. Lusters can also be earthy or dull.

Hardness The resistance a mineral has to being scratched is called its **hardness.** You know that your fingernail can scratch a wax candle easily, but it cannot scratch a metal spoon. This is because your fingernail is harder than wax, but softer than the spoon. Every mineral has a characteristic hardness. The hardest mineral known is diamond. A diamond can scratch all other minerals and can only be scratched by another diamond. Because of their hardness, diamonds are used in industry on saw blades, drill bits, and other cutting tools. Talc, on the other hand, is one of the softest minerals. Talc is used to make baby powder. What other soft mineral have you learned about already?

In order to give each mineral a measurable hardness, Friedrich Mohs, a German mineralogist, worked out a scale to rate the hardness of each mineral. The minerals in Mohs' scale of hardness are listed in Table 8-2. Each mineral assigned to the scale is a common mineral which represents many other minerals of the same hardness. The minerals are listed from softest (talc #1) to hardest (diamond #10). Hard minerals can scratch softer minerals. Therefore minerals with higher hardness numbers on Mohs' scale scratch minerals with lower numbers.

Figure 8-10 These minerals have nonmetallic lusters. *Top:* Fluorite is glassy. *Middle:* Talc is waxy. *Bottom:* Limonite has an earthy luster.

Table 8-2 Mohs' Scale of Hardness		
Hardness	**Mineral**	**Simple Test**
1	talc	easily scratched by a fingernail
2	gypsum	barely scratched by a fingernail
3	calcite	scratched by a copper penny
4	fluorite	easily scratched by a steel knife blade
5	apatite	barely scratched by a steel knife blade
6	feldspar	barely scratches glass; not scratched by knife
7	quartz	easily scratches glass and steel
8	topaz	scratches glass easily and scratches quartz
9	corundum	scratches topaz
10	diamond	hardest of all minerals, scratches all others

Figure 8-11 Talc can be scratched by a copper penny that has a hardness of 3 on Mohs' scale. What is the hardness of talc?

How do you find out a mineral's hardness? Go back and examine Table 8-2 carefully. You can use your fingernail, a copper penny, a knife blade or iron nail, and a piece of glass to find the hardness of most minerals. Suppose you have a mineral sample that you can easily scratch with a knife blade, but not with a copper penny. What is the sample's hardness? The hardness of the mineral being tested must be less than 4 if the knife blade leaves a scratch on the sample. (Remember that on Mohs' scale, the higher numbers are harder minerals, so the higher numbers scratch the lower numbers.) The hardness of the mineral must be greater than 3 if a penny will not scratch the sample. The hardness of the mineral is between 3 and 4, so you might say that it is about 3.5 on Mohs' scale.

What if the knife blade did not scratch the mineral? The next step is to try scratching the glass with the mineral. **CAUTION: Place the glass plate flat on a hard surface before scratching.** All minerals harder than 6 will scratch glass. Except for quartz, most minerals this hard are rare.

Cleavage and Fracture Another physical property of a mineral is the manner in which it breaks. Minerals that break or split along smooth surfaces are said to have **cleavage.** A cleavage surface is usually smooth and flat. Muscovite mica, shown in Figure 8-12 *(left)*, has one direction of cleavage and breaks apart like very thin sheets of paper. Sheets of muscovite are transparent enough that the mineral was once used in the Soviet Union in place of window glass. (Did you know that someone from Moscow is called a Muscovite?)

Galena [gə lē′ nə] is a mineral that has three directions of cleavage. If you hit a piece of galena with a hammer, it would break into small cubes. A cube is a shape with smooth surfaces in three directions. If you break each small galena cube, it will break into still smaller cubes, each having the same three directions of cleavage.

Figure 8-12 *Left:* Muscovite mica splits into single sheets because it has one direction of cleavage. *Right:* Galena has three directions of cleavage. It splits to form cubes.

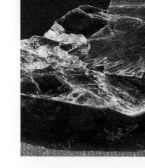

Figure 8-13 Other minerals break along uneven surfaces. *Left:* Quartz has curved, conchoidal fracture. *Right:* Some minerals with fibrous fracture are called asbestos.

Some minerals do not break smoothly in any direction. When a mineral breaks unevenly and leaves a jagged or irregular surface, it is said to have **fracture.** Quartz breaks like a chunk of glass, as shown in Figure 8-13 *(left).* This kind of fracture is called conchoidal [kän koid′ əl]. In this type of fracture, the rounded edges look like the inside of a shell. Minerals can also fracture into long thin fibers, so they are said to have a fibrous fracture. Some minerals with fibrous fracture are called asbestos, shown in Figure 8-13 *(right).*

Specific Gravity All minerals have a particular density. You know that density is the amount of matter in a given space. No matter how large two samples of a mineral are, they always have the same density. A mineral's density is sometimes measured by comparing its weight to the weight of an equal volume of water. This is called **specific gravity.** For example, the specific gravity of silver is 10.5. This means silver weighs 10.5 times more than an equal volume of water. Quartz has a specific gravity of 2.7. How does this compare to the weight of water?

You can also compare the densities of two minerals in the lab by hefting them. To **heft** is to test the weight of something by lifting it. Take two pieces of different minerals that are approximately the same size and hold one in each hand. You can tell which one has the greater density by judging which one feels heavier. For example, a sample of galena (which contains lead) feels heavier than an equal size sample of bauxite [bȯk′ sīt] (which contains aluminum). Lead is a much heavier metal than aluminum. Which do you think is more dense, galena or quartz?

Crystal Types You have already learned about crystals, their shapes, and how they form. If the crystals are large enough to be seen, the crystal shape can be used to help identify a mineral. Quartz crystals have six sides and triangular faces that meet at a point. Halite, galena, and pyrite all have cubic crystals.

Fact or Fiction?

Is the lead in a pencil really the element lead? No, it isn't! In fact, pencil lead contains no lead at all. Black, soft pencil lead is made from the mineral graphite. To make pencil lead, powdered graphite is mixed with small amounts of clay. Adding more clay makes pencil lead harder.

Why is pencil lead called lead? The first known pencils were made in England, where graphite was called "plumbago" or "black lead," even though it was not really lead. The name stuck, and is still used today.

Chewing on pencils is still not a good idea. You can't get lead poisoning from pencil lead, but you could still get sick from the lead or other poisons in the paint covering the pencil!

Table 8-3 Properties of Some Common Minerals

Mineral Name Composition	Hardness	Specific Gravity	Color	Cleavage Directions	Luster	Streak
Minerals with Metallic Lusters						
graphite C	1–2	2.2	black	1–very good	metallic to earthy	black
galena Pb, S	2.5	7.5	lead gray	3–very good	metallic	lead gray
copper Cu	2.5–3.0	8.9	copper red	none	metallic	metallic, orange red
gold Au	2.5–3.0	19.3	gold	none	metallic	yellow
silver Ag	2.5–3.0	10.5	silver	none	metallic	gray, silver
bornite Cu, Fe, S	3	5.1	bronze, purple, blue, black	none	metallic	grayish black
chalcopyrite Cu, Fe, S	3.5–4.0	4.2	brassy, yellow-gold	none	metallic	greenish black
hematite Fe, O	5.5–6.5	5.1	reddish brown to black	none	metallic	reddish brown
magnetite Fe, O	6	5.2	black	none	metallic	black
pyrite Fe, S	6.0–6.5	5.0	brassy yellow	none	metallic	black
Minerals with Nonmetallic Lusters						
talc Fe, H, Mg, O, Si	1	2.8	pale green, white, gray	1–good	pearly, greasy, dull	white
sulfur S	1.5–2.5	2.1	yellow	none	dull, resinous	yellow
gypsum Ca, H, O, S	2	2.3	colorless, white, gray, yellow	3–good	glassy to pearly, silky	colorless
muscovite mica Al, H, K, O, Si	2–2.5	2.9	colorless, shades of green, gray, or brown	1–very good	glassy, silky, pearly	white, colorless
halite Na, Cl	2.5	2.2	white, colorless	3–very good	glassy to dull	colorless
biotite mica Al, Fe, H, K, Mg, O, S	2.5–3.0	3.0	black, green, brown	1–very good	glassy, pearly	colorless

Mineral Name *Composition*	Hardness	Specific Gravity	Color	Cleavage Directions	Luster	Streak
Minerals with Nonmetallic Lusters (continued)						
calcite *Ca, C, O*	3	2.7	white, gray, yellow, colorless	3—very good	glassy	colorless
barite *Ba, O, S*	3.0–3.5	4.5	clear, white, reddish	3—good	glassy to earthy	white
dolomite *Ca, Mg, C, O*	3.5–4.0	2.9	colorless, white, pink, gray	3—good	glassy to dull	white
sphalerite *Zn, S*	3.5–4.0	4.0	brown	6—very good	glassy to dull	yellow
fluorite *Ca, F*	4	3.2	lt. green, blue, yellow, purple	4—good	glassy	colorless
apatite *Ca, Cl, F, H, O, P*	5	3.2	green, brown	1—poor	glassy	white
limonite *Fe, H, O*	4–5.5	3.8	yellow brown to brown	none	dull to glassy	yellow to brown
augite *Al, Ca, Fe, Mg, O, Si*	5–6	3.3	green	none	glassy	greenish gray
hornblende *Al, Ca, Fe, H, Na, Mg, O, Si*	5–6	3.2	dark green to black	2—good	glassy to silky	colorless
albite *Al, Na, O, Si*	6	2.6	grayish white	2—good	glassy	white
potassium feldspar *Al, K, O, Si*	6	2.7	white, gray, pink	2—good	glassy, pearly	white
olivine *Fe, Mg, O, Si*	6.5–7.0	3.9	olive green, grayish green	none	glassy	white, gray
garnet *variable*	6.5–7.5	3.9	red, brown, green, black	none	glassy to resinous	none
quartz *Si, O*	7	2.7	colorless, white, varied	none (conchoidal fracture)	glassy to dull	none
topaz *Al, F, H, O, Si*	8	3.5	clear, yellow, blue, pink	1—very good	glassy	none
corundum *Al, O*	9	4.0	clear blue, gray, brown	none	glassy to dull	none

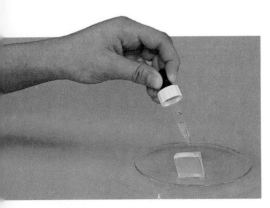

Figure 8-14 In an acid test, calcite reacts to dilute acid by giving off bubbles of carbon dioxide gas.

Figure 8-15 This calcite has the property called double refraction. Objects viewed through it have a double image.

Special Properties

So far you have learned about a mineral's physical properties. Minerals, because they possess a definite chemical composition, can be identified by chemical testing. Two of these chemical tests are simple enough to perform in your school laboratory. The acid test is used to see if a mineral is made of calcium carbonate. A drop of dilute hydrochloric acid placed on calcium carbonate will cause a chemical change. Bubbles of carbon dioxide gas form on the surface, causing it to fizz. This is a quick and easy way to identify the mineral calcite, which is made of calcium carbonate. You should always wear safety goggles and a lab apron when performing an acid test.

Flame testing can also be performed on powdered samples of minerals. As discussed in Chapter 7, the color you see in the flame can tell you if a given element is present. Although this does not identify the mineral itself, flame testing can offer a clue as to the mineral's composition.

There are several unique properties that are helpful in identifying certain minerals. For example, some minerals that contain iron are magnetic. Lodestone is a form of the mineral magnetite and is itself a natural magnet, capable of attracting iron. Some minerals' surfaces have a special feel to the touch. Graphite feels greasy; talc feels smooth, like a bar of soap.

Clear samples of calcite exhibit an unusual property. Look at Figure 8-15. What happens to the image of an object when viewed through a clear piece of calcite? Some minerals glow when placed under ultraviolet light. This is called fluorescence [flür es' ents]. Samples of fluorite, calcite, and barite are often fluorescent.

Lesson Review 8.2

6. Explain the difference between metallic and nonmetallic luster. Give an example of each.

7. What is meant by the hardness of a mineral? Name a very soft mineral and the hardest known mineral.

8. Calcite has two special properties having to do with light. Describe these two properties.

Interpret and Apply

9. Explain the difficulty in identifying an unknown mineral with the results of only one physical test.

A C T I V I T Y   8 . 2

IDENTIFICATION OF MINERALS

Purpose To identify common minerals by their properties.

Materials

numbered mineral samples	safety goggles
	lab apron
copper penny	streak plate
iron nail	hand lens
glass plate	

Procedure

1. Read all the instructions for this activity before you begin your work.

2. Copy the data table on a clean piece of paper. Put on your safety goggles and lab apron.

3. Go get one mineral sample. Record the sample number on the data table.

4. Observe and record the color of your sample.

5. Place the streak plate flat on the table. Rub the sample across the streak plate and record the color powder you see. **CAUTION: Always keep streak and glass plate flat on table when testing. Tile could break in your hand and cause a serious cut.**

6. Examine the surfaces of the sample. Write *cleavage* if the sample has broken along smooth surfaces, or *fracture* if it has broken unevenly. Assume you are not seeing crystal faces in these samples.

7. Test each sample for its hardness. Use your fingernail first, then go on to the penny, nail, and glass plate if needed. Record the hardness number from Mohs' scale (Table 8-2).

8. Observe how the mineral reflects light. Does it look like metal? Record *metallic* or *nonmetallic* in the data table.

9. Heft the sample. If necessary, compare it to another sample the same size. Record *light*, *medium*, or *heavy* under the "Heft" column.

10. Repeat steps 3 through 9 for each of the numbered mineral samples.

11. Once all the minerals have been tested, clean up all materials and wash your hands thoroughly.

Collecting and Analyzing Data

1. Compare your findings with the minerals in Table 8-3. Match the properties you found for the mineral with the properties in the chart that most resemble it. Write the correct name of the mineral in the last column of your data table.

Drawing Conclusions

2. What additional tests could have been performed? How would these tests be useful in identifying the minerals?

Data Table

Sample Number	Color	Streak	Cleavage/ Fracture	Hardness	Luster	Heft	Mineral Name

8.3 Mineral Resources

People have used minerals throughout history. Stone Age humans chipped crude tools and weapons out of the mineral flint. Later, during the Bronze and Iron Ages, people learned how to combine and process minerals to make products they needed. In this century, minerals have been the source of the radioactive elements needed for nuclear energy. The use of minerals is constantly adapted to society's changing needs.

Today minerals are used in many products that are part of your everyday life. Table 8-4 shows several minerals and their uses. Can you think of any other minerals used today?

Gems

When you browse through a jewelry store, you see many gemstones set in silver and gold. **Gems** are beautiful, rare, and valuable minerals that are cut and polished for jewelry. Diamonds, emeralds, rubies, and sapphires are the rarest gems and are therefore the most valuable. These are called precious stones, and have been worn as jewelry for centuries. Diamonds are hard enough to have industrial uses as well, including the familiar one shown in Figure 8-16.

Lesson Objectives

▶ **Distinguish** between precious and semiprecious gems.

▶ **Define** the term ore.

▶ **List** some common minerals and describe their uses.

▶ **Discuss** current mineral supplies and **evaluate** methods of conservation.

▶ **Activity** **Form a model** of a chemical technique for mining waste reclamation.

New Terms

gem
ore
smelting
nodules

Table 8-4 Common Mineral Uses	
Mineral	**Used in**
sulfur	matches, medicines, rubber, gunpowder, fertilizer
quartz	glass, watches, radios, televisions, radar instruments
feldspar	pottery, glass, scouring powder, porcelain
mica	electronic parts, glossy makeup, insulation, fake snow
calcite	medicines, toothpaste; also found in the building stones, marble and limestone
graphite	pencils, dry lubricant; also used in batteries as electrodes
halite	table salt, food preservatives, glass, paper, cardboard
gypsum	wallboard, plaster of Paris; also used in fertilizer
borax	soaps, household cleansers, porcelain, dyes, inks
talc	talcum powder, wire insulation, furnace linings, crayons, paints, soap

Other gems are not as rare and valuable. They are called semiprecious stones. This group includes such familiar gems as amethyst, turquoise, opal, zircon, and garnet. These gems are beautiful and durable, but are not as rare as the precious stones. The Chinese have carved figures and vases from the semiprecious stone jade for many centuries. Malachite is another stone often used for boxes and tabletops.

Ores

School buses, toasters, fillings in your teeth, and even your kitchen sink are all made from minerals mined from Earth. Many minerals contain important elements like iron, zinc, aluminum, and lead. Usually these elements are combined with other substances in the mineral and must be separated before they can be used. If a mineral contains enough of an element to make mining and separation profitable, it is called an **ore.** For example, there is enough aluminum in the mineral bauxite that it is worthwhile to mine it and remove the aluminum. Bauxite, therefore, is an ore of aluminum. Feldspar also contains aluminum, but not enough to make mining it profitable. Aluminum is used in a variety of products: cans, foil, airplanes, and lightweight motors.

Some other ores mined for their metals include limonite [lī′ mə nīt] and hematite. These are ores of iron. Iron is an important metal used to make steel. Galena is an ore of lead. Other metals derived from ores include copper, silver, gold, and chromium. Figure 8-17 *(left)* shows one way these ores are mined from Earth.

When an ore containing one of these metals is mined from Earth, the ore is often separated by a process called smelting. In **smelting,** ore is heated in a way that separates the metal from any unwanted substances. Smelting is only necessary when dealing with ores that contain a metal.

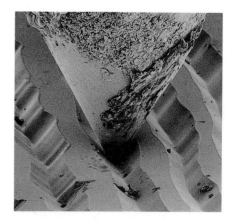

Figure 8-16 This electron microscope photo shows a diamond-tipped phonograph stylus in the groove of a record album.

Figure 8-17 *Left:* Copper ore is often mined from gigantic open pits, such as this one in Montana. *Right:* Usable metal is extracted from ore in the smelting process.

Many nonmetal minerals are ores as well. Halite and sulfur are used in many products. Since it is profitable to mine and sell halite and sulfur, they are considered to be ores. Some nonmetals can be used just as they come from the ground. The mineral gypsum is mined from large open pits and crushed to make plaster for walls. Perhaps you have used plaster of Paris in your art or science class. Plaster of Paris is made entirely from dehydrated gypsum. Talc and graphite are other nonmetal ore minerals.

Mineral Supplies

Your lifestyle depends on thousands of products made from Earth's mineral resources. As the population increases, the need for more mineral resources also grows. Most of the mineral deposits we depend upon were formed by processes acting on Earth over millions of years. Unfortunately that makes most minerals nonrenewable resources. That means once the supplies of these minerals are mined and used, there will be no more available. Even though the natural processes that formed these minerals are continuing to this day, they occur so slowly that it would take millions more years to replace what we have used.

Of course, the first step in using mineral resources is finding them. Early mineral exploration was limited to simply looking for ore on Earth's surface, where it could be easily seen. The ore deposits found in this way were usually so rich that removing the desired elements from the ore was simple. Unfortunately most of these rich, convenient surface deposits have been used up. Where else might ore deposits be found?

To increase current mineral supplies, geologists must explore deeper in Earth's crust to find new deposits. Imagine searching a park or a forest for a nickel buried one meter below the surface 100 years ago. Where would you begin? How do you find something you cannot see?

Many different methods are used to find deep mineral deposits. Topographic and geologic maps, showing the surface shape and the type of rock, can offer clues as to what is below the surface. Photos taken from planes and orbiting satellites can show large features that often go unnoticed on the ground. Holes are drilled and samples taken from great depths. Sometimes even the types of plants growing in an area, or the presence of metal ions in a pond or stream, can indicate the presence of minerals underground.

Other methods are based on mineral properties discussed in this chapter. Have you ever heard an echo? You know from an echo that sound bounces off objects and is reflected

Figure 8-18 The earliest human use of metal relied on finding native minerals, such as this copper, on or near Earth's surface.

back toward you. Buried minerals can do this too. Underground explosions are set off to create sound waves that travel deep into Earth's crust. The echoes that form when these sound waves bounce off buried mineral deposits can provide information about the location, shape, and size of the deposit. Small differences in the pull of gravity and magnetism can also be measured. An area with an unusually high or low gravity or magnetic measurement may have a large deposit of ore buried beneath it.

Even with the use of modern technology, it is hard for the supply of mineral resources to keep pace with demand. You may face mineral shortages in your lifetime. New sources of minerals must be found and explored. One new frontier for exploration is the ocean floor. Some metals, like manganese, copper, iron, and zinc are found as clumps or **nodules** on the ocean floor. These nodules, shown in Figure 8-19, are found 4000 to 6000 meters below the ocean's surface, making it difficult and expensive to recover them. Currently, nodules are being mined only on an experimental basis. Think about what you learned about ores. What would need to happen for nodules to become an ore for manganese? Could mining of nodules harm ocean life?

Figure 8-19 There may be 1.5 billion metric tons of manganese nodules like these on the Pacific Ocean floor.

ENVIRONMENTAL AWARENESS

Asbestos

Why are people so concerned about asbestos? Asbestos is a mineral form with thread-like fibers that separate easily. The fibers can be woven like wool or pressed into sheets. Until the late 1970's, asbestos was commonly used because it is flame-resistant and does not conduct heat or electricity very well. Many schools and theaters had stage curtains made with asbestos fibers to guard against fires. Because it resists heat, asbestos was used in the brake linings of cars and to insulate electrical wiring, motors, and hot-water pipes.

The actual fibers of asbestos are a hundred times tinier than your eyelash. During mining and manufacturing, these fibers break off and float in the air. The fibers also break off finished products. If inhaled, these tiny fibers get trapped in people's lungs and can cause cancer.

Because of the dangers of asbestos, many people feel it should no longer be used. Many towns are calling for the removal of asbestos from their schools and other public buildings. They believe other materials can be used as an asbestos substitute. Vermiculite is a material with similar insulating properties. Fiberglass can be used in shingles and floor tiles.

Other people believe asbestos removal causes more health problems than leaving it in place. Why would this be the case? ■

As technology advances, it seems possible that people in the future may be mining minerals from the ocean floor or in space. However, these ideas are still many years from becoming real mineral sources. You need minerals today and every day. What can be done to ensure the supply?

Research and Recycling

There are many ways minerals can be conserved to ensure enough supplies for the future. One way to conserve mineral supplies is to develop more artificial substitute materials. However, it is difficult to find substitute materials with all the unique properties many minerals have. Today plastics have replaced many metals once used in cars, machinery, and factories. What problems are there with using plastics to replace metals? Plastics are made from petroleum, which is also in short supply. Many plastics do not rot or decompose, and present a long-term waste disposal problem.

Better mining techniques and improved methods of recovering minerals from their ores can increase mineral supplies. Since some elements are hard to separate from their ore minerals, much is wasted. For example, copper ore is usually mined in large, open pits and then crushed and smelted. Much copper is left behind in the "waste rock" left at the end of the processing. If more copper could be taken from this waste rock, copper supplies would increase. This is called secondary recovery of mining waste.

Recycling of materials by industry, communities, and nations can help conserve Earth's mineral resources. Many recycling centers, such as the one shown in Figure 8-21, are now available for depositing cans, glass bottles, and scrap metals. These materials are reused to make new products without removing more minerals from Earth's crust. Recycling materials saves energy which, like certain minerals, is in increasingly short supply.

Figure 8-20 Some alternatives to minerals have drawbacks. Increased use of plastic has led to increased pollution.

Figure 8-21 Aluminum cans are recycled in many states. What are the advantages of recycling cans?

A C T I V I T Y 8 . 3

Lab Equipment

RECLAIMING MINING WASTE

Purpose To observe and evaluate a process to recover minerals from waste rock.

Materials

500 mL beaker	sandpaper
copper sulfate	iron nail
crystals	blue litmus paper
graduated cylinder	water
lab balance	lab apron
string	safety goggles

Procedure

1. Read all instructions for this activity before beginning your work.

2. Record your observations on a separate sheet of paper.

3. Put on your safety goggles and your lab apron.

4. Use the balance to measure 3 g of copper sulfate. Place the copper sulfate in your beaker. **CAUTION: Copper sulfate is poisonous. Do not handle.**

5. Cover the copper sulfate with 50 mL of water.

6. Observe and record the color of the solution. Dip a piece of blue litmus paper into the solution and record any change in the color of the litmus paper.

7. Use the sandpaper to make the nail's surface shiny. Tie a piece of string around the nail. Carefully lower the iron nail into the solution, leaving one end of the string hanging outside the beaker.

8. Observe the nail and the solution for 15 min. Record any change in color. Test the solution again with blue litmus paper. Record the results of the litmus test and any other observations.

9. Carefully lift the nail out of the solution using the string. Dispose of the nail, string, and solution following your teacher's instructions.

10. Before leaving the laboratory, clean up all materials and wash your hands thoroughly.

Collecting and Analyzing Data

1. What happened to the copper sulfate when you added water?

2. What happened to the color of the solution when the nail was added?

3. What substance began to coat the surface of the nail? How could you recognize it?

Drawing Conclusions

4. Copper sulfate is in the waste rock left from copper mining operations. How do you think the waste rock could be processed to recover this leftover copper?

5. Blue litmus paper turns pink when dipped into acids. What problems would there be if water from this mineral recovery procedure were emptied into a stream?

Cooperation between nations is necessary to conserve and recycle Earth's mineral resources. No country has, within its own borders, every type of mineral it needs. Figure 8-22 shows the uneven distribution of certain mineral deposits throughout the world. Countries must trade minerals they have for those they don't have in order to guarantee their economic survival. Communication between countries often exists because of the need to trade mineral resources. What might happen if one country controlled all the deposits of a mineral?

In this chapter, you have learned how Earth's chemistry forms minerals. You have learned how minerals are identified and how they are used. The next step in understanding Earth is to learn how minerals combine to form the solid substance called rock.

Figure 8-22 Major mineral resources are spread unevenly throughout the world. What material shown is not found in the United States?

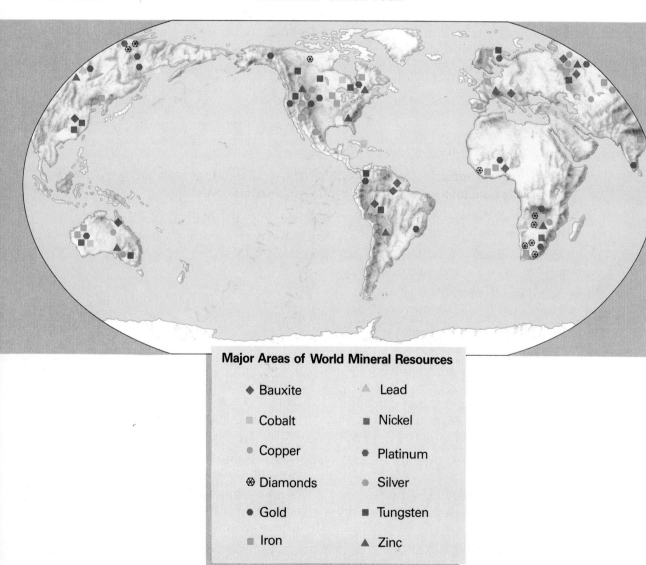

Major Areas of World Mineral Resources

◆ Bauxite	▲ Lead
▪ Cobalt	▪ Nickel
● Copper	● Platinum
⊗ Diamonds	● Silver
● Gold	▪ Tungsten
▪ Iron	▲ Zinc

Lesson Review 8.3

10. Name four minerals and give examples of how they are used.

11. What is an ore? Give two examples of ores mined for the metal they contain. Name one nonmetal ore.

12. List two differences between precious stones and semi-precious stones. Give examples of each.

13. What does the term *nonrenewable* mean? Why are mineral resources considered nonrenewable?

Interpret and Apply

14. Explain how modern technology has helped in the discovery of new mineral deposits.

15. Explain how returning an aluminum can to a recycling center helps conserve mineral resources. How does recycling also help conserve energy resources?

Chapter Summary

Read this summary of the main ideas in this chapter. If any are not clear to you, go back and review that lesson.

8.1 Minerals and Crystals

■ A mineral is a natural, inorganic, solid with a definite chemical makeup and a crystal structure.

■ A crystal is a definite arrangement of atoms that forms a repeated pattern within a mineral.

■ Crystals that form slowly will be much larger than crystals that form quickly.

8.2 Identifying Minerals

■ Minerals have physical and chemical properties that can be used to identify them.

■ Some physical properties of minerals can be observed directly, like color, luster, cleavage, and fracture.

■ Simple tests help identify a mineral's streak, hardness, and heft.

■ Some minerals can be identified by special properties, including magnetism, reaction to acid, and fluorescence.

8.3 Mineral Resources

■ Minerals are used in a variety of ways in your everyday life.

■ Many rare, valuable, and durable minerals are classified as gems. Precious and semi-precious gems are used in jewelry.

■ Ores are minerals that are mined and processed for a profit.

■ Continued supplies of nonrenewable minerals can be ensured by the use of exploration, recycling, and by cooperation among nations.

Chapter Review

■ Vocabulary

cleavage	magma
crystal	mineral
fracture	nodules
gem	ore
hardness	smelting
heft	specific gravity
luster	streak

■ Concept Mapping

Using the method of concept mapping described on pages 3–5, complete a concept map for minerals. Copy the incomplete concept map below. Then fill in the missing terms.

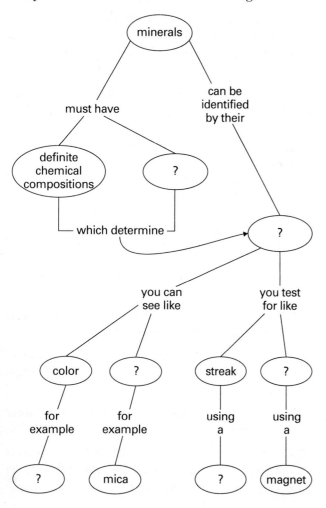

■ Review

Number your paper from 1 to 20. Match each term in List **A** with a phrase in List **B**.

List A

a. streak
b. hardness
c. smelting
d. acid test
e. cleavage
f. amethyst, opal, turquoise
g. ores
h. luster
i. gems
j. recycling
k. diamond
l. fracture
m. solid
n. crystal
o. nodules
p. halite
q. specific gravity
r. inorganic
s. evaporation
t. talc

List B

1. one method of crystal formation
2. the way a mineral reflects light
3. state of matter minerals must be in
4. refers to materials not made from living things
5. atoms or ions that are arranged in an orderly repeating pattern
6. the hardest mineral known
7. a powdered line left by a mineral
8. the ability of a mineral to resist scratching
9. when a mineral breaks along smooth, flat surfaces
10. general name for all minerals mined for profit
11. a mineral's weight compared to the weight of an equal volume of water
12. the softest mineral
13. test for the compound calcium carbonate
14. the mineral name for salt
15. when a mineral breaks along an uneven and rough surface

16. general name for all minerals cut and polished for use in jewelry

17. examples of semiprecious stones

18. clumps of mineral-rich deposits on the seafloor

19. a method of removing metals from an ore

20. one method to conserve mineral resources

■ Interpret and Apply

On your paper, answer each question using complete sentences.

21. Why is wood not considered a mineral?

22. Explain how the size of crystals can indicate where they might have formed.

23. If ice cream partially melts and is then put back in the freezer, where it slowly refreezes, it can become grainy and crunchy. Why do you think this happens?

24. Consider the following pairs of minerals. Choose the best chemical or physical property that would easily distinguish them:
    a. quartz and fluorite
    b. calcite and fluorite
    c. halite and calcite

25. What might be some advantages and disadvantages of mining minerals on the moon or other planets?

26. Some people believe a diamond is real if it scratches glass. Why can't you assume that scratching glass is an accurate test to identify a diamond?

27. Some mines across the country closed because it became too expensive to operate them. Other mines reopened because companies found they could make a profit. The ore mineral being mined does not change from year to year. Explain what might cause a company to close or reopen a mine.

■ Writing in Science

28. Imagine that your community has decided to start a program for recycling bottles, cans, and scrap metals. Bins will be provided for these materials. You have been chosen to write an information sheet about this program that will be mailed to every apartment and house in the town. Your writing will have two purposes: to inform people about the program and to persuade them to participate in it. Use your own ideas in addition to information that you have learned in this chapter.

■ Critical Thinking

You are assigned to explore Planet X. On your expedition, you discover an interesting new mineral that has the following properties:

Properties of Unknown Mineral from Planet X	
Color	bright red
Streak	clear
Luster	nonmetallic, glassy
Hardness	8
Specific Gravity	7
Breaks	conchoidal fracture
Crystal Shape	too small to see

29. What is this mineral's most interesting or unusual property?

30. What other tests could you run to learn more about this mineral?

31. What Earth mineral does this new discovery most resemble? Give evidence to support your answer.

32. Discuss the possible uses for this new mineral.

33. What are some of the things you would need to consider before you started to mine this mineral as an ore?

9 Rocks

Chapter Preview

Have You Ever WONDERED?

How did this strange-looking mass of rock form?

This is Devils Tower in Wyoming. It is over 260 meters high. Notice how the rock tower is divided into long, thin columns. An Indian legend says that a huge bear clawed these lines into the rock when he tried to climb it.

What you see are actually the remains of an ancient volcano. Devils Tower was once magma in the center of a volcano. The lines were formed as the magma slowly cooled and hardened to form rock. More cooling caused the new rock to shrink and crack into columns. Over millions of years, the surrounding volcanic cone of dust and cinders was carried away by wind and water, leaving behind the rock core you see today.

In this chapter, you will learn more about how rocks are formed and how they may be identified.

Observing Rocks

Where you are sitting right now could have once been covered by an ancient ocean, a flow of hot volcanic lava, or by the shifting sand dunes of a desert. How could you find out which one it was? The clues are found in the rocks outside. Geologists learn about Earth's past by studying rocks. Rocks can show you many things about the conditions present when the rocks were formed. For example, rocks can show you what the climate was like, or what plants and animals were alive at the time. Rocks can record the slow formation of mountains over millions of years or the instant changes caused by an earthquake.

Types of Rocks

You have probably discovered that not all rocks look alike. As you kick them along the ground, or toss them in the air, you notice they are different colors, sizes, and weights. What are rocks? How are they different from minerals?

A **rock** is a natural solid that is usually a mixture of different minerals. Just as there are many minerals, there are many kinds of rocks. Rocks are grouped or classified according to how they form. There are three different types of rocks. **Igneous** [ig' nē əs] rocks form when hot, molten rock cools and crystallizes into a solid. The second rock type is called sedimentary. **Sedimentary** [sed ə ment' ə rē] rocks form when pieces of rocks, shells, or the remains of plants and animals are squeezed and cemented together. The third type, **metamorphic** [met ə mȯr' fik] rocks, form when existing rocks are changed into new rocks by intense heat and pressure deep inside Earth.

How could you tell an igneous rock from a sedimentary rock? Because it is a mixture, a rock does not have special properties like the minerals tested in the last chapter. For example, a mineral has a definite density. Any two samples of that mineral will have the same density. The density of a rock, however, depends on what minerals are in it and how much of each mineral is present in that sample. Two samples of the same rock may have different densities because they contain different amounts of the same minerals. A rock's streak can also look different every time it is taken. Each time you rub the rock across a streak plate, you could be powdering a different mineral in the rock, or a different set of minerals all at once. The streak may not be the same.

The three rock types will be discussed in more detail later in this chapter. But first, let's learn some ways to describe rocks that are useful in telling them apart.

Lesson Objectives

▶ **Define** a rock and **explain** three ways rocks can form.

▶ **Describe** how to identify rocks by their characteristics.

▶ **Summarize** how size, shape, and arrangement of mineral matter determine a rock's texture.

▶ **Activity** **Observe** and **describe** properties of some common rocks.

New Terms

rock	metamorphic
igneous	grains
sedimentary	texture

Figure 9-1 Rocks provide valuable clues about the environments in Earth's past. Where was this rock deposited?

quartz

mica

hornblende

feldspar

Rock Characteristics

Did you ever gather small rocks to toss into a stream? Maybe you searched for smooth, flat rocks to skip along the surface of a lake or pond. From your experience, you know rocks can appear smooth or rough, shiny or dull, and can be many different colors. Just as minerals have mineral properties, rocks have certain rock characteristics that help you identify them.

Remember that a rock is a mixture of different minerals. Knowing which minerals make up a rock can help you identify and classify it. Some igneous rocks have crystals large enough for you to recognize the minerals that these rocks contain. Look at the photograph of granite in Figure 9-2. Can you recognize any minerals from last chapter? Quartz, mica, feldspar, and hornblende are some of the common minerals you might easily see in this igneous rock.

Some rocks are made of crystals. These crystals grow and lock together when the rock first forms, much like the way your heated solutions crystallized in Activity 8.1. Other rocks are made up of **grains**, which are small pieces of materials that have been broken apart and put back together again to form new rocks. Sometimes a grain is a piece of a mineral crystal. Sometimes a grain is a piece of some other rock. You may see that the grains are single pieces of sand or shells. The sedimentary rock, sandstone, is commonly made up of small quartz sand grains.

Texture is another way of describing a rock. What is texture? Before you answer, remember that scientists sometimes take words you use every day and reuse them in new and unfamiliar ways. In rocks, **texture** is the visual pattern made by the size, shape, and arrangement of the crystals or grains.

Figure 9-2 Granite is a mixture of many common minerals.

Figure 9-3 Sandstone is a rock made from grains of sand.

Texture is how the rock looks, not how it feels. Imagine looking at some fruit through the glass doors of a supermarket refrigerator. When you look at an orange, an apple, and a pineapple, you can see their different textures without having to feel their surfaces. The pineapple looks rough and has a pattern carved into the surface of its skin. The apple appears smooth. How does the orange compare? You have described texture just by looking at the fruit.

Coarse, *fine*, and *glassy* are terms used to describe rock textures based on the size of individual crystals or grains. If a rock has large, visible crystals or grains, it is said to have a coarse texture. A polished piece of granite has a surface that looks and feels smooth to the touch. If you described this same polished piece of granite, you would say its texture was coarse because it has large crystals.

Table 9-1 Rock Properties Based on Grain or Crystal Properties

Size	Shape	Arrangement
Fine (small) slate	Rounded conglomerate	Banded gneiss
Coarse (large) granite	Angular breccia	Nonbanded granite
Glassy (none visible) obsidian	Flattened meta-conglomerate	

Sandstone has a coarse texture if it is formed from large sand grains. On the other hand, tiny crystals or grains packed tightly together make a rock look smooth. Can you see individual grains or crystals in the picture of slate in Table 9-1? They are too small to see, and they give slate a fine texture. Molten rock that cools too quickly to develop crystals has a glassy texture. Obsidian, called natural glass, is an example of this.

There are ways to further describe a rock's texture. Grains, for example, can be described as rounded or angular based on their shape. *Angular* means that the edges have sharp corners. Compare the pictures of breccia [brech′ ə] and conglomerate in Table 9-1. Which rock has rounded grains?

Texture can also describe how the grains or crystals are arranged in a rock. Some rocks have their grains or crystals arranged in visible bands, which give the rock a layered appearance. Other rocks have no visible bands because they are a mass of interlocking crystals or grains. Look again at Table 9-1. Does the rock gneiss [nīs′] have bands?

The last characteristic used to identify rocks is color. The color of a rock can show you which minerals it contains. Light-colored rocks contain light-colored minerals like quartz, muscovite mica, feldspar, and calcite. Dark minerals, like hornblende, augite, and biotite form dark rocks. Some rocks, like granite, have a speckled appearance because they contain both light and dark minerals. Which other rocks in Table 9.1 are made of both light and dark minerals?

As you can see, rocks are made of various materials, and have different textures and colors. You will better understand why rocks have such different characteristics once you learn more about how and where the three main rock types form.

Fact or Fiction?

Do people sometimes think you have rocks in your head? Actually, you do. There are tiny particles called otoliths found inside your ears. They are made of calcite, the same mineral found in limestone and marble. These tiny "ear stones" in your head help you maintain your balance. They move in a fluid. As you change the position of your head, the otoliths move, hitting against delicate hairs. Striking these hairs triggers nerve impulses to your brain. Your brain then tells your body how to restore itself to the correct position. This is what you call your sense of balance.

Lesson Review 9.1

1. How is a rock different from a mineral?
2. Name three characteristics that help identify rocks.
3. What are some ways you might describe a rock's texture and how are those ways different?

Interpret and Apply

4. Compare the visible textures of the wicker basket, the glass vase, and the gelatin salad shown in Figure 9-4. Use the same terms you have used to describe rock textures, such as *coarse*, *angular*, and so on.

Figure 9-4

PROPERTIES OF ROCKS

Purpose To observe and describe the properties of some common rocks.

Materials
labeled rock samples
hand lens

Procedure

1. Read all the directions for this activity before you begin your work.

2. On your paper, make a data table like the one shown. Fill in the first two columns with the rock names and types provided by your teacher.

3. Carefully observe each rock sample. Use your hand lens when needed.

4. Observe the color of the sample. Write *light* or *dark* depending on the most common color of the grains.

5. Observe the rock's composition. Decide if the rock is one solid mass of interlocking crystals or is made of separate grains cemented together. Write *crystals* or *grains* in the data chart.

6. Observe the size of the grains or crystals in each sample. Write *large* if they can be seen easily. Write *small* if they are invisible or can only be seen with the hand lens. Record *none* if the rock looks like glass.

7. If your rock sample has grains, observe their shape. Record *angular* or *rounded* in the column marked *Shape* under *Crystal or Grain*. If your rock sample has crystals, record the names of any minerals you may recognize from Chapter 8.

8. Observe the arrangement of the grains or crystals. Decide if they are *banded* or *nonbanded*. Record your answer in the chart.

9. Before leaving the laboratory, clean up and put away all materials.

Collecting and Analyzing Data

1. Which properties were easiest to observe? Which were most difficult?

2. What two samples are most alike?

3. In what way was conglomerate similar to sandstone?

4. Using your chart, how can you distinguish granite from gneiss?

Drawing Conclusions

5. What combination of properties is found only in igneous rocks? Sedimentary? Metamorphic?

6. Explain why a rock with large crystals is probably not sedimentary.

Data Table						
Rock Name	**Rock Type**	**Color**	**Crystal or Grain**			
			Composition	**Size**	**Shape**	**Arrangement**

9.2 Igneous Rocks

All rocks that cool and crystallize from molten rock are called igneous. An igneous rock can form from lava that pours out of a Hawaiian volcano, or from magma cooling for centuries, kilometers below Earth's surface. You will see that the texture of igneous rocks largely depends on where and how quickly they crystallize. Why is this? You know that crystal size is part of what makes a rock's texture. You learned in Chapter 8 that crystal size is determined by how fast a solution is cooled. It takes longer for large crystals to form. The slower molten rock is cooled, the bigger its crystals will be and the more coarse its texture.

Intrusive Igneous Rocks

Igneous rocks that form from magma cooling inside Earth are called **intrusive**. Intrusive igneous rocks usually have a coarse texture because their large, visible crystals had time to form as magma slowly cooled deep below Earth's surface. Often you can see different minerals in an intrusive igneous rock as specks of different colors. For example, the use of a simple hand lens can show the minerals that make up the intrusive igneous rock granite.

Because it is hard and crystallized, granite is very resistant to the forces of nature. Granite can also be highly polished. These characteristics make granite an excellent building stone. You have probably seen it used in curbstones, buildings, and monuments. The faces in Mount Rushmore, shown in Figure 9-5, are carved from granite.

Lesson Objectives

▸ **Compare** the two types of igneous rocks.

▸ **List** and **describe** several common igneous rocks.

▸ **Activity** **Observe** and **measure** the differences between two common igneous rocks.

New Terms

intrusive
lava
extrusive

Figure 9-5 The faces on Mount Rushmore were carved from durable granite.

Figure 9-6 Gabbro is a dark, intrusive igneous rock. What is there about this rock that makes you think it is intrusive?

Although commonly found on Earth's surface, granite formed inside Earth. It is visible on the surface because the great forces that make mountains and move continents have lifted it up, and because other forces have removed kilometers of rock that were above it. It is believed that granite makes up the foundations of all the continents.

Gabbro [gab′ rō] is another intrusive igneous rock. Can you tell from Figure 9-6 that gabbro is intrusive? Like granite, gabbro has large crystals. Gabbro is darker in color and more dense than granite because it is made of darker, heavier minerals like augite, hornblende, and biotite.

Extrusive Igneous Rocks

Not all igneous rocks form below Earth's surface. **Lava** is magma that reaches Earth's surface during a volcanic eruption. Igneous rocks that form from cooled lava are called **extrusive** igneous rocks. Looking at Figure 9-7 (right), would you expect lava to cool faster or slower than magma? Lava is exposed to the air and water on the surface, which immediately start to cool the lava. Since the lava cools quickly, extrusive igneous rocks have tiny crystals. This gives them a fine-grained texture.

Basalt [bə sȯlt′] is the most common extrusive igneous rock. It is dull, black, and has the same mineral composition as gabbro. Hundreds of square miles of basalt are found in the states of Washington and Oregon, where they formed from ancient lava flows. Such a basalt flow is shown in Figure 9-7 (left). Islands like Hawaii, Japan, and Iceland are also made of basalt. Although the continental crust is mostly granite, the crust beneath the ocean floor is mostly basalt.

Figure 9-7 *Left:* The Columbia Plateau of Washington and Oregon is made of basalt layers, shown here exposed by the Columbia River. *Right:* Extrusive igneous rocks form when lava cools on Earth's surface.

Figure 9-8 Examples of extrusive igneous rocks, *Left:* Obsidian; *Middle:* Pumice; *Right:* Scoria

Sometimes lava cools so quickly that there is no time for crystals to form. Obsidian is called natural or volcanic glass because it has no crystals and looks like glass. As you can see in Figure 9-8 *(left)*, obsidian breaks with shell-like, conchoidal fracture. Ancient people used sharp-edged obsidian for spearheads and cutting tools.

Pumice [pəm′ əs] and scoria [skōr′ ē ə] are extrusive igneous rocks formed by rapidly cooling lava that is filled with escaping gases. Sometimes this lava cools so quickly that the gas bubbles are preserved as holes, frozen in stone. As a result, these rocks look like hardened sponges. Pumice can usually float in water because the trapped gases in the rock make it less dense than water. When pumice is ground up, it is used in scouring powders and soap. Small blocks of this rock are also used to sharpen knives. Scoria is a darker rock than pumice. What do you think might cause scoria's darker color? Scoria usually has larger holes than pumice, yet scoria is the heavier rock. This is because scoria is made of more dense minerals.

Lesson Review 9.2

5. Where do intrusive and extrusive rocks form?
6. Name some common igneous rocks and describe their uses.
7. Why do extrusive igneous rocks have fine or glassy textures?

Interpret and Apply

8. Explain why intrusive igneous rocks usually have larger crystals than extrusive rocks.
9. Compare the following information about intrusive and extrusive rocks: where they form, what material they form from, and their texture.

A C T I V I T Y   9 . 2   Lab Equipment

COMPARING TWO IGNEOUS ROCKS

Purpose   To observe and measure differences between granite and basalt.

Materials _____

graduated cylinder	rock samples
lab balance	hand lens
overflow can	water

Procedure

1. Read all directions for this activity before you begin your work.

2. On your paper, make a data table like the one shown.

3. Observe each rock sample using the hand lens. On the data table, fill in the color, texture, and minerals observed.

4. Measure the mass of each sample to the nearest tenth of a gram. Record mass on your data table.

5. Fill the overflow can with water and place it on a level surface so the excess water drains into a bowl or sink. Allow the water to finish draining. Hold your graduated cylinder beneath the overflow can as shown.

6. Carefully drop your sample into the overflow can. Catch the displaced water in your graduated cylinder. Read the volume in the graduated cylinder. This is the volume of the rock sample. Using this method, find the volume of the other sample. Write the volumes in the data table.

7. Calculate the density of each sample. Remember that density = mass/volume.

8. Before leaving the laboratory, clean up all materials.

Collecting and Analyzing Data

Data Table		
Sample	**Granite**	**Basalt**
Color		
Texture		
Minerals seen		
Mass		
Volume		
Density		

1. How does the crystal size in granite compare with that in basalt?

2. Which rock is more dense?

Drawing Conclusions

3. What is there about the textures you observed that can help you identify these two rocks as either intrusive or extrusive? Which is which?

4. Compare your density calculations with those of your classmates. Give reasons why your results might be different.

5. Give evidence from your observations to tell how intrusive igneous rocks are different from extrusive igneous rocks.

9.3 Sedimentary Rocks

Seventy-five percent of the rocks you see on Earth's surface are sedimentary rocks. These rocks form from sediment. **Sediment** is any material that settles to the bottom of a liquid. To understand sediment, think about the chocolate ooze you see at the bottom of a glass of chocolate milk. Maybe the milk was not stirred long enough, or perhaps you added more syrup to the milk than it could hold. In either case, the extra chocolate sank to the bottom where it was deposited as a flat layer. The chocolate became a sediment.

Geologists divide sedimentary rocks into three main types, based on the origin of the sediment from which they are formed. Sedimentary rocks that form from smaller pieces of other rocks are called **clastic rocks**. Sedimentary rocks made from the remains of things that were once alive are **organic rocks**. Minerals dissolved in water are deposited and left behind to form **chemical rocks**. Before examining these three sedimentary rock types in more detail, let's try to answer two questions. Where does all this sediment come from? How does it become a solid rock?

Formation of Sedimentary Rocks

The most common source of sediment in nature is the rock on Earth's surface. Rock that is exposed to air and water breaks down into smaller pieces or dissolves in a process called weathering. Weathering is a slow but continual process that breaks apart rock and reshapes the surface. You will learn more about the forces that cause weathering in Chapter 12. Boulders, quartz sand, mud, and clay are all sediments formed from weathered rock. So is the salt dissolved in sea water.

The running water in rivers and streams moves sediment from one place to another. This movement of sediment is called erosion. Wind and ice also erode sediment. Water's ability to move sediment depends on its speed. The faster the water moves, the bigger the particles it can carry or erode. In streams, boulders and cobbles are too big to be carried very far from their original source. Smaller sediments, like sand, silt, or clay, can be carried all the way to the ocean.

When water slows down, it loses its ability to carry sediment. This can happen when a river or stream flows into a large body of water, like a lake or ocean. When the water slows down, the sediment begins to fall to the bottom where it forms horizontal layers—like the chocolate left at the bottom of your glass. Over time, new layers of sediment are deposited on top of the older layers.

Lesson Objectives

▸ **Explain** how rocks are formed from sediments.

▸ **List** three types of sedimentary rocks and the sediments that form them.

▸ **Describe** some features of sedimentary rocks.

▸ **Activity** **Perform an experiment** that compares the settling rates of sediments.

New Terms

sediment	chemical rocks
clastic rocks	compaction
organic rocks	cementation

Figure 9-9 This muddy stream carries sediment to the ocean, where the fine silt and mud grains settle to the seafloor.

Figure 9-10 Sediment settles out of water to form flat layers.

As layers of sediment are deposited, the bottom layers are pushed on by the layers of sediment above. The buried sediments become squeezed together. The squeezing together of sediments to form rock, shown in Figure 9-11, is called **compaction**. Sediment can also be glued together to form rock in a process called **cementation**. Cementation occurs when mineral-rich water moves through the sediment. As minerals in the water crystallize between grains, they act as natural cements. Quartz and calcite are common cements. Compaction and cementation change sediment into sedimentary rock.

Figure 9-11 *Top:* In compaction, buried sediment is squeezed together by the weight of layers above to form a rock like shale. *Bottom:* In cementation, grains of sediment are glued together by minerals left behind by water.

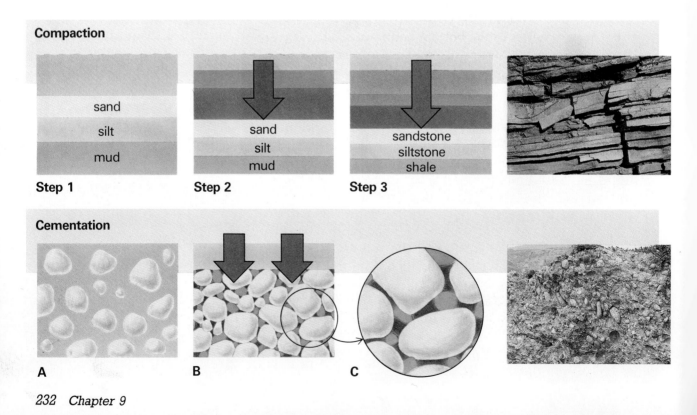

Compaction

sand	sand	sandstone
silt	silt	siltstone
mud	mud	shale
Step 1	**Step 2**	**Step 3**

Cementation

A   B   C

Clastic Rocks

The most common type of sedimentary rock is the clastic rock. As you recall, clastic sedimentary rocks are made of smaller pieces of other rocks. These pieces are called grains. The grain size of sediment determines the name of the rock. For example, the rock sandstone is made of sand-sized pieces of quartz, calcite, feldspar, or some other material. The larger the sand grains, the more coarse the sandstone's texture. Similarly, siltstone is made of silt-sized particles. Silt is smaller than sand. Silt feels gritty to the touch, but the individual grains are visible only with a microscope. Shale is a rock made of the tiniest clastic grains, which are called clay or mud. Siltstone and shale are fine-grained. When you use clay in art class, can you tell it is made of tiny grains? Clay grains are so small that clay feels smooth and slippery. The largest clastic grains, cobbles and pebbles, are found in the coarse-textured rock, conglomerate. Conglomerate usually contains clay and sand as well.

Do you remember that running water's ability to carry sediment is based on the speed of the water? This is one more thing you can use to figure out what conditions existed when the sediment in the rock was deposited. The pebbles and cobbles in conglomerate are so large that only a fast-moving stream or river can carry them far. On the other hand, the clay particles in shale are so small that they can stay suspended for days in water that is not visibly moving, such as a lake or lagoon. Very calm water is necessary for clay particles to settle to the bottom and form the thin layers that you now see preserved in shale, such as the sample shown in Figure 9-11.

Figure 9-12 The clay used in pottery is made of the smallest sediment weathered from rock.

Figure 9-13 The shape of rock fragments carried by water changes as they move farther from their source.

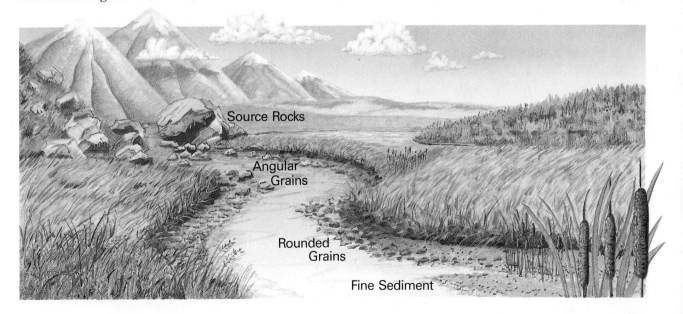

Source Rocks

Angular Grains

Rounded Grains

Fine Sediment

Figure 9-14 *Top:* Rounded grains are cemented together to form conglomerate. *Bottom:* Breccia contains angular grains.

As clastic grains are carried from their source to the ocean by the processes of erosion, their size and shape change. The farther the particles travel, the more rounded and worn they become. Fragments found near their source are more angular than those that traveled a great distance. Look at the samples of breccia and conglomerate in Figure 9-14. Which rock formed closest to the source of the sediment? Breccia is similar to conglomerate, except the large particles found in breccia are angular instead of rounded. The grains are angular because they were not moved far enough or weathered long enough to have their sharp edges worn down. The rounded shape of the pebbles in conglomerate tells you that they may have been deposited in a mountain stream or at a rocky beach. You know this because these are places where pebbles, rounded by the rapidly moving waters, are deposited today. Similarly, the rounded quartz grains you might find in a sandstone may tell you that the sand was deposited on an ancient beach or in a desert, since that is where you might find that sort of sand today.

Clastic grains also provide clues about their source. For example, a granite pebble in a bed of conglomerate can be traced back to a mountain of granite upstream. What would you expect to happen to the size of the granite pebbles in the conglomerate as you got closer to their source?

ENVIRONMENTAL AWARENESS

Preserving National Park Geology

When you go somewhere special, you probably want a souvenir to help you remember your trip. Souvenirs can be bought, but the ones with more meaning are the ones you find: a shell, an unusual-looking rock, or an interesting mineral. Did you realize that taking one of these natural souvenirs could be unlucky, harmful to the environment, or even illegal?

Hawaiians believe the goddess of volcanoes, Pele, puts a curse on people who take home volcanic rocks or black sand as souvenirs. Many people who disregard this warning later return their souvenirs to Hawaiian authorities with letters of apology and stories of bad luck that followed.

Even if you are willing to accept some bad luck, can you afford a souvenir that costs $10 000? That is the fine you might pay if you remove, destroy, or deface the rocks, minerals, or fossils in our national parks. The National Park Service has strict laws to protect the natural beauty and environment of these areas. Without these laws, the millions of park visitors, each taking away a little piece of rock, could quickly destroy geologic formations that took millions of years to form. ∎

Organic and Chemical Rocks

Organic rocks form from the sedimentary remains of plants and animals. Coal is one type of organic sedimentary rock. The most common organic rock is limestone. The "lime" in limestone is the mineral calcite. Calcite is dissolved out of rocks on land and carried by rivers to the oceans. Animals that live in shallow oceans, such as clams, mussels, sea snails, and coral, use calcite to make their shells. When these animals die, their calcite shells pile up on the shallow ocean floor, where they usually become broken and crushed by wave action. Eventually these materials become compacted and cemented into a fine-grained organic limestone.

Limestone only forms in a warm, shallow ocean. Scientists know that such oceans covered much of the United States because of the limestone deposits found here. Many buildings are built of limestone that came from Indiana. It is also a major ingredient in cement and mortar.

Other forms of organic limestone include coquina [kō kē′ nə] and chalk. Coquina is made from large fragments of shells. Figure 9-15 (right) shows a sample of coquina found along the beaches of Florida. Chalk is made of the calcite skeletons of microscopic marine animals.

Chemical sedimentary rocks form when sediments are deposited due to chemical changes. Such changes occur when ions dissolved in water combine to form new minerals. Some rocks, like halite and gypsum, form when large bodies of water evaporate. This can happen if a small bay or portion of an ocean is cut off from the main body of water. As more and more water evaporates over thousands of years, layers of minerals are deposited. Halite and gypsum deposits can be hundreds of feet thick and cover a wide area. Today chemical rocks are being deposited in places like the Great Salt Lake in Utah.

Figure 9-15 Examples of organic sedimentary rocks, *Left:* Limestone; *Right:* Coquina.

Figure 9-16 Limestone is used in common building materials. It is baked and crushed to form cement. Sometimes small pieces of limestone are added to cement to form concrete.

Figure 9-17 Layers of sedimentary rock have been exposed by weathering and erosion in the Grand Canyon.

Figure 9-18 *Left:* These ripple marks formed as gentle waves washed over a muddy beach. *Right:* Where were these mud cracks formed?

Sedimentary Features

One of the main characteristics of sedimentary rocks is that they occur in layers. This should not be surprising, since the original sediment was deposited as horizontal layers. These rock layers, called beds, can be seen because cementation and compaction have preserved the original differences in color, texture, and sediment size. The Colorado River has exposed sedimentary layers by carving out the Grand Canyon in Arizona, shown in Figure 9-17.

Sedimentary rocks can also contain fossils. Fossils are evidence of past plant and animal life. Sediment can bury dead plants and animals, protecting them from decay. The changed tissue or imprints of these plants and animals may be preserved when the sediment becomes sedimentary rock. Limestone usually contains many fossils of ancient sea animals. Shale can contain fossils of plants and animals buried in mud millions of years ago. Fossils not only help you determine what conditions were present when the sediment was deposited, but they also tell you when it was deposited. A sedimentary rock is as old as the fossils it contains.

Ripple marks and mud cracks can also be found in sedimentary rocks. Ripple marks form when water or wind moves constantly over soft sediments, such as sand or mud. Have you ever seen ripple marks at the beach or on the bottom of a fast moving stream? If these sediments become buried and someday turn into sedimentary rock, the ripple marks could be preserved. The ripple marks in the sandstone shown in Figure 9-18 *(left)* were formed millions of years ago. Mud cracks are formed when wet mud dries. As it dries, the mud contracts and cracks into pieces. You see this when muddy roads and puddles dry up. Mud cracks can also be preserved when mud becomes layers of shale.

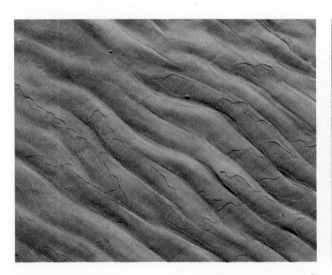

Environment of Deposition

Mudflat   Beach   Stream

clay → shale   sand → sandstone   pebbles → conglomerate

Clastic Sedimentary Rock

To geologists, reading sedimentary rock layers is like reading the pages of a history book. The rock layers tell where ancient deserts and oceans once existed. Was the environment a rocky shoreline or a mountain stream? Was the climate warmer thousands of years ago? What kinds of plants and animals lived in the early oceans? Sedimentary rocks help scientists answer these questions and learn about Earth's past.

Figure 9-19 Different types of sediment are deposited in different environments. You can often tell where the rock was formed by looking at the sedimentary features.

Lesson Review 9.3

10. Describe the processes that form a sandstone from sand.

11. What is the most common type of sedimentary rock? What is the source of its sediment?

12. Name and give examples of the three main types of sedimentary rocks. Where was each kind formed?

Interpret and Apply

13. Describe the conditions needed for a fine-textured clastic sedimentary rock to form.

14. Considering where limestone formed in the past, where would you expect to find limestones forming in the world today?

ACTIVITY 9.3   *Lab Equipment*

SETTLING RATES OF SEDIMENTS

Purpose To perform an experiment to determine whether size affects how fast sediment settles.

Materials

plastic tube	watch or timer
ring stand	small paper cup
burette clamp	sediment samples
water	

Procedure

1. Read all directions for this activity before you begin your work.

2. On your paper, make a data table like the one shown.

3. Fill the plastic tube with water, leaving the top 3 cm empty. Stand the tube upright in the ring stand and secure it with the burette clamp.

4. Take one pebble and drop it down the tube. Time how long it takes to reach the bottom. Repeat three more times. Record the four trial times in the data table and use them to calculate the average settling rate.

5. Repeat step 4 with the other sediment samples. Drop a piece or a pinch of the sample into the tube.

6. Empty the tube and sediments as instructed by the teacher. Never dump any sediments down the sink.

7. Refill the tube with water as in step 3.

8. Mix all four sediments in a paper cup and put them into the tube all at once.

9. Make observations and a sketch showing how the sediments appear in the tube as they settle, and on the bottom of the tube after they settle.

10. Clean up as in step 6. Remember, there should be no sediments in the sink.

Collecting and Analyzing Data

Data Table					
	Trial				
Sediment	**1**	**2**	**3**	**4**	**Average**

1. Which sediment settled to the bottom fastest? Which took the longest?

2. Describe what the sediment mixture looked like once it settled.

Drawing Conclusions

3. Which sample would travel the farthest in a river? Why?

4. Shale is a rock made from clay that deposited in a calm body of water. What did you observe that supports this idea?

5. What rocks would form from each layer in your mixture? What would have to happen for them to become rocks?

9.4 Metamorphic Rocks

Have you ever taken clay and formed it into a bowl in art class? To make it strong and durable, your clay pot was probably baked at high temperatures in a special oven called a kiln. Once baked, the soft clay changed into a different material. It became hard, brittle ceramic.

Like clay, rocks buried deep inside Earth can be changed into different rocks by great heat and pressure. This intense heat and pressure can cause changes in the appearance and mineral content of rocks that are buried deep in the crust. The new rocks that form are classified as metamorphic.

What effect does extreme pressure have on a buried rock? Imagine a bed of sedimentary rock already buried beneath Earth's surface. As new layers of sediment are deposited at the surface, lower layers of rock are pushed deeper into the crust. The addition of more and more layers of sediment and rock above increase the weight on a buried rock. The weight puts great pressure on the rock and causes the rock grains to squeeze closer together and flatten. This is the first metamorphic change to occur. Compare the appearance of the cars in Figure 9-20 to the rock grains. What caused the cars to look this way? Just as extreme pressure flattens these cars, so can pressure on rocks deep below the surface flatten their grains or crystals. The deeper the rock is buried, the greater the pressure on it becomes.

Extremely high temperatures deep within Earth also form metamorphic rock. At depths of 12 to 16 kilometers beneath the surface, temperatures can be between 200° C and 800° C. Under these conditions, rocks can change without being completely melted. This happens when the minerals are melted just enough so that their atoms or ions are free to form larger crystals.

Lesson Objectives

▸ **Explain** *how metamorphic rocks are formed.*

▸ **Describe** *characteristics of metamorphic rocks.*

▸ **Diagram** *the rock cycle.*

▸ **Activity** **Classify** *and* **identify** *some common rocks.*

New Terms

foliation
rock cycle

Figure 9-20 *Left:* The grains in this metamorphic rock have been flattened. *Right:* How do the rock grains compare with these cars in a junkyard?

Rocks can also be metamorphosed by heat from nearby magma or by the hot gases and liquids escaping from that magma. The heat from the magma bakes the rocks that come in contact with it. An example of a rock formed this way is hornfels, which forms when shale comes in contact with very hot magma.

The amount of metamorphism can depend upon several things: how deep the rock is buried, how much heat the rock is exposed to, and how long the rock has been under these conditions. At higher levels of metamorphism, the atoms in the rock's minerals may rearrange themselves into larger crystals. Often the atoms recombine and recrystallize into completely new minerals. Talc, soapstone, graphite, and garnet are minerals often formed in metamorphic rocks.

Characteristics of Metamorphic Rocks

Metamorphic rocks can be very different from the original rock. At certain depths, minerals recrystallize into long and slender shapes, or into flat shapes, that line up in one direction. This arrangement of minerals in parallel layers is called **foliation** [fō lē ā′ shən]. Foliated rocks look flaky and split into thin layers. The picture of slate in Figure 9-21 is an example of a foliated rock. What is it about slate that led to its use as chalkboards?

Figure 9-21 Heat and pressure change sedimentary rocks into metamorphic rocks.

shale

Heat
and
Pressure

slate

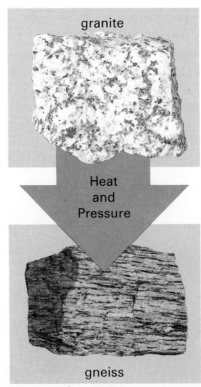

granite

Heat
and
Pressure

gneiss

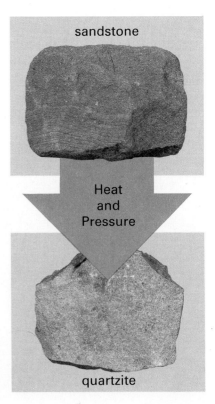

sandstone

Heat
and
Pressure

quartzite

Pressure can cause minerals to recrystallize into different mineral bands. For example, examine the picture of gneiss in Figure 9-21. All the light and dark minerals in gneiss have arranged themselves into a distinct pattern. This type of foliation is called *banded*.

Metamorphic rocks that are not layered are called non-foliated. These rocks do not break into flat sheets. They have a coarser, more crystalline texture than the rocks from which they formed. Figure 9-21 *(bottom right)* shows an example of the nonfoliated metamorphic rock quartzite.

Because their grains or crystals have been squeezed together more tightly, metamorphic rocks are usually stronger and more dense than their original form. Many metamorphic rocks can withstand the forces of weathering and are therefore used for building purposes.

Types of Metamorphic Rocks

As you know, there are many different kinds of sedimentary and igneous rocks. Exposure of these rocks to different levels of heat and pressure forms many different metamorphic rocks. Any rock can be metamorphosed. Even a metamorphic rock can be changed into a new metamorphic rock by more heat and pressure. Table 9-2 shows the five most common metamorphic rocks and the rocks from which they were formed.

Marble is a metamorphic rock made from limestone. Although the limestone has changed form, marble keeps the same chemical makeup. Both marble and limestone are made of calcium carbonate. Do you remember how to test for calcium carbonate from Chapter 8? Marble has a coarse, crystalline texture, and often has bands of colors. However, while it is banded, this is not the same as foliation. Marble is nonfoliated. Because of its strength and beauty when polished, marble is used in many monuments and buildings. Where else have you seen marble used?

Figure 9-22 Marble is both attractive and soft enough to be used in making statues.

Table 9-2 Metamorphic Rocks			
Rock	**Formed from**	**Texture**	
gneiss	granite, schist	coarse	foliated
slate	shale	fine	
schist	slate, basalt, granite	medium, coarse	
quartzite	sandstone	medium	nonfoliated
marble	limestone	coarse	

Figure 9-23 Slate was once used for roofing tiles and walkways because it is durable, colorful, and it splits into flat sheets.

Figure 9-24 Metamorphism has caused the mica grains in this mica schist to line up.

Most slate forms from shale. Like shale, slate splits easily into smooth, thin layers. This makes slate a fine-textured, foliated, metamorphic rock. Slate has a wide range of colors, such as blue, green, gray, brown, and red. Slate is used for "flagstone" walkways, roofs, and chalkboards.

Quartzite is formed by the metamorphism of sandstone. During metamorphism, the sandstone is compacted into a strong, durable rock with interlocking grains of quartz. This makes quartzite very resistant to weathering. Quartzite is often found forming sharp mountain ridges because it is not easily worn away.

Schists can form from many different rocks, such as shale, slate, and basalt. Schists represent severe metamorphism and the final stage of change for many minerals. Often the new rock is made mostly of mica. New minerals like garnet, staurolite, and kyanite can also be formed. For this reason, schists are usually named for the major mineral found in them. For example, there are mica schists, hornblende schists, and talc schists. Notice the shimmering appearance of the foliated mica schist in Figure 9-24. The mica crystals formed by metamorphism have been stretched and lined up in one direction.

The Rock Cycle

As you know, igneous rocks form from melted rock, like lava. As soon as the lava hardens, it begins to be broken down into sediment by weathering. Intrusive igneous rocks, which are formed below the surface from magma, may be pushed up to the surface by the forces which build mountains. Once a rock is at the surface, it too can be broken down into sediment by weathering. The sediment is deposited and forms sedimentary rocks. The sedimentary rock can become buried deeper and deeper inside Earth, where intense heat and pressure can change it into a metamorphic rock. When rocks are buried deeper within Earth, the pressure and temperatures become great enough to melt the metamorphic rock, changing it back into magma. This magma may eventually cool to form igneous rock again.

New rocks are always forming somewhere on Earth. Does that mean Earth is growing larger in size? Actually, even though new rocks are always forming, other rocks are being remelted and destroyed somewhere else. This constant recycling of rock materials makes up the **rock cycle.**

Look at the diagram of the rock cycle in Figure 9-25. Trace the events described above. You may notice some shortcuts and detours in the rock cycle. For example, sometimes metamorphic rocks are not remelted. Instead, they can be exposed on the surface and weathered to form sediment. Or they may become reburied even deeper underground, where greater heat and pressure changes them into different metamorphic rocks. Igneous rocks can be metamorphosed or remelted underground without ever being weathered at the surface.

The rock cycle is a continuous but slow process. Changes in rocks can take millions of years to happen. The land and rocks around you today may look quite the same next year or even a few hundred years from now, but think what they might be like millions of years from now.

Figure 9-25 The rock cycle. Arrows leading *toward* a rock type are processes by which that rock is formed. Arrows leading *away* from a rock type are processes that change that rock into some new product.

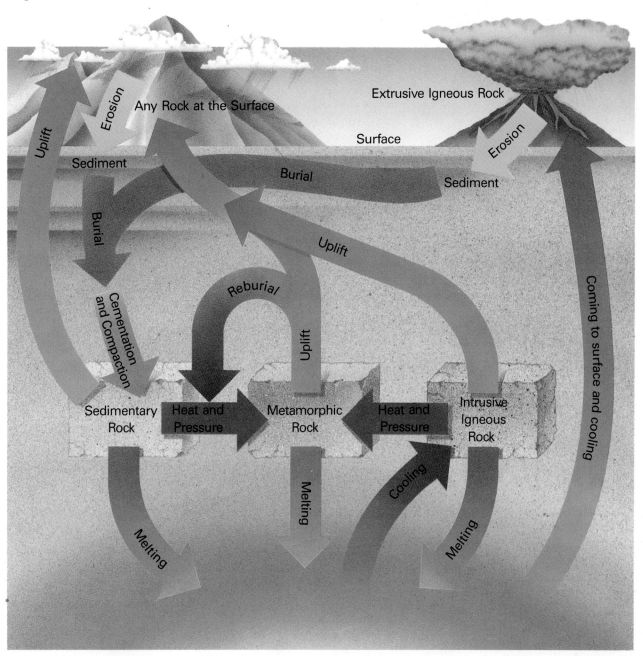

A C T I V I T Y 9.4 Lab Equipment

CLASSIFYING ROCKS

Purpose To classify and identify some common rocks.

Materials

numbered rock samples
colored pencils or crayons
dilute hydrochloric acid
hand lens

iron nail
safety goggles
lab apron

Procedure

1. Read all the directions for this activity before you begin your work.

2. On your paper, draw a data table like the one shown. Make the second and third column wider than the others.

3. Put on your safety goggles and lab apron.

4. Examine one rock sample at a time. Carefully draw the rock sample using the colored pencils. Record as many observations about the sample as possible. Be sure to describe the rock's texture and any minerals you might recognize.

5. If light-colored minerals are present, test with the dilute acid. Remember, if the rock fizzes when one drop of hydrochloric acid is applied, it is made of calcium carbonate.

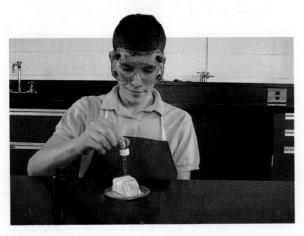

6. Rinse the sample with water and dry it with a paper towel. Rinse your hands.

7. Repeat steps 4 through 6 for the other rock samples.

8. Try to identify and record the name of the rock. Refer to the information in the chapter if necessary.

9. In the last column, record the type of rock it is. Write *igneous*, *sedimentary*, or *metamorphic*.

10. Before you leave the laboratory, clean up all materials and wash your hands thoroughly.

Collecting and Analyzing Data

Data Table				
Unknown Sample	Drawing of Sample	Observations	Rock Name	Rock Type
1				
2				

1. Which of the three main rock types was easier to identify? Why do you think so?

2. Which two rocks seemed most alike? Describe how they are similar.

3. What extrusive igneous rocks did you test? How do you know these samples were extrusive?

Drawing Conclusions

4. Relate the differences you observed between shale and slate with the different ways in which they are formed.

5. Explain how the textures you observed were helpful in identifying the rocks.

6. What might have caused the crystals in gneiss to line up or form bands of color?

Lesson Review 9.4

15. Explain two ways igneous or sedimentary rocks can become metamorphic rocks.

16. What are the major differences between foliated and nonfoliated rocks?

17. Draw a portion of the rock cycle that shows how quartzite could become sandstone again.

Interpret and Apply

18. List some uses of metamorphic rocks. Why are they suitable for these purposes?

19. Using the rock cycle, explain why scientists have been unable to find rocks as old as Earth.

Chapter Summary

Read the summary of the main ideas in this chapter. If any are not clear to you, go back and review that lesson.

9.1 Observing Rocks

■ A rock is a natural solid that is usually a mixture of minerals.

■ There are three types of rocks classified by how they form—igneous, sedimentary, and metamorphic.

9.2 Igneous Rocks

■ Igneous rocks form when melted rock cools and crystallizes.

■ Cooling of magma underground usually forms intrusive rocks with large crystals. Cooling lava on Earth's surface forms extrusive rocks with very small crystals.

9.3 Sedimentary Rocks

■ Sedimentary rocks are formed from sediment. Sediment is any material that settles to the bottom of a liquid.

■ Most sedimentary rocks form through the processes of weathering, erosion, deposition, compaction, and cementation.

■ Sedimentary rocks may form from clastic, organic, or chemically deposited sediments.

■ Sedimentary rocks are deposited in layers and can contain fossils. Sedimentary rocks offer information about past environments.

9.4 Metamorphic Rocks

■ Existing rocks that undergo extreme heat and pressure change to metamorphic rocks.

■ Minerals are rearranged into parallel layers in foliated metamorphic rocks. Some metamorphic rocks are nonfoliated.

■ Metamorphic rocks are dense and strong and can be used for building purposes.

■ Rocks undergo weathering, metamorphosis, remelting, and crystallization to form new rocks. Rock materials are continually recycled.

Chapter Review

■ Vocabulary

cementation
chemical rocks
clastic rock
compaction
extrusive
foliation
grains
igneous
intrusive

lava
metamorphic
organic rocks
rock
rock cycle
sediment
sedimentary
texture

■ Concept Mapping

Construct a concept map for rocks. Include at least five terms from the vocabulary list.

■ Review

On your paper, write the word or words that best complete each statement.

1. Rocks are classified into (two, three, five) main types.

2. Rocks are classified as igneous, sedimentary, or metamorphic according to (their size, mineral content, the way they form).

3. The size, shape, and arrangement of crystals in a rock is called its (texture, hardness, density).

4. All (igneous, sedimentary, metamorphic) rocks form from melted rock cooling and crystallizing.

5. (Intrusive, Extrusive) rocks form from slower cooling magma.

6. Most intrusive rocks have (small, large, no) crystals.

7. Lava hardens to form (igneous, sedimentary, metamorphic) rock.

8. Rocks break down into smaller pieces by the process of (erosion, weathering, deposition).

9. Most of the rocks found on Earth's surface are (igneous, sedimentary, metamorphic).

10. (Erosion, Cementation, Compaction) causes sediment to be tightly squeezed together into a sedimentary rock.

11. Water rich in calcite or quartz aids in the (compaction, cementation, deposition) of sediment.

12. (Clastic, Organic, Chemical) sediments form conglomerate, shale, and sandstone.

13. (Limestone, Conglomerate, Coal) forms in a warm, shallow ocean.

14. Halite and gypsum form by (evaporation, weathering, melting).

15. Fossils are usually found in (igneous, sedimentary, metamorphic) rocks.

16. Intense heat and pressure deep inside Earth forms (igneous, sedimentary, metamorphic) rocks.

17. Shale becomes (marble, gneiss, slate) when metamorphosed.

■ Interpret and Apply

18. Explain why fossils are usually found in sedimentary rocks, not in igneous or metamorphic rocks.

19. The word "igneous" comes from the Latin word *ignis*, meaning fire. Why do you think this name was chosen for igneous rocks?

20. Hawaii is a chain of volcanic islands. Explain why many of Hawaii's famous beaches have black sand.

21. Think about the rock cycle and how each type of rock forms. Which of the three types of rocks do you think formed first on Earth? Explain your answer.

22. Name a type of cookie. Explain what rock it most resembles and why.

23. How are grains different from crystals?

24. How can sedimentary layers be distinguished from one another?

25. You are building a house and want to use three different rocks in its construction. Which rocks would you choose and why?

26. Geologists who study sedimentary rocks are called "soft rock" geologists. Why do you think they use this term? What do you think they call geologists who mainly study igneous and metamorphic rocks?

27. These are symbols used by geologists to represent different rocks. Why do you think they chose the two symbols that represent sandstone and conglomerate?

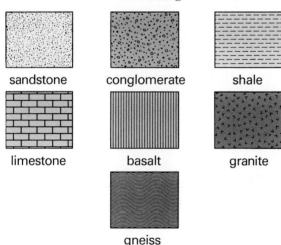

sandstone   conglomerate   shale

limestone   basalt   granite

gneiss

28. How are the symbols for granite and gneiss similar? How are they different?

29. Explain why the symbol for limestone looks like bricks. Create and draw a symbol that could represent marble.

■ Writing in Science

30. Describe the steps by which an igneous rock can become another igneous rock. Before you write, you will need to recall the different ways that this type of change can happen. Then you will need to list the steps for each way in the order in which they occur.

■ Critical Thinking

You are interviewing for a high-paying job as a geologist. But before you are hired, your potential employer decides to test your geology background. She shows you this cross section of an area 5 kilometers from end to end, located somewhere in the United States. The cross section shows rock layers to a depth of 0.3 km into the crust. Using the rock symbols from question 27 at left, try to get the job by answering her questions written below.

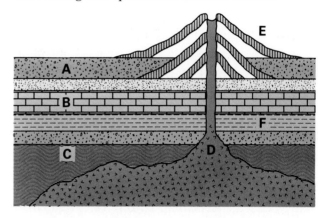

31. What four sedimentary rocks are shown in the cross section?

32. What kind of rock is labeled D? How did it form?

33. What type of environment existed immediately after the area was a swampy lagoon? How do you know this?

34. There is some concern that the field geologist has incorrectly identified rock D. A report lists D as having a medium texture. What is wrong with the texture and location of D?

35. Ore mineral deposits are often associated with contact metamorphism, which is metamorphism of rocks in contact with magma or lava. Where would you test for economic mineral deposits in this cross section? Although they are not shown, where else would you expect to find metamorphic rocks in the cross section?

STATE PASSES NEW LAW REQUIRING PEOPLE TO RECYCLE TRASH

Issue: *Should local governments require people to recycle their trash?*

In 1988, a garbage barge from Islip, New York, spent months looking for a place to dump its trash. Newspapers covered the story as port after port turned away the barge. Many people feel that their community should not have to accept someone else's garbage. This view is known as NIMBY—Not In My BackYard.

Each year, the United States throws out more than 200 billion kilograms of solid waste. About 80 percent of this trash is dumped in more than 5000 landfills. But in the last five years, thousands of landfills closed because they were full. As more landfills close, communities will have to set aside land for new landfills or find other ways to take care of their trash.

Some communities use incinerators to burn their garbage. But many people are against incinerators, which produce toxic ash that needs special disposal. Some states have passed mandatory recycling laws to reduce the amount of trash at its source. Mandatory recycling requires people to separate recyclable trash—such as paper, plastic, aluminum, and glass—from the rest of their garbage. Some communities send trucks to homes to pick up the recyclable trash. Other communities require people to bring trash to recycling centers. The recycling centers then prepare each kind of trash for resale to industry.

Mandatory recycling solves recycling's greatest problem—how to cheaply sort billions of kilograms of trash.

Many people feel that mandatory recycling is the only way to get most of the people to recycle their trash. In the United States, only 10 percent of the trash is recycled. In Japan and Germany, countries that are using mandatory recycling, more than 50 percent of all trash is recycled. Landfills in these countries do not fill up as quickly as in the United States.

Mandatory recycling saves money and energy. For example, recycled plastic costs about 30 percent less than new plastic. Making new aluminum cans out of old aluminum cans uses

95 percent less energy than smelting aluminum from ore. It is not surprising that many aluminum manufacturers support mandatory recycling laws.

The advantage of mandatory recycling is that the recycling center does not have to pay people to sort different colors of glass or types of plastic. Recycling centers can make a profit only by selling sorted materials to industry. In some communities, profits from mandatory recycling centers pay to dispose of trash that cannot be recycled.

Many people think recycling should be voluntary.

Some people think that mandatory recycling laws are too hard to enforce, and that many people will "cheat" rather than sort their trash. Pennsylvania's mandatory recycling law sets aside funds for advertising and education, with the hope that people will obey the law if they understand the need for recycling. Some communities with mandatory recycling require clear garbage bags so that "garbage police" can inspect the garbage. People who do not recycle are first given a warning. Repeat offenders pay a fine or perform a community service, but the fines rarely pay for the cost of garbage police.

Many people favor other ways of promoting recycling. Some communities charge people for each trash bag they put out. The more trash that people recycle, the less they have to pay for disposal of their trash. Other areas charge a fee for dumping recyclable materials in their landfills, and then use the money to pay for recycling. In many states, people pay a bottle deposit fee that is refunded when they return bottles or cans. These plans promote recycling without making it mandatory.

Act on the Issue

Gather the Facts

1. Use library articles and books listed in the *Readers' Guide to Periodical Literature* to learn more about recycling plastic. Because there are many different kinds of plastic, it can be difficult to recycle. Some companies are making biodegradable plastic—plastic treated to decompose over time in a landfill. Find out whether everyone agrees that biodegradable plastic really decomposes in landfills.

2. Use books and articles in the library to find out how mandatory recycling programs work in Germany or Japan. Write a short report on recycling in one of these countries.

3. Find out where your community's garbage goes. If your community has its own landfill, find out how much longer it is expected to remain open. If your community sends its garbage somewhere else, find out where it goes. Then research the options for recycling.

Take Action

4. Start a voluntary recycling program in your school. Decide which materials to collect and plan how to transport the materials to a local recycling center. Find a way to advertise the recycling program to students and teachers. How can the recycling program pay for itself? You may want to give awards to the people who collect the most recyclable materials.

5. Write to your state legislator and explain your position on mandatory recycling. Ask the legislator to explain his or her position on this issue. If your state does not have any recycling laws, ask if there are plans for new recycling legislation.

Science in Action

CAREER: *Geology Professor*

Bruce Simonson is a geology professor. He studies the oldest sedimentary rocks in the world. He also does research on the way sedimentary rocks form today.

When did you first become interested in rocks?

It goes way back to when I was a kid. I collected rocks and fossils, and my dad helped me identify them. When I went to college, geology was the only subject I could major in that let me do most of my work outdoors.

What does a geology professor do?

It's really two jobs in one. I teach geology to college students. In teaching, I try to interest students in earth science. I am teaching a course right now called Geological Hazards. It's about floods, earthquakes, volcanoes, landslides—things like that. A course like this can interest a student in becoming a geology major.

What's the other part of your job?

I also do research in sedimentology. For the past five summers, I've worked in Australia around some of the world's largest iron mines. The ancient sedimentary rocks I specialize in originally formed as muds at the bottom of ancient seas. They are so rich in iron that today they are used as iron ore.

What kind of training did you have in order to become a professor?

I went to college and graduate school, where I specialized in sedimentology. Many geologists who have the same training I have go to work for oil companies or the government. I decided, however, that I wanted to teach and to do research.

CAREER: *Asbestos-Removal Specialist*

Mike West and his father, James, started an asbestos-removal company five years ago. It is called West Environmental.

Why did you decide to go into asbestos removal?

Several years ago, the federal government realized that there was a lot of asbestos in schools, and that some of it was loose and flaking. This was a real health hazard to children and teachers. My father and I saw that there was going to be a need for companies that specialize in getting rid of asbestos.

Did you have to go to school to learn about asbestos removal?

I didn't go to college. But I've gone to a number of training courses to learn how to safely remove asbestos. I studied the state and federal regulations, attended training sessions, and finally passed the state certification requirements.

Working with asbestos must be dangerous. How do you protect yourself?

There are many things we do. At each site, we have to set up three rooms. There's the room where we actually work with asbestos. This room is sealed off from the rest of the building. The next room has a portable shower in it. That's where the workers wash after working in the asbestos room. The third room is a clean room. Each time the workers go into the asbestos room, they put on a clean, disposable suit. When they come out several hours later, they throw away their suits and then shower.

While they work, our workers wear breathing masks with very fine filters and a pump that traps the asbestos before they can breathe it in.

Will you be out of work when companies like yours have removed all the asbestos from schools?

Absolutely not. I think the government will require that asbestos be removed from all federal buildings next, and then from all state buildings. Eventually, it will have to be taken out of any building open to the public. But we're not taking any chances. Later this year, I'm going to take a course about surveying homes for radon!

HOBBY: Rock Collecting

Caroline Reynolds, age thirteen, collects rocks and minerals. She began collecting when her family built a summer home on a lake in northern Minnesota.

What kind of rocks do you find?

That's the fun thing about rock hunting on our lake. The area was once covered with glaciers that pushed down from places in Canada. As the glaciers moved south, they picked up all kinds of rocks and minerals and dumped some of them around our lake. Some of my rocks must have come from hundreds of miles away.

My favorite rocks to look for are agates. They're just a form of quartz, but they have beautiful bands of color. I've also found copper and petrified wood.

Do you collect rocks from other places?

Yes, I do. Last summer I went with my family to Colorado. In an old gold-mining town, I found a rock with flakes of gold in it! That's my favorite specimen.

Changes in Earth's Crust

You Know More Than You Think

You may be surprised at how much you already know about changes in Earth's crust. To find out, try to answer the following questions.

- *Where in the United States do earthquakes occur?*
- *How many volcanoes can you name?*
- *What happens to soil in a strong windstorm?*
- *What happens to water when you pour it on a houseplant or garden?*
- *What kind of landscape would have a lot of waterfalls?*

When you finish this unit, answer these questions again to see how much you have learned.

The smoothing down of pebbles and the building up of mountains are two examples of changes in Earth's crust.

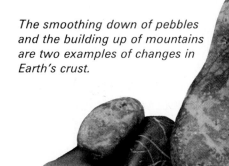

253

10 Plate Tectonics

Chapter Preview

Have You Ever WONDERED?

Why are some mountains taller than other mountains?

The Himalayan [him ə lā' ən] mountains of southern Asia are the highest mountains in the world. The world's highest mountain, Mount Everest, is found in the Himalayas. Everest is over 8800 meters high and is covered with snow and ice. The name *Himalaya* comes from the words meaning "house of snow."

The rocks that form the Himalayas were once at sea level. In fact, many of the rock layers were formed below sea level. Great forces have pushed the rock layers upward. The same forces have ripped the layers apart and crumpled the rocks together like a ball of paper. These forces are still working on the rocks, pushing Mount Everest higher every year.

The great forces that make mountains are caused by movements in Earth's crust. In this chapter, you will learn about the movements in the crust, and how those movements build the great mountains like the Himalayas.

10.1 *The Moving Continents*

Lesson Objectives

▶ *Describe* how the scientific method was used to develop the theory of continental drift.

▶ *Discuss* the types of data gathered to support the theory of continental drift.

▶ **Activity** *Form a model* of a supercontinent.

New Terms

Pangaea
continental drift
echo sounding

Have you ever put together a jigsaw puzzle like the one pictured in Figure 10-1? At first, the many shapes of the puzzle pieces can be confusing. It is hard to imagine that all those small pieces fit together to form one picture. With so many pieces, what do you do first? Before doing anything else, you must choose a method to solve the puzzle.

Different methods are used to solve a jigsaw puzzle. One method is trial and error. The trial-and-error method may provide a solution, but it will take a very long time. You probably use a shorter, more logical approach. You look for clues in the shapes and colors of the puzzle pieces. Pieces with straight edges are usually part of the puzzle border. If the picture is a landscape, perhaps you sort out the light blue pieces and assemble the sky. By observing and comparing shapes and colors, you search for pieces that are most likely to fit together. In a short time, you can solve the puzzle using this logical method and your skills of careful observation.

A jigsaw puzzle is like a puzzle in nature. In Chapter 1, you learned about a logical method of solving puzzles based on careful observations. It is called the scientific method. The first step is to gather data. Then you look for a pattern in your observations. Next, form a hypothesis to explain the observed pattern, and test the hypothesis with new observations. If the new observations fit the hypothesis, you can form a theory. The scientific method can be used to solve a simple puzzle or to answer puzzling questions about the world you live in.

Figure 10-1 The shape of jigsaw puzzle pieces sometimes provides valuable clues about how they fit together.

Jigsaw Puzzle Earth

"How is Earth like a jigsaw puzzle?" At first, this may seem like a silly question. Look at Figure 10-2. Notice the shape of the eastern coastline of South America. Now look at the western coastline of Africa. Is it possible that the continents once fit together like pieces of a jigsaw puzzle? A man named Alfred Wegener [vāg′ ə ner] asked that question about 80 years ago. Today the answer to his question seems to be yes.

Alfred Wegener was a meteorologist who used maps of the world in his study of weather and climate. The shapes of the continents became very familiar to him as he mapped world weather patterns. He knew that the coastlines of South America and Africa were very much alike in shape. Wegener was not the first person to notice how much alike the two coastlines were. He was, however, one of the first people to develop and test a scientific hypothesis based on his observations of the shapes of continents.

Wegener developed a hypothesis based on his observations. The hypothesis said that there was once one great continent made of all the land masses known today. He called that supercontinent **Pangaea** [pan jē′ ə], meaning "all lands." Wegener believed that Pangaea split apart long ago to form today's continents, and that the continents slid or drifted across the ocean floor to their present locations. Following the scientific method, Wegener's next job was to test his hypothesis by collecting more data.

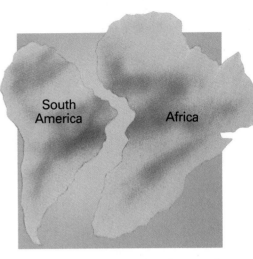

Figure 10-2 The similar shapes of South America and Africa sparked Wegener's imagination.

Figure 10-3 This is how Wegener assembled Pangaea, his theoretical supercontinent.

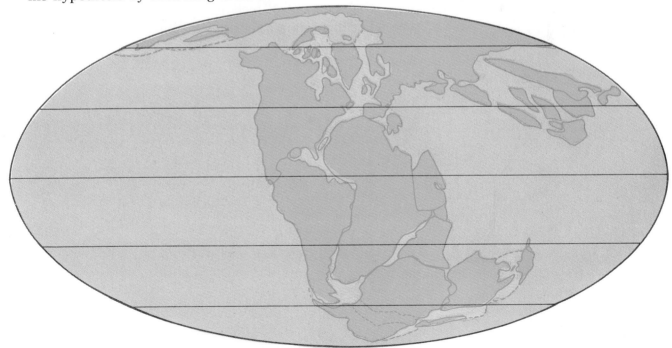

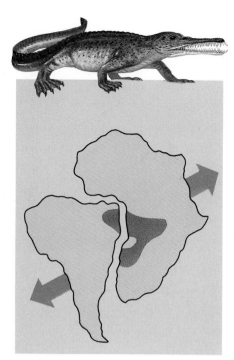

Figure 10-4 Fossils of the reptile *Mesosaurus* are found in areas that suggest South America and Africa were joined when the animal still lived.

Wegener Tests His Hypothesis

If you traveled to South America and Africa today, you could gather firsthand the same evidence Wegener found 80 years ago. You would find that many geologic features that end on the coast of South America match features beginning on the African coast. Mountains in Argentina seem to connect with mountains in South Africa. Diamonds are found in both South Africa and Brazil. Not only are the types of rocks on the two continents identical, but fossils in the sedimentary rocks are the same age.

Other fossil clues are even more interesting. The fossil remains of a small reptile called *Mesosaurus* were found in both Africa and South America. The *Mesosaurus* fossils in both continents are identical. This is very unusual. Animals that have evolved in different parts of the world usually have different characteristics. For example, the blue jays in England are different from the American blue jays. The chances are slim that *Mesosaurus* evolved in exactly the same way on two separate continents. Wegener concluded that the fossil animals and plants had evolved on a single land area. When Pangaea split and the continents drifted apart, the fossils were divided between the two continents. The same process split the rocks and mountain chains.

Data that Wegener gathered from other continents also supported his hypothesis. For example, coal beds in the Appalachian Mountains of North America matched coal beds in Britain. All the data seemed to fit. Wegener gathered his research and put it all together to form the theory of continental drift. **Continental drift** is the idea that the continents move from one part of Earth to another. It was now time for Wegener to present his theory to his peers.

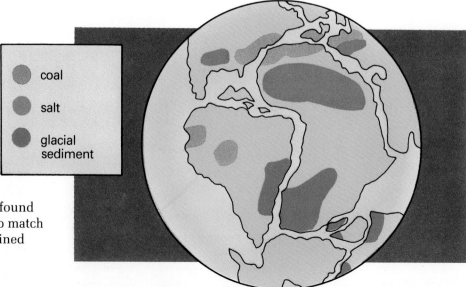

Figure 10-5 Similar rocks found on different continents also match when the continents are joined together.

coal

salt

glacial sediment

Continental Drift

Wegener published his continental drift theory in 1915 in a book called *The Origin of Continents and Oceans*. Publication of new theories is an important part of science. Let's say you discover a form of antigravity. You publish your theory and detailed descriptions of your research in a scientific journal read by other experts in gravity research. Some of them may choose to perform the same experiments you performed to see if they get the same results. Others may suggest new experiments. A theory is not accepted until scientists debate about it and are convinced the theory explains enough observations.

Unfortunately for Wegener, most people did not accept his theory during his lifetime. What force could be powerful enough to move continents? How could continents move over or through the solid rock of the ocean floor? Why would Pangaea break apart? Without answers to these questions, the theory of continental drift was actually laughed at in science meetings worldwide.

A discouraged Wegener returned to his work in Greenland. There he used an echo sounding technique to map ice layers. Small explosions set off on the surface send sound waves deep into the solid material, whether it is ice or rock. Some of the sound waves bounce off the layers and are received by microphones back on the surface.

Wegener died on that last expedition, attempting to make a 300-mile journey across Greenland in the winter of 1930. Twenty-five years later, oceanographers using echo sounding to map the ocean floor would find new evidence to revive both Wegener's theory and reputation.

Figure 10-6 Even today, exploration in Greenland can be cold and dangerous.

Lesson Review 10.1

1. What observation led Wegener to think that South America and Africa may once have been joined together?
2. How did Wegener use fossil and rock data to support his theory?
3. List the continents that were part of Pangaea.

Interpret and Apply

4. Wegener found fossils from a warm climate on continents with very cold climates. How can this be explained with the theory of continental drift?

THE CONTINENTAL PUZZLE

Purpose   To form a model on paper of a supercontinent.

Materials_____

copy of Figure 10-7
scissors
paste or tape
colored pencils

Procedure

1. Read all instructions for this activity before you begin your work.

2. There are three symbols for fossils in Figure 10-7. The types of fossils show that they were formed near the equator, the middle latitudes, and the poles. Color the fossil symbols using a different colored pencil for each of the three symbols.

3. The shaded areas on the continents in Figure 10-7 each represent one type of rock. Color these rock areas in the correct locations on your paper continents.

4. Use scissors to carefully cut your copy of Figure 10-7 along the border of each continent. **CAUTION: Scissors can be sharp. Use them with care.** The figures cut from the paper represent the approximate shape of the continents formed when Pangaea broke apart.

5. Place the continents on a piece of paper. Use the clues to move the continents until they form one large supercontinent. The pieces do not have to fit together exactly.

6. Attach the continents to the piece of paper using the paste or tape. Try to keep the pieces together in the shape of the supercontinent.

7. Before leaving the laboratory, clean up all materials and wash your hands thoroughly.

Collecting and Analyzing Data

1. Which two continents have the most obvious fit of their coastlines?

2. How were the fossil symbols helpful in deciding where to move the continents?

3. How did you use the types of rock as a guide in moving the continents?

4. Describe the order you followed in placing separate continents into the supercontinent.

Drawing Conclusions

5. Find a world map. Compared with the present locations of the continents on a world map, which continent has changed its position least?

6. A large mass of ice called a glacier once covered the parts of Pangaea nearest the South Pole. On what continents would you expect to see evidence of that glacier?

7. Why would the present shape of the continents not fit perfectly into the shape of a supercontinent?

8. Describe the direction each continent has moved to get from Pangaea to its present location.

Figure 10-7 Continents

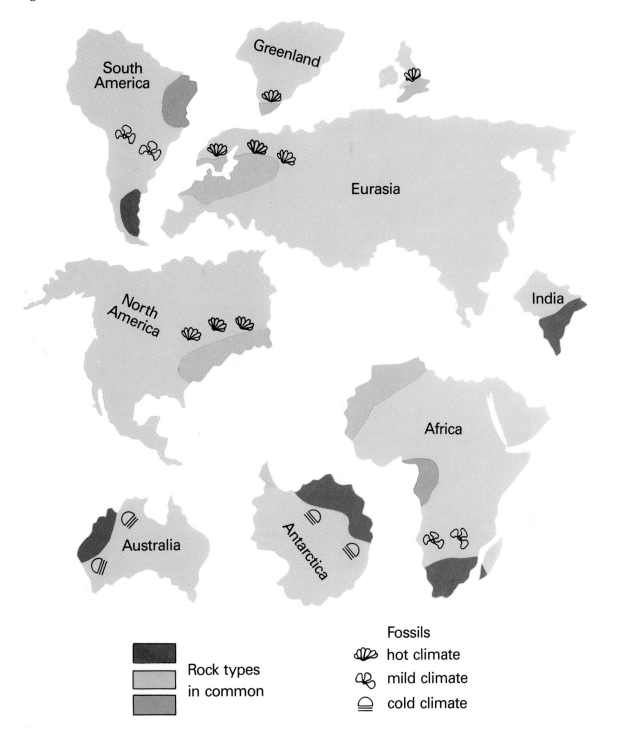

Rock types
in common

Fossils
- 🐚 hot climate
- 🐚 mild climate
- 🐚 cold climate

The Expanding Oceans

New Terms

echo sounding	trenches
mid-ocean ridge	lithosphere
rift	plate
seafloor spreading	asthenosphere

An interesting feature of the Atlantic Ocean was discovered by people laying telegraph cable more than 100 years ago. As workers lowered cable from ships to the ocean bottom, they measured water depth. Workers expected the ocean to be about the same depth from one side of the Atlantic to the other. Instead, they were surprised to find that the water was shallower in the middle of the ocean and deeper to either side. They had stumbled upon a fascinating discovery—an underwater mountain range.

New Evidence

The discovery of a mountain range at the bottom of the Atlantic Ocean opened a new frontier for exploration. Researchers needed better data to map and understand these strange new features.

Better depth readings were gathered using an echo sounding method like the one Wegener had used in Greenland. **Echo sounding** is the use of reflected sound to measure distance. The ship in Figure 10-8 is sending sound waves to the bottom of the ocean. The sound reflects off the seafloor and is received by microphones on the ship. The time between sending the sound and receiving its echo is used to calculate the depth of the ocean. As ships with echo sounders pass over the mountains, they collect depth data points. Points with the same depth are connected with a contour line. The contour lines are used to construct topographic maps. Instead of topography on land, these maps describe the shape of mountains under the oceans.

The second type of data gathered was the age of seafloor rocks. Ships collect ocean-floor rock and sediment samples using long pipes and special drills. Drill ships cut long cylinders of rock, called cores, from the seafloor. The age of sediment or sedimentary rock is found by carefully examining the fossils the cores contain. The age of igneous rock is found using methods you will learn about in Chapter 14. The age of an igneous rock indicates how long ago the hot magma or lava cooled and became solid rock.

A third type of data gathered is water temperature near the seafloor. Ships tow thermometers on the end of very long cables. These special thermometers measure the water temperature near the seafloor and send a signal to the ship where the temperatures are recorded. The data points are then recorded on maps, where they are connected to form temperature contour lines. Maps made with these data reveal areas of similar water temperatures along the seafloor.

Figure 10-8 An echo sounder on a ship measures water depth using sound waves.

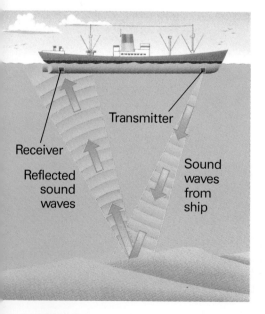

Transmitter

Receiver

Reflected sound waves

Sound waves from ship

MAPPING THE MID-ATLANTIC RIDGE

Purpose To interpret data which describe the Mid-Atlantic Ridge.

Materials
copy of Figure 10-9
pencil

Procedure

1. Read all instructions for this activity before you begin your work.

2. Figure 10-9 provides three sets of data collected from one part of the Atlantic Ocean seafloor.

3. Draw depth contour lines by connecting the identical depth symbols on your copy of Figure 10-9. There will be two contour lines for each depth.

4. Draw temperature contour lines by connecting the identical symbols showing water temperatures along the seafloor.

5. Connect identical age symbols with age contour lines.

Collecting and Analyzing Data

1. Use the depth contour lines to describe the shape of the mountain and the unusual feature found in its center.

2. The data you have mapped shows a part of the underwater mountain range called the Mid-Atlantic Ridge. Where is the youngest rock in the Mid-Atlantic Ridge?

Drawing Conclusions

3. What is the relationship between the age of the rock and the temperature of the water near the rock?

4. What is the pattern of change in the age of the rocks as you move away from the center of the ridge?

Figure 10-9 Atlantic seafloor data

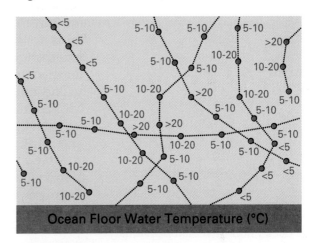

Ocean Floor Water Temperature (°C)

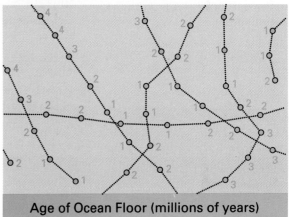

Age of Ocean Floor (millions of years)

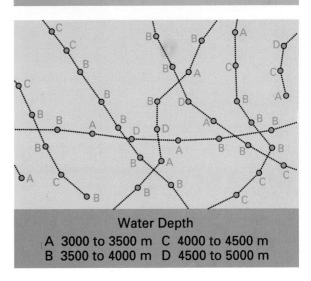

Water Depth
A 3000 to 3500 m   C 4000 to 4500 m
B 3500 to 4000 m   D 4500 to 5000 m

Seafloor Spreading

The map of seafloor topography shown in Figure 10-10 is the result of many years of collecting data. As you can see, the mountain range in the middle of the Atlantic Ocean is part of a much larger system of underwater mountains. Together these mountains make up the longest mountain range on Earth. These long, narrow chains of underwater mountains are called **mid-ocean ridges.** These ridges have a total length of about 74 000 kilometers. That length is almost twice Earth's circumference.

The mid-ocean ridge in the Atlantic Ocean is called the Mid-Atlantic Ridge. Compare the shape of the Mid-Atlantic Ridge with the coastlines of North America, South America, and Africa. What similarities do you see?

A very deep valley runs down the center of all mid-ocean ridges. That deep valley is called a **rift** valley. Water temperatures at the seafloor are usually only 2°C or 3°C, but can be much warmer near the mid-ocean ridges. Water temperatures in the rift can be as high as 20°C. Temperatures in the rift suggest that some source of thermal energy keeps the water warmer than usual.

Figure 10-10 Detailed mapping of the ocean floor revealed previously unknown underwater mountains and trenches.

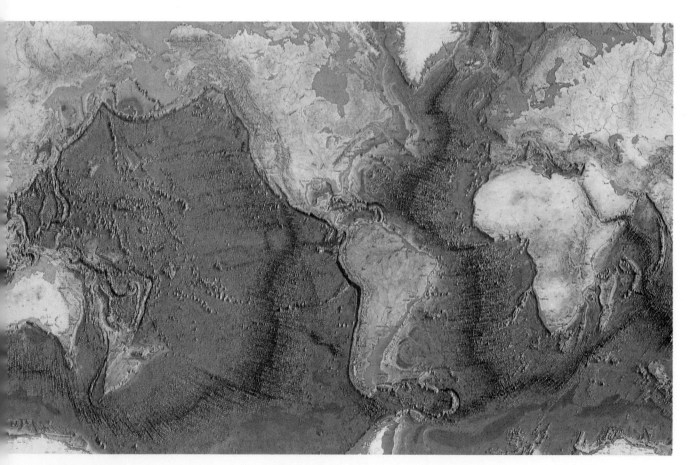

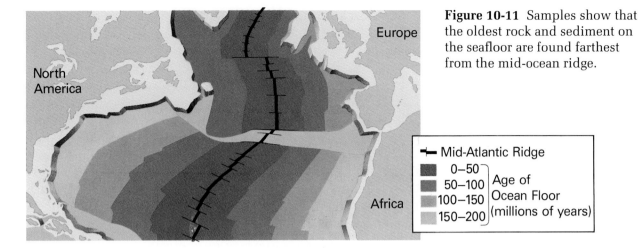

Figure 10-11 Samples show that the oldest rock and sediment on the seafloor are found farthest from the mid-ocean ridge.

Mid-Atlantic Ridge
- 0–50
- 50–100
- 100–150
- 150–200

Age of Ocean Floor (millions of years)

Think back to the age data from Activity 10.2. Where did you map the youngest rocks? The map in Figure 10-11 shows the ages of rocks and fossils found near the Mid-Atlantic Ridge. The youngest rock is found in the rifts. The oldest rock is found farthest from the rifts. Perhaps the heat source is hot magma coming up from deep within Earth and flowing out as lava at the rifts. How would this hypothesis explain that the youngest rocks are found at the rift?

Is there lava pouring out through the rifts as the rock age and water temperature suggest? By the 1960's, submarines were able to dive into the rift valleys of the Mid-Atlantic Ridge and photograph new rock being formed. The magma entering the rifts cools quickly because of the cooler ocean water. The cooled magma forms an unusual, fine-grained igneous rock called pillow lava, shown in Figure 10-12.

Pillow lava contains atoms of iron. The electrons in these iron atoms can be arranged into a magnetic pattern or code while the lava is still liquid. The location, shape, and strength of Earth's magnetic poles determine the magnetic code locked inside the rock. Sometimes the magnetic poles reverse, leaving the magnetic North Pole in the Southern Hemisphere. When the magnetic poles change their location, the magnetic code of new rock forming on the seafloor also changes. How might this data be useful?

The data gathered on mid-ocean ridges should lead you to the conclusion that the seafloor spreads apart. **Seafloor spreading** is the theory that seafloor crust forms at the mid-ocean ridges and spreads away from those ridges in opposite directions. Ocean crust forms constantly as magma forces its way up through the rifts in the mid-ocean ridges. As new rock forms in the rift, it splits apart and is pushed or pulled away from the ridge. Over time, older rock moves farther and farther away from the center of the ridge.

Figure 10-12 Pillow lava forms when magma cools quickly. This pillow lava formed underwater.

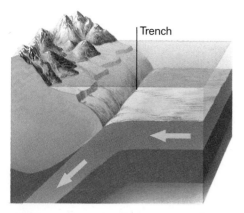

Trench

Figure 10-13 Seafloor crust is destroyed at trenches, where it is forced down into Earth's interior.

Figure 10-14 The lithosphere is divided into sections called plates. Plates usually contain both continental and oceanic crust.

Look back at Figure 10-10. Maps of the ocean floor do not only reveal the mountainous mid-ocean ridges. These maps also show a series of deep valleys, called **trenches,** near some continents and islands. The theory of seafloor spreading says that seafloor crust is destroyed at the trenches, where it is forced down into Earth's interior.

In many ways, the theory of seafloor spreading provides the answers Wegener needed to support the idea of continental drift. Earth's crust moves after all. Two questions remain to be answered. How are the movements of the continents connected to the movement of the seafloor? What is the great force needed to move the crust around like pieces of a jigsaw puzzle?

Plates

Are the continents moving or are the seafloors moving? Actually, they are both moving as connected sections of the solid, outer Earth. This solid layer is not made of the crust only. Studies of sound waves from earthquakes have shown that the uppermost layer of the mantle is also solid. The term **lithosphere** refers to all of the solid, outer Earth, including both the crust and upper mantle. The thickness of the lithosphere ranges from an average of 70 kilometers beneath the oceans to about 100 kilometers beneath the continents.

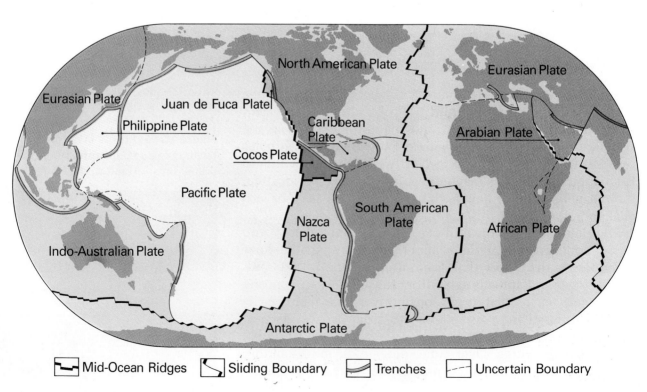

North American Plate

Eurasian Plate

Eurasian Plate

Juan de Fuca Plate

Philippine Plate

Caribbean Plate

Arabian Plate

Cocos Plate

Pacific Plate

Nazca Plate

South American Plate

African Plate

Indo-Australian Plate

Antarctic Plate

Mid-Ocean Ridges · Sliding Boundary · Trenches · Uncertain Boundary

The moving sections of lithosphere which contain both continents and seafloor are called **plates.** The mid-ocean ridges and deep trenches you saw in Figure 10-10 divide the lithosphere into 12 major plates and several smaller plates, shown in Figure 10-14. The largest plate is the Pacific Plate. Can you find the three smallest plates in Figure 10-14?

Seafloor crust and continent crust are very different. As you know, the crust that forms the seafloor is made of basalt. The crust that forms the continents is similar to granite. Granite is less dense than basalt. This means continents are less dense than the seafloor. Even though the crust thickness and composition are different on the seafloor and on a continent, they are very often part of the same plate. For example, the North American continent and the western half of the northern Atlantic Ocean seafloor are both part of the North American plate. When the North American plate moves, the seafloor and the land also move.

How does this large slab of solid rock move over the mantle without shattering? Look at Figure 10-15. Each plate of the lithosphere rests on a layer of rock called the asthenosphere [as then' ə sfir]. The **asthenosphere** is a hot layer of Earth's mantle that acts like putty. It is neither liquid nor solid. The plates of the lithosphere move on top of the flowing plastic asthenosphere and are pushed away from the mid-ocean ridges.

The puzzle pieces finally seem to fit. Only one question remains: What makes the plates move? The same type of movement makes the winds blow and causes cold, deep currents in the ocean. What is this type of movement?

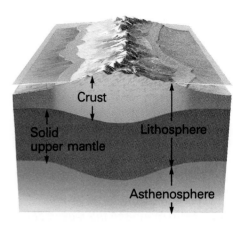

Figure 10-15 Plates are pieces of the solid lithosphere which move on top of the plastic asthenosphere.

Lesson Review 10.2

5. What is the relationship between a mid-ocean ridge and a rift?

6. List and describe the types of data used to develop the theory of seafloor spreading.

7. Why is the oldest seafloor crust found farthest from a mid-ocean ridge?

8. Compare the shoreline of the continent of North America with the border of the North American plate.

Interpret and Apply

9. How did the seafloor temperature and rock age data show that plates are not only being formed at the rift, but are also moving away from the rift?

10.3 *Plate Tectonics*

Lesson Objectives

▸ **Describe** the transfer of motion energy from magma to plates of the lithosphere.

▸ **Compare** diverging and sliding boundaries.

▸ **Explain** how the formation of faults is related to the movement of plates.

▸ **Activity** *Form a model* for heat and motion.

New Terms

plate tectonics	sliding
convection	boundary
diverging boundary	fault

Everyone has had the wrong answer to a math problem at one time. You may have used the right numbers and formulas, and perhaps you even followed the right steps, but still the answer was not correct.

Strangely, there are even times when you can get the right answer even though you used the wrong numbers. Alfred Wegener had good information, and he followed the scientific method. He thought that Earth's continents were once joined together as the supercontinent Pangaea. He thought Pangaea split apart and that the continents drifted away from each other like separated pieces of a jigsaw puzzle. As you have seen, Wegener had the right idea, but the wrong pieces of the puzzle. The sections of lithosphere called plates are moving, not the continents by themselves.

The theory that entire plates move is called **plate tectonics.** The word "tectonics" is taken from the Greek word, *tekton,* which means builder. Today plate tectonics is an accepted theory. It explains both the evidence Wegener used in describing continental drift and the evidence later used to describe seafloor spreading.

Clues found in rocks suggest that some plates have moved great distances over millions of years. For example, the kinds of fossils found in India show that it was once much closer to the South Pole. India is part of the Indo-Australian plate. Geologists usually place the Indo-Australian plate near Antarctica in models of Pangaea. As Pangaea split apart, the Indo-Australian plate moved thousands of kilometers to its present location. What caused this and other plates to move such great distances?

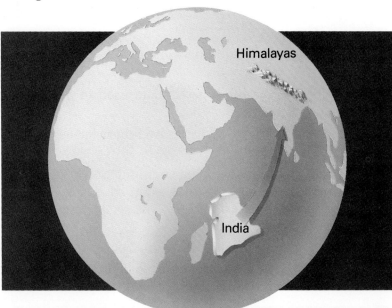

Figure 10-16 India has moved thousands of kilometers during the last 200 million years.

ACTIVITY 10.3

CONVECTION

Purpose To form a model to investigate the connection between heat and motion.

Materials

large Pyrex beaker	candle
ring stand and iron ring	matches
pot holder	clock or watch
ice-cold water	lab apron
cold food coloring	safety goggles

Procedure

1. Read all instructions for this activity before you begin your work.

2. On your paper, make a data table like the one shown. Put on your lab apron and safety goggles.

3. Place the ring stand and iron ring on a level table.

4. Place an unlit candle on the ring stand as shown. Move the ring so that the candle is about 5 cm below the ring and near one side. **Do not light the candle yet.**

5. Fill the beaker about three-fourths full with ice-cold water.

6. Carefully put the beaker of water on the iron ring. **CAUTION: Be sure to balance the beaker on the iron ring so that it does not tip over.**

7. Wait until the water is perfectly still. Add just two drops of food coloring to the water and observe. Record your observations.

8. Carefully light the candle without bumping into the beaker or table. **CAUTION: Keep hair, hands, and clothing away from the flame.**

9. Observe what happens to the colored water that is being heated by the flame. Record your observations.

10. Carefully blow out the candle and remove the beaker from the iron ring.

11. Before leaving the laboratory, clean up all materials and wash your hands.

Collecting and Analyzing Data

Data Table	
Procedure	**Observations**
add 2 drops of food coloring to cold water	
colored water heated over the candle flame	

1. Describe the change in the food coloring from the time you added it to the water to the time you lit the candle.

2. Diagram the movement of the food coloring after you lit the candle.

Drawing Conclusions

3. Is there a connection between thermal energy and motion? Support your answer with your data.

4. Air is a material that flows with this kind of motion. Explain why air conditioner vents are often on the ceiling and heating vents are often at floor level.

Heat

Figure 10-17 In convection, hot material rises and cold material sinks.

Figure 10-18 Convection within the mantle causes currents that move the overlying plates.

Convection

You remember from Chapter 7 that particles in a substance are more spread out in a gaseous state than in a liquid state. Heating a substance makes the particles move farther apart. There is less mass in the same volume. As heated water expands, it becomes less dense and rises to the surface.

The movement of a fluid because of density differences is called **convection.** A fluid is a form of matter that flows. Liquids and gases are both fluids. Any fluid moves by convection as long as one part is hotter and less dense than another part. The air in an oven or in the atmosphere can move by convection. Water in the oceans sometimes moves by convection. Where is there fluid below Earth's surface?

The discovery of magma rising into the rifts along ocean ridges explains why India has moved so far. Magma may be formed when the radioactive decay of unstable atoms heats the rock in Earth's mantle. The magma is less dense than the cooler surrounding solid rock and starts to rise toward the lithosphere.

Some of the magma flows out of a rift along a mid-ocean ridge. However, as you see in Figure 10-18, much of the magma spreads sideways underneath the lithosphere. As the magma moves beneath, some of its motion energy transfers to the plate. The plate is moved in the same direction.

The moving magma eventually cools as it spreads under the plate. This makes the magma more dense. It starts to sink back into the asthenosphere where it may be reheated. Eventually, the same magma may again rise up to a rift. This circular movement is called a convection cell or cycle.

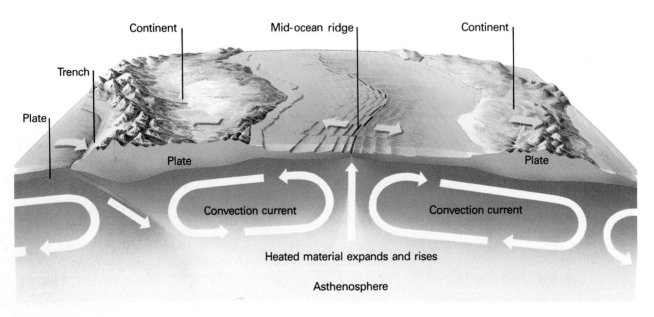

Continent   Mid-ocean ridge   Continent

Trench

Plate

Plate

Plate

Convection current   Convection current

Heated material expands and rises

Asthenosphere

10.4 *Mountain Building*

Would you be surprised if you found a fossil seashell in the Himalayas or in the Alps? The Himalayas and Alps are the highest mountains on Earth's surface. Himalayan mountain peaks, like Mount Everest in Nepal and K2 in India, are over 8000 meters above sea level. Fossils on those peaks are as far above the seafloor as any fossil can be. What force pushed up the rock containing these fossils high enough to form the world's tallest mountains?

Convection in the asthenosphere carries the plates along at a rate of only a few centimeters per year. Yet, when the plates collide, enough energy is released to crumple the plates into mountains or destroy them entirely.

Converging Boundaries

You have learned about diverging and sliding plate boundaries. There is a third type of plate boundary. If two plates coming from different directions meet head on, a **converging boundary** is formed. The plate edges that meet contain either continental crust or seafloor crust. The events that take place at the converging boundary depend on the types of crust that collide. There are three ways for plates to collide, as shown in Figure 10-21.

What happens when plates containing continental crust collide with plates containing seafloor crust? Remember, granite is less dense than basalt. When these two kinds of crust collide, the more dense seafloor crust plunges under the less dense continental crust. The movement of one plate beneath another plate is called **subduction**.

Lesson Objectives

▶ **Describe** three kinds of converging plate boundaries.

▶ **Discuss** subduction, folding, and uplift, and explain how they are related to the collision of plates.

▶ **Explain** how crust thickness is related to isostasy.

▶ **Activity** *Form a model* to represent isostasy in Earth's crust.

New Terms

converging boundary	anticlines
	plateau
subduction	craton
synclines	isostasy

Figure 10-21 The three types of convergent plate boundaries

Ocean-Ocean

Continent-Ocean

Continent-Continent

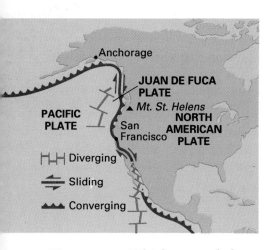

Figure 10-22 Which types of plate boundaries are present along the western coast of North America?

Look at the southern coast of Alaska in the map shown in Figure 10-22. The North American plate forms a converging boundary with the Pacific plate in this area. The Pacific plate moves northwest and collides with the North American plate. The Pacific plate is subducted beneath the North American plate. Where are two other places where subduction occurs along the North American plate?

A second kind of converging boundary occurs when plate edges made of seafloor crust collide. Both plate edges are made of basalt and have the same density. Because seafloor crust is usually thin, the two plates meet like two pieces of paper pushed together along a flat surface. The thin edges meet and then one slips beneath the other. One seafloor plate is subducted beneath the other.

The third kind of converging boundary happens when plate edges made of continental crust collide. Continental crust is thick, and little subduction occurs. Instead, the two plates fuse together to form a larger plate. Large sections of land have been added to the North American continent in this way. For example, much of Alaska has been added on to North America by plates colliding.

ENVIRONMENTAL AWARENESS

Burying Radioactive Waste

Imagine producing garbage that will not rot for thousands of years. Now imagine that this garbage is deadly poison. This should give you an idea of the problem society faces in disposing of radioactive waste.

Radioactive materials are used in electric power plants, hospitals, universities, and industry. The major problem with their use is that these materials lead to radioactive waste, which remains harmful even after thousands of years. How do you dispose of something this dangerous?

Present plans call for radioactive waste to be stored in mines deep inside Earth. This method has problems. Even at depths of several hundred meters, the waste can harm life if it is released into the environment.

What if containers of radioactive waste were buried in the trenches at subduction zones? What would happen? Sediment that fills the trenches would bury the containers. As subduction occurred, the waste would be carried down along with the seafloor crust. When the waste was subducted deep enough, it would melt along with the sediment and rock. It would be far from Earth's surface and no longer a threat to life.

Why is this not a good idea? The best containers start to fall apart after only thirty years. Remember that plates move very slowly. In thirty years, the containers would have moved less than a meter. They would break open long before being subducted and waste would poison the water. ■

Folded and Lifted Rock

What happens to rock layers when two plates collide? Colliding plates often behave like a moving rug hitting a wall. The moving rug crumbles, folds, and lifts up when it hits the wall. The layers of rock in plates also crumble, fold, and lift up when two plates converge. The changes are greatest when two pieces of continental crust collide. However, even subduction squeezes the rocks. The plate that is not subducted is pushed and compressed. Under this stress, the rocks in the crust either fold or break.

How do rocks become folded? Under most surface conditions, rocks are very rigid. They will break before they bend. Rock behaves differently underground where there is heat and pressure. If pressure is applied very slowly to rock layers, they bend instead of break. The collision of two plates provides this slow pressure as rocks are pushed together. The photograph in Figure 10-24 *(left)* shows two features of folded rock layers: synclines and anticlines. The **synclines** are the downward folds of rock layers. **Anticlines** are upward folds of rock layers.

The Appalachian Mountains provide excellent examples of folded rocks. You know that folding can result from two plates colliding. Look back at Figure 10-14. The Appalachians are near the east coast of the United States. Is that near a plate boundary? The Appalachians are evidence that North America collided with something before Pangaea broke apart. There may have been separate continents before there was ever a supercontinent. Pangaea could have formed when Eurasia and Africa collided with North and South America. During that collision, huge amounts of pressure squeezed the American continents, forming the synclines and anticlines of the Appalachian Mountains.

Locate the Alps on a world map. The Alps are a large chain of mountains in southern Europe. Which two plates do you think collided to form the Alps?

Figure 10-23 If a moving rug hits an obstacle, it starts to fold and buckle up.

Figure 10-24 Folding of rock layers creates synclines and anticlines.

Anticline

Syncline

Figure 10-25 *Top:* The Grand Tetons in Wyoming are fault-block mountains. *Bottom:* Fault-block mountains form when large pieces of crust are lifted along faults.

Figure 10-26 The Colorado Plateau was formed by the collision of the North American and Pacific plates.

The Himalayas formed when two sections of continental crust collided. After the breakup of Pangaea, India was a separate continent moving on a small plate. The Himalayas formed when India collided with the southern part of the Eurasian plate. India acted like a bulldozer. Rocks made of seafloor sediment lifted and folded. Unbelievably, the Himalayas will continue to grow as the Indo-Australian plate continues to push north into the Eurasian plate.

Sometimes rock layers do not bend. If the pressure on a rock is strong enough or quick enough, the layers of rock break along faults. If two plates are moving toward each other, separate sections of rock are pushed above the surrounding crust. If two plates are pulling apart, blocks of rock slide down along the faults, as shown in Figure 10-25 *(bottom)*. Some sections of the plate are left standing higher than the surrounding parts or are actually lifted up to form fault-block mountains. The Grand Teton Mountains in Wyoming, shown in Figure 10-25 *(top)*, are fault-block mountains. This type of mountain range is common in the four corners area of Utah, Colorado, New Mexico, and Arizona.

The Colorado Plateau of the southwestern United States is also an example of how plate collisions affect the land. **Plateaus** are flat, broad, raised areas of land. The Colorado Plateau is a lifted rock structure formed by the gentle buckling of the crust as the Pacific plate was thrust under the North American plate. Look at Figure 10-26. Is the Colorado Plateau located only in Colorado?

Many parts of continents are far from plate boundaries. These parts of continents are billions of years old. The oldest part of a continent is called the **craton** [krā′ tän]. Cratons are made of ancient igneous and metamorphic rocks which may be covered with younger sedimentary rocks.

Isostasy

The solid plates of the crust float on the more dense magma of the asthenosphere. As you recall, the magma is fluid because it melted within the hot, inner Earth. The balance of the plates floating on the asthenosphere is called **isostasy.** More dense rock, like basalt, sinks deeper into the asthenosphere. Less dense rock, like granite, floats higher.

Mountain ranges are built by uplifting and folding. Imagine what would happen to the crust under a mountain range as the mountains become larger. The sections of the crust beneath the mountain sink deeper into the mantle. If the mountain is worn away, the remaining crust is not as heavy and floats higher. The land lifts as it is worn away. The up-and-down movement of the crust caused by isostasy leads to further faulting.

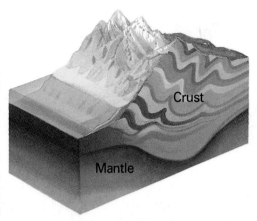

Figure 10-27 The crust beneath continents and mountains is thicker than oceanic crust and sinks deeper into the mantle.

Subduction and the Rock Cycle

Subduction is one step of the rock cycle you learned about in Chapter 9. A rock that plunges deep into Earth during subduction melts and becomes magma again. The convection cycle in the asthenosphere moves the magma in a great circle. The magma can eventually return to the surface at a diverging boundary, where it cools to become igneous rock and part of a new expanding plate. This convection cycle may take hundreds of millions of years.

Figure 10-28 The processes of plate tectonics can be linked to the rock cycle.

The movement of the plates can change a rock in other ways. The forces that fold a rock sometimes change it into metamorphic rock. Uplift may bring a rock up to Earth's surface where it weathers into sediment. Faults also develop in the rock layers.

Sometimes the movement of the plates causes sudden and violent changes in Earth's surface. Rocks suddenly break, or magma comes to the surface with great force. In the next chapter, you will learn more about these sudden changes as you study earthquakes and volcanoes.

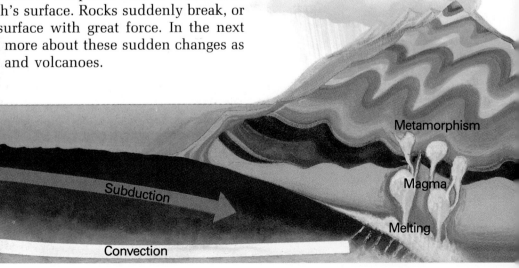

New igneous rock

Metamorphism

Magma

Rising magma

Subduction

Melting

Convection

A C T I V I T Y   1 0 . 4   General Supplies

A MODEL OF ISOSTASY

Purpose   To form a model showing how floating objects rise or sink.

Materials

plastic bucket	hammer
3 woodblocks	metric ruler
heavy nail	safety goggles

Procedure

1. Read all instructions for this activity before you begin your work.

2. On your paper, draw a data table like the one shown. Use a ruler and pencil to place millimeter marks along one edge of each block.

3. Put on your safety goggles.

4. Use the hammer to place a nail in the center of one side of one woodblock. **CAUTION: Be careful not to hit your fingers with the hammer.**

5. Fill the bucket about two-thirds full with water. Place the woodblock with the nail in the bucket as shown. If the block tips to one side, touch it with a pencil to help it float upright.

6. Measure and record the total height of the woodblock sticking out above the water.

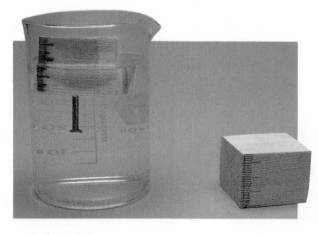

7. Measure and record the total depth of the woodblock below water.

8. Stack a second block on top of the first block. Repeat steps 6 and 7. Add a third block. Repeat steps 6 and 7.

9. Remove the third and second blocks, repeating steps 6 and 7 each time. Repeat step 5.

10. Before leaving the laboratory, clean up all materials and wash your hands thoroughly.

Collecting and Analyzing Data

Data Table			
Number of Blocks	**Depth Below Water**	**Height Above Water**	**Depth Height**
1			
2			
3			
2			
1			

1. For each part, divide the total depth of wood below water by the total height of wood above water to complete the chart.

2. How do the depth/height values for the blocks compare with each other?

3. What happens to the amount of wood below water as the height of the block stack increases?

Drawing Conclusions

4. Compare stacking blocks with the formation of a mountain by folding.

5. Compare the removing of woodblocks to a mountain being weathered and eroded by wind and water.

Lesson Review 10.4

16. Describe a converging boundary.

17. Why does subduction happen when a continental crust meets a seafloor crust?

18. List the changes that result from the collision of plates.

19. What is the relationship between the thickness of the crust and the depth the crust sinks into the mantle?

Interpret and Apply

20. How are fault-block mountains different from folded mountains?

21. Compare and contrast the formation of the Colorado Plateau with the formation of the Appalachian Mountains.

Chapter Summary

Read this summary of the main ideas in this chapter. If any are not clear to you, go back and review that lesson.

10.1 The Moving Continents

■ Wegener used the scientific method to develop the theory of continental drift.

■ Continental drift is the idea that the continents were once joined together as Pangaea, that they split apart, and that they drifted to their present positions.

■ Wegener's theory was not widely accepted because he did not provide an explanation of why or how the continents moved.

10.2 The Expanding Oceans

■ Four types of data support the theory of seafloor spreading.

■ New crust forms in rifts as the seafloor spreads away from the mid-ocean ridge.

■ Mid-ocean ridges and trenches divide the lithosphere into plates.

10.3 Plate Tectonics

■ Density differences, such as those found in fluids with different temperatures, lead to the movement called convection.

■ The heating of magma results in convection currents which cause plate movement.

■ Diverging boundaries form as plates move away from ocean ridges.

■ Sliding boundaries form as plates slide past one another.

10.4 Mountain Building

■ Plates coming from opposite directions meet to form converging boundaries.

■ The effects of plate movement include subduction, uplift, folding, and faulting.

■ Fault-block mountains result from the uplift of sections of crust divided by faults.

■ Plateaus form when large, broad sections of the crust are uplifted.

■ Thick crust sinks deep into the mantle.

Chapter Review

■ Vocabulary

anticline
asthenosphere
continental drift
convection
converging boundary
craton
diverging boundary
echo sounding
fault
isostasy
lithosphere

mid-ocean ridge
Pangaea
plate
plateau
plate tectonics
rift
seafloor spreading
sliding boundary
subduction
syncline
trench

■ Concept Mapping

Using the method of concept mapping described on pages 3–5, complete a concept map for plate tectonics. Copy the incomplete map shown below. Then fill in the missing terms.

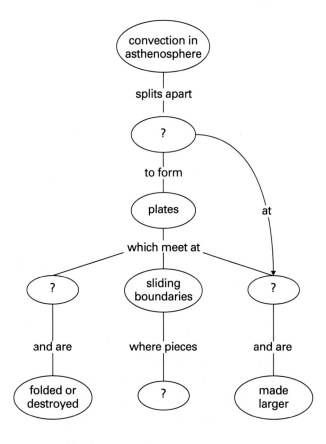

■ Review

On your paper, write the word or words that best complete each sentence.

1. Seafloor spreading only occurs at _____ boundaries.

2. The heating of magma creates a(n) _____ current.

3. Plate movement can cause the rocks in the crust to break along surfaces called _____ .

4. Wegener proposed the theory of _____ .

5. The Himalayas were formed when two pieces of _____ crust collided.

6. In _____ , rock is forced down toward the asthenosphere.

7. An upward fold in a layer of rock is called a(n) _____ .

8. The lithosphere is divided into sections called _____ .

9. A _____ is a long, narrow mountain range on the ocean floor.

10. The San Andreas fault zone is an example of a _____ boundary.

11. The plates move on top of a puttylike layer of the mantle called the _____ .

12. _____ is the balance between the crust and the mantle on which the crust is floating.

13. The movement of the plates relative to each other is called _____ .

14. *Mesosaurus* is a fossil reptile found in both Africa and _____ .

15. At a rift, rocks are _____ in age and water temperatures _____ than they are elsewhere on the seafloor.

16. Convection currents are caused by differences in the _____ of a fluid. A _____ fluid moves up, while a _____ fluid sinks.

Interpret and Apply

17. Some continents have cold climate fossils in one layer of rock and warm climate fossils in another layer. Use the theory of continental drift to help explain this observation.

18. Look back at Figure 10-11 and locate Iceland near the middle of the northern Atlantic Ocean. The youngest rocks are near Iceland's center. Where would the oldest rocks in Iceland be found? Explain your answer.

19. In the theory of continental drift, Wegener stated that continents slide along the seafloor. How does the theory of seafloor spreading differ from Wegener's theory of continental drift?

20. Use Figure 10-14 to predict how the size of the Atlantic and Pacific oceans will change in the next 100 million years.

21. As small ocean animals die, their skeletons fall to the seafloor at a constant rate. Assume the sediment from these skeletons is the same everywhere. Should the sediment thickness be greater near the mid-ocean ridge or near the trench? Explain.

22. Someday the heating of magma deep inside Earth will stop. How will this affect the movement of plates?

23. The oldest seafloor crust is only about 200 million years old. Earth is billions of years old. Why is there no older seafloor crust?

24. How would it be possible for the entire border of a plate to be a converging boundary?

25. Explain why it is important for scientists to publish the results of their research in scientific journals.

26. Sometimes people say that mountains have roots, like teeth. How is this idea related to isostasy?

Writing in Science

27. When writers compare two things, they explain how those things are alike and different. In a paragraph, compare the processes that formed the Himalayas with those that formed the Grand Tetons. Prepare to write by listing the similarities and differences between the two processes. Then decide how to organize your writing.

Critical Thinking

A geologist is trying to understand how the land in Virginia has formed and changed. He finds records of wells drilled to bring up samples from rock layers buried hundreds of meters underground. The table below provides data from three wells spaced 1 km apart.

Data Table			
	Age of Rocks in Millions of Years		
Depth	**Well 1**	**Well 2**	**Well 3**
0 m	150	100	50
250 m	200	150	100
500 m	250	200	150
750 m	300	250	200
1000 m	350	300	150
1250 m	400	300	100
1500 m	450	300	100
1750 m	500	350	150

28. How does the pattern in the age of the rock layers differ in Wells 1 and 2?

29. Which wells may have drilled through a folded layer of rock? Explain your answer.

30. How can folding explain an unusually thick layer of rock, such as the 300-million-year-old layer in Well 2?

31. If Well 3 were drilled another 250 m to a depth of 2000 m, what do you think would be the age of the rock at that depth? Explain how you got your answer.

Earthquakes and Volcanoes

Chapter Preview

*H*ave You Ever WONDERED?

Is it possible to outrun volcanic eruptions?

There are different kinds of volcanic eruptions. This man is sitting near a moving flow of lava. He isn't in danger because lava flowing from this volcano moves fairly slowly. In this Icelandic eruption, hot lava moved at less than 8 kilometers per hour. That's about how fast people go when they are walking rapidly.

You might not be able to outrun other eruptions. Some volcanoes produce lava that moves at speeds as high as 80 kilometers per hour. Other volcanoes explode, hurling out choking clouds of hot ash at speeds of hundreds of kilometers per hour. There is no way to outrun that kind of eruption.

People have to live with the possibility of natural disasters like volcanoes and earthquakes. In this chapter, you will learn how different types of volcanoes and earthquakes occur and how they may one day be predicted.

11.1 Earthquakes

Lesson Objectives

▶ *Distinguish* between normal, reverse, and strike-slip faults.

▶ *Describe* the sudden movements that result in earthquakes.

▶ *Compare* the motion and detection of different types of seismic waves.

▶ *Explain* the use of seismic waves in mapping Earth's interior.

▶ *Activity* **Form a model** of energy storage and release along a fault.

New Terms

earthquake	epicenter
normal fault	primary wave
reverse fault	secondary wave
strike-slip fault	surface wave
seismic wave	seismograph
focus	shadow zone

It's Saturday afternoon. You are sitting at the big desk in the family room doing homework. As you stand up to stretch, you hear a rumbling like distant thunder. The walls begin to shake. Quickly, you get under your desk. Books fall from the shelves. Pictures smash to the floor. The entire house seems to move from side to side. Then the shaking tapers off. You've just lived through another earthquake.

Some people say a small earthquake feels like a bulldozer is driving by. Have you ever watched a bulldozer in action? The bulldozer moves rock, soil, and almost anything else in its way. Soil usually moves easily and quietly as it is pushed. But a bulldozer may need to use the full force of its engine to break apart a thick sidewalk. As the sidewalk breaks, it produces vibrations. Some of these vibrations are felt as ground shaking. Other vibrations are heard as sound waves.

In a way, convection in the asthenosphere is like the bulldozer. Convection causes the solid plates of the lithosphere to move and break apart like the sidewalk. When the rock in the plates moves or breaks, energy is released in the form of vibrations, which shake the earth. The shaking of the ground caused by movement in the rocks is commonly called an **earthquake.**

Fault Types

Earthquakes occur when the rocks in the crust break or move. As you will recall, the rocks break and move along surfaces called faults. The rocks on either side of a fault move in different ways. The type of movement depends on the kind of forces that are acting on the rocks. Forces pull apart rocks, push them together, or make them move side by side. The three types of movement cause three main kinds of faults, as illustrated in Figure 11-1.

Figure 11-1 The three types of faults are the result of forces (blue arrows) pushing and pulling rock in different directions.

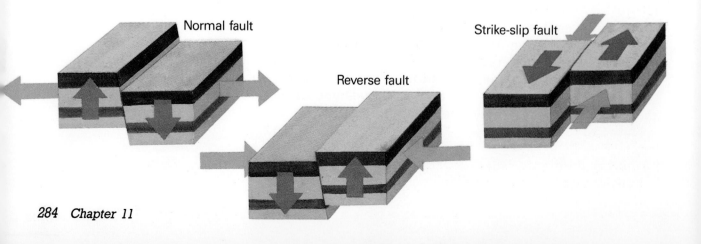

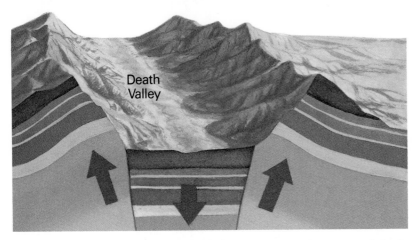

Death
Valley

Figure 11-2 *Left:* Death Valley formed when a section of crust between two normal faults dropped below sea level. *Right:* Normal faults

When forces pull apart rocks, they form the type of fault shown in Figure 11-1 *(left)*. This is a normal fault. A **normal fault** forms when the rocks above the fault surface move down. The forces needed to pull apart rocks occur at diverging plate boundaries. The fault-block mountains you read about in Chapter 10 formed along normal faults. The lowest spot on the North American continent, Death Valley in California, was also formed by normal faulting. Death Valley, shown in Figure 11-2 *(left)*, was formed when the western part of the North American plate stretched. The crust broke into pieces along normal faults, dropping the land in Death Valley to about 86 meters below sea level.

Sometimes forces push the rocks together, such as at converging plate boundaries. This pushing together, or compression, of the rocks forms a reverse fault, shown in Figure 11-1 *(middle)*. In a **reverse fault,** the rocks above the fault surface are pushed up over the rocks on the other side. Mountains also form by reverse faulting, as pieces of crust are forced up over other pieces, creating a stack of faulted blocks. The Alaska range in southern Alaska was formed by reverse faulting and the folding of rocks. This happened when the Pacific plate moved north and collided with the Alaskan section of the North American plate.

A **strike-slip fault,** shown in Figure 11-1 *(right)*, is where the rocks on either side of the fault slide past each other. The rocks on both sides of the fault can be part of the same plate, or they can be parts of different plates. What type of plate boundary has this kind of movement? The San Andreas fault is the best known fault in the United States. The San Andreas is one of several strike-slip faults along the west coast of North America, where the Pacific plate is moving past the North American plate.

The San Andreas and other West Coast faults are famous for their violent history of earthquakes and their potential for further destruction. Let's examine how plate movement is transformed into an earthquake.

ACTIVITY 11.1 General Supplies

ENERGY AND FRICTION

Purpose   To form a model of how energy is stored and released at a fault due to friction.

Materials _____

textbooks
string
table or desk top

Procedure

1. Read all instructions for this activity before you begin your work.

2. On your paper, draw a data table like the one shown.

3. Get about 70 cm of string. Tie one end of the string around the cover of a textbook, as shown.

4. Close the cover of the book and place it on a table or desk.

5. Gently pull on the string until the book starts to move. Describe how much the book resisted moving. Record your observations in your data table.

6. Return the book to its original position. Place a second book on top of the first book. Repeat step 5.

7. Return the two books to their original position. Add a third book. Repeat step 5.

8. Repeat step 5 using stacks of 4, 5, 6 and 7 books.

9. Clean up all materials before leaving the laboratory.

Collecting and Analyzing Data

Data Table	
Number of Books	**Observations of Book Movement**
1	
2	
3	

1. How could someone else tell how much you were pulling on the string just before each stack of books moved?

2. How much were you pulling on the string immediately after the books moved?

3. Imagine that your eyes were closed as you did this experiment. How would you know when the books moved?

Drawing Conclusions

4. What is the relationship between the amount of friction between the table and the book and the number of books in the stack?

5. What is the relationship between the amount of friction and the amount of force required to move the books?

6. What is the relationship between the amount of friction and the suddenness of the movement of the books?

7. The tabletop is a model of a fault. Relate the energy released when the books moved to the energy released when rocks move along a fault.

Seismic Waves

Some people are very good at snapping their fingers. They have learned how much pressure to use to build friction between their thumb and finger. The friction holds the thumb and finger together, even though they are being forced apart. This stores energy. When the thumb and finger suddenly move, the stored energy is released. Some of the released energy is in the form of vibrations that travel through the atmosphere to your ears. These vibrations are sound waves.

In Activity 11.1, you provided the force needed to move books across a tabletop. Friction made the books resist movement. The books finally moved when enough force was provided to overcome friction. Your books and tabletop were a model for what happens along a fault. The fault was represented by the surface of the tabletop. The rocks on either side of the fault were the books on one side and the table on the other. Rocks on either side of a fault move when forces pushing them become greater than the force of friction that keeps them in place.

Like the snapping fingers or the sudden jolt of the moving books, the movement of rocks along a fault releases stored energy as vibrations. This sudden movement causes the earthquake. A vibration produced by an earthquake is called a **seismic wave.**

Seismic waves are not released along the entire length of the fault. Some faults are many kilometers long. Seismic waves come from a point called the focus, illustrated in Figure 11-3. The **focus** is the true location of an earthquake and is usually found below Earth's surface. The focus is where the first major movement along the fault occurs. The point on Earth's surface directly above the focus is called the **epicenter.** The epicenter is the earthquake location you hear reported in the news.

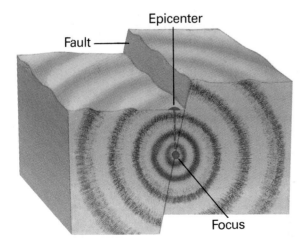

Figure 11-3 Seismic waves move out from the focus in all directions.

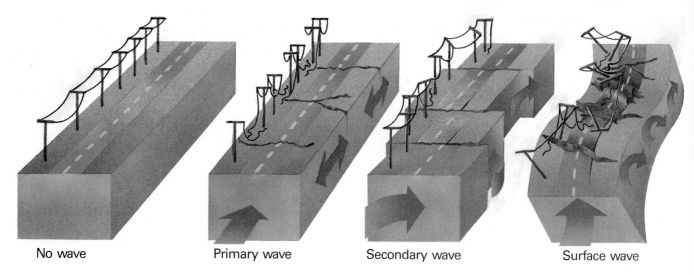

| No wave | Primary wave | Secondary wave | Surface wave |

Figure 11-4 The three kinds of seismic waves move through the earth in different ways.

An earthquake produces three different kinds of seismic waves, illustrated in Figure 11-4. **Primary waves** are seismic waves that cause matter to stretch and compress. These are the fastest seismic waves. Seismic waves that move matter from side to side are called **secondary waves.** They are called secondary waves because these seismic waves are slower than primary waves and arrive second at recording stations. The third type of seismic wave forms when primary and secondary waves combine at Earth's surface. **Surface waves** are seismic waves that cause a rolling motion in the rock and soil. Surface waves are similar to the ripples produced when you drop a rock into a pool of water.

Detecting Seismic Waves

Figure 11-5 A seismograph

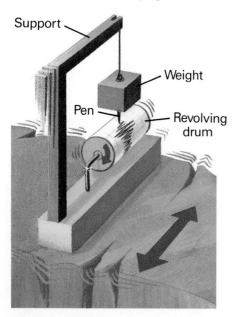

Support
Weight
Pen
Revolving drum

Seismic waves travel away from an earthquake in all directions. Seismic waves from the same earthquake are recorded at seismograph stations all over the world. A **seismograph** is an instrument that measures and records seismic waves. In a typical seismograph, such as the one shown in Figure 11-5, a piece of paper is attached to a rotating drum. The rotating drum is attached to a support that rests on Earth's bedrock, which is the solid rock beneath the soil. A pen attached to a heavy weight hangs above the paper. As the seismic waves from an earthquake arrive, they cause the bedrock to move, which moves the rotating drum. The pen stays still as the drum moves beneath it, and the movements are recorded on the paper. A clock on the drum allows you to determine the time at which each seismic wave arrived.

When a seismograph records seismic waves, seismologists work quickly to determine the location and strength of the earthquake. A seismologist is a person who studies the effects and causes of earthquakes.

Mapping Earth's Interior

Much of what you learn about Earth's interior comes from the careful study of seismic waves. Experiments show that primary waves travel through both solids and liquids. Secondary waves, however, only travel through solids. Liquids stop or absorb secondary waves. In an earthquake, both primary and secondary waves travel out from the focus in all directions. Look at Figure 11-6. Where are secondary waves recorded from the earthquake shown in the diagram? Secondary waves would be recorded at every seismograph station in the world if Earth were completely solid. They are not. The secondary waves are not recorded at seismograph stations on Earth's opposite side. These stations record no secondary waves because the waves are blocked by the liquid rock of Earth's outer core.

If Earth were completely solid, you would also expect to record primary waves all over the world. Primary waves travel through liquids, so they would not be stopped by the outer core. As you would expect, primary waves are recorded on the side of Earth opposite the earthquake. This is true no matter where the earthquake occurs. Yet there are places where primary waves are not recorded. Seismic waves bend when they cross a boundary between layers of material with different density. The bending of primary waves at the boundary between the mantle and outer core creates shadow zones in a small band on Earth's opposite side. A **shadow zone** is a region where seismic waves are not received.

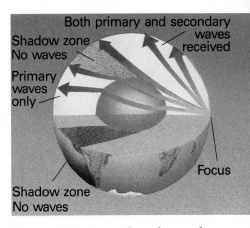

Figure 11-6 An earthquake sends seismic waves through Earth's interior. Areas in the shadow zone receive no seismic waves from that earthquake.

Lesson Review 11.1

1. What causes plate sections to lock together and then suddenly move?

2. The surface of a normal fault and a reverse fault look very much alike. Why do rocks slide down a normal fault and up a reverse fault?

3. Draw and describe the motion of a row of telephone poles as each kind of seismic wave moves beneath the poles.

4. Why do some seismographic stations receive both primary and secondary waves while others do not?

Interpret and Apply

5. Some people twist ice-cube trays to cause the ice cubes to break away from the tray. How is this action similar to an earthquake?

11.2 *Size and Effects of Earthquakes*

It was a Tuesday night in autumn, and people across the country were settling in to watch the third game of the World Series. In San Francisco, the ballpark was jammed with fans. Some were hoping to see the team from Oakland up its lead in the series; others wanted to see the San Francisco team start a comeback. Most people expected a good baseball game. But the game was not played that night. At 5:04 P.M. Pacific time, on October 17, 1989, the San Francisco Bay area was struck by a powerful earthquake while the rest of the country looked on in disbelief. Lasting only 15 seconds, the earthquake collapsed highways, damaged bridges, and swept buildings off their foundations. Many people lost their lives.

In the first couple of hours following the earthquake, the news from the affected area was sketchy. Electricity and phone service shut down. Because reporters were unable to reach towns outside of San Francisco, you would think that the reporters would not know where the earthquake actually occurred. Yet, within 90 minutes, the reporters knew both the location of the earthquake's epicenter and the earthquake's strength. If you're wondering where they got that information, it came from seismograph recordings. Let's look at how you can use seismic wave recordings to find an earthquake's location.

Figure 11-7 During the October 1989 earthquake, apartment buildings in San Francisco's Marina district were heavily damaged. Some were shaken off their foundations.

LOCATING AN EARTHQUAKE'S EPICENTER

Purpose To construct a map to show how earthquakes are located.

Materials

copy of Figure 11-8   pencil
drawing compass   metric ruler

Procedure

1. Read all instructions for this activity before you begin your work.

2. Use the latitudes and longitudes in the table to draw the seismograph station locations onto your map.

3. Use the compass to draw a circle around Station 1. **CAUTION: Compass point is sharp. Handle with care.** Place the center of the circle at the station. Use the map scale to make the radius of the circle equal to the distance from Station 1 to the earthquake.

4. Repeat step 3 for Stations 2 and 3.

Figure 11-8 Base map of western United States

Collecting and Analyzing Data

Data Table			
Seismograph Station Data			
	Location		**Distance from Earthquake**
Station	**Latitude**	**Longitude**	
1	45° N	120° W	1300 km
2	35° N	105° W	1200 km
3	40° N	115° W	750 km

1. Determine the latitude and longitude of the intersection of the three circles.

Drawing Conclusions

2. How many possible earthquake locations are there with information from one seismographic station?

3. How does information from other seismographic stations decrease the possible locations of an earthquake?

4. Why would information from a fourth station be unnecessary?

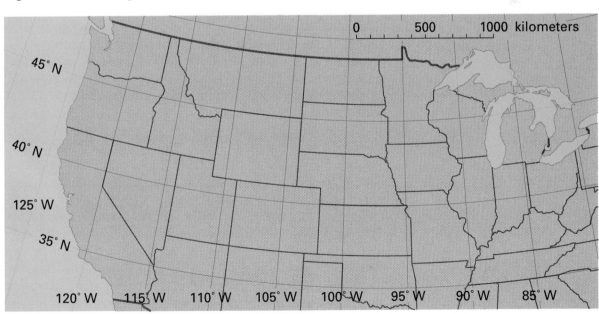

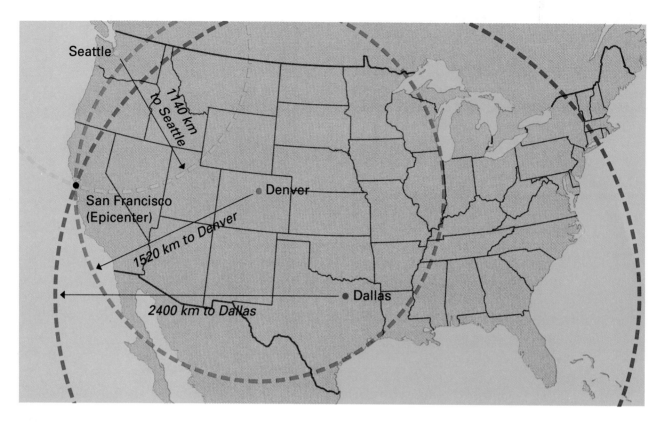

Seattle

1140 km
to Seattle

San Francisco
(Epicenter)

Denver

1520 km to Denver

2400 km to Dallas

Dallas

Figure 11-9 The radius of each circle is the distance from that seismograph to the epicenter. The point where all three circles meet is the epicenter.

Locating Earthquakes

Have you ever listened for thunder after seeing a flash of lightning? You see the lightning almost as soon as it happens. Light travels at a very high speed. The sound waves of the thunder travel more slowly. The extra time it takes for the slower sound waves to reach you is an indication of how far away the lightning was.

This same idea is used to find the distance from a seismograph to an earthquake. You know that primary waves travel faster than secondary waves. Primary waves arrive at a seismograph before the secondary waves. The time delay between the primary and secondary waves is used to determine how far the seismic waves traveled. This is the distance to the earthquake. However, the seismograph does not indicate from which direction the wave came. The seismograph only gives the distance to the earthquake. This is why you draw a circle with a radius equal to the distance to the earthquake. The earthquake may have occurred at any location on the circle. To pinpoint the earthquake's location, you need to get the information from two other seismograph stations, draw two more circles, and find the point of intersection, as shown in Figure 11-9. Once you have used seismograph data to determine the location of an earthquake, you can then determine the earthquake's strength.

Measuring Earthquake Strength

The strength of an earthquake depends on how much energy builds up along the fault before movement occurs. The most commonly used scale of earthquake strength was developed by a seismologist named Charles Richter. The **Richter scale** is a numerical description of the size of seismic waves produced by an earthquake. You find the Richter scale number by examining the size of the seismic waves recorded on the seismograph. An increase of 1 on the Richter scale represents a ten-fold increase in the size of seismic waves. For example, a tremor with a Richter value of 3 produces waves 10 times larger than a tremor with a value of 2. An earthquake with a Richter value of 4 produces waves 100 times larger than an earthquake with a value of 2. How much larger are the seismic waves from an earthquake with a Richter value of 7 than an earthquake with a value of 4? An earthquake with a Richter value greater than 7 is considered a major earthquake. In a major earthquake, most lives are lost when buildings collapse. Table 11-1 lists the strength and loss of lives from major historical earthquakes.

The largest earthquake ever recorded in the United States was the Alaskan earthquake of 1964. However, the largest earthquake in United States history occurred in 1811, before seismographs existed to record its effects. The largest earthquake occurred in the middle of the continent, near New Madrid, Missouri, away from any plate boundary. The largest of several New Madrid earthquakes had a strength estimated at 8.7 on the Richter scale.

Figure 11-10 Many people died when buildings collapsed during the 1985 earthquake in Mexico City.

Table 11-1 Great Earthquakes in History			
Year	Location	Richter Value	Deaths
1556	Shen-shu, China	—	830 000
1755	Lisbon, Portugal	8.8 est.	60 000
1906	San Francisco	8.3	700
1923	Tokyo, Japan	8.3	143 000
1939	Concepción, Chile	8.3	30 000
1964	Prince William Sound, Alaska	8.5	117
1976	T'ang-shan, China	8.2	242 000
1985	Mexico City, Mexico	8.1	25 000
1988	Spitak, Soviet Armenia	6.8	25 000
1989	San Francisco/Oakland	7.1	67

Predicting Earthquakes

Can earthquakes happen where you live? Two patterns might help you determine whether you are presently in any danger. The first is a pattern of location. The second is a pattern in the number of years between major earthquakes.

Most earthquakes occur along plate boundaries. You can see this pattern in the map of world earthquake locations in Figure 11-11. Earthquakes release the energy that is stored as plates move apart, collide, or slip beside each other. Notice that the largest number of earthquakes occurs along the border of the Pacific Ocean, where the Pacific plate and smaller plates are being subducted under other plates. This area of high earthquake activity is often called the Ring of Fire because so many volcanoes also occur there.

Figure 11-12 shows the areas in the United States with the greatest risk of a major earthquake. The southern California region, which is split by the San Andreas fault, is the most active seismic region in the United States. However, notice that New England, South Carolina, the Rocky Mountain states, and the Mississippi River valley area near Missouri all have potential risk for major earthquakes. These areas are at a greater risk because they have experienced large earthquakes in the past. The Mississippi River valley is at risk because scientists feel the New Madrid earthquake fault could move again.

Figure 11-11 Most earthquakes and volcanoes occur at plate boundaries. Compare this map with Figure 10-14.

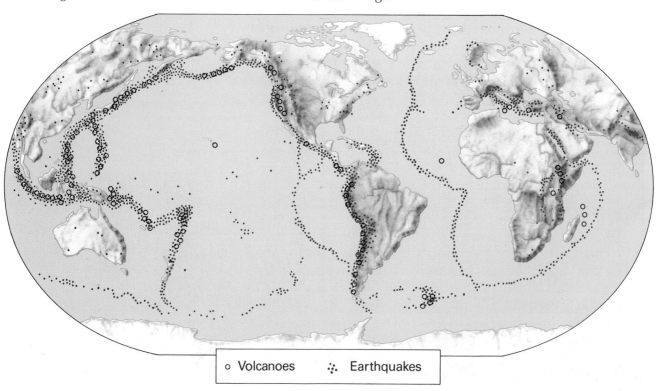

o Volcanoes   ∴ Earthquakes

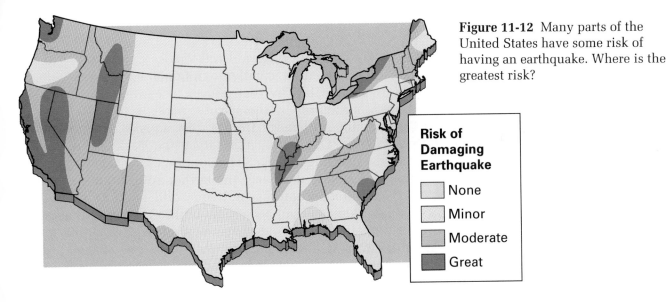

Figure 11-12 Many parts of the United States have some risk of having an earthquake. Where is the greatest risk?

Risk of Damaging Earthquake

None
Minor
Moderate
Great

Once you know where an earthquake might occur, the next thing you want to know is when it will occur. Faults seem to slip and release energy every so many years. In southern California, the San Andreas fault produces a major earthquake about once every 150 years. The last major earthquake in that region was in 1857. It is likely that there will be a major earthquake in southern California within the next 20 to 30 years. Knowing an earthquake will occur within 20 years is helpful for long-term planning. For example, many buildings in the San Francisco area were able to withstand the 1989 earthquake because they were built knowing such a quake would occur someday.

Some natural events may signal an impending earthquake. For example, land in the area of an earthquake may rise or fall dramatically. Movement along a fault, measured with sensitive lasers, may change. The number of microquakes in the area increases or decreases. The water level in wells may rise or fall. The soil releases larger amounts of radon gas. Animals often act strangely before an earthquake. One geologist in California attempts to predict earthquakes by graphing the number of missing pets listed in the local newspaper. These and other warning signs may one day be used to reduce the number of lives lost in an earthquake.

The best example of accurate earthquake prediction occurred in China. Chinese seismologists predicted an earthquake for February 4, 1975. More than 100 000 people left the Haicheng area. At 7:36 P.M. on the fourth, 90 percent of the buildings in Haicheng were damaged or destroyed by a major earthquake. The collapse of those buildings would have killed many of the residents. Unfortunately, the Haicheng prediction was a rare success.

Figure 11-13 This technician is installing a device that measures movement along a fault.

Figure 11-14 Even though this building did not collapse during the 1989 San Francisco earthquake, the bricks that fell off into the street could have hurt or even killed passers-by.

Earthquake Safety

Do people and buildings fall into cracks during an earthquake? Actually, faults usually do not open up to form wide cracks in the earth. The real danger of earthquakes is the shaking of structures by the seismic waves.

The amount of damage from an earthquake depends on many factors. Obviously, the larger the earthquake, the greater the possible damage. The amount of damage from an earthquake usually decreases the farther away from the epicenter you are. Structures built on solid bedrock usually suffer less damage than structures built on loose sediment. Unfortunately, many cities have expanded by building on landfills. During an earthquake, this loose soil shakes like jelly. The increased shaking leads to more damage in a building.

Even solid rock reacts differently to seismic waves. Do you remember the New Madrid earthquake? The tremors were felt all the way to Canada because the rocks in the eastern United States are able to conduct vibrations so well. Figure 11-15 shows areas that would have similar amounts of ground shaking from the same size earthquake. Which would affect the larger area, an earthquake located in California or in Missouri?

There are other dangers from an earthquake. Fire destroyed many buildings during San Francisco's 1906 earthquake. Fires started when natural gas pipelines broke. The fires could not be stopped because water pipes leading to fire hydrants had also broken. Bridges and highways may collapse or become unstable. Dams may collapse, unleashing water that floods towns. Storage tanks for oil or chemicals may be damaged, threatening water supplies.

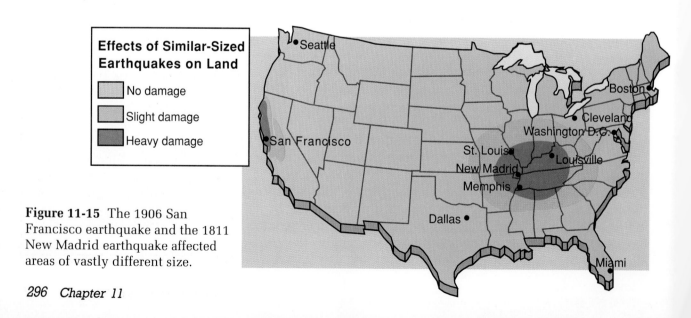

Effects of Similar-Sized Earthquakes on Land

☐ No damage
☐ Slight damage
■ Heavy damage

Figure 11-15 The 1906 San Francisco earthquake and the 1811 New Madrid earthquake affected areas of vastly different size.

In an ideal world, no one would live where they would be in danger from an earthquake. However, millions of people choose to live near mountains and oceans with active fault zones. One way to prepare for an earthquake is to build structures that will resist damage from seismic waves. Another is to store water, food, medical supplies, batteries, and anything else needed in an emergency. In a way, preparing for an earthquake is no different than preparing for a hurricane or other natural event.

What should you do if there is an earthquake? Your first concern is to protect yourself from falling objects. If you are outside, run to a clearing, away from buildings and power lines. This may sound easy to do, but many earthquake veterans say that it is hard to walk when the land under your feet is moving. They say that walking in an earthquake is like walking on a trampoline. If you are inside a building, you can protect yourself in two ways. If you are near a door, leave the building. You can also seek a safe place inside the building. Standing in a doorway or getting under a strong table or desk will help protect you from falling objects. After the earthquake is over, get to a safe area away from damaged buildings. Smaller earthquakes, called aftershocks, often occur after the main earthquake. Aftershocks are large enough to bring down buildings that were damaged in the main earthquake.

Figure 11-16 These students are earthquake-proofing their classroom. Why are they moving these heavy objects to a lower shelf?

ENVIRONMENTAL AWARENESS

Building for the Big One

As bad as the 1989 Bay Area earthquake was, it could have been much worse. The reason more lives were not lost is that San Francisco is well prepared for earthquakes. In San Francisco, new buildings must be built to withstand major earthquakes without collapsing. Old buildings must be upgraded to meet the new standards. Buildings that do not collapse are safer during earthquakes.

How do you earthquake-proof a building? A building or home should be securely attached to its foundation. This allows the home to move with the shaking foundation instead of sliding off the foundation and collapsing. Better yet, the building should be built on or attached to bedrock. You should avoid building on soft sediment or landfill, which makes the effects of seismic waves stronger.

Tall buildings are designed to bend and sway during an earthquake. Shorter buildings are made very rigid, so that they cannot bend and break. Some buildings are put on cushions and rollers, so that the ground will move under them. ■

Figure 11-17 This damage was caused by a tsunami that hit Resurrection Bay, Alaska after the Alaskan earthquake of 1964.

Tsunamis

An underwater earthquake or volcanic eruption produces a seismic wave that travels through water instead of rock and soil. The huge water wave produced by underwater Earth movements is called a **tsunami** [sü näm′ ē]. Tsunamis are sometimes incorrectly called tidal waves, even though they are not caused by tides.

Like other seismic waves, a tsunami is very destructive. A tsunami has a height of less than 1 meter as it travels across deep ocean water. At that height, the tsunami can pass under boats unnoticed. However, as the tsunami approaches land, its height increases dramatically as the water depth decreases. As it comes ashore, the tsunami becomes a towering wall of water, up to 50 meters high.

The size and speed of a tsunami make it extremely dangerous. A tsunami can reach speeds of 600 kilometers per hour. This means the tsunami can sweep over entire islands and coastal areas before there is any warning. In the Pacific Ocean, where there is no large land mass to stop or weaken the wave, tsunamis sometimes travel thousands of kilometers before striking land. Minutes after the great Alaskan earthquake of 1964, a tsunami hit the Alaskan coast, destroying buildings and leaving boats stranded on land. Eight hours after the earthquake, the tsunami that started in Alaska hit Crescent City, California, drowning ten people.

The number of earthquakes around the Pacific Ocean carries with it the constant threat of tsunamis. To protect lives and property, a warning system has been set up in coastal areas and for the Pacific islands to alert people if a tsunami is likely to occur.

Lesson Review 11.2

6. How is the difference in speed of primary and secondary waves useful to a seismologist?

7. Why do earthquakes cause so much damage?

8. List four things being looked at as possible tools for predicting earthquakes.

Interpret and Apply

9. The 1964 Alaskan earthquake caused damage and loss of life in Alaska and all along the Pacific Ocean border. How did this earthquake do so much damage to areas far from its epicenter?

11.3 Volcanoes

It's eerie to think that the ground can burst open and begin spouting jets of molten rock, ash, sulfurous gases, and steam. Yet that is exactly what happens every day. Somewhere in the world there is a volcano erupting. A **volcano** is an opening in Earth's crust where magma reaches Earth's surface. Most people have no idea what it would be like to live next to a volcano. The people of Iceland and Hawaii know. They live on a group of islands formed by volcanic eruptions.

Types of Volcanic Eruptions

The people who live in Iceland live at a site of rift eruption. Rift eruption occurs at diverging boundaries where plates spread apart. As the plates spread, hot magma comes up through the rifts to reach Earth's surface. The combination of rifting and eruption results in the seafloor mountain chain called the mid-ocean ridge. In some cases, the ridge is built up enough to become islands, such as Iceland or the Azores.

The lava in rift eruptions usually has the composition of the rock, basalt. Basaltic lava is thin and does not contain much dissolved gas. As you know, rift eruptions below sea level form pillow lava. In a rift eruption above sea level, the basaltic lava sometimes sprays into the air where it cools to form hard fragments of extrusive igneous rock. These pieces of ash, cinder, and rock are all called **tephra.** Sometimes the tephra buries nearby buildings, as shown in Figure 11-18. Other times, the thin basaltic lava quietly flows out of the rift and spreads across the land. This lava forms the basalt flows you read about in Chapter 9.

▶ **Distinguish** between rift, hot spot, and subduction boundary eruptions.

▶ **List** and **describe** the features of volcanoes.

▶ **Give examples** of methods for predicting volcanic eruptions.

▶ **Activity** **Interpret data** that describe the change in the features of Mount St. Helens.

New Terms

volcano	composite cone
tephra	sill
cinder cone	dike
shield cone	

Figure 11-18 Volcanic eruptions, such as this one in Iceland, are both beautiful and dangerous. These houses have been buried by black tephra.

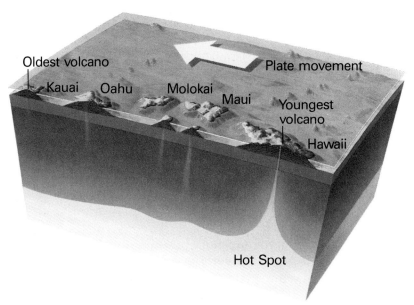

Oldest volcano
Kauai   Oahu   Molokai
                              Maui
Plate movement
Youngest
volcano
Hawaii

Hot Spot

Figure 11-19 *Left*: An eruption of Kilauea on the island of Hawaii; *Right*: The Hawaiian Islands have formed as the Pacific plate moves over a hot spot. Each island takes millions of years to form.

Figure 11-20 The oceanic plate and seafloor sediments, subducted at a trench, melt and rise back to Earth's surface as thick, gas-filled magma.

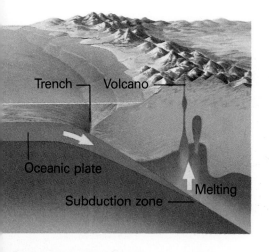

Trench   Volcano

Oceanic plate

Subduction zone   Melting

The volcanoes of Hawaii are a good example of a second type of eruption. Hawaiians live on islands created by one of Earth's hot spots. Like rift eruptions, hot spots have basaltic lava. Unlike rifts, hot spots can be thousands of kilometers from a plate boundary. A hot-spot eruption occurs when a stream of magma melts its way up through a plate.

What, do you think, would be evidence for hot-spot eruptions? In Figure 11-19 (right), notice that the Hawaiian Islands are a chain of old volcanoes. The oldest volcanic islands are at the northwest end of the chain. Each island in the Hawaiian chain formed as the Pacific plate moved northwest over the hot spot. As the plate moved, the old volcano moved off the hot spot and stopped erupting. A new volcano started forming over the hot spot. This process is still going on today. A new Hawaiian island is forming to the southeast of the main island of Hawaii. There is also a hot spot under Yellowstone National Park, where its thermal energy powers the Old Faithful geyser.

The third type of volcanic eruption is by far the most common. About 80 percent of all volcanic eruptions occur near converging plate boundaries where subduction takes place. The explosive eruptions that occur at subduction boundaries are often dramatic and deadly.

When the ocean floor basalt is subducted, it is covered with thick layers of wet sediment. The thermal energy deep underground melts and mixes the basalt and the solid sediment. Heating also evaporates the water and burns plant and animal remains. Gases made in the process mix with the magma. This new magma has a composition more like granite and is much thicker than the basaltic magma.

Why are subduction boundary eruptions more explosive than other eruptions? These eruptions are explosive because they involve a different kind of magma than rift or hot-spot eruptions. Think about which is easier to drink through a straw, water or a thick milkshake. Thick fluids do not flow easily. It is more difficult to force thick, gas-filled, granitic magma through an opening than it is to force thin, basaltic magma through the same opening. Hot, granitic magma, which is filled with gas, is less dense than the surrounding rock; the magma rises up toward Earth's surface through any available path. But like the thick milkshake in the straw, the thick magma does not flow easily. Pressure builds until the entire top of the volcano explodes. This pressure buildup is what caused Mount St. Helens to erupt in May 1980.

In spite of warnings and predictions, the eruption of Mount St. Helens in Washington state still surprised everyone with its suddenness and power. In one day, the eruption released as much energy as would be released by exploding a small nuclear bomb every second for nine hours. The eruption blew away the north side of the mountain, leaving a large crater. A cloud of steam and tephra rushed out from the volcano at speeds between 100 and 400 kilometers per hour, knocking down entire forests of trees over 25 kilometers away.

Mount St. Helens is one of many volcanoes in a chain of mountains called the Cascade range. The Cascades extend from California to Canada. These volcanoes have erupted for millions of years as the Juan de Fuca plate has been subducted beneath the North American plate. Eruptions in the Cascade range are historically similar to the eruption at Mount St. Helens. Crater Lake in Oregon, shown in Figure 11-22, is all that remains of an ancient volcano called Mount Mazama. An eruption 6600 years ago destroyed Mount Mazama, leaving a water-filled crater.

Figure 11-21 The explosive eruption of Mount St. Helens sent broken rock, ash, and mud as far as 300 kilometers away.

Figure 11-22 Crater Lake was formed when water filled the crater left by an ancient subduction boundary eruption.

Table 11-2 Great Volcanic Eruptions in History		
Volcano	**Year**	**Amount of Tephra Ejected (km³)**
Mazama	4600 B.C.	40.0
Vesuvius	A.D. 79	2.7
Fuji	A.D. 1500	1.3
Tambora	A.D. 1815	80.0
Krakatoa	A.D. 1883	20.0
Katmai	A.D. 1912	30.0
St. Helens	A.D. 1980	4.0

Mount Mazama was not the largest volcanic explosion known. The eruption of Tambora, described in Table 11-2, threw so much tephra and sulfuric acid droplets into the atmosphere that they blocked out sunlight for months, reducing world temperatures. The following year has been called a year without summer. In New England, it snowed in June and began to frost as early as late August. Mary Shelley spent her summer vacation in Lake Geneva, Switzerland, where it was too cold and dreary to go outdoors. Instead, she stayed inside and wrote the novel *Frankenstein*.

Volcano Features

The different types of volcanic eruptions often lead to different kinds or shapes of volcanoes. An explosive eruption blasts lava into the air, where the lava cools rapidly. The cooled lava falls back to the ground as tephra. Usually the heaviest pieces of tephra fall nearby. The lighter pieces of ash are carried farther from the volcano. As the eruption continues, the tephra builds a mountain with steep sides. A volcanic mountain built of tephra is called a **cinder cone.**

Figure 11-23 There are three basic types of volcanic cones.

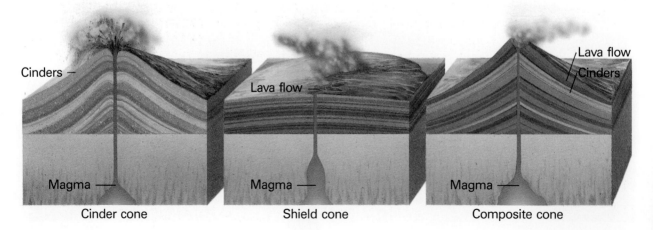

Cinders

Lava flow

Lava flow

Cinders

Magma

Magma

Magma

Cinder cone

Shield cone

Composite cone

When thin, basaltic lava erupts, it flows over Earth's surface. As each layer of lava cools, another layer of hot lava flows over it. The layers of lava cooling on top of each other build a shield cone. A **shield cone** is a volcanic mountain with a broad base and gently sloping sides. The Hawaiian Islands are shield cones built up from the ocean floor.

Sometimes volcanoes go through periods of both explosive and quiet eruptions. Explosive eruptions produce tephra. Once the volcano has released trapped gases, it may start to erupt more quietly. Quiet eruptions produce layers of lava. A mountain made up of layers of both lava and tephra is called a **composite cone.** Mount St. Helens, Mount Fuji in Japan, and Mount Vesuvius in Italy are all composite cones.

Some features associated with volcanoes lie hidden beneath Earth's surface. These features form when magma near a volcano forces its way between or through older rock. The magma then cools to form intrusive igneous rock. These features are illustrated in Figure 11-25. A **sill** is a sheet of igneous rock that is parallel to and in between layers of older rock. For a sill to form, the magma must have been forced between layers of older rock. This process also forms the dome-shaped laccolith. A **dike** is a sheet of igneous rock that cuts through layers of older rock. The largest intrusive igneous rock feature is the batholith. Batholiths can cover an area tens of thousands of square kilometers across.

Figure 11-24 Mount Redoubt, in Alaska, is a composite volcano that erupted in December 1989.

Figure 11-25 Some igneous rock structures are formed by the intrusion of magma into rocks underground. Is the lava flow an intrusive feature?

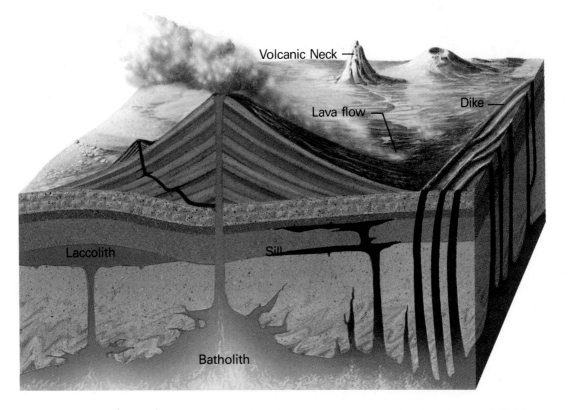

Volcanic Neck

Lava flow

Dike

Laccolith

Sill

Batholith

THE ERUPTION OF MOUNT ST. HELENS

Purpose   To interpret data that shows the shape of Mount St. Helens before and after the 1980 eruption.

Materials

Figures 11-26 and 11-27
metric ruler

Procedure

1. Read all instructions for this activity before you begin your work.

2. Locate the camp in the southwest corner (lower left) of the map in Figure 11-26. Measure and record the shortest distance from the camp to the 1750-m contour line. Continue that line and measure the distance to the 2000- and 2250-m contour lines.

3. Repeat step 2 using the map in Figure 11-27.

4. Observe and record the general shape on the 1750-m contour line on each map.

5. On a separate sheet of paper, draw the approximate shape of the 1750-m contour line of each map. Then draw the approximate shapes of the 2000- and 2250-m contour lines on the drawing started in step 4.

Collecting and Analyzing Data

1. Compare the values in step 2 with the values in step 3.

2. How do the shapes of the 1750-, 2000-, and 2250-m contour lines on the map in Figure 11-26 differ from the same contour lines on the map in Figure 11-27?

3. In which sections of your map drawings are the contour lines the same?

Drawing Conclusions

4. Which side of Mount St. Helens changed the most during the 1980 eruption?

5. How do the maps show that the eruption destroyed a section of the mountain peak?

6. The land directly north of the eruption increased elevation only slightly as a result of the eruption. What must have happened to the lava produced in the eruption?

Figure 11-26 Mount St. Helens, before 1980 eruption

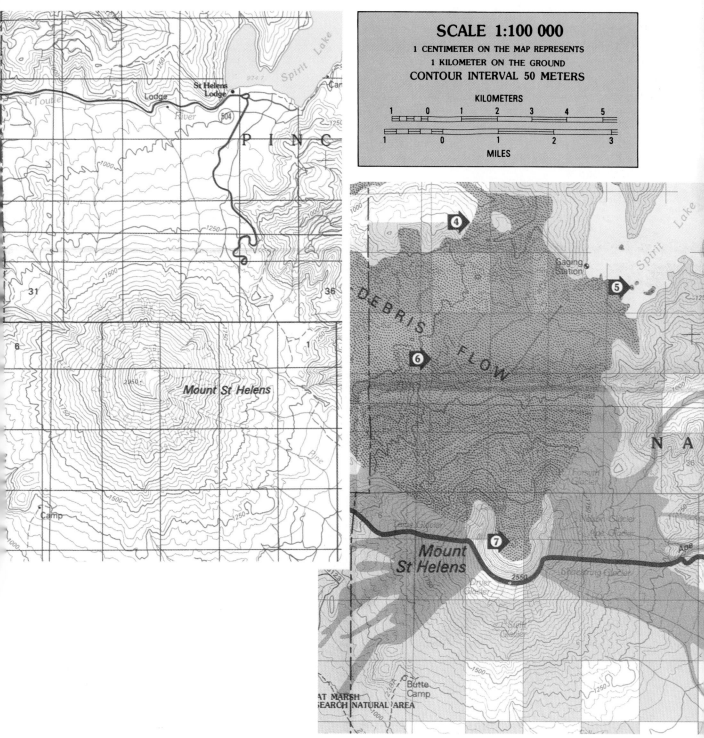

SCALE 1:100 000

1 CENTIMETER ON THE MAP REPRESENTS
1 KILOMETER ON THE GROUND
CONTOUR INTERVAL 50 METERS

KILOMETERS

MILES

Figure 11-27 Mount St. Helens, after 1980 eruption

Figure 11-28 These scientists are measuring lava temperatures at the site of a recent eruption.

Figure 11-29 Methods for predicting eruptions: *Left:* Portable seismographs; *Right:* Watching for changes in elevation within the Mount St. Helens crater

Predicting Eruptions

How do you know if you are in any danger from a volcanic eruption? Let's say you live near a known volcano, such as one of the mountains in the Cascade range. The first thing you might want to do is find out as much as you can about the volcano's history. Much of the history is taken from layers of rock that record the volcano's past eruptions. It is possible to examine layers of rock to determine how often the volcano erupts. These layers may also tell you what kind of eruption to expect, and what areas are usually affected.

The next thing to look for is activity. For example, steam venting from the side of the volcano is a sign that heat could be building up inside the mountain. One of the best signs of activity to look for is the presence of small earthquakes. As magma moves up beneath the volcano, it causes small earthquakes. Seismographs record the locations of the earthquakes and their frequency. An increase in the number and size of earthquakes beneath the volcano may be a sign that magma is approaching Earth's surface.

As the magma gathers beneath the volcano, it sometimes makes the volcano increase in height or bulge out on one side. Changes in elevation are a sign of activity, as is the tilting of the land. Tilting is detected by a tiltmeter. The tiltmeter senses when the land starts to tilt, the same way a tilt device in a pinball machine detects when someone picks the legs off the floor. Modern tiltmeters, such as the ones used on Mount St. Helens, use lasers.

Today the land near Mount St. Helens is turning green again. As you will learn in the next chapter, the processes that change rock to soil work continually to hide the effects of natural destruction.

Lesson Review 11.3

10. Compare the three types of volcanic eruptions and give examples of where each occurs.

11. How does a shield cone differ from a composite cone?

12. Compare and contrast a sill and a dike.

13. Describe the use of a tiltmeter in predicting a volcanic eruption.

Interpret and Apply

14. What role does plate tectonics play in each type of volcanic eruption?

15. Describe how the composition of erupting lava determines whether an eruption is quiet or explosive.

Chapter Summary

Read this summary of the main ideas in this chapter. If any are not clear to you, go back and review that lesson.

11.1 Earthquakes

■ Earthquakes are vibrations of Earth as sections of rock suddenly move along faults.

■ Normal, reverse, and strike-slip faults are produced when sections of rock stretch, collide, or slide along each other.

■ Earthquakes result in primary, secondary, and surface seismic waves.

■ Seismic waves are used to map Earth's interior. This is how geologists know Earth's outer core is liquid.

11.2 Size and Effects of Earthquakes

■ Data points from three different seismograph stations are needed to locate an earthquake's epicenter.

■ The Richter scale describes the size and energy of seismic waves.

■ Most death and injury in an earthquake result from falling objects.

■ Until ways are found to accurately predict earthquakes, the best thing to do is prepare for them.

■ Tsunamis are large ocean waves caused by underwater landslides, earthquakes, or eruptions.

11.3 Volcanoes

■ Volcanic eruptions occur at rifts, hot spots, and subduction boundaries.

■ The composition of magma and the amount of dissolved gases it contains determine how explosive an eruption will be.

■ Sometimes magma hardens to form deposits of intrusive igneous rock beneath Earth's surface.

■ Bulges in Earth's crust or an increase in earthquake activity may signal a volcanic eruption.

Chapter Review

■ Vocabulary

cinder cone
composite cone
dike
earthquake
epicenter
focus
normal fault
primary wave
reverse fault
Richter scale
secondary wave

seismic wave
seismograph
shadow zone
shield cone
sill
strike-slip fault
surface wave
tephra
tsunami
volcano

■ Concept Mapping

Construct a concept map for earthquakes. Include the following terms: *primary waves, secondary waves, surface waves, seismographs,* and *damage.* Use additional terms as you need them.

■ Review

Number your paper from 1–15. Match each term in List **A** with a phrase in List **B**.

List A

a. composite cone
b. earthquake
c. sill
d. radon
e. hot-spot eruption
f. primary wave
g. Richter scale
h. shield cone
i. secondary wave

j. seismograph
k. shadow zone
l. strike-slip fault
m. subduction boundary eruption
n. microquakes
o. tsunami

List B

1. a giant ocean wave sometimes caused by earthquakes and volcanoes

2. seismic waves that move rock and structures from side to side

3. an area on Earth's surface where seismographs do not receive seismic waves

4. a volcanic mountain with layers of both lava and tephra

5. occurs when a stream of magma melts its way up through the solid plate

6. a fault where rocks slide sideways past each other

7. shaking of the ground caused by sudden movements of plate sections

8. a seismic wave that travels through liquid

9. a horizontal mass of igneous rock that is formed beneath Earth's surface

10. an instrument used to detect seismic waves

11. gas released from soil in greater quantity just before an earthquake

12. only has explosive, gas-filled lava

13. a volcanic mountain formed by layers of lava

14. the small earthquakes sometimes recorded before major earthquakes or volcanic eruptions

15. a scale that describes the size and strength of the seismic waves recorded on a seismograph

■ Interpret and Apply

On your paper, answer each question using complete sentences.

16. The land in Yellowstone National Park has risen almost a meter during the last 100 years. What geologic event may happen at Yellowstone Park in the future? Explain your answer.

17. Why do the chances of an earthquake along a fault increase as time passes since the last quake rather than decrease?

18. What will happen to the distance between two opposite walls as primary waves move through the room?

19. You can use a microscope to study a piece of uncooked spaghetti as it is being bent. What might you observe in the area of the bend just before the hard spaghetti snaps? How is this similar to the events leading up to an earthquake?

20. Both rift and subduction boundary eruptions occur at plate boundaries. How do they differ?

21. In the 1960's, the pumping of liquid waste into underground disposal wells in Colorado triggered small earthquakes. How could the movement of oil, water, or magma into a fault zone trigger an earthquake?

22. Seismographs could one day be placed on other planets, just as they have already been placed on the moon. If a planet has no shadow zone, what can be concluded about its interior?

23. How are energy waves produced by lightning similar to the waves produced by earthquakes?

24. In what way does the speed of plate movement over a hot spot change the size of mountains produced during hot spot eruptions?

25. Tell how a volcanic eruption is a part of the rock cycle.

■ *Writing in Science*

26. A student was preparing to write a paragraph explaining the events that lead up to earthquake damage. The student brainstormed the following list of events:

   ■ sudden movement of rocks at focus
   ■ destruction of buildings, etc., at epicenter
   ■ movement of seismic waves out from focus
   ■ buildup of energy from friction

   Arrange these details in correct order. Then use them to write a paragraph.

■ *Critical Thinking*

Seismologists use distance-time graphs like the one shown below to determine the distance to an earthquake epicenter. In the graph, the distance that primary and secondary waves travel is indicated along the horizontal scale. The time needed for each type of wave to travel a certain distance is indicated along the vertical scale. Use the graph to answer the following questions.

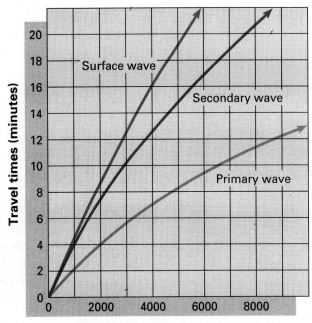

Distance to epicenter (kilometers)

27. How much time is needed for a primary seismic wave to travel a distance of 5000 kilometers?

28. How far does a secondary wave travel in the same amount of time?

29. What will be the difference in arrival times of primary and secondary waves if both waves must travel 5000 kilometers?

30. What happens to the difference in arrival times as the distance traveled increases?

31. How far will the waves have traveled if the time delay between the two wave types is about three minutes?

12 *Weathering and Soil*

Chapter Preview

Have You Ever WONDERED?

Why are some stone monuments hard to read?

Next time you're walking around town, take a look at the writing carved into some buildings, statues, and on stones in cemeteries. You will probably see that some stones have clear, sharp inscriptions. By comparison, other stones have inscriptions that are difficult to read. Compare the kind of rock each monument is made from. Does the kind of rock seem to affect how the inscription looks? If the monuments have dates on them, compare the ages of the monuments to their appearance. Are the older monuments always harder to read than the newer ones?

Rock is not as unchanging as you may think. In Chapters 10 and 11, you learned about forces that build up land and mountains. In this chapter, you will learn about processes that wear down land and mountains. Both time and the kind of rock involved determine the results of these weathering processes.

12.1 Weathering

Did you know that entire mountain ranges like the Appalachians, the Rockies, and the Alps will eventually disappear? It will not be earthquakes or other sudden events that move the mountains. The mountains will crumble because of slow and steady processes going on today that you may not even notice.

You learned in Chapter 9 that granite forms when magma cools deep beneath Earth's surface. A process breaks and wears solid granite into smaller, separate boulders, like the ones in Figure 12-1. Given more time, that same process will break down the boulders too. Eventually, only sand grains and clay will be left. The process of weathering breaks rocks apart when they are exposed to air, moisture, plants, animals, and changes in temperature and pressure. Like granite, most rocks form beneath Earth's surface. But when rocks are raised up to the surface by plate activity, they are exposed to weathering processes. You will study the two main types of weathering, mechanical and chemical.

Mechanical Weathering

How can you change a piece of chalk? If you break the chalk into smaller pieces, each piece has the same chemical composition as the large piece. **Mechanical weathering** breaks down rocks into smaller pieces without changing their chemical composition. You compared physical and chemical changes in Chapter 7. Mechanical weathering is a physical change that takes place in nature. Water, pressure changes, motions, and plants all lead to mechanical weathering.

Lesson Objectives

▸ *Identify* causes of mechanical and chemical weathering.

▸ *Contrast* materials that result from mechanical and chemical weathering.

▸ *Relate* the rate of weathering to environmental conditions.

▸ **Activity** *State a conclusion* about the effect mechanical weathering has on the rate of chemical weathering.

New Terms

mechanical weathering	abrasion
ice wedging	chemical weathering
exfoliation dome	carbonic acid

Figure 12-1 Weathering has reduced the size and changed the shape of these masses of rock.

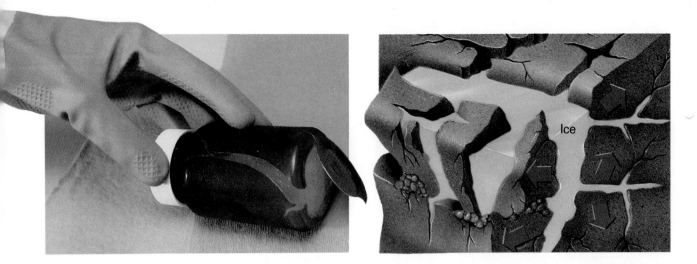

The bottle in Figure 12-2 *(left)* was filled with water and left in a freezer. If you have ever left a soft drink in the freezer too long, you probably got the same results. When water freezes, it expands. Freezing water breaks rocks in a process called **ice wedging.** When solid rock reaches Earth's surface, it develops tiny cracks throughout. Rainwater and melting snow seep into the tiny cracks. As you look at Figure 12-2 *(right)*, think of the rock cracks as containers filled with water. If it gets cold enough, the water in the cracks freezes and expands, making the cracks wider. Later, the ice melts and the water runs out of the cracks or evaporates. When it rains, more water gets into the cracks and freezes, making the cracks larger. As this process repeats, the rock splits along the cracks.

Mechanical weathering also happens when the pressure on a mass of rock changes. Imagine you are sitting on a sponge. Your weight puts enough pressure on the sponge to compress it. How does the sponge change as you stand up? When surface rocks wear away, the pressure decreases on the rocks below, and cracks form. Granite is one example of a rock that weathers due to this process. As the rock over granite is removed, the granite expands, just as the sponge expands when you stand up. Thin, curved sheets of granite break off at the surface. The rock mass left behind is a rounded shape called an **exfoliation dome.** Figure 12-3 shows an exfoliation dome in Yosemite National Park in California. Exfoliation domes occur in many other places, for example, Stone Mountain, Georgia.

Have you ever chipped a rock by throwing another rock at it? This is an example of **abrasion,** which occurs when rocks hit or grind against each other. In nature, abrasion is common where wind, running water, and moving ice carry small bits of rock and sand. As the rocks move along, they hit against each other and break off pieces.

Figure 12-2 As water freezes, it expands. *Left:* The force of freezing water broke this bottle. *Right:* In nature, water enters cracks in rocks and then freezes, widening the cracks.

Figure 12-3 As rock pieces flake off at the surface, a rounded hill remains. What is this kind of hill called?

Figure 12-4 What will happen to the rocks and pavement as the trees and grass continue to grow?

Plants and animals also cause weathering. As roots grow in rock cracks, the roots wedge the rock apart. Plants of all sizes, from small mosses to large trees, cause mechanical weathering in this way. You have probably seen grass grow in cracks in the pavement, as shown in Figure 12-4 (right). Burrowing animals, such as insects, earthworms, and gophers, dig holes and tunnels that allow air and water to pass through the soil to the bedrock below. When air and water reach the bedrock, weathering begins, even though the rock is not yet on the surface.

Each of these mechanical weathering processes—ice wedging, pressure release, abrasion, and plants and animals—has the same effect on the rock. The rock breaks into smaller pieces but keeps its same chemical composition.

Chemical Weathering

Figure 12-5 shows a piece of chalk placed in vinegar. Notice how the chalk slowly crumbles away as bubbles come off. When you simply break chalk, you end up with smaller pieces of chalk. With vinegar, however, the atoms that make up chalk combine with atoms in the vinegar to form new chemical substances. The equation below describes the chemical changes as pure chalk and vinegar react.

$$CaCO_3 + 2HC_2H_3O_2 \longrightarrow Ca(C_2H_3O_2)_2 + CO_2 + H_2O$$

chalk + vinegar $\longrightarrow$ calcium + carbon + water
acetate   dioxide

In **chemical weathering,** the minerals in a rock change into new minerals. Often the new minerals are weaker than the original minerals, and the rock crumbles. Most chemical weathering is caused by water. Sometimes water alone works on the rock. Other times, water combines with oxygen or carbon dioxide from the air to weather the rock. The rock granite contains the mineral feldspar. When water comes into contact with feldspar, water and feldspar combine to

Figure 12-5 The chalk is being dissolved, or chemically weathered, by the acid.

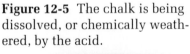

form clay minerals. Clay minerals, which are soft and have tiny grains, crumble apart and fall out of the granite. Figure 12-6 shows feldspar and a clay mineral that formed from feldspar. Compare the two minerals. What properties tell you that the clay mineral is not the same as feldspar?

Have you ever seen a rusty nail? Rust forms from chemical weathering as iron in the nail combines with oxygen and water. The mineral hematite forms when minerals with iron, such as pyrite and magnetite, combine with oxygen. Hematite commonly has a reddish color. Notice the color of the rock layers in Figure 12-7. The red color shows that iron minerals in the rocks have combined with oxygen to form hematite. The reddish-brown mineral limonite forms when both water and oxygen combine with iron minerals. Hematite and limonite crumble more easily than the minerals from which they form.

Acids in water and from growing plants also cause chemical weathering of minerals. In nature, water combines with carbon dioxide and forms a solution of **carbonic acid.**

$$H_2O + CO_2 \longrightarrow H_2CO_3$$
$$\text{water} + \text{carbon} \longrightarrow \text{carbonic acid}$$
$$\text{dioxide}$$

The carbonated water in soft drinks is carbonic acid. In nature, carbon dioxide enters water from the air and from decaying plants in the soil. Water that contains carbonic acid seeps into cracks in bedrock and weathers the rock. Carbonic acid partially dissolves some minerals, such as feldspar and mica. Carbonic acid forms clays with the undissolved parts of those minerals. Carbonic acid completely dissolves the mineral calcite. When cracks in limestone or other calcite-containing rocks fill with carbonic acid, hollow caves in the rock layers result.

Figure 12-6 Often, chemical weathering changes one mineral into another. *Top:* Feldspar; *Bottom:* Kaolinite, which forms from the chemical weathering of feldspar

Figure 12-7 The rock layers contain iron. What has caused the rocks to turn red?

Figure 12-8 Lichens release acids that dissolve minerals from rock. Lichens and other plants, such as mosses, use the dissolved minerals as they grow.

Plants and acid rain also contribute acid that weathers minerals. Figure 12-8 shows lichens [lī′ kənz] growing on a rock. Lichens release acids that slowly dissolve some minerals, breaking the rock into smaller pieces. Acid rain occurs when raindrops combine with pollutants from cars, factories, and power plants.

Usually, both mechanical and chemical weathering happen at the same time. For example, a plant root growing in a rock crack both wedges the rock apart and dissolves minerals in the rock. Water in a rock crack both splits the rock apart as it freezes, and reacts with the rock's minerals.

Rate of Weathering

It may take more than 1000 years to weather away 1 centimeter of a limestone layer. Yet limestone weathers more quickly than many other kinds of rock. The rate at which a rock weathers depends on three main conditions: the climate, the minerals in the rock, and the amount of rock exposed.

Climate is an area's average weather conditions over a long period of time. Chemical weathering happens most quickly in moist climates with warm temperatures year-round. Warm temperatures speed up the rate at which water and acid combine with minerals. In fact, most chemical weathering takes place in warmer climates. Mechanical weathering happens most quickly in moist climates where the temperature falls below freezing part of the year. Can you explain why these conditions speed up mechanical weathering?

The minerals that make up a rock also affect the rate at which the rock weathers. If you put salt and sand in water, the salt dissolves fairly quickly, while the sand hardly dissolves at all. Likewise, some minerals weather more quickly

Fact or Fiction?

Do all liquids expand as they freeze? No, they do not. Water is unique in that it contracts as it first cools, but expands just before it freezes. Beverages like juice and milk are mostly water and also expand as they freeze. Other liquids, like mercury and alcohol, continue to contract as they cool to their freezing points. You might know mercury and alcohol as the liquids used in thermometers. Why isn't water used in thermometers?

than others. For example, carbonic acid dissolves calcite much more quickly than it dissolves feldspar. Carbonic acid hardly affects the mineral quartz. As a result, granite, which contains feldspar and quartz, weathers slowly compared to limestone, which is made of calcite.

Mechanical weathering helps speed up chemical weathering by changing the rock surface and shape. For example, if you place a piece of chalk into vinegar, the vinegar starts dissolving the sides and ends of the chalk. If you then break the chalk into four pieces, there are more surfaces for the vinegar to attack. Likewise, if mechanical weathering breaks a rock into smaller pieces, chemical weathering has more surfaces to work on. Mechanical weathering often produces sharp-edged rock pieces. Chemical weathering attacks sharp edges more quickly than smooth surfaces. As the corners and sharp edges wear down, rounded boulders develop.

Time also affects how much a rock weathers. Weathering begins as soon as air, moisture, temperature changes, and pressure changes affect the rock. The longer the rock is exposed to weathering—that is, the longer the rock is at or near the surface—the more weathering that takes place. Which will probably be more weathered, granite that has been exposed for 1000 years or granite that has been exposed for 10 000 years, if they are in the same climate?

As weathering destroys rocks, it helps create one of Earth's most important resources—soil. In the next two lessons, you will learn about this precious resource, how it forms, and how to protect it.

Figure 12-9 How many surfaces does the unbroken rock have? How many surfaces does the rock have after it has broken into four pieces?

Lesson Review 12.1

1. Describe one example each of water causing mechanical weathering and water causing chemical weathering.

2. Describe the differences between materials left behind after mechanical weathering and those left behind after chemical weathering.

3. List and explain some conditions that cause weathering to happen more quickly.

Interpret and Apply

4. Would you expect weathering to occur quickly or slowly where you live? Which type of weathering probably happens more quickly? Support your answer with information about climate and rock type in your part of the country.

RATE OF WEATHERING

Purpose   To state a conclusion about the effect of mechanical weathering on the rate of chemical weathering.

Materials

2 250-mL beakers	vinegar
clock or watch	lab apron
mortar and pestle	safety goggles
2 Alka Seltzer tablets	plain paper
2 2-cm pieces of chalk	graph paper
water	

Procedure

1. Read all directions for this activity before you begin. Copy the data table. Put on your safety goggles and lab apron.

2. Pour 200 mL of water into each beaker.

3. Carefully crush one of the seltzer tablets, using the mortar and pestle. Empty the mortar onto a piece of plain paper.

4. At the same time, drop the uncrushed seltzer tablet into one beaker of water and pour the crushed tablet in the other beaker. Observe and record the time in seconds (s) needed for each tablet to dissolve.

5. Empty, clean, and dry the two beakers. Then pour 20 mL of vinegar into each beaker. **CAUTION: Keep vinegar off your skin and out of your eyes. Wash spills and splashes immediately.**

6. Crush one piece of chalk with the mortar and pestle. Empty the mortar onto a piece of plain paper.

7. At the same time, drop the uncrushed chalk into one beaker of vinegar and the crushed chalk into the other beaker. Observe and record the time to dissolve.

8. Before leaving the lab area, clean up all materials and wash your hands.

Collecting and Analyzing Data

Data Table		
	Dissolving Time (s)	
Substance	**Uncrushed**	**Crushed**
Seltzer Tablet		
Chalk		

1. Make a bar graph comparing the time it took each item to dissolve.

2. Which kind of weathering did you demonstrate when you crushed the samples? When you dissolved them?

3. Which dissolved more quickly, the uncrushed materials or the crushed materials?

Drawing Conclusions

4. How did crushing the seltzer tablet and chalk affect the number of surfaces exposed to chemical weathering?

5. How does mechanical weathering help speed up chemical weathering?

12.2 Soil Resources

Have you ever thought of dirt as being important for your survival? Many people use the term *dirt* when they really mean *soil*. Soil may be the most important product of weathering. Fruits, vegetables, and grains come from plants that grow in soil. Most meat comes from animals who feed on plants that grow in soil. Without soil, you would have little to eat.

Soil is a mixture of weathered rock and humus. **Humus** [hyü′ məs] is a dark-colored substance made of small bits of decaying plants and animals. Soil forms as rock weathers and as plants grow and decay. Because weathering is a slow process, soil takes thousands of years to form.

The rock that weathers to form soil is called the soil's parent material. Mechanical and chemical weathering break the parent material down into sand- and silt-sized particles and into clay minerals. Soils are classified into two groups, depending on the source of their parent material. In some places, bedrock is the parent material and **residual soils** develop. In other places, wind, moving water, or ice has carried in soil or parent material from somewhere else. A **transported soil** either came into an area from somewhere else, or it formed from parent material that came from somewhere else. The northeastern and midwestern United States have transported soils. About 10 000 years ago, glaciers and wind carried the parent materials for these soils from Canada to the United States.

Lesson Objectives

▶ **Contrast** the parent materials of residual and transported soils.

▶ **Compare** soil materials in the A, B, and C horizons.

▶ **Relate** characteristics of various soil types to the area in which the soil forms.

▶ **Activity** *Observe and describe* materials in different soil samples.

New Terms

humus	topsoil
residual soil	leaching
transported soil	subsoil

Figure 12-10 Most of the food you eat comes from the soil.

Soil Profiles

If you dig a hole, you will notice that the soil below is different from the soil on the surface. In Figure 12-11 *(left)*, notice the soil layers in the hole. Each of these layers is called a soil horizon. Soils that have had a chance to develop fully usually have three horizons. From top to bottom, they are called the A, B, and C horizons. Below the C horizon is unweathered parent material. All the horizons together make up the soil profile.

The A horizon is made up of **topsoil,** which contains more humus than the other horizons. The weathered rock material in topsoil is mostly sand and silt particles. Water seeping through the A horizon carries most of the clay down to the B horizon. Water also carries down dissolved minerals in a process called **leaching.**

The mixture of humus, sand, and silt makes topsoil fertile—good for growing plants—and helps it absorb water. The most productive farms are in areas with thick topsoil. As you will see later, wind and moving water often remove valuable topsoil.

As you dig deeper, you come to sticky soil that is packed harder than the topsoil above. This is the B horizon, and you are digging in subsoil. **Subsoil** contains the minerals and sticky clay that were washed down from the A horizon. Figure 12-11 *(right)* shows a close-up comparison of topsoil and subsoil. The B horizon has a lighter color than the A horizon, because subsoil contains little humus. Because subsoil lacks humus and sand, it is infertile and easily waterlogged. What do you think would happen to crop growth on a farm that had only subsoil left?

Below the subsoil of the B horizon is the C horizon. If you dig this deep, you will find partly weathered parent material lying on top of the bedrock or transported material.

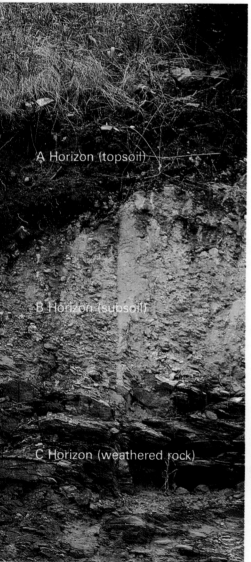

Figure 12-11 *Left:* Mature soil profiles have three horizons. *Right:* The dark color of topsoil is due to humus. What materials make up subsoil?

A Horizon (topsoil)

B Horizon (subsoil)

C Horizon (weathered rock)

A C T I V I T Y 1 2 . 2 General Supplies

OBSERVING SOIL

Purpose To observe and describe materials in soil samples.

Materials

2 or more different samples of soil
hand lens or microscope
plain white paper
lab apron

Procedure

1. Read all instructions for this activity before you begin your work.

2. On your paper, draw a data table like the one shown. Then put on your lab apron.

3. Sprinkle a small part of one sample onto a white sheet of paper. In your data table, describe the color of the sample.

4. Examine the particles of the sample with a hand lens or low-power microscope.

5. Draw a diagram of the particles you see in the soil sample.

6. Pinch the soil sample to see if the particles tend to stick together or if they stay loose.

7. Squeeze the sample in your hand. Describe any changes in the soil.

8. Return or discard the soil sample as directed by your teacher.

9. Repeat steps 3–8 for each soil sample.

10. Before leaving the lab area, clean up all materials and wash your hands thoroughly. IMPORTANT: Do not put any soil in the sink.

Collecting and Analyzing Data

Data Table			
Sample Number	1	2	3
Color			
Diagram			
Other Observations			

1. Are all the soil samples the same color?

2. Did you recognize any organic material in the soil when you used the hand lens? If so, what was it?

3. When you squeezed the soil samples, did they stick togther or fall apart?

Drawing Conclusions

4. Why do you think one of the soil samples was darker than the others?

5. Would one of the samples absorb water better than the others? Why?

6. Which soil sample do you think would be best for growing plants? Which of your observations helped you decide?

Soil Types

Soil profiles and composition differ around the world. The soil that exists where you live depends mainly on time and climate. Residual soils demonstrate how time affects soil profiles. The longer weathering has gone on, the thicker a residual soil profile becomes. Recall that the B horizon forms as clays and other minerals leach down from the A horizon. In areas where soil has been developing for many thousands of years, the B horizon is thick. If the topsoil is only a few thousand years old, then the B horizon is thin or absent.

Transported soils may develop in a different way. Remember that glaciers dropped sediments over parts of the United States several thousand years ago. Some of these deposits were soil that had formed elsewhere. The thick topsoil of today's Midwest first developed somewhere else, then was moved in by glaciers and wind.

ENVIRONMENTAL AWARENESS

Reducing Soil Pollution

When you hear the word *pollution*, do you think first of dirty air and water? Did you know that soil pollution is also a concern? Every year, United States farmers and gardeners use more than 10 billion kilograms of fertilizers and almost 400 million kilograms of pesticides. These chemicals increase crop production, but they also build up in the soil, and may enter underground water supplies. Studies have shown a link between some herbicides and higher rates of cancer.

Fortunately, some methods of fertilizing and protecting crops are less dangerous. You are probably familiar with ladybugs and praying mantises, which feed on common garden pests. Diatomaceous earth, a natural dust, contains microscopic particles that cut up the skin of slugs and root maggots. Ask about these and other alternatives when you go to the garden supply store. ■

Climate has an important effect on soil type because climate controls chemical weathering. A tropical rain forest, like the one in Figure 12-12 *(left)*, produces a lot of humus as the plants die and decay. You may think that the topsoil must be very fertile, but it is not. The heavy rainfall washes away most of the humus and minerals. Normally, decaying plants replace the lost topsoil. Today many acres of rain forest are being cleared for farming. For a year or two, the soil produces good crops. But without the forest to replace the humus, crops quickly use up soil nutrients. When crops no longer grow, farmers clear another area of forest. Soil in the areas left behind is infertile and unprotected.

In some climates, including many parts of the United States, temperatures change with the yearly seasons. Less rain falls than in tropical areas, and chemical weathering occurs more slowly. The soil profile is thinner than in tropical areas, but the topsoil is usually fertile. With less rainfall, the humus and minerals stay in place. Soils that develop in these areas usually make good farmland.

In dry climates, such as the southwestern United States, chemical weathering is slow and soil profiles are thin. Because of the lack of rainfall, few minerals leach from the A horizon. When farmers water dry-climate soils, as shown in Figure 12-13, the soils produce crops well. However, after several years, dissolved minerals in the water may build up in the topsoil and harm crops.

Soil profiles are also thin in areas at high latitudes and at high elevations. In these areas, the ground is frozen during most of the year. Little chemical weathering occurs and soil develops slowly. Often, the surface is bare rock without soil.

Figure 12-12 *Left:* Tropical rain forest plant growth suggests that the soil is fertile. *Right:* In reality, rain forest soil is not very fertile.

Figure 12-13 Irrigation helps farmers take advantage of the fertility of desert soils.

Figure 12-14 Fertilizing, shown here, and crop rotation both help preserve soil fertility.

Preserving Soil Fertility

You and everyone you know depend on soil for food and many other products. Thus, it is important to keep soil fertile and intact. Growing plants remove minerals and nutrients from the soil. When farmers harvest crops, they remove soil nutrients along with the plants. Farmers replace soil nutrients through fertilizing and crop rotation. Fertilizers are substances added to the soil to replace nutrients and make the soil more productive. Figure 12-14 shows a field being fertilized.

In crop rotation, farmers alternate the kind of crop grown in a field each year. Crop rotation works because different kinds of plants use up and replace different minerals and nutrients in the soil. For example, corn takes nitrogen from the soil. If you plant corn every year, then the soil becomes infertile. Alfalfa returns nitrogen to the soil. By planting a field in corn some years and in alfalfa other years, farmers balance the amount of nitrogen in the soil.

Loss of nutrients is not the only danger to soil. Without proper protection, soil may wash away in rain or blow away in the wind. Soil loss can have devastating effects on food supplies and on farmers' lives. In Lesson 12.3, you will find out ways that people protect soil from these dangers.

Lesson Review 12.2

5. Describe the main difference between the parent materials of residual and transported soils. Give an example of a residual soil and of a transported soil.

6. Sketch a soil profile. Label and describe the properties of each soil horizon.

7. Name three conditions that affect soil formation. Explain why soils form more quickly in warm, moist climates.

8. Why is it important to protect soil fertility? Name two ways to preserve soil fertility.

Interpret and Apply

9. Temperatures in the eastern and midwestern United States are similar, but the eastern section gets more rainfall. Which area would you expect to have the thickest soil profile? Explain your answer.

10. Comparing the same two parts of the country as in question 9, what other factors could affect the thickness of the soil profile?

12.3 Mass Movements and Soil Conservation

So far, you have learned how weathering breaks solid bedrock into smaller pieces and leaves them on the surface. In a process called **mass movement,** gravity pulls loose, weathered materials downhill. In Figure 12-15, gravity pulled weathered rock pieces to the bottom of the cliff. Mass movement forms piles of rock or soil at the bottom of slopes.

All mass movements result from gravity. Many mass movements happen when heavy rains or melting snow make rocks and soil slippery. Some mass movements, such as landslides, are rapid and dramatic. Other mass movements, such as creep, are slow and hard to notice.

Rapid Movements

The term landslide describes any rapid downhill movement of rocks, soil, or other weathered material. Landslides are most common in places with steep slopes, such as mountains. Loose materials on steep slopes are unstable, which means it does not take much to knock them off the slope. Often, landslides are set off by earthquakes or heavy rains. The sudden shock of an earthquake knocks unstable rocks and soil off a slope and sends them rapidly downhill as a landslide. Heavy rains make rocks and slopes slippery, just as rain makes roads and sidewalks slippery for walking. As the soil soaks in the rain, it becomes heavier. At some point, the soil becomes too heavy and slippery for friction to hold it in place, and a landslide occurs.

Lesson Objectives

▶ **Describe** the causes of mass movement.

▶ **Compare** conditions for rapid movement with conditions for slow movement.

▶ **List and describe** methods of protecting the soil.

▶ **Activity** *Identify and control variables* that affect mass movement.

New Terms

mass movement	slump
mudflow	soil creep

Figure 12-15 Gravity pulled these boulders downhill in a process called mass movement. What processes could have broken the boulders off the rock mass?

Figure 12-16 How is the movement of soil different in these two kinds of mass wasting? *Left:* A mudflow; *Right:* A slump

Mudflows usually happen on hillsides that do not have enough plants to hold the soil. Heavy rain soaks into the bare soil and forms slippery mud. If the mud gets wet enough, it flows quickly downhill like a liquid and picks up more soil along the way. Mudflows are fast, powerful, and dangerous. Figure 12-16 *(left)* shows the results of a mudflow.

In a **slump,** large chunks of rock or soil break off the side of a slope and slide downhill. Figure 12-16 *(right)* shows a chunk of soil that has slumped. Often, slumps occur in places where a strong, weather-resistant layer lies over weaker materials. As the less resistant materials weather, cracks form in the slope. The whole block of rock and the materials beneath slide downhill.

Slow Movements

Not all mass movements happen quickly. Earthflow is a slow downhill movement of mud. Like a mudflow, an earthflow often occurs after heavy rain. Unlike the soils in a mudflow, the soils affected by earthflows have plants growing in them. The plants slow the movement of the mud. Instead of rapidly sliding down the slope, earthflows gradually slip downhill.

The slowest type of mass movement, **soil creep,** occurs on steep, soil-covered hillsides. Freezing and thawing, animals, and water loosen soil particles. As the particles loosen, gravity pulls them slowly downhill. Soil creep is so slow that you do not actually notice any movement. You can tell if soil creep has happened by the effects it has. After several years, soil creep makes fenceposts, poles, and other objects lean downhill. The tree trunk in Figure 12-17 shows an effect of soil creep. Can you explain how soil creep caused the tree trunk to have this unusual shape?

Figure 12-17 Soil creep is a slow process. Its effects show where it takes place.

ACTIVITY 12.3   General Supplies

OBSERVING MASS MOVEMENT

Purpose To identify and control some of the variables that affect mass movement.

Materials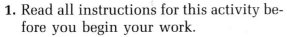

dry soil   ice-cream stick
water   lab apron
shallow pan   safety goggles
meterstick

Procedure

1. Read all instructions for this activity before you begin your work.

2. On your paper, make a data table like the one shown. Put on your lab apron and safety goggles.

3. Cover the bottom of the pan with a thin layer of soil.

4. Raise one end of the pan 2 cm at a time until the soil just begins to slip downslope.

5. Record the height of the end of the pan at the moment the soil begins to move down the pan.

6. Spread the soil over the bottom of the pan again.

7. Repeat steps 4–6 three more times.

8. Add just enough water to turn the soil to mud. Stir the mixture with the ice-cream stick to make sure all of the soil is wet.

9. Repeat steps 4–7, using the mud in the pan.

10. Before leaving the lab area, clean up all materials as directed by your teacher and wash your hands. IMPORTANT: Do not put any soil in the sink.

Collecting and Analyzing Data

Data Table					
Material	Height for Each Trial (cm)				
	1	2	3	4	Average
Dry soil					
Mud					

1. Calculate the average height that the material began moving for dry soil and for mud. Record the average in your data table.

2. Did the dry soil begin moving at the same pan height in each trial?

3. Did the mud begin moving at the same height in each trial?

4. Why is it important to test each sample more than one time?

5. Which material moves downslope more quickly, soil or mud?

Drawing Conclusions

6. How does the variable water affect the movement of the soil?

7. Why do you think the water affects the movement of the soil?

Figure 12-18 *Left:* Contour plowing helps hold soil in place; *Right:* Terracing makes it possible to farm steep slopes.

Preventing Soil Loss

Whenever you see dust in the wind or a muddy stream, you are seeing lost soil. Wind and rain move tons of topsoil each year. During the Dust Bowl of the 1930's, windstorms carried away more than 300 million (300 000 000) metric tons of soil. Because of the Dust Bowl, hundreds of people went bankrupt and had to find new jobs. Natural events and poor farming practices both caused the Dust Bowl disaster. Ever since the Dust Bowl, the Soil Conservation Service has taught good soil conservation practices to farmers.

Planting windbreaks is a good way to help prevent soil loss. Wherever wind blows along large, flat, smooth surfaces, it can pick up large amounts of soil. Planting trees or hedges around a field forms a windbreak that slows down the wind.

Any time it rains, water running over the surface washes soil into streams and rivers. Running water removes soil most easily from hills, where gravity helps. Several methods slow down water and reduce soil loss. In contour plowing, farmers plow along the contour lines of a hill, rather than straight up and down. Figure 12-18 *(left)* shows the results of contour plowing on a hill. The rows that follow the contours act as small ridges and slow down the water flow. Terracing is another method that slows soil loss. As you can see in Figure 12-18 *(right),* terracing is building level places into a hillside.

In strip crop farming, rows of corn alternate with a grassy crop, such as alfalfa. Corn does not hold soil well by itself because there are so many spaces between corn rows. In strip crop farming, the strips planted with a grassy crop help slow water movement and hold soil.

No-till farming is a fairly new soil conservation practice. In no-till farming, farmers leave stalks on the surface when they plant new crops. The stalks shown in Figure 12-19 hold the soil in place during windstorms and rainstorms. No-till

Figure 12-19 The remains of last year's crop, when left on the soil, help prevent soil loss.

farming also requires smaller machinery that goes over the soil just once. The less compressed soil absorbs rain, instead of being washed away by it.

The Dust Bowl may seem unimportant today, more than half a century later. However, droughts in the late 1980's threatened to cause another Dust Bowl anywhere that soil conservation practices were ignored. It is tempting to think that past disasters can never happen again. But the only way to help prevent such disasters is to plan ahead.

Lesson Review 12.3

11. Name the force that causes all mass movements.

12. Construct a table comparing landslides, mudflows, slumps, earthflows, and soil creep. Include the headings *Speed, Slope Steepness, Moisture, Other Conditions.*

13. Describe three methods of preventing soil loss. Why is it important to follow these methods?

Interpret and Apply

14. Which types of mass movement could occur where you live? List reasons for your answer.

Chapter Summary

Read this chapter summary. If any ideas are not clear, review that lesson.

12.1 Weathering

■ Mechanical weathering breaks rock down into smaller pieces that have the same mineral makeup.

■ Chemical weathering forms new minerals as it breaks the rock into smaller pieces.

■ The rate of weathering depends on climate, rock type, and surface area.

12.2 Soil Resources

■ Residual soils form from the local bedrock. Transported soils either form in one place and are carried to another, or form from transported parent material.

■ Mature soil profiles have three horizons. The A horizon contains topsoil. The B horizon contains subsoil. The C horizon is partly weathered parent material.

■ Climate and time are two important factors in the development of different types of soil.

12.3 Mass Movements and Soil Conservation

■ A mass movement occurs when gravity pulls weathered material downhill.

■ Landslides and mudflows are rapid mass movements. Earthflows and soil creep are slower mass movements.

■ Contour plowing, no-till farming, and windbreaks help reduce soil loss.

Chapter Review

■ Vocabulary

abrasion

carbonic acid

chemical weathering

exfoliation dome

humus

ice wedging

leaching

mass movement

mechanical
   weathering

mudflow

residual soil

slump

soil creep

subsoil

topsoil

transported soil

■ Concept Mapping

Using the method of concept mapping shown on pages 3–5, construct a concept map for *weathering*. Include these terms: *mechanical weathering, chemical weathering, water, ice wedging, abrasion, exfoliation, carbonic acid.* Use other terms as you need them.

■ Review

Match each term in List **A** with the most appropriate phrase in List **B.**

List A

a. soil

b. landslide

c. soil horizon

d. leaching

e. parent material

f. topsoil

g. residual soil

h. weathering

i. crop rotation

j. subsoil

k. humus

l. mass movement

m. transported soil

n. chemical weathering

o. ice wedging

p. soil creep

q. carbonic acid

r. abrasion

s. strip crop farming

t. no-till farming

List B

1. process that breaks bedrock down into smaller pieces

2. carbon dioxide dissolved in water

3. rock from which soil forms

4. process that changes minerals into new minerals while breaking down a rock

5. decaying plant and animal material in soil

6. large mass of weathered material rapidly slipping downhill

7. dissolved minerals being carried down to the B horizon

8. any movement of weathered material, fast or slow, caused by the pull of gravity

9. very slow downhill movement of soil

10. soil that has formed from the bedrock directly beneath it

11. soil in the A horizon

12. soil that formed in one location and was carried to a new location

13. one of the layers in a soil profile

14. caused by water expanding as it freezes

15. a combination of weathered rock particles and humus

16. planting different kinds of crops in a field in alternate years

17. row crops alternated with grassy crops in the same field at the same time

18. leaving the remains of last year's crop on top of the soil

19. soil of the B horizon

20. bits of rock that are carried by the wind or moving water wearing down other rocks

■ Interpret and Apply

On your paper, answer each question.

21. At the end of a cold and wet winter, it is common for parts of streets and highways to be crumbled. Describe how this could happen. Tell which kind of weathering might be responsible.

22. Tell whether each of the following is similar to mechanical or chemical weathering.
    a. An old car gets rusty.
    b. A tree is cut for lumber.
    c. A tree dies and decays.
    d. A window shatters when a baseball hits it.

23. Explain how it might be possible for the following soil profiles to develop.
    a. A horizon directly on top of bedrock
    b. A and C horizons, but no B horizon
    c. B and C horizons, but no A horizon

24. What could you look for in a C horizon that would tell you whether a soil was residual or transported?

25. What differences in grain size would you expect to find between the A, B, and C horizons in a soil profile?

26. The photograph below shows layers of rock exposed in a canyon. Which layer weathers the slowest? How can you tell? Why would some rock layers in the canyon weather faster than others?

■ Writing in Science

27. Mountain soils are usually thin. Write a paragraph explaining why this is the case. Before you write, you will need to identify the processes that affect the amount of soil found on mountains. Then decide how each process affects the situation.

■ Critical Thinking

The photos below show Cleopatra's Needle, a stone monument that stood in Egypt for 3400 years before it was moved to New York City about 100 years ago. The first photograph shows how the monument looked about the time it was moved from Egypt. The second photo shows how the monument looks now.

28. While the monument was in Egypt, do you think it had weathered much from when it was first carved? How can you tell?

29. Compare the photos. How did the monument change in 100 years?

30. From the evidence in the photographs, compare the rates of weathering in Egypt and in New York City.

31. What is the main factor causing the difference in weathering rates of the two locations?

32. What type of mechanical weathering occurs in New York that does not occur in Egypt?

33. Explain the difference in the chemical weathering of the monument while it was in Egypt and since it has been in New York.

34. Besides moving Cleopatra's Needle, what effect does human activity have on the weathering of the monument?

13 Erosion and Deposition

Chapter Preview

Have You Ever
WONDERED?

What happens to the water after a rainfall?

Think about the last heavy rain you watched. Water ran all over the roads, the ground was wet, and puddles covered low-lying areas. What happened to the water after the rain ended? The process of evaporation provides part of the answer. However, when it rains, a lot of the rainwater never gets the chance to evaporate. Some of the water flows downhill over the surface, eventually joining a stream. The remaining water seeps into the ground. As the water moves over the surface or underground, it carries away weathered rock. Later, the water leaves the weathered material in a new place. For example, water moving underground formed the beautiful limestone cavern shown at left. In this chapter, you will learn more about how water, wind, and ice affect Earth's crust.

13.1 *The Action of Groundwater*

Lesson Objectives

▶ **Contrast** the processes of erosion and deposition.

▶ **Relate** the passage of groundwater to the properties of earth materials.

▶ **Describe** the results of erosion and deposition by groundwater.

▶ **Activity** *Form and test a hypothesis* that compares porous materials with different grain sizes.

New Terms

erosion   porous
deposition   permeable
groundwater

By now, you have a good understanding of how earth materials affect each other. Based on your understanding, what do you think is happening to the area shown in Figure 13-1? Form your hypothesis before you read further.

Defining Erosion and Deposition

In Chapter 12, you learned how weathering by water, wind, and other agents breaks down solid rock into smaller pieces. By now you also know that breaking down rock is only part of the process. **Erosion** is the process in which water, wind, and other agents carry away sediments. While weathering breaks down materials on Earth's surface, erosion moves those materials from one place to another. The soil in Figure 13-1 has been eroded by running water. Was your hypothesis about Figure 13-1 correct? What evidence in the photo led you to your hypothesis?

Although the land in Figure 13-1 has lost soil, the soil has not disappeared. Eventually, the running water drops the soil in a new place. **Deposition** is the process in which water, wind, or ice drops sediments in a new location. Erosion removes sediments and wears down surface features. Deposition drops sediments and builds up surface features.

The effects of erosion may be as small as wind carrying dust across a ball field or as large as the slow carving of a deep canyon. The effects of deposition may be as small as dirt washed onto your sidewalk or as large as a sandy beach. As you study this chapter, watch for examples of erosion and deposition where you live.

Figure 13-1 What Earth process could have formed these gullies?

Figure 13-2 A porous material has room for water between its grains. *Left:* Water fills the spaces between the marbles. *Right:* Many soils are porous.

Groundwater

In Figure 13-1, you saw an example of the effects of water eroding Earth's surface. Water also weathers, erodes, and deposits materials below Earth's surface. Remember the rainwater seeping into the ground at the beginning of the chapter? Water that has seeped below Earth's surface is called **groundwater.** You are used to thinking of water as it occurs on Earth's surface, in streams and ponds. However, there are few underground streams, even though Earth has much more groundwater than surface water.

To understand how water exists underground, look at the container of marbles in Figure 13-2 *(left).* The marbles fill the container, but there is space for water between the marbles. A **porous** material has spaces, or pores, between its grains. Most weathered materials, such as sand and soil, are porous. Pores and cracks in earth materials store most of Earth's groundwater.

For water to actually seep into porous materials, the pores must be connected. Any material that water can seep into is a **permeable** material. The marbles and the soil in Figure 13-2 are permeable. However, when water seeps into fine-grained sediments, such as clay and silt, the water clogs up the pores. Therefore, wet clay is not permeable, even though it is porous.

The terms *porous* and *permeable* describe rocks as well as soil. Sandstone is an example of a porous, permeable rock. Sandstone often contains liquid resources such as crude oil or groundwater. (You will learn more about these resources in Chapters 16 and 21.) Other rocks, such as granite and most limestone, are not porous. However, if bedrock that is not porous has cracks, then water seeps in through the cracks. If limestone bedrock has cracks running through it, is the limestone permeable?

Figure 13-3 Even though this granite is not porous, cracks make it permeable.

ACTIVITY 13.1   *Lab Equipment*

MEASURING PORE SPACE

Purpose To test a hypothesis that compares porous materials with different grain sizes.

Materials

3 250-mL beakers
100-mL graduated cylinder
3 sizes of beads or marbles,
  sorted by size
water
lab apron

Procedure

1. Read all directions before you begin. Copy the data table onto your paper.

2. Form a hypothesis by answering the following question. Which has more pore space: a material with large grains or a material with small grains?

3. Put on your lab apron. Fill each beaker to the 200-mL mark with different size beads or marbles. In your data table, record the volume of beads or marbles in each beaker. The beads or marbles represent sediment grains.

4. Pour exactly 100 mL water into the graduated cylinder.

5. Carefully pour water from the graduated cylinder into the beaker with the smallest size grain. Stop pouring when the water just covers the grains.

6. Observe and record the volume of water left in the cylinder. Subtract your measurement from 100 mL to find out how much water it took to fill the pores. Record this value as volume of pores.

7. Repeat steps 4–6 for the other grain sizes in the other beakers.

8. Before leaving the lab area, clean up all materials and wash your hands.

Collecting and Analyzing Data

Data Table			
Grain Size	Volume of Grains (mL)	Volume of Pores (mL)	Pore Space (%)
Small			
Medium			
Large			

1. The pore space in a material is expressed as a percent. Follow steps a, b, c to calculate the percent of pore space for each grain size.

   a. Divide the volume of the pores by the volume of the grains.

   b. Multiply your decimal answer by 100 to change it to a percent.

   c. Record the pore space percentage in your data table.

2. Why was it important to know how much water you started with before you poured water into the beakers?

3. Why was it important to avoid splashing water while you poured it into the beakers?

4. Compare the percent of pore space of the different grains. Which size grain had the most pore space?

Drawing Conclusions

5. Do your activity results support your hypothesis?

6. Predict what would happen to the percent of pore space if you mixed large grains and small grains together. If you have time and your teacher's permission, test your prediction.

Figure 13-4 The results of ground-water erosion and deposition are obvious in this cavern.

Groundwater Erosion and Deposition

As groundwater seeps down, it weathers and erodes soil and rocks. The amount of rock that groundwater weathers depends on the water's acidity and temperature. Carbon dioxide dissolves in water, forming carbonic acid. The more carbonic acid groundwater has, or the warmer the ground-water is, the more rock it erodes. Likewise, groundwater deposits sediments when it loses acid or cools.

Figure 13-4 shows a cavern, one of the most spectacular effects groundwater has on rocks. Figure 13-5 illustrates how a limestone cavern forms. Carbonic acid dissolves the lime-stone, which is mostly calcite. When the moving ground-water carries away dissolved calcite, it leaves a small hole in the limestone. The hole becomes a cavern as the acid slowly erodes more of the limestone. Most caverns include several rooms connected by tunnels. The Big Room in Carls-bad Caverns, New Mexico, is as large as 47 football fields. The Big Room's ceiling is more than 87 meters above the cave floor—high enough to hold a 22-story building.

Figure 13-5 Caverns form as groundwater gradually dissolves and carries away limestone. Where in the cavern does groundwater deposit limestone?

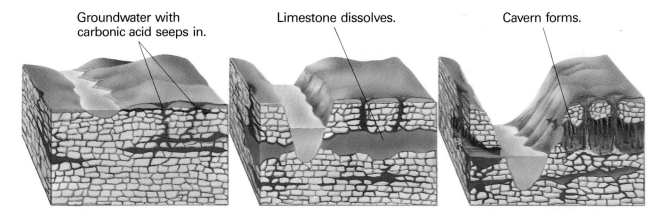

Groundwater with carbonic acid seeps in.

Limestone dissolves.

Cavern forms.

Figure 13-6 As water from this hot spring cools, it deposits minerals that were dissolved in it.

Weirdly-shaped stone features, like the ones in Figure 13-4, are examples of groundwater deposits. Imagine a drop of water on a cavern ceiling. Water in an open cavern loses carbon dioxide to the air, like an open soft drink going flat. As the groundwater loses carbon dioxide, it loses carbonic acid. With less acid, the groundwater cannot keep all of the calcite dissolved. Some of the calcite crystallizes onto the cavern ceiling. The water drop falls and another water drop takes its place, adding to the calcite deposit. Over thousands of years, a cone-shaped stalactite forms. As the water drops splash on the floor below, they lose even more carbon dioxide. This process is like your soft drink going flat as you pour it quickly. More calcite crystallizes, and a calcite stalagmite forms on the cavern floor.

Temperature changes also cause groundwater to deposit weathered materials. Groundwater warms up if it seeps deep beneath Earth's surface or if it comes near igneous rock that has not cooled completely. Warm groundwater dissolves a larger amount of most minerals than cool groundwater does. When the heated groundwater flows out at the surface in a hot spring, the water cools and deposits minerals around the spring, as shown in Figure 13-6.

If you live near limestone caverns or hot springs, you probably drink weathered and eroded minerals every day. Often, water resources in these areas are hard. Hard water contains a large amount of dissolved minerals. You will learn more about water resources in Chapter 21.

Lesson Review 13.1

Figure 13-7 Underwater stalactites and stalagmites

1. Explain how the processes of erosion and deposition are different.

2. What do the terms *porous* and *permeable* mean?

3. Name two changes in groundwater that cause it to deposit minerals.

4. Briefly describe how groundwater forms caverns. Use the words *erosion* and *deposition* in your answer.

Interpret and Apply

5. Explain why groundwater rarely carries solid, undissolved grains through tightly-packed sediments.

6. Figure 13-7 shows stalagmites and stalactites covered by water. Was the water there while these features were forming? Give reasons for your answer.

13.2 The Action of Surface Water

You can probably name some of the processes that formed the canyon in Figure 13-8. For example, what process pulls rocks down into the canyon? What process weathers sandstones by dissolving the cement? Running water erodes the weathered material and deposits it farther down the canyon. Running water erodes and deposits sediments everywhere it flows. How quickly erosion occurs and the features that form as a result depend on the amount of water and the kind of rock in the area.

Streams and Drainage Basins

Running water erodes more weathered material than groundwater, ice, or wind. Rivers and streams are common examples of running water. Rainwater is another example. Any rainwater that does not sink into the soil or evaporate flows downhill over the surface as **runoff**. Runoff erodes steep slopes and bare, unprotected areas like the soil in Figure 13-1. Eventually, runoff soaks into the ground or flows into a stream. The word *stream* refers to a place where water runs most of the time. You might call a small stream a brook or a creek. You call a large stream a river. Can you name some creeks or rivers in your area?

The place where a stream begins to flow is its source. The water that feeds a stream comes from rainfall, melting snow and ice, groundwater, and lakes. The bottom of a stream, under the water, is the streambed. The stream's mouth is where the water flows out of the stream, usually into another stream, a lake, or an ocean.

Figure 13-8 Running water caused most of the erosion that formed this canyon.

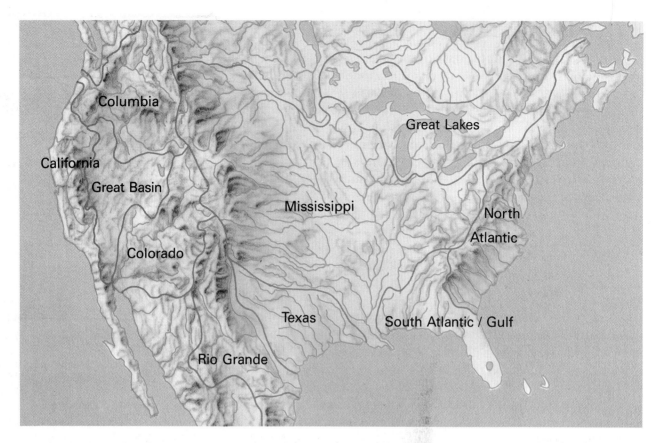

Figure 13-9 Major drainage basins in central North America

Small streams join to form larger streams and rivers. Generally, the water from all the streams in an area flows into one main river. The land that drains into a river and its streams is called the **drainage basin** of that river. The map in Figure 13-9 shows some of the major drainage basins in North America. Notice how much of the United States drains into the Mississippi River drainage basin. Because so many streams flow together, events in one part of the drainage basin sometimes affect other parts. For example, what might happen to the volume of water in the Mississippi River if the Ohio River valley has a drought?

Stream Erosion

Drainage basins form as streams erode Earth's surface. The shape of a drainage basin and the time it takes to form depend on erosion by running water. As a stream flows, it picks up and carries gravel, sand, and clay from its bed. As this material drags and scrapes along the bottom, more material erodes from the streambed and from its sides.

All of the sediment that a stream carries is called the stream's load. A stream carries its load three ways: suspension, bed load, and solution. Figure 13-10 *(left)* illustrates these three processes. Grains that are light enough to hang in the water, such as clay and silt, move in **suspension.** Suspended material may make a stream look muddy. The size of the grains that are in suspension depends on the speed of the stream. A swift stream may carry sand in suspension. However, where the stream slows down, the sand sinks to the streambed.

Large sand grains, pebbles, and boulders make up the stream's bed load. The stream pushes or rolls its bed load along the streambed. Sand grains appear to bounce along the bottom as the stream picks them up and then drops them a short distance downstream. You can observe this process yourself in a clear stream.

Dissolved minerals, such as chemically weathered calcite, stay dissolved as they travel downstream. Recall from Chapter 7 that dissolved materials form a solution in water. Thus, dissolved minerals travel in solution. Materials in solution come from chemical weathering of the stream's bed and from groundwater.

The total amount of sediment a stream can carry depends on two factors: the speed of the flowing water and the amount of water in the stream. Imagine that one escalator in a shopping mall moves twice as fast as another escalator. Which escalator could carry more people in an hour? In the same way, a fast-moving stream can carry more sediment than a slow-moving stream of the same size. The speed of a stream depends mostly on the steepness of its slope and on the amount of water in it. The amount of water in the stream affects its carrying ability in another way. Think of it this way: Which could carry more people, a bus or a compact car? Likewise, a large river can carry more sediment than a small creek flowing at the same speed.

Fact or Fiction?

Does the Missouri River flow into the Mississippi River or is it the other way around? On a map, find the place where the two rivers join. North of that point, the Missouri is about 3700 km long, while the Mississippi is only about 1900 km long. Some people argue that the lower part of the Mississippi should be renamed the Missouri. What do you think of this idea?

Figure 13-10 *Left:* Streams carry sediments three different ways. *Right:* What process rounded the pebbles in this stream?

From stream source

Suspension

Bed load

To stream mouth

Solution

ACTIVITY 13.2

STREAM SLOPE AND SPEED

Purpose To measure the effect of a stream's slope on its speed.

Materials

trough or gutter	ring stand with 2
cup	rings
funnel	shallow pan
meterstick	water
clock or watch	lab apron

Procedure
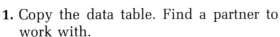

1. Copy the data table. Find a partner to work with.

2. Put on your lab apron. Set up your equipment as shown in the figure.

3. Measure and record the trough length and trough height in cm.

4. Decide who will be the timer and who will be the pourer. When the timer says "go," pour water through the funnel. The pourer says "stop" when the water just reaches the end of the trough. Repeat until you have done 4 trials.

5. Raise the rings to make the trough steeper. Measure and record the height in cm. Complete 4 trials for the new height by repeating step 4.

6. Raise the trough again. Record the height of the trough. Complete 4 trials for the new height.

Collecting and Analyzing Data

1. To calculate the slope of the trough in each position, divide the height of the trough as it rested on the ring stand by the length of the trough. Record the slope for each height in your data table.

2. Find the average time of the four trials for each trough height. Then, find the average speed by dividing the length by the average time for that height.

Drawing Conclusions

3. How does the water speed change as the trough slope increases?

4. Did the water flow down the trough in a straight line? If it did not, how might this variable affect your results?

5. Imagine there were sediments in the trough. Which slope do you think would result in the most erosion?

Data Table								
Height of Trough (cm)	**Length of Trough (cm)**	**Slope (height/length)**	**1**	**2**	**3**	**4**	**Avg.**	**Avg. Speed (cm/s)**

Stream Deposits

As streams slow down, the largest grains settle first. The smallest grains settle last. Streams slow when they reach level ground or when they flow into another body of water.

To understand the effect of changing slope on a stream, think about coasting down a steep hill on a bicycle. When you get to the bottom of the hill, your bicycle slows down as the ground levels out. Figure 13-11 (top) shows a place where a stream comes out of a steep mountain valley onto level ground. This stream ends at an **alluvial fan,** a triangle-shaped deposit of sediments on the dry ground. Alluvial fans form where streams flow onto a desert floor.

If a stream flows into a calm body of water, like a lake or ocean, the stream deposits sediments. A **delta** is a deposit of sediments in a body of water at a stream's mouth. Deltas can be shaped like a triangle or like a bird's foot. Figure 13-11 (bottom) shows the delta at the mouth of the Mississippi River. The shape forms because the stream is so slow that it must branch out to move all the water.

Streams also slow down if they overflow. Floods usually occur during heavy rains or while snow melts quickly in the spring. During a flood, a stream flows faster and carries more sediment. As the stream overflows and spreads out, it slows down. Figure 13-12 shows two features that form when a river overflows. The large-grained sediments, which are deposited first, form long ridges, or **levees,** along both sides of the river. As the water flows farther from the river, it slows down even more and deposits finer-grained sediments. A **floodplain** is a wide, flat area of small-grained sediments on either side of a river.

Floods cause an average of 3 billion dollars of property damage each year. Since 1973, towns that do not plan ahead for floods do not receive flood cleanup money from the United States government. Planning ahead for a flood includes not building on floodplains and providing places for flood water to flow safely.

Figure 13-11 *Top:* An alluvial fan; *Bottom:* The Mississippi River delta

Figure 13-12 As streams overflow, they slow down and deposit sediments. Where would you expect the coarsest sediments to be?

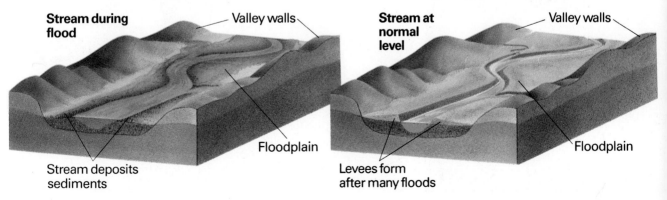

Stream during flood — Valley walls — Floodplain — Stream deposits sediments

Stream at normal level — Valley walls — Floodplain — Levees form after many floods

Changes in a Stream Valley

As you grow older, you go through stages of change or development. The terms *young*, *mature*, and *old* describe the general pattern a stream follows as it develops. However, some young streams are older than some old streams—you will learn why a little later.

You can recognize a stream's stage by its properties. A stream's slope affects its properties at each stage. Figure 13-13 *(left)* illustrates the properties of a young river. Usually, when a river or stream is young, its source is much higher than its mouth. The river valley has a steep slope. The fast-flowing stream has a rough bed, which river rafters know means rough water, rapids, and waterfalls. Most of the erosion takes place on the riverbed, rather than on its sides. The river forms a deep, narrow, V-shaped valley, like the one in Figure 13-13 *(left)*.

As the river matures, erosion smooths out most rapids and waterfalls. Figure 13-13 *(right)* shows a mature stream valley. When the slow river comes to a place that is difficult to erode, it flows around that place. A stream flowing through a curve flows faster on the outside of the curve and slower on the inside. Thus, the river erodes sediment on the outside of the curve. The river deposits sediment on the inside of the curve. This process forms a larger curve, or **meander** [mē an′ dər], in the river. A meandering river erodes the sides of its valley, forming a flood plain.

When the river has eroded its bed so much that its slope is very slight, the river is in its old stage. An old river flows slowly and hardly erodes its bed. Its valley is wide and flat, as shown in Figure 13-14 *(left)*. An old river's meanders become large, looping curves. During floods, the river may cut off a meander to form an oxbow lake.

Figure 13-13 *Left*: A young river flows swiftly and has steep valley walls. *Right*: A mature river flows more slowly and forms a floodplain.

Remember that the terms *young*, *mature*, and *old* do not describe the real age of the stream. The Colorado River has been flowing for millions of years. But the Colorado River is still youthful because it still has a steep slope, and it is still eroding its bed. By comparison, the Mississippi River has been flowing for thousands of years, much less time than the Colorado River. However, the Mississippi is mature and even old in some places. The Mississippi's gentler slope and softer riverbed are the reasons it is more mature than the Colorado. Think about streams and rivers where you live. Are the streams young, mature, or old? How does the slope of the land in your area compare to the stage the streams are in?

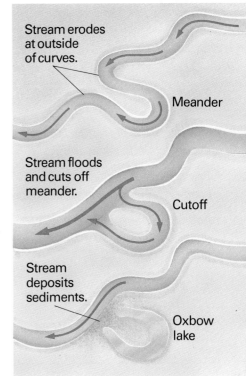

Figure 13-14 *Left:* An old river flows very slowly and has a wide, flat valley. *Right:* Floods may cut off a meander, forming an oxbow.

Lesson Review 13.2

7. Name three sources of water that feed streams.

8. Describe the three ways in which a stream carries sediment.

9. Name two stream properties that determine the amount of sediment it can carry.

Interpret and Apply

10. On your paper, write the letters A–D. Write the term that correctly describes the feature labeled in Figure 13-15.

11. A stream that flows into another stream does not form a delta at its mouth. Explain why this is true.

12. Compare the size of grains that could be carried by streams in each stage of development.

Figure 13-15 Diagram of a river

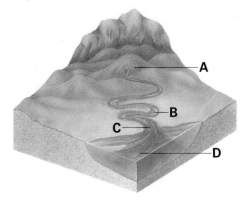

▶ **Compare** *valley glaciers and continental glaciers and the erosional features left by both.*

▶ **Contrast** *deposits left by ice with deposits left by meltwater.*

▶ **Describe** *land features caused by wind erosion and wind deposition.*

▶ **Activity** **Interpret data** *about glacial landforms on a topographic map.*

New Terms

glacier
moraine
eskers

Far up on a mountain in the Rockies, the climbers scratch and pick their way over the ice. With axes and spikes they cling to the sometimes slippery surface. They set up ropes to cross giant cracks that plunge deep into the ice. The sport of climbing glaciers is only for the well-prepared.

Glaciers

The glacier the climbers are on, like all glaciers, started out as tiny snowflakes. If last winter's snow did not melt, then it would pile up as new snow fell on the old snow. On high mountains and at latitudes near Earth's poles, this is exactly what happens. A **glacier** is a large mass of ice that exists all year and moves over Earth's surface. There are two kinds of glaciers: valley glaciers and continental glaciers.

Valley glaciers form in high mountain areas with low air temperatures. The shade of steep valley walls protects snow from melting in the sun. As the snow piles up deeper, the snow below is compressed into ice grains. Due to gravity, the ice grains slip downhill past each other. Every day, a valley glacier moves downhill a few centimeters or more.

Continental glaciers form at polar latitudes. Unlike valley glaciers, continental glaciers cover millions of square kilometers of land. During the last ice age, continental glaciers covered much of the northern United States. Today, the only continental glaciers are in Greenland and in Antarctica. Continental glaciers are so large that the weight of ice pressing down at the center pushes out the edges.

Figure 13-16 *Left:* Valley glaciers occur on mountain slopes in cold climates. *Right:* Continental glaciers cover whole landmasses.

Glacier Erosion

You are probably used to thinking of ice as clean, pure cubes from your freezer. However, glacier ice is more like ice lying next to the road in winter, which has sand frozen into it. Like water and wind, glaciers pick up and carry sediments from the surface. Beneath a glacier, the trapped sediments grind away at the land. Both kinds of glaciers carry sediments in sizes ranging from fine, dusty grains to boulders as large as houses.

Erosion by Valley Glaciers A valley glacier commonly moves down a steep, V-shaped valley that a stream carved earlier. A valley glacier fills its valley from wall to wall. Moving down the mountainside, the glacier scrapes and flattens the valley bottom and cuts away at the sides, reshaping the valley. When the ice melts, the valley left behind is U-shaped, like the one in Figure 13-17 *(left)*. If two valley glaciers move side by side, they leave a sharp ridge between them. You can recognize mountain areas that were shaped by valley glaciers by sharp ridges and peaks like the ones behind the valley in Figure 13-17 *(left)*.

Erosion by Continental Glaciers Continental glaciers are thick enough to cover entire mountain ranges. As a continental glacier moves, it scrapes over the tops of the mountains. Like sandpaper smoothing a piece of wood, rocks and grains in the ice rub over the land surface. Instead of making features on Earth's surface steeper, as valley glaciers do, continental glaciers tend to level the surface. However, large rocks or boulders scraping over the rock may leave long scratches like the ones in Figure 13-17 *(top right)*.

Figure 13-17 *Left:* Valley glaciers leave sharp peaks and U-shaped valleys. *Bottom right:* Continental glaciers leave smooth, rounded land surfaces. *Top right:* These scratches were carved by a continental glacier.

Glacier Deposits

Both kinds of glacier eventually deposit the sediments they carry. Most deposition takes place at the glacier's leading edge, called its ice front. If more snow falls than melts each year, the ice front may appear to move forward. If less snow falls than melts, the ice front may appear to move backward as it melts. If the amount of snowfall equals snow melt, the ice front stays the same. Whatever the ice front is doing, remember that the glacier itself is always moving forward.

Unsorted Glacier Deposits Glaciers carry sediments of all sizes and drop them, unsorted, at the ice front. Unsorted sediment deposited by glaciers is called till. The ridge of till that builds up as ice melts at an ice front is a **moraine.** In till, sediments from tiny clay grains to huge boulders all lay together. Much of the northeastern United States is covered by a layer of till. The well-known stone walls of the Northeast are rocks that farmers dug out of the soil and piled into long rows to get them out of the way.

ENVIRONMENTAL AWARENESS

Recreational Erosion

Have you seen or ridden on a four-wheel-drive or all-terrain vehicle (ATV)? Many people enjoy riding these vehicles through the desert, on beaches, up hills, or through small streams. Many of these places erode easily. Off-road vehicles churn up soil, loosening it in some places and compacting it in others. Plants that would hold soil in place cannot grow where ATV's travel. ATV trails become stream channels when it rains, and the rushing water erodes the soil. In dry areas, wind easily carries away the loose, unprotected soil.

It is estimated that there are about 6 million off-road vehicles in the United States, with as many as 45 million people enjoying them. Some people think that off-road vehicles should be banned from areas that erode easily. Other people feel they should

be allowed to ride off-road vehicles wherever they like. Is there a solution that balances protection of the land with the desires of the riders? What do you think should be done about this situation? ■

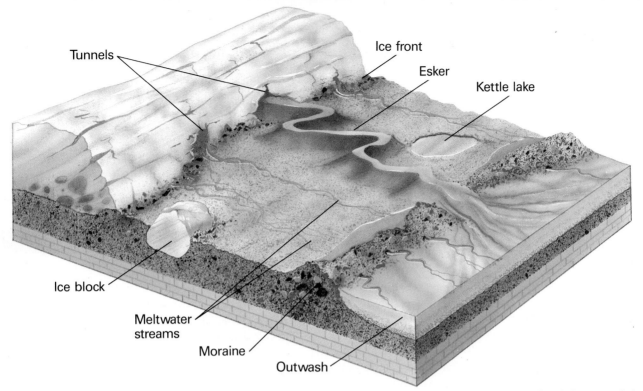

Tunnels

Ice front

Esker

Kettle lake

Ice block

Meltwater streams

Moraine

Outwash

Sorted Glacier Deposits Meltwater at the ice front forms streams that flow away from the glacier. The streams carry away some of the smaller sediments. As you know, running water sorts sediments by size as it deposits them. Sediment that was sorted by streams flowing out of melting glaciers is called outwash. Water runs within a melting glacier as well as in front of it. The meltwater carves tunnels under the ice and deposits sediments in the tunnels. When the glacier melts, the sorted sediments in the tunnels remain as long, narrow ridges called **eskers.**

Glacial Lakes Minnesota is known as the Land of 10 000 Lakes. Glaciers formed many lakes in Minnesota and in other northern states. Large blocks of ice, covered with sediments, sometimes break off at the ice front. The sediments protect the ice block from the sun, so the block melts slowly. When the buried ice block melts, a water-filled pit, or kettle lake, stays behind. Figure 13-19 shows kettle lakes.

Glacial erosion and melting worked together to form the Great Lakes. A continental glacier moved over the area and deepened and widened river valleys there. As the glacier melted, it put less weight on the land. As the weight decreased, the land rose. Some of the rivers were cut off from the ocean. The valleys filled with water.

If you live in a northern state, look for glacial landforms where you live. You can watch for glacial landforms as you walk or ride around your area. You can also look for them on a topographic map.

Figure 13-18 Kinds of deposits left by a melting glacier

Figure 13-19 These two kettle lakes were left behind after ice blocks from a glacier melted.

ACTIVITY 13.3

MAP OF GLACIAL LANDFORMS

Purpose To interpret data about glacial landforms on a topographic map.

Materials

photo (Figure 13-20)
portion of topographic
  map of Voltaire,
  North Dakota
  (Figure 13-21)

metric ruler
paper
pencil

Procedure

1. Review the information about topographic maps on pages 54–57. As you do this activity, refer to Appendix D on page 624 for map symbols.

2. Examine the topographic map portion in Figure 13-21. The map shows an area that was once covered by a continental glacier.

3. Refer to the map in Figure 13-21 to answer questions 1–10. Refer to descriptions of glacier deposits on pages 348–349 as needed.

Collecting and Analyzing Data

1. What is the contour interval of this map? Where did you find this information?

2. Describe the general shape of the land area shown in the map. Are the slopes steep or gentle? Are there any hills? Explain how you used the map information to determine land shape.

3. Use your ruler and the map scale to find the greatest diameter of Stink Lake.

4. Name the kind of stream feature that lies directly east of Westgaard Cemetery.

5. Did the river at the top of the map form before or after the glacier melted? How do you know?

Drawing Conclusions

6. Keep in mind that a continental glacier melted in this area. Think of an explanation for the many depressions in this area.

7. Name the kind of glacier feature that forms long ridges like the ones on either side of the two lakes.

8. Would you expect the sediments in the long ridges to be sorted by size or unsorted? Explain the reason for your answer.

9. Explain why a contour interval of 80 feet would not be useful on this map.

10. Compare the area shown in the map in Figure 13-21 with the area shown in the photo in Figure 13-20. Is it possible that a continental glacier shaped the area in the photo? What evidence in the photo supports your answer?

Figure 13-20 Landscape in part of Midwestern United States

Figure 13-21 Portion of topographic map of Voltaire, North Dakota

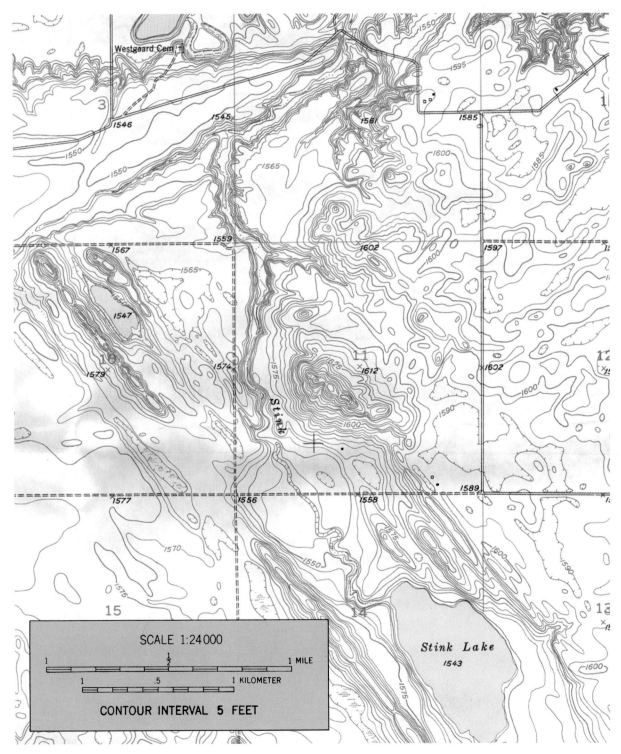

SCALE 1:24000

1   ½   1 MILE

1   .5   1 KILOMETER

CONTOUR INTERVAL **5** FEET

Figure 13-22 How did wind erosion make this rock thinner at the base than at the top?

Wind Erosion and Deposition

Have you ever gotten dust or sand in your eyes on a windy day? If so, then you are familiar with the wind's ability to carry sediments. Wind carries sediments most easily in places where sediments are small and dry and where there are few plants to hold the grains in place. Where do you think these conditions are common? Wind carries grains the size of clay, silt, and fine sand. Like the grain sizes carried in streams, the grain size that wind carries increases with wind speed. Because most wind-blown sediments travel just above the ground, wind abrasion weathers rock nearest the ground.

When the wind slows down, it deposits its sediments, just as streams do. Changes in the weather and windbreaks such as trees, mountain ranges, and buildings slow the wind and cause it to drop sediments.

Sand dunes, like the ones in Figure 13-23 (right), are wind deposits. Sand dunes form where there is sand and a fairly constant wind. Deserts, sandy ocean shorelines, and the shores of some large lakes have these conditions. The size and shape of a sand dune depend on the amount of sand and on the speed and direction of the wind.

Sand dunes gradually move, or migrate, over the surface. Figure 13-23 (left) illustrates sand dune migration. The wind blows sand grains up the side of the dune that faces the wind, forming a gentle slope. When a sand grain reaches the top of the dune, it falls down over the other side, forming a steeper slope. As thousands of sand grains continually blow up one side of the dune and down the other, the entire dune gradually moves downwind.

Figure 13-23 *Left:* Sand dunes gradually move in the direction of the wind. *Right:* Which way does the wind in this area usually blow?

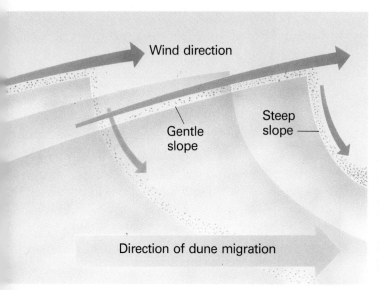

Wind direction

Gentle slope

Steep slope

Direction of dune migration

Lesson Review 13.3

13. Compare the size, location, and motion of a valley glacier with a continental glacier.

14. Contrast the shape of features eroded by valley glaciers with features eroded by continental glaciers.

15. Describe how you can tell whether sediments were deposited by ice or by running water.

16. What kind of conditions allow wind erosion to be most effective?

Interpret and Apply

17. Not all mountains on Earth have valley glaciers. Think of two reasons why this is true.

Chapter Summary

Read this summary of the main ideas in this chapter. If any are not clear to you, go back and review that lesson.

13.1 The Action of Groundwater

■ Erosion moves and carries weathered materials. Deposition leaves the weathered materials in a new place.

■ Porous materials contain spaces, or pores, between their grains. Permeable materials allow water to pass through them.

■ Groundwater erodes and deposits rock as it passes through cracks and pores. Groundwater deposits minerals when it cools, evaporates, or loses acid. Caverns are examples of groundwater erosion and deposition.

13.2 The Action of Surface Water

■ Rain, groundwater, melting snow, and runoff all feed streams. The land area that drains into a stream is its drainage basin.

■ Running water carries sediment in three ways—suspension, bed load, and solution.

■ Streams deposit sediments when they slow down. Alluvial fans, deltas, levees, and flood plains are all formed by stream deposits.

■ A stream valley goes through stages of development as the stream erodes its bed.

13.3 The Action of Ice and Wind

■ Glaciers are large masses of ice that erode the land as they travel over Earth's surface.

■ Generally, valley glaciers leave sharp features, while continental glaciers leave smooth, polished features.

■ Where glacier ice deposits sediments directly, grain sizes are mixed together. Where meltwater streams deposit sediment, grains are sorted by size.

■ Wind erosion and deposition take place in dry places with few plants. Sediments carried by the wind weather surfaces by abrasion. Sand dunes are common wind deposition features.

Chapter Review

■ Vocabulary

alluvial fan
delta
deposition
drainage basin
erosion
esker
floodplain
glacier

groundwater
levees
meander
moraine
permeable
porous
runoff
suspension

■ Concept Mapping

Using the method of concept mapping described on pages 3–5, make a concept map for sediments. Include the following terms in your map: *erosion, deposition, groundwater, streams, glaciers, wind.* Use additional terms as you need them.

■ Review

On your paper, write the word or words that best complete each statement.

1. _____ is the process in which sediments are picked up and carried.

2. Sediments are dropped in a new location in the process of _____.

3. When a stream erodes its bed sideways, it begins to develop curves, or _____.

4. A _____ material has spaces between its grains.

5. A _____ material allows groundwater to pass through.

6. _____ erosion occurs in dry areas with little plant cover.

7. Deposits that contain mixed sizes of sediments were probably dropped by _____ rather than streams.

8. A _____ is a large, hollow space formed by groundwater erosion beneath Earth's surface.

9. Erosion by _____ glaciers rounds off the tops of mountains.

10. Water dripping from a cave ceiling leaves a cone-shaped deposit called a _____.

11. _____ is the name for sediments that were deposited by meltwater from a glacier.

12. A stream's _____ is the place where the stream flows into another body of water.

13. When a stream has a muddy appearance, it means that it is carrying small sediments in _____.

14. Streams usually erode their beds downward the most when they are in the _____ stage of development.

15. Some heavy sediments move along the stream bottom as part of the stream's _____.

16. A _____ forms where a stream drops its load as it flows into a calm body of water.

17. _____ is rainwater that moves downhill over the ground surface.

18. Ridges of sediment deposited on either side of a stream as it overflows are called _____.

19. As a stream gradually slows down, it sorts and deposits its sediments according to their _____.

20. A _____ glacier moves down the slope of a mountain.

■ Interpret and Apply

On your paper, answer each question.

21. You are with a group of people exploring a cavern. You come to a small room that has a shallow, flowing stream covering the cavern floor from wall to wall. Hundreds of small stalactites hang from the ceiling, but there are no stalagmites on the floor. Explain to the others why there are no stalagmites in this room.

22. The same sediments in the same stream can be carried as bed load or in suspension. Explain how changing conditions in the river make this possible.

23. You observe a large rounded boulder in an open field. What evidence would you look for to determine if the boulder was deposited by a glacier?

24. Describe the changes that would occur in the mature Mississippi River valley if sea level dropped 100 meters at its mouth.

25. The photograph below shows a pothole, a feature that is common in the beds of very fast-flowing streams with whirlpools. Based on your observations of the photograph and on your knowledge of streams, explain how the pothole formed.

26. For thousands of years, farmers in the Nile River flood plain in Egypt relied on yearly floods to deposit new fertile soil. Then the Aswan Dam was built upstream. Now, farms downstream from the dam are less productive. Explain how the dam keeps fertile sediment from reaching the farms.

27. Along some rivers, people have added material to build up the tops of natural levees. Explain why people would do this. Include a diagram with your answer.

■ *Writing in Science*

28. Find an example of deposition in your neighborhood or other place that you are familiar with. Write a detailed, accurate description of what you see. Then analyze all the things that might have caused the deposition. Look for examples of deposition in the following places:

    a. in cracks in sidewalks or rocks
    b. along the banks of streams
    c. at the bottom of rain gutters
    d. at the base of steep hills or walls

■ *Critical Thinking*

The photograph below shows a wing dam in a river. Most wing dams extend only partway into the river. The purpose of a wing dam is to change the river flow by directing more water down the middle of the stream.

29. What happens to the speed of the stream along the bank near the wing dam?

30. Predict which parts of the river will have greater erosion and which will have greater deposition, due to the wing dam.

31. What effect does the wing dam have on the speed of the water near the center of the stream, beyond the end of the dam?

32. What would the wing dam do to the rate of erosion in the middle of the river?

33. How do the effects of the wing dam help boats on the river?

FLOODS SWEEP THROUGH SOUTH; DISASTER RELIEF COSTS BILLIONS

Issue: *Who should pay for the damage caused by natural disasters in high-risk areas?*

On September 21, 1989, hurricane Hugo slammed into the South Carolina coast. Hugo was one of the worst storms ever to hit the mainland United States. More than 65 000 people were left homeless, and property damage reached over $8 billion. Then, while the President was considering how much federal aid to give to Charleston, South Carolina, an earthquake struck San Francisco on the opposite coast. The October 17 earthquake measured 7.1 on the Richter scale. Sixty-four lives were lost, and property damage was estimated at more than $10 billion.

A house damaged by flooding

These are only two examples of natural disasters that strike every year, causing billions of dollars in damage. Most people agree that the federal government must aid people struck by unexpected disasters such as hurricanes. But many people are against government aid in areas where people know a disaster will strike sooner or later. They think that people in these high-risk areas either should buy disaster insurance or pay for losses out of their own pockets. But other people argue that only the federal government can afford to pay for the damages caused by natural disasters. These people feel that the whole country should share the cost.

The greatest danger to human life in an earthquake comes from buildings, roads, and bridges that collapse. Although the state government pays to maintain these structures, the federal government sends relief after a big earthquake strikes. California had only $1 billion set aside for emergencies when the 1989 earthquake struck. Without federal aid, many buildings could not have been rebuilt until years after the earthquake.

In the past, the federal government has always helped people during disasters.

Some natural disasters are more predictable than earthquakes. Each year, many rivers flood in the spring, destroying homes and businesses. Barrier islands, located offshore from beaches, are affected by erosion every time a big storm hits. Beachfront houses on these islands are slowly swept off their foundations. Most insurance companies feel it is too risky to offer flood insurance in these areas. In the past, the government provided federal flood insurance to help people when no other insurance was available. But in recent years, the government has held back flood relief when the damage was predictable. In 1983, for example, Congress passed the Coastal Barrier Resources Act. This law prevents the use of federal funds for building on barrier islands. The government simply does not have enough money to rebuild houses after every big storm. Unfortunately, many homeowners who cannot afford to rebuild on their own will lose their homes forever.

Many people cannot afford the high cost of disaster insurance.

Some people think that people who build in high-risk areas are taking advantage of the government, knowing that they will be bailed out in a disaster. If the federal government does not help people in high-risk areas, then people will have to pay for damages themselves or rely on private insurance. But many people cannot afford disaster insurance because it is so costly. The government hopes its new policy will encourage people to relocate to safer areas. But many people feel it is unfair to force people to move away from areas they have lived in for many years.

Insurance companies are hard hit when a disaster strikes because many people make claims all at once. Insurance companies protect themselves from heavy losses in several ways. They build up funds in years when there are few disasters. Then in bad years, such as 1989, they have the money to pay large claims. Insurance companies also raise insurance rates in the years following a bad year. This passes the cost of rebuilding on to their customers. In the long run, whether the federal government or private insurance companies pay, the costs of damages from natural disasters are shared by many people.

Act on the Issue

Gather the Facts

1. Use library books and articles listed in the *Readers' Guide to Periodical Literature* to find out more about recent laws concerning federal flood insurance. Which states have sponsored bills in Congress? Who pays for the cost of the insurance? Find out what compromises were made to pass these laws.

2. In many high-risk areas, money is spent to prevent damage from natural disasters. Use library books and articles to find out how buildings, roads, and bridges are reinforced to make them earthquake-proof. Contact the United States Army Corps of Engineers to find out more about the government's role in flood prevention. You may want to do more library research to find out which kinds of disasters are likely to occur in your area.

3. Look in library books and articles to learn more about large-scale projects to fix erosion damage on beaches and barrier islands. Find out where coastal erosion is a problem, and what it costs to restore an entire beach. Then research whether state, federal, or private funds were used to complete these projects.

Take Action

4. Imagine that you are an insurance expert asked to testify before Congress. Give two arguments you would use to convince Congress to overturn the Coastal Barrier Resources Act. Consider both the long-term and short-term effects of restoring federal flood insurance in high-risk areas. Then write to your representatives in Congress and ask them where they stand on this issue.

Earth Through Time

You Know More Than You Think

You may be surprised at how much you already know about Earth and time. To find out, try to answer the following questions.

- What is a fossil?
- Are any large dinosaurs alive today?
- What is the oldest object you can name?
- Name some fuels that people use as energy sources.
- Can you think of ways to conserve energy?

When you finish this unit, answer these questions again to see how much you have learned.

Earth's story is written in its rocks.

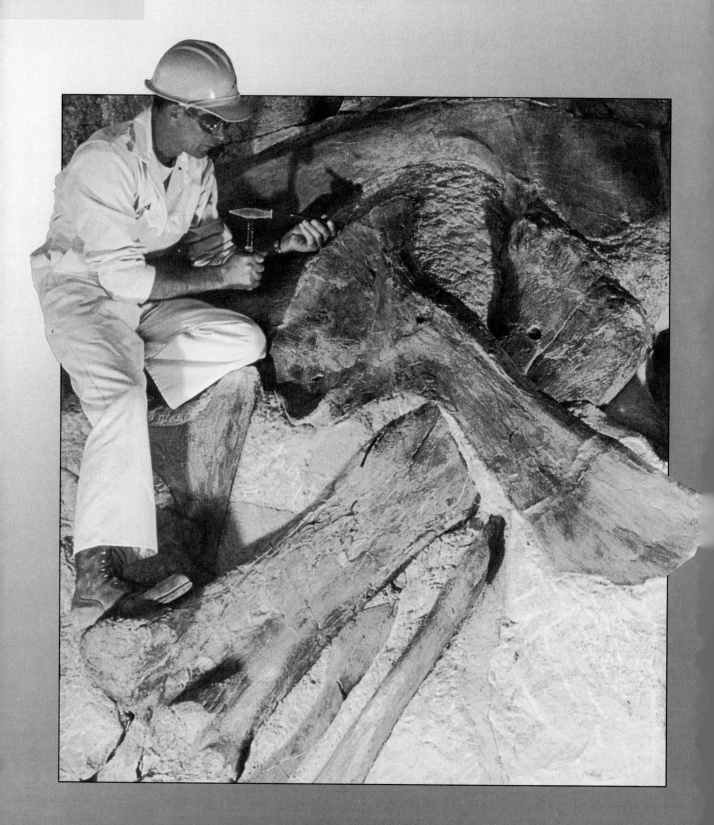

Chapter Preview

Have You Ever WONDERED?

Why do some rocks contain so many fossils while other rocks contain none?

Notice that the rock in the photograph contains a large number of fossil dinosaur bones. When you look at most other rocks, however, you find no fossils at all. Several conditions determine the number of fossils in a rock. As you might expect, one factor is the number of living things that were in the area when the rock was forming. The rock in the photograph contains many fossils because the rock formed where many animals were living and dying. A second factor is the way the rock forms. Fossils are more likely to form when plants or animals are buried soon after they die. Sediments like mud and sand bury the organisms as the sediments are deposited in lakes, streams, and oceans. As a result, sedimentary rocks are more likely to contain fossils than other rock types. In this chapter, you will learn more about how fossils form and what they tell us about changes on Earth.

14.1 The Fossil Record

Lesson Objectives

▸ **Describe** processes of fossil formation.

▸ **Compare** fossil remains with trace fossils.

▸ **Summarize** the ways that fossils indicate changes in living things and their environments.

▸ **Activity** **State a conclusion** about how two types of fossils form.

New Terms

carbonized fossils	paleontologist
mold	trace fossils
imprints	natural
cast	selection

No one was around 4 600 000 000 (4.6 billion) years ago to actually see Earth form. So how can scientists estimate the age of Earth? As you will learn in this chapter, scientists have developed methods to figure out the ages of rocks in Earth's crust. The oldest rocks you see today are not the original rocks that formed when Earth cooled and contracted. Heat, pressure, and other factors have changed the original rocks into different rocks. Earth itself must be older than the oldest rocks.

In Chapter 9, you learned that fossils, the evidence of past life, help determine the ages of sedimentary rocks. In this lesson, you will take a closer look at how fossils form and what they tell about the rock.

Fossil Formation

Imagine that you take a trip to northern Siberia, near the Arctic Circle. As you travel along on your dogsled, you find what looks like an elephant frozen in the ice. You know that elephants do not live near the Arctic Circle today. Your discovery turns out to be a fossil of an extinct relative of today's elephants. The extinct elephant, called a mammoth, lived in the Arctic region thousands of years ago.

Two factors determine whether or not a dying organism becomes a fossil. First, fossilization is more likely if the remains are buried soon after the organism's death. When most plants and animals die, their remains are left on top of the ground. There bacteria, which are simple one-celled organisms, cause the remains to decay. Or carnivores, animals that eat other animals, might eat the remains, like those of the zebra in Figure 14-1. If an organism dies in or near a body of water, sediment might bury the organism's remains. This burial slows down the process of decay. Burial also protects the remains from predators.

Figure 14-1 Because the lions eat most of its bones, this zebra will probably not become fossilized.

The second factor that determines whether remains become a fossil is hard parts. Shells, bones, teeth, or wood are more likely to be fossilized than the organism's soft parts. However, scientists have found some fossils of simple organisms that had only soft parts. Whether the parts are hard or soft, the preservation process determines the type of fossil that forms.

Original Remains   Original remains are fossils that are unchanged from the time of death. Usually, original remains are the teeth or bones of an animal. Sometimes, however, an entire organism, including the soft parts, has been preserved. A sticky substance such as natural tar, tree sap, quicksand, or even lava traps an animal's body. The substance hardens around the body, protecting the soft parts from decay. Because the fossil includes soft parts, it tells scientists more about the organism than other types of fossils.

Freezing is another process that can cause complete preservation. That is why you store some foods in the freezer. People have found the frozen remains of several types of Ice Age animals, such as mammoths. Figure 14-2 shows a mammoth on display in a museum. The skeleton, teeth, internal organs, skin, and hair were all preserved. When scientists dissected one specimen, they found undigested grasses from the mammoth's last meal frozen in its stomach.

Replaced Remains   Burial slows down but does not stop the decay of an organism's soft parts. The hard parts remain much longer, up to several million years. The organic material making up a bone, tooth, shell, or piece of wood slowly dissolves. Minerals that are carried by groundwater, such as calcite, quartz, or pyrite, gradually replace the missing material. The replacement process leaves behind a mineral copy, called replaced remains, of the original hard part. Most dinosaur "bones" that people have found have actually been replaced by minerals. Petrified wood, shown in Figure 14-3, is another good example of replaced remains.

Carbonized Fossils   Have you ever used carbon paper? You place it between two sheets of paper and write on the top sheet. The carbon paper leaves a copy of your writing on the bottom sheet. Some fossils are "carbon copies" of the original organism. A carbonized fossil of a leaf forms after the leaf is buried in mud. While the mud is turning to shale, the leaf changes chemically until only the carbon is left. The carbon leaves a thin film on the shale, called a **carbonized fossil,** shaped exactly like the leaf. Sometimes the carbonized fossil is so detailed that you can see the outlines of leaf cells through a microscope.

Figure 14-2 This mammoth, on display in a Soviet museum, was preserved in Arctic ice for several thousand years.

Figure 14-3 Can you see the tree rings in this petrified log?

Figure 14-4 *Left:* This imprint was preserved when soft mud turned into rock. *Right:* The mold of this trilobite fossil is on the right, while the cast is on the left.

Molds, Imprints, and Casts Figure 14-4 *(right)* shows a cavity in a rock. The cavity, called a **mold,** formed when a shell that was in the rock dissolved completely. Sometimes flat objects like the fern leaf in Figure 14-4 *(left)* leave **imprints** in soft sediment. An imprint is similar to a mold, but shallower. Groundwater seeps into and deposits minerals in some molds. The deposited mineral forms a **cast** of the shell. Figure 14-4 *(right)* shows the cast that formed from the mold in the figure.

Trace Fossils Have you ever seen footprints preserved in a cement sidewalk? The footprints are a record of that person's presence left in the sidewalk. Figure 14-5 shows dinosaur footprints preserved in sedimentary rock. From the footprints, a **paleontologist** [pā lē ən tol′ ə jist], a scientist who studies fossils, can estimate the size of the dinosaur. The burrows of worms and insects are also sometimes preserved in sedimentary rocks. Footprints and burrows are examples of **trace fossils,** a record that an animal leaves while it is still alive instead of after it dies.

Figure 14-5 These dinosaur footprints are located in Cameron, Arizona.

ACTIVITY 14.1

MAKING FOSSILS

Purpose To state a conclusion about how two types of fossils form.

Materials

lab apron	paper towels
safety goggles	modeling clay
paper cup	plaster of Paris
spoon	solution of Epsom salts
piece of yarn	water
tweezers or tongs	seashells

Procedure

1. Read all instructions for this activity before you begin your work. Put on your lab apron and safety goggles.

2. Flatten the modeling clay. Firmly press the shell into the clay.

3. Carefully remove the shell without disturbing the clay. Examine the surface of the clay.

4. Put a small amount of plaster of Paris and water in the paper cup. Mix the plaster and water with the spoon. The mixture should be almost as thick as stick glue. You need just enough to fill the impression you made in the clay. IMPORTANT: Do not put any plaster of Paris in the sink.

5. Spoon the plaster mixture into the impression in the clay. Set the mixture aside and allow the plaster to harden. While the plaster hardens, continue with step 6.

6. Use tweezers to dip your piece of yarn into the solution of Epsom salts. Allow the yarn to absorb some of the solution. Take the yarn out and lay it on the paper towel to dry.

7. After the plaster has hardened, remove it from the clay. Examine the plaster.

8. After the yarn has dried, pick it up and observe it closely for any changes.

9. Before leaving the laboratory, clean up all materials and wash your hands.

Collecting and Analyzing Data

1. How is the impression similar to the shell you pressed into the clay? How is it different?

2. How is the piece of hardened plaster similar to the original shell? How is it different?

3. How did the structure of the yarn change after you soaked it in the solution and then let it dry?

Drawing Conclusions

4. Which type of fossil does the impression you made in the clay represent?

5. Which type of fossil does the hardened plaster represent?

6. In what type of place would you expect fossils like the clay mold and the plaster cast to form?

7. Epsom salts are like a mineral. What fossilization process do the steps with the yarn represent?

8. How does your yarn "fossil" differ from actual fossils formed this way?

Figure 14-6 These fossils were found in mountains high above sea level. Where do you think the animals actually lived?

Information from Fossils

Fossils give you much information about past life and about changing environments on Earth. Fossil bones can reveal an animal's approximate size and shape and how the animal moved. Teeth indicate the kind of foods the animal ate. Clues like these help you to determine what the organism was like. In addition, a fossil allows paleontologists to describe the environment in which the organism lived. Scientists compare the fossil to similar organisms living today. Where do you think the fossilized animals in Figure 14-6 lived? The fossils were actually found in a rock layer high above sea level. Fossils of tropical plants have been found in Antarctica. These fossils show that the environment changed sometime in the past. The movement of the continents might explain some of these environmental changes.

Fossils also tell you that living things have changed over time. The fossil record shows that many organisms that thrived in the past no longer exist. Likewise, many of today's more complex plants and animals did not exist in the past. The oldest fossils found so far are about 3 500 000 000 years old. These are fossils of simple one-celled organisms that resemble bacteria. These organisms, which lived in the oceans, may be one of the earliest forms of life.

ENVIRONMENTAL AWARENESS

Concerned Citizens Help Protect a Fossil Site

In the 1800's, a site containing fossils of Ice Age animals such as giant ground sloths, peccaries, and mastodons was discovered a few kilometers south of St. Louis, Missouri. By the early 1900's, the fossilized bones of as many as 60 mastodons had been taken from the site. The area was recognized as a major fossil site, but in the 1970's, the land was put up for sale.

Local citizens became concerned that the remaining fossils would be destroyed or covered by buildings on the site. The citizens began a drive to raise money to buy the land and preserve it as a park.

Local students raised money in several ways. Students from one school district raised over $8000 by going door to door. A fifth grade class held a walkathon from their school to the fossil site, collecting $500 in pledges. Students wrote hundreds of letters to the governor and the state legislature asking for help in saving the area. Eventually people succeeded in raising over $560 000. With this money, the state Department of Natural Resources purchased 418 acres containing the fossil beds. This land is now preserved as Mastodon State Park, and research on the fossils continues. ■

Over the years, living things became larger and more complex. Eventually, some forms of life spread from the oceans to the land. The fossil record shows several times when many species died out. Other forms of life developed and took the place of the extinct organisms.

Fossil evidence suggests that life-forms have changed over time as a result of natural selection. In **natural selection,** a species changes over time because some individual organisms are better adapted to their environment than other individuals. The better-adapted organisms live longer and produce more offspring similar to themselves. Individual organisms that are less adapted to the environment do not live as long and thus produce fewer offspring. Imagine an island that has a population of mice. Some of the mice have heavier coats of fur than others. The climate gets colder for a period of time. The mice with the heavy coats are better able to survive cold temperatures. As a result, the mice with heavy coats survive longer and produce more offspring than the mice with light coats. After several generations, most of the mice have heavy coats. For a long time, scientists considered natural selection to be a slow, steady process. But the fossil record shows that forms of life have sometimes changed suddenly after long time periods with little change. Scientists continue to study fossils and changes in modern organisms to determine how natural selection happens.

Fossils tell you not only about past life and changes in Earth's environments, but also about the rocks themselves. In the next lesson, you will learn more about how fossils help geologists date rocks.

Figure 14-7 Which of these moths is more likely to be eaten by a bird?

Lesson Review 14.1

1. Why are complete, unchanged remains of plants and animals uncommon?

2. How do trace fossils differ from other fossil types?

3. Describe the theory of natural selection.

Interpret and Apply

4. How would the types of fossils found in a 2 000 000 000-year-old layer of rock compare with fossil types found in a 2 000 000-year-old layer of rock?

5. Suppose you found some fish fossils while climbing high in the Rocky Mountains. What could you conclude about the type of environment present when the fossils formed?

14.2 Relative Dating

Lesson Objectives

▶ **Trace** a rock-forming sequence by using geologic principles.

▶ **Compare** three types of unconformities.

▶ **Determine** the meaning of gaps in the rock record.

▶ **Determine** the relative ages of rocks by comparing similar rock layers in different locations.

▶ **Activity** **Interpret data** from geologic diagrams.

New Terms

relative age	key bed
uniformitarianism	index fossil
unconformity	geologic
correlation	column

Look at the cars in Figure 14-8. You might not know the exact year each car was built, but you could probably arrange the cars in order of age. You can do the same thing with layers of rock. By studying the positions of rock layers, you can determine the order in which the layers formed. The **relative age** of rock layers lists the layers in order of age. Geologists determine the relative ages of rocks by studying fossils and by using several principles of geology.

Geologic Principles

Geologic principles are general rules that come from observations of the rock and simple logic. You will learn about the principles of uniformitarianism, original horizontality, superposition, cross-cutting relationships, and included fragments. Some of the terms might sound complicated, but the ideas behind them are fairly simple.

Principle of Uniformitarianism Early geologists thought that all the geologic features on Earth had formed quickly. For example, these geologists thought that a single earthquake could raise an entire mountain range. Then, in 1795, James Hutton, a Scottish geologist, presented a different idea. He noticed that processes like erosion, deposition, and uplift were slowly changing Earth's surface. He thought that the same slow processes also changed Earth's surface in the past. His idea, known as **uniformitarianism** [yü ni fōr mi ter′ ē ə niz m], means that geologic processes occurred in the past in the same way as they do today.

Figure 14-8 Can you arrange these cars in order of age?

Principle of Original Horizontality Sediments are almost always deposited in flat, horizontal layers. When you see sedimentary layers that are not horizontal, you know that a later geologic event must have tilted them. For example, compression of the rocks may have cracked the layers and tilted them gradually.

Principle of Superposition Is your school or other familiar building built of bricks? When you look at such a building, notice that the bricks are layered row upon row. Which row of bricks do you think the builders laid first? Geologists realized that they could answer the same questions about layers of sedimentary rock. The principle of superposition states that younger rock layers were deposited on top of older rock layers. Knowing this, you can figure out the relative ages of each layer in a set of sedimentary rocks. Which layer in Figure 14-9 is the oldest?

Using the principle of superposition is simple when the rock layers are horizontal or almost horizontal. But sometimes the folding processes you learned about in Chapter 10 turn over the rock layers. Figure 14-10 shows that the oldest layers are on top if the rocks turn over completely. In this case, you would have to look at other features in the rocks to figure out which layer is really the oldest. For example, you might find older fossils in the higher of two rock layers. This might indicate that the layers have been turned upside down. Other features in the rock can give you clues about what has happened to the rock layers. For example, suppose you find preserved mud cracks on what appears to be the bottom of a rock layer. Since mud cracks always form on top of a sediment layer, you know that the layer has been overturned.

Figure 14-9 Which of these layers is the oldest? Which is the youngest?

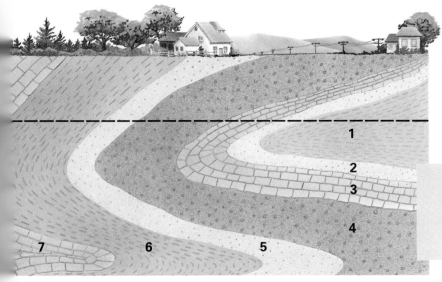

Figure 14-10 These layers are numbered from oldest (Layer 1) to youngest (Layer 7). After the surface has eroded down to the dashed line, however, the fold makes Layer 1 appear to be the youngest.

Shale
Sandstone
Conglomerate
Limestone

Figure 14-11 This basalt dike cuts across older bedrock.

Figure 14-12 The tilted layers were eroded before the horizontal layers were deposited on top, forming an angular unconformity.

Principle of Cross-Cutting Relationships Recall that igneous dikes form as hot magma moves into cracks in rocks and then cools. Figure 14-11 shows an example of an igneous dike. What can you say about the relative age of the bedrock in the picture compared to the age of the dike that cuts across it? The bedrock had to be there before the dike formed. The principle of cross-cutting relationships tells you that igneous structures are younger than the rock they cut across. The principle of cross-cutting relationships also applies to faults. Faults are younger than the rock they cut across.

Principle of Included Fragments Think about a chocolate chip cookie. Which was made first, the cookie or the chocolate chips? Some rocks contain pieces, or fragments, of other rocks. Recall from Chapter 9 that conglomerate contains pebble-size pieces of older rock that are cemented together. The principle of included fragments states that the pebbles in the conglomerate are older than the layer of conglomerate itself.

Breaks in the Rock Record

Look again at the layers of sedimentary rock in Figure 14-9. You might think that as soon as one layer was deposited, the next layer was immediately added on top. Sometimes layers are deposited one right after the other. However, uplift and erosion may have interrupted the deposition of sediments. A break in the rock record is called an unconformity. An **unconformity** represents a period of time when rocks were above sea level. Rainwater, ice, and wind eroded the rocks. No new layers of sediment were deposited. Later the climate changed or the surface was covered by water or ice. The water deposited new layers of sediments on the eroded surface. The land surface you see outside will become an unconformity later if water deposits new sediments on the land. The rocks above an unconformity are always younger than the rocks below it.

Three types of unconformities can develop according to this general process. Figure 14-12 shows an angular unconformity, the easiest type of unconformity to identify. Can you tell why it is called angular? The layers you see in the lower part of the photograph were deposited horizontally under water. Then geologic forces tilted the layers. The uplifted ends of the layers were eroded. Some time later, the rocks sank again and water covered the rocks. The water deposited new horizontal layers of sediments on top of the eroded surface.

Sometimes level layers are eroded and then covered by new sediments. In this case, the unconformity is called a disconformity. Disconformities are difficult to recognize because the layers above and below the disconformity are parallel. The third type of unconformity is a nonconformity. A nonconformity results when sedimentary rocks are deposited on top of eroded igneous or metamorphic rocks.

Unconformities in the rock record tell you that information about the geologic history of an area is missing. Still, unconformities do give you some information about past uplift, erosion, and sinking of the area.

Correlation of Rocks

Geologic principles and observations of unconformities tell you the general order of events that produced the rocks in a certain location. You can also determine the relative ages of rocks by comparing rocks from different locations. The layers of rock on either side of a canyon match up with one another. By examining two layers opposite each other on the canyon walls, you would find that they are actually the same layer. The layer was cut in half as the rock eroded. The process of matching rock layers from different locations is called **correlation.**

Correlating rocks that are more widely separated requires more information. Geologists look for a **key bed,** which is a widespread layer that is easy to recognize. Layers of volcanic ash are common key beds. Tracing a key bed from one place to another can help you figure out the relative ages of other rocks in the region. When you identify a key bed in two different locations, you know that the rocks below the key bed in both places are older than the rocks above the key bed. Often, you can recognize a key bed in locations separated by hundreds of kilometers. Do you know of an area in the United States where the ash from a volcanic eruption might later form a key bed?

Index fossils also help you to correlate rock layers. An **index fossil** is the remains of a living thing that was widespread but existed only for a few million years of Earth's history. Rock layers that contain the same index fossil are about the same age. Trilobites are examples of good index fossils. Trilobites were animals that once lived on the bottoms of shallow oceans all over the world. The fossil record shows that trilobites existed for about 350 000 000 years. However, some kinds of trilobite were widespread for only a short period of time. Finding fossils of a specific kind of trilobite in widely separated rock layers tells you that those rock layers formed at about the same time.

Fact or Fiction?

Did King Kong actually exist? Fossil bones of a giant ape have been discovered in Vietnam. Scientists call the ape *Gigantopithecus.* Measurements of the fossils indicate that the plant-eating ape may have been as much as 4 meters tall. Scientists are searching for evidence that *Gigantopithecus* lived in southeast Asia at the same time as early humans. Scientists think that *Homo erectus,* an ancestor of modern humans, may have hunted the large ape to extinction.

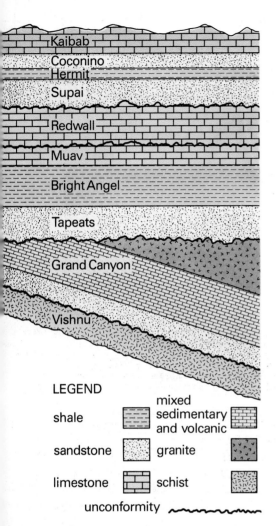

Kaibab
Coconino
Hermit
Supai
Redwall
Muav
Bright Angel
Tapeats
Grand Canyon
Vishnu

LEGEND

		mixed
shale		sedimentary and volcanic
sandstone		granite
limestone		schist
unconformity		

Figure 14-13 *Left:* The geologic column for the Grand Canyon; *Right:* Can you locate each layer in the Grand Canyon?

After you have found the relative ages of the rocks in an area, you can draw up a geologic column. A **geologic column** shows the complete stack of rock layers in order of age. Figure 14-13 shows a portion of a geologic column for the Grand Canyon. The legend gives the symbols for the different kinds of rock. You can correlate geologic columns from different areas by using key beds and index fossils. From your correlation, you can put together a column for a larger area.

Geologists have determined the actual ages of many key beds and index fossils. Thus, the presence of a key bed or index fossils in a rock layer tells you how many years ago the layer formed. In the next lesson, you will learn how geologists measure the actual ages of rocks.

Lesson Review 14.2

6. Explain how to use the principle of superposition to determine the relative ages of a series of sedimentary rock layers.

7. Why is a disconformity more difficult to recognize than an angular unconformity?

8. What geologic processes might leave a break in the rock record?

Interpret and Apply

9. A layer of rock contains the same index fossil as another layer 500 kilometers away. The first layer is covered by a key bed of volcanic ash, but the second layer is not. Explain how this might have happened.

ACTIVITY 14.2

Paper & Pencil

RELATIVE DATING

Purpose   To interpret data from geologic diagrams.

Materials _____

pencil	diagrams in Figures
paper	14-14 and 14-15

Procedure

1. Study Figures 14-14 and 14-15. The diagrams contain some rock layers that are the same age.

2. Use the principles you learned in this lesson to list the layers, faults, episodes of erosion, and intrusions in Figure 14-14 in the order they occurred.

3. Repeat step 2 for Figure 14-15.

Collecting and Analyzing Data

1. How do you know that the order of events you listed for Figure 14-14 is correct?

2. In Figure 14-15, which way did the rocks move on each side of the fault? How can you tell?

3. How do you know whether the fault in Figure 14-15 occurred before or after the rock layers were deposited?

4. Did the igneous dike in Figure 14-15 form before or after the fault? How do you know?

5. Which kind of unconformity is shown near the top of Figure 14-15?

Drawing Conclusions

6. Which diagram represents the area that has had the most geologic activity overall? How can you tell?

7. Can you tell which diagram represents the longest period of time? Explain your answer.

8. Which layer in Figure 14-14 might have formed at the same time as layer W in Figure 14-15? How can you tell?

9. Can you be sure whether the dike in Figure 14-15 formed before or after the conglomerate layer T? Why or why not? What about the granite at the bottom of Figure 14-14?

Figure 14-14

Figure 14-15

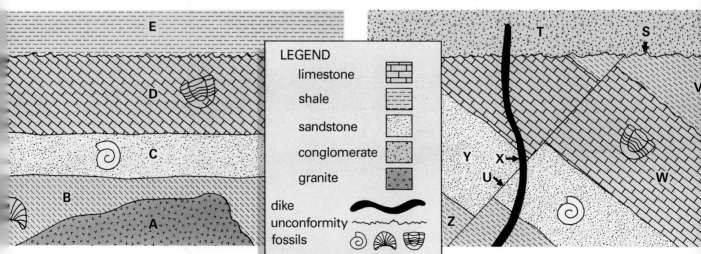

LEGEND

limestone	
shale	
sandstone	
conglomerate	
granite	
dike	
unconformity	
fossils	

14.3 Absolute Dating

Lesson Objectives

▶ **Describe** methods of determining the age of Earth.

▶ **Describe** the process of radioactive decay.

▶ **Compare** the advantages of different kinds of radioactive dating.

▶ **Activity** **Form a model** for the half-life of a radioactive substance.

New Terms

absolute age
radioactive decay
isotopes
half-life

Relative age lists layers of rock in order of age, but it does not tell you the actual age of the rocks. The **absolute age** of a rock is its age in years. Absolute age tells how long ago the rock formed. The absolute ages of rocks help geologists determine the age of Earth.

People have long wondered about the age of Earth. Ancient Greek philosophers assumed that Earth had existed forever. Centuries ago the Chinese believed that everything in the universe, including Earth, was destroyed and recreated every 24 000 000 years. In Ireland in the 1600's, a well-known official calculated that Earth was created at 9 A.M. on October 26, 4004 B.C. In those days, scientists had not yet developed methods to measure the age of Earth.

Methods of Estimating Earth's Age

In the 1800's, several scientists did attempt to determine Earth's absolute age. One group of scientists measured how fast sediments like those in Figure 14-16 are deposited. They also measured the total thickness of the sediments. By combining these two pieces of data, they estimated Earth's age to be 96 000 000 years. A second method used the idea that all the salt in the oceans originally came from rocks on the land. First, scientists calculated the total amount of salt in the ocean. Then they divided the total by the amount of salt they thought the rivers added each year. Scientists using the second method figured that Earth was 80 000 000 to 90 000 000 years old. Can you think of reasons why these two methods do not give an accurate age for Earth?

Figure 14-16 If you measured the rate at which sedimentary layers like these are deposited, could you accurately estimate Earth's age?

In the 1860's, a British scientist named William Thomson estimated Earth's age by measuring how fast Earth had cooled since its formation. Thomson announced that Earth had formed between 20 000 000 and 40 000 000 years ago. However, Thomson assumed that no heat had been produced in Earth since it first formed. But in the early 1900's, scientists discovered that radioactive elements in rocks release large amounts of energy. This energy heats up the core of Earth. The discovery of this heat source meant that Thomson's age for Earth was incorrect. However, radioactive elements were eventually used to measure the age of Earth accurately.

Radioactive Decay

You learned in Chapter 7 that all matter is made of atoms. The number of protons in an atom's nucleus determines the atom's atomic number and the kind of element. For most atoms, the atomic number stays constant. But the number of protons in the atoms of some elements changes. When this happens, a new element forms. Look at the periodic table on pages 182–183. Imagine that an atom of uranium loses 2 protons. What new kind of atom does the uranium atom become? The process in which one element changes into another element as the number of protons in its atoms changes is called **radioactive decay.** The new type of atom that forms from radioactive decay is called a decay product.

Isotopes of an element have the same number of protons but different numbers of neutrons. Many elements have isotopes that are radioactive. Figure 14-17 compares a carbon-12 atom with an atom of carbon-14. The numbers 12 and 14 represent the total number of protons and neutrons in the nucleus. Both isotopes of carbon have 6 protons. Carbon-12 atoms have 6 neutrons. Carbon-14, a radioactive isotope of carbon, has 8 neutrons. Most carbon found on Earth is carbon-12. Carbon-14 is present in small quantities.

As radioactive decay occurs, the atom gives off particles. One type of particle some radioactive elements give off is called an alpha particle. An alpha particle consists of two protons and two neutrons from the nucleus of the radioactive atom. The decay product has two fewer protons than the original element. Look at the periodic table on pages 182–183 again. What is the decay product when radon gives off an alpha particle? In other types of radioactive atoms, a neutron breaks apart into two new particles. One particle is given off. The particle left behind in the nucleus is a proton. The decay product has one more proton and one less neutron than the original radioactive element.

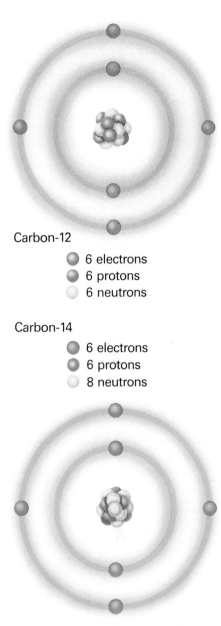

Carbon-12

- 6 electrons
- 6 protons
- 6 neutrons

Carbon-14

- 6 electrons
- 6 protons
- 8 neutrons

Figure 14-17 Carbon-12 and carbon-14 each have six protons, but carbon-14 has two extra neutrons.

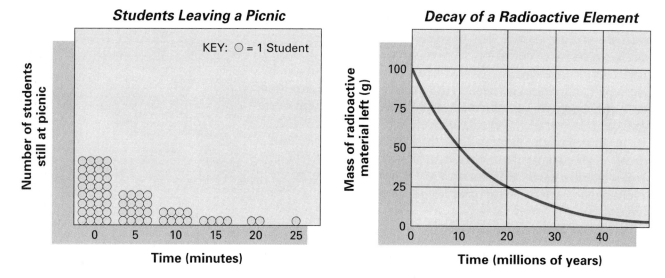

Students Leaving a Picnic

KEY: ◯ = 1 Student

Number of students still at picnic

Time (minutes)

Decay of a Radioactive Element

Mass of radioactive material left (g)

Time (millions of years)

Figure 14-18 *Left:* If four students are left at the picnic, how long ago did the students begin leaving? *Right:* If a rock contains 12.5 grams of radioactive material left from the original 100 grams, how old is the rock?

In the early 1900's, scientists discovered that radioactive elements decay at predictable rates. A radioactive element's **half-life** is the period of time needed for half of the element to change to the decay product. Imagine 32 students at a picnic. Every 5 minutes, half of the students leave the picnic. The students who have left the picnic have "decayed." In other words, the half-life of the picnic crowd is 5 minutes. Figure 14-18 *(left)* is a graph showing the decrease in the number of students over a period of time. After 5 minutes, there would be 16 students left at the picnic. If you know the original number of students and the number of students remaining at the picnic, you can use the graph to tell how long ago students began leaving. In other words, you can figure out when the decay process began.

Age of Rocks

Many igneous rocks contain small amounts of radioactive material. The radioactive element began to decay when the rock first cooled from magma or lava. By comparing the amounts of the original element and its decay product, you can find out how long ago the rock formed. Use the graph of an imaginary radioactive element in Figure 14-18 *(right)* to work the following example. What is the half-life of the imaginary element? Suppose that a rock sample contained 100 grams of the radioactive element when it first formed. Now the rock contains 12.5 grams of the element. How long ago did the rock form? This method of determining absolute age is not usually used for sedimentary or metamorphic rocks. The age of a sedimentary or metamorphic rock as measured by radioactive decay is the age of its included fragments, not the age of the rock itself.

Table 14-1 shows half-lives and decay products for several radioactive elements. The long half-lives of uranium and rubidium make them useful for measuring the ages of Earth's oldest rocks. Potassium can be used for younger rocks because it has a shorter half-life. Potassium is also useful because it is found in a greater number of rocks than uranium or rubidium. Carbon-14 is often used to determine the age of original organic remains in rocks. Because of its short half-life, carbon-14 is useful in determining the ages of plant and animal remains that are less than 100 000 years old. Because most rocks are older than 100 000 years, carbon-14 is not used to determine the ages of most rocks.

The ages of rocks from many parts of the world have been measured by means of radioactive dating. Figure 14-19 shows the oldest rocks found so far. These rocks come from northwestern Canada. They have been dated at 3 960 000 000 years of age. But Earth itself is older than these rocks. As a result of plate movements, erosion, and deposition, the rocks that formed as Earth itself formed no longer exist.

In Chapter 4, you learned some theories about the formation of the moon. Most astronomers think that the moon and Earth formed at about the same time. Compared to Earth's surface, the surface of the moon has changed very little since it first formed. It is possible that some rocks on the moon are as old as the moon itself. If the moon and Earth formed at about the same time, the age of the oldest moon rocks would be about the same as Earth's age. Because of this idea, scientists used radioactive dating on moon rocks collected by the *Apollo* astronauts. Based on the age of the oldest rocks brought back from the moon, 4 600 000 000 years is now the accepted age for Earth.

As scientific knowledge has increased, estimates of Earth's age have changed several times in the past few centuries. Radioactive dating of lunar rocks brought back by the *Apollo* astronauts has given the most recent value of 4 600 000 000 years. But it is possible that new technology or the discovery of even older rocks will cause scientists to change their estimates once again.

Figure 14-19 One of the world's oldest rocks.

Table 14-1 Some Radioactive Elements		
Radioactive Element	**Final Decay Product**	**Half-Life (years)**
uranium-238	lead-206	4 500 000 000
potassium-40	argon-40	1 300 000 000
rubidium-87	strontium-87	49 000 000 000
carbon-14	nitrogen-14	5 730

ACTIVITY 14.3

General Supplies

RADIOACTIVE DECAY

Purpose To form a model for the half-life of a radioactive substance.

Materials

box with lid	pencil or marker
100 flat toothpicks	graph paper

Procedure

1. Read all instructions for this activity before you begin your work.

2. Copy the data table onto your paper. Make room for at least 15 entries.

3. Use your pencil or marker to put a mark on one side of the box.

4. Place the 100 toothpicks in the box. Write *100* in your data table for Shake 0.

5. Place the lid on the box and shake the box for 3 s.

6. Open the box. Imagine that you can extend the line of each toothpick from the round end to the pointed end toward one of the sides of the box. Remove all the toothpicks that are pointing toward the marked side of the box.

7. Count the toothpicks that are left in the box. Record this number in your data table for Shake 1.

8. Repeat steps 5 through 7 until the box is empty.

Collecting and Analyzing Data

Data Table	
Shake	**Number of Toothpicks Left**
0	
1	
2	
3	
4	

1. Graph the information in the data table on a graph like the sample graph shown here.

2. How many shakes were needed to remove all of the toothpicks? To remove 50 toothpicks?

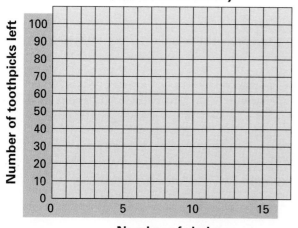

Radioactive Decay

Number of toothpicks left (y-axis: 0, 10, 20, 30, 40, 50, 60, 70, 80, 90, 100)

Number of shakes (x-axis: 0, 5, 10, 15)

Drawing Conclusions

3. Compare your toothpick model with radioactive decay. What do the original 100 toothpicks represent?

4. What do the toothpicks you removed represent?

5. Let each shake represent 1 000 000 years. What is the half-life of the element?

6. Suppose that a rock sample began with 100 undecayed radioactive atoms. If there are 25 undecayed atoms in a rock, how old is the rock?

Lesson Review 14.3

10. Describe how the cooling rate of Earth was used to measure the age of Earth. Explain why this method gave an incorrect value for Earth's age.

11. Describe the two types of changes that can occur in the nucleus of a radioactive atom during decay.

12. In what way does an atom of carbon-14 differ from an atom of carbon-12?

13. What is the accepted value for the age of Earth? How was this value determined?

Interpret and Apply

14. Give two reasons why carbon-14 would not be useful in determining the age of an igneous rock.

Chapter Summary

Read this summary of the main ideas in this chapter. If any are not clear to you, go back and review that lesson.

14.1 The Fossil Record

■ Fossils represent a small fraction of the organisms that have existed on Earth.

■ Organisms are more likely to become fossilized if they have hard parts and are buried soon after death.

■ A trace fossil is a record left behind by an organism while it was still alive.

■ Fossils indicate both changes in the types of life that have existed on Earth and past changes in the environment.

14.2 Relative Dating

■ Relative age tells whether one event occurred before or after another event.

■ Geologic principles can be used to determine the order in which some geologic events occurred.

■ Unconformities represent missing information from the rock record.

■ Rocks from one area can be correlated with rocks from another area by using index fossils and key beds.

14.3 Absolute Dating

■ Absolute age is the actual age in years of a geologic event, rock, or fossil.

■ The number of protons in the nucleus of a radioactive element changes, producing an atom of a different element.

■ The presence of radioactive elements in an igneous rock enables scientists to determine the age of the rock.

■ Carbon-14 is useful for dating organic remains in rocks that are less than 100 000 years old.

■ Radioactive decay of elements in lunar rocks has allowed scientists to estimate the age of Earth as 4 600 000 000 years.

Chapter Review

■ Vocabulary

absolute age
carbonized fossils
cast
correlation
geologic column
half-life
imprints
index fossil
isotopes

key bed
mold
natural selection
paleontologist
radioactive decay
relative age
trace fossil
unconformity
uniformitarianism

■ Concept Mapping

Using the method of concept mapping described on pages 3–5, complete a concept map for the rock record. Copy the incomplete concept map shown below. Then fill in the missing terms.

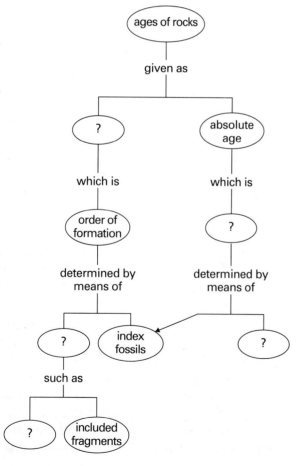

■ Review

Number your paper from 1 to 20. Match each term in List **A** with a phrase in List **B**.

List A

a. absolute age
b. radioactive decay
c. isotopes
d. half-life
e. paleontologist
f. natural selection
g. relative age
h. unconformity
i. correlation
j. key bed
k. index fossil

l. uniformitarianism
m. cross-cutting relationships
n. superposition
o. included fragments
p. proton
q. decay product
r. imprint
s. original remains
t. trace fossil

List B

1. tells that a rock layer is older than one layer but younger than another, without giving exact age in years

2. principle that says an igneous dike is younger than the rocks it cuts across

3. process where atoms of an element change into atoms of another element

4. principle that says that the oldest layer is on the bottom of a series of rock layers

5. principle that states that better-adapted organisms are more likely to survive and reproduce

6. atomic particle that determines which element an atom makes up

7. any break in the rock record

8. atoms of an element that contain the same number of protons but different numbers of neutrons

9. actual age of a rock in years

10. scientist who studies fossils

11. matching of rock layers of the same age

12. shallow impression left in sedimentary rock by a flat organism

13. fossil of an organism that lived for a geologically short period of time over a large area

14. widespread layer that allows geologists to match rock layers in different areas

15. time needed for half of the original amount of a radioactive element to decay

16. principle that says that pebbles in conglomerate are older than the conglomerate

17. preservation of a complete organism

18. preserved footprints or burrows

19. new element that forms from radioactive decay

20. principle that says geologic processes today are the same as in the past

■ Interpret and Apply

On your paper, answer each question using complete sentences.

21. A deer drowns while crossing a stream. Describe how the deer might be fossilized.

22. Fossils of tropical plants have been found in Greenland. What do these fossils tell about past climates in this cold region?

23. While observing some sedimentary rock layers, you find an index fossil in one of the lower layers that is younger than a fossil in one of the upper layers. Explain what might have happened to the layers.

24. Explain why an unconformity is considered a break in the rock record.

25. How did the discovery of heat-producing radioactive elements in Earth's crust affect scientists' estimates of Earth's age?

26. How does the amount of a radioactive element compare to the amount of its decay product over a period of time?

27. You find a carbonized fossil in shale. How could you determine the age of the shale?

■ Writing in Science

28. What trace fossils of present-day humans might be found two million years from now? Describe what the trace fossils would look like. What could future paleontologists learn about modern humans by studying these fossils?

■ Critical Thinking

Use your understanding of radioactive decay and the decay graph for carbon-14 below to answer the following questions.

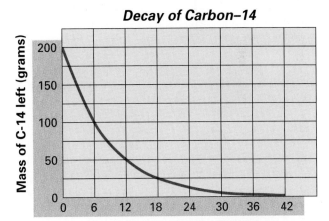

Decay of Carbon–14

29. If a tree trunk that originally contained 200 grams of carbon-14 now contains 12.5 grams, how long ago did the tree die?

30. Scientists find a piece of wood left over from an ancient campfire. The wood originally contained 6.25 grams of carbon-14. The wood comes from a tree that died 6000 years ago. How much carbon-14 is left in the wood?

31. Some pieces of partially cooked grain containing carbon-14 are found near the wood mentioned in question 30. The grain originally contained 0.48 gram of carbon-14. When the grain is discovered, it contains only 0.12 gram of carbon-14. Could this grain have been cooked in the campfire built from the wood? How do you know?

15 Earth's History

Chapter Preview

*H*ave You Ever WONDERED?

Were the dinosaurs cold-blooded, slow-moving reptiles?

Recently, some paleontologists have disagreed with this description. Careful study of dinosaur bones suggests that some dinosaurs were warm blooded. Closely-spaced nesting sites may indicate that some dinosaurs cared for their young for a time after birth. Dinosaur footprints show that some of the plant eaters traveled in herds. Adult dinosaurs surrounded the young in the center of the herd. Have you ever noticed that you take longer steps when you run than when you walk? The distance between some dinosaur footprints is large enough to show that the dinosaurs could run quite fast. These pieces of evidence suggest that some dinosaurs were more like warm-blooded mammals and birds than like modern reptiles.

15.1 *Precambrian Earth*

Lesson Objectives

▶ **Describe** how Earth may have formed.

▶ **List** the divisions of the geologic timetable.

▶ **Compare** Earth's early atmosphere with today's atmosphere.

▶ **Describe** early forms of life.

▶ **Activity** **Observe** and **describe** how liquids of different densities separate into layers, as molten materials may have separated in early Earth.

New Terms

geologic timetable	epochs
eras	stromatolites
periods	invertebrates

Imagine that there were no calendars or clocks. If someone asked you how long ago the Declaration of Independence was signed, what would you tell them? What if you wanted to know how long you slept last night? These questions would be hard to answer without a method of timekeeping. People use calendars and clocks to keep track of time and events. The year's calendar is divided into units of time called months, weeks, and days. The calendar tells you that Washington's birthday is in February, the first day of spring is in March, and so on. Geologists also use a calendar. The geologists' calendar marks important events during Earth's history. In this lesson, you will learn about the early history of Earth and the geologic timetable.

Formation of Earth

According to one theory, the solar system formed about 4 600 000 000 (4.6 billion) years ago from a cold, rotating cloud of dust and gas. At first, Earth had no atmosphere or oceans. If you cut Earth open, you would find that its interior contained a mixture of iron and lighter materials. According to the theory, heat from compression and radioactive decay in Earth's interior raised its temperature. Much of Earth's interior melted. In any mixture of liquids, denser materials sink and less dense materials rise. Figure 15-1 shows the denser iron and nickel sinking to Earth's core. Heated gases and steam erupted through the new crust. Heat from radioactive decay in Earth's core makes the plates of Earth's crust continue to move and to change.

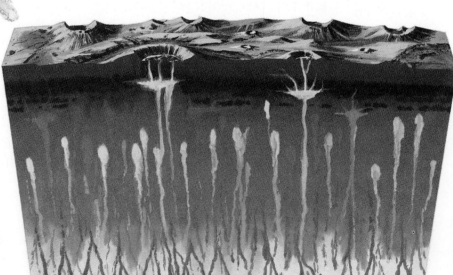

Figure 15-1 Dense material sank to Earth's core during an early stage in Earth's formation.

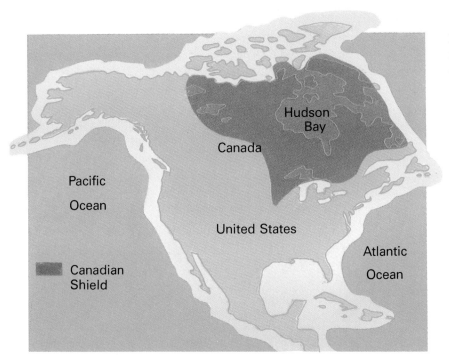

Figure 15-2 The Canadian Shield is the ancient Precambrian center of the North American continent.

Geologic Timetable

You learned in Chapter 14 that Earth's age is about 4 600 000 000 years. Many changes in Earth's surface and in forms of life on Earth have occurred during that time. To keep track of these changes, geologists use a special type of timetable. The **geologic timetable** in Table 15-1 divides Earth's history into units of time. The longest units of time in the geologic timetable are **eras.** The eras are divided into **periods.** The periods are divided into **epochs.** Major changes in the fossil record mark the beginning and end of each time unit. The change is usually the disappearance of one kind of life from the fossil record and the appearance of another. The eras' names refer to the kinds of life in the fossil record during those times. The Archeozoic (beginning life) and Proterozoic (early life) eras are sometimes combined into Precambrian (before Cambrian) time. *Paleozoic* means "ancient life," *Mesozoic* means "middle life," and *Cenozoic* means "recent life." Notice that the more recent units of time are shorter than the older units. Shorter divisions are possible because the recent fossil record is more complete. The recent fossil record shows more changes in life-forms than the early fossil record.

Today's continents formed around central masses of Precambrian rock. The map in Figure 15-2 shows the Canadian Shield, the largest mass of Precambrian rock in North America. Precambrian rocks are also visible in other uplifted and eroded areas. Such areas include parts of the Rocky Mountains, the Appalachians, the Ozarks, and the Grand Canyon.

Figure 15-3 Precambrian rocks like these are visible in several areas of the United States.

Table 15-1 The Geologic Timetable

Era	Period	Epoch	Began (Years Ago)	Events
Cenozoic	Quaternary	Recent	11 000	Humans dominant
		Pleistocene	2 000 000	Ice ages, early humans, mammoths
	Tertiary	Pliocene	7 000 000	Mammals develop further
		Miocene	23 000 000	Alaska joined to Asia, more mammals
		Oligocene	38 000 000	Land mammals reach large size
		Eocene	53 000 000	Ancestors of modern mammals
		Paleocene	65 000 000	Many new mammals
Mesozoic	Cretaceous		136 000 000	Dinosaurs disappear, flowering plants and trees appear
	Jurassic		195 000 000	Large dinosaurs
	Triassic		230 000 000	First dinosaurs, Pangaea begins to split apart

(continued at top of next page)

Table 15-1 continued

Era	Period	Epoch	Began (Years Ago)	Events	
Paleozoic	Permian		280 000 000	Mass extinctions, continents join to form Pangaea	
	Pennsylvanian		310 000 000	Coal swamps	
	Mississippian		345 000 000	Crinoids abundant, First reptiles	
	Devonian		395 000 000	First amphibians	
	Silurian		435 000 000	First land animals and plants	
	Ordovician		500 000 000	First vertebrates (Fish)	
	Cambrian		570 000 000	Trilobites abundant	
Proterozoic	Precambrian time		2 500 000 000	First jellyfish	
Archeozoic			3 800 000 000	Bacteria, one-celled organisms	
Formation of Earth			4 600 000 000	Earth contracts, heats up	

Earth's Ancient Atmosphere

As Figure 15-4 illustrates, the gases that escaped through volcanoes in the crust of young Earth formed the early atmosphere. If you had visited Earth at that time, however, you could not have breathed the atmosphere for long. Earth's ancient atmosphere did not contain the same gases as today's atmosphere. The ancient atmosphere probably contained many of the same gases that modern volcanoes give off. These gases include carbon dioxide, carbon monoxide, sulfur dioxide, water vapor, hydrogen, nitrogen, and some other gases. Scientists have found evidence that Earth's ancient atmosphere contained no oxygen. Rocks older than 3 000 000 000 years contain iron but no iron oxide (rust). If there had been any oxygen in the atmosphere, it would have combined with iron in the rocks to form iron oxide. Early plantlike bacteria took in carbon dioxide and released oxygen into the lower atmosphere. Thus, early life played a role in changing Earth's atmosphere.

The water vapor in the atmosphere eventually condensed into clouds that produced rain. Since Earth was still hot, the rain evaporated back into the atmosphere. More clouds formed and more rain fell. As Earth continued to cool, rain stayed on the surface as liquid water. The water filled the low areas of Earth's crust and formed the original oceans. Geologists have found marine sedimentary rocks that are 3 800 000 000 years old. These rocks show that some oceans had formed within Earth's first billion years.

Figure 15-4 The gases of Earth's early atmosphere probably came from volcanoes.

DENSITY OF LIQUIDS

Purpose To observe and describe how liquids of different densities separate into layers, as molten materials may have separated in early Earth.

Materials

2 graduated cylinders	water
lab apron	vegetable oil
safety goggles	glycerin

Procedure

1. Read all instructions for this activity before you begin your work. Put on your lab apron and safety goggles.

2. Pour 2 mL of water into one of the graduated cylinders. Pour 2 mL of vegetable oil into the other graduated cylinder.

3. Add the water to the vegetable oil as shown in the figure. Observe the mixture of water and vegetable oil.

4. Repeat step 3, using the glycerin. You should now have all three liquids in the same graduated cylinder.

5. Examine the mixture. Draw a diagram of their arrangement on your paper.

6. Put your finger over the top of the graduated cylinder and shake it to mix the liquids. Put the graduated cylinder on the table. Do not touch the cylinder for at least 5 min.

7. After 5 min have gone by, draw another diagram of the arrangement of the liquids.

8. Before leaving the laboratory, clean up all materials and wash your hands thoroughly.

Collecting and Analyzing Data

1. What happened when you poured the water into the vegetable oil?

2. What happened when you poured the glycerin into the mixture?

3. In your first diagram, what is the order of the liquids from top to bottom?

4. How did the arrangement of the liquids change after you shook them?

5. Look at your second diagram. What happened to the mixed liquids after you let them sit for 5 minutes?

Drawing Conclusions

6. Why did the liquids arrange themselves in the order you observed?

7. Did the liquids separate completely again after you shook them? If you had let the liquids sit for a longer period of time, how would their arrangement have changed?

8. On the basis of this activity, write a sentence describing how liquids of different densities in the interior of young Earth would have arranged themselves.

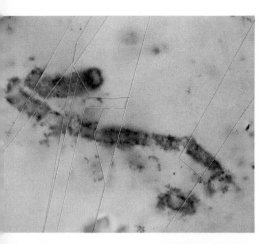

Figure 15-5 *Top:* This fossil bacterium is 3 500 000 000 years old. *Bottom:* These modern stromatolites are bacteria colonies cemented together by limestone layers.

Early Life

Scientific evidence suggests that life began in Earth's ancient oceans. Experiments show that simple organic molecules may have formed when sunlight and lightning acted upon the gases of the early atmosphere. These molecules collected in the oceans to form cells. The cells were similar to modern bacteria that cannot produce their own food. Eventually, some cells developed the ability to make their own food and to reproduce.

People have found few Precambrian fossils. The oldest fossils ever studied are about 3 500 000 000 years old. Figure 15-5 *(left)* shows one of these fossils, which look like modern bacteria. Some plantlike bacteria formed limestone mats called **stromatolites** in shallow, warm oceans. Fossil stromatolites look very much like the modern stromatolites in western Australia shown in Figure 15-5 *(right).* As time went on, single-celled organisms became more complex. Finally, animals without backbones, called **invertebrates,** developed in the oceans. Worms and jellyfish are examples of invertebrates that developed during Precambrian time. Precambrian fossils show little detail because these invertebrates contained only soft parts.

Precambrian time began when Earth formed 4 600 000 000 years ago and ended about 570 000 000 (570 million) years ago. In all, Precambrian time is more than 85 percent of the history of Earth. In the next lesson, you will learn how geologists decided when Precambrian time ended. You will also learn how Paleozoic Earth differed from Precambrian Earth.

Lesson Review 15.1

1. List the three most recent eras of geologic time. What type of change on Earth does the name for each era represent?

2. How did Earth's core become the densest part of Earth?

3. What gas that is necessary for human survival was not present in the early atmosphere? How did this gas eventually get into the atmosphere?

4. Give a reason why there are so few Precambrian fossils.

Interpret and Apply

5. Where did the water in Earth's oceans come from?

15.2 *The Paleozoic Era*

How did geologists decide that Precambrian time ended and the Paleozoic Era began 570 000 000 years ago? Rocks of the early Paleozoic Era contain many more fossils than Precambrian rocks. During the Paleozoic Era, life spread from the oceans to the continents. The continents themselves changed greatly due to plate motions. The stage was set for further changes after the Paleozoic Era ended.

Expansion of Life

Why do Paleozoic rocks contain more fossils than Precambrian rocks? One reason is that more living things actually existed by the beginning of the Cambrian Period. The main reason, however, is that invertebrates with hard parts had evolved. Some invertebrates developed the ability to grow shells. Table 15-1 shows that the Cambrian fossil record includes large numbers of shelled trilobites. The trilobites were 2 to more than 45 centimeters long. Cambrian rocks also contain fossils of brachiopods, shelled animals that you might mistake for clams. The fossils in Figure 15-6 *(right)* are brachiopods. Brachiopods still exist in some parts of the ocean today.

By the Ordovician Period, primitive fish had evolved. The Ordovician fish were early **vertebrates,** which are animals with backbones. During the Silurian Period, plants finally spread from the oceans onto land. The plants became food for some types of animals, which also spread to the land. People have found fossils of spiders and millipedes, the earliest known land animals, in Silurian rocks. Fish continued to evolve during the Devonian Period. Figure 15-6 *(left)* shows a fossil of a Devonian fish. Primitive lungfish, which can breathe air, appeared during the Devonian Period. Some lungfish had fins strong enough to lift themselves out of the water onto land. The first amphibians probably evolved from lungfish during the Devonian Period. Large ferns and pine trees grew on land during the Devonian Period.

Lesson Objectives

▶ *Identify* the major forms of life in each Paleozoic period.

▶ *Trace* the movement of the continents and geological activity during the Paleozoic Era.

▶ *Activity* *Form a model* representing the time span of Earth's history.

New Term

vertebrates

Figure 15-6 *Left:* Fish were the dominant life-form during the Devonian Period. *Right:* Ther were many brachiopods during the Cambrian Period.

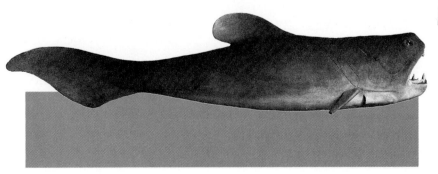

Figure 15-7 Crinoids, which are animals that attach themselves to the seafloor, were common during the Mississippian Period.

Fossils of the earliest known reptiles appear in Mississippian rocks. Many fish and other types of animals, like the crinoid in Figure 15-7, still lived in the oceans. Amphibians increased in number. During the Pennsylvanian Period, great forests and swamps, like those in the model shown in Figure 15-8, covered parts of the eastern United States. Coal formed when the plants in the swamps died and were buried under sediments. Fossils of insects show that they reached enormous sizes. Dragonflies had wingspans as wide as card tables, and some cockroaches were as long as an ice cream stick.

At the end of the Permian Period, 90 percent of all marine species and many land species disappeared from the fossil record. Geologists have concluded that these organisms died out altogether. What change would have been great enough to cause such a widespread extinction? Changes in climate, the usual weather pattern for an area, probably caused the extinctions. The climate over most of the land became very dry and cool. Some areas had an ice age. The disappearance of warm, shallow-sea environments killed many marine organisms. Tropical land plants did not survive the colder temperatures. Some species of plants and animals, however, survived into the Mesozoic Era.

Figure 15-8 A Pennsylvanian swamp

ENVIRONMENTAL AWARENESS

Mass Extinctions

The fossil record shows that several mass extinctions have occurred during Earth's history. During mass extinctions, many species have become extinct at the same time. Several possible causes, including the motions of continents and asteroid impacts, led to changes in the environment. Climate, food sources, sea level, and landscapes all changed. Some organisms died out because they were not able to adapt to their new environments.

Are changes in environment occurring today? Will more species become extinct? The answer to both questions is yes. But today, human activities are speeding up the changes. Pollution of Earth's air, land, and waters has endangered many species. The burning of millions of acres of rain forest has destroyed not only the trees but also many other forms of life in the forest. Humans have built roads, farms, and cities on much of Earth's surface. Do you think humans will become part of a mass extinction in the future? How should humans change their activities in order to prevent another extinction? ■

Geologic Changes

If you had a satellite image of Earth during the Cambrian Period, you would be able to see several continents. However, they would not look like today's continents. In Chapter 10, you learned that the continents move as the plates of Earth's crust move. During the early Paleozoic Era, most landmasses were located near the equator. These landmasses included the future continent of North America. What kind of climate do you think North America had at that time? Shallow seas covered parts of North America at various times during the Paleozoic Era.

Other landmasses collided with North America several times during the Paleozoic Era. During the Ordovician Period, a landmass collided with eastern North America. This collision began to lift sections of the Appalachian Mountains. In the Silurian Period, shallow seas covering North America evaporated. What minerals do you think the evaporating water deposited during the Silurian Period? North America collided with two other landmasses late in the Devonian Period. One landmass was probably part of Europe. This landmass hit northeastern North America. The collision lifted the northern Appalachian Mountains still higher. The other landmass hit western North America, raising the early Rocky Mountains.

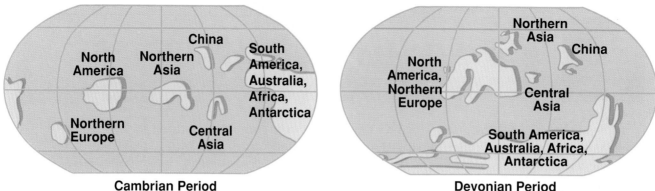

Cambrian Period　　　　　　　**Devonian Period**

Figure 15-9 The continents of the Paleozoic Era looked different from today's continents.

The last collision occurred during the late Mississippian Period. The combined continents of Africa and South America collided with North America. This final mountain-building event raised the central and southern Appalachians. By the end of the Pennsylvanian Period, mountains ringed the entire southern border of North America. The same collision raised a series of mountain ranges in the American Southwest. During most of the Mississippian and the Pennsylvanian, however, many parts of western North America remained under the sea. The sea deposited great amounts of sediment.

By the late Permian, all of the continents had come together to form the single supercontinent Pangaea. Since the large inland part of Pangaea was far from the ocean, the climate was dry. One enormous ocean covered most of Earth's surface area. Later, Pangaea split apart. The continents gradually moved to their present positions.

Lesson Review 15.2

6. Compare the dominant ocean animals during the Cambrian Period and Devonian Period.

7. Where on the globe was North America located at the beginning of the Paleozoic Era? Where was North America at the end of the Paleozoic Era?

8. What final geologic event lifted the Appalachian Mountains near the end of the Paleozoic Era?

Interpret and Apply

9. What changes in climate occurred at the end of the Paleozoic Era? How did geologic changes affect the oceans, causing the extinction of many animals there?

ACTIVITY 15.2

THE GEOLOGIC TIME SCALE

Purpose To form a model representing the time span of Earth's history.

Materials

5-meter strip of calculator tape	meterstick pencil

Procedure

1. Read all instructions for this activity before you begin your work.

2. Draw a short line across one end of the tape. Label the short line *Today*.

3. Mark a point 1 m from the line labeled *Today*. Label this mark *1 000 000 000 years ago*. Divide the entire tape into 1-m-long sections. Label your last mark *5 000 000 000 years ago*.

4. Earth formed 4 600 000 000 years ago. Using a scale of 1 cm = 10 000 000 years, the formation of Earth is 40 cm from the mark labeled *5 000 000 000 years ago*. Measure this length and mark it. Label the mark *Formation of Earth*.

5. Mark the boundary for each period, era, and epoch on the tape. Measure each length from the line labeled *Today* on your tape.

6. Mark the correct position for each event listed in the table below.

Table of Events

Event	Number of Years Ago	Distance on Tape (cm)
End of recent ice age	10 000	0.001
First humans	3 800 000	0.38
Extinction of dinosaurs	65 000 000	6.5
First mammals	200 000 000	20
First dinosaurs	230 000 000	23
First reptiles	340 000 000	34
First fish	480 000 000	48
Early trilobites	560 000 000	56
Oldest fossils	3 500 000 000	350
Oldest rocks	3 960 000 000	396

Collecting and Analyzing Data

1. Which era requires the longest length on the tape? Which era requires the shortest length on the tape?

2. On which end of the tape did you have the most difficulty marking the events?

3. How far from the *Today* end of the tape did you mark the *Formation of Earth*?

Drawing Conclusions

4. Why is the Precambrian part of the tape so empty while the *Today* end of the tape is so crowded?

5. Was there actually nothing going on during Precambrian time? Explain.

6. What percent of geologic history does Precambrian time represent?

7. How does the length of time that humans have been on Earth compare to the length of time dinosaurs were on Earth?

15.3 *The Mesozoic Era*

Lesson Objectives

▸ **Describe** the motion of the continents during the Mesozoic Era.

▸ **List** some forms of life that developed during the Mesozoic Era.

▸ **Summarize** scientists' theories for the extinction of the dinosaurs.

▸ **Activity** **Identify** and **control** **variables** that might affect the flight length for a flying reptile.

New Terms

Laurasia   reptile
Gondwanaland mammal

If you visited Earth at the beginning of the Mesozoic Era, you would find the continents still combined into one large landmass, Pangaea. The continental climate was cold and dry. Many Paleozoic life-forms no longer existed. As a result, new species developed and spread over Pangaea.

Separation of the Continents

About 200 000 000 years ago, Pangaea began to split into the continents that exist today. The series of maps in Figure 15-10 shows how the continents would have looked as they separated. First, Pangaea separated into two large continents during the Triassic Period. The landmasses that eventually became North America, Europe, and Asia composed the northern continent, called **Laurasia.** The southern continents of South America, Africa, Antarctica, and Australia made up **Gondwanaland.** During the Jurassic and Cretaceous periods, Laurasia and Gondwanaland broke apart into today's continents. Slowly the continents moved toward their present positions.

Figure 15-10 The continents began moving toward their present positions during the Mesozoic Era.

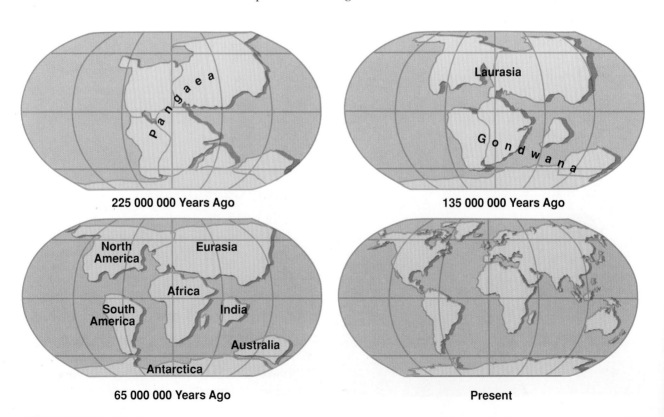

225 000 000 Years Ago

135 000 000 Years Ago

65 000 000 Years Ago

Present

Age of Reptiles

During the Mesozoic Era, reptiles gradually spread over the continents. **Reptiles** have some advantages over amphibians that allow reptiles to live greater distances from water. Most amphibians must spend time in water to keep their bodies moist. Amphibians must lay their eggs in water so that the eggs do not dry out. The scale-covered skin of a reptile helps to keep its body from losing moisture. Reptile eggs are also covered by a shell that prevents them from drying out. As a result, reptiles do not need to lay their eggs in water.

Rocks formed during the Mesozoic Era contain fossils of many kinds of reptiles. Today's alligators, crocodiles, turtles, snakes, and lizards evolved from the early reptiles. Some reptiles even developed the ability to fly. Reptiles also evolved into some of the most impressive animals that ever existed—the dinosaurs.

When you think of dinosaurs, do you think first of large ones like the 15-meter-long *Tyrannosaurus rex* in Figure 15-11 or the 22-meter-long *Apatosaurus* in Figure 15-12? Did you know that some dinosaurs were no larger than a chicken? Dinosaurs of all sizes existed during the Mesozoic Era. Some, like the *Tyrannosaurus*, were meat eaters. Others, like *Apatosaurus*, were plant eaters. The first small dinosaurs appeared during the Triassic Period. Larger species developed during the Jurassic and Cretaceous Periods. Throughout the Mesozoic Era, new kinds of dinosaurs appeared while others became extinct. Figure 15-13 shows examples of dinosaurs from two Mesozoic periods. If you were on Earth during this time, would you have seen a *Tyrannosaurus* attacking an *Apatosaurus*? As a group, dinosaurs dominated life on Earth for 165 000 000 years. The last dinosaurs disappeared 65 000 000 years ago.

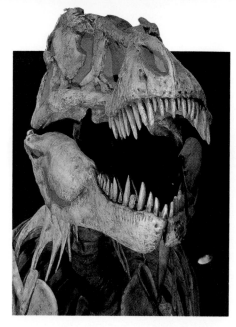

Figure 15-11 *Tyrannosaurus rex*, a large meat-eating dinosaur, lived during the Cretaceous Period.

Figure 15-12 *Apatosaurus*, a large plant-eating dinosaur, became extinct by the end of the Jurassic Period.

What caused the extinction of the dinosaurs? To some scientists, the fossil record shows that the dinosaurs died off gradually over several million years. According to one theory, increased volcanic activity filled the atmosphere with dust and ash. Less sunlight could pass through the dusty atmosphere. As a result, many plants died. Then plant-eating dinosaurs starved to death. Finally, meat-eating dinosaurs died out because their food source was gone. Dust blocking the sun's energy could also have cooled Earth's climate. If the dinosaurs were cold blooded, they might not have adapted to the colder climate.

Another theory traces the cause of the dinosaur extinction to a worldwide drop in sea level. As a result, climates on the continents became more severe. Since many life-forms, including the dinosaurs, could not adapt to the climate changes, they became extinct.

Another theory states that dinosaurs became extinct within just a few years. A large amount of iridium, an element that is rare on Earth, exists in a thin layer of late Cretaceous rock. Geologists hypothesize that a large asteroid containing iridium hit Earth at the end of the Mesozoic Era. The gigantic impact of the asteroid threw dust into the atmosphere. The heat from the impact set large forest fires. The fires added smoke to the dust in the atmosphere. The smoke and dust blocked the sun's light for a long period of time, causing widespread destruction of life-forms on Earth. Some paleontologists think that the dinosaurs were already dying out by this time and the asteroid just finished them off. Is any one of these theories correct? Possibly a combination of events led to the extinction of the dinosaurs.

Figure 15-13 *Left: Stegosaurus* was a plant-eating Jurassic dinosaur. *Right:* Dinosaurs like *Maiasaura* were Cretaceous plant eaters.

ACTIVITY 15.3 *General Supplies*

DESIGNING A FLYING REPTILE

Purpose To identify and control variables that might affect the flight length for a flying reptile.

Materials

drinking straws	colored pencils
paper clips	meterstick
paper	tape

Procedure

1. Read all instructions for this activity before you begin your work.

2. Copy the data table onto your paper.

3. You and your classmates will vary wingspan, head length, and tail length in making a model of a flying reptile. Your teacher will help you choose reasonable values for each variable. Record all values in your data table.

4. Connect straws with paper clips to make a body and wing frame for your reptile. Use the paper or cardboard to make the wings, head, and tail. You may also color your model.

5. Carry out four flight trials for your model reptile to measure the flight length to the nearest cm. Record your measurements in your data table.

Collecting and Analyzing Data

1. Average the four flight lengths for your flying reptile. Record the average in your data table. Subtract the shortest average flight length from the longest average flight length for all students who used different values of the same variable.

2. Compare your difference to the differences for the other two variables. List the differences from smallest to largest.

Drawing Conclusions

3. Before you did the activity, which variable did you think would affect flight length the most?

4. Which variable did affect the model reptiles' flight lengths the most? Which variable affected flight length the least?

5. What advantage does the ability to glide long distances offer a flying reptile?

6. Scientists have found fossils of large flying reptiles in sediments that were once an ocean bottom. Offer an explanation for the deaths of these flying reptiles.

7. Scientists found bones of flying reptiles in Texas with wingspans of 15 meters. Do you think that such a large wingspan helped the reptile fly? Explain your answer.

Data Table	
Constants	
Variable	
Trial no.	**Flight length (cm)**
1	
2	
3	
4	
Average	

Figure 15-14 This fossil of *Archaeopteryx* was found in what is now Germany.

Other Mesozoic Life

Reptiles were the dominant kind of life during the Mesozoic Era, but they were not the only kind. Although mammals did not become large until the Cenozoic Era, they first appeared during the Triassic Period. **Mammals** are warm-blooded vertebrates with skin that is covered by hair or fur. Because of these characteristics, mammals can adapt to many kinds of environments. Birds also appeared during the Jurassic Period. The fossil of *Archaeopteryx* in Figure 15-14 shows that the animal had teeth and claws like a meat-eating dinosaur and feathers like a bird. Fossils show that wings developed from front legs, and feathers developed from reptile scales. Today's birds probably evolved from dinosaurs.

Important changes in plant life also occurred during the Mesozoic Era. Flowering plants developed during the Cretaceous Period. If you could have visited a Cretaceous forest, you would have seen many trees that are found in forests today. Maples, oaks, and other trees appeared during the Cretaceous Period. Grasses, fruit trees, and many of today's vegetables date back to the Mesozoic Era. These plants make up much of the food supply for mammals. How do you think the number of mammals changed as flowering plants spread across the land? The spread of mammals and the extinction of the dinosaurs and other life-forms mark the end of the Mesozoic Era and the beginning of the Cenozoic Era.

Lesson Review 15.3

10. How did the position of the North American continent change during the Mesozoic Era?

11. What was the dominant form of life in the Mesozoic Era?

12. Name one group of plants and one group of animals on Earth today that were on Earth during the Mesozoic Era.

13. Give two theories held by paleontologists for the extinction of the dinosaurs.

Interpret and Apply

14. According to fossil evidence, Earth's climate remained very mild during the Mesozoic Era. Suppose Earth's climate had cooled for several million years shortly after both reptiles and mammals appeared. How do you think life might have developed differently during the rest of the Mesozoic Era? Give reasons for your answer.

15.4 *The Cenozoic Era*

During the early Cenozoic Era, Earth began to take on its present-day appearance. Plant and animal life developed into some forms that you can recognize today. Because the Cenozoic Era is more recent, the Cenozoic fossil record is more complete than the fossil record for other eras. Geologists have divided the Tertiary and Quaternary periods of the Cenozoic into epochs. Geologists have given the epochs individual names, which appear in Table 15-1. The fossil evidence shows that many changes in landscape, climate, and life-forms occurred from one epoch to the next.

Continuing Continental Movement

You have learned that Pangaea, the supercontinent, broke apart during the Mesozoic Era. During the Cenozoic Era, the continents reached their current positions. As a result of plate motion, volcanic and earthquake activity continue today. The motions of the North American, Juan de Fuca, and Pacific plates cause volcanism and earthquakes in the American West. Africa collided with Europe, pushing up the Alps. India collided with Asia, raising the Himalayan Mountains. Today the Indian plate is still moving, causing major earthquakes and lifting the Himalayas still higher.

During the Cenozoic Era, many parts of Earth cooled and ice ages occurred. Much of North America was covered by thick glaciers during the most recent ice age. Some forms of life survived the changes in climate. Which survivors came to dominate Earth during the most recent epoch of the Cenozoic Era?

Figure 15-15 The Sierra Nevada Mountains in California are still rising due to motions of the North American and Pacific Plates.

Age of Mammals

After the dinosaurs became extinct at the beginning of the Cenozoic Era, few large animals lived on the land. Mammals were still quite small, about the size of a squirrel. The mammals took advantage of the increasing food supply of flowering plants. As the number of plant-eating mammals increased, so did the number of meat-eating mammals. Mammals gradually increased in size during the Cenozoic Era. An example is an early horse called *Hyracotherium*. In the early Cenozoic Era, *Hyracotherium* was only about the size of a small dog. By the time of the Oligocene and Miocene epochs, some grazing animals had reached very large sizes. *Indricotherium*, shown in Figure 15-16, stood 5 meters high at the shoulders, making it the largest land mammal of all time. Mammals spread to the sea and air during the Cenozoic Era. Can you name some examples of mammals that live in the sea or the air today?

Sea level fell and rose several times during the Cenozoic Era as the result of ice ages. As glaciers trapped ocean water as ice, sea levels dropped. Land bridges allowed animals to migrate from one continent to another. Horses, which developed first in North America, migrated to Asia and Europe. Mammoths like those in Figure 15-17 *(right)* were types of elephants that spread from Africa to Asia to North America. When the glaciers melted, the sea level rose again. Water covered the land bridges, stopping the animal migrations. Australia remained isolated from the other continents throughout most of the Cenozoic. As a result, mammals developed there that are found nowhere else in the world. What are some of Australia's unique mammals?

Figure 15-16 *Indricotherium* was a gigantic ancestor of the modern rhinoceros.

Indian rhinoceros   Human   Indricotherium

Figure 15-17 *Left:* A Neanderthal family. *Right:* A woolly mammoth.

Mammals of all sizes were abundant during most of the Cenozoic Era. But by the end of the last ice age, about 10 000 years ago, many large mammals had become extinct. *Indricotherium* and mammoths were gone from all the continents. Some scientists link the extinctions of the large mammals to the rise of a mammal that still dominates Earth today—humans. Humans are primates, like apes. What makes humans different from other primates? Humans have larger brains and walk upright on two legs. The early humanlike primates are called **hominids.**

The species that includes modern humans is called *Homo sapiens.* Figure 15-18 shows a hominid called *Australopithecus*, a possible ancestor of *Homo sapiens*. How does *Australopithecus* appear different from today's humans? Look at an example of a Neanderthal in Figure 15-17 *(left)*. Neanderthals were also members of the species *Homo sapiens.* However, Neanderthals became extinct about 30 000 years ago. Modern humans, who appeared about 90 000 years ago, were excellent hunters. Large numbers of fossils found in some prehistoric hunting sites indicate that humans may have killed many more animals than they needed. Some scientists have hypothesized that humans hunted many of the large mammals to extinction.

Earth itself and life on Earth changed greatly during each era of geologic history. What changes do you think might occur in the future? Where will the continents be 50 000 000 years from now? How long will humans dominate Earth? Will they last as long as the dinosaurs did? How are humans changing Earth in ways other animals did not? Will earth science students of the future be reading about you?

Figure 15-18 *Australopithecus*, an early hominid

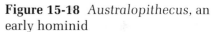

MAPPING THE SPREAD OF HUMANS

Purpose To interpret data about the migration of humans across Earth.

Materials

map of early human migration	pencil paper

Procedure

1. Read all instructions for this activity before you begin your work.

2. Use the map below to determine the order in which the continents were inhabited by humans.

Collecting and Analyzing Data

1. On which continent did the first humans appear?

2. On which continent did humans arrive last?

Drawing Conclusions

3. How long did humans take to inhabit all the continents?

4. Humans lived in both the continents of Asia and Europe by 500 000 years ago. Which of the two continents do you think humans reached first? Explain your answer.

5. Where did the humans who reached North America come from originally? How were they able to get to North America?

6. Evidence suggests that many large animals gradually became extinct, starting at the northern part of North America. The extinctions ended near the southern tip of South America about 8000 years ago. Use the map to explain the extinction pattern in the Americas.

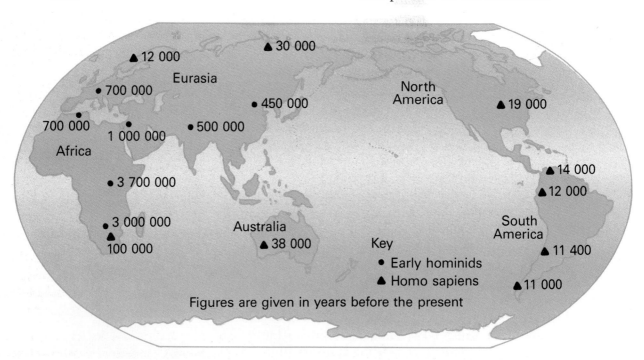

Figures are given in years before the present

Lesson Review 15.4

15. List an area where mountain building is still occurring today.

16. Compare and contrast Cenozoic and Mesozoic mammals.

17. List two ways early hominids differed from the apes.

18. What climate changes occurred during the Cenozoic Era?

Interpret and Apply

19. Suppose that there had been no ice ages during the Cenozoic Era. How might that have affected the sea level and the development of life in North America?

Chapter Summary

Read this summary of the main ideas in this chapter. If any are not clear to you, go back and review that lesson.

15.1 Precambrian Earth

■ The original atmosphere came from volcanic gases and contained no oxygen. Water vapor from volcanic gases condensed and fell as rain, forming the oceans.

■ Eras, periods, and epochs divide Earth's history on the geologic timetable.

■ Simple one-celled organisms, the first form of life, appeared in the oceans 3 500 000 000 years ago.

15.2 The Paleozoic Era

■ The continents moved together to form the supercontinent Pangaea.

■ Earth's climate was warm and moist during most of the Paleozoic Era. At the end of the era, most of Earth was cool and dry.

■ Life spread from the oceans to the land during the Paleozoic Era. Many species became extinct at the end of the era.

15.3 The Mesozoic Era

■ Pangaea began to split apart in the early Mesozoic Era. The climate became warm and humid as oceans surrounded the continents.

■ During the Mesozoic Era, reptiles spread across Earth. Dinosaurs were the dominant form of life. Mammals, birds, and flowering plants also appeared.

■ Dinosaurs became extinct at the end of the Mesozoic Era. Several theories explain the extinction.

15.4 The Cenozoic Era

■ After the dinosaurs were extinct and flowering plants were common, mammals became larger and dominated Earth.

■ Several ice ages occurred during the Cenozoic Era. As sea levels dropped, animals migrated from one continent to another across land bridges.

■ Humans are a type of primate. The oldest human fossils are about 3 800 000 years old.

Chapter Review

Vocabulary

epoch	Laurasia
era	mammal
geologic timetable	period
Gondwanaland	reptile
hominid	stromatolite
Homo sapiens	vertebrate
invertebrate	

Concept Mapping

Construct a concept map for Earth's history. Include the following terms: Earth's history, life-forms, eras, Mesozoic, Cenozoic, periods, Cambrian, Tertiary, Triassic.

Review

On your paper, write the word or words that best complete each statement.

1. The longest unit of time on the geologic timetable is the _____ .

2. The _____ Era is the present era of Earth's history.

3. Earth had oceans by the time it was _____ years old.

4. The gases of the original atmosphere and the water in the oceans came from _____ .

5. The early atmosphere contained little or no _____ , the gas necessary for the development of animal life.

6. Life began in Earth's _____ .

7. The oldest fossils are plantlike bacteria that formed limestone mats called _____ .

8. By the end of the Paleozoic Era, the continents had moved together to form one large continent called _____ .

9. Paleozoic fossils are more abundant than Precambrian fossils because Paleozoic invertebrates had developed _____ .

10. Fish first appeared in the _____ Period.

11. The dominant invertebrate in the Cambrian oceans was the _____ .

12. Some fish developed the ability to breathe air. These fish developed into the first _____ .

13. Pangaea began to separate during the early _____ Era.

14. _____ were the largest vertebrates living on Earth during the Mesozoic Era.

15. Dinosaurs became _____ by the end of the Mesozoic Era.

16. From the fossil record, it appears that today's _____ are descendants of the dinosaurs.

17. _____ developed during the Cretaceous Period.

18. Several _____ occurred during the Cenozoic Era, causing sea levels to rise and fall.

19. In the Cenozoic Era, _____ took the place of dinosaurs as the largest vertebrates.

20. The earliest humanlike primates are called _____ .

Interpret and Apply

On your paper, answer each question, using complete sentences.

21. Precambrian time makes up about 85 percent of Earth's history. Why has Precambrian time not been divided into shorter periods and epochs?

22. By looking at a yearly calendar, you know when the next week or month begins. Can you look at the geologic timetable to find out when the next era will begin? Explain your answer.

23. If Earth had not heated up soon after it formed, how might its interior be different than it actually is?

24. Suppose that Earth did not have any volcanoes early in its history. How would today's atmosphere be different? How would the absence of volcanoes have affected the development of life?

25. Why did animals develop after plants developed?

26. If large swamps had not existed in the eastern part of North America during the Pennsylvanian Period, what major energy source would not be found there today?

27. Each of today's continents has different plants and animals that are found naturally only on that continent. How would life on Earth be different if Pangaea had not split apart?

28. If the dinosaurs died out because Earth's climate became cooler, then how were the mammals able to survive?

29. Fossils of mammoths have been found in ocean-bottom sediments off the coast of North America. How is it possible that large mammals like mammoths were living in those areas?

30. Mammals have existed since the beginning of the Mesozoic Era. However, mammals remained small in both size and number until after the development of flowering plants. Explain why.

31. How would North America look different today if no landmasses had collided with it during the Paleozoic Era?

■ Writing in Science

32. Imagine that you are able to travel backward in time. You are a scientist on an expedition traveling to one of the following eras—Paleozoic, Mesozoic, or Cenozoic. Write a story about the expedition. Use your imagination, but also include realistic details about the era based on information in this chapter.

■ Critical Thinking

The map shows the part of Pangaea that became North America during the Mesozoic Era. The arrows show the direction North America moved as it separated from Africa.

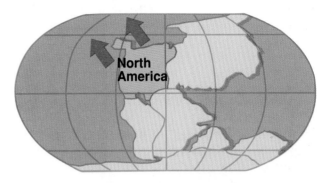

33. Explain why mountain ranges of the western United States began to rise during the Mesozoic Era.

34. Lava flows covered parts of the eastern United States shortly after Pangaea broke apart. Explain why.

35. North America is moving in roughly the same direction today. What future changes might occur in the mountain ranges of the West?

36. Even though North America is still moving in the same direction today, there are no new lava flows in the eastern part of the country. Where are the new lava flows occurring that are related to North America's movement?

16 Earth's Energy Resources

Chapter Preview

Have You Ever WONDERED?

Why is the biggest hill at the beginning of a roller coaster ride?

Do you think they plan it that way to make you as nervous as possible? Actually, roller coasters are designed to save energy. The people who operate roller coasters do not want to pay for a lot of energy to pull you all the way around the track. If you listen carefully as they tow the cars to the top, you can hear the sound of motors working. Once you are at the top, the motors are no longer needed. Now that you are at the highest point on the track, you have enough energy to travel all the way to the end. Gravity does the rest.

Earth's supply of energy is a valuable resource. You hear much talk about the need to conserve energy because energy resources are limited and costly. In this chapter, you will learn about Earth's energy resources, and how the use or misuse of those resources will affect your future.

16.1 Fossil Fuels

Lesson Objectives

▶ **Describe** how fossil fuels form and how they are used.

▶ **Discuss** the environmental problems caused by human use of fossil fuels.

▶ **List** possible new sources of fossil fuels.

▶ **Activity** **Observe** and **describe** methods used to recover oil.

New Terms

natural resources	natural gas
fossil fuel	crude oil
hydrocarbon	petrochemicals
coal	strip mining
petroleum	oil shale
	tar sand

Earth supplies you with materials you need to live. These materials include such things as water, food, air, minerals, building materials, fibers for clothing, and sources of energy. Materials taken from Earth for human use are called **natural resources.**

There are two types of natural resources, renewable and nonrenewable. Renewable resources are things that nature replaces almost as fast as they are used up. For example, food and trees are renewable because they can often be grown again on the same land. Water is a renewable resource, because it evaporates from the oceans and returns to Earth as rain. Renewable resources, if managed and cared for properly, will always be there for you to use because they are being replaced fast enough to meet demand.

Nonrenewable resources are not replaced quickly enough by nature to maintain their supply. Ores, which supply metals and other important minerals, are nonrenewable. You read about these important resources in Chapter 7. Even though some metal is recycled, very little new metal is being added to Earth's crust.

Many of Earth's valuable energy resources are nonrenewable. Energy sources, such as coal, petroleum, natural gas, and uranium, are used to produce thermal and electric energy worldwide. Once these nonrenewable energy sources are used, they are gone. What natural resources do you see in Figure 16-1? Which are renewable? Which are nonrenewable?

Figure 16-1 Some natural resources are renewable. Others are nonrenewable.

A fuel is a substance that produces thermal energy when burned. A **fossil fuel** is made of the partly decayed remains of plants and animals that died long ago. Fossil fuels, such as coal, petroleum, and natural gas are hydrocarbons. A **hydrocarbon** is a compound that contains the elements hydrogen and carbon. As you read this lesson, try to remember that almost 90 percent of the energy used in the United States comes from nonrenewable fossil, hydrocarbon fuels. These same fuels are also in shorter and shorter supply. Does this create problems for your future?

Coal

Coal is an organic sedimentary rock. Coal is also a solid fossil fuel. The United States has just over 30 percent of the world's known recoverable coal reserves. Much of that coal is found in the Appalachian states, such as Pennsylvania, Kentucky, Ohio, and West Virginia. Coal is also abundant in Illinois. Western states, such as Montana and Wyoming, also have coal, but it does not give off as much energy when burned.

Coal is used to produce electricity and in making steel. Most coal formed from plants that lived in swamps millions of years ago during the Paleozoic era. When the plants died, they fell over into the water or were quickly buried. Burial helped prevent the plants from decaying. Thick layers of dead plants built up. Shallow seas later covered the plant layers with layers of sand and mud. Underground, heat and pressure slowly changed the plant matter into coal, as illustrated in Figure 16-2.

The buried plants change into a substance called peat. Peat is not coal. Peat is a brown substance in which you can still see mosses, leaves, and twigs. Peat still forms today in bogs and swamps. Some people dry peat and use it for fuel. However, peat is not a clean-burning fuel.

Under more pressure, peat changes into a harder, more compact substance called *lignite*. Lignite is a soft, brown coal. Lignite, under still more pressure and heat, becomes soft, black, *bituminous coal*. Under still greater pressure, the bituminous coal sometimes changes into a hard, black, shiny coal called *anthracite*. This step-by-step change from lignite to bituminous to anthracite coal is called the coal series. With each new type of coal formed, the carbon content increases. Peat, for example, is only about 60 percent carbon. Anthracite is about 94 percent carbon. The more carbon there is in coal, the more thermal energy the coal releases when burned. Which fuel would release more energy, lignite or bituminous coal?

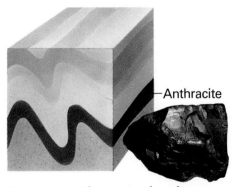

Figure 16-2 The types of coal are formed as stages in a process of compaction and change.

Petroleum and Natural Gas

Fossil fuels did not only come from land plants. Oceans are filled with tiny plants and animals. When organisms living in ancient oceans died, they fell to the seafloor and became buried under layers of sand and mud. Over time, heat and pressure changed the organisms into hydrocarbons. **Petroleum** is a liquid hydrocarbon. You probably call petroleum *oil*. A gaseous hydrocarbon is called **natural gas.** Like oil, natural gas forms from marine organisms. Unlike oil, natural gas can also form from coal that has been under great heat and pressure.

Once they are formed, oil and gas seep into the pore spaces in nearby rock. This porous rock is usually sandstone or limestone. Porous rocks often contain water. Because oil and gas are less dense than water, they move upward through the cracks and pores in the rock. The oil and gas move to the top of the water layer. Maybe you have seen vegetable oil floating at the top of your salad dressing. Even if you shake the bottle, the oil will return to the top every time.

The oil and gas move upward until they reach a rock they cannot pass through. Figure 16-3 *(left)* shows how oil and gas have been trapped beneath an impermeable layer of shale in an anticline. A well, drilled through the shale into the sandstone, lets the oil and gas out of the trap. Oil and gas can also be trapped by faulting. Look at Figure 16-3 *(right).* The oil and gas moved up through the tipped layer of permeable sandstone until they reached the fault. What is there on the other side of the fault that traps the oil?

Sometimes the oil and gas are under enough pressure that they flow to the surface. Sometimes the oil must be pumped out. Even after pumping, some oil may remain stuck in the rock's pores. New methods recover more oil from previously pumped oil traps.

Figure 16-3 Two types of hydrocarbon traps: *Left:* Anticline trap; *Right:* Fault trap

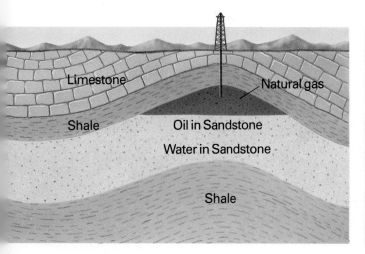

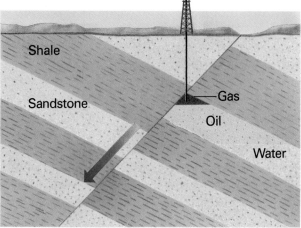

A C T I V I T Y   1 6 . 1   Lab Equipment

RECOVERING OIL

Purpose To observe and describe methods used to recover oil from the ground.

Materials

100-mL graduated cylinder
plastic bottle with a spray pump
clear plastic tubing
clean pebbles

cold and hot water
vegetable oil
liquid detergent
safety goggles
lab apron

Procedure

1. Read all instructions for this activity before you begin your work.

2. On your paper, make a data table like the one shown.

3. Put on your safety goggles and lab apron.

4. Set up a model oil well like the one shown. Add 100 mL of oil to your well.

5. Pump as much oil out of the well as you can. Record in your data table the number of mL you were able to recover.

6. Dispose of the oil in your graduated cylinder.

7. Add 50 mL of cold water to the bottle. Observe what happens. Try again to pump oil out of the well. Allow the oil and water in the graduated cylinder to separate. Record the amount of oil recovered in the data table. Pour out the contents of the graduated cylinder.

8. Repeat steps 6 and 7 using 50 mL of hot water.

9. Repeat steps 6 and 7 using 50 mL of hot water and 8 drops of liquid detergent.

10. Before leaving the laboratory, clean up all materials and wash your hands thoroughly.

Collecting and Analyzing Data

Data Table	
Method	**Oil Recovered (mL)**
Oil	
Oil and Cold Water	
Oil and Hot Water	
Oil, Hot Water, and Detergent	

1. How much oil was recovered by pumping just the oil alone?

2. Did the oil move when you added the cold water? Where did the oil go?

3. Were you able to recover more oil when you added the cold water?

4. How much oil did you recover with the hot water? How much oil did you recover when the detergent was added?

Drawing Conclusions

5. Can pumping alone remove all the oil from an oil well? What evidence do you have to support your answer?

6. Did the detergent make it easier to pump oil from the well? Why do you think this is true?

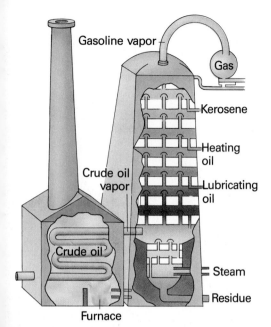

Figure 16-4 Crude oil is separated into different products at a refinery.

Using Natural Gas and Petroleum

Natural gas is a mixture of many useful hydrocarbons in the gas state. People use natural gas because it burns cleaner than other fossil fuels. Natural gas is easy to transport and use. The most common natural gas is methane. Methane is used mostly for home heating and cooking. Propane is another natural gas, which is used in some homes and for camp stoves.

Petroleum pumped from a well is called **crude oil.** Crude oil is usually a useless mixture of hydrocarbons until it is separated, or refined, into different products. At an oil refinery, the crude oil is heated until it becomes a mixture of hydrocarbon vapors. The vapors from the crude oil go into a tall, thin tower like the one shown in Figure 16-4. As the vapor cools, each hydrocarbon in crude oil condenses back to a liquid at a certain level in the tower and is collected. In Figure 16-4 (top), which products collect at the bottom? Gasoline, kerosene, and jet fuel are all products taken from crude oil at a refinery.

Many forms of transportation use petroleum as fuel. Oil-burning furnaces heat homes. Many electric power plants use oil. However, fuel is not the only use of petroleum. Many products you use every day are made from petroleum. Some of the more obvious products include petroleum jelly, lubricants, wax, and asphalt. Some petroleum products are less obvious. How many products in Figure 16-5 did you know were made with petroleum? Plastics, synthetic fibers, Plexiglas, vinyl, and aspirin are all petrochemicals. **Petrochemicals** are chemical compounds made from petroleum or natural gas. What effect would using less of these materials have on the demand for petroleum?

Figure 16-5 Many common products and packages are made of petrochemicals.

Oil Supply and Demand

The type of fuel a society uses depends on several things. The fuel should be plentiful, easy to transport, clean to burn, and should produce as much energy as possible. Sometimes societies switch from one fuel to another. In the 1800's, coal replaced wood as a fuel because coal released twice the energy when burned. The automobile caused a great demand for petroleum products, as did the change to oil for home heating. Oil burned cleaner than coal and could easily be piped into homes.

To satisfy the increased demand for oil, the United States increased its oil exploration and production. The biggest oil traps in the United States were soon found and drained. By the 1960's, it became cheaper and easier to buy petroleum from other countries. Today almost half of the oil used in the United States is imported. How does this affect political relations with the countries that export the oil?

Although the United States makes up only 6 percent of the world's population, it uses 30 percent of the world's petroleum. Why do Americans use so much oil? Today more people live outside of cities and depend on their cars for transportation. Greater use of cars has increased the demand for gasoline. Many home appliances require large amounts of electricity. That electricity often comes from oil-burning power plants. Petrochemicals, like plastic and synthetic fibers, have replaced products that were once made of wood, metal, glass, and cotton. What other changes have increased the need for oil?

Maintaining your modern lifestyle requires the use of billions of barrels of petroleum each year. The world could run out of petroleum by the year 2080 if use continues at the present rate. The United States may run out of its own petroleum much sooner. How would this affect you? What can you do to lessen the demand for fossil fuels?

Environmental Concerns

Burning fossil fuels causes major environmental problems. In addition to hydrogen and oxygen, fossil fuels can also contain unwanted elements like sulfur. Sulfur burns to form a smelly, polluting gas called sulfur dioxide. If you have ever smelled the exhaust from a school bus, you know how choking sulfur dioxide is. The sulfur dioxide produced by burning fossil fuels joins with water vapor in the air to form acid rain. Acid rain ruins crops, increases chemical weathering on buildings and roads, and kills fish in the lakes and streams of northeastern United States and Canada.

Figure 16-6 One reason the United States uses so much oil is that there are so many cars.

Figure 16-7 Burning coal in electrical power plants, such as this one in Arizona, can release pollutants into the air.

Figure 16-8 *Top:* This land in Pennsylvania is currently being strip-mined. *Bottom:* The land above this strip mine in West Virginia has been returned to its original condition.

Burning fossil fuels also adds carbon dioxide to the air. Carbon dioxide traps thermal energy in Earth's atmosphere. The trapped energy may be making Earth warmer. The warming of Earth's atmosphere due to trapped energy is called the greenhouse effect. The greenhouse effect will be discussed further in Chapter 20.

Coal mining causes other environmental problems. The traditional way to mine coal is to dig an underground shaft. Today coal deposits found close to the surface are strip-mined. **Strip mining** is a process by which an ore is mined after all the soil and rock above it have been removed. After the coal is exposed at the surface, large machines dig out the coal. Strip mining, however, can cause pollution. The sulfur-rich waste from strip mining is often washed into streams and nearby soil. The sulfur combines with water to form acids. Acids poison streams and ponds and ruin valuable farmland. Laws now require mining companies to restore land after they have finished mining the coal. Figure 16-8 shows how a strip-mined area was restored. Making land useful again is called land reclamation.

Future Sources

Geologists are always looking for new deposits of fossil fuels. Oil companies now drill many wells looking for petroleum beneath the ocean floor. However, there is concern that offshore drilling platforms, like the one in Figure 16-9, can leak oil and seriously harm fishing areas. Spills from oil tankers have also taken their toll on the environment.

Figure 16-9 Offshore wells, such as these being drilled in Cook Inlet, Alaska, have produced petroleum and natural gas from beneath the ocean floor.

One future source of petroleum might be oil shale. **Oil shale** is a rock that contains trapped petroleum. There are vast deposits of oil shale in Colorado, Utah, and Wyoming. To remove the oil, the oil shale must be crushed and heated until the oil turns to gas. Unfortunately, this process uses a large amount of water. Water is not plentiful in the states where oil shale is found. Using modern technology, oil shale is too costly to be a worthwhile energy source.

Another source of oil might be tar sand. **Tar sand** is a mixture of sand, water, and tar. Tar is a black, sticky form of petroleum, similar to asphalt. Large deposits of tar sand are found in Alberta, Canada. Removing tar from these sands requires huge amounts of water, equipment, and energy. Like oil shale, the process is still too costly. Billions of barrels of oil are locked in oil shale and tar sand.

Figure 16-10 Oil shale contains so much oil that the rock burns.

As petroleum supplies become more scarce, coal could become a more important source of energy. If the United States keeps burning coal at the present rate, there is enough coal left in this country to last more than 300 years. Although coal is the most abundant fossil fuel, it unfortunately contains more sulfur than other fossil fuels. Converting coal into a gas or liquid may someday allow coal to be used like natural gas or petroleum. These new forms of coal are called synthetic fuels. Synthetic fuels contain less sulfur and cause less pollution.

Although fossil fuel supplies may be increased with more exploration, or by using new sources, these are only temporary solutions. Fossil fuels are a nonrenewable resource. Substitutes must be found to fill future needs.

Lesson Review 16.1

1. How does coal form?
2. Draw an oil trap. Explain how the oil and gas gather inside the sandstone.
3. What are petrochemicals? Give examples.
4. What makes coal the dirtiest fossil fuel to burn?
5. Name and discuss two future sources of petroleum.

Interpret and Apply

6. Oil shale and tar sands could be called ores of petroleum. Think back to the definition of an ore. What will determine whether or not oil shale and tar sands are used to provide petroleum?

16.2 Earth's Alternate Energy Sources

Lesson Objectives

▶ **Discuss** the two forms of nuclear energy.

▶ **Diagram** ways to use geothermal energy.

▶ **List** some advantages and disadvantages of nuclear and geothermal energy.

▶ **Activity** *Form a model* of nuclear fission and fusion.

New Terms

nuclear energy
fission
fusion
geothermal energy

Figure 16-11 Where does the electricity come from that is used to light these buildings in Chicago?

Everyone thinks about the future. You probably have some ideas about your life a few years from now. Perhaps you have thought about what car you would like to buy. You may have even decided on the car's color and model or the type of stereo system it will have. Do you ever think about your future energy needs? What good is a beautiful car if there is no gasoline to make it go? As fossil fuels become more scarce, important decisions about energy will become harder to make.

Some fuels are used as a source of thermal energy, such as the charcoal burned to barbecue hot dogs or the natural gas used to heat a house. Other sources are used for transportation. However, most energy sources are used to make electric energy. Think of how many ways you use electric energy in your home. Electric energy, or electricity, is convenient to use. It is easily transported through wires from power plants to your home. Many power plants burn fossil fuels to produce electricity. Thermal energy from the burning fuels changes water into steam. Steam turns the blades of a generator, where the energy of motion is changed into electricity.

There are ways to make steam and electricity without using fossil fuels. Any source of energy other than fossil fuel is called an alternate energy source. Like fossil fuels, alternate energy sources have benefits and problems.

Nuclear Energy

One alternate energy source already provides 18 percent of the United States electricity. That electricity comes from power plants that run on nuclear energy. **Nuclear energy** is released when the nucleus of an atom is changed. There are two ways to change the nucleus to produce energy. One way that the nucleus is changed is by a process called fission. **Fission** is the splitting of the nucleus of an atom.

In a power plant, fission takes place inside a nuclear reactor. The fuel used in fission is a form of the element uranium, called uranium-235. The nucleus of this radioactive atom splits easily. Fission releases large amounts of energy. Remember that the breakdown of radioactive material inside Earth gives off thermal energy. However, inside Earth, the process happens slowly over millions of years. In a nuclear reactor, the splitting process is speeded up to release a lot of thermal energy quickly.

As shown in Figure 16-12, the first uranium nucleus splits to form lighter elements, three neutrons, and large amounts of thermal energy. The three neutrons each go on to split other uranium nuclei. These nuclei split and give off neutrons that go on to split other nuclei. This continuous process is called a chain reaction. You can create a chain reaction by standing a line of dominoes close together. What happens when the first one is knocked over?

In a nuclear reactor, the energy from fission changes water into steam. The steam turns electric generators. The control rods, shown in Figure 16-13 *(left)*, slow down or stop the chain reaction. The control rods work by absorbing the neutrons that keep the reaction going.

There are advantages and disadvantages to nuclear energy. A small amount of uranium generates large amounts of electricity. Unlike burning fossil fuels, nuclear power does not add smoke, sulfur, or other pollutants to the atmosphere. However, uranium is a nonrenewable energy resource. If used at the present rate, the United States supply of uranium will only last about 30 years.

There are other problems with the use of nuclear energy. Fission creates radioactive waste. This waste releases radiation that harms living cells. Think back to Chapter 14 and the discussion of radioactive age dating. Do radioactive materials stop being radioactive in a short amount of time? The fission waste must be stored away from living things for thousands of years. The waste must never leak out of the storage area. This means storing the waste in a dry place, far from people, and in an area free of faults and earthquake activity. Presently the United States does not have such a storage place for waste. A pilot project to bury waste in a salt formation 2000 feet below the desert surface in New Mexico has been delayed.

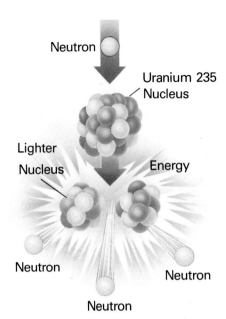

Figure 16-12 In fission, a nucleus is split to form a lighter nucleus plus free neutrons. The free neutrons split other nuclei to cause a chain reaction.

Figure 16-13 *Left:* The thermal energy released in the reactor core is used to make steam. The steam is used to generate electricity. *Right:* Workers in nuclear power plants must protect themselves from radiation.

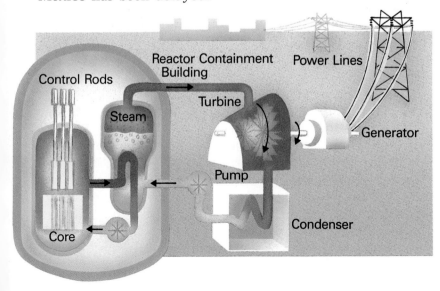

The safety of nuclear power plants concerns many people. Despite safeguards, accidents occur where reactors release radioactive materials into the atmosphere or water. Once radioactive material is released, it can be carried far from the reactor in a matter of days. Small amounts of radioactive material were released in 1979 at the Three Mile Island reactor in Pennsylvania. A much greater amount of radioactive material was released by the Chernobyl reactor in the Soviet Union in 1986.

Fusion is another nuclear process. **Fusion** is the process of joining together the nuclei of small atoms. Like fission, fusion creates great amounts of energy. In Chapter 6, you learned that fusion occurs in the sun and causes the sun to shine. In the sun, the nuclei of four hydrogen atoms join together to form a nucleus of the heavier element, helium. On Earth, the form of hydrogen needed for fuel is common in sea water. Fusion would also produce little radioactive waste. Why then do all nuclear power plants use fission instead of fusion?

Fusion requires temperatures of millions of degrees. The hottest magma in Earth's mantle is less than 2000°C. Even if these temperatures can be reached here on Earth, how do you contain the super-hot fuel? Reports in 1989 that researchers had achieved fusion at low temperatures caused much excitement. However, there is controversy about the data, and research continues.

Geothermal Energy

Thermal energy that comes from inside Earth is called **geothermal energy.** As you know, thermal energy inside Earth is caused by the breakdown of radioactive materials. The magma formed below the surface heats surrounding rock and groundwater. The water may reach the surface as hot water or steam. Sometimes the water or steam comes shooting out as a geyser, such as the one shown in Figure 16-14. This thermal energy can be used as an alternate source of energy.

The size of the area, rock temperature, and amount of water in the ground determine how geothermal energy is used. In some areas, geothermal steam is used to turn a generator. The Geysers plant uses natural steam to produce more than half of San Francisco's electricity. In other areas, rising hot water is piped directly into buildings for heating. Many homes in Boise, Idaho, are heated this way. Geothermal hot water is also used for heating in Iceland, Italy, and New Zealand. From your knowledge of plate tectonics, why do you think Iceland has so much geothermal energy?

Figure 16-14 Heating of water inside Earth causes eruptions of hot water and steam. These eruptions are called geysers.

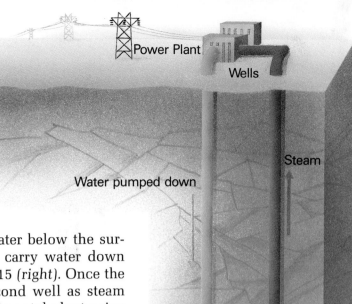

Some geothermal areas lack natural water below the surface. In these areas, a well is drilled to carry water down into the hot rock, as shown in Figure 16-15 (right). Once the water is heated, it returns through a second well as steam and is used to make electricity. An experimental plant using this type of geothermal energy is located in Fenton Hill, New Mexico.

Geothermal energy is a safe energy source that requires no fuel and produces little pollution. Unfortunately, geothermal sources exist only in areas where hot spots are near the surface. Other than rare exceptions, like Hawaii, these areas are usually limited to land along active plate boundaries. Often these areas are not near cities. The electricity must be carried long distances from the plants to more populated areas. Problems also occur when hot water or steam dissolve large amounts of minerals from rocks. These minerals must be removed from the water before they contaminate water supplies or eat away at costly equipment.

Figure 16-15 *Left:* At this power station in New Zealand, geothermal steam is converted into electricity. *Right:* If water is not naturally present underground, it can be pumped down into hot rock to make steam.

Lesson Review 16.2

7. Compare the process of fission to fusion.

8. Explain how thermal energy produced in a nuclear power plant is used to make electricity.

9. What are the drawbacks of using nuclear fission as a source of energy?

10. How is geothermal energy used as an energy source?

Interpret and Apply

11. Explain why geothermal areas are not heavily populated.

12. Discuss two ways to dispose of radioactive waste that were not mentioned in this chapter. What do you think are the disadvantages and cost of each method?

NUCLEAR FISSION AND FUSION

Purpose   To form a model of nuclear fission and fusion.

Materials

small clear plastic cup	plastic knife
alcohol/water mixture	safety goggles
vegetable oil	lab apron
spoon	

Procedure

1. Read all instructions for this activity before you begin your work.

2. On your paper, make an observation chart like the one shown.

3. Put on your safety goggles and your lab apron.

4. Fill the plastic cup halfway to the top with the alcohol/water mixture. **CAUTION: This mixture is flammable. Do not get it near a flame.**

5. Bring one spoonful of oil as close to the surface of the liquid as you can. Carefully tip the spoon and slide the oil into the cup. The oil should sink to the bottom of the cup.

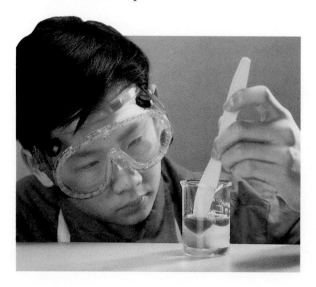

6. Carefully add more water a few drops at a time. Add water until your oil blob is floating in the middle of the cup. The oil blob represents a model of an atomic nucleus.

7. Gently push the plastic knife against the sides of your model nucleus. Try to make your model nucleus split in two. Record your observations.

8. Using the knife, gently try to put the two newly formed model nuclei back together. Record your observations.

9. Before leaving the laboratory, clean up all materials and wash your hands.

Collecting and Analyzing Data

Data Table	
Process	**Observations**
Splitting (fission)	
Joining (fusion)	

1. What happened when you tried to put the two nuclei back together?

2. Do you think the nucleus could split or join together by itself? Explain.

3. Which process was easier with your oil drop, fission or fusion?

Drawing Conclusions

4. How did your methods of splitting your model nucleus compare with those used by scientists to split uranium nuclei?

5. Why would it be easier for you to accomplish fusion with your model than it would be for scientists with hydrogen nuclei?

16.3 Alternate Energy Sources from the Sun

Have you ever tried to eat a chocolate bar on a hot summer day? What happens if you don't eat it fast enough? Sunlight is a constant source of energy. Almost all energy on Earth first comes from the sun. The plants and animals that formed fossil fuels got their energy from sunlight millions of years ago. The sun's energy causes winds to blow and evaporates water to form clouds. Since plants use sunlight to grow, all the foods you eat contain stored energy from the sun.

Solar Energy

Energy from the sun used for heating or lighting is called **solar energy.** Solar collectors change the sun's radiant energy into thermal energy. Solar collectors are large boxes with clear plastic or glass tops. Water, moving through pipes inside the box, is heated when the collector is placed in the sun.

Why does the inside of a solar collector get hot? The sun's radiant energy is changed to thermal energy when it is absorbed by an object. You have felt this if you have ever tried to sit on a vinyl car seat that has been in the sun all day. Sunlight and other forms of radiant energy pass through the car windows. The radiant energy is absorbed by the material inside the car. The radiant energy is changed into thermal energy, which heats the air inside the car. The hot air cannot escape through the glass. The car gets very hot inside. The sun's radiant energy heats the solar collector in the same way it heats the air inside the car. The hot air then heats the water inside the collector.

Lesson Objectives

▶ **Describe** ways solar energy is used.

▶ **Explain** how wind, water, and biomass provide energy.

▶ **Summarize** the advantages and disadvantages of using energy sources from the sun.

▶ **Activity** **Perform an experiment** to compare how different types of biomass fuels burn.

New Terms

solar energy
photovoltaic cell
hydroelectric
biomass
gasohol

Figure 16-16 Why are solar collectors put on rooftops?

Figure 16-17 *Left:* A passive solar home; *Right:* The Carrisa Plains power station in California produces electricity using photovoltaic cells.

Figure 16-18 Windmill farms, such as this one in California, use generators to change wind into electricity.

Solar collectors are used to heat water for washing clothes, bathing, or heating homes. Some solar collectors use pumps and motors to move water through the system and back to storage tanks. Houses equipped with such machinery are called active solar homes. The term *active* refers to the moving parts needed to use solar energy in this way.

A passive solar home is one that is built to use solar energy without the need for any equipment with moving parts. The entire house in Figure 16-17 *(left)* is a solar collector. Sunlight enters large glass windows that face the sun. Concrete, brick, stone, or water are used to store energy absorbed during the day and then to release it at night. How could you keep the house in Figure 16-17 cool in the summer?

A **photovoltaic cell,** or solar cell, changes light into electricity. You might own a calculator or small video game that runs on solar cells. In Carrisa Plains, California, over 10 000 of these cells produce electricity for thousands of homes in the area. However, such solar cell panels are costly.

Wind Power

Wind is an indirect form of solar energy. The sun's energy causes air to move, producing wind. Wind has been a source of energy ever since the Egyptians sailed their boats up the Nile River over four thousand years ago. In Europe, windmills have been used for centuries to grind grain and pump water. Today modern wind machines turn generators to make electricity.

Wind is safe, renewable, and nonpolluting. Once equipment is installed, wind energy is free. However, these wind machines are costly. The batteries needed to store power in case the wind does not blow are also expensive. Wind machines work best in areas where winds blow fairly consistently. For this reason, wind power is best used on mountains or near the seashore.

Figure 16-19 The energy from running water has been used in mills for centuries.

Water Power

Have you ever thrown a twig into a stream and watched it get carried away? Moving water, like moving air, has energy you can use. Energy from moving water is another form of solar energy. Water continuously evaporates from the oceans and falls back to Earth as rain. As water moves downhill and back to the sea, it has energy. Remember the roller coaster ride at the beginning of this chapter. Just as gravity gave you energy to continue the ride, water has energy from gravity as it moves downhill.

For centuries, waterwheels have been used to turn millstones to grind grain or to run machines in factories. Today water is used to make electricity. Using moving water to make electricity is called **hydroelectric** power. Dams along major rivers, like the one shown in Figure 16-20, create reservoirs where water is stored and then released to lower levels when electricity is needed. Hydroelectric plants provide only 8 percent of present electricity needs.

Ocean tides are also used to generate electricity. Dams are built in areas where large tides enter narrow bays. Electricity is produced by channeling the rushing tidal water through generators. A tidal power plant operates at the mouth of the La Rance River in France. Another tidal plant at Annapolis Royal in Nova Scotia, Canada, is being tested to see if the famous Bay of Fundy tides can be used to make electricity.

Another experimental energy source is *Ocean Thermal Energy Conversion* (OTEC). Floating OTEC plants would generate electricity by using the differences found in ocean water temperature. Surface water in the tropics is warm enough to boil liquid ammonia trapped in pipes. The ammonia gas turns electric generators. The gas then condenses back into liquid ammonia as it is piped near cold, deep ocean water. An experimental OTEC plant is producing electricity off the coast of Hawaii.

Figure 16-20 Hydroelectric power is clean and nonpolluting, but it is limited by the availability of water. What else determines where hydroelectric power is used?

Figure 16-21 Biomass is a renewable resource. *Top:* The average American produces nearly a ton of trash each year. Much of that trash is burnable biomass. *Bottom:* Wood is a more common form of biomass.

Biomass

When you toast marshmallows over a campfire, you use an energy source called biomass. The term **biomass** describes any plant or animal material. Biomass includes wood, other plant parts, animal waste, and even trash. Since all living things get their energy from the sun, biomass is another way to use stored solar energy.

Sometimes biomass materials are chemically changed into fuels. Grains, such as wheat and corn, are changed into alcohol and mixed with gasoline to make a fuel called **gasohol.** Gasohol reduces the amount of gasoline used in cars.

Biomass materials are also burned directly. A power plant in Hawaii burns sugarcane waste to produce electricity. In Vermont, some power plants burn wood chips. Vermont also has an experimental power plant that uses a more unusual form of biomass. This plant gets electricity by burning methane gas produced from cow manure shipped in from farmers.

What benefits would there be in burning trash to make electricity? If you empty the trash at home, you know how quickly trash piles up. Towns and cities are having problems finding suitable ways to dispose of millions of tons of trash each year. Much of this trash is burnable biomass. There are several power plants in Massachusetts that burn trash as fuel. However, burning trash can release toxic materials into the air. Until ways are found to make alternate forms of energy clean and inexpensive, society will continue to rely on fossil fuels.

Lesson Review 16.3

13. Discuss two ways solar energy is used to heat homes.
14. How can the rain falling on a mountain be used to make electricity?
15. List the advantages and disadvantages of using wind as a source of energy.
16. What is gasohol? How is it used?

Interpret and Apply

17. Some scientists worry that large OTEC plants could harm ocean life by warming the deep ocean water. How does an OTEC plant heat the water at depth?
18. In North America, passive solar homes are built with most of their windows facing south. Why?

USING BIOMASS AS FUEL

Purpose To perform an experiment to compare how biomass fuels burn.

Materials

safety goggles	aluminum foil
lab apron	clay
shelled peanuts	straight pins
minimarshmallows	graduated cylinder
wood splint	thermometer
test tube	matches
wire spiral	water

Thermometer
Test tube
Aluminum foil
Wire spiral
Pin
Clay

Procedure

1. Read all instructions for this activity before you begin your work.

2. Make a data table like the one shown.

3. Put on your goggles and lab apron.

4. Cover the spiral of wire with aluminum foil as shown. Leave an opening for a door. Set the test tube in the top of the wire spiral.

5. Stick the tip of the pin into the peanut and stand it in a piece of clay as shown. **CAUTION: Pinpoints are sharp.**

6. Pour 10 mL of water into the test tube. Measure the temperature of the water. Record the temperature in your data table.

7. Light the peanut with a match. When the peanut starts to burn, place it under the test tube as shown. **CAUTION: Never reach over an exposed flame. You may get burned.**

8. When the peanut is finished burning, measure and record the water temperature. Pour out the water.

9. Observe any odors or residues left behind. Observe if any smoke is produced. Record your observations.

10. Repeat steps 5–9 using the minimarshmallow and the wood splint.

11. Clean up and return all materials as instructed by your teacher. Wash your hands thoroughly before leaving the lab.

Collecting and Analyzing Data

Data Table				
	Temperature (°C)			
Sample	**Start**	**Final**	**Change**	**Observations**
peanut				
marsh-mallow				
wood				

1. Did all three samples heat the water equally? Why or why not?

2. Which sample caused the most smoke?

3. Which samples left material behind when they burned?

Drawing Conclusions

4. Which sample would you least want to use as an energy source? Explain.

5. Compare the advantages and disadvantages of using biomass as a fuel.

16.4 *Energy Conservation*

Lesson Objectives

▸ **Evaluate** *the reasons for conserving energy.*

▸ **Outline** *ways to conserve energy in your home, at work, and while traveling.*

▸ **Explain** *why buildings use insulation.*

▸ **Activity** **Construct graphs** *that compare energy transfer in different insulating materials.*

New Terms

insulation

How long do you stand in front of the open refrigerator just to see what is in there? Do your parents get upset when they find the television on and nobody watching it? Are the lights in your classroom left on even when no one is there? Most people waste energy without realizing it. Dwindling fuel supplies and higher costs make it important for everyone to conserve energy. By conserving energy, fossil fuel supplies will last longer, and there will be more time to develop alternate energy sources.

The chart in Figure 16-22 shows how energy is used in the United States. How can the United States use less energy? What can you do as an individual to use less energy? This lesson will show you how to conserve energy.

Transportation

Much of the energy used is for transportation. Transportation uses 27 percent of the energy in the United States. People now use less energy for transportation by driving less. Many people are joining carpools, riding bicycles or mopeds, or walking. Many commuters use public transportation, such as trains, subways, or buses to get to work.

Motorists can get better gas mileage and use less gasoline in a number of ways. A car with a well-tuned engine and properly inflated tires uses less fuel. Combining trips and errands cuts down on unnecessary travel. Cars use more fuel at higher speeds. Motorists save gas by driving at the posted speed.

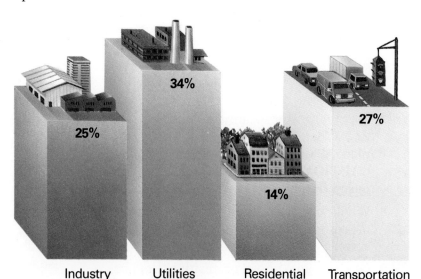

Figure 16-22 The biggest uses of energy in the United States are for transportation and to produce electricity.

25%   34%   14%   27%

Industry   Utilities   Residential   Transportation
            Producing   and
            Electricity Commercial

Carmakers have become more energy conscious. They make smaller, lighter cars with better-designed engines. Cars built today use much less fuel than older cars. In fact, manufacturers must pay a gas-guzzler tax on new cars that do not meet basic government standards set for gas mileage. Cars in the future may burn even less gasoline. However, the supply of petroleum will run out someday. What kind of fuels could cars of the future use?

Figure 16-23 *Left:* Riding a bike to work saves energy by taking cars off the road. *Right:* Many people use mass transit to commute to and from work.

Saving Electricity

There are many ways your family can save energy at home. For example, turning off the lights or television when you leave the room is an easy way to save energy. Fluorescent lights also save energy. These tube-shaped bulbs are common in schools and offices because they use less electricity than regular light bulbs. Do you have any fluorescent lights in your home?

Hot-water heaters use either natural gas or electricity. Using less hot water saves energy. Running dishwashers and washing machines only when they are full also saves energy. Taking short showers instead of baths also helps. Why do you think this saves energy?

Sometimes simple planning saves energy. Look at how your kitchen is arranged. Refrigerators should not be next to stoves. Why would moving the refrigerator save energy? Most household appliances are sold with tags that tell how much energy they use in a given amount of time. This allows shoppers to compare the energy use of several models before making a purchase. Using less energy saves money. In some cases, the money saved on your electric bill by using a more efficient appliance is enough to pay you back the appliance's original cost.

Figure 16-24 Replacing normal light bulbs with fluorescent bulbs reduces the amount of electricity used by a lamp.

Figure 16-25 Infrared photography reveals where thermal energy leaks from a house. Lighter colors indicate warmer areas.

Figure 16-26 Installing insulation saves money by preventing energy loss through the sides of this water heater.

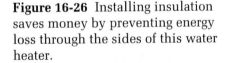

Heating and Cooling Your Home

Energy keeps your home warm in winter and cool in summer. Sometimes that energy is wasted. In winter, thermal energy escapes through the roof, doors, and windows. In summer, thermal energy enters your house from outside. To be comfortable, you either turn up the furnace or turn on the fan or air conditioner. The less you use heating and air conditioning systems, the more energy you conserve.

Your home probably has insulation in the walls and roof to prevent the transfer of thermal energy. **Insulation** is a substance that slows the flow of thermal energy. The best insulation is trapped air. Trapped air cannot move and transfer thermal energy. Materials that trap the most air make the best insulators. For example, you know that a fluffy down jacket or quiltlike coat will keep you very warm. These materials insulate you by wrapping you in a blanket of trapped air. Layered clothing keeps you warm because it creates small, unconnected layers of trapped air.

Many homes are insulated with pink fiberglass blankets. Other houses may be insulated with shredded paper material or plastic foam boards. Thermal energy still gets in or out of a house through doors and windows. Where is thermal energy escaping from in the house shown in Figure 16-25? Weather stripping helps keep out unwanted hot and cold air. Adding storm windows or sheets of plastic over existing windows helps create trapped air spaces that further insulate your home. On cold nights, closing curtains and pulling down shades help keep your house warm. Many people turn down their thermostat at night, dress warmly, and use more blankets. These are simple ways to conserve energy at home. What other ways can you think of?

Energy and Industry

Industry uses many of the same energy-saving methods used in your home. Wasted energy costs money, and that can make a business less profitable. Lighting, heating, and cooling systems in factories and office buildings are designed to reduce energy use. Computers in large buildings are used to adjust thermostats, fans, and vents. Some companies process their own waste materials for sale or reuse. Others burn waste and use the thermal energy to run their plants.

Recycling is a great energy saver. For example, it takes about 20 times more energy to get aluminum from ore than from used aluminum cans. For this reason, many beverage companies pay for returned aluminum cans. Is there a recycling center for aluminum cans in your community? Recycling raw materials not only saves energy, but it also saves Earth's mineral resources.

The longer current fuel supplies last, the longer the world has to develop new, alternate energy sources. The best way to make current supplies last is through conservation. Perhaps someday there will be a clean, cheap, abundant new source of energy. However, for now, conserving energy is the cheapest and easiest way to deal with the world's current energy problems.

ENVIRONMENTAL AWARENESS

The Automobile

Imagine the government passing a law that forbids you to own and operate a car. Could that ever happen? Should it?

During fuel shortages in the 1970's, motorists waited in long lines at gas stations to fill their tanks. In some parts of the country, people were allowed to buy gasoline only on certain days of the week. Many European countries banned driving on Sundays. Could this happen again?

In the United States alone, there are over 139 million cars. Transportation currently uses 64 percent of the petroleum produced or imported. That is over 7 million barrels of nonrenewable oil used per day.

The car is also this country's biggest source of air pollution. Over 60 percent of air pollution is from car exhaust. Car exhaust adds deadly carbon monoxide gas to the atmosphere, as well as nitrogen oxide and other harmful gases. Cars also send tons of solid materials into the air. Tiny particles of rubber from tires, cancer-causing asbestos fibers from brake linings, and all sorts of metal particles are added to the air by cars.

Transportation in the future may not include the car as you know it. Maybe the car you most admire will be seen only in a museum along with the remains of the dinosaurs. ∎

A C T I V I T Y   1 6 . 4

Lab Equipment

INSULATION

Purpose Construct graphs to compare energy transfer in different insulating materials.

Materials

4 small, metal juice cans, same size and color	colored pencils
	graph paper
	newspaper
4 thermometers	aluminum foil
clock or timer	large plastic foam
warm water	cup and lid
masking tape	safety goggles

Procedure

1. Read all instructions for this activity before you begin your work.

2. On your paper, make a data table like the one shown.

3. Put on your safety goggles.

4. Wrap one can in a layer or two of aluminum foil. Leave an opening in the top of the can so that it can later be filled with water.

5. Wrap the second can in ten layers of newspaper. Secure the newspaper with a small piece of masking tape.

6. Put the third can inside the foam cup. Leave the fourth can uncovered.

7. Fill each of the four cans with warm water. Carefully place a thermometer into each can. Put the lid on the foam cup, allowing the thermometer to stick through.

8. Record the starting temperature of each can in your data table.

9. Read and record the temperature in each can every 2 minutes for 12 minutes more.

10. Clean up all materials and wash your hands before leaving the laboratory.

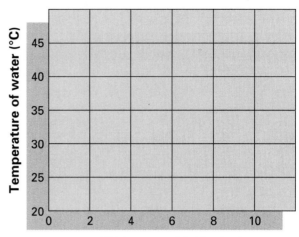

Time passed (minutes)

Collecting and Analyzing Data

Data Table				
Time passed (minutes)	**Temperature of Water:**			
	Foil	Paper	Foam	None
start (0)				
2				

1. Construct a graph of temperature versus time. Use a different color line for each can. Make a key to identify which color stands for which insulator.

2. According to your graph, which can cooled the quickest? Which can had the smallest decrease in temperature?

3. Does insulation prevent the loss of thermal energy? Explain.

Drawing Conclusions

4. Which substance would best insulate your home in winter? Would you choose the same substance to insulate your home in summer? Explain.

5. Would hot chocolate stay warmer in a plastic foam cup, a paper cup, or a metal cup? Which cup would be easier for you to hold? Explain fully.

Lesson Review 16.4

19. Why is it important to conserve energy?

20. What are some ways to save electricity in your home?

21. Explain how recycling saves energy.

22. How does insulation work?

Interpret and Apply

23. Why do people wrap hot-water heaters with foam?

24. Nonrenewable energy sources will one day run dry. Why is it still important to conserve energy now?

Chapter Summary

Read the summary of the main ideas in this chapter. If any are not clear to you, go back and review that lesson.

16.1 Fossil Fuels

■ Coal, petroleum, and natural gas form from plants and animals. They are called fossil fuels.

■ Fossil fuels are nonrenewable.

■ Petroleum and natural gas are mixtures of hydrocarbons found in rocks below Earth's surface.

■ Tar sands and oil shale may be sources of petroleum in the future.

16.2 Earth's Alternate Energy Sources

■ Most energy sources are used to produce electricity.

■ Nuclear fission occurs when an atomic nucleus is split. Fusion occurs when four nuclei join together.

■ Small amounts of radioactive fuel release large amounts of energy.

■ Radioactive waste is dangerous for thousands of years.

■ The different types of geothermal energy depend on the amount of water and the temperature beneath the surface.

16.3 Alternate Energy Sources from the Sun

■ Solar collectors change the sun's radiant energy into useful thermal energy. Photovoltaic cells change light into electricity.

■ Wind, water power, and biomass are renewable energy sources that get their energy from the sun.

■ Wind and running water are both used to make electricity.

■ Biomass is an energy source using plant and animal materials.

16.4 Energy Conservation

■ There are ways to reduce the need for energy in all areas of energy use.

■ Energy conservation makes fossil fuels last longer and allows time for new sources of energy to be developed.

■ Insulation is a substance that slows the flow of thermal energy.

Chapter Review

■ Vocabulary

biomass
coal
crude oil
fission
fossil fuel
fusion
gasohol
geothermal energy
hydrocarbon
hydroelectric
insulation

natural gas
natural resources
nuclear energy
oil shale
petrochemicals
petroleum
photovoltaic cell
solar energy
strip mining
tar sand

■ Concept Mapping

Construct a concept map for alternate energy sources from the sun. Use the terms *sun, wind, photovoltaic cell, biomass,* and *light.* Use additional terms as you need them.

■ Review

Number your paper from 1 to 20. Match each term in List **A** with a phrase from List **B.**

List A

a. fusion
b. radioactive waste
c. geothermal
d. acid rain
e. biomass
f. gasohol
g. photovoltaic cell
h. insulation
i. coal
j. tidal power

k. fission
l. petrochemicals
m. transportation
n. anthracite
o. strip mining
p. generator
q. natural resources
r. crude oil
s. recycling
t. oil shale

List B

1. turning this machine makes electricity
2. last stage in the coal series
3. splitting the nucleus of an atom
4. mixture of gasoline and alcohol

5. energy source using thermal energy from inside Earth
6. saves the energy needed to smelt raw ore
7. can only be used in narrow bays or inlets
8. using plant and animal materials for energy
9. used to convert light into electricity
10. fossil fuel containing the most sulfur
11. substance that slows the flow of thermal energy
12. largest use of petroleum
13. all materials supplied by Earth
14. biggest problem with fission as an energy source
15. petroleum mixture taken out of the ground
16. plastics, vinyl, synthetic fibers
17. joining four nuclei of hydrogen together
18. simplest way to mine coal
19. a future oil source found in Colorado, Wyoming, and Utah
20. environmental problem caused by burning coal

■ Interpret and Apply

On your paper, answer each question using complete sentences.

21. Explain how today's energy needs have caused more environmental problems than there were 100 years ago.

22. A well is drilled into the top of an anticline. Natural gas flows from the well for several months. Then the well starts to flow crude oil. Finally, the well is pumped and starts to produce nothing but water. Explain why the substances changed.

23. Describe how an orange is a mass of stored solar energy.

24. A certain solar hot-water system costs $7000 to install in your home. The money you save on energy bills would pay for this cost after 15 years. Discuss whether or not you would install the system. What factors would affect your decision?

25. Evaluate the benefits and disadvantages of laws that would require everyone to recycle their trash.

26. Explain why the United States must import oil and what problems importing so much oil has caused.

27. Describe ways in which you could design your future home to be more energy efficient.

28. Explain why solar homes in the northern hemisphere are built with their windows or solar collectors facing south. What additional benefit would there be in building a passive solar home partially buried in the side of a hill?

29. Suppose researchers found a way to use gold as a fuel. Would gold be a renewable energy source? What would determine how rapidly homes or industry would accept burning gold as a fuel?

■ *Writing in Science*

30. Persuasive writing tries to convince readers that a particular point of view is correct. Newspaper editorials are one type of persuasive writing. Imagine that your community must decide whether or not to let a fission nuclear power plant be built within its boundaries. Decide how you feel about this issue. Then write an editorial, such as you might see in your local newspaper, expressing your point of view. Before you write, list the reasons you will use to support your viewpoint.

■ *Critical Thinking*

Two students are building a solar collector. They need to find out what color to paint the inside of the collector. They put the same volume of water in three identical cans. They paint each can a different color. The colors used are black, yellow, and silver. The students then place the cans in the sun.

When they start, the water in all three cans is 20°C. Every five minutes, the students measure the temperature of the water in the cans. The graph below shows the students' results. Use the graph to answer questions 31–36.

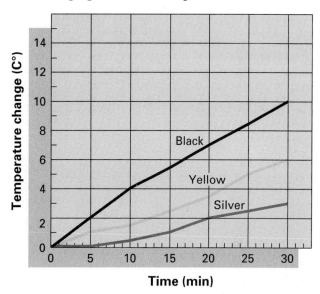

31. Which can had the greatest change in temperature?

32. Which can had the least change in temperature?

33. Try to explain why the silver can did not get as warm as the others.

34. What color should their solar collector be?

35. According to the graph, what colors would you recommend people avoid wearing in summer?

36. Predict where the color blue would fall on this graph. Design an experiment to test your hypothesis.

FOSSIL FUELS MAY RUN OUT IN YOUR LIFETIME

Issue: *What is the best way to manage the world's limited energy resources?*

Imagine what life would be like without natural gas to cook your food, oil to heat your home, or gasoline to fill up the family car. While this might sound farfetched, it could happen in your lifetime. Fossil fuels are non-renewable resources. Scientists predict that the world's petroleum will be gone by the year 2080. Coal, the most abundant fossil fuel, will be used up in about 300 years.

Satellite photographs of city lights at night show the unequal use of Earth's energy. Undeveloped countries appear dark, while developing nations have some city lights. Developed countries, with only 20 percent of the world's people, use more than 70 percent of the world's energy. But each year, developing countries use more energy as their populations go up and they try to improve their standard of living. In comparison, energy use in developed countries has not gone up in the last 15 years. Developed countries fear that their energy conservation efforts are being offset by the growth of developing countries.

Developing nations do not have money to invest in energy-efficient technology.

Some people feel that developing countries should use fossil fuels more efficiently. Developing countries use coal for much of their energy needs because it is the cheapest fossil

This artist's view of city lights is based on satellite images

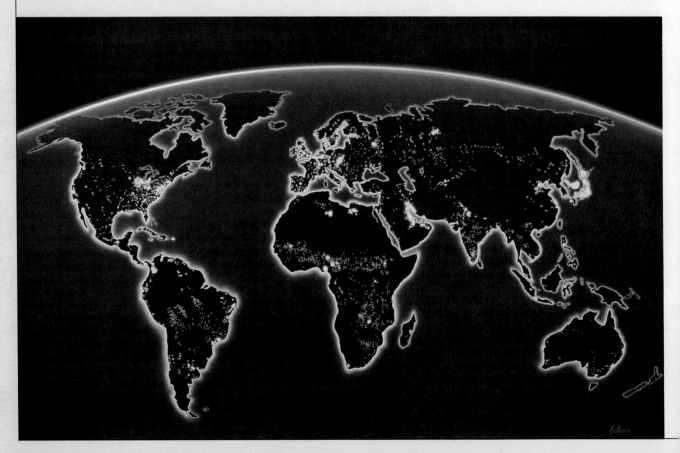

fuel. In China, for example, up to 75 percent of the energy comes from coal. Compare this to developed nations, which use coal for only 20 to 30 percent of their energy. Unfortunately, coal is the least efficient fossil fuel.

Many developing countries feel that it is more important to improve their standard of living than to conserve energy. They can improve their standard of living only by increased production, but this requires more energy. New energy-efficient machines could help these countries to save money in the long run. But many developing countries do not have money to invest in this new technology.

Developed countries are saving energy with new efficient machines that get more work out of a given amount of fuel. For example, the average car can travel about 6 kilometers per liter of gasoline. The most efficient cars can travel 27 kilometers on the same amount of fuel. New models of refrigerators, furnaces, and air conditioners also are more efficient. But many people still use older machines that are not as efficient.

Developed countries use 70 percent of the world's energy.

Some people think that developed nations could be doing more to save energy. For example, many European countries have a large tax on gasoline to discourage people from wasting it. In the United States, however, the gasoline tax is small. Many people feel that a large gasoline tax is unfair because it hurts poor people more than the wealthy. But other people feel that a gasoline tax is the only way to get more fuel-efficient cars on the road.

Energy conservation is the best way to make fossil fuels last longer. But as nonrenewable energy sources are used up, people will have to turn more to renewable resources. At present, renewable resources such as solar, geothermal, hydroelectric, and wind energy supply less than 5 percent of the world's energy. Many people feel that all countries must work together to develop these renewable resources for the future.

Act on the Issue

Gather the Facts

1. Use library books and articles listed in the *Readers' Guide to Periodical Literature* to learn more about world supplies of oil, coal, and natural gas. For each of these resources, find two estimates for when they will run out. What factors explain differences between the estimates?

2. Use books and articles in the library to find out how much people in other countries pay in gasoline tax. Find out what those countries do with this money. Think of two ways the United States could use gasoline tax money to conserve energy.

Take Action

3. Take an opinion poll in your school or your community. Start by writing a list of five questions. Each question should have two possible answers. Do people think that there is going to be a shortage of gasoline in the 1990's? Which is more important, finding new sources of energy or finding ways to conserve energy? Should the government give tax breaks to encourage using renewable energy sources such as solar energy? Share the results with your class.

4. Make up a fact sheet of ways people can conserve nonrenewable energy sources in their daily lives. Organize the fact sheet into categories such as travel, using electricity, and using hot water. Emphasize how easy it is to save energy.

Science in Action

CAREER: Quarry Superintendent

Fred Patterson has worked in the sandstone quarries of northern Ohio for 40 years.

What was your first job in the quarry?

I was seventeen when I became a quarry-man. The quarrymen use derricks to lift 10-ton blocks of sandstone out of the pit.

What else did you do before you became a superintendent?

I've had just about every job in the quarry. I ran one of the channeling machines that makes the first cuts in the sandstone. They cut blocks that are 30 feet long and 13 feet 6 inches wide. I've also been a driller. The drillers break up those big blocks into smaller ones. I've also worked on the company railroad, moving the blocks from the pit to the mill, where the stone is cut into still smaller pieces.

How did you learn to do all these things?

In the quarry, the men are divided up into groups. The group leader is responsible for teaching each worker. It takes about five years to learn all about sandstone quarrying. It's like learning to be a carpenter.

What do you like best about your work?

Sandstone is one of nature's gifts. We take it out of the ground and sell it to people who use it to make things that will last many lifetimes. The stone from our quarries is some of the finest in the world.

How much longer will you be able to take sandstone from these quarries?

The first sandstone was brought out in the 1840's. At the rate we are bringing it out today, I would guess that it will last another hundred years.

CAREER: Petroleum Prospector

Emma Jennings works for an oil company as a petroleum geologist.

What are you looking for when you go out into the field?

Not all oil is buried. I have been doing a lot of work in Colorado and Wyoming the past several years looking for oil shale. Oil shale is a rock that contains something called kerogen, which we can process into oil. Some oil shale is at the surface. My job is to locate it, and then try to determine how much oil shale is buried below the surface.

Are there other ways of looking for the rocks that may contain kerogen?

The first thing we do is look at aerial photographs of an area. We even use photographs from *Landsat*.

If the kerogen is inside the rock, how will your company ever get it out?

As you said, the oil is actually inside the shale. To get the oil out, companies will have to mine the oil shale and then remove the oil. To remove the oil, the oil shale must be crushed, processed, and heated to temperatures of almost 500°C. Since the price of oil from wells is still fairly low and the cost of removing oil from oil shale is high, the process is not economical.

What kind of training did you have for your job?

I majored in geology in college. While I was still in college, I was lucky to have two summer internships working for the oil company that I work for now. Those summer jobs really helped me decide that this is the job for me.

HOBBY: Exploring Ponds and Streams

Noni Gordon, a high school student, became interested in limnology after taking an ecology class at her school. Limnology is the study of lakes, ponds, and streams.

It's fairly unusual to take ecology in high school. Why did you take ecology?

My school has a terrific ecology teacher. I signed up for the class because of her reputation. The school, Lake Ridge Academy, has its own pond. We can study the pond

and the plants and animals without ever leaving school grounds.

Other than exploring the pond, did you take many field trips?

That's the best part of the course. As part of our work, we took a trip to one of the islands in Lake Erie. We spent the whole day measuring things like the turbidity or muddiness of the water and the water temperature at different depths.

On another trip, we went canoeing on Old Woman Creek, a wildlife sanctuary on the southern side of Lake Erie. In the late fall, birds coming from Canada rest and feed at the creek before migrating farther south. We went there because there have been a lot of changes in the habitat since a turnpike was built. The road changed the drainage, making a lake out of the creek. As a result, many of the plants and animals died off.

Will you study ecology in college?

Absolutely. I really like the outdoors. I want to learn more about ecosystems. Then again, I am also interested in journalism. Maybe I will combine those interests someday as a science writer or editor.

UNIT 6

The Atmosphere

You Know More Than You Think

You may be surprised at how much you already know about the atmosphere. To find out, try to answer the following questions.

- *How many kinds of precipitation can you name?*
- *What happens to the bathroom mirror when you take a hot shower?*
- *Which would have cooler weather, a place near the equator or a place near the South Pole?*
- *How might air become polluted?*
- *What is a desert?*

When you finish this unit, answer these questions again to see how much you have learned.

Frost forms when the temperature and the moisture are right for it.

441

17

Earth's Atmosphere and Wind

Chapter Preview

*H*ave You Ever
WONDERED?

Why is the sky blue?

Look outside right now. What color is the sky? Possibly it is brilliant blue. If you sat on the moon instead of on Earth, you would look out into a black sky with stars, even in the daytime. Looking at the sun from the moon would be like looking at a glaring streetlight on a dark night here on Earth. Why do Earth and the moon give you different views of the sky?

The earth is covered by an air film so thin that it is like the skin on an apple. But you know that air itself is colorless, not blue. What makes the sky look blue? You learned in Chapter 6 that light from the sun is a mixture of all the colors of the rainbow. White light from the sun hits gas molecules on its way through the atmosphere to the earth. These molecules are just the right size to scatter blue light waves in all directions. Because you see blue waves coming from all directions, the entire sky looks blue.

What gases make up the atmosphere? How does sunlight affect the atmosphere? What makes the wind blow? You will find answers to these and many other questions about the atmosphere in this chapter.

New Terms

troposphere
stratosphere
mesosphere
thermosphere

On July 26, 1959, Lieutenant Colonel William Rankin was forced to bail out of his jet plane at an elevation of 16 kilometers. Immediately, Rankin felt a blast of freezing air rush past him. As he plunged toward Earth, he felt his body swell like a balloon. He struggled to stay conscious despite a lack of oxygen. After falling for 20 seconds or so, he reached the towering top of a thunderstorm. No sooner had his parachute opened when upward blasts of air slammed him away from the earth. Winds in the seething thunderhead bounced Rankin up, down, and sideways through sheets of rain and volleys of hail. After this incredible half-hour journey, he landed in a tree, swinging from his parachute lines. He had survived a ride through the atmosphere!

Layers of the Atmosphere

Suppose you made Colonel Rankin's journey in reverse. This time you travel safely enclosed in a rocket. Your rocket is equipped to measure outside air temperature and density. Use the chart shown in Figure 17-1 to follow your progress. Place the bottom edge of a blank piece of paper on the horizontal line at 0 kilometers. This elevation line represents Earth's surface. Mark the gauges for temperature and density on the bottom edge of your paper. You begin your voyage from your launch pad at the bottom of the troposphere. Move the paper up slowly as you imagine your rocket taking off.

The air temperature outside decreases as your rocket climbs. At an elevation of 12 kilometers, the temperature levels off at about −56°C. More than 75 percent of the weight of the atmosphere and almost all of the world's weather is below you. You have just traveled through the **troposphere,** the lowest layer of the atmosphere and the layer in which life exists. The temperature remains constant for a while as your rocket rises. Eventually the air temperature begins to rise again and levels off at 0°C by the time you reach 50 kilometers. You have passed through the **stratosphere.**

After you leave the stratosphere, 99 percent of the air is below you, but there are two more layers to come. As you pass through the **mesosphere,** the temperature falls again. The sky outside is black instead of blue. The temperature reaches its lowest point, −90°C, at an elevation of 80 kilometers. Here the air is very thin. Your rocket passes into the **thermosphere** as the temperature rises for the last time. Ions that reflect radio waves from Earth are found in the lower thermosphere. The ions disrupt your radio contact with the ground as you pass through.

Figure 17-1 A journey through the atmosphere

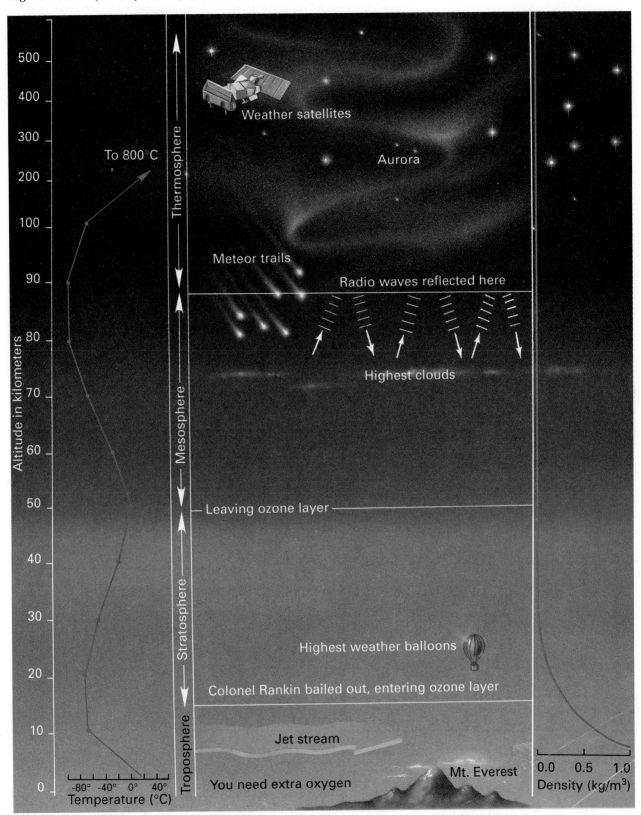

Altitude in kilometers

500
400
300
200
100
90
80
70
60
50
40
30
20
10
0

To 800°C

Thermosphere

Mesosphere

Stratosphere

Troposphere

Weather satellites

Aurora

Meteor trails

Radio waves reflected here

Highest clouds

Leaving ozone layer

Highest weather balloons

Colonel Rankin bailed out, entering ozone layer

Jet stream

Mt. Everest

You need extra oxygen

-80° -40° 0° 40°
Temperature (°C)

0.0   0.5   1.0
Density (kg/m³)

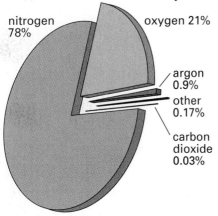

Elements in Earth's Atmosphere

nitrogen 78%

oxygen 21%

argon 0.9%

other 0.17%

carbon dioxide 0.03%

Figure 17-2 No other planet in the solar system has the same mixture of gases as Earth.

It is difficult for you to decide when your trip through the atmosphere ends. Beyond the thermosphere lies a region where gas molecules are so far apart that they blend into space. At 600 kilometers, you decide to return home to the bottom of the troposphere. You leave your rocket asking several questions. As you moved closer to the sun, why did the air temperature in the troposphere go down rather than up? Why did the temperature increase in the stratosphere? In order to answer these questions, you need to know about the gases and particles that make up the atmosphere.

Composition of Air

Air is a mixture of gases. Figure 17-2 shows that air consists mostly of nitrogen and oxygen molecules, with tiny amounts of carbon dioxide, argon, and other gases. This proportion of gases is the same up to the bottom of the thermosphere. Above that level, air gases separate by their densities. The least dense gas, hydrogen, blends from the top of the atmosphere into space.

ENVIRONMENTAL AWARENESS

A Hole in the Sky

In 1985, British scientists in Antarctica reported a surprisingly large decrease in stratospheric ozone. NASA satellite data confirmed that the hole in the ozone over Antarctica was sometimes as large as the United States. A comparison of past ozone levels showed the hole was growing.

Why is the ozone disappearing over Antarctica? Traces of human-made chlorine compounds were found over both the South and North Poles after years of experiments. These compounds, produced by chemicals called chlorofluorocarbons (CFC's), destroy ozone. In 1987, representatives from 24 nations met in Montreal and agreed to cut back on CFC's, which are used in some spray cans and in air conditioners. ∎

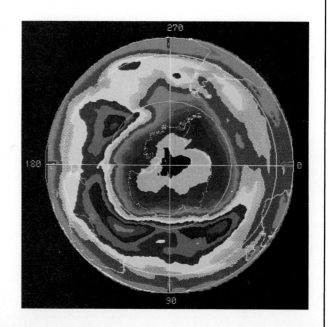

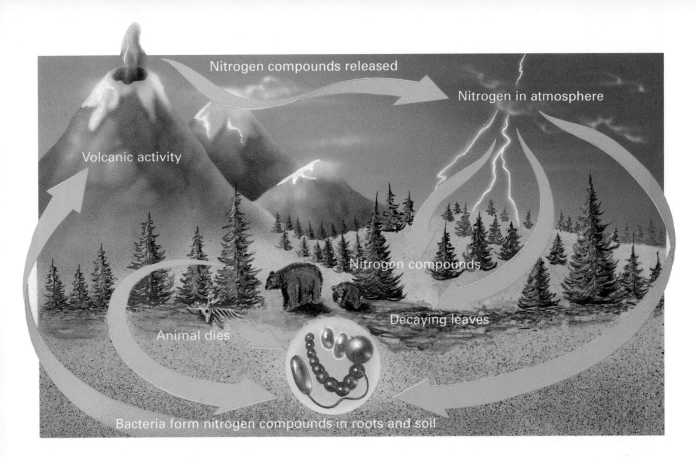

What is the most common gas in air? You might say oxygen, because that is the gas you need to stay alive. Actually, nitrogen makes up 78 percent of air. Nitrogen is just as important as oxygen to all living things. Nitrogen is one of the building blocks of plant and animal tissue. Plants and animals cannot use nitrogen directly, however. Fortunately, lightning causes nitrogen to change to a form that can be absorbed by plants, as shown in Figure 17-3. Oxygen, at 21 percent, is the second most common gas in air. Oxygen allows plants and animals to release their food energy. Plants also produce oxygen as they make food. On a sunny day, the leaves of a full-grown maple tree can release 20 kilograms of oxygen into the air. This is enough oxygen to keep you breathing for five days! Green plants use carbon dioxide and sunlight to make their own food. Although less than one percent of air is carbon dioxide, it has an important effect on Earth's surface temperature. You will learn more about this effect in Lesson 17.2. Another component of air, water vapor, varies in amount from 0.01 to about 3 percent of the air. Without water vapor in the air, there would be no clouds or rain, and no life as you know it. Like carbon dioxide, water vapor helps to control Earth's surface temperature. Chapter 18 discusses the role of water in the atmosphere in detail.

Figure 17-3 The nitrogen cycle. Nitrogen returns to the atmosphere when plants and animals decay.

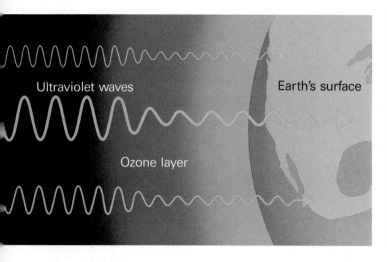

Figure 17-4 *Left:* The ozone layer absorbs most ultraviolet radiation from the sun. *Right:* What effect does ultraviolet radiation have on people who stay out in the sun a long time?

Do you recall that the stratosphere warmed up on your rocket journey? This temperature increase occurs when the gas ozone absorbs ultraviolet radiation. Ozone is a special form of oxygen that has three oxygen atoms in a molecule. Ozone protects life on Earth by absorbing 99 percent of the sun's ultraviolet radiation. Your body needs a small amount of ultraviolet radiation. Too much ultraviolet radiation, however, can cause severe sunburn or skin cancer.

Nitrogen, oxygen, carbon dioxide, water vapor, and ozone are all gases. But air also contains solid particles. Smoke from volcanoes, forest fires, factories, and automobiles, as well as salt from seawater, blowing soil, pollen, and meteor dust are all found in the air.

Lesson Review 17.1

1. List and describe the layers of the atmosphere.
2. List the five main components of air. Which of these are gases?
3. Explain the importance of each component of air for living things.

Interpret and Apply

4. You identify the gases in a sample of atmosphere from another planet. How could you tell whether plants and animals from Earth might be able to survive there?
5. An area of tropical rain forest larger than New York State is cut or burned each year. What effect does this large-scale removal of trees have on the amount of carbon dioxide in the air?

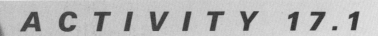

ACTIVITY 17.1   Lab Equipment

PARTICLES IN THE AIR

Purpose To interpret data from particle counts in the air near your home.

Materials

glass microscope slide	plastic wrap
rubber band	microscope
clear tape	ruler
paper cup	

Procedure

Part A

1. Read all instructions for this activity before you begin your work.

2. Make sure that the glass slide is clean. Write your name, class, and date on the paper cup.

3. Place the slide in the cup and take it home. At home, cut a piece of clear tape as long as the slide. Place the tape on the slide, sticky side up. Fasten the ends of the tape to the slide with two smaller pieces of tape.

4. Find a place outdoors about 1 m above ground level where you can lay the slide flat. Leave the slide there, sticky side up, for 24 hours in dry weather.

5. Record the location of the slide and the date and time you put it outdoors.

6. After 24 hours, put the slide back in the cup. Cover the cup with plastic wrap and secure it with the rubber band. Record the time you brought the slide indoors and the weather conditions during the time it was outside. Bring the slide back to school.

Part B

7. Place the slide under a microscope set at $100\times$. Without moving the slide, count all the particles you see. Record your total count.

8. Move the slide so that you are looking at a second microscope field that does not overlap the first. Count the particles and record your count again. Repeat the procedure for two more fields.

Collecting and Analyzing Data

1. Find your average number of particles by adding the numbers from your four microscope fields and dividing by four.

2. Multiply the average number of particles by 62, which will give you the total particle count in 1 square centimeter.

3. Compare your results with those of your classmates. Find a class average for particles per square centimeter.

4. Record your class results on a map of your town or school district.

5. Why should all samples be collected from the same height and for the same length of time?

Drawing Conclusions

6. Where do you think the particles on your slide came from? Give evidence for your answer from your map.

7. Compare your average count to the one obtained by the classmate who lives closest to you. How can you explain the difference in the two counts?

8. How might the weather affect your count?

17.2 The Sun and the Atmosphere

The energy from our star, the sun, travels 150 million kilometers to the earth in 8 minutes. Because of the earth's small size and enormous distance from the sun, only half of one billionth of the total energy given off by the sun reaches Earth. This tiny amount of energy and its interaction with the atmosphere makes Earth unique.

Solar Energy and the Atmosphere

In Chapter 6, you learned that energy from the sun travels through space in the form of radiation or waves. White sunlight consists of all of the colors of the rainbow. The sun also produces several forms of radiation that your eye cannot see, including infrared and ultraviolet radiation. They are outside the narrow band of visible radiation. All types of waves together form the solar spectrum.

The sun does not give off equal amounts of visible, infrared, and ultraviolet radiation. Most of the sun's energy is in the visible and short wave infrared parts of the spectrum. The sun radiates much less long wave infrared and ultraviolet radiation, and even less in the other regions of the spectrum.

What happens when the sun's radiation passes through the thin film of air surrounding the earth? Figure 17-5 shows what happens to this radiation.

Lesson Objectives

▶ **Discuss** the effects of the atmosphere on incoming solar radiation.

▶ **Compare** incoming solar radiation to the radiation given off by Earth.

▶ **Explain** how Earth's atmosphere behaves like a greenhouse.

▶ **Activity**   **Form a model** for the heating of Earth's atmosphere.

New Terms

energy balance
greenhouse effect

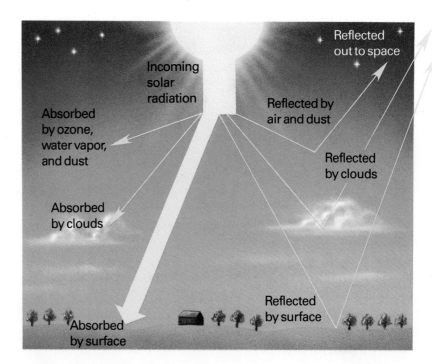

Figure 17-5 Radiation from the sun is both absorbed and reflected by the atmosphere and the earth.

Some incoming waves are reflected into space and never reach the earth. You can see white swirls in Figure 17-6 because clouds reflect light from the sun. Other waves do not reach Earth's surface because gases like carbon dioxide and ozone absorb them. When gases absorb radiation from the sun, the atmosphere warms up a little. Only about half of the sun's radiation actually reaches the earth.

So far, the sun's radiation has caused little heating of the air. When the radiation reaches the surface, a small portion is reflected, while the rest is absorbed. If you walk barefoot on a dark-colored driveway on a sunny summer day, your feet feel the effects of this absorbed radiation. Most of the absorbed energy is finally radiated back into space. Fortunately, the amount of energy that arrives from the sun is roughly equal to the energy given off into space by the earth. This **energy balance** keeps the surface temperature of Earth stable over time. Slight changes in the energy balance of Earth may lead to long-term climate change.

Greenhouse Effect

Radiation from Earth heats the atmosphere, while radiation from the sun has little heating effect. There are two reasons for this. The first is that Earth's radiation is different from the sun's radiation. This is not surprising, because Earth is not as hot as the sun. The sun gives off mostly visible and short wave infrared radiation, while Earth gives off only long wave infrared radiation. Second, certain gases in the atmosphere absorb specific waves of radiation. How can these two factors explain why air at the bottom of the atmosphere is warmer than air near the top?

To answer this question, recall a time when you got into a car on a sunny day, and then jumped out quickly because the air inside the car was very hot. Why was the air inside the car so much hotter than the air outside? Visible and short wave infrared radiation from the sun passed through the closed windows of the car. The inside of the car, including the seats, warmed up as it absorbed some of this radiation. The warm seats, like the warm earth, gave off long wave infrared radiation. The glass windows absorbed a little of the long wave infrared radiation. The air inside the car absorbed some long wave infrared radiation as well. The warm seats and the absorbed infrared radiation heated up the air. Since the air was trapped, it could not mix with cooler air outside the car. As the hot air and sunlight made the seats get hotter, the trapped air became hotter as well. Did you open a window? If so, you let air move through the car, and the car cooled off.

Figure 17-6 How can you tell that sunlight is being reflected in this picture?

Fact or Fiction?

Winning a million dollars may happen to you "once in a blue moon," which means not very often. Can the moon really be blue? During a large forest fire in Alberta, Canada, in 1950, people from Ontario to Europe saw a blue moon and sun for many days. Unlike molecules of air gases that scatter blue light, certain sizes of smoke and dust particles scatter red and yellow light, allowing blue light to pass through. By the time the white light from the moon reaches your eye, much of the red and yellow light has been scattered out. Blue light is the strongest of the remaining light, so the moon appears blue.

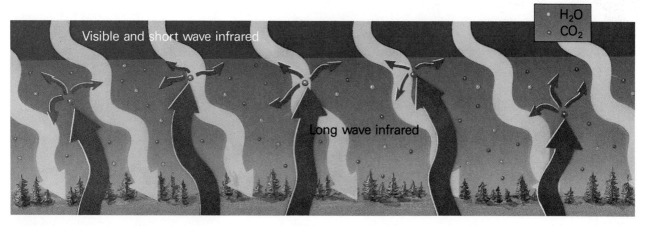

Visible and short wave infrared

H₂O
CO₂

Long wave infrared

Figure 17-7 Water vapor and carbon dioxide in the troposphere absorb and give off infrared radiation from the warm earth.

Because a greenhouse also traps heated air, this process is called the **greenhouse effect.** Carbon dioxide, water vapor, and other gases in the atmosphere act somewhat like the walls and windows of a greenhouse. Figure 17-7 shows that these gases allow visible radiation to pass through. However, these gases absorb much of the infrared radiation given off by Earth. The atmosphere warms up because of the absorbed energy. The warm atmosphere also gives off infrared radiation, which in turn heats the earth further. If these "greenhouse gases" did not act as Earth's thermal blanket, the earth would be similar to the moon. Daytime and nighttime temperatures would vary as much as 200°C. The overall surface temperature would be 15°C colder. What would happen if the amount of carbon dioxide and water vapor increased?

Lesson Review 17.2

6. How does radiation from the sun differ from radiation given off by Earth? What is the reason for this difference?

7. List and describe at least three ways sunlight is affected by the earth's atmosphere.

8. How do carbon dioxide and water vapor affect radiation given off by Earth?

Interpret and Apply

9. Why is it dangerous to leave a pet in a car with closed windows, especially in a sunny location?

10. Molecules of air gases scatter blue light from the sun more than red light. Dust and water vapor scatter all visible light waves equally. What color would you expect the sky to be on a very humid day? On a dry day? Explain your answers.

ACTIVITY 17.2 *General Supplies*

THE GREENHOUSE EFFECT

Purpose To form a model for the heating of the earth's atmosphere.

Materials

2 clear plastic shoe-boxes and lids
2 thermometers
3 index cards
masking tape
scissors
colored pencils
graph paper
6-cm high pile of newspaper
dark soil

Procedure

1. Read all instructions for this activity before you begin your work.

2. Use the scissors to cut one index card in half. Loosely fold one half of one index card around the bulb of each thermometer. Tape in place.

3. Add 2 cm of dark soil to each box.

4. Fold each uncut index card in half widthwise. Stand each folded card crosswise in the middle of each box as shown in the diagram.

5. Prop a thermometer upside down against each folded index card. The thermometer bulbs should be near the top of the box. Record the temperatures on the thermometers.

6. Close one box with a lid. Tape the lid in place. Leave the other box open.

7. Place each box in full sunlight on top of a 3-cm high pile of newspapers.

8. Record the temperature in each box every minute for 15 minutes.

9. Before leaving the laboratory, clean up all materials and wash your hands thoroughly.

Collecting and Analyzing Data

Data Table		
Time	Box Temperatures	
(min)	Covered (°C)	Uncovered (°C)
0		
1		
2		

1. Set up a graph with time in minutes on the horizontal axis and temperature on the vertical axis. Plot data for both boxes on the same graph. Use a different color for each line.

2. From your graph, which box heated up more rapidly?

Drawing Conclusions

3. Why did one box heat up more than the other?

4. If glass, waxed paper, or aluminum foil were used for the lid on the box, what would be the results?

5. Which box is more like a model of Earth's atmosphere? Why?

6. In what way is Earth's "greenhouse effect" different from the box?

New Terms

air pressure
temperature
parcel of air
mercury
  barometer

aneroid
  barometer
millibar

The next time you go outside, hold out your hand palm side up. Look up into the atmosphere. The air pressing on the palm of your hand extends from your skin to the edge of outer space, over 600 kilometers straight up. How much air is pressing on 1 square centimeter of your hand? The column of air over 1 square centimeter of your palm weighs about as much as a 1-liter bottle of your favorite soft drink. The weight of air on a unit area is called **air pressure.**

Why Air Pressure Varies

Three factors affect the weight of air pressing on a surface. One of these factors is elevation. Recall that the density of air decreases rapidly as you move away from Earth. When you go up in an elevator, your ears sometimes pop as they adjust to a decrease in air pressure.

Imagine a tall stack of peanut butter sandwiches. The sandwich at the bottom of the stack is squashed by the weight of all the sandwiches above. A sandwich in the middle holds up less weight and is therefore less squashed. Like the sandwiches, the air at the bottom of the column is squeezed by the air on top of it. Molecules of air gases at the bottom of the column are much closer together than molecules at a higher elevation. Because the molecules at the bottom of the atmosphere are so close together, there are more of them to press on your palm. The air pressure is higher at the bottom of the air column.

Air temperature also affects air pressure. The **temperature** of air depends on the average speed of its molecules. The higher the air temperature is, the faster its molecules are moving. Suppose you had a bag of air and placed it in the sunlight. The temperature of the air in the bag would increase. The molecules would move faster and spread out more. The bag would expand a little. But what happens to air in the atmosphere?

Think of a small volume or "package" of air that has the same temperature throughout. Meteorologists call such a volume a **parcel of air.** For example, a small mass of cool air over a pond is a parcel of air. A small mass of warm air over a nearby parking lot is another parcel of air. Because the molecules in the warm-air parcel are more spread out, there are fewer molecules in the warm air than in the cool air. The weight of the warm air is less than the weight of the cool air. As a result, the warm air exerts less pressure on the parking lot than the cool air exerts on the water. The higher the air's temperature, the lower the pressure.

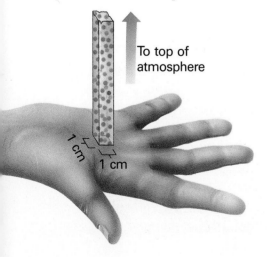

Figure 17-8 The weight of air on a unit area is called air pressure.

To top of atmosphere

1 cm
1 cm

How does the amount of water vapor in the air affect air pressure? Water molecules are lighter than molecules of oxygen or nitrogen. If lighter water molecules replace some of the heavier molecules in a parcel of air, the total weight of the air is less. The more water vapor there is in the air, the lower the air pressure.

Measuring Air Pressure

Have you ever sipped milk into a straw and then put your finger over the top? You can lift the straw, and the milk does not fall out. Because air is a gas, it pushes in all directions. Air pushes up on the bottom of the column of milk in the straw. You prevent air from pushing down just as hard from the top of the straw by putting your finger over the end. If you used a longer straw, the straw would hold more milk. If your straw were long enough, the milk's weight would be large enough to overcome the upward push of the air pressure. At this point, milk would run out of the straw.

Meteorologists solve the problem of the long straw by using a denser liquid. The denser the liquid is, the shorter the column of liquid needed to balance the air pressure. Mercury is a dense, readily available liquid. The level of the mercury inside the tube rises and falls with the air pressure like the height of the milk in the straw. This device, shown in Figure 17-9, is called a **mercury barometer.**

If you have a barometer in your home, it is probably a smaller, safer type called an aneroid barometer. An **aneroid barometer** contains a pancake-shaped metal can without much air in it. Figure 17-10 shows a diagram and a photo of an aneroid barometer. The air squeezes the metal can in an aneroid barometer. Changes in air pressure cause slight changes in the size of the can, which are made visible by a series of levers.

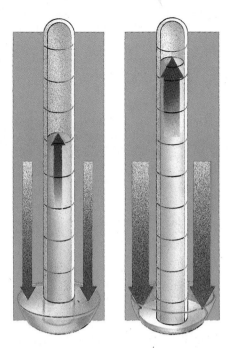

Figure 17-9 When the air pressure increases, more liquid is forced up into the tube of a mercury barometer.

Figure 17-10 An aneroid barometer

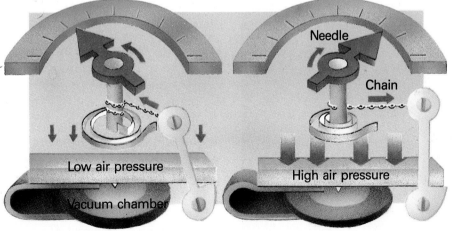

Needle

Chain

Low air pressure

Vacuum chamber

High air pressure

Table 17-1 Units for Measuring Air Pressure		
Inches of mercury	Millibars	Millimeters of mercury
31.00	1050.0	787
30.00	1015.9	762
29.92	1013.2	760
29.53	1000.00	750
29.00	982.1	737

The average sea-level height of the mercury column in a mercury barometer is 760 millimeters. Therefore, the average barometric pressure at sea level is 760 millimeters, or 29.92 inches. Meteorologists also express barometric pressure in millibars. A **millibar** is a unit of pressure that is related to the actual weight of air pressing on a 1 square centimeter area. The average sea-level value for atmospheric pressure is 1013.2 millibars. Table 17-1 compares different units of air pressure.

Lesson Review 17.3

11. What causes air pressure? Why is air pressure greater at sea level than at higher elevations?

12. Describe how air pressure changes when
    a. temperature is increased.
    b. elevation is increased.
    c. water vapor is decreased.

13. Describe two different types of barometers and explain how each works.

14. Explain why milk would not be a good liquid to use in a barometer.

Interpret and Apply

15. Suction cups on a stuffed animal's feet allow you to stick it to a car window (Figure 17-11). As a suction cup is pushed down, air is forced from the underside of the cup. Explain why the stuffed animal doesn't fall.

16. At sea level, a barometer reads 1013 millibars. At an elevation of 100 meters above sea level, the barometer reads 1003 millibars. Predict the barometer reading in Death Valley, which is 100 meters below sea level. Assume that the air's temperature and water vapor content are the same in all locations.

Figure 17-11

ACTIVITY 17.3

THE EFFECTS OF AIR PRESSURE

Purpose To observe and describe the effects of air pressure on a beverage can.

Materials _____

empty aluminum	apron
beverage can	tongs
hot plate	shallow pan
safety goggles	water

Procedure

1. Read all the instructions for this activity before you begin your work.

2. Put on your safety goggles and apron.

3. Turn on the hot plate to the highest setting.

4. Pour water into the shallow pan to a depth of a few centimeters.

5. Add about 10 mL of water to the empty beverage can. Place the can on the hot plate.

6. Watch until you see condensation rising from the can. **CAUTION: Do not allow all of the water to boil away from the can.**

7. Turn off the hot plate. Quickly pick up the can and move it over the shallow pan. **CAUTION: Use tongs to handle the hot can.** Turn the can upside down and immediately set it down in the water.

8. Observe the can. What do you see and hear? Slowly lift up the can. Record all of your observations.

Collecting and Analyzing Data

1. What did you observe while the can was being heated?

2. What happened to the can after you placed it in the water?

Drawing Conclusions

3. Was the beverage can really empty before you put the water in? List the contents of the can after you put the water in.

4. How did the air pressure outside the can compare to the air pressure inside the can when you started the activity? What evidence do you have?

5. When you heated the can and its contents, what changes do you think took place inside the can? What evidence do you have of these changes?

6. When you cooled the can and its contents under water, what changes do you think took place inside the can? Answer in terms of air pressure and give evidence.

7. Compare and contrast the can and an aneroid barometer.

17.4 Winds

Lesson Objectives

▶ *Relate* winds to convection currents in the atmosphere.

▶ *Identify* instruments used to measure wind speed and direction.

▶ *Identify and describe* the major wind and air pressure belts in the Northern Hemisphere.

▶ *Explain* how the Coriolis effect influences world winds.

▶ *Activity* *Measure* the effect of latitude on the heating of a globe.

New Terms

wind	trade winds
local winds	prevailing
anemometer	westerlies
Coriolis effect	polar easterlies
doldrums	polar front
horse latitudes	jet stream

Even on a hot summer day, you can often find a refreshing cool breeze near an ocean or lake. What causes the breeze and what happens to it at night? In this lesson, you will learn what causes many types of winds.

Convection Currents

Have you ever observed bubbles of gas in a soft drink? Because the gas bubbles are less dense than the liquid around them, they rise in the liquid. A similar thing happens to bubbles of air in the atmosphere. Air in contact with the warm ground is heated. Cool air surrounds the warm parcel. Because the gas molecules in the warm air are more spread out, the warm air is less dense than the cool air. You have already learned that warm air exerts less pressure than cool air. The warm air parcel will begin to rise through the cool air, like a bubble in the drink. As the warm air rises, cooler and denser air moves in from the side to replace the warm air. Eventually the cool air is heated and also rises. The cycle starts again as shown in Figure 17-12.

Air in motion because of density and pressure differences forms a convection current. You learned in Chapter 10 that slow convection currents in semimolten rock are thought to move continents. Convection currents in the atmosphere cause air to move. Air in motion is called **wind.**

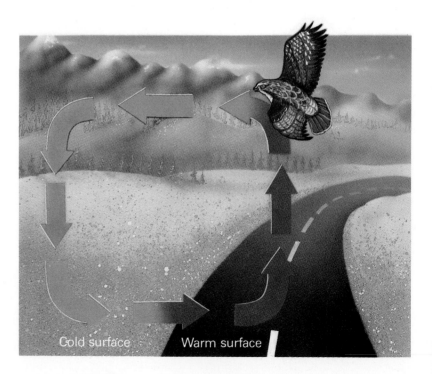

Cold surface   Warm surface

Figure 17-12 Many birds ride bubbles of rising hot air, called thermals, in convection currents.

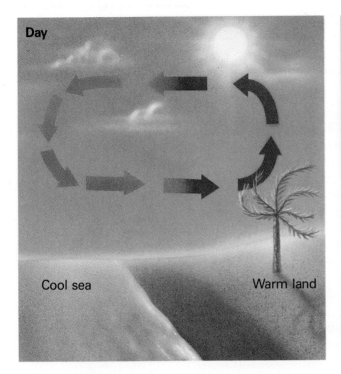

Day

Cool sea

Warm land

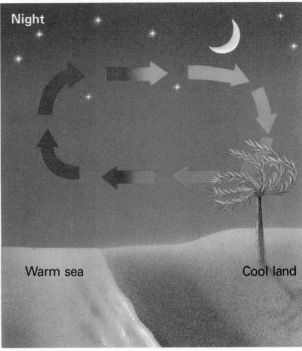

Night

Warm sea

Cool land

Local Winds

All winds, whether dust devils in a parking lot or world-scale winds, result from air pressure differences. Air pressure differences are caused by uneven heating of Earth's surfaces. Soil heats faster than water. Dark-colored land heats up faster than light-colored land. These heating differences set up **local winds,** which affect small areas. Steadier winds occur where expanses of water and land meet.

A sea breeze, illustrated in Figure 17-13, is an important example of a local wind. A sea breeze results from a temperature difference between land and water. During the daytime, the land is warmer than the water. High-pressure air falls over the water and low-pressure air rises over the land. At night, the land cools off faster than the water. Now the high-pressure and low-pressure areas switch places. The wind, called a land breeze, blows from land to sea. Local winds are important to airline pilots, sailors, fishers, and many other people.

Perhaps you have noticed that winds always move from high-pressure areas toward low-pressure areas. Have you ever blown up a balloon and then let the air out? The air in the balloon was at a higher pressure than the normal air outside it. When you let the balloon go, the high-pressure air inside the balloon moved toward the lower-pressure air outside. All winds, whether from balloons or on a world scale, blow from high pressure toward low pressure.

Figure 17-13 *Left:* A sea breeze blows during the daytime. *Right:* A land breeze blows at night.

Two properties of wind are of interest to meteorologists: wind direction and wind speed. Winds are named for the directions from which they blow. For example, a southwest wind comes from the southwest. A wind vane turns in the wind and points in the direction from which the wind is coming. An **anemometer** catches the wind in cups that are attached to a rotating axle. The faster the axle rotates, the higher the wind speed. Examples of a wind vane and an anemometer are shown in Figure 17-14. You can also estimate wind speed by observing everyday objects moving in the wind. Even the smallest wind makes smoke plumes curve, while whole trees bend in very strong winds. Use the Beaufort Scale in Table 17-2 to find the wind speed outside your room today.

Figure 17-14 Which instrument is the wind vane? Which is the anemometer?

Table 17-2 Beaufort Scale for Estimating Wind Speed		
Description of wind speed in forecast	Wind speed in km/h	Effects of wind
Calm	less than 1	Smoke rises straight up
Light	1–5	Smoke drifts
	6–11	Leaves rustle, wind felt on face
	12–19	Leaves and small twigs in constant motion
Moderate	20–28	Raises dust, dry leaves; moves small branches
Fresh	29–38	Small trees in leaf start to sway; whitecaps on inland waters
Strong	39–49	Large branches in motion; umbrellas hard to hold
	50–61	Whole trees in motion; walking against wind difficult
Gale	62–74	Twigs break off
	75–88	Slight damage to buildings
Strong gale	89–117	Trees uprooted; much damage
Hurricane	over 117	Extreme damage

A C T I V I T Y   **17.4**   *General Supplies*

TEMPERATURES AROUND THE GLOBE

Purpose To measure the effect of latitude on the heating of a globe.

Materials _____

scissors · black paper
globe or basketball · lamp with
3 thermometers · 250-W bulb
tape

Procedure

1. Read all of the instructions for this activity before you begin your work.

2. Copy the data table onto your paper.

3. Read your approximate latitude and longitude from the globe. Record it in the data section.

4. ☠ Set the globe in the center of a table. Cut out three small pieces of black paper. Tape one piece loosely across the bulb of each thermometer. **CAUTION: If a thermometer breaks, do not touch it. Notify your teacher.**

5. Attach a thermometer in each of the following locations along your line of longitude: equator, your latitude, North Pole. Be sure that the thermometers will not shade each other when the light is on.

6. Place a lamp about 30 cm from the globe's equator as shown in the figure. The light bulb should be at the same height as the equator. The North Pole of the globe should tilt away from the lamp.

7. Check to make sure that the initial readings of the three thermometers are the same.

8. Turn on the lamp. At the end of 3 min, record the temperature at the equator, your location, and the North Pole.

Collecting and Analyzing Data

Data Table		
Location	**Latitude (° N)**	**Temperature (°C)**
equator		
your school		
North Pole		
Your longitude:		

1. At which latitude was the temperature reading highest? Lowest?

2. What is the connection between latitude and temperature?

Drawing Conclusions

3. How does the angle of the sun's rays at the pole compare with the angle at the equator? How does the angle of the sun's rays affect the temperature?

4. On the same day, there may be a large temperature difference along the same line of longitude. Give the most important reason for this difference.

5. Your latitude does not change, but the average temperature of the air outside your school varies from summer to winter. How can you account for this change of temperature?

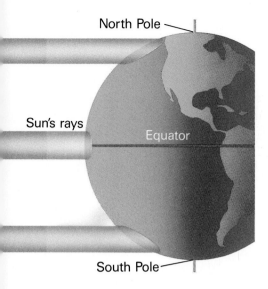

Figure 17-15 The sun's rays are spread out more at higher latitudes and heat the earth less there.

Coriolis Effect

Have you watched a TV commercial showing people playing in the warm Caribbean Sea while you shivered in a blizzard? Uneven heating of the earth is more than just the local heating differences between beach and water. The whole planet is heated unevenly by the sun. Recall from Chapter 3 that the sun appears to be lower in the sky in the winter than it is in the summer because of the tilt of the earth's axis. Figure 17-15 shows that solar radiation falls more directly on the equator than it does on the poles.

Earth's rotation affects all objects moving over it. Suppose you try to throw a baseball directly south to a friend in Quito, Ecuador, which is near the equator. Assume for the moment that you throw a super-human fastball. An astronaut would see the ball travel in a straight line. While the ball is in the air, Quito moves east because of the earth's rotation. The ball misses Quito and splashes into the Pacific Ocean. You would say that the ball curved off course to the right. A curve seen by earthbound observers in the path of an airborne object is called the **Coriolis effect.** The Coriolis effect is a result of Earth's rotation.

The Coriolis effect influences moving air. Like the baseball, when polar air travels south, the earth moves to the east as the air is moving over it. Winds in the Northern Hemisphere curve to the right, while winds in the Southern Hemisphere curve to the left.

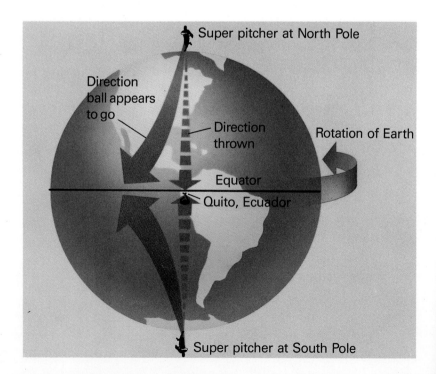

Figure 17-16 The super pitcher's fastball curves off course due to the Coriolis effect.

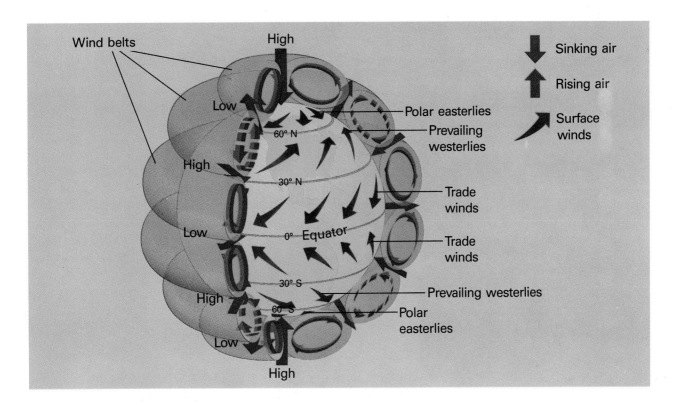

Wind belts

High

Low

60° N

High

30° N

Low

0° Equator

High

30° S

60° S

Low

High

Polar easterlies

Prevailing westerlies

Trade winds

Trade winds

Prevailing westerlies

Polar easterlies

Sinking air

Rising air

Surface winds

World Wind Belts

The pattern of the world wind belts was discovered by recording the average wind direction near the earth's surface over a period of years. Figure 17-17 shows the belts. Belts of winds blowing from the same direction most of the time occur within certain latitude regions on the globe.

Find the equator in Figure 17-17. Warm air rises near the equator, forming a band of low pressure. Air moving straight up would not do much to move the tall ship in full sail in Figure 17-18. To sailors of earlier times, the area of rising air at the equator was known as the **doldrums,** perhaps from the word *dull.*

Trade Winds Figure 17-17 shows that rising air over the equator spreads north and south. The rising air also cools as it moves away from the warm surface. At about 30° N latitude, the air moving north has cooled. Some air sinks back toward Earth's surface and piles up. This sinking air forms a band of high pressure at 30° N called the **horse latitudes.** At the surface, some of the sinking air moves from the horse latitudes back toward the equator, forming a large convection current. To a person on Earth, the wind comes from the northeast due to the Coriolis effect. These steady northeast winds, now called the **trade winds,** carried Columbus and other adventurers to the New World.

Figure 17-17 The pattern of global winds.

Figure 17-18 The captain of this tall ship needs to know about world wind patterns.

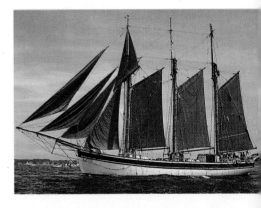

Earth's Atmosphere and Wind 463

Prevailing Westerlies Some of the sinking air at 30° N moves south to the equator, but some also moves northward. Winds between about 40° N and 60° N curve to the northeast. These winds are called the **prevailing westerlies.** Most of the weather patterns that travel across the United States move from west to east on the prevailing westerlies.

Polar Easterlies At the North Pole, very cold, dense air sinks, causing a high-pressure area. The sinking air spreads out and moves south. The winds in this region come from the northeast and are called **polar easterlies.** Cool air moving south from the pole in the region of polar easterlies meets warm air moving north from 30° N latitude. The two masses of moving air collide along a boundary called the **polar front.** There is nowhere else for the air to go but up. The air rises at approximately 60° N latitude, forming a band of low pressure. Rising air at the polar front eventually cools and moves north to the pole to be recycled.

Jet Streams

In the 1940's, pilots flying near the top of the troposphere reported winds with speeds up to 135 meters per second (300 miles per hour). These fierce winds, called **jet streams,** seemed to blow in narrow riverlike bands from west to east. Today you may fly from New York to San Francisco in six hours, but the return trip may take only five hours, thanks to a boost from the eastward-flowing jet stream.

Jet streams are found between neighboring air masses with strong temperature differences. In the Northern Hemisphere, the polar front jet stream forms where cold polar air meets warmer air from the south. Clouds along a subtropical jet stream are shown in Figure 17-19 *(right).*

Figure 17-19 *Left:* The polar-front jet stream. *Right:* Clouds stretch along a subtropical jet stream over Egypt.

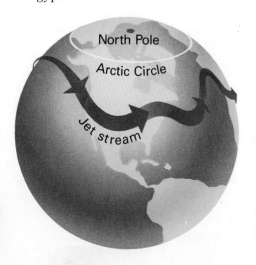

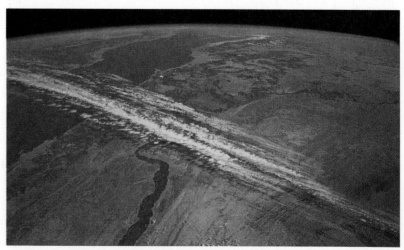

Lesson Review 17.4

17. Describe the motion of air in a convection current.

18. What are two instruments for measuring wind?

19. How does the heating of Earth depend upon latitude?

20. How does the Coriolis effect change the path followed by a baseball thrown from the North Pole?

21. Describe the three major wind belts of the Northern Hemisphere. How are Southern Hemisphere winds different?

Interpret and Apply

22. Mountaintops heat more quickly than valleys on a sunny day, and cool more quickly than valleys at night. Predict wind patterns at a mountainside cabin over 24 hours.

23. In what season would polar jet streams be strongest?

Chapter Summary

Read this summary. If any ideas are not clear, review that lesson.

17.1 Earth's Atmosphere

■ Air layers are distinguished by changes in temperature. Temperature decreases with elevation in the troposphere and mesosphere, but increases in the stratosphere and thermosphere.

■ Air is a mixture of gases, including nitrogen, oxygen, carbon dioxide, water vapor, and ozone, plus solid particles.

17.2 The Sun and the Atmosphere

■ Most of the sun's energy is in the visible-light and short wave infrared region of the spectrum.

■ Clouds and air reflect and absorb about half of the sun's radiation before it reaches the earth's surface.

■ Most of Earth's infrared radiation is absorbed by carbon dioxide and water vapor.

17.3 Air Pressure

■ Air pressure is the weight of air on a given surface area.

■ Air pressure decreases as elevation, temperature, and the amount of water vapor in the air increase.

17.4 Winds

■ Convection currents form when low-density warm air rises and is replaced by higher-density cool air. Sea and land breezes result from local uneven heating.

■ Winds blow from high-pressure areas toward low-pressure areas. Winds are named for the direction from which they blow.

■ The Coriolis effect is the curving of winds caused by the rotation of the earth.

■ There are three major wind belts in each hemisphere.

■ Jet streams are narrow riverlike high-speed winds near the top of the troposphere.

Chapter Review

■ Vocabulary

air pressure
aner iometer
aneroid barometer
Coriolis effect
doldrums
energy balance
greenhouse effect
horse latitudes
jet streams
local wind
mercury barometer
mesosphere

millibar
parcel of air
polar easterlies
polar front
prevailing westerlies
stratosphere
temperature
thermosphere
trade winds
troposphere
wind

■ Concept Mapping

Using the method of concept mapping described on pages 3–5, complete a concept map for wind. Copy the incomplete concept map shown below. Then fill in the missing terms.

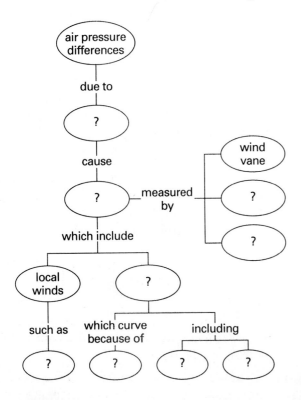

■ Review

On your paper, write the word or words that best complete each statement.

1. The protective ozone layer is found in the (stratosphere, troposphere, thermosphere).

2. Air is (a chemical compound, a mixture, the same throughout the atmosphere).

3. (Carbon dioxide and oxygen, carbon dioxide and water vapor, nitrogen and oxygen) absorb infrared radiation from Earth.

4. The most abundant gas in air is (oxygen, nitrogen, water vapor).

5. The weight of air on an area of one square centimeter is called air (pressure, temperature, weight).

6. As elevation increases, air pressure (increases, decreases, stays the same).

7. A(n) (thermometer, anemometer, barometer) is used for measuring air pressure.

8. Most solar energy is radiated in the (long wave infrared, short wave infrared and visible, ultraviolet) region of the spectrum.

9. (Ozone, Nitrogen, Hydrogen) prevents the most ultraviolet radiation from reaching Earth's surface.

10. The process by which air moves because of density differences is (convection, absorption, radiation).

11. In general, wind moves from (high to low pressure, high to low temperature, high to low latitude).

12. Wind is caused by the (uneven heating of Earth, motion of air in the thermosphere, motion of ocean waves).

13. Compared to water, land heats and cools (at the same rate, slower, faster).

14. Wind speed is measured by a(n) (wind vane, thermometer, anemometer).

15. Winds curve to the right or left because of (differences in temperature, rising air, the Coriolis effect).

16. Narrow bands of fast-moving winds high in the troposphere are called (polar easterlies, jet streams, trade winds).

17. Air over the equator is (low-pressure air, low-temperature air, high-density air).

■ *Interpret and Apply*

On your paper, answer each question.

18. Venus receives twice the radiation from the sun that Earth receives. The atmosphere of Venus is mostly carbon dioxide. Its rocky surface has no water. Venus rotates much more slowly than Earth, and in the opposite direction. Discuss possible wind patterns on Venus.

19. You have just taken a shower and the bathroom is full of hot, moist air. If you suddenly open the bathroom door, which way will the wind blow (a) at the floor level and (b) at the top of the door?

20. Earth reflects about 35 percent of incoming sunlight. Scientists have measured these percentages of light reflected from the moon and other planets: moon—7%, Venus—76%, Mars—16%, Jupiter—73%, Saturn—76%. Try to explain why these numbers vary so much. Think first of how Earth's portion of sunlight is reflected. Refer to Chapter 5 for information about other planets.

21. A white car with a black interior has been parked in the hot sun for several hours. Would the temperature inside the trunk of the car be the same as in the passenger area? Explain your answer.

22. In the late fall, ice forms first at the edge of a pond. In the spring, the first ice to melt is at the edge of the pond. Why?

■ *Writing in Science*

23. First drafts often need to be revised. Read the following first draft that a student wrote to explain how temperature affects pressure. Check to make sure that the explanation is accurate and complete. Then make any necessary corrections.

The higher the temperature of a parcel of air, the higher its air pressure will be. This relationship can be explained by the movement of the gas particles that make up air. These particles move faster at higher temperatures than at lower temperatures.

■ *Critical Thinking*

Gliders are motorless planes that depend entirely on air currents to keep them up. The glider pilot in the diagram is planning her flight on a sunny day. The pilot observes a lake, a plowed field with dark soil, and light-colored rocks in her flight area.

24. How is the temperature of the air in contact with the surface affected by each feature?

25. If the pilot flew directly across the landscape, what path would her plane take? Explain your answer.

26. Suppose the pilot wanted to try a moonlight flight. How would her flight be different? Explain your answer.

Water in the Atmosphere

Chapter Preview

Have You Ever WONDERED?

How heavy is a cloud?

Clouds floating in the sky look very light and fluffy. Have you ever walked outside while it was foggy? Fog is a cloud at ground level. Feeling fog on your face might leave you with the idea that a cloud is practically weightless. The weights of the tiny droplets that make up clouds add up, however. A small puff of a cloud in a summer sky can contain enough water to fill a bathtub—more water than you could lift. Clouds that produce thunderstorms can contain millions of tons of water, enough to cause serious flooding.

If clouds are so heavy, why don't they fall? Why don't all clouds produce rain? Why are fogs close to the ground but most clouds much higher? These and many other questions about water in the air will be answered in this chapter.

18.1 Evaporation, Condensation, and Humidity

Lesson Objectives

▶ **Contrast** the processes of evaporation and condensation.

▶ **Describe** the saturation of air with water vapor.

▶ **Relate** relative humidity and temperature.

▶ **Calculate** relative humidity.

▶ **Activity** **Measure** relative humidity of the air by using two thermometers.

New Terms

saturated
relative humidity

Water is easy to see in a pond with sparkling wavelets or in a snowfall that makes bushes glisten like white frosting. But not all water is visible. Have you ever observed someone washing a chalkboard with water? The water on the board is gone in a short time. Where does the water go?

Evaporation and Condensation

From Chapter 7, you recall that the process by which a substance changes from a liquid to a gas is called evaporation. What happens during the evaporation of water from a chalkboard? Liquid water molecules on the board are moving around. But they are still loosely linked to each other. Most of the water molecules are not moving fast enough to break free from other water molecules. A few of them, however, are traveling very fast and are close to the surface of the water. These faster molecules are able to break free of the liquid water to join other gas molecules in the air. When enough of the water molecules have evaporated, you begin to notice that the water on the board is disappearing.

The molecules of water vapor are moving fast in all directions. A few of them are even diving back into the liquid. Some molecules of water are leaving, and others are joining the liquid all the time. When more molecules join the liquid than leave, condensation is taking place, as shown in Figure 18-1 (left). Condensation also occurs when water vapor molecules collide and stick together to form droplets in the air. Figure 18-1 (middle) illustrates evaporation. It occurs if more

Figure 18-1 Condensation is occurring in the beaker on the left. Evaporation is occurring in the beaker in the middle. What is occurring in the beaker on the right?

Condensation

Evaporation

Saturation

molecules leave the water than join the water. If you compare the number of molecules leaving with the number joining, you can tell whether the water is evaporating or condensing.

What happens if you put a lid on a container full of water, like the aquarium in Figure 18-2? The number of water molecules returning to the water eventually becomes equal to the number leaving. The space above the water is said to be **saturated** with water vapor because condensation just balances evaporation. No more water can evaporate. The liquid level in the tank stays the same. Water droplets form a mist on the inner walls of the tank. If the lid is removed, some of the water vapor escapes and the space is no longer saturated. It is now possible for more water to evaporate. The level of liquid inside the aquarium goes down.

On certain days, water on a wet chalkboard evaporates more slowly than on other days. Why is this so? On some days, the air contains more water vapor than on other days. If the air contains a lot of water vapor, fewer water molecules enter the air. It is also more likely that the molecules of water vapor will collide with one another and stick to the chalkboard. When molecules join together on a surface like the chalkboard or in the air, they condense back into a liquid. The board dries more slowly.

Figure 18-2 How can you tell that the air inside the fish tank is saturated?

Temperature and Saturation

On a day when the air is nearly saturated with water vapor, the wet chalkboard dries very slowly. There is a way to make the water evaporate faster, however. Aim a hair dryer at the board or turn the heat up in the classroom. As you increase the temperature of the board, the average speed of the water molecules on the board increases. At higher speeds, two things happen. First, more water molecules have enough speed to escape from the liquid to become a gas. Evaporation occurs faster. Second, water vapor molecules are moving faster at the higher temperature. It is more difficult for them to stick together or to the board as they whiz by each other. Condensation slows down. If there is enough liquid water available, however, condensation will increase until it equals evaporation. The air will once again be saturated.

Temperature determines how much water vapor is possible in saturated air. The graph in Figure 18-3 shows how much water vapor is possible in a cubic meter of air at different temperatures. A cubic meter of air at 30°C can contain a maximum of about 30 grams of water vapor. A cubic meter of air at 10°C, however, can contain only about 9 grams of water vapor. The lower the temperature, the less water vapor is needed to saturate the air.

Figure 18-3 As the temperature increases, more water vapor is needed to saturate air.

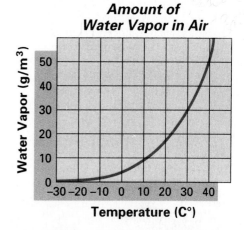

Figure 18-4 The juggler's balls represent water molecules. *Left:* lower temperature; *Middle:* higher temperature; *Right:* during a temperature reduction

To understand why the amount of water vapor in saturated air is related to temperature, imagine that you are watching a juggler like the one shown in Figure 18-4. The juggler catches as many balls as he tosses up. When the juggler tosses balls in the air slowly, only a few balls are in the air at any one time. In this comparison, the balls represent molecules of water. The small number of balls in the air is like the small number of water vapor molecules in low-temperature air at saturation. If the juggler speeds up and tosses the balls with more energy, he can keep more balls in the air. Saturated air at a higher temperature contains more molecules of water vapor. The juggler must collect some balls if he slows down. In a similar way, some of the water vapor condenses into a liquid if saturated air cools.

Relative Humidity

Have you ever felt uncomfortably hot on a summer day, like the athlete in Figure 18-5? Has your hair gotten curly or gone straight? Someone may have said to you, "It's not the heat, it's the humidity." Humidity is the amount of water vapor in the air. But water vapor makes your skin feel damp and sticky only when the air is close to being saturated. You would get a better idea of how uncomfortable the air is by measuring its relative humidity. The **relative humidity** compares the amount of water vapor actually in the air to the largest amount of water vapor possible in air at that temperature. The relative humidity is expressed as a percent.

How is relative humidity determined? Suppose that the temperature of the air in your room is 18°C. From Figure 18-3, you see that a cubic meter of air at 18°C would be saturated if it contained 15.0 grams of water vapor. The air in your room, however, actually contains only 7.5 grams of water vapor for every cubic meter. The relative humidity would be calculated as follows:

$$relative\ humidity = \frac{7.5}{15.0} = 0.50 \times 100 = 50\%$$

You could say that the air contained 50% of the water vapor possible at that temperature. The relative humidity shows how close the air is to being saturated. What is the relative humidity when the air is saturated with water vapor?

Evaporation is a cooling process. Have you ever wondered why damp washcloths always feel so cold or why you feel chilled when you step out of a shower? Recall that the faster molecules leave the surface of liquid water and become water vapor. When the faster molecules leave, the average speed of the remaining molecules decreases. When the average speed of molecules decreases, the temperature of the material becomes lower. The liquid water remaining on the washcloth has a lower temperature after evaporation begins. The water begins to remove thermal energy from the cloth, so that the temperature of the cloth decreases also. For evaporation to continue, thermal energy must be taken from both the liquid and its surroundings. Since evaporation is a cooling process, what do you think happens to the temperature of the water and its surroundings when water vapor condenses? Figure 18-6 illustrates the energy changes in both processes.

Figure 18-5 This athlete's body is overheated. Do you think that the relative humidity is high or low?

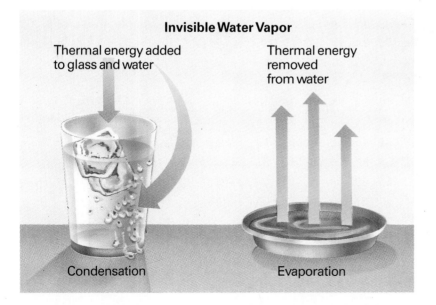

Invisible Water Vapor

Thermal energy added to glass and water

Thermal energy removed from water

Condensation

Evaporation

Figure 18-6 *Left:* When water vapor condenses, energy is added to the glass and the water inside it. *Right:* When water evaporates, thermal energy is removed from the water and its surroundings.

Lesson Review 18.1

1. Define *evaporation* and *condensation*.
2. Describe what happens at the surface of liquid water when the space above it is saturated with water vapor.
3. Define *relative humidity*.

Interpret and Apply

4. If the air temperature is 10°C and there are 6 grams of water vapor in 1 cubic meter of air, what is the relative humidity? Use Figure 18-3.
5. An old-fashioned way of finding wind direction is to wet a finger in your mouth and hold it up in the wind. The direction the wet side of your finger is facing when it feels coldest is the wind direction. Explain why this method works.

Table 18-1 Relative Humidity (%)

Dry-bulb temperature (°C)																				
	1	2	3	4	5	6	7	8	9	10	11	12	13	14	15	16	17	18	19	20
0	81	64	46	29	13															
2	84	68	52	37	22	7														
4	85	71	57	43	29	16														
6	86	73	60	48	35	24	11													
8	87	75	63	51	40	29	19	8												
10	88	77	66	55	44	34	24	15	6											
12	89	78	68	58	48	39	29	21	12											
14	90	79	70	60	51	42	34	26	18	10										
16	90	81	71	63	54	46	38	30	23	15	8									
18	91	82	73	65	57	49	41	34	27	20	14	7								
20	91	83	74	66	59	51	44	37	31	24	18	12	6							
22	92	83	76	68	61	54	47	40	34	28	22	17	11	6						
24	92	84	77	69	62	56	49	43	37	31	26	20	15	10	5					
26	92	85	78	71	64	58	51	46	40	34	29	24	19	14	10	5				
28	93	85	78	72	65	59	53	48	42	37	32	27	22	18	13	9	5			
30	93	86	79	73	67	61	55	50	44	39	35	30	25	21	17	13	9	5		
32	93	86	80	74	68	62	57	51	46	41	37	32	28	24	20	16	12	9	5	
34	93	87	81	75	69	63	58	53	48	43	39	35	30	28	23	19	15	12	8	5

The column header row spans: **Difference between dry-bulb and wet-bulb temperatures (°C)**

FINDING RELATIVE HUMIDITY

Purpose To measure the relative humidity of the air.

Materials

safety goggles	water
lab apron	cardboard
2 thermometers	book
2 15- to 20-cm	index card
pieces of string	tape
2 gauze pads	medicine dropper

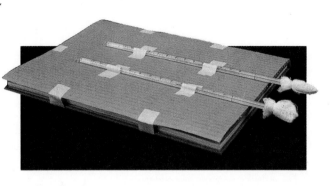

Procedure

1. Read all the instructions for this activity before you begin your work.

2. Put on your safety goggles and lab apron. Copy the data table onto your paper.

3. Tie a gauze pad around the bulb of each thermometer with the string.

4. Tape the thermometers to the cardboard and the cardboard to the book, as shown in the figure. Place the book in the middle of the table.

5. Thoroughly wet the gauze on *one* of the thermometers with the medicine dropper. This is the wet-bulb thermometer. The thermometer with the dry gauze is the dry-bulb thermometer. Immediately record both temperatures at 0 minutes in the data table.

6. Continuously fan both thermometer bulbs with the index card. After 1 minute, record the temperature for each thermometer. Continue fanning and taking readings each minute until there is no further change in temperature.

7. If your teacher permits, repeat the experiment in another location.

8. Before leaving the laboratory, clean up all materials and wash your hands.

Collecting and Analyzing Data

Data Table				
Location:				
Time (min)	**Temp. (°C) (dry)**	**(wet)**	**Dry – Wet (°C)**	**Rel. Hum. (%)**
0				
1				
2				

1. Subtract the lowest wet-bulb reading from the corresponding dry-bulb reading. Record this difference in the fourth column of your data table.

2. Look at Table 18-1. Find the dry-bulb reading on the left side of the table. Find the difference between your wet- and dry-bulb readings at the top of the table. Locate the place where the two columns meet. Read the relative humidity and record it in your data table.

Drawing Conclusions

3. Explain why the readings for the two thermometers differed the way they did.

4. If you did the experiment in a second location, compare the relative humidity values you obtained. What do they tell you about the air in the two locations?

18.2 *Types of Condensation*

Have you ever picked up a piece of warm toast from a plate and noticed droplets of water on the plate like those in Figure 18-7? Water in the hot bread evaporated and then changed back to a liquid on the cold plate. The water vapor condenses on your plate for the same reason that dew and clouds are formed.

Dew Point

Water droplets form on the outside of an icy glass of your favorite drink, especially in humid weather. In this case, the droplets on the glass came from water vapor that condensed as the air next to the glass cooled. Cooling the air slows down the water vapor molecules in it, making it easier for them to stick together and form a liquid on the glass. The **dew point** is the temperature at which the air becomes saturated with water vapor. As you learned in the last lesson, condensation and evaporation are balanced when the air is saturated. Condensation exceeds evaporation and forms visible droplets when the temperature falls slightly below the dew point.

The dew point is affected by how much water vapor is in the air. One sample of air with a relative humidity of 100% is at its dew point. A second sample of air at the same temperature but at a relative humidity of 50% contains half as much water vapor. For the sample with 50% relative humidity to become saturated, it must cool off. As the temperature of the second sample decreases, its relative humidity goes up. Eventually the relative humidity reaches 100%. The sample is saturated with water vapor. The sample's temperature at saturation is its dew point. Since the second sample had to cool in order to reach saturation, its dew point is lower than the dew point of the first sample.

You may have heard a meteorologist on a local TV newscast give the dew point after a hot summer day. The dew point tells you how humid that day was. If the dew point was close to the air temperature, there was a lot of water vapor in the air. The relative humidity was high. However, a dew point much lower than the air temperature means that the relative humidity was low.

Dew point is reported on official Weather Service maps rather than relative humidity. Why is this so? The temperature of air changes over 24 hours. But relative humidity varies with temperature. In air with a given amount of water vapor, the relative humidity changes with the time of day, but the dew point stays the same.

Lesson Objectives

▸ **Explain** how dew and frost form.

▸ **Describe** the role of condensation nuclei in cloud formation.

▸ **Contrast** the processes for forming fog and dew.

▸ **Activity** **Measure** the dew point.

New Terms

dew point	condensation
dew	nuclei
frost	fog

Figure 18-7 Water vapor from the hot toast condenses into water droplets on the cool plate.

A C T I V I T Y   1 8 . 2   *General Supplies*

FINDING THE DEW POINT

Purpose   To determine the dew point of air in different locations.

Materials

safety goggles	paper towels
lab apron	plastic cups
shiny can	room-temperature water
thermometer	ice chips
stirring rod	table salt

Procedure

1. Read all the directions for this activity before you begin your work.

2. Put on your safety goggles and lab apron.

3. Copy the data table onto a separate piece of paper.

4. Breathe on the shiny can to observe the tiny water droplets formed when water vapor from your breath condenses on the can. Draw a line in the droplets. Watch them evaporate.

5. ☠ Find the temperature of the air. Record the air temperature in the data table. **Caution: If a thermometer breaks, do not touch it. Notify your teacher.**

6. Fill the can halfway with the water.

7. Be sure that the outside of the can is dry. Place the thermometer in the water.

8. Add ice chips gradually. Stir with the stirring rod until a mist appears on the sides of the can. Quickly record the temperature, which is approximately the dew point.

9. If no mist appears on the can by the time the temperature is 0°C, add a small amount of salt to the mixture and continue to stir. Observe the can for signs of moisture.

10. Repeat steps 6–8 to verify your measurement in the classroom. Record your second value in the data table.

11. If you have time and your teacher approves, find the dew point outside.

Collecting and Analyzing Data

Data Table		
Location:		
Trial	**Air Temperature (°C)**	**Dew Point (°C)**
1		
2		
Average		

1. Did you get the same results for each trial when you found the dew point for classroom air? Why or why not?

2. Calculate the average dew point reading for each location.

Drawing Conclusions

3. Why was it easier to get condensation on the can from your breath than from the air in the room?

4. Explain any differences between the dew points of inside and outside air.

Figure 18-8 *Top:* The droplets of dew on this butterfly are evaporating in the morning sun. *Bottom:* Why does frost sometimes form instead of dew?

Dew and Frost

Have you ever gotten your feet soaked on a clear morning as you played sports on a grassy field? During the day, the field is heated by the sun's radiation. If the night is clear, the warm land continues to give off infrared radiation after the sun sets. After a while, the ground surface cools. The thin film of air next to the ground may eventually cool slightly below the dew point. Water condenses on the coldest part of the ground, which is often grass. Condensation on the earth's surface is called **dew.** Sometimes the dew point reached by the air above the grass is below freezing. In this case, water vapor in the air changes directly to ice crystals, called **frost.** This beautiful crystal form of water is shown in Figure 18-8 *(bottom).* Perhaps you have seen frost forming on the walls of your freezer at home.

Fog

Suppose you have a cold bottle of soft drink. As you twist off the lid, you may notice a fog forming in the neck of the bottle. You have just made a cloud. A cloud is a collection of tiny liquid droplets formed when a parcel of air has cooled slightly below its dew point. For water vapor to condense into liquid droplets, two conditions are needed. The air temperature must be just below its dew point, and there must be a surface on which vapor can condense. These conditions are needed whether the droplets condense on your glass, inside the bottle, or on the grass.

Particles that serve as condensation surfaces for cloud droplets are called **condensation nuclei.** Condensation nuclei are so small that the largest of them is only one-tenth the diameter of a human hair. In 1 cubic centimeter of air, there may be as many as 10,000 such particles. Water molecules stick to a condensation nucleus until they blend to form a droplet.

What produces these particles? One clue comes from a salt shaker. On humid days, salt is hard to shake. Water vapor condenses easily on salt particles and makes them stick to each other. Droplets of salty water from the ocean evaporate, leaving tiny salt particles in the air. Other tiny surfaces that take up water include sulfate or nitrate particles formed by the burning of fossil fuels and from volcanoes. Such particles can dissolve in cloud droplets and eventually produce acid rain. You will learn more about acid rain in Lesson 18.4. Water vapor can also condense on particles that do not dissolve, such as meteor dust and soil. Winds distribute many types of small particles.

Figure 18-9 How did this fog in San Francisco form?

Dew forms when cooling affects only a thin film of air in contact with the ground. Water droplets condense on grass and other cold objects on the ground. If there is a slight breeze, however, the cooling effect spreads upward. Water droplets condense on condensation nuclei and form a layer many meters high, called a **fog.** Fog can appear at night when warm air from an ocean or lake moves over cooler land, like the San Francisco fog in Figure 18-9. The droplets are large enough and close enough together to form a cloud at ground level. Cooling of the land on a clear night can also result in fog. When the water droplets are heated by the sun in the morning, they evaporate, and the fog is said to "burn off."

Lesson Review 18.2

6. How are dew and frost formed? Use the term *dew point* in your answer.

7. What is a condensation nucleus? How do condensation nuclei help to form water droplets?

8. State the two conditions for the formation of cloud droplets.

Interpret and Apply

9. You may have heard someone say that car windows "fog up" on a cold day when several people are in a car. Is "fog up" the correct term? Explain.

10. One kind of smog is a combination of smoke and fog. Smogs in London, England, became less dense when the burning of high-sulfur coal was outlawed in 1950. Why was there less smog after 1950?

18.3 *Clouds*

Lesson Objectives

‣ *List* and *describe* three ways for clouds to form.

‣ *Identify* clouds by observing their shape and altitude.

‣ *Describe* how different types of clouds form.

‣ **Activity** *Observe* and *describe* the formation of clouds.

New Terms

cumulus	cirrus
nimbus	alto-
stratus	

All clouds, from the miniature fog that comes from your mouth on a cold day to a towering thundercloud, result from the cooling of water vapor. In the last lesson, you learned one way for air to form a cloud. Fog forms when circulating air cools rapidly at the ground level. Air containing water vapor can also cool enough to produce clouds in two additional ways. First, air containing water vapor forms a cloud as it is forced up over a mountain. As the air moves up the face of the mountain, its temperature decreases slightly below the dew point. The second and most common condensation process, however, does not need mountains. Convection and expansion within the atmosphere often cool air below its dew point.

Cooling Due to Expansion

Recall from Chapter 17 that a parcel of air is a small volume of air with similar temperature and humidity throughout. Suppose a parcel of warm, moist air rises or is lifted from ground level into the atmosphere. The atmospheric pressure on the parcel becomes less as the air rises. The decreasing pressure allows the particles of air to spread apart. Because of this expansion, air particles slow down. Slower speeds mean a lower temperature, so the temperature of the parcel decreases. As long as no condensation occurs in the rising parcel, its temperature decreases by about 1°C for each 100-meter increase in altitude.

The diagram in Figure 18-10 shows what happens to a parcel of air as it rises and cools. Eventually its temperature decreases slightly below the dew point. Water vapor from the parcel condenses into a visible cloud of droplets. Cloud formation begins at the same level in the atmosphere for all rising parcels that have the same dew point. The height of the flat bottom of a cloud is close to the level at which the rising parcel reaches its dew point.

If evaporation is a cooling process, what happens as a result of condensation? When water vapor is changed to a liquid, thermal energy is released. The process of condensation heats up the space around the water vapor. The same amount of thermal energy that was absorbed during evaporation is released when condensation takes place. Huge amounts of energy are transferred in the atmosphere this way. The air where the cloud is forming is heated by the process of condensation. The parcel of air continues to rise and more water vapor condenses as it cools again. The cloud begins to take on a tall, puffy shape.

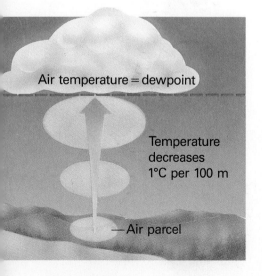

Figure 18-10 As an air parcel rises, it expands and cools. When it cools to just below the dew point, water vapor condenses and forms a flat-bottomed cloud.

Air temperature = dewpoint

Temperature decreases 1°C per 100 m

—Air parcel

Cloud Types

The shape, size, height, and motion of clouds give clues to what the invisible air is doing. The ancient Greeks thought clouds looked like the "sheep of the gods." Modern observers have divided clouds by their shape into three basic groups: cumulus, stratus, and cirrus.

Cumulus clouds are the white puffy clouds that look like cauliflower. The word *cumulus* means "heap." Cumulus clouds generally form from rising parcels of warm, moist air. Sun shining on a patch of dark volcanic rock or even a large parking lot can set up such rising parcels. In fair weather, you may see small cumulus clouds that appear in late morning grow larger by afternoon. Each bump on the "cauliflower" is formed by a new parcel of air. Some clouds only last 15 minutes before they evaporate. Water vapor in other rising air parcels continues to condense and new clouds form. On a hot day when plenty of water vapor is available, a cumulus cloud can grow large enough to produce rain. Huge cumulonimbus clouds often become thunderstorms. The word **nimbus** attached to a cloud name indicates that the cloud is producing rain or snow.

Air rising vertically from the ground results in the formation of puffy cumulus clouds. But warm, moist air can also slide slowly up over cool air or sloping ground as if on a slanted roof. The moist air can also cool due to radiation or through contact with a cool surface. If any of these things happen, the clouds form gray layers called **stratus** clouds. Stratus clouds can spread out in a large enough sheet to cover the whole sky. They often bring rain or drizzle and are usually found at altitudes below 2 kilometers.

Figure 18-11 This cumulonimbus cloud developed rapidly over a period of only 20 minutes.

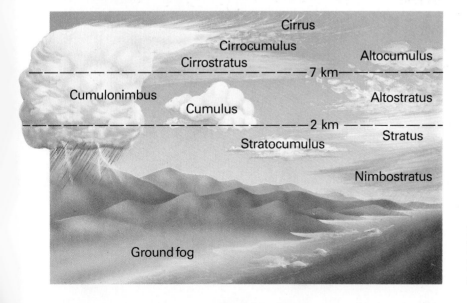

Figure 18-12 Clouds are grouped by shape and altitude. Usually, you would not see all types of clouds in the sky at once.

Cirrus clouds are thin, wispy clouds with an altitude over 7 kilometers. Since air at that altitude is well below the freezing point of water, cirrus clouds are made entirely from ice crystals.

Some cloud names are combinations of names for the basic shapes. For example, *stratocumulus* is the name for cumulus clouds that spread out in a layer. *Cirrocumulus* is the name given to high clouds that look like many tiny puffs of cotton. Other cloud names indicate height. **Alto-** in front of a cloud name indicates that the cloud is at a middle height of 2 to 7 kilometers. Altocumulus clouds look somewhat like cirrocumulus, but are nearer the ground.

Figure 18-13 Cloud Types. The weather predictions given are general. Wind directions refer to a range rather than to the exact direction stated. For example, *east* means "any direction from northeast to southeast."

HIGH CLOUDS (above 7 km)

Cirrus: wispy white streaks made of ice crystals
Weather Prediction: precipitation in a day or two if becoming thicker with east winds

Cirrocumulus: thin white puffs that can look like ripples or fish scales
Weather Prediction: precipitation within a day if becoming thicker with east winds

Cirrostratus: translucent white veil across much of sky, creating halo around sun or moon
Weather Prediction: precipitation within a day if lowering to altostratus with east winds

MIDDLE CLOUDS (2 to 7 km)

Altocumulus: white or gray patches with shadows, like a sheep's back
Weather Prediction: steady precipitation within a day if becoming thicker with east winds

Altostratus: gray or bluish sheet covering sky, through which sun can shine as bright patch
Weather Prediction: precipitation within half a day with east wind, then warmer and more humid followed by clearing

Lesson Review 18.3

11. Describe three ways for air containing water vapor to cool enough to produce clouds.

12. Name and describe the three basic cloud shapes.

13. Compare stratocumulus and cirrocumulus clouds.

Interpret and Apply

14. Why do cumulus clouds often disappear at night?

LOW CLOUDS (below 2 km)

Stratocumulus: gray rolls or rounded masses
Weather Prediction: precipitation if becoming thicker

Stratus: dull gray sheet, can cover entire sky
Weather Prediction: east winds bring heavy precipitation, west winds bring drizzle

Nimbostratus: low, dark, thick layer that blots out sun
Weather Prediction: steady precipitation for a day with east wind, for a few hours with west wind

VERTICALLY FORMED CLOUDS

Cumulus: separated fluffy clumps with flat gray bottoms
Weather Prediction: fair sunny weather unless thickening

Cumulonimbus: towering thunderheads that can reach into the stratosphere and darken the sky
Weather Prediction: heavy rain, lightning, thunder, strong winds, and possibly hail and tornadoes

CLOUD IN A BOTTLE

Purpose To observe and describe the formation of a cloud.

Materials

3 2-L plastic beverage bottles	graduated cylinder
flashlight or projector	matches
	lab apron
safety goggles	ice water
	warm water

Procedure

1. Read all of the directions for this activity before you begin your work.

2. Put on your safety goggles and lab apron.

3. Darken the room so that you can just see your equipment.

4. Leave one bottle empty. Add 50 mL of ice water to one bottle and 50 mL of warm water to the other. Tighten the cap on each bottle. Shake each bottle a few times. Shine a light in each bottle. Look for tiny cloud droplets in the air inside the bottle. Record your observations.

5. Squeeze each bottle hard, then release it. Shine the light into each bottle and look for droplets once again. Record your observations.

6. ■ Light a match and blow it out. **CAUTION: Keep hair and clothing away from an open flame.** Remove the caps from the bottles. Allow some smoke from the match to enter each bottle. Cap the bottles tightly. Repeat step 5 and record your results.

7. After 15 minutes, try making clouds again without opening the bottles or adding smoke. Record your results.

8. Before leaving the laboratory, clean up.

Collecting and Analyzing Data

1. What is the effect of the following on the formation of clouds in a bottle?
   a. squeezing, then releasing the bottle
   b. presence of water
   c. temperature of water
   d. presence of smoke

2. Describe what happened when you repeated the experiment after 15 minutes.

Drawing Conclusions

3. Explain what happened to the water vapor and other air gases when you squeezed and released the bottle.

4. Explain why the temperature of the water affects the formation of clouds.

5. Why does smoke in the bottle affect the formation of a cloud? How might different particles, such as chalk dust or ground-up table salt, affect cloud formation? If your teacher approves, you may test your predictions.

6. Why were your results different after 15 minutes?

7. From your answers to questions 1–4, where would you expect to find the most clouds in Earth's atmosphere?

18.4 *Precipitation*

Most clouds that pass over you do not produce rain. Why doesn't rain fall out of all clouds? What conditions are necessary in order for rain, snow, and other types of precipitation to form? **Precipitation** is the name for any liquid or solid form of water that falls from the atmosphere to the earth. Dew and frost are not considered precipitation because they do not fall. The type of cloud and the air temperature below the cloud help to determine what type of precipitation reaches the ground.

Forming Precipitation

Once water vapor in a rising parcel of air cools and condenses, a cloud of water droplets forms. The cloud droplets are only a small fraction of a millimeter in diameter. Since cloud droplets are tiny enough to be held up by small air currents, clouds are not considered precipitation either. The only difference between a cloud droplet that doesn't fall and a raindrop that does fall is size. The larger the drop, the faster it falls. In order for a cloud droplet to become heavy enough to fall, it must become larger. This is not as easy as it sounds. Condensation on cloud droplets slows down as the droplets grow to be 0.02 millimeters across. An average raindrop is 2 millimeters across, one hundred times larger than a cloud droplet. Figure 18-14 compares the sizes of several different types of droplets. How does a cloud droplet gain enough weight to fall?

Lesson Objectives

▶ **Describe** two ways for cloud droplets to become raindrops.

▶ **Name** and **describe** five forms of precipitation.

▶ **Describe** the process by which acid rain forms.

▶ **Summarize** the three stages in the development of a thunderstorm.

▶ **Activity** **Identify** the factors that control the speed of raindrops.

New Terms

precipitation	hail
drizzle	updrafts
rain	downdrafts
snow	lightning
sleet	thunder
acid precipitation	rain gauges

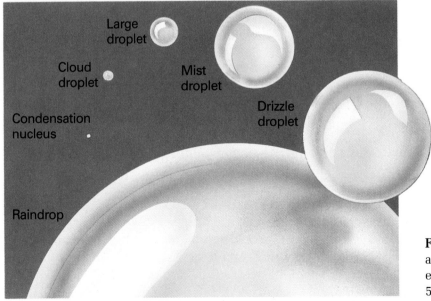

Figure 18-14 The relative sizes of a condensation nucleus and different sizes of droplets, all magnified 500 times.

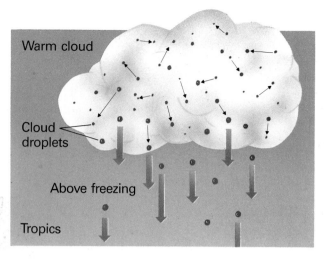
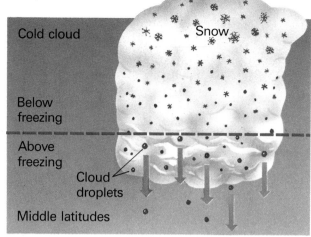

Figure 18-15 *Left:* In a warm cloud, cloud droplets collide and merge to form raindrops. *Right:* Subfreezing temperatures in a cold cloud cause snow to form. The snowflakes melt into raindrops as they fall through a warmer air layer near the ground.

Figure 18-16 In this standard rain gauge, rain enters a measuring tube.

In some clouds formed near the tropics, the temperature of cloud droplets is above the freezing point of water. Such a "warm" cloud is shown in Figure 18-15 *(left).* Air currents bounce cloud droplets of many sizes around within the cloud. Some droplets catch up with others and blend with them. When a droplet becomes large enough, it begins to fall. Small, slowly falling droplets are called **drizzle.** If more droplets combine, the droplets become larger and fall faster. These larger droplets are **rain.** One raindrop may contain as many as a million cloud droplets. The falling raindrops grow larger as they collide with more cloud droplets.

Most rain clouds in the middle latitudes north of 30°N are at least partly below freezing, however. These cold clouds, shown in Figure 18-15 *(right),* contain tiny ice crystals as well as liquid water cloud droplets. Ice crystals attract water vapor from evaporating cloud droplets, adding to the size of the crystal. When crystals in the cloud become large enough, they fall and are called **snow.**

Snow forms in most middle-latitude clouds even in the summer. Why are reports of snow falling in the summer rare? If the air through which a snowflake falls is above the freezing point of water, the snowflake melts. The precipitation reaching the ground is rain. If the air between the cloud and the ground is below freezing, snowflakes reach the earth without melting. The opposite process occurs when rain falls through air that is colder than the freezing point of water. The raindrops freeze into solid grains of ice called **sleet** before hitting the ground.

Precipitation is measured with a **rain gauge.** In the case of snow, depths are measured directly, then averaged. Fallen snow is mostly air. When melted, as much as 30 centimeters of powdery snow may result in only 1 centimeter of water. Ten centimeters of wet snow, the kind that makes good snowballs, may produce 1.5 centimeters of water.

Acid Precipitation

Soft drinks contain a weak acid called carbonic acid. It forms when carbon dioxide gas is dissolved in the water of the drink. Pure rainwater is also a weak acid. Natural substances in the air react with cloud droplets and precipitation. For example, you know that air contains small amounts of carbon dioxide. As in a soft drink, this carbon dioxide dissolves in pure rainwater and makes it slightly acidic. But recently, rain in Northeastern states has been ten times more acidic than pure rainwater.

Rain, snow, or sleet that is more acidic than pure rainwater is called **acid precipitation.** Acid rain is the best-known type of acid precipitation. The burning of coal, oil, and gasoline produces large quantities of sulfur and nitrogen oxides. These gases react with water vapor and other chemicals in the air to form acids. Scientists agree that most acid rain forms in this way. Some acid rain forms when water vapor condenses around sulfate or nitrate particles, which are also given off by burning coal and oil. The particles dissolve in the cloud droplet, forming acids. A cloud droplet or raindrop can collect more gas and particles after it forms. Once on the ground, the water from acid precipitation causes much damage to animals, plants, and buildings. You will learn more about the effects of acid rain in Chapter 21.

Figure 18-17 One source of sulfur and nitrogen compounds

ENVIRONMENTAL AWARENESS

Testing Rainwater Acidity

When rain falls in Poughkeepsie, New York, dozens of amateur scientists rush out of school. Students at Poughkeepsie Day School test the acidity of the rainwater with acid-indicator paper. After the students record the test results, their findings are telephoned into a national organization. In 1988, some of the rain in Poughkeepsie was as acid as a cola drink.

Volunteers in over 300 other locations also measure how acid the rainwater is. The organization that collects their test results is the National Audubon Society's Citizen's Acid Rain Monitoring Network. A monthly map shows data from all the locations in the network. The map helps participants keep track of changes in acid rain across the United States. The tests are not as reliable as those done in laboratories. However, the tests do provide data for the citizens' hometowns. Local newspapers and television stations often ask citizen rainwater testers to report their results. Rainwater testers keep people informed about rainwater acidity in their communities, which prompts them to take action. ■

Figure 18-18 Notice the layers that make up this hailstone.

Thunderstorms

Right now about 1800 thunderstorms are taking place all over the world. A thunderstorm is a small-scale storm in which there is always lightning, often heavy rain and high winds, and sometimes hail and tornadoes. The massive cloud of a thunderstorm, called a thunderhead, is a cumulonimbus cloud.

In a thunderhead, frozen raindrops or ice crystals can grow into hailstones like the one shown in Figure 18-18. Frozen raindrops become **hail** by picking up onionlike layers of ice. These layers form as air currents bounce the hail around inside a thunderhead for a relatively long time.

The life of a thunderstorm can be divided into three stages, as shown in Figure 18-19. In the first stage, hot land surfaces cause large numbers of warm, moist air parcels to rise rapidly. These upward-moving air currents are called **updrafts.** Huge quantities of water vapor quickly condense to form large cumulus clouds up to 10 kilometers in height. The condensing water vapor gives off a lot of thermal energy. This thermal energy heats up the cloud and causes even more convection. The higher the air rises, the colder it gets. When the top part of the cloud is above the freezing level, ice particles form in its top section.

The second stage in the life of a thunderstorm begins when drops and ice crystals become so large that the strong updrafts in the cloud cannot support them. The drops fall to the bottom of the cloud. The great height of these clouds gives drops and crystals more chances to collide and grow

Figure 18-19 The three stages in the development of a thunderstorm

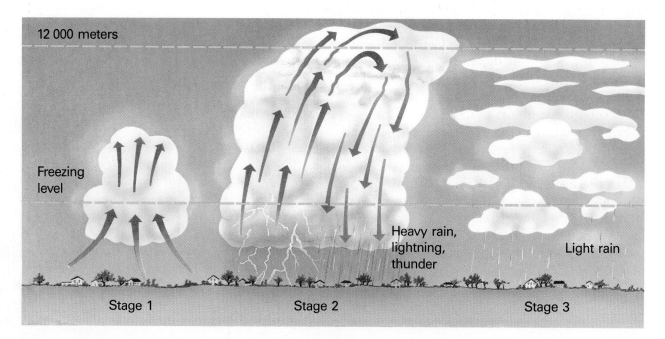

12 000 meters

Freezing level

Heavy rain, lightning, thunder

Light rain

Stage 1

Stage 2

Stage 3

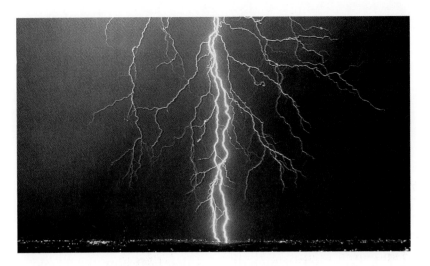

larger. Rain and hail begin to pour from the cloud as if it has burst. As the enormous numbers of raindrops fall, they create a **downdraft** of air. When the air reaches the ground, it divides and blows sideways like a stream of water hitting the bottom of a tub. Powerful winds bend trees toward the earth. As raindrops fall, some evaporate, and the air cools. This is the most violent stage of the storm. Lightning flashes, like those in Figure 18-20 *(left)*, split the air. Crashes of thunder follow the lightning. In the third stage, the downdrafts finally cut off the upward motion of air from the ground that feeds moisture to the cloud. Precipitation stops. The cumulonimbus cloud breaks apart. Finally, the cloud evaporates.

Have you ever felt a spark when you touched a doorknob after walking across a wool rug? These sparks are like lightning on a small scale. Ice crystals and water drops inside the cloud pick up opposite electric charges. Air currents separate the ice from the water. Because of the separation, the top and bottom of the thunderhead become oppositely charged. The ground under the cloud also becomes charged. When the charge becomes large enough, a giant spark called **lightning** passes through the air. Air in the path of the spark may become several times hotter than the surface of the sun. The flash you see is the glowing air.

The intense heating of air during a lightning stroke causes the air to expand explosively. This loud sound is called **thunder.** Since sound travels much more slowly than light, there is a delay between the time you see lightning and the moment you hear the thunder. You see lightning almost the instant it happens. But sound takes about 3 seconds to travel 1 kilometer. If you want to know the distance to a lightning flash in kilometers, count the seconds between flash and thunder and divide by three.

Fact or Fiction?

Perhaps you have heard the old expression, "Lightning never strikes the same place twice!" Unfortunately, this is not true. Since lightning always chooses the path of least resistance, it may strike the same place several times. If you do a little research, you may find that certain tall buildings in your area have been struck on more than one occasion. Scientists estimate that lightning strikes the earth millions of times each day. The odds are high that it will strike the same place twice.

ACTIVITY 18.4

THE FORMATION OF RAINDROPS

Purpose   To identify the factors that determine the speed of raindrops.

Materials

waxed paper
spray bottle
safety goggles
water

Procedure

1. Read all the instructions for this activity before you begin your work. Put on your safety goggles.

2. Spray water onto the waxed paper with the spray bottle. Try to make drops of different sizes, including tiny mist droplets.

3. Tip the paper slightly. Record your observations on the speeds of drops of various sizes.

4. Try to make one drop collide with another. Describe what you see. Record any change in the speed and size of the drop after the collision.

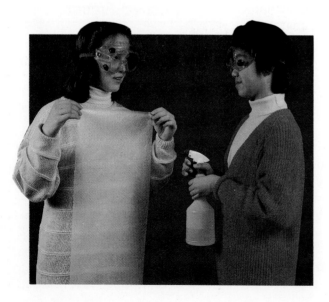

5. Tip the paper back and forth. Observe the general effect on the sizes of all the drops.

6. Before leaving the laboratory, clean up all materials and wash your hands thoroughly.

Collecting and Analyzing Data

1. Which drops rolled fastest on the waxed paper? Slowest? Answer in terms of drop size.

2. What effect did the collision between two drops have on their speed?

Drawing Conclusions

3. Which droplets behaved most like cloud droplets? Explain your answer.

4. The wax on the paper prevented some droplets from falling. What prevents droplets from falling in a cloud?

5. Suppose you used a longer piece of waxed paper to represent a taller cloud. How would your results change?

6. What conditions improve the chance of large raindrops forming from droplets in a cloud?

7. If one side of your waxed paper were below freezing, what would happen to the drops on the paper if you continued moving them back and forth? What type of precipitation can form in a similar way in a cumulonimbus cloud?

8. If you have time, measure the width of a few of the drops on your paper. The next time it rains, catch a few drops on waxed paper and measure them. How do your artificial raindrops compare to the real thing?

Lesson Review 18.4

15. Describe five forms of precipitation.
16. Describe the three stages in the development of a thunderstorm.
17. How does lightning produce thunder?
18. How does acid rain form?

Interpret and Apply

19. How does warm-cloud precipitation form differently from cold-cloud precipitation?
20. Explain why thunderstorms are usually short-lived.
21. Lightning that is seen but not heard is called *heat lightning*. When would you be able to see heat lightning?

Chapter Summary

Read this summary of the main ideas in this chapter. If any are not clear to you, go back and review that lesson.

18.1 Evaporation, Condensation, and Humidity

■ Saturation occurs when the numbers of molecules leaving and returning to a liquid are the same.

■ Relative humidity compares the amount of water vapor actually present in the air to the largest amount of water vapor possible in air at that temperature.

■ During evaporation, thermal energy is absorbed from the surroundings.

18.2 Types of Condensation

■ Dew point is the temperature at which air is saturated with water vapor.

■ A cloud forms when a parcel of air has been cooled slightly below its dew point.

■ Water vapor condenses on surfaces or on condensation nuclei.

18.3 Clouds

■ Rising air expands because air pressure decreases with altitude. The expansion cools the air.

■ The three basic cloud shapes are cumulus (fluffy), stratus (layered), and cirrus (wispy). Clouds are further classified by altitude and by their production of precipitation.

18.4 Precipitation

■ Precipitation is the liquid or solid form of water that falls from clouds.

■ The form of precipitation that reaches the ground depends on the type of cloud and the temperature of the air below the cloud.

■ Acid precipitation forms when sulfate or nitrate particles dissolve in cloud droplets.

■ Lightning is a giant spark that leaps from one place to another during a thunderstorm. Thunder is the sound made by rapidly expanding air.

Chapter Review

■ Vocabulary

acid precipitation	lightning
alto-	nimbus
cirrus	precipitation
condensation nuclei	rain
cumulus	rain gauge
dew	relative humidity
dew point	saturated
downdrafts	sleet
drizzle	snow
fog	stratus
frost	thunder
hail	updrafts

■ Concept Mapping

Construct a concept map for cloud formation. Include the following terms: clouds, height, shape, cloud droplets, alto-, cumulus, stratus, condensation nuclei, water vapor, sulfate particles, sea salt particles. Use additional terms as you need them.

■ Review

On your paper, write the word or words that best complete each statement.

1. The process in which more molecules leave a liquid than return to it is called _____.

2. When more water molecules return to a pool of liquid water than leave it, _____ is occurring.

3. When the number of molecules leaving a liquid is equal to the number of water molecules that return, the air above the liquid is said to be _____.

4. If relative humidity is low, evaporation takes place _____ than if relative humidity were high.

5. In the process of evaporation, _____ is removed from the surroundings.

6. After air falls below its _____, water vapor condenses from the air.

7. _____ forms when a thin film of air next to the ground cools past a dew point below the freezing point of water.

8. Cloud droplets form only if they can condense on _____ present in the air.

9. As a parcel of air rises in the atmosphere, it _____, causing its temperature to drop.

10. Cumulus clouds are formed by the process of _____, while stratus clouds form by the sideways movement of air.

11. If a cloud produces rain or snow, the word _____ is added to its name.

12. _____ are very high ice-crystal clouds that are sometimes influenced by the jet stream.

13. _____ is formed in warm clouds when cloud droplets collide with each other.

14. _____ clouds form vertically, and sometimes reach as high as the stratosphere.

15. Precipitation falling through a layer of freezing air between a cloud and the earth is likely to be _____.

16. Cloud droplets that form around particles produced by the burning of coal and oil become _____ rain.

17. _____ can form inside thunderclouds when air currents keep droplets and ice crystals moving around inside the cloud.

18. A thundercloud breaks up when enough rain falls, creating _____ from the cloud.

19. _____ _____ are used to measure amounts of rainfall.

20. An electrical spark in a cumulonimbus cloud creates _____.

21. Thunder is caused by the violent expansion of _____ after a lightning stroke.

■ *Interpret and Apply*

On your paper, answer each question.

22. Over 700 jets fly in the narrow airspace between Detroit, Michigan, and Des Moines, Iowa, each day. Since the increase in air traffic, there have been 53% more cloudy days. How can you explain this?

23. What do you think the relative humidity inside a cave with a river flowing through it would be like? Explain your answer.

24. Calculate the relative humidity of air at 15°C containing 2.4 grams of water vapor per cubic meter. Refer to Figure 18-3 in solving this problem.

25. Air conditioners take in hot, humid air, cool it off, and blow it into an enclosed space inside a building. If you walk underneath an air conditioner outside, it may drip water on your head. Where did the water come from?

26. Samples of rain or snow taken at the beginning of a storm are often more acidic than samples taken near the end. Why do you think this is true?

27. How far away is a thunderstorm if it takes one second for thunder to reach you from a lightning flash?

28. Using the three stages of thunderstorm formation, predict the season during which thunderstorms should be most common. Explain your prediction.

■ *Writing in Science*

29. When you compare two things, you explain both how they are like each other and how they are different. Write a comparison of the processes of forming snow and sleet. Prepare to write by listing the similarities and differences between the two processes.

■ *Critical Thinking*

Suppose the air temperature in the school parking lot is 20°C. The dew point is 10°C. Puddles in the lot evaporate, causing a parcel of warm, humid air to rise. The rising air condenses into a cloud like the one shown here.

30. Why is the bottom of the cloud flat?

31. If air cools 1°C for each 100 meters it rises, how far would the air rise before reaching the dew point?

32. Dew point actually decreases slightly with altitude. How would that affect the height at which clouds start to form?

33. After water vapor begins to condense, the air parcel cools at the rate of 0.6°C for each 100 meters as it continues to rise. Why is the cooling rate lower after condensation begins?

34. What type of cloud would form over the parking lot? Justify your answer.

19 Weather

Chapter Preview

Have You Ever WONDERED?

What is it like inside a tornado?

Will Keller, a Kansas farmer, found out when he looked out of his underground shelter. He saw three swirling tornadoes dangling from an eerie greenish-black cloud. One tornado lifted off the ground as it passed overhead. When Will looked up inside the tornado, he saw a calm space one third as wide as a football field. Clouds in the spinning walls crackled with lightning. The end of the funnel-shaped cloud screamed and hissed. A stove and parts of a house were spinning around in the tornado.

Other witnesses have described the noise of a tornado as being "like a million bees," "like a freight train," or "like a squadron of jet planes." Scientists do not completely understand how a tornado forms. They do know that the energy source that powers a tornado is the same source that causes all weather—the sun. In this chapter, you will learn more about all types of weather and how you can predict them.

19.1 *Air Masses and Fronts*

When you leave an air-conditioned store on a hot day, you feel the difference in two masses of air, indoors and outdoors. All over Earth's surface, collisions between much larger masses of air cause weather.

Air Masses

You might expect air temperature to go down steadily as you travel away from the equator. When early meteorologists mapped air properties, they had a surprise. Their maps showed broad areas, now called **air masses,** with about the same temperature and humidity throughout. Air masses form when air stays over the same land or water surface for days or weeks. During that time, the air takes on the temperature and humidity of the surface. Two conditions must be true before air masses form.

1. There must be the same kind of surface over millions of square kilometers—for example, the surface of a continent or ocean.

2. The air must be calm, so it does not move away from the land or water surface over a period of days.

Air masses are named for the temperature and humidity conditions of their source area. Figure 19-1 shows that cold, dry air masses form over Canada. What kind of air masses form over the Pacific Ocean off the coast of Mexico?

Lesson Objectives

▶ **Relate** air mass properties to the conditions under which an air mass forms.

▶ **Contrast** conditions at different kinds of fronts.

▶ **Interpret** isobars to predict the motion of air in high- and low-pressure areas.

▶ **Locate** weather data on a station model.

▶ **Activity** **Interpret data** on a weather map to locate air masses and fronts.

New Terms

air masses	high-pressure
cold front	area
warm front	low-pressure
stationary front	area
occluded front	station model
isobars	

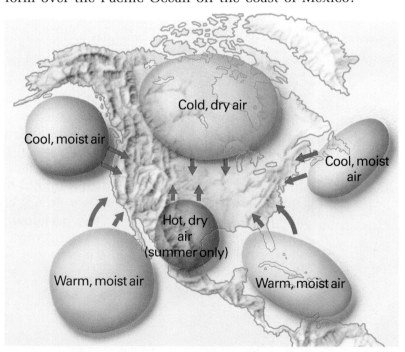

Figure 19-1 Air masses form when air takes on the temperature and humidity of the surface it covers.

Fronts

When air masses meet, they form a sharp boundary called a front. Fronts most often form at middle latitudes, that is, at latitudes between 30° N and 60° N, and between 30° S and 60° S. Fronts can be thousands of kilometers long. At a front, the masses may shove each other, sort of like bumper cars do. The name of a front depends on the air mass that won the shoving match. There are four kinds of fronts, each with its own kind of weather.

Cold Fronts Imagine cold, dense air pushing against warm, less dense air, as shown in Figure 19-2 *(left)*. The cold, dense air bulges in along the ground, forcing the warm, less dense air ahead of it to rise quickly, forming a **cold front.** The rising warm air at a cold front produces cumulus clouds and sometimes thunderstorms.

Warm Fronts A **warm front** forms when a warm air mass pushes into a cold air mass. Along a warm front, the warm, less dense air rides up a gently sloping wedge of the cold, denser air. The warm air gradually cools. If the warm air mass is also moist, layered clouds may form.

Stationary Fronts A **stationary front** results when neither air mass pushes into the other. If the warm air mass is also moist, layered clouds form along the stationary front. A stationary front can stay in the same place for days. When this happens, the weather stays the same for days.

Occluded Fronts If a cold front catches up with a warm front, two cold air masses trap a warm air mass above the ground. This condition, called an **occluded front,** occurs in some low-pressure systems. You will learn more about low-pressure systems in the next lesson.

Figure 19-2 Air masses meet at fronts. *Left:* A cold front; *Right:* A warm front

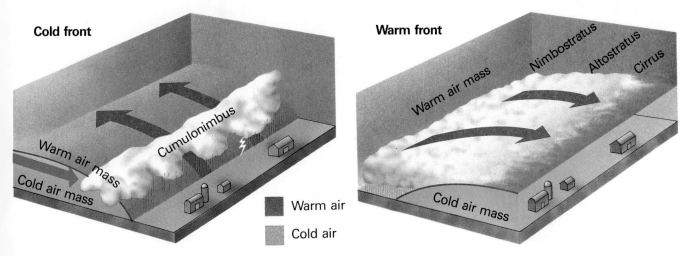

Pressure Changes along Fronts

Most air masses form in areas with high air pressure. Recall from Chapter 17 that air sinks and spreads out at 30° N, 30° S, and at the poles. This sinking air forms the worldwide high-pressure belts that you learned about. In high-pressure belts, air piles up over continents and oceans. More molecules hit against each other as they rush around in the air at the bottom of the piles. As the molecules hit each other, the air warms slightly. This warming decreases the relative humidity of the sinking air. The dry, sinking air in the high-pressure belt produces few clouds and little wind. However, if the air is over an ocean, the humidity may rise.

You can find areas of high pressure using a map of air pressure data. First, you would draw **isobars,** which are lines connecting points of equal pressure. The isobars may form patterns of rings within rings, like the ones in Figure 19-3. In a **high-pressure area,** the isobars show higher pressure readings as you move toward the center of the pattern. Find a high-pressure area in Figure 19-3. The center of a high-pressure area, called a high, is labeled *H* on the map. **Low-pressure areas** are places where the isobars show lower air pressure as you go toward the center of the pattern. Unlike high-pressure areas, which tend to be in air masses, low-pressure areas often go along with fronts. The center of a low-pressure area, called a low, is labeled *L* on a map.

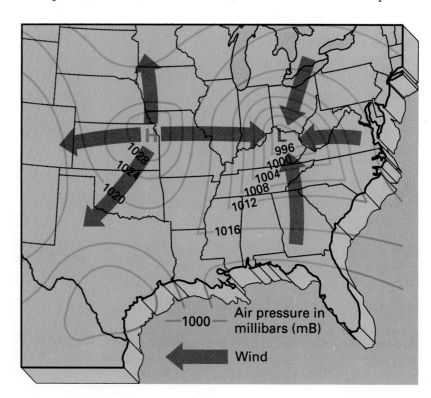

Figure 19-3 How do the isobars show you the centers of the high- and low-pressure areas?

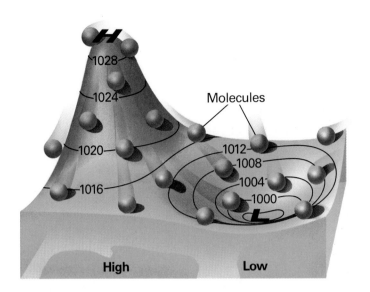

1028
1024
1020
1016
1012
1008
1004
1000
Molecules
High   **Low**

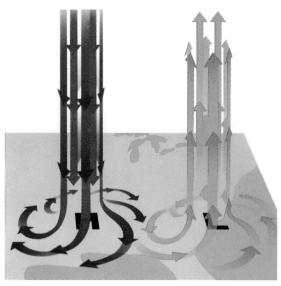

Figure 19-4 *Left:* A model that predicts wind direction near highs and lows; *Right:* Because of Earth's rotation, actual wind directions differ from the model.

The pattern of isobars may remind you of the contour lines you learned about in Chapter 2. Comparing isobars to contour lines can help you understand how air moves near highs and lows. Recall that contour lines on a topographic map show changes in the elevation as you travel across the land. Isobars show changes in air pressure as you travel through air masses and fronts. Think of high-pressure areas on an isobar map as mountains of air 3 to 6 kilometers tall and perhaps 1000 kilometers across, as shown in Figure 19-4 *(left)*. The center of the high-pressure area would be the peak of the air mountain. Air moves away from the center of the high in all directions. Think of objects moving down a slope from a mountain peak. The air moving away from the high-pressure area forms winds. Think of low-pressure areas as depressions, or shallow bowl-shaped valleys of air. Winds move toward the center of a low, just as objects would roll toward the bottom of a bowl. Winds blow away from the centers of high-pressure areas but toward the centers of low-pressure areas.

Air mountains and bowls, like many science models, do not completely explain real observations. For example, air does not really form peaks and valleys with surfaces that wind blows across. Wind directions also differ from the model. Compare the wind directions predicted by the model in Figure 19-4 *(left)* to actual wind directions, shown in Figure 19-4 *(right)*. As air moves away from a high or toward a low, Earth's rotation makes it swirl. In the Northern Hemisphere, air swirls around a high-pressure area in a clockwise direction. In the Northern Hemisphere, air swirls around a low-pressure area in a counterclockwise direction. In the Southern Hemisphere, the opposite is true. How does air move around highs and lows in the Southern Hemisphere?

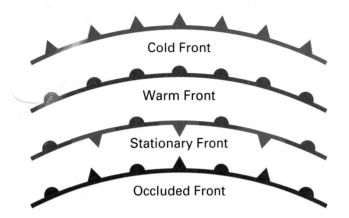

Wind Speed Symbols		
Symbol	Miles/Hour	Kilometers/Hour
◎	Calm	Calm
──	1 – 2	1 – 3
＼	9 – 14	14 – 22
＼	15 – 20	23 – 32
＼	55 – 60	88 – 96

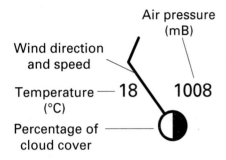

Figure 19-5 On a weather map, station models show weather conditions. Front symbols show where air masses meet.

You can locate the fronts between two air masses by comparing the temperature, pressure, and wind data for many locations. On a map, these data appear in a kind of shorthand called a **station model.** Figure 19-5 shows a station model and weather front symbols. In the station model, the shaded part of the circle shows how cloudy it is at that station. The temperature is listed at the upper left of the circle. Air pressure is at the upper right. A line on the circle points in the direction the wind is coming from. You can find the fronts by looking for sharp differences in temperature between two stations that are near each other. By looking for similar temperature differences, you can find the front over many kilometers.

Lesson Review 19.1

1. Give an example of conditions under which an air mass would form and describe the air mass that would form.

2. Make a table to contrast a cold front and a warm front. Include the headings *Weather, Movement of Air Masses, Symbol on Map,* and *Diagram.*

3. What is an isobar? Describe the pattern of isobars in a high-pressure area and a low-pressure area.

4. Contrast the motion of air in a high-pressure area with the motion of air in a low-pressure area in the Northern Hemisphere.

Interpret and Apply

5. Weather in the middle of an air mass is not always clear. Think of some conditions under which clouds or fog could form in a cold, dry air mass and in a warm, humid air mass.

MAPPING WEATHER FRONTS

Purpose   To interpret data on a weather map to locate air masses and fronts.

Materials

weather map in Figure 19-6
copy of Figure 19-6
colored pencils

Procedure

1. Compare the pressure readings on the isobars on your map. Find the low and label it *L*.

2. Figure out where the two air masses are. Compare the temperatures in the station models in each air mass. Then label each air mass as a cold air mass or a warm air mass.

3. Now study the map to find places where the temperature is very different between two stations. On your map, draw the boundary lines between cold and warm temperatures.

4. These are fronts that are moving from west to east. Figure out the correct name for each front and then label it using the symbols and colors in Figure 19-5. Add a legend to your map.

Collecting and Analyzing Data

1. Look at the wind directions in the station models. Describe the general direction of the winds compared with the low and the fronts. (Remember that wind indicators point into the wind.)

2. Are temperatures throughout an air mass exactly the same? Can you describe a pattern in any differences?

Drawing Conclusions

3. Explain how you figured out the correct label for each front.

4. How cloudy are stations near the fronts compared with stations away from the fronts? Explain these data, using what you know about weather in air masses and at fronts.

Figure 19-6 Portion of a weather map

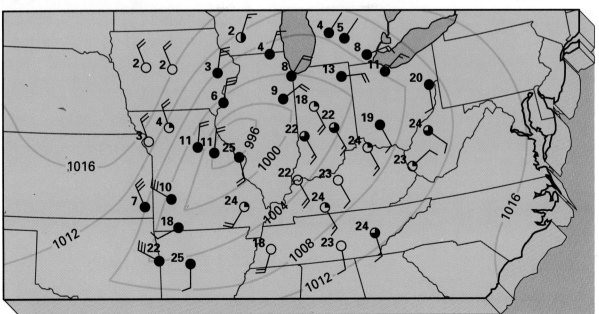

19.2 *Forecasting the Weather*

Lesson Objectives

▶ *Outline* the development and motion of a low-pressure system.

▶ *Relate* changes in weather to the passing of a low-pressure system.

▶ *List* the types of weather data used to make a weather map.

▶ *Describe* how weather service data are used to forecast weather and *discuss* the reliability of these forecasts.

▶ *Activity* *Predict* changes in weather as a low-pressure system passes.

New Terms

low-pressure system

When was the last time you wondered about the weather? Perhaps you were looking forward to a game or picnic. Often, you can predict the weather for your area for the next few hours by observing weather conditions. Already you can recognize cloud types, measure temperature, wind speed and direction, and interpret these data to find highs, lows, and fronts. The next step in weather forecasting is to find out how a low-pressure system develops.

Low-Pressure Systems

Generally, the weather over much of the United States changes every few days. This is because so much of the United States lies at middle latitudes, where low-pressure areas often form. The polar front is the boundary between the cap of cold air from the North Pole and the band of warm air from the tropics. Both air masses are high-pressure areas. In Figure 19-7, cold air that has piled up at the North Pole spills south on northeast winds. Warm air from the subtropics moves north on southwest winds. All that air moving toward the same place has nowhere to go but up. The rising air forms a long line of low pressure.

As long as air in one mass moves parallel to air in the other, nothing much happens. A stationary front forms. However, if the air is disturbed, then it begins to swirl, as illustrated in the second part of Figure 19-8. Mountains, changes in surface temperatures, or changes in the upper atmosphere can all disturb air. In the Northern Hemisphere, the disturbed air swirls counterclockwise toward a central point, forming a low-pressure area. Clouds form as the rising air of the low cools below its dew point. Rain or snow may result.

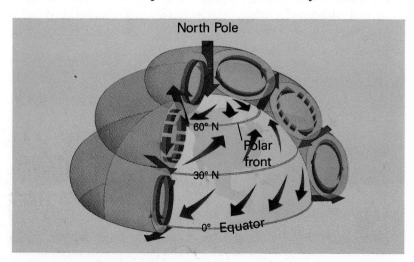

Figure 19-7 What kind of pressure area forms at the polar front?

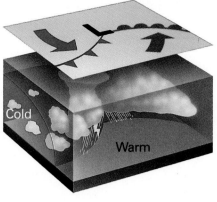
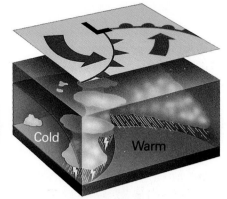
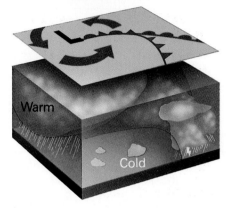

Around the low-pressure area, the cold and warm air masses start their shoving matches, as shown in the second and third parts of Figure 19-8. On the western side of the low, a cold front forms as the cold air mass bulldozes into the warm air mass. On the eastern side, the warm air mass slides up over the cold air mass and forms a warm front. The low-pressure area together with its fronts is called a middle latitude **low-pressure system.**

Low-pressure systems are the reason weather changes so often at middle latitudes. Have you ever watched a small whirlpool drift from the end of an oar or paddle? The water spins in the whirlpool. The whole whirlpool also moves away from the oar. In the same way, an entire low-pressure system moves away from where it began. Jet streams and prevailing winds generally move low-pressure systems eastward across North America.

As the low-pressure system moves, it also changes. After a few days, the cold front catches up with the warm front. The cold air pushes the warm air up from the ground, as shown in Figure 19-9. This condition is an occluded front. Many types of clouds and heavy precipitation can occur at occluded fronts. An occluded front cuts off fresh supplies of warm moist air. Thus, the low-pressure system begins to fall apart. From birth to death, the low-pressure system has lasted a week or so.

Figure 19-8 As a low-pressure system develops, a cold front and a warm front form.

Occluded Front

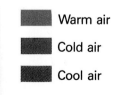

Warm air

Cold air

Cool air

Figure 19-9 At an occluded front, a warm air mass is caught up above two cold air masses.

A C T I V I T Y   1 9 . 2

INTERPRETING WEATHER MAPS

Purpose   To predict changes in weather as a low-pressure system passes.

Materials
maps in Figures 19-10, 19-11, 19-12

metric ruler
colored pencils

Procedure

1. Copy the data table onto your paper.

2. Locate the station models for Chicago, Illinois, and Des Moines, Iowa, on each map. Record the temperature, wind direction, and cloud cover for each day.

3. On the March 16 map, the black X-marks show where part of the cold front was on March 15 and 16. The green X-marks show where part of the warm front was on these days. Use these marks to measure the distance each front moved in one day. Use the map scale to convert your measurements to km.

Figure 19-10 March 15

Collecting and Analyzing Data

Data Table						
	Chicago			Des Moines		
Condition	15th	16th	17th	15th	16th	17th
Temp. (°C)						
Pressure (mB)						
Wind Direction						
Cloud Cover						

1. Draw lines on your data table to divide data from before and after a front.

Drawing Conclusions

2. Is the warm front moving as fast as the cold front? Explain your answer.

3. Predict the weather for March 18 for Raleigh, North Carolina.

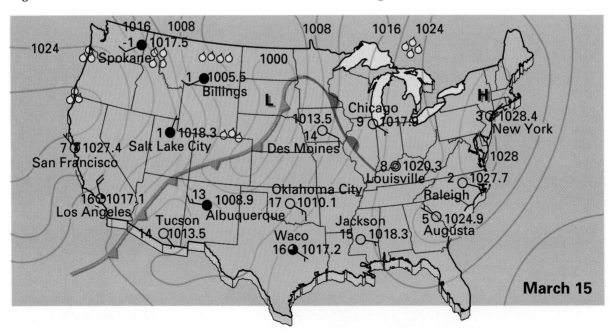

March 15

Figure 19-11 March 16

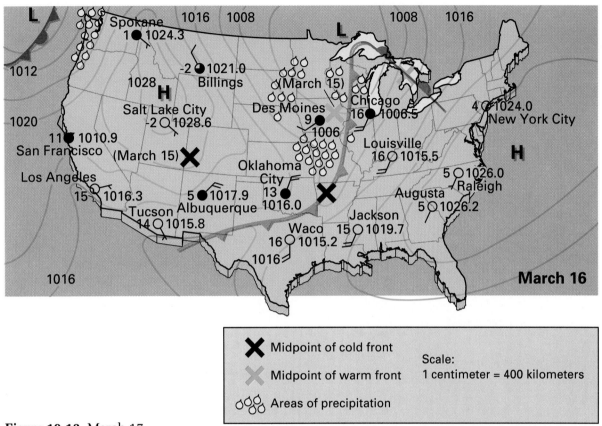

Figure 19-12 March 17

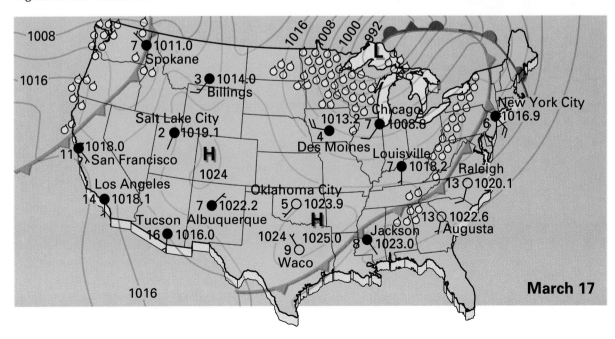

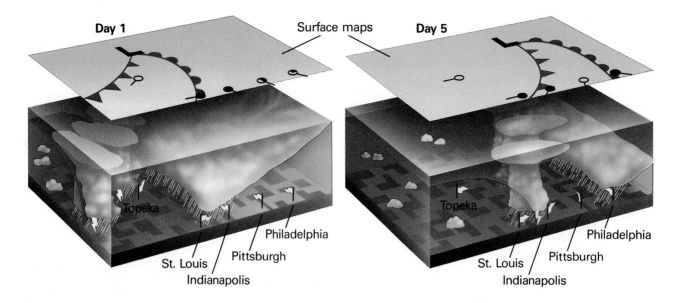

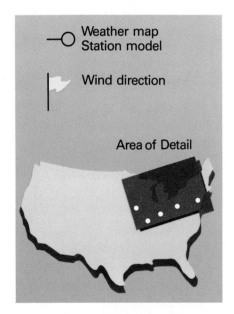

Figure 19-13 As low-pressure systems move across the country, they bring weather changes.

Low-Pressure System Weather

As the fronts in a low-pressure system pass over your area, weather changes in a predictable pattern. Figure 19-13 shows a cross-section of a low-pressure system as it passes over some cities. Imagine you are in St. Louis, Missouri. The weather pattern you would observe can be described as follows.

First Day The air is cool, the air pressure is high, and the wind is from the southeast. You notice a few wispy cirrus clouds at noon. During the afternoon, a veil of cirrostratus clouds moves in, giving the sun a halo. Later, a sheet of low stratus clouds cover the sky. The temperature rises, the air pressure falls steadily, and it starts to rain. The warm front has arrived. In Figure 19-13, which cities are under the warm front on the first day?

Second Day In the morning, it is still raining. Then the wind shifts to the southwest. The temperature continues to rise, and the sky clears. The warm front has passed.

Third and Fourth Days The weather is warm and humid. The sky is whitish-blue, with scattered cumulus clouds. You are in the warm air mass.

Fifth Day The warm, humid weather continues until suddenly, the western sky fills with storm clouds. The thunderstorm lasts an hour. The cold front has arrived. The storm ends and the sky clears. The temperature falls, the air pressure rises suddenly, and the wind shifts to the northwest. You are in the cold air mass. From Figure 19-13, can you predict the weather for the next day in Pittsburgh?

The weather just described for St. Louis is an example of a typical weather pattern as a low-pressure system passes. Of course, the actual weather is not that easy to predict. The exact weather pattern you observe depends on three variables: where you are compared to the central low, what direction the low-pressure system is moving, and the speed the system is moving. The average low-pressure system in North America moves from west to east at 800 to 1200 kilometers per day. As the system passes through, the wide air masses determine your weather for more days than the narrow fronts do. While high-pressure areas usually bring calm, clear skies, fronts often bring stormy weather.

Collecting Weather Data

The National Weather Service receives ground-level data from over 10 000 weather stations around the world. The data include temperature, air pressure, wind direction, wind speed, dew point, cloud cover, and precipitation. Radio, telegraph, and teletype are used to transmit the data.

The National Weather Service also uses data gathered far above the ground. Twice a day, weather balloons are released into the upper atmosphere. Satellites record images of Earth from space. Satellite data of ocean areas are of special value, because few ground-level observations are made on the ocean. You may have seen satellite images replayed at high speed to look like a movie of the day's weather.

Figure 19-14 *Top:* Weather at a front; *Bottom:* Weather in an air mass

Figure 19-15 This computer map of a low-pressure system was made from weather data. Can you tell where the weather fronts are?

Figure 19-16 This meteorologist is using a computer model to analyze the weather.

The National Weather Service also makes maps that predict the future position of weather fronts. A weather service computer is programmed to compare the position of fronts in the past few hours or days. The program forecasts where the front will move next. Then, the computer prints out a weather map for the near future. Such maps predict temperature, wind direction, precipitation, and the motion of low-pressure systems for any time from 12 hours to 10 days ahead. Of course, the 12-hour forecasts are more accurate than the 10-day forecasts.

The same computer map goes out several times a day to all radio and television stations, newspapers, airports, and private weather services. If everyone gets the same map, why do you hear different weather forecasts? The weather data the computer program receives are incomplete, because data are not collected in every possible location. The computer is too small to hold the models needed for very accurate forecasts. What computers can do is compare large amounts of data very quickly. Humans still need to interpret the data on the computer map.

A meteorologist adjusts the National Weather Service forecast for local conditions. Local conditions can include mountain ranges, ocean currents, or the heating effect of a large city. However, even the best information and experience do not guarantee an accurate forecast. Usually, if a forecaster correctly predicts the weather for the next few days, 70 percent of the time, he or she is doing a good job.

Lesson Review 19.2

6. Sketch a low-pressure system as it would appear on a weather map. Add a key to explain symbols.

7. Describe how a low-pressure system develops in the Northern Hemisphere. Include the direction in which the system moves.

8. List the types of data needed to make a weather map. How are these data collected?

9. Why are local meteorologists needed to interpret the National Weather Service forecasts?

Interpret and Apply

10. An old folk saying claims, "Halo around the sun or moon, rain or snow soon." How accurate would this forecast be? Refer to Figure 18-13 on pages 482–483 if needed.

19.3 *Severe Storms*

Skillful weather forecasts save lives and money. Farmers need to know when to protect crops from frost. Ski resort owners need to know whether to make snow. Ship and plane pilots need safe routes around storms.

Severe storms, such as thunderstorms, tornadoes, and hurricanes, are all areas of low pressure. The simple ingredients for a severe storm seem quite innocent: sun, water, and air, and perhaps Earth's rotation. You recall from Chapter 18 that thermal energy from the sun evaporates water from Earth's surface. As water vapor condenses to form clouds, thermal energy is then given off. When large amounts of water vapor condense in a short time, a burst of thermal energy follows. The energy burst heats the air in the cloud. The heated air can rise to great heights, producing even more clouds. The heated air causes lower pressure and stronger winds. The lower pressure pulls in more warm, moist air and the storm begins to build itself up.

Lesson Objectives

▸ **Describe** conditions under which thunderstorms, tornadoes, and hurricanes form.

▸ **Compare** the characteristics of tornadoes and hurricanes.

▸ **Activity** **Form a model** of a tornado.

New Terms

squall line	hurricane
tornado	storm surge

Thunderstorms

In Chapter 18, you learned that thunderstorms can form by convection when warm, moist air rises over hot ground. Usually, these convection thunderstorms last an hour or so. Other conditions can form a line of thunderstorms, called a **squall line,** just ahead of a cold front. Often, these thunderstorms can last several hours and become quite intense. If a thunderstorm has wind gusts of over 80 kilometers per hour and hail at least 2 centimeters across, it is classified as a severe thunderstorm. Thunderstorms can cause serious flooding and other damage.

Tornadoes

The unpredictable behavior and high winds of a tornado make it one of nature's most deadly storms. A **tornado,** or twister, is a violent, funnel-shaped storm that comes down from a cold front thunderstorm. The air pressure in the center of a tornado is extremely low. This low pressure can cause wind speeds that may be as high as 350 to 500 kilometers per hour. Meteorologists estimate tornado wind speeds from the size of objects that tornadoes have picked up. Like a giant vacuum cleaner, these whirling windstorms have picked up trains and houses and set them down hundreds of meters away. Tornadoes have even plucked chickens and pulled blankets off a bed and up a chimney!

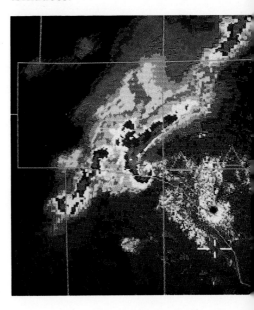

Figure 19-17 Radar technology is useful for tracking storms. This storm over Oklahoma has tornadoes.

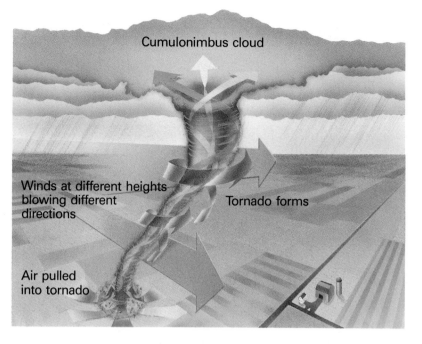

Cumulonimbus cloud

Winds at different heights blowing different directions

Tornado forms

Air pulled into tornado

Figure 19-18 *Left:* A tornado; *Right:* A model of how a tornado forms; *Bottom:* Tornadoes can destroy some homes while leaving others untouched.

How do such intense funnels start? Tornadoes almost always begin in severe thunderstorms. However, not all severe thunderstorms cause tornadoes. Tornadoes form in areas where a fast-moving layer of cool, dry air flows over a layer of warm, moist air. No one can predict exactly where a tornado will form, but there is a good model for how a tornado forms.

Figure 19-18 *(right)* shows a diagram of a tornado forming. At the base of a thundercloud, an updraft of air begins to spin. Under the right conditions, the air spins faster as it moves toward the center of the spinning area. You have seen this effect if you have watched a figure skater spinning. As the skater brings her arms closer to her body, she spins faster. A very low pressure area forms at the center of the moving air. The pressure is so low that the swirling air quickly expands and cools below its dew point. Cloud droplets form and swirl with the air. Debris and soil picked up by the wind mix with the cloud droplets.

A tornado follows an unpredictable path for a very short time and distance. It may move 6 kilometers or more in its short life—often, less than 10 minutes. A tornado may touch down for a minute or more, or it may skip around. The photo in Figure 19-19 *(bottom)* shows the twisting path one tornado took through a neighborhood in Oklahoma. Although its winds are very fast, the tornado itself moves about 40 to 65 kilometers per hour. This is about the same speed as a car on an average road (not on a highway). But many tornadoes move much faster, travel hundreds of kilometers, and last for hours.

Figure 19-19 Even in Tornado Alley, an area in Oklahoma and Kansas, your chances of being struck by a tornado are once in every 250 years.

Although tornadoes happen all over the world, ideal tornado conditions exist in the central part of the United States. This area, shown in Figure 19-19, is called tornado alley. Tornado alley averages 300 twisters each year. Heating conditions make tornadoes most common in spring and summer. At this time, warm, humid air often moves in from the Gulf of Mexico. Cooler, drier air from the Rocky Mountains moves in from the west at high altitudes. The high-altitude air traps the warm, moist air at ground level. Thunderstorms and tornadoes often result.

ENVIRONMENTAL AWARENESS

Storm Safety

You can help keep family and friends safe in a severe storm. First, get a portable radio with good batteries. Follow the storm information on the radio. You can also take the following steps:

For Thunderstorms Indoors, turn off appliances. Do not use the phone. Stay away from windows, electric outlets, and water. Outdoors, avoid tall trees or buildings in open areas. Crouch down or get inside a car. Do not touch anything metal.

For Tornadoes Go to a cellar or crawl under a sturdy piece of furniture in an interior room or in the southwest corner of a room. Outdoors, get away from water. Lie flat in a ditch. Cover your head.

For Hurricanes Indoors, before the storm, store fresh water and check batteries. Outdoors, board up windows and pick up loose objects. During the storm, stay indoors away from windows. Do not go outdoors, even if the storm seems to stop. ■

ACTIVITY 19.3 *General Supplies*

MODELING A TORNADO

Purpose To form a model of a tornado and to compare it with a real tornado.

Materials

plastic soft drink bottle with cap (0.5-L or 1-L)	liquid dish detergent
	table salt
	pencil or pen
water	sand

Procedure

1. Read all instructions for this activity. Copy the data table onto your paper.

2. Fill the bottle most of the way with tap water. Add a small drop of dish detergent, a pinch of salt, and a pinch of sand. Tightly cap the bottle.

3. To practice making a model of a tornado, hold the bottle upright and move your hand in circles. The water should form a whirlpool.

4. Now move your hand in counterclockwise circles. Observe and record the direction the whirlpool is swirling and the whirlpool's effect on the sand.

5. Move your hand in clockwise circles. Observe and record the direction of the whirlpool and the effect on the sand.

6. Move your hand counterclockwise again, but slowly. Gradually increase the speed. Observe and describe how the speed of your hand affects the speed of the "tornado" whirlpool.

7. Before leaving the lab area, clean up all materials and wash your hands. DO NOT PUT ANY SAND IN THE SINK.

Collecting and Analyzing Data

Data Table	
Hand Motion	**Effect on Model**
Counterclockwise	
Clockwise	
Slow	
Fast	

1. What connection is there between the direction you move your hand and the direction of the whirlpool in your tornado model?

2. What connection is there between the speed you move your hand and the speed of your tornado model?

3. Where did the force come from that made your tornado model spin? Do tornadoes form from this same kind of force in nature? Explain.

Drawing Conclusions

4. Compare your tornado model with a real tornado. How are the tornado model and a tornado alike in shape, size, and motion? How are they different?

Hurricanes

In the Pacific, it's called a typhoon. In the Philippines, it's called a baguio. Another name for it is tropical cyclone. Most Americans call a large low-pressure storm with steady winds over 120 kilometers per hour a **hurricane.** Because of their size, hurricanes are the most destructive of all severe storms. Figure 19-20 *(right)* shows hurricane Hugo, which struck several southern states in 1989. The clouds around Hugo show the spiraling, counterclockwise winds of a hurricane. At the center of a hurricane is an area of relative calm called the eye. Find Hugo's eye in Figure 19-20 *(right)*.

The strongest winds in a hurricane are on the walls around the eye. Wind speeds there reach up to 300 kilometers per hour. These screaming winds can uproot trees and rip buildings apart. Hurricanes also bring heavy rains, usually 10 to 24 centimeters per storm. Hurricane rain comes from the ocean, where rising air lifts billions of metric tons of water vapor to form clouds.

Many hurricanes that reach North America begin in the Atlantic Ocean off the coast of Africa. Here, in late summer and fall, the sun evaporates huge volumes of water into the air. As you know, moist, rising air can lead to thunderstorms. A hurricane can form when large groups of thunderstorms occur in a low-pressure area over the warm ocean. High-level air pressure changes may make the low spin faster, causing an air pressure drop. As air pressure drops, wind speeds increase. By this time, the storm is moving toward North America. Winds blowing over frothy waves make more water vapor move up into the storm.

Figure 19-20 *Left:* How is the air at a hurricane's eye different from the air around the eye? *Right:* This satellite image of Hurricane Hugo shows Hugo's eye and swirling clouds.

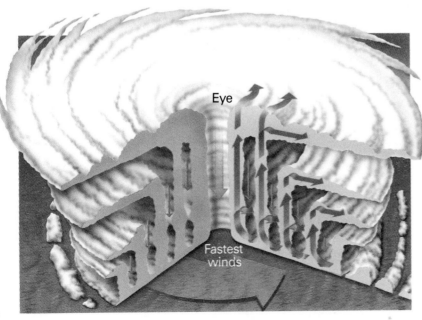

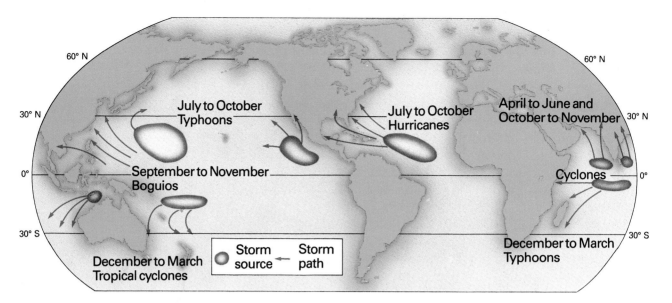

Typhoons July to October

September to November Boguios

July to October Hurricanes

April to June and October to November

Cyclones

December to March Tropical cyclones

December to March Typhoons

Storm source ← Storm path

60° N   60° N
30° N   30° N
0°   0°
30° S   30° S

Figure 19-21 Where do most hurricanes that reach the United States form?

Figure 19-22 Improved hurricane forecasting has saved many lives. However, as this photo taken after Hurricane Hugo shows, hurricanes still damage property.

Figure 19-21 shows the path of hurricanes around the world. As a hurricane moves over land or cool water, it loses its source of warm humid air and dies.

Hurricanes generally move 500 kilometers per day and can be active for weeks. Thus, hurricane damage is greater than destruction from thunderstorms or tornadoes. The most severe damage is caused by rapid sea-level rises. Hurricane winds whip up mounds of water and pile them against the shore in a **storm surge.** Sea level can rise as much as 6 meters during a hurricane. How high is this compared to your classroom?

In 1900, a storm surge flooded Galveston, Texas, demolished the city, and killed 5000 people. Little more than 50 years later, Hurricane Carla roared across the same area, yet no one died from the storm. Because of improved hurricane predictions, people were able to leave the area before Hurricane Carla hit. You can protect yourself from severe storms by following the advice of a radio announcer.

Strange though it seems, if there were no hurricanes, even more lives might be lost. In many parts of the world, hurricanes bring rainfall needed for crops and drinking water.

The balance between rainfall and drought is just part of the process you call weather. Recall from Chapter 17 that the sun and atmosphere together balance the energy at Earth's surface. Weather is nature's way of spreading around the sun's energy. Water vapor transfers thermal energy from tropical air toward the poles. Wind belts and weather systems circulate air over Earth's surface. Tropical air helps form the powerful winds of hurricanes and tornadoes. All of these processes are involved in making weather. How is the sun's energy affecting the weather where you are today?

Lesson Review 19.3

11. What is a squall line? What kind of front will follow a squall line?

12. Describe the conditions that can lead to tornadoes.

13. Describe these features for both tornadoes and hurricanes.
    a. where each forms
    b. how long each lasts
    c. their sizes
    d. their wind speeds
    e. air pressure at their centers
    f. overall damage they do
    g. how predictable they are

Interpret and Apply

14. If a thunderstorm passes at night, is it more likely caused by local convection currents or by a cold front? Explain your answer.

Chapter Summary

Read this chapter summary. If any ideas are not clear, review that lesson.

19.1 Air Masses and Fronts

■ An air mass is a large body of air with about the same temperature and humidity throughout.

■ Fronts are the boundaries between air masses. Cold fronts, warm fronts, stationary fronts, and occluded fronts have their own motions, properties, and weather.

■ Isobars connect points of equal air pressure on a weather map. In the Northern Hemisphere, air moves clockwise away from the center of a high, and counterclockwise toward the center of a low.

19.2 Forecasting the Weather

■ In the Northern Hemisphere, low-pressure systems form along the polar front and move from west to east. Low-pressure systems bring characteristic weather patterns.

■ Information needed for a weather map includes temperature, air pressure, wind direction, wind speed, cloud type, cloud cover, and precipitation.

■ The National Weather Service processes weather data by computer to produce weather maps. Meteorologists interpret the maps to forecast local weather.

19.3 Severe Storms

■ Thunderstorms, tornadoes, and hurricanes are all areas of low pressure. Tornadoes and hurricanes rotate counterclockwise.

■ A tornado is a small, violent storm lasting a few minutes that can form in severe thunderstorms. Tornadoes are destructive and move unpredictably.

■ A hurricane forms over tropical oceans when large amounts of evaporating water lead to heavy thunderstorms near lows. Hurricanes are large, destructive storms with high winds, heavy rain, and storm surges.

Chapter Review

■ Vocabulary

air mass
cold front
high-pressure area
hurricane
isobars
low-pressure area
low-pressure system

occluded front
squall line
station model
stationary front
storm surge
tornado
warm front

■ Concept Mapping

Use the method of concept mapping described on pages 3–5 to make a concept map for a low-pressure system. Include the following terms on your map: *warm front, cold front, stratus, cumulonimbus, air pressure, temperature,* and *wind direction.* Use additional terms as you need them.

■ Review

On your paper, write the word or words that best complete each sentence.

1. A huge body of air that has about the same temperature and humidity throughout is a(n) (cold front, low-pressure system, air system, air mass).

2. A mass of warm air moving into a mass of cold air is a (warm front, cold front, high-pressure area).

3. A pressure area that often causes precipitation is a(n) (high, low, isobar).

4. (Cumulonimbus, Nimbostratus, Cirrus) clouds are the first clue that a warm front is coming.

5. A (weather station, station model, radar wave) is a shorthand way to show weather data.

6. In the United States, low-pressure systems generally move from (west to east, south to north, east to west).

7. Changes in air pressure, temperature, and wind are common (in an air mass, in a high-pressure area, under a passing front).

8. A (computer, barometer, psychrometer) helps forecasters process data.

9. Temperature, air pressure, and cloud cover are all data used to make a(n) (isobar, isotherm, weather map).

10. To provide the most accurate forecast, (computers, radar waves, meteorologists) must read the computer maps from the National Weather Service.

11. (Low-pressure systems, Thunderstorms, Hurricanes) can form both by convection in an air mass and along cold fronts.

12. Hurricanes form (over warm water, along cold fronts, at the polar front).

13. Fast, violent, and short-lived best describe a (warm front, hurricane, tornado).

14. All severe storms have (high temperature, low pressure, hail).

15. Huge, destructive, wet, week-long describe a (cold front, warm front, hurricane).

16. In the Northern Hemisphere, air in all low-pressure areas rotates (clockwise, counterclockwise, either way depending on the temperature).

17. A line that connects points of equal air pressure readings is an (isotherm, isobar, isotope).

18. In a Northern Hemisphere high-pressure area, winds curve (clockwise away from the center, counterclockwise toward the center, clockwise toward the center).

19. At the center of a low-pressure area, air is (rising, sinking, moving sideways).

20. Most low-pressure systems in the Northern Hemisphere begin at the (equator, North Pole, polar front).

■ Interpret and Apply

On your paper, answer each question.

21. On your paper, copy the list of weather features given below the weather map. Next to each feature, write the letter of the label that corresponds to it.

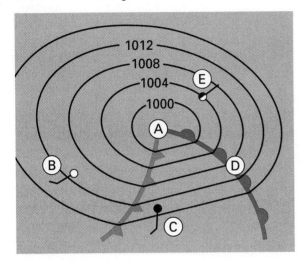

warm front   sunny city
northeast winds low-pressure area
warm air mass

22. This rule for locating storms has saved many ships: "In the Northern Hemisphere, stand with the wind at your back. The lowest air pressure is in front of you, slightly to the left." Explain why this rule works. Include a diagram.

23. Explain why this statement is true: "The sun causes both fair and stormy weather."

24. Describe the temperature and humidity of an air mass that would form dew, and one that would form thunderstorms.

25. Look at the predictions in Figure 18-13 on pages 482–483. Which predictions describe the passing of a warm front? Which describe the passing of a cold front?

26. List three jobs that rely on accurate weather forecasts. Discuss the reasons for your choices.

■ Writing in Science

27. Imagine that you write a newspaper column called Ask the Scientist. One day you receive the following letter:

Dear Ask the Scientist:
 I've heard that if a hurricane stops suddenly, you should stay indoors. This seems crazy to me, since if the storm is over, you should be able to go out. If it is a good suggestion, could you explain why?
      Wynn D. Weather

Write a reply to Wynn D. Weather.

■ Critical Thinking

In a temperature inversion, a layer of warm air lies over a layer of cooler air. A temperature inversion has formed over the city below.

28. Explain the layer of smoke and haze lying close over the city.

29. Air sinks in a high-pressure area. How does this information help explain why a high can lead to a temperature inversion?

30. In winter, the ground temperature is usually cool. In summer, the reverse is true. During which season would temperature inversions be more common? Explain.

31. Why are long-term temperature inversions dangerous to your health?

The Atmosphere and the Environment

Chapter Preview

Have You Ever WONDERED?

Why do some mountaintops have snow all year?

Mount Kilimanjaro rises out of the East African plains near the equator. Climbing Kilimanjaro is like taking a trip from the equator to the poles. You pass through a lush tropical forest on the lower slopes of the mountain. As you climb higher, the trees are shorter. Then there are no trees, only carpets of low-growing alpine flowers. Near the summit, glaciers form cliffs 30 meters high. The snowfields on the glacier last all year, even though Kilimanjaro is near the equator. Kilimanjaro's peak is 5889 meters above sea level. At that elevation, the climate is cooler.

Kilimanjaro's glaciers may soon disappear. For 200 years, its ice fields have been shrinking. Why is the climate on Kilimanjaro so cold? Why is its climate changing? In this chapter, you will learn about climates and why climates change.

Lesson Objectives

▶ *Define* climate *and* compare *the three major climate types.*

▶ *Discuss* the effect of latitude, elevation, bodies of water, and landforms on climates.

▶ *Outline* several theories about past climate changes and *give evidence* for each.

▶ **Activity** *Measure* conditions to identify microclimates and *verify results.*

New Terms

climate	microclimates
tropical	ice age
polar	feedback process
temperate	

Figure 20-1 Climate varies with latitude and elevation. *Left:* January in Maine; *Right:* January in Florida

If you could choose a spot to spend an all-expenses-paid winter vacation, where would you go? The students in Figure 20-1 have based their choices on climate. In January, the snow-skier in Maine braves temperatures near −5°C. The water-skier in Florida enjoys temperatures near 18°C. Temperatures vary from day to day, but these temperatures are typical for those places in January. For a given location, **climate** describes typical weather patterns over a period of years. The two conditions that are used to describe climate are patterns in temperature and precipitation.

Climate and Temperature

A place's temperature is affected by latitude, elevation, and distance from large bodies of water. For the skiers in Figure 20-1, latitude is the main reason for the January air temperatures they enjoy. You recall from Chapter 17 that the sun's energy strikes Earth more directly at latitudes nearer the equator. Florida is closer to the equator than Maine is. The heating effect of the sun is greater in Florida.

Because latitude affects surface temperatures, latitude also affects air mass temperatures. Climate types are grouped by the air masses that most affect their weather. Figure 20-2 illustrates how latitude affects the three major climate types. **Tropical** climates are affected most by warm air masses. The average yearly temperature in tropical climates is about 18°C or higher. In **polar** climates, cold air masses are most common, and the average temperature is about 10°C or lower. Warm and cold air masses both affect **temperate** climates. Middle latitudes have temperate climates. Temperate climates have average temperatures between those of tropical

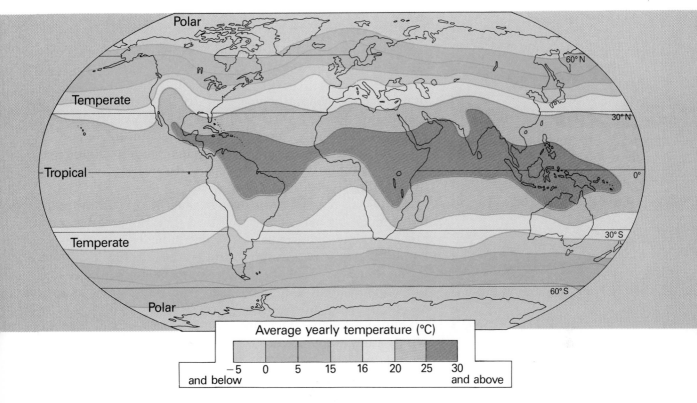

Average yearly temperature (°C)

−5 and below	0	5	15	16	20	25	30 and above

and polar climates. The difference between summer and winter temperatures in temperate climates is much greater than in tropical or polar climates.

Elevation affects temperature. St. Louis, Missouri, and Denver, Colorado, have similar latitudes. Yet the average yearly temperature in St. Louis is 13°C, while Denver's average is only 10°C. Recall from Chapter 17 that the higher you go in the troposphere, the lower the air temperature. St. Louis has an elevation of 162 meters above sea level. Denver has an elevation of 1610 meters. Denver is cooler than St. Louis because Denver has a greater elevation.

The third factor that determines air temperature is distance from an ocean or sea. Water temperatures change more slowly than land temperatures. Thus, coastal areas are generally warmer in winter and cooler in summer than inland areas. Seattle, Washington, and Bismarck, North Dakota, are at about the same latitude. But their temperature patterns are different because Seattle is near the ocean, while Bismarck is inland.

Oceans affect the temperature of nearby land areas in another way. A warm ocean current, the Gulf Stream, flows close to the east coast of the United States. The Gulf Stream makes the climate of the East Coast slightly warmer than it would be for its latitude. Likewise, cool ocean currents make climates cooler than they would be otherwise.

Figure 20-2 Latitude has a major effect on climate. In which climate zone does most of the United States lie?

Climate and Precipitation

Another important condition that describes climate is precipitation. Latitude affects precipitation. Recall that clouds most often form in rising, low-pressure air. Sinking, high-pressure air is generally clear and dry. In Figure 20-4, notice that many deserts, areas with less than 25 centimeters of precipitation yearly, have latitudes of about 30° N and 30° S. At these latitudes, sinking air means that few clouds form and little rain falls. Thirty degrees north and south are sometimes called the desert latitudes.

Humid air masses form over oceans. If prevailing winds move moist air masses over an area, then the area has more rain and snow than usual for its latitude. The southeastern United States is in a desert latitude. Yet rain levels are high in the Southeast because winds carry moist air masses from the Gulf of Mexico. In India, seasonal wind patterns carry moist air over land, causing heavy monsoon rains.

Landforms can affect precipitation. In Oregon, westerly winds carry moist air from the ocean over the Coast Range mountains, as illustrated in Figure 20-5. The mountains force the air to rise and cool. Clouds form, removing moisture from the air. As the air sinks and warms on the eastern side of the mountains, it becomes even less humid. Precipitation at Tillamook, Oregon, is higher than at Portland, Oregon, which is east of the Coast Ranges. What happens to rain patterns as air moves over the Cascade Range?

If you have a garden, you have probably noticed maps on seed packages. The maps show when to plant seeds in different parts of the country. Climate limits the types of plants that grow in a certain location. For example, palm trees grow best in tropical climates.

Figure 20-3 *Top:* A dry climate; *Bottom:* A humid climate

Figure 20-4 World map showing yearly precipitation

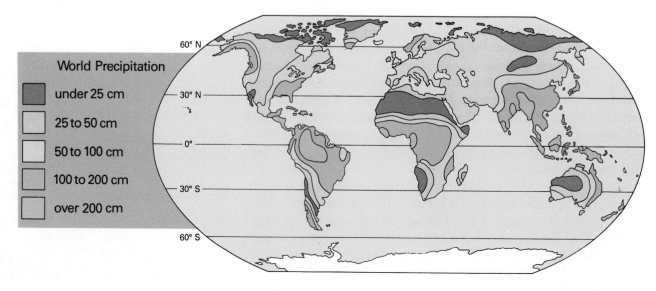

World Precipitation

- under 25 cm
- 25 to 50 cm
- 50 to 100 cm
- 100 to 200 cm
- over 200 cm

60° N
30° N
0°
30° S
60° S

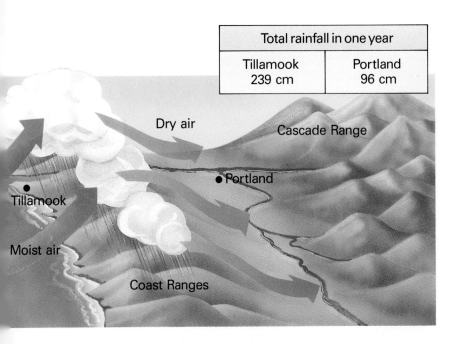

Total rainfall in one year	
Tillamook 239 cm	Portland 96 cm

Dry air

Cascade Range

● Portland

Tillamook

Moist air

Coast Ranges

Figure 20-5 Prevailing winds force moist ocean air up over the mountains in western Oregon. This results in more rain on the western mountain slopes.

Temperature differences affect plants on a local scale too. Small areas with distinct temperature and moisture patterns are called **microclimates.** For example, buildings and blacktop in cities absorb more solar energy than grassy areas do. A city creates its own microclimate that is warmer than nearby farmland. A microclimate can be even smaller than a city. The shady side of a tree trunk allows algae and moss to grow. Humid spaces between your toes can encourage athlete's foot fungus to grow. Cities, tree trunks, and toe spaces are all examples of microclimates.

Climate Change

Figuring out Earth's past climates is like working a jigsaw puzzle without its picture. Human history helps complete a tiny portion of the puzzle. Plants, oceans, glaciers, and rocks provide older evidence. For example, rings in bristlecone pine trees give clues about rain, drought, fires, and earthquakes in the Southwest for the past 8000 years. Plant pollen in ancient lake beds shows that, 11 000 years ago, Georgia and East Texas had climates like central Canada has today. Material trapped in glaciers tells about the atmosphere for the past 100 000 years. Fossils in some ocean sediments show temperatures for the past half million years. The rock record provides a few puzzle pieces that are even older.

Climate clues show that, for most of the past million years, Earth has been cooler than it is now. There are clues for several periods when continental glaciers were common. An **ice age** is the name for a period during which glacial ice covers a large part of Earth.

Figure 20-6 This scientist is slicing open a core of glacial ice to study it. The special clothing protects the ice sample from the scientist's breath and skin.

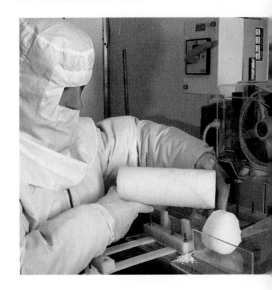

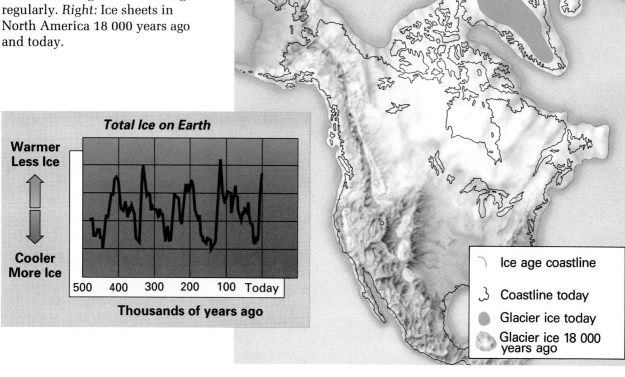

Figure 20-7 *Left:* Data suggest that the amount of glacier ice changes regularly. *Right:* Ice sheets in North America 18 000 years ago and today.

Total Ice on Earth

Warmer
Less Ice

Cooler
More Ice

500 400 300 200 100 Today

Thousands of years ago

Ice age coastline

Coastline today

Glacier ice today

Glacier ice 18 000 years ago

The last ice age reached its peak about 18 000 years ago. At that time, ice covered 30 percent of Earth. In between ice ages, ice sheets melt back. You live in one of the periods between ice ages. There are continental glaciers on Earth today, but they are not as large as during an ice age. Look at the temperature patterns shown in Figure 20-7 *(left).* From these data, do you think there will be another ice age?

Causes of Climate Change

What causes climate change? Incoming energy from the sun usually balances outgoing energy from Earth. If the energy in or the energy out changes, Earth's temperature and its climates also change. Changes in the sun's energy, Earth's motions, and Earth's atmosphere may all affect climate.

During an unusual period from 1645–1715, there were no visible sunspots, meaning that the sun gave off less energy. The lack of sunspots occurred in the middle of an unusually cold period on Earth. Some researchers think there is a connection between sunspots and climate change. Others say that it is just a coincidence.

The shape of Earth's orbit changes from more circular to more oval. This change happens in a cycle lasting about 100 000 years. Evidence suggests that ice ages happen in

Fact or Fiction?

Imagine a desert scene. Do you think of a hot, sandy place? Deserts do not have to be sandy or even hot. In fact, some desert areas lie over oceans, and others are frigid. One definition of a *desert* is a place that has less than 25.4 cm of precipitation per year. High-pressure belts, at the poles and at 30° N and S latitude, extend over both land and water. Sinking air at these latitudes results in less than 25.4 cm of precipitation per year. This means that by this definition, oceans and ice caps can be deserts!

cycles of about 100 000 years. This coincidence has led to the hypothesis that Earth's motions affect climate. Earth's axis also changes—sometimes it tilts more than 23½°, sometimes less. When Earth's orbit is circular and its tilt is less than 23½°, an ice age may begin. Summer may be cooler and winter may be warmer. Snow would still fall during warmer winters, but it would not melt during cooler summers. However, scientists do not all agree that changes in Earth motions could cause ice ages.

Earth's atmosphere may affect the energy balance. In 1816, people wore winter coats to July fourth parades, and snow still lay on the ground in June. This unusual summer happened the year after a volcano erupted. Some volcanic gases form acid droplets in the atmosphere. The droplets and dust may have blocked the sun's energy.

Changes in temperature can actually cause changes in temperature. For example, suppose lower temperatures mean that more snow is left on the ground. Snow reflects the sun's energy away from Earth. Earth heats less with more snow on it. Lower temperatures mean that snow stays on larger areas of the ground. More snow reflects more energy. In this way, a small change in the snow on the ground could lead to a major climate change. This is an example of a feedback process. In a **feedback process,** a change results in an effect that then causes more change. Feedback processes may cause climate changes.

Scientists agree that no single cause explains all climate changes. However, studying past climates can help explain how today's climates may be changing.

Figure 20-8 If volcano dust reaches the upper atmosphere, it may block the sun's energy. Lower worldwide temperatures may result.

Lesson Review 20.1

1. What is climate? Name two conditions that describe climate.
2. List three factors that affect temperature patterns in an area. Explain the effect of each.
3. List three factors that affect precipitation patterns in an area. Explain the effect of each.
4. List some evidence that suggests climates have changed.
5. Describe three possible causes of climate change.

Interpret and Apply

6. Places on the eastern shores of the Great Lakes receive more snow and rain than places on the western shores. Explain why this is true.

ACTIVITY 20.1   General Supplies

COMPARING MICROCLIMATES

Purpose   To identify a microclimate by measuring its conditions, and to verify the results of the measurements.

Materials

small paper plate	cellophane tape
pencil	wet- and dry-bulb
half an index card	thermometers
scissors	(from Activity 18.1)

Procedure

1. Read all instructions for this activity before you begin your work. Make two data tables like the one shown.

2. To make a wind speed device, poke a pencil through the small paper plate. **CAUTION: Do not poke the pencil into your hand.** Tape half an index card around your pencil so the card moves freely. Mark and label the plate as shown in the figure. To measure wind speed, turn slowly until the index card catches some wind. Record the mark the card moves to.

3. Choose two places to take measurements. One place should be on asphalt or concrete. The other place should be grassy or near trees.

4. For three days, measure and record the temperature, relative humidity, and wind speed just above the ground in both locations. Be sure to do the following:

   ▪ Use the thermometers to find relative humidity as described in Activity 18.1.

   ▪ Make your measurements at about the same time of day, in the air just above the ground.

   ▪ If you are in a sunny place, shade the thermometers with a piece of cardboard before making measurements.

Collecting and Analyzing Data

Data Table for _____ Location			
Date/Time	Temperature (°__)	Relative Humidity (%)	Wind Speed
Average			

1. Find the average temperature, relative humidity, and wind speed for each location. Record the averages.

2. How are the average readings for the two locations different?

3. Why was it important to take your readings at the same time of day?

Drawing Conclusions

4. What role might wind speed have in determining temperature? In determining relative humidity?

5. Did you notice any evidence that microclimates affected plants or animals in the two locations?

20.2 Air Pollution

Have you ever seen a hazy cloud of air over a city or highway? Has the air ever made your eyes burn? Does anyone in your family have lung problems? Do you use sunscreen more often because of possible changes in the ozone layer? If you answer yes to any of these questions, you have been affected by changes in the atmosphere. Many of these disturbing changes are caused by air pollution.

Air pollution affects you on two levels: regional and global. Regional air pollution affects an area the size of a city, state, or even several states. Global air pollution affects the atmosphere all over the world, no matter where the pollution came from.

If you ask several people, "What is polluted air," you may get several answers. The Environmental Protection Agency (EPA) uses this definition when it brings polluters to court: "Polluted air contains contaminants in sufficient quantity and for a long enough time to be harmful to plants, animals, or property. Such contaminants are called **pollutants**." The term *contaminant* means "something that makes the air unfit to use." Air pollutants include solids, liquids, and gases.

Regional Air Pollution

At some time, you have probably seen dust particles moving in a ray of sunlight. Dust is a common example of a particulate. **Particulates** [pər tik′ yə ləts] are solid particles or liquid droplets that are small enough to hang in the air. Table 20-1 on page 528 lists examples of particulates.

You can see and avoid some particulates, such as those in thick smoke. However, many gas pollutants are invisible and odorless. Three quarters of all regional air pollutants, by weight, are gases. Table 20-1 lists and describes several common gas air pollutants and their effects.

Lesson Objectives

▸ **Define** polluted air *and* **apply** *the definition.*

▸ **List** *regional and global air pollutants and their major sources.*

▸ **Compare** *the effects of regional and global air pollution.*

▸ **Activity** **Perform an experiment** *to compare air pollutants from several sources.*

New Terms

pollutants
particulates
smog
greenhouse gases
global warming
chlorofluorocarbons

Figure 20-9 Examples of particulates, magnified; *Left:* car exhaust, *Middle:* backyard dust, *Right:* power-plant particulates

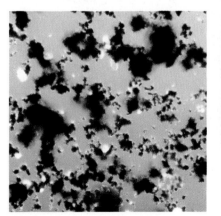  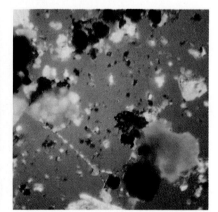

Table 20-1 Regional Air Pollutants

Pollutant and Description	Sources (*indicates greatest human-made sources)	Effects
particulates: solid particles or liquid drops	Natural: volcanoes, soil erosion, fires Human-made: *factories, *power plants, worn tires and brakes 	dirty surfaces; haze; blocking of sun's energy; lung disease
carbon monoxide: colorless, odorless gas made of C, O	Natural: forest fires Human-made: *car, bus, and truck exhaust, factories, home furnaces, cigarettes 	dizziness; headache; death if high levels
sulfur dioxide: colorless gas, choking odor, made of S, O	Natural: volcanoes, oceans Human-made: *power plants, ore smelting 	damages plants and animals, forms acid rain when dissolved in water
nitrogen dioxide: brownish gas made of N, O	Natural: lightning, soil bacteria Human-made: *car, bus, and truck exhaust, *high-temperature factory furnaces 	irritates eyes and lungs, forms acid rain when dissolved in water
hydrocarbons: group of gases made of H, C	Natural: fragrant plant oils Human-made: *spilled gasoline, *factories, oil burners, cigarettes, spray cans 	form smog, cause cancer

In Table 20-1, notice that each substance has natural as well as human sources. If a substance is natural, how can it be a pollutant? To answer this question, first think about the definition of polluted air. Polluted air has enough of a pollutant to make the air unfit to use. However, normal amounts of substances are not pollutants. Natural cycles remove normal amounts of substances from the air. For example, the nitrogen cycle, illustrated in Figure 17-3 on page 447, removes some nitrogen dioxide from the air. Natural sources of nitrogen dioxide, such as lightning, are spread out over large areas. In contrast, human sources of nitrogen dioxide, such as city traffic and factories, are close together. Near cities, natural cycles cannot remove nitrogen dioxide fast enough, and the air becomes polluted.

Pollutants can combine and form new pollutants. For example, **smog** results when energy from the sun causes a chemical reaction between nitrogen oxides and hydrocarbons. Generally, nitrogen oxides and hydrocarbons do not occur together naturally. However, these two pollutants often occur together in cities. From Table 20-1, what sources can you name for nitrogen oxides and hydrocarbons?

One of the most harmful gases in smog is ozone. Surprisingly, ozone, which protects you as a layer in the stratosphere, pollutes the air at ground level. Ozone irritates your eyes, nose, and throat. Ozone can cause asthma, stunt plant growth, and damage rubber, nylon, and other materials. Some schools cancel recess when ozone levels are high. Ozone at ground level also adds to the greenhouse effect.

Figure 20-10 Some of the air pollution from this source is visible. However, almost 80 percent of all air pollution is invisible gases.

Reducing Regional Pollution

Each year the United States dumps about 130 million metric tons of pollutants into the air. That amount is more than half a metric ton for every person in the country. Transportation—cars, trucks, planes, and other vehicles—causes 47 percent of these pollutants. Electric power plants and heating contribute another 30 percent of air pollutants. Factories add another 14 percent.

National and local governments have taken steps to reduce pollutants from cars. In some states, cars must pass a pollution test every year. Cars made for sale in the United States since 1974 have pollution-control devices. Most of these cars also run on unleaded gasoline. Cars made since 1989 must travel at least 27 miles (43 kilometers) on each gallon (3.8 liters) of gasoline. Even higher mileage standards are planned for the future. By burning less gasoline, cars give off fewer pollutants. Can you think of some ways you can help reduce pollution from cars?

A C T I V I T Y 2 0 . 2   *Lab Equipment*

AIR POLLUTANTS

Purpose   To perform an experiment that compares air pollutants.

Materials

500-mL Pyrex beaker	5 half sheets of
small metal jar lid	plain white paper
paper towel	matches (from your
wool cloth	teacher)
wood shaving	scouring powder
petroleum jelly	lab apron
	safety goggles

Procedure

1. Read all instructions for this activity. Bring all materials outside on a calm day. Put on your apron and goggles.

2. Place a 3- by 3-cm square of paper towel on the jar lid. Write *paper towel* on one of the half sheets of paper. Place the lid in the center of the paper.

3. Obtain a match from your teacher. Carefully light the paper towel. **CAUTION: Keep hair and clothing away from an open flame.** Quickly cover the burning paper with the beaker.

4. Observe the towel as it burns. Observe the color of the smoke and any moisture and particles on the beaker. Carefully observe the odor by gently waving a little smoke toward your nose from a distance. Examine the paper from under the beaker. Save the paper from under the beaker as part of your data.

5. Clean the beaker and lid with scouring powder at the wash station, as directed by your teacher. Dry the beaker and lid.

6. Label a second half-sheet of paper *petroleum jelly*. Place the lid on the paper. Carefully smear a little petroleum jelly on a 3- by 3-cm square of paper towel.

7. Place the towel on the lid. Light the paper towel and quickly place the beaker over the lid. Observe, record, and wash up as you did before.

8. Repeat step 7 for wool and wood. Do not burn any other materials without your teacher's permission.

9. When you finish, clean up all your materials and bring them back indoors.

Collecting and Analyzing Data

1. Which samples gave off moisture when burned? Describe your evidence.

2. Which samples gave off solids as they burned? Describe your evidence.

3. Which samples do you think gave off other gases when burned? Describe your evidence.

Drawing Conclusions

4. Which samples do you think caused the most pollutants? Be sure to check the definition of *polluted air*. In your answer, list the evidence you have.

Global Air Pollution

Carbon dioxide in the atmosphere has increased 25 percent since the end of the 1800's. During that time, cars and factories have increased and forests have decreased. Figure 20-11 illustrates the carbon cycle. In the carbon cycle, trees and other plants take in carbon dioxide as they make food. After trees are cut down, they no longer use carbon dioxide. Instead, cut trees give off carbon dioxide as they decay or burn. Cars and factories release carbon dioxide as they burn fuel.

Carbon dioxide is one of several **greenhouse gases,** which are gases that help heat the atmosphere. Greenhouse gases include carbon dioxide, water vapor, ozone in smog, methane, and nitrous oxide. You might use methane at home as natural gas. Nitrous oxide forms when fuels burn. The increasing amounts of greenhouse gases concern many people. Unlike regional pollutants, which affect small areas, greenhouse gases affect people worldwide. The term **global warming** describes predicted temperature increases due to an increase in greenhouse gases. Researchers fear that rapid global warming may cause harmful changes.

Some air pollutants are not part of any natural cycle. **Chlorofluorocarbons,** [klōr' ō flür' ō kär benz] or CFC's, are a group of chemicals containing chlorine, fluorine, and carbon. CFC's push liquids or powders out of some spray cans. CFC's are also used in the coils of refrigerators and air conditioners. In factories, CFC's clean computer parts and puff up some plastic foam products. CFC's enter the atmosphere from these spray cans, factories, and leaky air conditioners.

Figure 20-11 Plants, animals, soil, and the oceans are all part of the natural carbon cycle. How are human activities adding more carbon dioxide to the atmosphere?

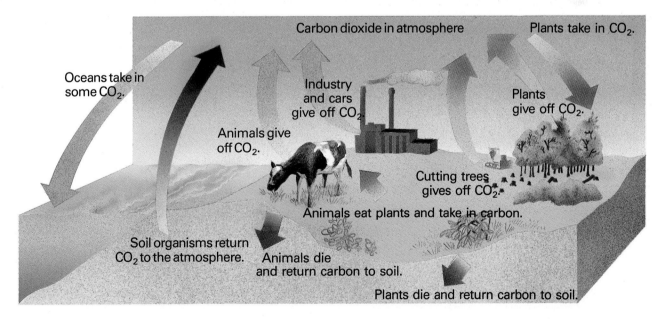

Carbon dioxide in atmosphere

Plants take in CO$_2$.

Oceans take in some CO$_2$.

Industry and cars give off CO$_2$.

Plants give off CO$_2$.

Animals give off CO$_2$.

Cutting trees gives off CO$_2$.

Animals eat plants and take in carbon.

Soil organisms return CO$_2$ to the atmosphere.

Animals die and return carbon to soil.

Plants die and return carbon to soil.

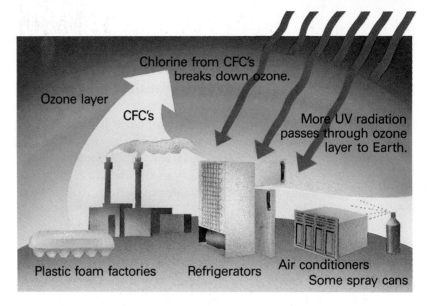

Figure 20-12 When CFC's reach the stratosphere, they break down and release chlorine, which destroys ozone.

CFC's may be weakening the ozone layer in the stratosphere. You learned in Chapter 17 that the ozone layer prevents ultraviolet radiation from reaching Earth. In the stratosphere, ultraviolet radiation releases chlorine from CFC's. Chlorine from CFC's destroys ozone molecules. Less ozone means less protection from ultraviolet radiation. The Environmental Protection Agency predicts that ozone loss will cause millions of people to get skin cancer. Not only that, but CFC's are 10 000 times more effective than carbon dioxide at trapping heat. Thus, CFC's also add to the greenhouse effect. The United States banned the use of CFC's in spray cans in the 1970's. CFC's are still used in factories, refrigerators, and air conditioners. Many nations plan to reduce these chemicals, or get rid of them, by the year 2000.

Lesson Review 20.2

7. Define the term *polluted air*.

8. List the five most common regional air pollutants and mention their major sources.

9. How can ozone be harmful in some locations and helpful in others?

Interpret and Apply

10. Some people argue that CFC's and carbon dioxide are not air pollutants. After all, no one knows whether CFC's are harmful to breathe, and carbon dioxide is necessary for life. Do you agree or disagree with their reasoning? Support your answer with information from this lesson.

20.3 *Preserving The Atmosphere*

What determines your final adult height? Perhaps your parents are tall or short. Your diet or health may have something to do with it. It is difficult to know exactly what your final height will be. Earth scientists face a similar problem when they try to predict climate change.

Predicting Climate Change

Scientists compare climate patterns from past years to predict climate for future years. The graph in Figure 20-13 shows that Earth's average temperature has increased over the past century. Does this mean that Earth is warming up? It is difficult to know for sure. The pattern in ice age data, shown in Figure 20-7 *(left)*, suggests Earth should be cooling. But that pattern is based on data from the distant past. Human activities, like factories and cars, started affecting climate about 100 years ago. Not enough data have been collected to be sure about climate patterns today.

In recent years, scientists have designed computer programs that imitate climates on Earth. These **climate models** are based on known data about Earth's climates. Climate models help predict changes caused by changing conditions. For example, suppose you add carbon dioxide to the atmosphere in a climate model, then run the program. The program imitates how today's climates would change if more carbon dioxide were added to the atmosphere.

Some conditions are too poorly understood to be put into climate models. For example, ocean water absorbs carbon dioxide from the atmosphere. But greenhouse warming may make oceans give off carbon dioxide, just like a warm soft drink going flat. More carbon dioxide from the ocean would mean more greenhouse warming—another example of a feedback process.

Lesson Objectives

▸ **Discuss** the difficulties in predicting climate change.

▸ **List** possible effects of global warming due to greenhouse gases.

▸ **Describe** some actions you can take to slow down climate change.

▸ **Activity**   **Graph data** for sea-level rise and **predict** future sea-level changes.

New Term

climate model

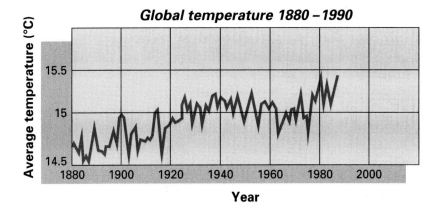

Global temperature 1880 – 1990

Average temperature (°C) / Year

Figure 20-13 Why is it important to look at the temperature change over a period of many years, rather than just a few years?

The Atmosphere and the Environment **533**

Figure 20-14 The roles of oceans and clouds in climate change are not yet well understood.

Warmer ocean water can also lead to more clouds. Clouds are difficult to deal with in climate models. High cirrus clouds allow the sun's energy in but prevent energy from leaving, which would warm Earth. On the other hand, low clouds reflect the sun's energy and could cool Earth. There are not enough data yet to predict whether oceans and clouds would make Earth warmer or cooler.

Effects of Global Warming

Climate models predict that if today's trends continue, Earth's average temperature would rise by 1 to 5 Celsius degrees by the year 2050. Five degrees may seem small, but small changes have large effects. An increase of only 3°C would give San Francisco an average temperature like San Diego has today. New York would be as warm as Atlanta. Boston would be as warm as Washington, D.C.

No one knows exactly how global warming would change Earth. One likely effect is that glacial ice would melt, adding water to the oceans. If warming trends continue, sea level could rise as much as 80 centimeters by the year 2050. Some coastal cities could end up below sea level.

Polar temperatures are predicted to increase more than temperatures near the equator. If polar temperatures rise, the polar front could shift. If the polar front shifted, storms may occur further north. Less rain might fall at middle latitudes. Much of North America could be drier—perhaps too dry to farm.

Figure 20-15 If global warming occurs, then glaciers may melt, causing a rise in sea level.

GRAPHING SEA-LEVEL CHANGES

Purpose To predict future sea-level changes, based on a graph of recent patterns of change.

Materials
graph paper   colored pencil or pen
pencil   ruler

Procedure

1. Read all the instructions for this activity before you begin your work.

2. On your graph paper, set up your graph. Label your horizontal axis *Year* and make the scale from 1900 to 2050. Label your vertical axis *Change (cm)* and make the scale from 0 to 50.

3. Plot the data from the data table onto your graph. Remember to plot years on the horizontal axis and sea level on the vertical axis.

4. Connect the data points on your graph.

5. Place one end of your ruler on the graph at 1900. Move the other end of your ruler until about half of the data points are above the ruler and about half are below. Use the colored pencil to draw a straight line. Extend the line to the year 2050. This line shows the general trend of sea-level change.

Collecting and Analyzing Data

1. Does sea level seem to be increasing or decreasing at New York City?

2. About how much did sea level rise between 1900 and 1985?

3. Calculate the average sea-level rise for New York City for the period 1900 to 1985. To do this, divide the rise in cm by the number of years.

Data Table Sea-Level Rise at New York City Compared to 1900	
Year	Rise (cm)
1900	0
1905	0
1910	6
1915	6
1920	9
1925	6
1930	6
1935	9
1940	15
1945	15
1950	12
1955	18
1960	18
1965	18
1970	24
1975	18
1980	18
1985	24

Drawing Conclusions

4. Rivers entering the ocean dump sediments offshore from New York City. These sediments press down Earth's crust. How might these sediments affect sea level in New York City?

5. Use your graph to make a prediction for sea level in 2000. Explain.

6. Make a prediction for 2050. Are you as sure about this prediction as you are about the one for 2000? Explain.

7. How could changes in human activity affect the rate of sea-level rise between now and 2050? Explain your answers.

8. What changes in your behavior or lifestyle could help slow the rate of sea-level rise in the future? Explain.

Slowing Global Warming

Humans are causing climate change faster than they can find out how climate works. Today no one knows for certain what the effects of greenhouse gases will be. Even so, people have to decide today what to do, because tomorrow may be too late. These decisions can cost billions of dollars. For example, should low-lying cities such as New Orleans start building sea walls? If the cities wait long enough to be sure sea levels are rising, floods could come before sea walls are built. Even though more research is needed, there are simpler actions that nations and individuals can take now to slow global warming.

Many of the ways to reduce greenhouse gases also conserve fuel. For example, if cars, factories, and appliances are more efficient, there will be less air pollution and less fuel use. Some governments plan to require fuel efficiency for items made and used in their nations. Some companies are working to develop nonpolluting energy sources, such as solar and wind power. Other companies are looking for chemicals to replace CFC's. The Environmental Awareness feature lists some ways you can help slow global warming.

The possible results of rapid global warming and ozone loss are frightening. However, concern about the atmosphere brings together scientists, government workers, and citizens from all over the world. People are beginning to see the need to work together to save their common planet, Earth.

Figure 20-16 You can help slow global warming in a number of ways.

ENVIRONMENTAL AWARENESS

Reducing Global Warming

Students in San Jacinto, California, are helping to slow global warming. They collected 76 dollars for the New Forests project. This organization provides tree seeds to people in developing countries. Students at their "sister school" in a Philippine village will start the 3500 tree seeds in class, and then take the young trees home to plant. In addition to absorbing carbon dioxide, the new trees will provide food, fuel, and erosion control for the village.

You can help slow global warming in other ways. Reduce greenhouse gases by using less fossil fuel. Walk, ride a bike, or take a bus instead of a car for short trips. Turn off appliances when you are not using them. Fossil fuel energy is used to make cans, bottles, paper, and other products you use. Often, less fuel is needed to reprocess materials that you recycle. Remember that living trees absorb carbon dioxide and help reduce greenhouse warming. ■

Lesson Review 20.3

11. How are climate models useful for predicting climate change?

12. Explain why climate models are not completely reliable for predicting climate change. Give an example to support your answer.

13. List three possible effects of global warming.

14. Explain why there is concern about global warming even though its effects are not yet fully understood.

Interpret and Apply

15. Describe three actions you could take to help slow global warming. Explain why each action would help reduce global warming.

Chapter Summary

Read this summary of main ideas in the chapter. If any are not clear to you, go back and review that lesson.

20.1 Climate

■ Climate describes the weather patterns in an area over a period of years. The two conditions used to describe climate are temperature and precipitation.

■ Latitude, elevation, and distance from large bodies of water all help determine the climate of an area.

■ Evidence suggests that Earth's climates have changed throughout its history. Theories for explaining climate change include changes in the sun's energy, changes in Earth's motions, volcanoes, snow cover, and the greenhouse effect.

20.2 Air Pollution

■ Polluted air contains contaminants in enough quantity and for a long enough time to be harmful to living things or property.

■ Regional pollution affects part of Earth's surface. Major sources of local air pollutants include vehicles, homes, factories, forest fires, and volcanoes.

■ Global air pollution affects all of Earth. Carbon dioxide, water vapor, CFC's, methane, surface ozone, and nitrous oxide each contribute to the greenhouse effect. CFC's also destroy ozone in the stratosphere.

20.3 Preserving The Atmosphere

■ Climate change is difficult to predict because there are not enough data, and some variables are unknown.

■ Climate models suggest that global warming will affect Earth. Some possible effects of global warming include rising sea levels, shifting weather patterns, and changes in farmland productivity.

■ Global warming could be slowed by efficient energy use, use of alternate energy sources, recycling, and replacement of CFC's with less harmful chemicals.

Chapter Review

■ Vocabulary

chlorofluorocarbon
climate
climate model
feedback process
global warming
greenhouse gas
ice age

microclimate
particulates
polar
pollutant
smog
temperate
tropical

■ Concept Mapping

Use the method of concept mapping described on pages 3–5 to complete a concept map for *global warming*. Use at least five terms from the vocabulary list. Use additional terms for concepts and links as you need them.

■ Review

Number your paper from 1 to 23. On your paper, write the word or words that best complete each sentence.

1. Temperature and precipitation patterns over a long period determine a place's _____ .

2. Lower temperatures result when you increase your _____ or your latitude.

3. The shady floor of a forest is an example of a(n) _____ .

4. Tree rings, glacier layers, and ocean floor sediments all provide evidence that Earth's climates have _____ .

5. Earth's surface temperature depends on a(n) _____ between energy coming in from the sun and energy going out to space.

6. _____ climates are affected mostly by warm air masses from near the equator.

7. A(n) _____ is a period during which glaciers cover a large part of Earth.

8. Volcanic eruptions, _____ , and _____ are possible natural causes for climate change.

9. The largest source of regional air pollution in the United States is _____ .

10. Most of the United States is affected by both warm and cold air masses and thus has a(n) _____ climate.

11. _____ release chlorine, which is thought to destroy ozone in the stratosphere.

12. Energy from the sun causes nitrogen oxides and hydrocarbons to combine to form _____ .

13. A(n) _____ is a substance that can cause harm to living things or property.

14. Carbon dioxide from human activity is considered to be a(n) _____ , because natural cycles cannot remove it from the air quickly enough to prevent harm.

15. A(n) _____ is a pollutant that occurs as solid specks or liquid droplets.

16. _____ is a gas that protects Earth as a layer in the stratosphere but is a pollutant at ground level.

17. Using cars less often, saving energy, planting trees, and recycling are all ways to reduce the _____ effect.

18. Carbon dioxide, water vapor, methane, CFC's, and nitrous oxide are all examples of _____ gases, which are gases that cause global warming.

19. Sea-level rise, shifts in weather patterns, and drought may all result from the effects of _____ warming.

20. A(n) _____ is one in which a change to a system can result in even more change.

21. The roles of oceans and _____ are examples of variables that are too complicated to predict for future climates.

22. Living trees take in _____ and thus help reduce global warming.

23. Belts of sinking, high-pressure air with few clouds result in _____ climates at 30° N and 30° S latitudes.

■ *Interpret and Apply*

On your paper, answer each question.

24. Choose the statement that best expresses current predictions about global warming. Then explain your reasons for choosing that statement.

 a. Earth's temperature will definitely increase by 5 Celsius degrees by the year 2050.
 b. Greenhouse warming will probably occur due to greenhouse gases already in the atmosphere.
 c. Oceans will probably absorb carbon dioxide, and thus prevent greenhouse warming.

25. What effect could global warming have on the number of hurricanes formed each year? Explain your answer.

26. City drivers stuck in tunnels in rush-hour traffic sometimes complain of dizziness and occasionally have accidents as a result. Why does this happen? What pollutant is probably involved? How could drivers avoid these problems?

27. As you climb a high mountain, you see plant zones change in much the same way as if you were traveling toward the poles. What might happen to plant patterns on a mountain as a result of global warming?

28. A few years ago, people who live in a rain forest protested the cutting of rain forest trees. They were told by an official of their government, "If cutting rain forest causes warmer weather and less rain, it will benefit my golf game." What arguments could you use to persuade the government official to limit the cutting of rain forest trees?

29. In 1975, the United States government funded a study of Africa's climate during the last ice age. A senator criticized this study as a waste of taxpayers' money. Do you agree or disagree? Support your answer with evidence and examples.

■ *Writing in Science*

30. Writers need to consider who will be reading what they have written. Imagine that you are writing about air pollution. You want to convince people to reduce their use of fossil fuels. Choose one of the following groups of people and write an explanation that emphasizes how air pollution can affect those people.

 a. farmers
 b. people who live along the seacoast
 c. residents of large cities.

■ *Critical Thinking*

Read the following political advertisement and answer questions 31–34.

Power For Your Hometown

Your vote on whether to build the Lottawatts coal power plant can affect your world tomorrow. You may have heard that gases from a coal power plant cause global warming. The fact is, gases from a coal power plant, such as carbon dioxide, are natural substances. It's also a fact that your car gives off some of the same gases that a coal power plant gives off. Coal power plants might actually help cool Earth by giving off particulates, which reflect solar radiation. Thus, your vote for the Lottawatts power plant could help balance global warming and cooling, while bringing power to your hometown.

31. What opinion about the new power plant is presented in the advertisement?

32. List two facts in the advertisement. Do you agree that the facts support the opinion?

33. The advertisement states that carbon and nitrogen compounds are natural. Is it logical to conclude that natural compounds cannot cause global warming? Explain.

34. Think of some ways you could gather more facts and opinions about coal power plants before you decided how to vote.

SCIENTISTS SHOW LINK BETWEEN DEATH OF FORESTS AND ACID RAIN

Issue: *How should the United States reduce pollution that causes acid rain?*

Trees all across the Northeast are dying. Needles on the spruce and fir trees turn brown and fall off. Eventually, the forests look almost as though a fire had swept through. What causes the death of so many trees? Many scientists think the culprit is acid rain.

Acid rain is caused by pollutants such as sulfur dioxide (SO_2) and nitrogen oxides (NO and NO_2). These gases dissolve in cloud droplets to form sulfuric acid and nitric acid. Sulfur dioxide and nitrogen oxides are given off by cars, power plants, and factories that burn fossil fuels. The only way to stop acid rain is to reduce this pollution.

Acid rain causes far-reaching damage. Over time, acid rain can react with city buildings, slowly eating them away. Acid rain causes soil, streams, and lakes to become more acidic.

In the worst cases, acid rain has killed animals and plants in affected waters. Scientists think acid rain is destroying forests that are downwind of industrial areas in Europe, the United States, and Canada.

New technologies can reduce fossil-fuel pollution by more than 50 percent.

The best way to reduce pollution that causes acid rain is to burn less fossil fuels. Hydroelectric and nuclear power plants produce electric power without giving off pollutants that cause acid rain. Cities can reduce car pollution by expanding their mass transportation systems. Other options include electric cars and cars that run on gasoline substitutes that are less polluting.

When fossil fuels must be burned, there are several ways to reduce pollution. Catalytic converters remove nitrogen oxides from car exhausts. A new law requires carmakers to reduce car pollution by 60 percent before 1996. Power plant and factory smokestacks can be cleaned by "scrubbers," which remove 90 percent of the sulfur dioxide. New "clean-coal" power plants burn coal more efficiently. This reduces the amount of nitrogen oxides given off by 50 percent.

Unfortunately, all of the solutions to the acid rain problem cost a lot of money. Carmakers do not want to spend huge sums designing better catalytic converters and cars that run on gasoline substitutes. They argue that cars already are 96 percent cleaner than they were in the 1970's, when pollutant controls first were required. It will cost power companies billions of dollars to build clean-coal power plants and refit old power plants with scrubbers. Ultimately, the costs will be paid for by the consumer.

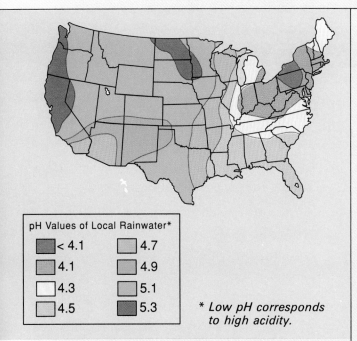

pH Values of Local Rainwater*

■ < 4.1		□ 4.7	
▨ 4.1		▨ 4.9	
□ 4.3		▨ 5.1	
□ 4.5		■ 5.3	

* Low pH corresponds to high acidity.

At present, only half of the coal-burning plants in the United States have pollution controls. Scrubbers could be added to existing power plants and factories within the next 15 years. But scrubbers only reduce the amount of sulfur dioxide given off. Clean-coal power plants reduce the pollution from both sulfur dioxide and nitrogen oxides. But it may take 50 years to replace all of the old power plants with clean-coal power plants.

Efforts to reduce acid rain are costly and will take many years.

Politics will play an important part in the solution to the acid rain problem. In the United States, midwestern states have big coal-burning plants that contribute to acid rain. However, the acid rain falls mostly in the Northeast. People from these two areas disagree about who should pay for reducing pollution and how soon it must be done.

Acid rain also is an international problem. Pollution from the United States causes up to 75 percent of the acid rain in Canada. In 1989, the United States signed a pact with Canada to reduce pollution. Acid rain often crosses borders in Europe, where many countries are close together. In the coming decades, countries will have to work together to solve the problems of acid rain.

Act on the Issue

Gather the Facts

1. Use library books and articles listed in the *Readers' Guide to Periodical Literature* to find out more about United States acid rain laws. Which states sponsored bills in Congress? Who pays for the cost of reducing pollution? Find out what compromises were made to pass these laws.

2. Use books and articles to find out more about how scrubbers reduce pollution from power plants and factories. How much do scrubbers cost? Is there any problem with the solid waste they produce? Write to the Environmental Protection Agency for more information.

Take Action

3. You are a member of Congress. Debate a bill that requires all 50 states to share the cost of putting scrubbers in power plants in the Midwest. Some students will represent midwestern states; others will represent northeastern states. A third group can represent states that are not directly involved. Decide how you will vote on this bill, and defend your position.

4. Make a poster that tells people how they can reduce pollution from their cars. For example, a well-tuned car will produce fewer pollutants. Emphasize that people can help the acid rain problem right now.

Earth's Water

You Know More Than You Think

You may be surprised at how much you already know about water. To find out, try to answer the following questions.

- What is the main difference between ocean water and fresh water?
- Where does your drinking water come from?
- How many oceans can you name?
- Can you think of any products you use that come from the ocean?
- Why don't ocean waves wash away all the beach sand?

When you finish this unit, answer these questions again to see how much you have learned.

Most of Earth's water is salty. Only a small amount of Earth's water is useful as a resource.

21 Freshwater Resources

Chapter Preview

*H*ave You Ever
WONDERED?

How did rain forests get their name?

Hundreds of years ago, people thought that trees made it rain. Christopher Columbus claimed that the afternoon rains in the lush forests of the West Indies were caused by the trees. In a way, Columbus was right. Recent studies of the Amazon Basin in Brazil show that 75 percent of the water taken in by trees is returned to the atmosphere. This is enough water vapor to produce clouds. When the clouds become thick enough, rain falls back on the trees, completing the cycle.

Trees are not the only source of the water vapor that forms rain clouds. Oceans, lakes, and even puddles contribute water to the atmosphere. It's a good thing they do. Without a continual supply of fresh water, there would be no life on Earth. In this chapter, you will learn about Earth's freshwater resources and how they are used.

21.1 Surface Water Resources

Lesson Objectives

▶ **Trace** the paths of the water cycle and **describe** the changes water goes through in that cycle.

▶ **List** ways in which lakes form and **describe** how lakes die.

▶ **Explain** how acids and bases are related to the pH scale.

▶ **Activity** **Measure** the acidity of freshwater samples.

New Terms

water cycle
pH scale

Imagine that you are hot and thirsty after a gym class. You push the button at the water fountain for a drink, but no water comes out. Only then do you see the sign below the fountain which reads, "Contaminated water. Fountain no longer in use." What is wrong with the water? Isn't clean, fresh water always available? In order to answer these questions, you need some information about how water changes as it moves from the earth to the atmosphere and back again.

The Water Cycle

For a planet mostly covered with water, Earth has a short supply of water suitable for drinking. Of all the water on Earth, only 3 percent is fresh. Of that 3 percent, more than two thirds is locked in the form of glacial ice. This leaves less than 1 percent of Earth's water available as a liquid to meet the freshwater needs of plants, animals, and humans.

Each day a million million (1 000 000 000 000) metric tons of Earth's water changes to water vapor. Most water vapor in the air evaporates from the ocean, lakes, rivers, and from the soil. A smaller amount of water vapor comes from plants and animals. For example, the leaves of one large oak tree release up to 150 000 liters of water into the air each year.

The air containing water vapor cools as it rises through the atmosphere. The water vapor condenses into clouds. If enough cloud droplets join together, the water falls back to

Figure 21-1 How often do you drink from a water fountain? What if you went to get a drink and no water came out?

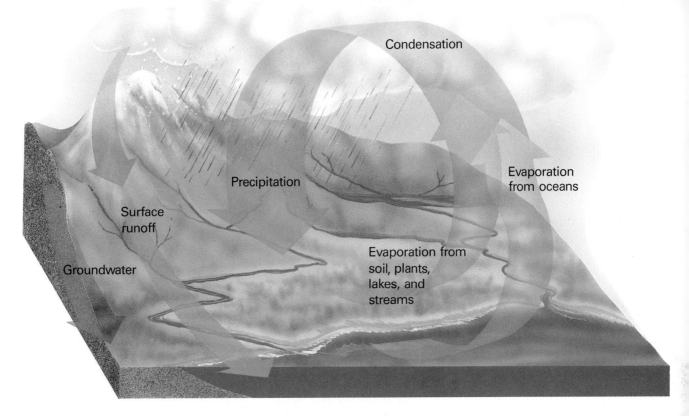

Condensation

Precipitation

Evaporation from oceans

Surface runoff

Evaporation from soil, plants, lakes, and streams

Groundwater

Earth as some form of precipitation. Most of the precipitation, about 70 percent, evaporates from the ground where it falls. Some of the rain sinks into the ground, where it becomes groundwater. Some of the rain runs off along the ground's surface into rivers and lakes and returns to the ocean, where it is eventually turned back into water vapor. This continuous recycling of Earth's water is illustrated in Figure 21-2. The process by which water evaporates from Earth's surface, condenses into clouds, falls as precipitation, and then evaporates again is called the **water cycle.**

For Earth as a whole, the amount of water that returns to the ground as precipitation is the same as the amount that evaporates. The small amount of water broken down into hydrogen and oxygen each year is replaced by new water from volcanic eruptions. In effect, there is no new water in the water cycle. Almost all the water that has ever been on Earth is still on Earth today. The water you drink today is perhaps the same water that a dinosaur drank long ago.

Pure, fresh water is still available because of the process of evaporation. When salt water evaporates, the salt is left behind. Only pure water leaves as water vapor. The same thing happens with polluted water in a river. Fresh water evaporates, and most pollutants are left in the remaining liquid water. However, as water vapor condenses, it can absorb or dissolve new pollutants, such as those that cause acid rain.

Figure 21-2 The water cycle

Figure 21-3 As the water in this stream evaporates, what becomes of the pollutants?

Figure 21-4 This lake in Alberta, Canada, was formed when glacial moraine dammed a mountain valley.

Fresh Water at the Surface

When you think of fresh water on Earth's surface, perhaps you think of the rivers and streams you studied in Chapter 13. Where else is fresh water being stored at Earth's surface? Some streams do not empty into other streams or into the ocean. Instead, they drain water into a lake. A lake is a body of water that fills an enclosed depression in Earth's surface. A pond is a smaller version of a lake, formed when water fills a smaller, shallower depression or basin.

The basins that allow water to collect and form lakes are caused by a wide variety of processes. Lakes are a common feature in those parts of the United States that were covered by glaciers in the last ice age. In areas where groundwater has weathered out caves beneath the surface, the ground sometimes collapses. Many ponds in Kentucky and Missouri are water-filled sinkholes. Blocking a river or stream creates a lake or pond. A dam might form when there is a landslide, or it could be built by humans.

Lakes and ponds have life cycles in much the same way as rivers. When it first forms, a lake contains pure, fresh water and little life. Plants and animals begin to live in the lake as it grows older. The organic material from the plants and animals provides nutrients for other life to grow. However, a lake is not a permanent feature. Sediment and organic material eventually fill the basin. After a length of time, ranging from a few decades to several thousand years, the lake disappears. The products of human activity, such as increased erosion from nearby development, can often shorten the life span of these bodies of fresh water.

Acid Lakes and Streams

Have you ever made lemonade from frozen concentrate? The lemonade tastes tangy because it contains citric acid. You know that the more water you add to the concentrate, the less tangy the lemonade tastes. The citric acid becomes less concentrated when you add water. Something that is less concentrated is also called dilute.

Acids are compounds that release hydrogen ions when dissolved in water. Bases are compounds that release hydroxide ions when dissolved in water. A hydroxide ion is made of one oxygen atom and one hydrogen atom. Bases are also described as alkaline. The **pH scale,** shown in Figure 21-5, is a rating system used to describe the concentration of hydrogen ions in a solution. The pH scale has a range of 0 to 14. A solution with a pH equal to 1 is a very strong acid. A strong acid contains a large amount of hydrogen ions and a small amount of hydroxide ions. A solution with a pH of 6 is a weak acid. The lower the pH, the stronger the acid. At the opposite end of the pH scale, the strongest base has a pH of 14. A strong base contains a small amount of hydrogen ions and a large amount of hydroxide ions. Strong acids and bases react easily.

A value of 7 on the pH scale is neutral, which means that a liquid with a pH of 7 is neither acid nor base. You might think that pure rainwater would be neutral. However, even the purest rain is a weak acid. From Chapter 12, you know that when carbon dioxide in the atmosphere dissolves in water vapor, it forms carbonic acid. Pure rainwater is dilute carbonic acid and has a pH of about 5.6. Acid rain is defined as rain that has a pH lower than 5.6.

Figure 21-5 On the pH scale, acid rain is anything lower than 5.6. Rain with a pH of 1.5 has been measured in Wheeling, West Virginia.

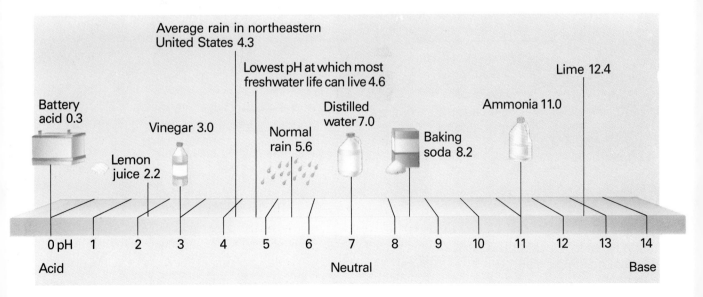

Average rain in northeastern United States 4.3

Lowest pH at which most freshwater life can live 4.6

Lime 12.4

Battery acid 0.3

Vinegar 3.0

Distilled water 7.0

Ammonia 11.0

Normal rain 5.6

Lemon juice 2.2

Baking soda 8.2

0 pH   1   2   3   4   5   6   7   8   9   10   11   12   13   14

Acid   Neutral   Base

Another important thing to know about acids and bases is that they have the ability to neutralize each other. In neutralization, mixing an acid and a base tends to make the resulting mixture closer to neutral on the pH scale.

Is acid rain neutralized after it reaches Earth's surface? Some of the acid rainwater runs into streams, ponds, or lakes. The rest sinks into the ground. The acid rainwater reacts with the rock and soil as it trickles through. Soils are related to the rocks from which they are formed. If the rocks or soil are natural bases, which are called alkaline, then some of the acid in the water is neutralized.

Some rocks and soil are more alkaline than others. Limestone and soils made from limestone are able to neutralize dilute acids. Granite, gneiss, and the soils that result from them are poor at neutralizing acid. When acid rainwater flows through these materials and into lakes and ponds, the water remains acid.

Lakes and streams become acid when the acid rainwater in them is not neutralized. The map in Figure 21-6 shows areas of the United States where the ground is least able to neutralize acid precipitation. For example, the Northeast and the Rocky Mountains are sensitive to acid because they have granite and soils formed from granite.

What is the effect of acid in lakes and streams? Small water animals, such as fish, frogs, snails, and insects, cannot survive in water with a pH of much less than 5. Cities often take their drinking water from these same lakes and streams. Drinking a dilute acid will probably not harm your health. However, acids have the ability to dissolve and corrode many things they come in contact with, such as toxic lead.

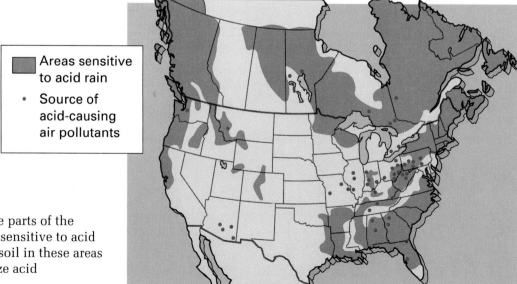

Areas sensitive to acid rain

• Source of acid-causing air pollutants

Figure 21-6 Some parts of the country are more sensitive to acid rain. The rock or soil in these areas does not neutralize acid effectively.

In some places, powdered limestone is being added to the lakes in an attempt to make the lake less acid. Each time water from an acid lake or stream goes through the water cycle and becomes rain, there is another opportunity for the water to be less acid. However, acid lakes and streams have little chance to become healthy again until acid rain is reduced. Some progress has been made in lowering the amount of sulfur and nitrogen oxides spewed out by cars and power plants, but further cuts need to be made.

Figure 21-7 *Left:* The top fish is normal. The bottom fish was caught in the same lake after the lake was artificially made more acid (pH 5.0). *Right:* Powdered limestone is being added to this lake to help neutralize the acid from acid rain.

Lesson Review 21.1

1. How is salt water from the ocean changed to fresh water by the water cycle?
2. What is acid rain? Use information from the pH scale in your answer.
3. What effect does acid rain have on water in lakes and streams? What happens to animals as a result?
4. What changes can result in the formation of a lake?

Interpret and Apply

5. Why are acid lakes and streams becoming more of a problem in the Northeast?
6. Animal life slowly returned to several ponds on Cape Cod after ground limestone was added to them, as illustrated in Figure 21-7. Explain why this might work. Do you think that this is a good solution to the problem of acid rain? Explain the reasons for your opinion.

A C T I V I T Y   2 1 . 1

TESTING THE ACIDITY OF FRESH WATER

Purpose To measure the acidity of freshwater samples.

Materials

samples of fresh water
distilled water
wide-range pH paper
  1–11 and color chart
narrow-range pH paper
  3.0–6.0 and color chart
small containers
masking tape

Procedure

1. Read all directions for this activity before you begin your work.

2. Copy the data table onto your paper.

3. Select several clean, dry containers. Obtain enough of each liquid sample so that there is enough to test with the paper. Use the masking tape to make a label for each sample. Record the sample source and the date each sample was taken in your data table.

4. Test each water sample with a strip of the narrow-range pH paper. Follow the directions on the dispenser. Record the pH number on your data table. Use a new strip of paper for each sample.

5. If the reading for your sample is not on the narrow-range chart, repeat the test using the wide-range pH paper and a new sample of the water.

6. Test a sample of distilled water and record the pH in your data table.

7. Rinse the test containers with distilled water. Clean up all materials and wash your hands thoroughly.

Collecting and Analyzing Data

Data Table		
Sample Source	**Date Sample Taken**	**pH**

1. Draw a pH scale similar to Figure 21-5. Label where each sample from your tests falls on this scale.

2. Which samples were most acid (lowest pH)? Which were least acid or even alkaline?

3. Compare the pH values for similar samples taken on different dates.

Drawing Conclusions

4. Would you consider the precipitation you measured to be acid precipitation?

5. Were all the rain or melted snow samples the same pH? Try to explain any similarities or differences.

6. In which part of the water cycle do samples become acid? Explain what might cause this.

7. Compare the acidity of the precipitation samples to the acidity of surface water samples. Explain the similarities or differences.

21.2 *Groundwater Resources*

Imagine hearing that the fish in a nearby lake are unsafe to eat because they contain a deadly concentration of some chemical. Where did the chemical come from? As weeks pass, you read in the newspaper that the water in streams flowing into the lake is clean, yet the lake itself is polluted with this chemical. The source of the problem is finally located. Workers digging 2 kilometers from the lake find drums of hazardous industrial waste, buried deep underground. The drums, buried nearly 30 years ago, are leaking deadly chemicals into the groundwater. But how does the pollution of the groundwater affect the water in a lake 2 kilometers away?

In Chapter 13, you learned that some of the rain that falls in a drainage basin soaks into the pore spaces of the soil and rock of Earth's surface. More of Earth's fresh water is stored beneath the surface as groundwater than is stored in all the lakes and rivers in the world. This makes groundwater an important freshwater resource.

Lesson Objectives

▸ *Explain* how changes in the amount of groundwater affect the water table.

▸ *Diagram* and label the parts of an aquifer, a well, and a spring.

▸ *Give an example* of how pollutants get into groundwater.

▸ **Activity** *Form a model* of water movement in an aquifer.

New Terms

zone of saturation	aquifer
water table	spring
zone of aeration	recharge
wetland	toxic

Figure 21-8 The fluorescent dye poured into this stream in Mammoth Cave National Park, Kentucky, is carried underground into a cave. The dye will be tracked to determine how quickly groundwater moves.

The Water Table

Think about what would happen if you started pouring water into a bucket of sand. The bucket fills with water from the bottom upward, just as it would without the sand. Gravity pulls the water down through the sand until the water reaches the bottom of the bucket. The water cannot pass through the bucket, because the bucket is impermeable. The water fills the pore spaces in the sand. If you keep pouring water into the bucket, you fill more and more of the spaces. Eventually, you can fill all the spaces between sand grains with water. The sand is saturated with water. If you add more water, the bucket will overflow.

How does this model of groundwater relate to what happens inside Earth? Look at Figure 21-9. The water that falls to Earth soaks into the ground and is pulled downward by gravity until it reaches an impermeable layer. This impermeable layer may be a bed of shale, or unweathered, nonporous bedrock. The water, unable to continue soaking downward, starts to fill the pores in the rock or soil. The area of rock or soil where the pores are completely filled by groundwater is called the **zone of saturation.** The top of the zone of saturation is called the **water table.** As more water soaks into the ground, the zone of saturation gets thicker and the water table rises, getting closer to Earth's surface.

Not all groundwater is stored in the zone of saturation. Some water is left behind in the soil and rock as the water moves downward. This water is trapped where grains are in contact and is therefore not pulled downward by gravity. This water is only removed by evaporation or by plant roots. The layer of rock or soil above the water table is called the **zone of aeration** [ar ā′ shən]. *Aerate* means "to add air to something."

Figure 21-9 The water table separates the zone of aeration from the zone of saturation. In which zone are the pore spaces filled with water?

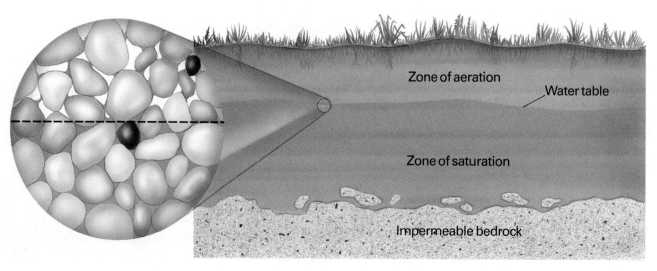

Zone of aeration

Water table

Zone of saturation

Impermeable bedrock

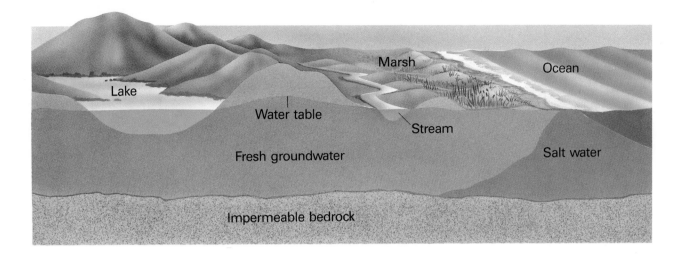

Groundwater and surface waters, such as streams and lakes, are related to each other as illustrated in Figure 21-10. In a drought, water evaporates from the soil surface. The dry soil absorbs groundwater from below. The water table drops. Since the water table and the surface of streams and lakes is the same surface, the surface water levels also drop. Sometimes water flows out of the ground into a stream, causing the stream to continue flowing even though there has been no rain in the drainage basin for days or even weeks.

If there is an abundance of rain, the water table rises. The water level in the lakes and streams also rises, due to runoff. If there is too much rain over a short period of time, the pore spaces in the ground can completely fill and the rain runs off into the streams. This often leads to flooding.

One land feature that minimizes flooding is a wetland. A **wetland** is an area that is covered with shallow water or that has wet soils. Wetlands include swamps, marshes, and bogs. For many years, people thought that wetlands were useless. Wetlands were drained or filled in to make way for houses and malls. But wetlands absorb excess water and release it slowly, making flooding less likely. Wetlands also provide rich environments for wildlife.

Using Groundwater

Groundwater collects in any soil or rock that is both porous and permeable. A rock that is very porous but not very permeable, such as shale, takes the water in, but does not allow it to move quickly through the pore spaces. In order to use groundwater, you need to be able to get it out of the rock. You need to find a saturated layer of rock that is both very porous and permeable. Such a layer of rock is called an aquifer. An **aquifer** is an underground deposit of sand, gravel, or rock through which water passes easily.

Figure 21-10 The water table comes out at Earth's surface as the surface level of lakes and streams. What would happen to the water table if it did not rain for a long period of time?

Figure 21-11 Wetlands, such as this area near Reelfoot Lake in Tennessee, are important habitats for wildlife.

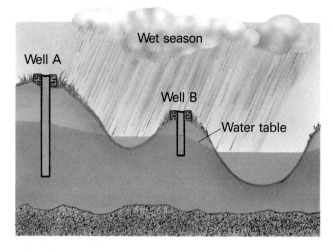

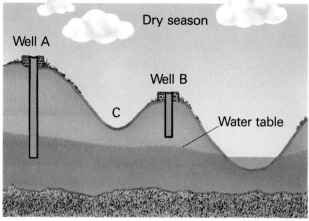

Figure 21-12 The water table drops during the dry season. Which well has water only part of the year? What feature is present at Location C during the wet season?

Figure 21-13 This sinkhole in Winter Park, Florida, was caused by overpumping groundwater.

About one fourth of the water used in the United States comes from aquifers. You use groundwater if the water in your school or home is pumped from a well. Think back to the bucket of sand and the water. You have saturated the sand almost to the top of the bucket. If you were to poke your finger into the sand and then pull it out, water would partly fill the hole. This hole is like a water well dug into an aquifer. The water level in the hole is the top of the water table. Locate the well in Figure 21-12. What happens to the water in the rest of the aquifer when water is removed from the well? In an aquifer, the water table drops as water is withdrawn unless more water is put back in. Rainfall can refill, or **recharge,** an aquifer. If rainfall recharges an aquifer as fast as water is pumped out by wells, the water table stays at the same level. Serious problems occur when more water is removed from an aquifer than comes into it. On the Texas High Plains, so much water has been pumped out that many wells have gone dry as the water table dropped.

Overuse of groundwater creates problems apart from reducing the available water. Groundwater helps support the weight of the soil above it. When the water table is greatly lowered, the surface of the ground sometimes sags and buckles. In parts of Texas, California, and Florida, land surfaces have dropped 5 meters or more as groundwater was removed. Sometimes this leads to large depressions in the land, such as the one shown in Figure 21-13. These depressions caused by the land collapsing are called sinkholes.

Many people think that water flows underground in fast-moving rivers. Except in caves, this is rarely the case. Most groundwater flows slowly through the pore spaces or cracks in the rock, moving between 1 meter a day to 1 meter a year. Groundwater may travel many kilometers before it appears at Earth's surface. A **spring** is a place where groundwater flows out onto Earth's surface.

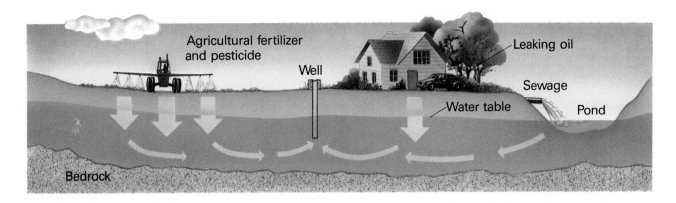

Figure 21-14 How many different pollutants might be found in water from this well?

Protecting Groundwater

It is difficult to understand the need to take care of water you cannot see. Even though wetlands and soil remove some impurities in groundwater, other pollutants remain. Pesticides, industrial waste, sewage, gasoline leaking from underground storage tanks, and contaminated water leaking from landfills all find their way into groundwater. Substances that are harmful to living things are called **toxic.** Toxic waste in groundwater is very difficult to remove. One service-station storage tank leaking only one gallon of fuel per day can ruin a volume of water that would supply 50 000 people. How many people are polluting the groundwater in Figure 21-14?

Is groundwater a renewable resource? If groundwater is used up faster than it is naturally replaced, the answer is no. In some ways, people mine groundwater, just as they mine ores. What methods of conserving mineral resources might work with freshwater resources?

Lesson Review 21.2

7. Under what conditions would the water table in an aquifer be higher than normal? What could cause the water table to be lower than normal?

8. Sketch an aquifer in which one well has water and another is dry.

9. How does groundwater become polluted? Give some examples of pollutants in groundwater.

Interpret and Apply

10. In the winter, salt is often used to melt ice from sidewalks and roads. About one fourth of the well water in Massachusetts has unusual amounts of salt. Explain.

ACTIVITY 21.2

WELLS AND GROUNDWATER

Purpose To form a model showing the movement of water in an aquifer.

Materials

pencil
fine plastic screening,
  15 cm x 9 cm
2 rubber bands
water
clear beaker or
  other container

dry, coarse sand
  mixed with gravel
1 plastic straw
metric ruler
cup

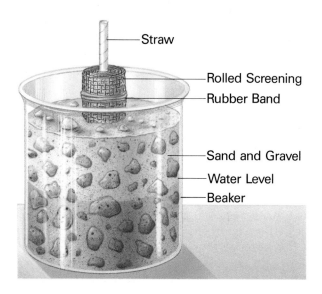

Procedure

1. Read all the instructions for this activity before you begin your work.

2. Copy the data table onto your paper.

3. Roll the screening around a pencil. Place rubber bands on either end of the screen cylinder so that it is about 1 cm in diameter. Remove the pencil.

4. Place the screen cylinder upright in the center of the beaker. Fill around the cylinder with sand and gravel.

5. Pour water into the sand and gravel until you can see the water level halfway up the beaker. Measure the depth of the water level from the surface of the sand and gravel. Record this in the data table.

6. Dip the straw into your screen well. Be sure the straw touches the bottom of the beaker. Place your finger on top of the straw. Lift the straw and place the water from your well in a cup. Observe any changes in the water level. After withdrawing 10 strawfuls of water, measure and record the water level in the sand again. Repeat, removing 10 more strawfuls of water. Measure the water level.

7. Before leaving the laboratory, clean up all materials and wash your hands.

Collecting and Analyzing Data

Data Table	
Time	**Depth of Water Level**
Beginning	
After 10 strawfuls withdrawn	
After 20 strawfuls	

1. How did the water level change when water was taken out of the well?

2. In what ways does your model behave like an aquifer? In what ways is it different?

Drawing Conclusions

3. Suppose toxic waste is buried in the sand. How would this affect your well? Think of some ways this problem could be avoided.

4. In your model, how do you know where the water table is? Predict what would happen to the water table if water was taken from two wells at the same time.

21.3 Water—A Limited Resource

Is there enough fresh water for everyone to use? To answer this question, you must compare the fresh water available to the amount used. You know that the amount of usable fresh water on Earth is small compared to the total amount of water. It still must seem to you that there is enough fresh water to meet your needs. You turn on the tap and water comes out. Even water data suggest that there should be enough water. The United States' average rainfall of 76 centimeters per year provides about 30 000 liters of fresh water a day for each person in the country. This volume makes it seem like a lot of water is available.

Water Use and Distribution

How much water do you use a day? You use more water than you think. Your body only needs about 3 liters of drinking water a day to stay healthy. However, that is not the only way you use water. The average person uses another 300 liters of water a day around the house. That water is used to wash dishes and clothes, take showers or baths, and to carry away waste from your bathroom. Three hundred liters may seem like a lot of water, especially if you multiply that by the number of people in your family or in your class. Yet these numbers do not show the true volume of the water you use every day.

Most of the water you use each day does not actually pass through your house as liquid water, but rather in the form of the products you use. The food you eat requires water to grow. For example, it takes 3000 liters of water to grow enough beef for one lunchtime hamburger. Not only do cattle drink water every day, but they also eat grain that was grown on land irrigated with water.

You also need the water that is used by industry to manufacture products. Sometimes water is used in the product itself or it is part of the manufacturing process. Industry also uses water to cool and clean the factories. It takes over 60 liters of water to make one aluminum soft-drink can. An incredible 600 000 liters of water are required to process the steel used to make one car.

If you add the water used to manufacture goods and produce food to the water you use in your home, you would find that you use about 8000 liters of fresh water a day. That is enough water over the course of a year to fill a column 1 meter square and nearly 3 kilometers tall. As the population grows, and as people buy more manufactured goods, the demand for fresh water increases.

Lesson Objectives

▶ **Discuss** limits on the amount of fresh water available.

▶ **Describe** the effect of common pollutants on fresh water.

▶ **List** ways you can reduce your demand for water.

▶ **Activity** **Evaluate** the need for water in two areas.

New Terms

hard water
sewage

Figure 21-15 One and a half trillion liters of fresh water are used each day in the United States.

Industry 54%

Farming 35%

Home 11%

Figure 21-16 This aqueduct is part of the Central Arizona Project. It transports water from the Colorado River to Phoenix and the rest of central Arizona.

If the same amount of rain fell everywhere in the United States, there would be enough water for everyone. Yet the western part of the country, which has 60 percent of the nation's land area, gets only 25 percent of the total rainfall. As you know from your study of weather and climate, rain does not fall at the same rate year-round. In North America, most precipitation falls in the winter and spring. Much of this water evaporates or runs off into rivers and streams. In order to save this wet-season water for use in the dry season, many communities build artificial lakes called reservoirs. The water stored in reservoirs is used when rainfall is less abundant.

Shortages are also caused by uneven demand for water. Cities need far more water than is found locally. Some of New York City's water travels through huge tunnels from reservoirs in the Catskill Mountains, 200 kilometers away. Heavily populated southern California relies on aqueducts that carry fresh water from northern and central California, and from the Colorado River to the east.

Water Quality

Some water is of poor quality. Natural pollutants may make water harmful to use. Groundwater can dissolve ions of calcium and magnesium from rock or soil it passes through. Water that contains too much dissolved calcium and magnesium is called **hard water.** Hard water is not harmful to drink, but it causes other problems. When you add soap to hard water, it is difficult to get a rich lather. The dissolved materials are deposited inside water pipes and hot-water heaters, making them work less efficiently. Sediment is also a natural water pollutant. Soil eroded from the land collects in surface waters. The sediment can smother fish, and prevent sunlight from reaching freshwater plants.

Figure 21-17 The dissolved material in hard water can be deposited inside water pipes.

In addition to natural pollutants, water can become polluted with human-made toxic substances, such as pesticides and industrial waste. Another toxic water pollutant is sewage. **Sewage** is wastewater from drains and toilets. The human and animal waste in sewage contains disease-causing germs. In towns where the sewers are connected to the storm drains, the sewage also contains toxic metals and oil washed from the roads.

What happens when sewage is dumped into a river? Sometimes the river can cleanse itself. If there is only a small amount of sewage, it becomes diluted in the water. The plant and animal waste starts to decay in the water. The bacteria that cause the decay take in oxygen as they feed on the waste. In a bubbling river, the oxygen used up by the bacteria is replaced, and the quality of the water returns to normal. However, if there is too much decaying sewage, the oxygen level of the water drops quickly, killing fish and other organisms. Sewage is a much more serious problem when it enters the groundwater. There is less oxygen in groundwater and fewer bacteria to break down the organic pollutants. This makes it very difficult for groundwater to clean itself once it becomes polluted.

In many communities, sewage is sent to a treatment plant where it goes through several steps to remove harmful materials. First, large particles are strained out of the sewage. Smaller solids are allowed to settle out in holding tanks. Bubbling oxygen through the remaining liquid or trickling it over rocks helps bacteria break down any remaining plant and animal wastes. Chlorine is added to the water in many places to kill harmful germs. Other chemicals are sometimes added to remove other harmful organic or inorganic substances.

Figure 21-18 Adding oxygen to water or sewage helps bacteria break down waste. Here water is being aerated by trickling the water over a bed of rocks.

Figure 21-19 Phosphates, such as those found in some household detergents, can cause water plants like this algae to grow too much.

Some pollutants are difficult to remove from water using current treatment methods. Toxic materials found in industrial waste, such as mercury, lead, and dioxin, are not removed by normal sewage treatment processes. These chemicals are harmful even in small quantities. Some of these difficult-to-remove toxic pollutants may come from your own kitchen or garage.

Phosphate is another pollutant that is difficult to remove from sewage. Phosphates and excess fertilizer draining from farmers' fields both cause rapid growth in water plants. Look at Figure 21-19. This water is packed with algae, a type of water plant. This algae may become so abundant that some other water plants die from lack of light. When a large amount of the algae and other plants dies and decays, bacteria use up the oxygen in the water. Many fish and other organisms can die from lack of oxygen.

Not all water pollutants are actual substances. Thermal energy is also a water pollutant. Water from streams and lakes is used to cool electric power plants by absorbing excess thermal energy. Nuclear power plants, in particular, use tremendous amounts of water to cool reactors. When the warmer water is put back into the streams or lakes, it harms the plants and animals living there.

ENVIRONMENTAL AWARENESS

The Return of the Salmon

It was an exciting day when the salmon returned to Pigeon Creek. Pigeon Creek flows behind a school in Everett, Washington. For 20 years, the water in the creek had been so polluted that salmon no longer used the creek to breed. In the mid-1980's, kids from the school "adopted" the creek. They removed tons of trash from the creek. The kids convinced local home and business owners to be more careful about allowing pollutants to run into the creek.

Once the creek was clean, the next step was to get salmon eggs from the State Fishery. The students raised the young fish in tanks at school. Each June, the students re-leased young salmon into Pigeon Creek. In 1988, the salmon returned to Pigeon Creek and laid eggs. The students plan to keep up their work to be sure that the salmon will keep coming back. ■

Using Water Wisely

Water often seems plentiful until times of drought, but you now know fresh water is a limited resource. What can be done to insure a plentiful supply of clean water? One way is to use less water. Study Table 21-1. Estimate the amount of water you use each day for these activities. How much would you use if you tried to save water?

Table 21-1 Water Used in Common Activities		
Activity	**Normal Use**	**Water-Saving Use**
Shower (5 minute)	Normal-flow shower head, 95 L	Low-flow shower head, 53 L
Tub Bath	Full tub, 137 L	Lower water level, 38 L
Brushing Teeth	Tap running, 38 L	Wet brush, rinse briefly, 2 L
Toilet Flushing	Normal, 19–27 L	Weighted bottles in tank, 15–23 L
Dish Washing (hand)	Tap running, 114 L	Using basin, 19 L
Dish Washing (machine)	Full cycle, 61 L	Short cycle, 27 L

There are other ways to use less water. Many older cities lose 30 percent of their water through leaky pipes before it is even delivered to users. The same type of waste goes on in your own home. You might be surprised by how much water is lost through one leaky faucet. A dripping faucet leaks as much as 400 liters of water per day.

Another way to increase the amount of fresh water available is to use the same water several times. Many industries now find it easier to reuse or recycle the wastewater from their plants. This saves money and reduces the risk of polluting local water sources.

Before, when you turned on the faucet or pulled the plug in the bathtub drain, perhaps you never thought about where water comes from or where it goes. Now you know that fresh, clean water is a vital but a limited resource. Today's fresh water is all that Earth will ever have. Your actions and decisions today affect the quantity and quality of water available in your future.

Figure 21-20 Wise use of water includes management of household toxic waste. Citizens of Bellevue, Washington, hold an annual Waste Collection Day. This waste will be disposed of safely, instead of being poured down the drain and becoming a pollutant.

ACTIVITY 21.3 *Paper & Pencil*

MAKING DECISIONS ABOUT WATER USE

Purpose   To evaluate water needs in a real situation.

Procedure

1. Read the following information about two regions where water use is a critical issue.

   California   California produces half of the country's fresh fruits and vegetables, mostly on irrigated land. Millions of people live in the Los Angeles-San Diego area. Southern California's farms, industries, and people all need water. Huge aqueducts carry water to this area from northern California and from the Colorado River. In the future, California will have less water available from the Colorado River, because Arizona plans to use more water from the Colorado River before it reaches California. One solution is to pipe water from dams on the Columbia River in the northwestern United States. Large sums of federal tax money would be required to pay for the pipeline.

   Columbia River Area   The amount of water flowing out of the Columbia River each day is four times the daily amount used by California. Dams on the Columbia and its surrounding rivers provide about one third of the hydroelectric power in the United States. The development of the aluminum-processing industry in the Northwest depends heavily on this electric power. Water available to hydroelectric dams decreases as water is taken from the rivers for other purposes. Water from the Columbia irrigates fruit-producing areas. Native Americans and others interested in fishing want to keep some streams available for salmon.

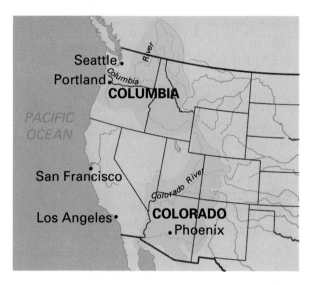

2. Divide into two groups. One group will represent California. The other group will represent the Columbia River. Within your group, discuss the water-related needs of people from your area.

Collecting and Analyzing Data

1. Create some characters to role-play a debate with the other group. Use information from the readings. Try to build the strongest case for your side.

2. At the end of the debate, take a class vote on the following question: Should a water pipeline be built from the Columbia River to southern California?

Drawing Conclusions

3. How did you decide which side to vote for? Did your classmates agree on which group's needs were most important?

4. Suggest ways for each group to reduce water needs in their area.

5. Do you think the federal government should settle disagreements about water use? List reasons for your opinion.

Lesson Review 21.3

11. Describe three conditions that limit the amount of fresh, clean water available.

12. Describe how wastewater is treated to remove pollutants.

13. Which pollutants are the most difficult to remove from wastewater?

14. What are some of the major uses of water in the United States?

Interpret and Apply

15. Find out where your tap water comes from and where it goes after it leaves your drain. Draw a sketch of the water cycle in your area that includes this information.

16. How much water do you use in one day? Make a list of the ways that you could cut down on your use of household water. How much could you save per day? Refer to Table 21-1 to make your estimates.

Chapter Summary

Read this summary of the main ideas in this chapter. If any are not clear to you, go back and review that lesson.

21.1 Surface Water Resources

■ Only 3 percent of Earth's water is fresh. Only 1 percent is available for you to use.

■ Water in the water cycle continually evaporates from land. As the water evaporates, it leaves behind impurities.

■ Lakes fill depressions caused by a variety of processes.

■ Rocks with low neutralizing ability cause some areas to be sensitive to acid rain.

21.2 Groundwater Resources

■ Water is closer to the surface when the water table is high. As water is removed from an aquifer, the water table lowers.

■ An aquifer consists of porous and permeable materials that allow groundwater to freely move through them.

■ Groundwater becomes polluted when toxic materials seep into the aquifer. Polluted groundwater is difficult to clean.

21.3 Water—A Limited Resource

■ Water supplies are limited by both the supply of water at a location and by the demand on what water is available.

■ Water can be recycled if contaminants are removed. Some pollutants, but not all, can be removed by treatment with bacteria and oxygen, as well as with chemicals.

■ There are many simple ways to conserve fresh water in your everyday life.

Chapter Review

■ Vocabulary

aquifer
hard water
pH scale
recharge
sewage
spring

toxic
water cycle
water table
wetland
zone of aeration
zone of saturation

■ Concept Mapping

Using the method of concept mapping described on pages 3–5, complete a concept map for pollutants in fresh water. Copy the map below. Then fill in the missing terms.

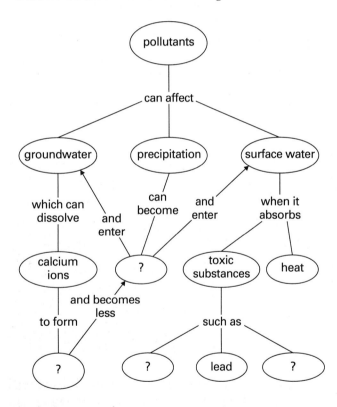

■ Review

On your paper, write the word or words that best complete each statement.

1. Fresh water in nature is considered acid if it has a pH of (greater than 7, less than 5.6, less than 7).

2. (Precipitation, Runoff, Abrasion) is not part of the water cycle.

3. When an acid is mixed with the right amount of an alkaline material, the result is (neutralization, acid rain, damage to water life).

4. Many lakes in the northern United States formed as the result of (water filling craters, glacial erosion, faulting).

5. The part of Earth that is filled with groundwater is called the (water table, zone of aeration, zone of saturation).

6. Swamps and bogs are examples of a(n) (aquifer, wetland, zone of aeration).

7. If you take water out of an aquifer faster than it can be recharged, the water table (rises, stays the same, falls).

8. For a well to have water, the bottom of the well must be (below the water table, in a recharge area, in an impermeable material).

9. Materials that harm living things are (always human made, generally gases, toxic).

10. Groundwater can become contaminated by (household chemicals, sand and gravel, impermeable materials).

11. Differences in rainfall and (population, temperature, elevation) are often the most important reasons why fresh water is piped from one area to another.

12. Most of the fresh water you need for your daily life is used for (drinking water, washing and waste disposal, making products or food).

13. You can increase the amount of available fresh water with the least damage to the environment by (damming more rivers, conserving water, building more sewage treatment plants).

14. When sewage decays, (nitrates, toxic chemicals, bacteria) take(s) in oxygen.

◼ Interpret and Apply

On your paper, answer each question using complete sentences.

15. Some land in Houston, Texas, is 3 meters lower than it was earlier this century. Houston, a city that has grown quickly in the last 20 years, is located over an aquifer. What is the most likely cause for the lowering of the land?

16. Describe the roles that plants and animals have in the water cycle.

17. Your neighbor has just changed the motor oil in his car. Should he bury the dirty oil in sandy soil? Why or why not? If not, what should he do with the oil?

18. What would be the best time of day to water your garden if you want to conserve water? Suggest other ways to reduce the need for water for plants around the home.

19. In Arizona, many homeowners choose to have natural desert landscaping rather than large, green lawns. Explain how this practice helps to conserve water.

20. Two lakes are close to each other. One is acid. The other is close to neutral. The acid lake has a small drainage basin and thin soil. The neutral lake has a larger drainage basin and deeper soil. Explain why the lakes' acidity differs.

◼ Writing in Science

21. As water from the Colorado River moves over fields, three quarters of it evaporates. The rest of the water is returned to the river, where it is used again. Over a period of time, salt builds up in the soil irrigated with this reused water. Write an explanation of why this salt buildup occurs. Use the following terms in your explanation: *water cycle, groundwater,* and *evaporation.*

◼ Critical Thinking

Imagine that the following announcement appears in your local newspaper:

New Shopping Mall Hailed

The Waterville Development Corporation announced plans today to build the Melody Marsh Shopping Center. Many local residents welcome the filling of the mosquito-infested marsh to make way for the mall. Plans call for over 25 fashionable stores and a 12-pump service station. Parking will be conveniently located in the large lot adjoining the mall. Citizens with comments about the plans for the new mall are encouraged to attend a meeting at City Hall, Tuesday night at 7:30 P.M.

Use the above information and the diagram below to answer questions 22–24.

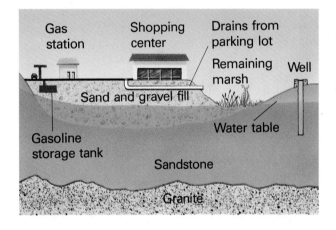

22. Study the plans for the new mall. How will the plans affect the amount of water entering the aquifer?

23. What water-pollution problems do you foresee if the mall is built?

24. People who live near the marsh drink well water pumped from the aquifer near their houses. How might the building of the mall affect these people?

22 *Ocean Resources*

Chapter Preview

Have You Ever WONDERED?

Why is the ocean salty?

If you have ever accidentally swallowed a mouthful of water while swimming in the ocean, you know the taste is much saltier than drinking water. Where did the salt come from?

Materials that form salt enter the ocean in many ways. Rivers carry dissolved materials to the ocean from chemically weathered rocks on land. Water seeps into cracks in the ocean crust and dissolves minerals from the rocks. Ions from gases produced by undersea eruptions dissolve in sea water. All these materials combine in the ocean to form different kinds of salt.

Is the salt in the ocean the same kind of salt you put on popcorn? Are some parts of the ocean saltier than others? You will find the answers to these and many other questions in this chapter.

22.1 *Earth's Oceans*

New Terms

sea
salinity
thermocline

Whether you live near it or far away, the ocean affects your life. The ocean provides you with resources, such as food, fresh water, minerals, and energy. The ocean also changes the atmosphere. No matter where you live, the ocean has affected today's weather. Temperatures on land would be much colder in winter and hotter in summer without the ocean's warming and cooling effect on air masses.

Even as the ocean has a great effect on human lives, human actions also greatly affect the ocean. How do you think that people change the ocean?

Oceans and Seas

Seen from space, Earth is mostly a striking blue color. Ocean waters cover 71 percent of Earth's surface. In fact, you could sail around the world and never set foot on dry land. Figure 22-1 shows how 97 percent of all water on Earth connects into one huge, continuous ocean. Geographers, however, refer to Earth as having four separate oceans. Locate the four major oceans in Figure 22-1. The Pacific Ocean is the largest, followed by the Atlantic, Indian, and Arctic oceans. The Pacific Ocean covers one third of Earth's surface. The Pacific is so large that you could fit all of the continents inside its boundaries and still have an area larger than the Arctic Ocean left over.

You probably know the names of seas not shown in Figure 22-1. A **sea** is a smaller area of water usually considered part of a major ocean. For example, the Caribbean and Mediterranean seas are part of the Atlantic Ocean.

Figure 22-1 Earth's oceans and seas

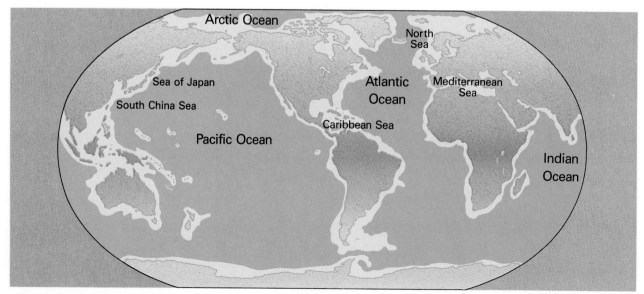

Composition of Sea Water

If you decided to make sea water, what ingredients would you need? Sea water is like a soup containing most of the natural elements you learned about in Chapter 7. The biggest part of sea water is pure water. You would need large amounts of hydrogen and oxygen to make the pure water needed for your soup. Your recipe would also call for over 60 other elements. Sea water even contains tiny amounts of different metals, including gold, copper, and uranium.

Those 60 other elements found in sea water combine to form the materials called salts. Salts are an important ingredient in your seawater soup. Materials dissolved from the ocean crust, rocks weathered on land, and undersea eruptions all add elements to ocean water. These elements combine to form salts. The chart in Figure 22-2 shows the kinds of salt in sea water. Notice that sodium chloride is the most abundant salt in sea water. You may remember that sodium chloride is common table salt. What is the second most abundant salt in sea water?

The amount of dissolved salts in sea water is its **salinity**. The average salinity of sea water is 35 parts per thousand. This means that if you evaporated 1000 grams of sea water, 35 grams of salt would be left behind, as shown in Figure 22-3. There are 35 parts of salt in every 1000 parts of sea water. How much salt would be left in a beaker if you evaporated 2000 grams of average sea water?

Not all sea water has the same salinity. The salinity of sea water usually ranges from 33 to 37 parts per thousand. The higher the salinity, the more dense the water. Even if you have trouble floating on your back in a freshwater lake, you might be able to float in salty ocean water. Since salt water is more dense than fresh water, objects float higher in the ocean than they would in a river or lake.

Pure water 96.5%

Salts 3.5%

Most Abundant Salts in Seawater

Salt	Parts per thousand
sodium chloride	27.2
magnesium chloride	3.8
magnesium sulfate	1.7
calcium sulfate	1.3
potassium sulfate	0.9
calcium carbonate	0.1
magnesium bromide	0.1

Figure 22-2 Dissolved materials, called salts, make up 3.5 percent of the average sample of sea water.

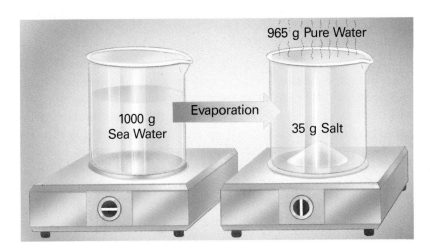

965 g Pure Water

1000 g Sea Water

Evaporation

35 g Salt

Figure 22-3 If you evaporate 1000 grams of average sea water, 35 grams of salt will be left behind.

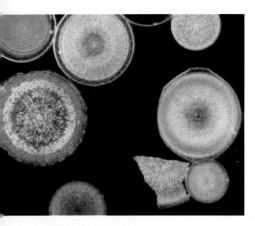

Figure 22-4 Microscopic plants, such as these diatoms, provide oxygen to sea water and are the base of the ocean's food chains.

What could cause sea water in some areas to be saltier than the average? In some areas, such as the Mediterranean Sea, the weather is warm and dry. There is little rainfall and much evaporation. As water evaporates, it leaves salt behind. The remaining water has an above average salinity of about 40 parts per thousand. In polar regions, salt water slowly freezes into sea ice. Although the ice traps some salt, much of the salt is left behind, increasing the salinity of the remaining water. There are also places where ocean water is less salty than the average. This happens when rivers, melting ice, or heavy rainfall add fresh water to the ocean.

Your seawater soup is not complete until you add dissolved gases. All gases found in air are also found dissolved in sea water. These gases mix into ocean water at the surface. Underwater volcanic eruptions also add gases to the water. Much of the oxygen in the water comes from plants. Plants produce oxygen when they use sunlight to make food. This sunlight does not reach much deeper than 200 meters into the ocean water. It should not surprise you that ocean plants live mostly in shallow water. The oxygen these plants produce adds to the oxygen needed by other forms of life in the ocean and on land. Would you expect to find more or less dissolved oxygen in deep ocean water?

Temperature also affects the amount of dissolved gases in sea water. Warm water holds less dissolved gas than cold water. Cold, dense water near the poles sinks and carries oxygen down to the deep ocean, where animals use the oxygen to live.

Water Temperature and Pressure

The ocean is divided into three layers based on water temperature. These layers are shown in Figure 22-5. The sun is the major source of thermal energy in the oceans. The warmest water is found nearest the surface, in the top few hundred meters of water. The warm water is less dense and tends to stay near the surface. This is called the mixed layer. The mixed layer forms when winds, waves, and ocean currents mix the heated surface waters with colder water from below. Sunlight cannot penetrate ocean water below a few hundred meters. Below that point, water temperatures drop rapidly. The ocean layer where temperature changes rapidly is called the **thermocline.** At what depth does the thermocline end? As you see in Figure 22-5, water below the thermocline is very cold. Even near the equator, the temperature at the bottom of this layer is rarely higher than 5°C. The cold, dense water at this level is always near freezing, unless it is near a hot spot or mid-ocean ridge.

Figure 22-5 Why does water temperature usually decrease with depth?

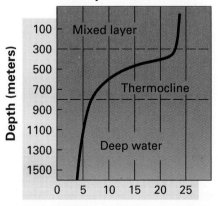

Ocean Temperature Zones

Depth (meters)

Mixed layer

Thermocline

Deep water

100
300
500
700
900
1100
1300
1500

0   5   10   15   20   25

Average water temperature (°C)

The temperature of ocean water decreases with depth. Pressure, however, increases with depth. You know from your study of air pressure in Chapter 17 that the weight of the atmosphere presses on you as you stand at Earth's surface. The average air pressure at sea level is expressed as one atmosphere. When you dive below the ocean's surface, you have the weight of the atmosphere pressing on you, plus the added weight of water. For every 10 meters deeper you dive, the pressure on you increases one atmosphere. Pressures at deep ocean depths are very high. Divers must carry equipment that supplies their lungs with air at the same pressure as the water surrounding them. Even with special equipment, scuba divers cannot safely go deeper than 100 meters. The average depth of the ocean is 4000 meters.

Figure 22-6 *Left:* This hard-shell diving suit protects divers from the extreme pressures and temperatures of the deep ocean. *Right:* Water samples are taken by lowering sampling devices from research ships.

Lesson Review 22.1

1. Starting with the smallest one, rank the four major oceans of Earth based on their size.
2. How much salt is in 3000 grams of average sea water?
3. How is the thermocline different from the mixed layer?
4. Explain why the Mediterranean Sea is saltier than the rest of the Atlantic Ocean.

Interpret and Apply

5. Some people call Earth's atmosphere an ocean of air. Make a table comparing the real oceans with the atmosphere. Include the headings *Composition*, *Pressure*, and *Temperature*.

ACTIVITY 22.1

Lab Equipment

SALINITY AND FLOTATION

Purpose To observe and describe the effect of salinity on floating objects.

Materials

1 paper drinking straw	metric ruler
	pen or pencil
500 mL beaker	lab balance
tap water	balance papers
table salt	safety goggles
graduated cylinder	lab apron
paper clips	

Procedure

1. Read all the instructions for this activity before you begin your work. Copy the data table on your paper.

2. Put on your safety goggles and lab apron.

3. Use the ruler to draw a line down the center of the straw. Mark this line in 1-mm intervals. Number every fifth line.

4. Fold over the bottom few centimeters of the straw and attach 2 or 3 paper clips.

5. Pour 500 mL of water into your container. Carefully float the straw in the water with the folded end down. Slide the paper clips up or down slightly until the straw floats upright. Record in your data table under *0 g* the number on the scale at which your straw floats.

6. Remove the straw from the water. Use your balance to measure out 5 g of salt. Add the salt to the water and stir with the stirring rod. Float the straw in the water and use your data table to record the number at which it floats.

7. Repeat step 6 four more times.

8. Before leaving the laboratory, clean up all materials and wash your hands thoroughly.

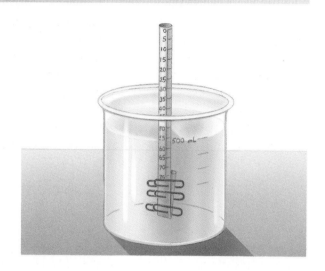

Collecting and Analyzing Data

Data Table	
Amount of Salt (g)	**Reading on Straw**
0	
5	
10	

1. Make a line graph of your data. Use *Amount of Salt* as the horizontal axis, and *Reading on Straw* as the vertical axis.

2. Does the straw float higher or lower in a salt solution?

3. Did the straw rise the same amount each time 5 grams of salt were added?

Drawing Conclusions

4. Using your graph, predict the level at which the straw would float if you added 10 more grams of salt.

5. What would happen to a ship sailing from a river into the open ocean?

6. How would water temperature affect the reading on your straw?

574 *Chapter 22*

22.2 Exploring the Ocean Floor

For hundreds of years, the ocean floor was more of a mystery than the moon's surface. Astronomers could see features on the moon's surface with a telescope. No one could see the surface of the ocean floor. No one even knew what was beneath the water's surface. Tales of sea monsters were more common than hard fact. However, in this century, modern technology and equipment have revealed much about the oceans. New discoveries about the ocean floor have helped geologists understand the processes that shape Earth.

Early Exploration

Early oceanographers could only study the ocean from the water's surface. Today this would be like trying to study Earth's surface from a plane that is flying over thick cloud cover. In 1872, a British ship called the *H.M.S. Challenger* was outfitted as a floating laboratory. For four years, the *Challenger*'s scientists took water and sediment samples using only simple jars and nets. The crew calculated water depth by lowering a weighted wire until it hit bottom. A depth measurement taken by lowering a wire is called a **sounding.** With simple equipment, the *Challenger* collected enough information about the oceans to establish oceanography as a new field of science.

Modern Methods

How would you go about exploring the ocean today? Weighted drop lines have been replaced by electronic echo sounders. You may remember echo sounding from Chapter 10. The echo sounder was first used by a German research ship, *Meteor*, in 1927. Echo sounders were used in the 1950's to make ocean floor maps that revealed features formed by plate movements. Unlike soundings taken with a weighted line, a ship does not have to stop to take an echo sounding. The echo sounder takes continuous soundings as the ship sails along. Other data are used to make seafloor maps. Maps of seafloor age and water temperature help determine the location and rate of seafloor spreading.

Side-scan sonar is another device used to map the ocean floor. Instead of sending its sound waves straight down, like an echo sounder, the side-scan sonar sends out sound waves in many directions. It gives a much wider picture of the ocean floor. Side-scan sonar was first developed to find enemy submarines. Today you can use it to map the ocean floor, or to locate shipwrecks or schools of fish.

Lesson Objectives

▸ *Contrast* today's ocean exploration with past methods.

▸ *Describe* the features of the ocean floor and **explain** how they form.

▸ *Summarize* how coral reefs form.

▸ Activity *Construct a graph* to show ocean floor features.

New Terms

sounding	turbidity
cores	currents
submersible	continental rise
continental shelf	abyssal plain
continental slope	seamount
submarine	guyot
canyon	atoll

Figure 22-7 This image of the ocean floor was made from side-scan sonar information.

Figure 22-8 Maps made from satellite data reveal seafloor topography beneath the oceans. This image of the Atlantic Ocean was taken by the satellite called *Seasat*.

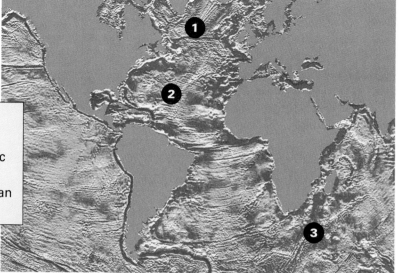

1. Reykjanes Ridge
2. Mid-Atlantic Ridge
3. Indian Ocean Ridge

Figure 22-9 Researchers examining cores

Your most complete map of the ocean floor would come from satellite data. Figure 22-8 shows a map made from information collected by the satellite *Seasat*. Satellite signals cannot pass through the water to the ocean floor. The satellites can, however, make very accurate measurements of their height above the ocean surface. The surface of the water bulges up slightly over underwater mountains and dips down over trenches. The satellite reads the smallest difference in the water's surface.

Maps and pictures tell you a lot about the ocean floor, but actual samples provide much more information. How do you get samples of sediment from the ocean floor? You could use a mechanical device like the grab sampler. A grab sampler grabs sediment off the ocean floor.

Many samples today are collected using a huge hollow drill. The drill brings long cylinders of sediment and rock, called **cores,** to the surface. You can better understand core samples if you make one yourself. Plunge a plastic straw straight down into a frosted layer cake. When you carefully remove the straw and cut it open, you will see a core sample. The *Glomar Challenger*, a modern research vessel named for the original British ship, drilled many ocean floor cores. These cores give data about marine life, ocean currents, and the rate at which sediment builds up on the ocean floor. Cores of sediment are sometimes taken with a gravity or dart corer. A gravity corer is a hollow, weighted tube, open at one end and attached to the ship by a cable at the other end. When the gravity corer is dropped over the side of a ship, it plummets through the water and sticks into the seafloor. The tube fills with sediments, which are then recovered when the corer is pulled back to the surface.

Why can't you gather samples and make observations in person? Remember that a scuba diver can only comfortably go as deep as 100 meters. Most of the ocean is much deeper than 100 meters. To visit the seafloor, you need a submersible. A **submersible** is a small submarine used for undersea research. The *Alvin* is a well-known battery-powered submersible. Perhaps you saw *Alvin* in the news when it was used to explore the wreck of the *Titanic*. The *Titanic* was an ocean liner that hit an iceberg and sank in 1912. *Alvin* carried a smaller robot submarine, named *Jason Jr.*, that was able to go inside the *Titanic* and take pictures.

One problem with submersibles is that they spend most of their diving time getting to and from the ocean bottom. One solution to this problem is for researchers to use a device like *Argo. Argo* is an underwater sled that operates without people on board. *Argo* is towed across the ocean bottom by a ship on the surface. As it is towed, *Argo's* cameras send television pictures to the ship above.

Figure 22-10 Submersibles, such as *Alvin*, allow scientists to explore deep ocean areas.

Ocean Floor Features

Imagine taking a trip through the world's oceans in a submersible that could travel very fast, stay down for days, and go as deep as you wanted. Figure 22-11 is a diagram showing many features found on the seafloor. Let's say your trip starts from a port city on the left side of the diagram. As you travel out to sea, the first part of the seafloor you would see is a broad, gently sloping extension of the continent called the **continental shelf.** The continental shelves were formed when glaciers from the last Ice Age melted. The added water in the oceans caused sea level to rise, flooding the edges of the continents. These flat underwater parts of the continents are the shelves.

Figure 22-11 Ocean floor features

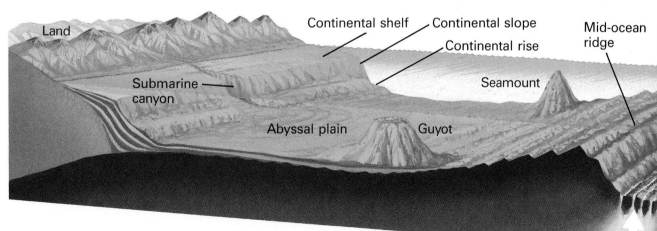

Land

Continental shelf Continental slope Mid-ocean ridge

Continental rise

Submarine canyon

Seamount

Abyssal plain Guyot

At the edge of the continental shelf, your submersible would journey down a steep surface to the deep ocean basin. The boundary between the continental shelf and the ocean basin floor is called the **continental slope.**

You might be surprised to find your submersible hovering over an underwater valley. A deep valley or canyon carved into the continental shelf and the continental slope is called a **submarine canyon.** Some submarine canyons are wider and deeper than the Grand Canyon. Some submarine canyons are extensions of the river valleys formed on land. Other canyons are formed by turbidity currents. A **turbidity current** is a fast movement of sediment-filled water. These currents are like underwater landslides. Some turbidity currents may go as fast as 30 kilometers per hour. The water in these currents is full of sand and mud, which makes it a good agent of erosion. Why would the amount of sediment in the water make a difference in how much erosion occurs? Which would scratch your skin more, being hit by a large wave of water or being hit by a large wave of water carrying sand and mud? Turbidity currents take sediment from the continental shelf and dump it out in front of the continental slope. The sand and mud deposited by the current forms a gentle, sloping surface at the base of the continental slope called the **continental rise.**

As you come down off the continental rise, your submersible is now traveling along the ocean basin floor. Here the water is an average of 4 kilometers deep. Much of the ocean basin floor is covered by large, flat areas of sediment called **abyssal plains.** Turbidity currents carry fine-grained sediment from the continental shelf. The fine sediment spreads out across the ocean basin floor, filling in low spots and covering low hills. This results in the very flat abyssal plains. These plains are the most level areas on Earth.

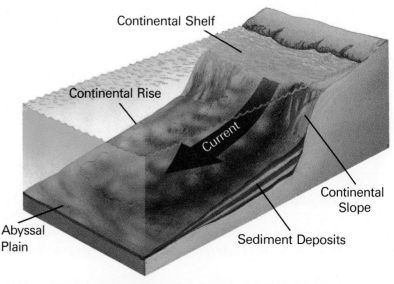

Figure 22-12 Turbidity currents move huge amounts of sediment down the continental slope.

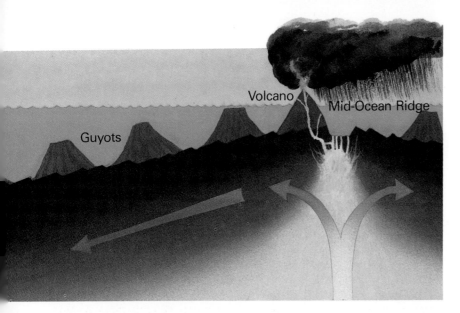

Your submersible would also take you to large mountains growing up from the deep ocean basin floor. These mountains are really underwater volcanoes. Some volcanic mountains emerge from the water as islands. Other than Hawaii, what volcanic islands do you recall from Chapter 11?

Not all underwater volcanoes are tall enough to come out of the water. An underwater volcano rising from the seafloor is a **seamount.** Some seamounts look as if they have had their tops chopped off. The tops of these seamounts were once near the ocean's surface, where they were eroded by waves. An underwater volcano which has had its top flattened by wave erosion is called a **guyot** (gē′ ō).

If the guyot was once near enough to the ocean's surface to be eroded, why is it so far underwater now? This is another piece of evidence in support of plate tectonics. Look at Figure 22-13. The volcano originally formed near a divergent boundary. The water depth was less, and the top of the volcano was soon worn down by the waves. The top became flat. As the plates spread apart, the volcano moved farther and farther from the mid-ocean ridge. As it moved away, the volcano sank deeper into the water.

As your underwater journey continues, you could also explore the mid-ocean ridges. Mid-ocean ridges form at divergent plate boundaries. Magma pushes up where the two plates pull apart. *Alvin's* crew found 350°C hot springs bubbling out of a rift valley in the eastern Pacific. The water was so hot that the rods holding thermometers nearly melted. Strangely, these hot springs are surrounded by giant tube worms and clams, shown in Figure 22-14 *(bottom)*. Most ocean life depends on sunlight. These hot-spring organisms, however, get energy from bacteria. These bacteria are able to produce energy from hydrogen sulfide in the hot water.

Figure 22-14 *Top:* The hot water pouring from vents at mid-ocean ridges contains so much dissolved material that it looks like smoke coming from a chimney. *Bottom:* Strange organisms, like the giant tube worm, feed on bacteria present at mid-ocean ridge vents.

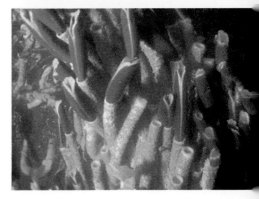

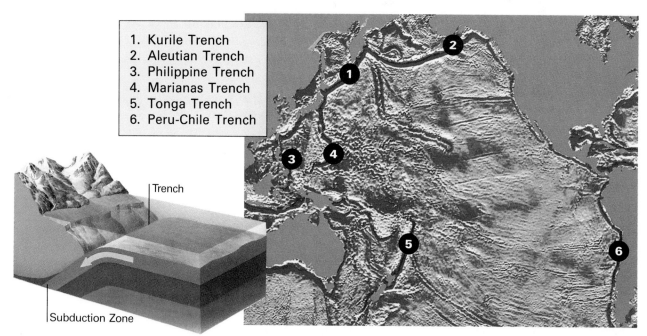

1. Kurile Trench
2. Aleutian Trench
3. Philippine Trench
4. Marianas Trench
5. Tonga Trench
6. Peru-Chile Trench

Figure 22-15 Trenches, such as those shown in this *Seasat* image of the Pacific Ocean, form when an ocean plate is subducted beneath another plate.

Figure 22-16 The coral reef is built by tiny marine organisms. Why is life so abundant around a coral reef?

Some parts of the ocean are too deep for most submersibles to explore. In Chapter 10, you learned that trenches form where one plate is subducted beneath another. Trenches are 2 to 4 kilometers deeper than the nearby seafloor. Many of the deepest trenches are around the edges of the Pacific Ocean. For example, the Marianas Trench, located southeast of Japan, contains the deepest spot known on Earth, called Challenger Deep. The bottom of Challenger Deep is over 11 kilometers below sea level. That means the pressure of the water on a human body would be about 1100 times what the body experiences on Earth's surface. The longest trench is the Peru-Chile Trench. This trench is located along the entire western coast of South America. It stretches for 5900 kilometers. The Peru-Chile Trench is formed by the subduction of the Nazca Plate beneath the South American Plate.

Coral Reefs

Many of the bright, colorful fish you see in pet stores come from coral reefs. Reefs are built by large groups of tiny organisms living in warm, shallow oceans. These organisms use the calcite dissolved in sea water to make their shells. The most common organism building the reef is the coral. When corals and other organisms die, new corals build their shells on top of the older shells. Reefs develop as layer upon layer of coral shells are added. The warm, shallow water needed for reef growth occurs in the Caribbean Sea, around some volcanic islands in the South Pacific, and in other areas near the equator.

Fringing reef

Barrier reef

Lagoon

Atoll —

Lagoon

Sediment

Figure 22-17 shows three forms of coral reefs. These three forms may represent stages in the development of a reef. A reef that grows close to land is a fringing reef. Corals do not survive in water that is not fairly clear. Sediment washing off the island makes the water near shore cloudy. The coral reef grows out and away from the land to stay in clear water. This process soon forms a reef separated from land by a shallow lagoon. This type of reef is called a barrier reef. Perhaps you have heard of the Great Barrier Reef of Australia. It is about 2000 kilometers long. Some coral reefs grow around sinking volcanic islands. If the island sinks and the reef continues to grow, it may form a circular coral reef called an **atoll.**

Figure 22-17 The three types of coral reef are formed as the volcanic island sinks and the coral continues to grow upward into shallow water.

Lesson Review 22.2

6. Briefly describe how the following undersea vessels are used: *Alvin, Jason Jr.,* and *Argo.*

7. What information can you learn from a sediment core?

8. Describe the process that turns a seamount into a guyot.

9. What ocean floor features form as a result of plate tectonics?

Interpret and Apply

10. Compare the seamounts and submarine canyons found on the ocean floor with similar topographic features on land. Describe how the processes that formed these ocean and land features are similar.

11. Sea level has changed many times in Earth's geologic past. What effect would sea level change have on coral reefs?

ACTIVITY 22.2

MAPPING THE SEAFLOOR

Purpose   Construct a graph from soundings that shows ocean floor features.

Materials

bucket or tub	graph paper
coarse wire mesh	pencil
water	35 cm string
food coloring	small weight
metric ruler	lab apron
assorted small objects	

Procedure

1. Read all instructions for this activity. Put on your lab apron.

2. Trace an outline of the top of your bucket on a large piece of graph paper.

3. Use several small objects to make a model of ocean floor features in the bottom of the bucket.

4. Carefully add water to the bucket until it is half full. Add food coloring to the water until you cannot see the model.

5. Exchange buckets and graph paper with another team in the room.

6. Place the wire mesh over the top of the bucket as shown. Each square hole should correspond to one square on the piece of graph paper.

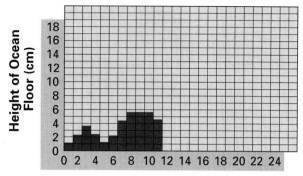

Squares on Sample Line A

(y-axis: Height of Ocean Floor (cm) — 0, 2, 4, 6, 8, 10, 12, 14, 16, 18)
(x-axis: 0 2 4 6 8 10 12 14 16 18 20 22 24)

7. Tie the weight to the string. Lower the weight through one of the holes in the mesh. When you feel the weight touch bottom, measure the length of string remaining above the mesh. Calculate the height of the ocean floor by subtracting your measurement from 35 cm and then subtracting this number from the depth of the bucket. Record this height on your graph paper.

8. Choose a line of squares in the wire mesh across the bucket. This will be line A. Take soundings in each square along this line. Record the depths.

9. On the second piece of graph paper, set up a graph like the one shown above. Use your data from the first sheet of graph paper to plot a profile of line A.

10. Drain water out of your bucket. Compare your profile to the model.

11. Clean up all materials.

Collecting and Analyzing Data

1. Did your profile resemble the model?

2. How could you change the procedure to determine the shape of the ocean floor more accurately?

Drawing Conclusions

3. What are the disadvantages of using this method to map the deep ocean floor?

22.3 Using Ocean Resources

If you were asked to imagine a farmer at work, would you think of someone riding a tractor or milking cows? Would you think of someone in scuba gear? Today there are farmers who harvest fish and seaweed from acres of ocean water. Food has always been an important ocean resource. The ocean is also a source of minerals, fresh water, and energy. People treasure the ocean's natural beauty, as well as depend on the ocean for recreation and transportation.

Will the ocean always be able to provide these resources? This lesson will explain in more detail what ocean resources are. You will also see how these resources are currently being threatened by human activity, and what is being done to manage and protect them.

Recreation and Food

The oceans are used like massive highways between continents. Ships transport products, such as cars and oil, from one continent to another. The oceans are also crowded with recreational users like swimmers and boaters. Many businesses and jobs along the coasts depend on healthy, clean beaches for a successful tourist season. In 1988, many beaches in the northeastern United States were closed when medical waste began to wash ashore. Other beaches have been closed when sewage dumped into the ocean made the water unhealthy for swimmers. What problems are caused when beaches are closed due to pollution?

Lesson Objectives

▶ **Discuss** ways the ocean provides food and recreation.

▶ **Describe** some products and energy sources of sea water.

▶ **Evaluate** current concerns about ocean pollution.

▶ **Activity** **Perform an experiment** to compare methods used to clean up an oil spill.

New Terms

kelp
krill
desalination

Figure 22-18 The ocean has many recreational uses.

Figure 22-19 The ocean is also a source of food.

About 90 percent of the food taken from the ocean is fish. Problems arise when too many fish are removed from an area before the fish population can reproduce itself. This situation is called overfishing. Overfishing has become such a serious problem partly due to modern fishing methods and partly due to an increasing demand for food. Almost 99 percent of all seafood comes from waters above the continental shelf. The broad continental shelf off of New England, known as George's Banks, is one of the world's richest fishing grounds. In recent years, the supply of fish caught on George's Banks has dropped due to overfishing. Overfishing for just one year could mean poor fishing in that area for many years to come.

In recent years, fish farming has grown to become a major industry. Oysters have been farmed in Chesapeake Bay and in Japan for over a century. In Maine and in the Pacific Northwest, farmers purchase baby salmon. The farmers raise the salmon in large floating pens until they reach a marketable size. Salmon have been successfully farmed this way in Norway and in British Columbia, Canada, for many years. Fish farming methods like this could increase food supplies without problems of overfishing.

What other seafood do people eat? Clams, oysters, lobsters, shrimp, and even seaweed are all used as food. **Kelp,** a fast-growing seaweed shown, is harvested for food, iodine, and potassium. Kelp is also a source of algin, used in making salad dressing, ice cream, medicines, and cosmetics.

In the future, you may be eating the same food some whales eat. **Krill** is a tiny, shrimplike creature that lives in the water off Antarctica. Blue whales eat over 4 metric tons of krill each day. Krill are a good source of protein. The Japanese use krill in noodles and rice cakes.

Figure 22-20 *Left:* Kelp can grow as much as two thirds of a meter each day. *Right:* Small shrimplike krill are used as an ingredient in processed foods.

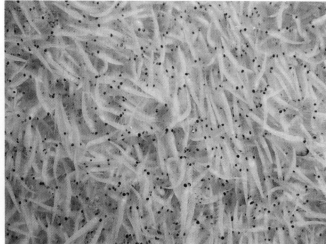

Sea Water

You have learned that sea water contains important minerals. The most common salt, sodium chloride, has been used for thousands of years. Salt was highly valued in ancient Greece and Rome, where it was sometimes used as money. In fact, the word *salary* comes from the Latin word for *salt money*. Over half the world's supply of magnesium comes from sea water. Other metals may someday be mined from the nodules found on the ocean floor.

The most useful part of sea water may be the water itself. Have you ever seen a movie where people adrift on the ocean for days are dying of thirst? You cannot drink salt water. However, limitless supplies of fresh water can be made from salt water through the process of desalination. **Desalination** is the process of removing salt from sea water. Sea water is piped into large glass-topped containers, where the sun heats and evaporates pure water. At night, when the roof cools, the fresh water condenses and collects in another container. Some plants desalinate water by passing it through a membrane that removes the salt. Many dry countries and islands too small to collect enough rainwater depend on desalination for fresh drinking water. In the United States, there are desalination plants in Key West, Florida, and Freeport, Texas. Unfortunately, fresh water produced by desalination is expensive. Saudi Arabia, a country that is rich in energy but that has little fresh water, has even proposed towing icebergs from the Antarctic to use as a source of fresh water. Why would the water in an iceberg be fresh?

Figure 22-21 Salt can be removed from sea water by simple evaporation.

Energy

Think back to the ocean energy sources you learned about in Chapter 16. Companies drill for oil on the continental shelf. OTEC power plants use thermal energy in the mixed layer to make steam and generate electricity. Some countries use the tides as energy sources. In addition to these sources, there are new ideas for using the oceans as energy resources.

The energy in waves is even greater than the energy in tides. Large waves could be used to rock large floats. The rocking motion would be used to turn generators and produce electricity. Figure 22-22 shows what such a power plant might look like.

The ocean might also provide burnable biomass fuels. Kelp can be harvested and decomposed in airtight tanks to produce methane, a type of natural gas. However, farming enough kelp to meet current natural gas needs would take an area tens of thousands of square kilometers in size.

Figure 22-22 An artist's idea of a future wave-powered electrical generating plant

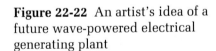

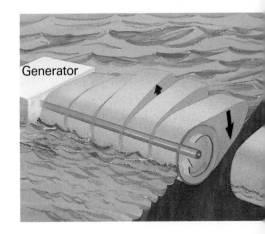
Generator

Environmental Concerns

It would be wrong to suggest that the ocean is only important because of the resources taken from it. The ocean is a major part of the world environmental system. You know, for example, how the oceans affect weather and climate. Did you know that green ocean plants supply most of the oxygen in Earth's atmosphere? Ocean life forms also help remove carbon dioxide from the atmosphere. Carbon dioxide contributes to the greenhouse effect, which causes global warming. A threat to ocean life may easily threaten life on land.

Every day it becomes clearer how human activity threatens the ocean environment. Chemical dumping is just one example. For years, industry dumped hazardous materials, such as cyanide, lead, and mercury, into the ocean from the land. Fish and shellfish absorbed these harmful metals and chemicals. Birds and mammals that ate the poisoned fish were also poisoned. In Japan, people died or became seriously ill from eating fish that contained high levels of mercury. In 1972, many countries passed strict laws to reduce chemical dumping and restrict the use of pesticides.

Figure 22-23 Plastic dumped into the ocean does not decay. As the seal grows, this noose of plastic will slowly choke him to death.

ENVIRONMENTAL AWARENESS

Oceans and Oil

Do you remember Alaska's horrible oil spill in 1989? The tanker, *Exxon Valdez*, ran aground, spilling over 38 million liters of oil into the waters of Prince Edward Sound. The oil spill covered an area larger than Rhode Island. Even with massive clean-up efforts, the effects of the oil on the bay's environment will last for decades.

Oil tanker spills are not the only source of oil pollution. Oil is released accidentally from offshore oil wells. Oil from leaking pipelines or from automobiles is continuously carried by rivers to the ocean. Some oil even leaks naturally from the ocean floor.

Oil floats on the water's surface. The oil gets carried to the beaches by currents and waves. All levels of the ocean's food chain are affected by oil. For example, when sea birds get oil on their feathers, they can no longer fly or keep themselves warm. As a result, thousands of birds die.

How can oil pollution be stopped? Because of public pressure, new oil tankers are being built stronger to resist damage and contain oil leaks. New methods are being used to unload and clean out tankers. You can help stop oil pollution in your life. When your family car gets an oil change, where does the old oil go? Many garages now recycle the used oil they remove from car engines. Some people want to stop offshore drilling and seek other sources of energy in order to protect the environment. How would you vote on such issues? ∎

The use of nuclear energy has created the problem of nuclear waste disposal. By 1982, thousands of metric tons of radioactive waste had been sealed in concrete and steel drums and dropped into the northeastern Atlantic Ocean. The United States no longer dumps its nuclear waste this way. However, many other countries continue to use the ocean to dispose of radioactive wastes.

Do you pollute the ocean? Even if you live far inland, you may not realize that many of your unwanted materials reach the ocean. Leftover cleansers you use in your home and pesticides used in your backyard may wash down rivers and into the ocean. The plastics you use every day also pollute the ocean. Plastics get carried downriver to the oceans or are dumped there with other garbage. Plastic does not easily rot or decay. Biologists estimate 100 000 marine animals and 2 million sea birds are killed every year by eating or becoming entangled in plastic. Eleven states have already passed laws banning the use of the plastic rings that hold beverage cans together. Some schools, like Sisson Elementary School in Mount Shasta, California, have stopped their annual practice of releasing balloons into the atmosphere. The balloons fall into the ocean, where they are sometimes mistaken for food. Birds and fish that swallow the balloons later die.

There are many problems with ocean pollution. It is not yet known what effects pollutants will have on future life. Some parts of the ocean far from human activities already show signs of pollution. Why is pollution more concentrated in certain ocean areas? Are there places where waste dumping would be less harmful? In the next chapter, you will read about movements of ocean water. The circulation of ocean water around Earth has many benefits. In the case of spreading pollution, it also has its disadvantages.

Figure 22-24 The *Exxon Valdez* oil spill in 1989 affected 800 miles of Alaskan coastline.

ACTIVITY 22.3   *General Supplies*

OIL SPILLS

Purpose To perform an experiment to compare methods used to clean up oil spills.

Materials

shallow pan	paper towel
water	cotton ball
vegetable oil	tweezers
ice cream bar sticks	sand
paper cup	liquid detergent
feather	safety goggles
medicine dropper	lab apron

Procedure

1. Read all the instructions for this activity before you begin your work.

2. List your observations on a separate piece of paper. Label your cup, *Recovered Oil.*

3. Put on your safety goggles and lab apron.

4. On a flat, level surface, fill one end of the pan with sand. Create a small beach about one fourth the length of the pan and about 3 cm deep.

5. Fill the remaining portion of the pan with water as shown.

6. At the end of the pan opposite the beach area, dip the long edge of an ice cream bar stick in and out of the water once every few seconds. This should create waves on your beach.

7. Carefully pour 20 mL of vegetable oil into the water between the popsicle stick and the beach. Observe how the oil behaves in the water.

8. As the oil spill spreads out, stick your finger in the center. Observe what happens when your finger is removed.

9. Put the feather into the oil spill. Describe what happens to the feather.

10. Try to prevent the oil spill from reaching your beach. Record your observations.

11. Put two drops of liquid detergent on part of the oil spill. Observe what happens.

12. Use the wooden sticks, cottonball, paper towel, and dropper to recover as much oil as possible. Use tweezers to handle the paper and cotton. Dispose of used items and oil in the paper cup. Write down any observations.

13. Before leaving the laboratory, clean up all materials and wash your hands.

Collecting and Analyzing Data

1. What happened to objects like the feather and your finger when they were dipped in the oil?

2. What effect did the detergent have on the oil?

3. Which materials absorbed oil? Which material absorbed the oil most easily?

4. Describe any problems you had trying to remove the oil from the water.

Drawing Conclusions

5. What effects do winds and wave action have on cleaning up an oil spill?

6. Do you think it would be easier to remove the oil from the water or the beach? Explain your answer.

Lesson Review 22.3

12. Name some ways to solve the problems caused by overfishing.

13. List and describe some products taken from the ocean.

14. Explain how you can help prevent ocean pollution.

Interpret and Apply

15. What jobs are directly affected by ocean pollution?

16. Explain why the continental shelves are more likely than the deep ocean basin to suffer environmental problems.

17. Magnesium and bromine are currently being taken from sea water. Gold is not. What determines which elements are mined from the ocean water?

Chapter Summary

Read the summary of the main ideas in this chapter. If any are not clear to you, go back and review that lesson.

22.1 Earth's Oceans

■ There are four major oceans. The largest ocean is the Pacific.

■ Sea water contains over 60 elements. Sodium chloride is the major salt in the ocean.

■ The average salinity of sea water is 35 parts per thousand. Salinity increases in areas with high levels of evaporation. Salinity decreases in areas where fresh water enters the ocean.

■ Sea water temperature decreases with greater depth. Water pressure increases with greater depth.

22.2 Exploring the Ocean Floor

■ Today oceans are mapped using echo sounders, side-scan sonar, and satellites.

■ Submersibles and remote-controlled robots provide data about the deep ocean.

■ The continental shelf is a broad extension of the continents. The edges of the continental shelf and slope are cut by canyons.

■ The deep ocean basin is made mostly of flat abyssal plains. Other features include seamounts and guyots.

■ The mid-ocean ridges and the trenches are ocean features formed by plate movement.

■ Coral reefs form in warm, shallow ocean water.

22.3 Using Ocean Resources

■ The ocean is a source of food, energy, and minerals. It is also used for transportation and as a place for recreation.

■ New food sources, fish farming, and fishing boundaries are ways to avoid problems caused by overfishing.

■ Desalination is used to change salt water into fresh drinking water.

■ Ocean pollution can seriously reduce and endanger the oceans as a resource.

Chapter Review

■ Vocabulary

abyssal plain
atoll
continental shelf
continental slope
cores
desalination
guyot
kelp
krill

salinity
sea
seamount
sounding
submarine canyon
submersible
thermocline
turbidity current

■ Concept Mapping

Construct a concept map for sea water. Include the following terms: *density, dissolved gases, pure water, salinity,* and *temperature.* Use additional terms as you need them.

■ Review

Number your paper from 1 to 22. Match each term in list **A** to a phrase in list **B**.

List A
a. atoll
b. pressure
c. thermocline
d. salinity
e. continental shelf
f. desalination
g. Atlantic Ocean
h. turbidity currents
i. oil and chemicals
j. abyssal plain

k. *Alvin*
l. *H.M.S. Challenger*
m. kelp
n. overfishing
o. Pacific
p. sodium chloride
q. calcite
r. guyot
s. krill
t. temperature

List B
1. most common mineral taken from water by organisms to build a reef
2. largest ocean on Earth
3. types of ocean pollution
4. large, flat area of the deep ocean floor
5. underwater stream carrying mud and sand
6. amount of dissolved salt in sea water
7. temperature layer of the ocean
8. shrimplike creatures eaten by whales
9. removing more fish than are replaced by reproduction
10. a form of seaweed used for food and which may be used as biomass
11. seamounts flattened by wave erosion
12. decreases with depth
13. first floating laboratory to explore and study oceans
14. area rich in fish, oil, and natural gas
15. increases with depth
16. second largest ocean and still growing
17. removal of salt from sea water
18. major salt in sea water
19. submersible used to explore the ocean floor
20. ring-shaped coral reef

■ Interpret and Apply

On your paper, answer each question using complete sentences.

21. Explain how the formation of guyots from volcanoes supports the theory of seafloor spreading.
22. A tidal pool is a small pocket of sea water left on the shore when the tide goes out. As you walk along a rocky shore on a sunny day, you see two tidepools. Tidepool *A* is much farther from the ocean than Tidepool *B*. Discuss how you think they would compare in temperature, salinity, and dissolved oxygen.
23. River water contains much dissolved calcium. Even though rivers empty into the ocean, the amount of calcium in sea water is fairly low. Where does the calcium go once it enters the ocean?

24. Suppose you wanted to spend a week's vacation on the surface of the moon and then stay a week on the ocean floor. Explain how your two vacation homes would be similar. What supplies would you need to bring for both vacations?

25. Discuss what would happen if there were enough pollution floating on the ocean's surface to block sunlight from the water.

26. What are the benefits of using tides and wave movement as energy sources?

27. Explain why many turbidity currents probably start at the mouth of a river.

28. Sound travels at 1500 meters/second in sea water. It took 12 seconds for an echo sounder to send and receive a sound wave. What is the depth of the water?

29. What ocean floor feature must the ship in question 28 be over?

30. Would a ship float higher in the Mediterranean Sea or at the mouth of the Mississippi River? Explain your answer.

■ Writing in Science

31. Most first drafts need some revision. Read the following first draft of a paragraph explaining why the salinity of ocean water can vary. Then revise it. Pay particular attention to whether the information is accurate and related to the topic.

> *Several factors can change the salt content of ocean water. When ocean water freezes, most of its salt stays in the surrounding water. Water in very cold areas can thus have fairly high salinity. Cold ocean water can also hold more oxygen than warm water. In warm areas where there is little rainfall, much ocean water evaporates. This evaporation reduces the salt concentration. When freshwater flows into the ocean, the salinity in that area decreases.*

■ Critical Thinking

Australia's Great Barrier Reef is being overrun and damaged by starfish. The starfish eat the tiny reef-building organisms and leave behind an empty coral skeleton. There are two hypotheses to explain the problem:

■ Shell collecting and modern game fishing on the reef have reduced the numbers of natural predators that eat starfish eggs. Without predators to limit their numbers, too many starfish develop.

■ The growth in the starfish population is part of a natural cycle. The number of starfish will increase until the food supply is gone, and then the number of starfish will decrease rapidly.

Using the above information, answer questions 32–34.

32. You drill a core into the reef. Close examination of the core shows that the reef has undergone starfish attacks several times in the last 10 000 years. Which hypothesis does this support? Explain.

33. What other data should you collect to try to find out if the large starfish population is part of a natural cycle?

34. Divers have been injecting starfish with poison to control their numbers. Explain how these efforts to control the starfish population affect conclusions based on starfish population data.

23 Waves and Currents

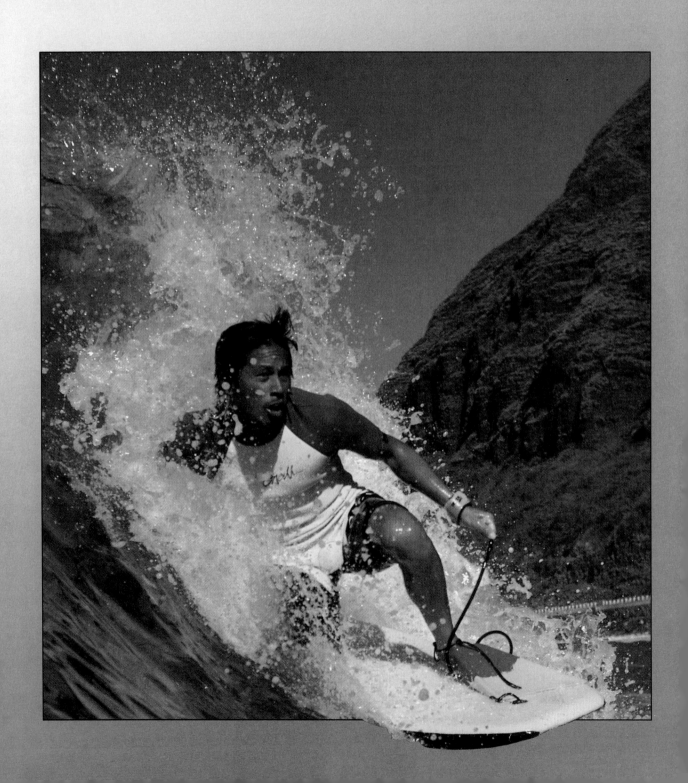

Chapter Preview

Have You Ever WONDERED?

How do surfers ride waves?

Sitting offshore, a surfer on a surfboard waits patiently for just the right wave to come along. When that wave finally approaches, the surfer paddles like crazy to stay just in front of the wave. The wave starts to break. The surfer stands up and rides down the wave's front slope as the wave rushes toward land. By balancing and turning from side to side, the surfer gets a very long ride before the wave washes up onto the beach.

Surfers study the movement of ocean water and winds to figure out when surfing will be best. In this chapter, you will learn about waves and other movements of ocean water. Perhaps this information will help you "catch a wave" someday.

23.1 *Ocean Waves*

Lesson Objectives

▸ **Explain** *how waves are formed and* **diagram** *their features.*

▸ **Discuss** *why waves break when they reach shore.*

▸ **Activity**   **Perform an experiment** *to study how waves affect shorelines.*

New Terms

crest   swells
trough   breaker
wave height

It's fun to spend time at an ocean beach. Have you ever noticed how the beach changes from day to day? Even the waves aren't always the same. One day the waves are so small that you could jump over them as they roll up onto the sand. The next day, the waves may be larger and crash against the same beach with a deafening roar. These waves are too big to jump. Perhaps you tried to "catch" these waves with your body or a board. It's the same beach and the same ocean on both days, yet the waves have changed. How do waves form and why do they change?

Wave Features

You already know one way that waves form in the ocean. In Chapter 11, you learned how underwater earthquakes, landslides, or volcanoes sometimes create the large waves called tsunamis. Like the circular ripples that spread out when you throw a pebble into a puddle, the tsunami waves spread out from their source, carrying off energy in all directions.

You are also familiar with other types of waves. The energy given off by the sun, such as light, X rays, and infrared radiation, is all in the form of waves. Sound travels as waves. Seismic waves move energy from an earthquake through solid rock. Even the wave that fans do at a sporting event seems to transfer energy from one location to another. What do these waves have in common with the waves you have seen at the beach?

Figure 23-1 The ocean is a fun and exciting place to spend the day.

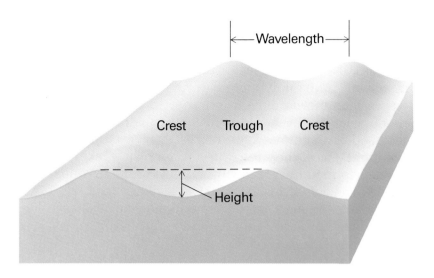

Wavelength

Crest   Trough   Crest

Height

Figure 23-2 The parts of a wave

All waves share the same basic parts, as shown in Figure 23-2. The **crest,** like the crest of a mountain, is the highest part of a wave. The low spot between two crests is called a **trough.** The distance from one crest to the next, or from the bottom of one trough to the next, is called the wavelength.

Imagine sitting in a boat on the ocean with waves passing beneath you. As the crests and troughs pass by, your boat moves up and down, over and over again. This is the rhythmic motion that makes some people seasick. The vertical distance between the bottom of the trough and the top of the crest is called the **wave height.** The greater the height of the wave, the more energy it contains.

Wind and Waves

Where does the energy come from that causes waves in the ocean? When you try to cool hot soup by blowing on it, you are demonstrating the way ocean waves form. Blowing on soup forms small waves on the soup's surface. Similarly, wind causes waves by blowing across the surface of water. How is the energy in moving air put into the water? In some places, the air pushes down on the water as the wind moves forward. The air that pushes down makes a small dent in the water's surface. As more air comes along, it hits the side of the dent, giving it a shove. It is the transfer of energy from millions of these little shoves that forms waves.

Wave height and wavelength depend on the amount of energy put into the water by the wind. Three things determine how much energy the wind is able to transfer to the water: the speed of the wind, how long the wind blows, and the distance of open water the wind blows across. Increasing any one of these three things adds more energy to the water, which makes the waves bigger.

Figure 23-3 In a storm, large waves toss ships around and may even flip the ships over.

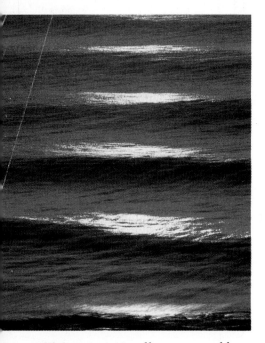

Figure 23-4 Swells are caused by storms far out at sea.

Very light winds create small ripples on the water's surface. If the wind continues to blow, or if the wind's speed increases, the ripples develop into bigger and bigger waves. Ocean waves are rarely more than 15 meters high, but strong storm winds can produce waves over 30 meters high. That's taller than a six-story building! People usually think of waves forming only in ocean water. Waves also form in lakes. What conditions are needed for waves to form in a lake?

Waves formed by strong storm winds in the middle of the ocean travel great distances before striking land. As these waves move farther from the storm, their shape changes. The waves develop more rounded crests and become the same size. These waves are called **swells.** As they move, swells develop a pattern resembling ridges on a potato chip.

Motion of Waves

Waves formed in the water by wind travel in the same direction as the wind. However, it is not the water itself that is moving. Instead, the wave's energy is moving. Remember what happens in an earthquake. The energy released as seismic waves travels hundreds of kilometers, often through solid rock. The rock is not traveling at all. The energy moves through the rock.

If you have ever tried to recover a beach ball thrown far from shore, you may notice it bobs up and down as each wave passes under it. Even though the wave is moving toward shore, the ball seems to stay in the same place. To understand this better, look at Figure 23-5. Like the beach ball, water particles move up and slightly forward on the crest of a wave. Once the crest passes, the water particles drop back slightly into the trough. The water particles actually travel a circular path and end up close to where they started.

Figure 23-5 Water particles move in a circle as a wave passes, much like this floating object moves in a circle.

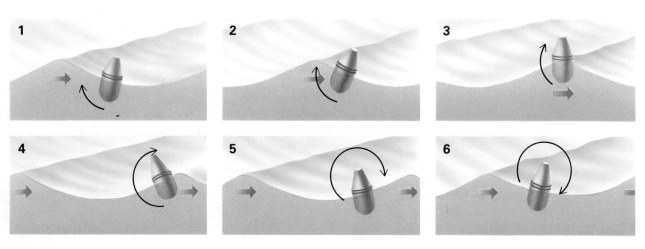

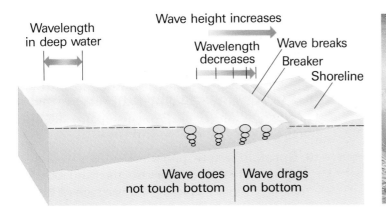

Figure 23-6 *Left:* Breakers form when waves reach shallow water. *Right:* Where waves break or topple over is often called the surf zone.

Beneath the surface, the size of the circles that water particles travel gets smaller as you go deeper. In fact, if you dive under the water to a depth equal to half the wavelength, you would barely know there are waves passing above you. All of the wave's energy is traveling between that depth and the water's surface.

The shape and motion of a wave do not remain the same. Look at Figure 23-6 *(left).* As the wave nears shore, the water particles circling below the surface begin to drag along the shallow ocean bottom. The dragging causes the wave to lose energy and slow down. As waves slow down, they get closer together and grow in height. The tops of the waves outrun the bottoms, which are still dragging along the ocean bottom. Soon the crest is leaning forward so far that it cannot hold itself up. The crest falls over, sending foamy water rushing up the beach. A collapsing wave is called a **breaker.**

Lesson Review 23.1

1. What factors determine the size of a wind-formed wave?
2. Sketch and describe how a wave's features change as it becomes a breaker.
3. Diagram the motion of a water particle in a wave.

Interpret and Apply

4. Explain why people riding in a submarine that is traveling 50 meters beneath the surface do not have to worry about the movement of waves.
5. Discuss why Hawaii, an island in the middle of the Pacific Ocean, has some of the largest waves for surfing.
6. Explain why larger waves form in an ocean rather than in a pond or reservoir.

ACTIVITY 23.1

General Supplies

WAVES

Purpose Perform an experiment to study how waves affect shorelines.

Materials

plastic shoebox	pen or pencil
metric ruler	4 heavy blocks
water	pencil shavings
plastic straw	

Procedure

1. Read all instructions for this activity before you begin your work.

2. Copy the diagram onto your paper.

3. Carefully pour enough water into your shoebox to reach a depth of 1 cm.

4. Place a pen or pencil under the end of the shoebox as shown. Allow 2–3 minutes for the water to become still.

5. Using your straw, gently blow air across the surface of the water. Use your copy of the diagram to sketch in Box A the wave pattern you observe.

6. Repeat step 5, but this time, blow through the straw as hard as you can. Sketch your observations in Box B.

7. Place the blocks in the shoebox as shown in Box C. Repeat step 5.

8. Rearrange the blocks to resemble the diagram for Box D. Repeat step 5. Sketch the wave pattern in Box D.

9. Sprinkle a few pencil shavings in the water at the center of the shoebox. Gently blow air across the surface of the water. When they reach the back of the shoebox, continue blowing. Sketch the path of the shavings in Box E.

10. Before leaving the laboratory, clean up all materials.

Collecting and Analyzing Data

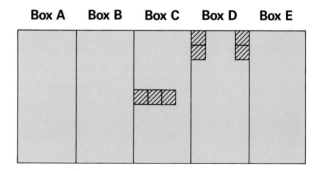

Box A   Box B   Box C   Box D   Box E

1. Describe the pattern of waves approaching the far end of the box, which represented a shoreline.

2. What happened to the waves when you blew as hard as you could?

3. Look at your results for Box D. Are waves concentrated at areas that stick out into the ocean or in areas that are set back, such as a bay or inlet?

Drawing Conclusions

4. Many coastal communities build large barriers across a harbor. What purpose do you think these barriers serve?

5. Explain why land jutting into the ocean erodes faster than land set back from the ocean.

23.2 Ocean Currents

Does this story sound familiar? A person stranded on a desert island writes a note, puts it in a bottle, and tosses the bottle out to sea. The bottle is miraculously found hundreds of kilometers from the island. A ship or plane is sent to the island, and the person is rescued. Could this really happen? How could the bottle travel so far?

Many items, such as bottles, driftwood, plant seeds, and trash have been carried great distances by ocean currents. You have learned about convection currents and currents of air. Ocean currents are parts of the ocean where the water flows in one direction. In a way, an ocean current is like a stream, except that instead of flowing over the land, the ocean current flows through more water.

Surface Currents

The surface currents moving through the oceans are gigantic in scale. Figure 23-7 shows the pattern of these surface currents. Notice how the warm and cold surface currents form large loops of circulating water. In Chapter 17, you learned how the heating of air together with Earth's rotation sets up global wind patterns. The movement of global winds over Earth's oceans creates large currents of moving water near the ocean's surface.

Lesson Objectives

▶ **List** and **describe** three types of ocean currents.

▶ **Explain** how different types of ocean currents form.

▶ **Discuss** how the ocean currents affect weather, climates, and ocean life.

▶ **Activity** **Form a model** of a density current.

New Terms

El Niño
upwelling
longshore current
rip current

Figure 23-7 Major currents in Earth's oceans

Major currents in Earth's oceans
➡ Warm water current ➡ Cold water current

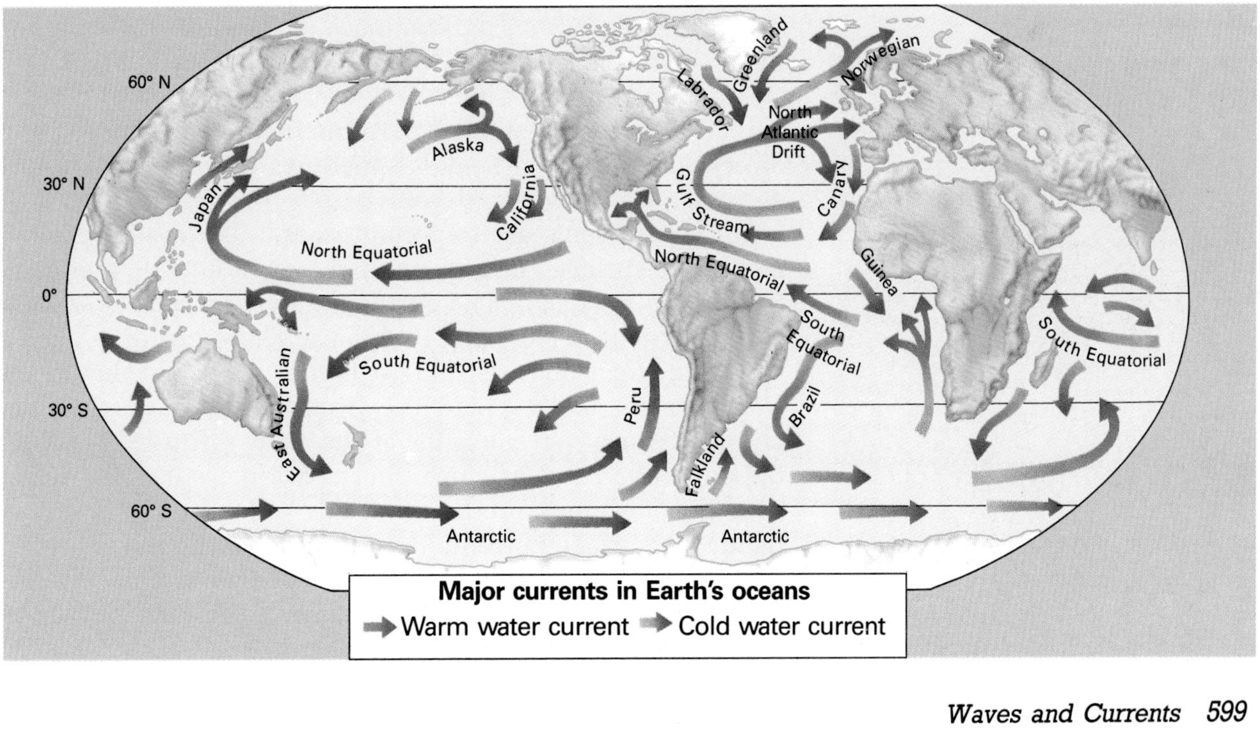

It is clear that winds have something to do with causing the surface currents. You learned that wind hitting the water adds the energy that causes waves. You also learned that the energy is what moves in waves, not the water itself. There is another way that wind adds energy to ocean water. When wind moves over the ocean, there is friction between the air and water. The friction causes the layer of water closest to the surface to start moving.

Unlike waves, currents do not keep moving in the same direction. Look again at Figure 23-7. Some surface currents form where warm water north and south of the equator is pushed westward by the trade winds. As those currents travel toward the west, they begin to turn toward one of Earth's two poles. The currents turn because of the Coriolis effect. As Earth rotates beneath the moving water, the current appears to turn. Currents in the Northern Hemisphere turn toward the right. Currents in the Southern Hemisphere turn toward the left. Whether flowing north or south, these currents move along the edges of a continent until they are pushed eastward by the prevailing westerly winds. Currents are pushed eastward until they approach land again and turn toward the equator to complete the cycle. This process forms the giant looped pattern you see in Figure 23-7.

The Gulf Stream

The Gulf Stream is a fast-moving surface current that carries 100 times more water than all of Earth's rivers combined. However, the Gulf Stream is not a simple, single stream. Figure 23-8 shows a satellite image of the Gulf Stream along the Atlantic coast. In the image, warm water appears red, and cooler water is blue. As you can see, the Gulf Stream is really a series of smaller currents that change speeds and directions, split apart, and sometimes form small circling currents.

Surface currents are important in maintaining Earth's climate. The surface currents act like a giant heating and cooling system for Earth. The currents moving from the equator carry warm water toward the poles. These currents have a warming effect on coastlines at higher latitudes. Due to the Gulf Stream, Iceland and the British Isles have a milder climate than other countries at the same latitude. The Gulf Stream warms the air above it. The warmer air mass moves over the land and produces milder weather. On the other hand, the surface currents that move from the poles toward the equator carry cold water. These currents cool areas along coastlines that would normally have a warmer climate at that latitude.

Figure 23-8 In this infrared satellite image, the warm water of the Gulf Stream appears as the colors red and orange.

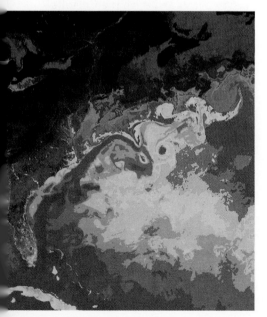

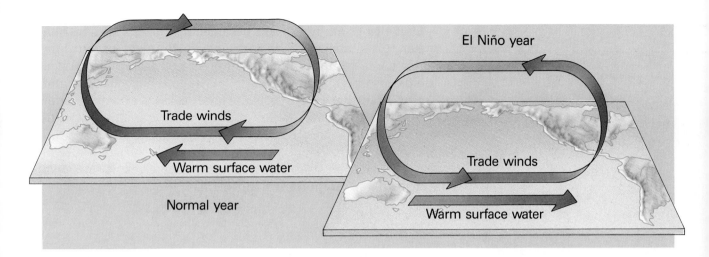

Trade winds

Warm surface water

Normal year

El Niño year

Trade winds

Warm surface water

El Niño

The connection between surface currents and weather is not always a good thing. One warm surface current in the Pacific Ocean, called **El Niño,** is the cause of weather-related disasters all over the world. During 1982 and 1983, El Niño was blamed for storms, flooding, and droughts worldwide. Hurricanes pounded Hawaii and Tahiti. Tens of thousands of people in Mississippi, Louisiana, and Florida evacuated their homes because of flooding, while northern states saw blizzards with record-breaking snowfalls.

The unusual thing about El Niño is that it flows against the trade winds that cause it. El Niño moves warm water toward the east, not toward the west. Look at Figure 23-9. Every five years or so, the trade winds in the Pacific Ocean become stronger than normal. The stronger winds push more surface water westward than usual. The water piles up in the western Pacific basin. When the trade winds die down, the warm water begins to slowly flow back across the Pacific, opposite the normal direction of flow. Several months later, after slowly moving back across the Pacific, El Niño arrives off the coast of South America.

Upwelling

In some areas, such as the west coast of South America, wind-driven currents carry water away from land. As the warm water moves away from the land, cold water rises up from the ocean floor to replace the warm water. Look at the diagram in Figure 23-10. Like a conveyor belt, the cold water continually replaces the water that moves away. This cold, upward current, usually found along the western coast of continents, is called an **upwelling.** Upwellings are found off the western coasts of California, Australia, and Africa.

Figure 23-9 A change in the trade winds causes El Niño.

Figure 23-10 Winds along the coast, combined with the Coriolis effect, drive surface water away from the shore. Cold water from below then rises up to replace the surface water.

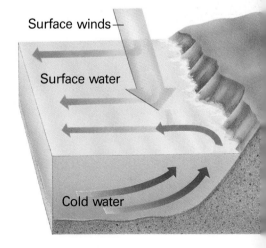

Surface winds

Surface water

Cold water

Figure 23-11 Upwellings provide rich fishing grounds.

Upwellings are important because they bring nutrient-rich water to the surface. The nutrients in the cold ocean floor water come from plants and animals that have died. When the plants and animals die, they settle to the ocean floor and decay. Like the humus in soil, this decayed organic matter is used by growing plants and animals. Wherever an upwelling brings these nutrients to the surface, you will find an abundance of plankton. Many forms of ocean life feed on the plankton and on each other. As a result, areas of upwelling are important fishing areas.

Density Currents

Some ocean currents have nothing to do with wind. These currents are formed by density differences in the water and are called density currents. Do you remember how a convection current works? Hot material is less dense than cold material. The hot material rises, and the cold material sinks. Sea water that is colder than the water around it has a greater density. The cold water sinks and forms a density current. Cold-water density currents form in the polar regions where cold winds and freezing temperatures make sea water cold and dense. This cold water sinks to the ocean floor and moves slowly toward the equator. Some of this cold, dense water remains circulating in the deep ocean basins for as long as one thousand years.

Another way to form a density current is to change the salinity of sea water. The more dissolved salt that is in the water, the greater the density. Look at the circulation of water in Figure 23-12. The saltier water in the Mediterranean Sea sinks to the bottom. As salty water continues to sink, it gets pushed out along the bottom of the Mediterranean Sea into the Atlantic Ocean through the narrow Straits of Gibraltar. Less salty water from the Atlantic Ocean flows into the Mediterranean to replace the water that has flowed out.

Figure 23-12 A density current moves saltier water from the Mediterranean Sea out along the bottom of the ocean floor into the Atlantic Ocean.

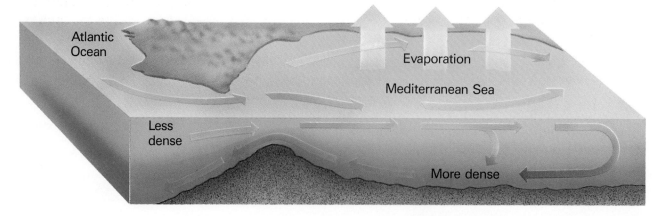

DENSITY CURRENTS

Purpose To form a model of a density current.

Materials

plastic shoebox	paper cup
water	strip of cardboard
salt	spoon
food coloring	lab apron
graduated cylinder	pencil
masking tape	

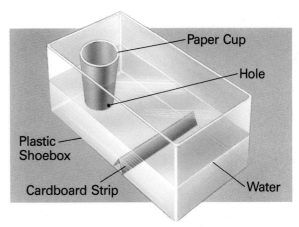

Procedure

1. Read all directions for this activity before you begin your work.

2. Put on your lab apron.

3. Insert the precut cardboard strip tightly against the bottom center of your shoebox as shown in the diagram. Tape the strip to the shoebox if necessary.

4. Carefully fill the box with water until the water is 3 cm deep.

5. Put 150 mL of water in the paper cup. Add a rounded spoonful of salt and 4 drops of food coloring. Stir with the spoon.

6. Carefully place the cup into one end of the shoebox. Use the pencil point to punch one small hole at the bottom of the cup on the side facing the cardboard strip. This will allow the colored water to pour out. Immediately observe what happens below the surface of the water by getting at eye level with the bottom of the box.

7. Observe the flow of colored water until all movement has stopped.

8. Before leaving the laboratory, clean up all materials and wash your hands thoroughly.

Collecting and Analyzing Data

1. On a clean sheet of paper, sketch the flow of the colored water as you saw it happen in the shoebox. Use arrows to indicate the direction of movement.

2. Why did the salt water move along the bottom of the shoebox?

3. Describe what happened when the salt water reached the cardboard barrier.

4. What happened to the salt water that reached the far end of the box?

Drawing Conclusions

5. Discuss what could cause the density current between the Mediterranean Sea and the Atlantic to stop flowing.

6. Explain how some sea water becomes trapped in deep ocean basins for thousands of years.

7. Predict what would happen if you used ice water in the paper cup instead of salt water. Explain your prediction.

Shoreline Currents

Think of a day you have spent at the beach. You went into the water directly in front of your beach blanket for a swim. When you decided to come out of the water, your blanket was gone. But it wasn't gone. After searching, you found your blanket farther up the beach. Did someone move the blanket or did you move while you were in the water? You had no way of knowing, but an ocean current had moved you down the beach.

Another type of ocean current is formed when waves approach the land. You may think that waves always move straight in toward the beach, with the breakers lined up parallel to the shoreline. Actually, waves often strike the beach at an angle. When the wave breaks, the water washes up onto the beach. The water and any sand the water picks up move up the beach in the same direction that the wave moves. Although the water and sand are pushed up the beach at an angle, they slide back into the sea in a straight line. The next wave can carry the same water and sand back up onto the beach to repeat the entire process. Figure 23-13 (right) shows the zig-zag pattern that develops from this constant movement. This pattern causes the water to move parallel to the shore. A current that moves along the shoreline is called a **longshore current.** Longshore currents carry and deposit sand along a shoreline.

There are other local currents that can pull you out to sea. On steep beaches, the water that washes up onto the beach rushes back into the sea very quickly. This forms a current called an undertow. An undertow can knock your feet out from under you and pull you into deeper water.

Figure 23-13 *Left:* Waves often approach the shore at an angle. *Right:* Waves striking the shore at an angle produce a longshore current.

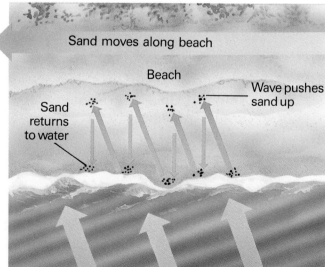

Sand moves along beach

Beach

Wave pushes sand up

Sand returns to water

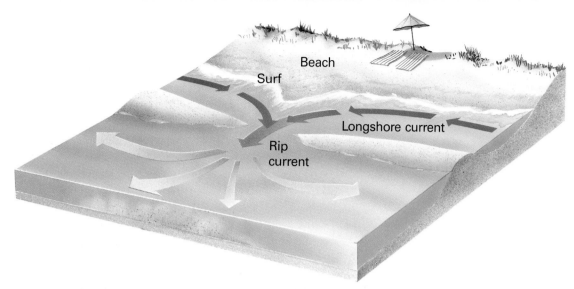

Beach

Surf

Longshore current

Rip current

Figure 23-14 Rip currents develop where two longshore currents meet and water is moved out into the open ocean.

An even stronger current forms when waves pile more water along the shore than can be returned to the ocean. When the water finally returns to the ocean, it rushes straight out from the shoreline at speeds of up to 5 kilometers per hour and for distances of a kilometer or more. This is illustrated in Figure 23-14. This strong, narrow surface current flowing out from shore is a **rip current.** Rip currents are very dangerous. A swimmer caught in a rip current should not try to swim toward land. By swimming parallel to the beach, the swimmer can cross out of the rip current and then swim safely back to shore.

Shoreline currents move both water and sand along the shoreline, forming and destroying beaches and other shoreline features. Why are some beaches sandy and others rocky? The next lesson will explain how ocean waves and currents form the different features you see along the shore.

Lesson Review 23.2

7. List and describe three types of ocean currents.

8. Describe two ways density currents form.

9. Explain how a surface current can alter an area's climate.

10. What is an upwelling and why is it important?

Interpret and Apply

11. Discuss how El Niño causes a worldwide increase in food prices.

12. Explain why the water at a beach in Southern California is much colder than the water at a beach in South Carolina, even though the latitude in both places is the same.

23.3 *Shoreline Features*

New Terms

sea cliff	beach
wave-cut terrace	spit
sea cave	barrier island
sea stacks	

If you have ever built a sand castle on a beach, you know how temporary shoreline features are. The sand castle you build in the morning gets washed away in the afternoon, as the tide comes in and waves wash higher and higher onto the beach. Although the sand castle is no longer there, the sand still exists. The same water that destroyed your work has taken the sand and deposited it elsewhere.

Features of Erosion

Changes along a shoreline happen quickly. One reason for such rapid changes is that the waves are so good at weathering and eroding the shoreline. Sea water chemically weathers the rocks. The water enters cracks and dissolves or changes the rock's minerals. Mechanical weathering occurs when the waves pound the shoreline with tremendous force. The energy carried in the waves is transferred to the rocks. The waves smash into the shoreline over and over again. This splits and breaks rock into smaller pieces. Broken pieces of rock are then hurled back against the shoreline, weathering the remaining rock. Over time, the ocean carves the shoreline into the features you see today.

One feature formed by wave action is a sea cliff, shown in Figure 23-15. A **sea cliff** is a steep portion of land or rock eroded by waves. You have probably seen cans of soup stacked on a supermarket shelf. What happens if someone pulls out a can from the bottom of the stack? The cans above the new gap fall with a crash and roll all over the floor. Waves form sea cliffs along the shoreline in a similar way.

Figure 23-15 The repeated pounding of powerful waves on a rocky shoreline is a strong agent of weathering and erosion.

Sea cliffs form where land juts out into the ocean. Large waves from strong storms pound against the land head on. At first, a small cliff forms when a notch is eroded or cut into the base of the piece of land. As waves cut the notch deeper into the base of the new cliff, they remove the support for the overlying rock. Without support, the rock from above falls into the sea.

The rocks that pile up at the base of the sea cliff are broken into smaller sediment and moved toward the ocean. Waves continue to cut the notch into the land, and the cliff is worn back. A wide, flat area forms in front of the cliff. This flat, underwater area in front of the sea cliff is called a **wave-cut terrace.** In Figure 23-16, wave-cut terraces are visible above sea level. This tells you that either the sea level has fallen or that the land has been lifted up out of the water.

Sea cliffs are not the only features formed by erosion along the shoreline. Sometimes a large hole in the sea cliff, called a **sea cave,** is formed when the waves cut under a cliff made of hard rock. The sea cave deepens and widens as waves continue to rush in and out. If the cave is cut into a narrow piece of land, the cave can be cut all the way through. This leaves an arch of rock where the cave once was. This is called a sea arch. Like the notch under a sea cliff, a sea arch leaves a gap under the remaining rock. Without support, the sea arch can collapse. When the arch collapses, tall columns of rock, called **sea stacks,** are left standing out away from the sea cliff.

The time it takes for these features to form depends on the type of rock that is being eroded. Soft rocks, like limestone and chalk, are worn away as much as a meter a year. For example, old maps show that certain parts of the English coast have worn back several kilometers in the last 2000 years. Harder rock, like granite, may show little effects of erosion after the same amount of time.

Figure 23-17 This sea arch in Oregon will soon collapse, leaving a sea stack standing away from the eroding sea cliff.

Figure 23-18 Beaches are not always made of white sand. *Left:* This beach in Mexico is made of pebbles. *Right:* The black sand beaches in Hawaii are made of weathered pieces of volcanic rock.

Figure 23-19 Sand deposited out from the shoreline by longshore currents forms a spit.

Features of Deposition

Erosion is not the only shoreline process. The pieces of rock weathered and eroded from the shoreline are moved along and deposited somewhere else. The deposition of this sediment forms new shoreline features.

If more sediment is washed up on shore than is taken away, a beach forms. A **beach** is a deposit of sediment along a shoreline. Beaches are often made of sand-size grains of quartz. Some beaches are made from other sediment. Coral reefs and seashells break apart to form sand. Florida and many tropical areas have beaches made of shell fragments. Hawaii is famous for its beaches made of black sand weathered from volcanic rocks. If a beach is steep, it may be covered with pebbles. A steep beach has a strong undertow, which carries away finer sediment, such as sand.

As rivers deposit sediment into the ocean, longshore currents carry and distribute the sediment along the shoreline. When the longshore current slows down, it deposits the sediment. You can think of the beach as a large conveyer belt of sand. Rivers entering the ocean add sand at one end of the beach. Longshore currents move the sand along the beach. Finally, at the other end, the sand is often dumped into a submarine canyon and carried along the seafloor to deeper water.

Longshore currents also deposit sand away from the shoreline. If waves do not carry the sand toward land, a sandbar forms. Some sandbars form offshore. Others form where the shoreline moves away from the longshore current, such as at a bay or inlet. These sandbars are like pieces of the beach that stick out into the water. A sandbar that has one end attached to land is called a **spit.** Figure 23-19 shows a spit extending into the water. Tidal currents sometimes shape the spit so that it resembles a long hook.

ENVIRONMENTAL AWARENESS

Beach Erosion

As beaches adjust to rising sea level, lines of houses are collapsing into the sea due to erosion by currents and waves. On Kure Beach, North Carolina, First Street no longer exists. The houses built on Second Street have become beachfront property as the beach erodes toward land.

In an effort to protect property and lives, millions of dollars have been spent to save beaches from erosion. Expensive seawalls temporarily stop storm waves from reaching homes and property, but cause the beach to become steeper and lose sand more rapidly. Towns losing their beaches to erosion have built structures out into the sea to trap sand carried by longshore currents. These structures, called jetties, often trap the sand needed at other beaches down the coast, which then begin to erode more rapidly.

How can you save the beaches? If you live near the ocean, you may want to participate in the planting of dune grass. With proper care, perhaps the beaches will be there for you to enjoy for many years to come. ∎

Barrier Islands and Salt Marshes

Many sandbars are not attached to land at all. A **barrier island** is a huge sandbar that lies parallel to the shoreline and that has been built up above sea level by waves and currents. Steady winds blowing toward shore may push the sand on these islands into tall dunes. If undisturbed, dune grass may take root and help trap more sand. The growth of sand dunes helps strengthen the island and protect it from erosion. However, even with the dune grass, sand is continually removed and replaced.

There are over 300 barrier islands in the United States, from the coast of southern Maine to Florida and along the Gulf coast to southern Texas. Some well-known communities are built on barrier islands: Galveston, Texas, Florida's Miami Beach, Atlantic City in New Jersey, and Hatteras, North Carolina. If you were to look at a barrier island from a great height, you would notice that the ocean side of the island has been worn smooth by the waves and currents.

SHORELINE FEATURES

Purpose   To interpret data about shoreline features from a topographic map.

Materials

copy of Figure 23-20
pen or pencil
metric ruler
colored pencils

Procedure

1. Read all instructions for this activity before you begin your work.

2. Obtain a copy of Figure 23-20 from your teacher.

3. Figure 23-20 is a map of Point Reyes, California. Carefully look over the map and use it to complete questions 1–10.

Collecting and Analyzing Data

1. What feature did longshore currents form in Drake's Bay? Draw red arrows on your map to indicate the direction you think the current is flowing.

2. Draw green arrows to show where you think waves are hitting the shoreline the hardest. Explain your choice.

3. What shoreline feature is Point Reyes and how did it form?

4. There are many small features off the coast of Point Reyes, such as Chimney Rock. This rock stands alone and resembles a chimney. Identify this type of feature and explain how it formed.

5. Draw marsh symbols on the area of your map where you predict a marsh may form. Explain your choice.

6. Has more sand been deposited seaward of Point Reyes Beach or Drake's Beach? Explain the reasons for your answer.

Drawing Conclusions

7. Explain how you know that Limantour Spit was formed after the sea cliff at Drake's Head.

8. Discuss how this shoreline map might change if there were a sudden rise in sea level.

9. Would you expect this area to be an important nesting ground for mammals and birds? Explain your answer.

10. Discuss why some areas of Point Reyes National Seashore have features formed by deposition, while other areas have features formed by erosion.

Figure 23-20 Topographic map, Point Reyes, California

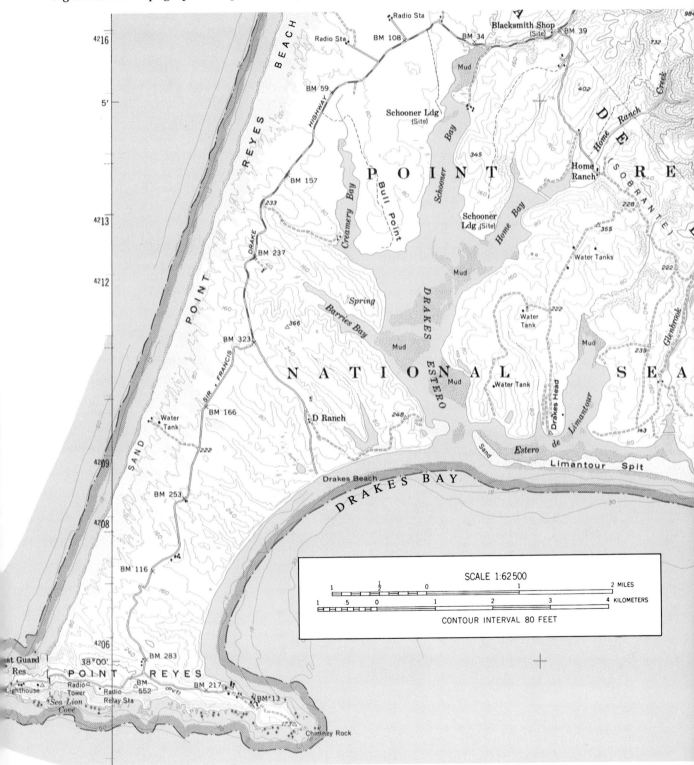

SCALE 1:62 500

CONTOUR INTERVAL 80 FEET

Figure 23-21 Barrier islands, such as Padre Island in Texas, help protect the coast from strong storms. What might happen to the barrier island during a hurricane storm surge?

Most barrier islands are not the result of longshore current deposition. Instead, they formed when sea level rose after the last ice age. As sea level rose, the ocean flooded a low coastal plain. The sand dunes that stood at the edge of the ancient shoreline were moved toward land by the waves and have continued to move toward land as sea level has risen over the past 10 000 years.

Barrier islands protect the coast. Without the barrier islands to absorb wave energy, hurricanes and other major storms could cause billions of dollars more damage to coastal towns than they already do.

Unfortunately, houses, apartments, roads, and shopping centers have been built on many barrier islands, which has led to serious erosional problems. Dunes are sometimes leveled for construction or because they block the view of the ocean. Human activity, like riding dirt bikes or even walking on the dunes, can also lead to increased erosion. Destroying the dunes weakens the island's ability to absorb the energy of large storm waves.

There are other reasons to preserve the barrier islands. Barrier islands offer nesting areas for birds and turtles. Behind the barrier island, where rivers dump sediment into the quiet protected water, a low, flat salt marsh forms. Salt marshes provide nesting grounds for many birds and mammals. The salt marsh is also considered the nursery of the sea, because many fish and shellfish use this area to breed.

The oceans and shorelines are great resources. At the shoreline, where humans meet the ocean, choices about the oceans' future are being made every day. How are the oceans to be protected? How should Earth as a whole be managed? You are an active participant in those decisions.

Figure 23-22 Why are salt marshes so important?

Lesson Review 23.3

13. Describe three ways that waves erode a shoreline.

14. Where does the sand on a beach come from?

15. What features on a shoreline indicate sea level has changed in the past?

16. Explain how barrier islands form and explain why they are important to coastal cities.

Interpret and Apply

17. Discuss the advantages and disadvantages of building a home on a barrier island.

18. Figure 23-23 is a cross section of a rocky shoreline. List the labeled features in the order they occurred and describe how they were formed. Where did the sediment labeled G come from?

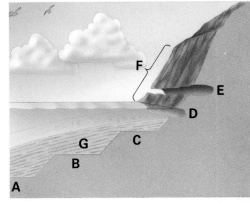

Figure 23-23 Profile of a sea cliff

Chapter Summary

Read the summary of the main ideas in this chapter. If any are not clear to you, go back and review that lesson.

23.1 Ocean Waves

■ Wind blowing over sea water forms ocean waves. All waves have similar features.

■ Water waves move energy from one place to another, but do not move the water itself.

■ Wave size is determined by how long, how hard, and how far wind blows over the water.

■ Waves break as they come near shore because the water within the wave slows down as it starts dragging across the sea bottom.

23.2 Ocean Currents

■ Surface currents, driven by global winds, form large loops around the ocean basins.

■ Density currents are caused by differences in ocean water temperature and salinity.

■ Upwellings bring cold, nutrient-rich water to the surface.

■ Longshore currents carry and deposit sand parallel to the shore.

23.3 Shoreline Features

■ Waves erode sea cliffs, sea caves, arches, and stacks along a shoreline.

■ Sediment from rivers, weathered coastal rock, and from broken seashells is deposited to form beaches, sandbars, and barrier islands.

■ Barrier islands protect the mainland from large storms. Destruction of sand dunes increases erosion of barrier islands.

■ Salt marshes are important breeding grounds for many sea and land animals.

Chapter Review

■ Vocabulary

barrier island   sea cliff
beach   sea stack
breaker   spit
crest   swells
El Niño   trough
longshore current   upwelling
rip current   wave-cut terrace
sea cave   wave height

■ Concept Mapping

Construct a concept map for shoreline features. Include at least five terms from the vocabulary list.

■ Review

Number your paper from 1 to 15. Match each term in List **A** with a phrase from List **B**.

List A

a. crest
b. breaker
c. barrier island
d. salinity differences
e. wind
f. longshore
g. Gulf Stream
h. wave-cut terrace
i. trough
j. El Niño
k. sea stack
l. wavelength
m. upwelling
n. rip current
o. salt marsh

List B

1. a sandbar parallel to the shoreline and above sea level

2. a current that pulls swimmers out to sea

3. the distance between two wave crests

4. a warm surface current moving north along the eastern United States coast

5. the major cause of surface waves and currents

6. a problem-causing warm surface current in the Pacific Ocean

7. the lowest part of a wave

8. causes a density current between the Atlantic Ocean and Mediterranean Sea

9. the nursery of the sea

10. a current that moves parallel to the shoreline

11. a column of rock along a seashore

12. a wave that falls forward onto a beach

13. the highest part of a wave

14. shoreline features that mark changes in sea level

15. a cold, rising current rich in nutrients

■ Interpret and Apply

On your paper, answer each question using complete sentences.

16. You notice that larger-than-normal waves are breaking along the beach. Explain how the large waves might indicate that stormy weather is coming.

17. Discuss how old leaking containers of radioactive waste in one seafloor location could become a worldwide problem.

18. Discuss what questions you might want answered before you bought a house atop a sea cliff like the one shown below.

19. If you rush up the school stairs too quickly, you may fall forward and drop your books all over the steps. Compare this action to a wave breaking on a beach.

20. Discuss why waves have taller crests at a steep-sloped beach.

21. Describe what might happen to a shoreline if a major river flowing toward it were dammed upstream.

22. Explain why boats tied to a dock bob up and down.

23. Some people view salt marshes as wasted coastal areas because the marshes have little immediate economic value. Describe the problems that would be created if marsh areas were filled in to build vacation homes or other structures.

24. People living on a barrier island have decided to build an artificial barrier to trap the sand carried by longshore currents. Describe the effects this barrier will have on other barrier islands farther down the shoreline.

■ Writing in Science

25. Persuasive writing tries to convince readers that a particular opinion is correct. Good persuasive writing uses facts and examples to support the opinion. In addition, it considers opposing viewpoints and tries to point out their weaknesses.

    Suppose the government of a seaside community is thinking of passing a law that would prevent the construction of buildings on dunes. Make a list of reasons why such a law might be a good idea. Also list arguments against the law. Then decide whether or not you think this proposed law would be a good idea, and write a composition arguing in favor of your opinion. Be sure to explain the weaknesses of the opposite point of view.

■ Critical Thinking

You own a large sailboat and want to take a great sailing vacation. You buy a map of Atlantic Ocean surface currents to help plan your trip. This map is shown below. You want to visit the following places: the west coast of Africa, England, New York City, the Greek Islands, Portugal, Puerto Rico, and Iceland. Use the map and the above information to answer the following questions about your trip.

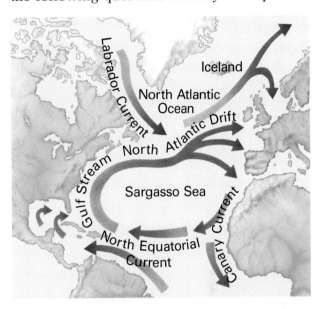

26. Your sailboat has a motor, but you would rather not use it. List the order of your destinations for the most fuel-efficient trip if you set sail from Miami, Florida.

27. Your raincoat should come in handy in London, since you hear the weather there is drizzly and foggy. Explain how ocean currents affect the London weather.

28. If your vacation time is cut short, which stop will you leave out to save the most travel time?

29. What hazards should you be careful of as you near the Labrador current?

30. What harm would there be in dumping your trash overboard once you are in the middle of the ocean?

DROUGHT HITS; FARMERS REFUSE TO GIVE UP WATER TO CITIES

Issue: *Should the federal government end subsidies of irrigation projects in the West?*

In California, the drought of 1988 set off a water "war" between urban dwellers and farmers. To conserve water, the government restricted water usage in cities. People could only water their lawns for a short time each day. Washing cars was not allowed. In Sacramento, "water police" patrolled neighborhoods to make sure people were obeying the restrictions. But urban dwellers complained that some of the water used to irrigate crops should be diverted to their cities. The farmers, however, claimed they needed all of the water for their crops.

Sprinkler irrigation is used in many western states to water crops.

Much of the western United States is arid or semiarid, which means there is too little rainfall for farming. To get farmers to settle in the West, the federal government started irrigation projects in the early 1900's. Since 1902, the Federal Bureau of Reclamation has built hundreds of dams, canals, and reservoirs in 17 western states. This system provides water for farmers, industries, and cities. But the government gives special funds, or subsidies, to farmers to encourage them to use water for irrigation. These subsidies make water much cheaper for farmers than for other groups. People in Los Angeles pay about $230 per 100 000 liters of water. Farmers nearby pay as little as $10 for the same amount of water. Some farmers could not survive without these subsidies.

Critics claim that irrigation subsidies just help farmers increase their profits.

Many urban dwellers feel that the irrigation subsidies are unfair. In California, the fast growth of cities is putting pressure on the water supply. At present, farmers use 85 percent of the water available to California. The rest goes to cities and industries. Most of the state's water supply is in northern California, but 90 percent of the population is in cities in the south. Many of the state's canals were built to bring water south to the Los Angeles area. Developers feel that the cities cannot grow without increasing their water supply. But farmers fear they will lose some of their water if more canals are built.

Many people think that the government should stop paying irrigation subsidies to farmers. They claim that the farmers use more water than they need to for the sake of higher profits. Crops like rice, cotton, and alfalfa are not suited to arid climates because they need large amounts of water. California farmers grow these crops because they can make a large profit. Critics of subsidies argue that if farmers had to pay the full price for water, they would plant crops that need less water. Then there would be enough water for everyone.

Farmers claim that the growth of cities in California is hurting the state.

Critics also point out that large-scale irrigation in California is harming the environment. Irrigation increases the amount of salt in the soil. All water carries small amounts of dissolved salts. As the water moves through the soil, it evaporates, leaving the salts behind. Over time, salt builds up in the soil. This is called salinization, and it is harmful to most crops. Irrigation also reduces the water flow in streams. This has destroyed the fish populations in some areas of California. Salmon spawning in the Central Valley, once the second largest spawning ground in the country, has gone into a serious decline.

California farmers are quick to point out that the rest of the country benefits from their crops. California supplies about half of the country's fruit and vegetables, and much of its beef. Many farmers feel that this justifies the use of federal money to pay for irrigation subsidies. The subsidies help farmers to stay in business, without having to worry as much about crop failure in a drought. Without irrigation, many farmers would have lost their farms in the drought of 1988. This would have driven up food prices for the whole country.

In some cases, the way cities use water for development is worse for the environment than irrigation is. For example, Los Angeles has diverted water from Mono Lake for more than 50 years. As a result, Mono Lake is slowly drying up. Most groups agree that if nothing is done, much of the wildlife around Mono Lake will die within twenty years.

Many Californians think that the fast growth of cities is hurting the quality of life in their state. They feel that urban dwellers use water selfishly, for washing cars, watering lawns, and filling swimming pools. In the coming years, farmers, industries, and cities will have to work together to better manage their water resources.

Act on the Issue

Gather the Facts

1. Fights over access to water occur throughout the western United States. Look in books and articles listed in the *Readers' Guide to Periodical Literature* to find out how people in other western states feel about irrigation subsidies. Write a two-paragraph summary of how this issue affects a state other than California. In each paragraph, give one side's arguments and the reasons they give to support their view.

2. Use library books and magazine articles to find out about at least three methods farmers use to conserve water used in irrigation. For each method, find out what the costs are and whether the method affects productivity.

Take Action

3. Write to your State Department of Agriculture. Ask if your state is considered an arid, semi-arid, or humid state. Find out if farmers in your state use irrigation and sprinklers. In addition, ask what the main crops are. Find out whether your state has a plan for water distribution in the event of a drought.

Science in Action

CAREER: Meteorological Technician

Herman Washington is a weather specialist with the National Weather Service.

What does a meteorological technician do?

My primary job is to observe the weather. I go outside, look at the sky, and identify the kinds of clouds and their altitude. I estimate the percent of the sky that is covered by clouds. I also use instruments to tell the temperature, dew point, air pressure, wind speed and direction, and humidity.

Who uses this information?

We send the information to the airport first—to the control tower, flight services, and all of the airlines. The information also goes out to every other weather station in the country.

How often do you take these measurements?

We take most of them at least once an hour. The readings are taken at the same time so that National Weather Service maps can be compiled showing things like lines of high or low pressure. The maps are made from points that come from many different weather stations.

How did you first become interested in observing and forecasting the weather?

I joined the Air Force after I finished high school in 1956. They trained me to be a weather forecaster. I was a weather forecaster in the Air Force for 23 years.

CAREER: Environmental Educator

Stephanie Kaza is Education Coordinator at the Botanical Garden of the University of California at Berkeley.

What is a botanical garden?

It's a place where people grow plants for research and education. It's like a museum, but everything in it is alive and growing. At our botanical garden in Berkeley, we have many species of California plants, as well as plants from around the world.

What do you like best about your job?

I love being in contact with the natural world. Plants and animals can teach us so much. I especially like working with seventh and eighth graders.

What special projects are going on at the Botanical Garden right now?

I am very excited about our creek restoration project. There's a creek flowing through the garden and into Berkeley. Until recently, the creek was polluted. Most of it ran underground through conduits. People didn't know that a creek flowed through their neighborhood. We've received funds to clean up the creek, bring it above ground, and replant it with native plants.

It sounds like your job involves more than just plants.

Absolutely. To work in conservation, it is very important to also understand how people make decisions and, ultimately, laws. Laws are only a reflection of how we relate to the environment.

HOBBY: Computer Networking

Katie Barofsky is an expert on telecommunication. As a participant in the National Geographic Kids Network, she uses a computer to share acid rain data from her school in Wausau, Wisconsin, with thousands of students all over the world.

What is the Kids Network?

Each classroom in the network has a computer. All the computers are linked by phone lines to the main computer in Washington, D.C. We then "talk" to kids in the other schools by writing letters on our computer and sending the letters to the main computer. There are now more than 500

schools in the network. The schools are all over the United States and Canada, and there is even one school in Moscow!

Explain the acid rain project.

We wanted to find out how acid the rain is here in Wisconsin and compare it with rain tested at schools in other parts of the United States. The first thing we had to do was collect data. We made a rain collector from an old coffee can. After we collected the water, we tested its pH with a strip of short-range litmus paper.

Each week we entered our data into the main computer where other schools could call it up on their own computers. We could also get a map on our computer showing readings from all the other schools.

What do you like best about the acid rain project and the computer network?

When we looked at the data from other parts of the country, we found out that some areas really do have acid rain. Readings from schools in the Northeast, for example, were between 4.0 and 4.5. That's pretty acid. I feel with the computer we are doing real science. We didn't know the answers. We found the answers ourselves.

Laboratory Safety Rules

General Safety Rules

1. Locate and learn to use all laboratory safety equipment.
2. Never eat, drink, chew gum, or apply cosmetics in the lab. Do not store food or drinks in the lab area.
3. Never do a lab activity unless your teacher is present.
4. Read all parts of an activity before you begin. Pay special attention to safety **CAUTIONS.** Follow your teacher's directions completely.
5. Never run, push, play, or fool around in the lab.
6. Keep your work area clean and uncluttered.
7. Turn off all electrical equipment, water, and gas that is not in use, especially at the end of the lab period.
8. Always clean your equipment and work space after you finish a lab activity.
9. Dress properly for the laboratory:
   a. Wear safety goggles when using chemicals, hot liquids, lab burners, or hot plates.
   b. Wear a lab apron when using chemicals or hot materials.
   c. Wear plastic gloves to handle preserved specimens or poisonous, corrosive, or irritating chemicals.

Using Heat and Fire Safely

10. Be careful when using heat or fire:
    a. Never leave a hot plate, lit Bunsen burner, or other hot object unattended.
    b. Never reach over an exposed flame or heat source.
    c. Use a clamp, tongs, or heat-resistant gloves to handle equipment that has been heated.
    d. Use only Pyrex glassware for heating.
    e. When heating in an open container, point the open end away from yourself and others.
    f. Never heat a closed container. Expanding gases may explode the container, injuring you and others.

Using Chemicals Safely

11. Use care when working with chemicals:
    a. Never touch or taste substances in the laboratory except as directed by your teacher.
    b. Never smell substances without specific instructions. Avoid inhaling fumes directly.
    c. Never return unused chemicals to the stock bottles.
    d. Always wash your hands with soap and water after working with chemicals or samples from outside, such as soil, rocks, pond water, etc.

Using Laboratory Equipment Safely

12. Use care when working with laboratory equipment:
    a. Never use chipped or broken glassware.
    b. Keep your hands away from sharp or pointed ends of scissors or compass points.
    c. Do not force glass tubing or thermometers into a rubber stopper or twist the glass once it is in a stopper.
    d. Do not aim the mirror of a microscope directly at the sun. Direct sunlight can damage your eyes.

Using Electrical Equipment Safely

13. Be careful when using electrical equipment:
    a. Make sure the area around the electrical equipment is dry and free of flammable materials. Never touch electrical equipment with wet hands.
    b. Do not let cords dangle over a table edge.

Reporting Accidents

14. Take care to report accidents:
    a. Report *all* accidents or injuries and *all* breakage or spills to your teacher.
    b. If a chemical gets into your eyes or spills on your skin or clothing, wash it off immediately with plenty of cool water while calling to your teacher.
    c. Clean up all spills immediately.
    d. Use a dustpan and a brush to pick up broken glass.
    e. If a thermometer breaks, do not touch the broken pieces with your bare hands. Notify your teacher.

Safety Outdoors

15. Dress properly for the weather and for where you are going.
    a. Wear shoes or boots that support your ankles if hiking up and down hills.
    b. If there is a risk of getting ticks or mites, wear clothing that covers your legs and arms.
16. Avoid glass collection containers. Use plastic, paper, or cloth containers.
17. Avoid potentially dangerous plants and animals.
18. Stay with your group. Listen for further instructions from your teacher.
19. Be respectful of others' property.

SI Units of Measurement

The *Systeme Internationale*, or SI, is a system of measurement used worldwide. SI developed from the metric system. SI has been the official system of measurement for scientists since 1960. Most countries also used SI units in everyday life. You may have noticed that some items in the grocery are now marked with SI units. The United States is one of the last countries in the world to adopt SI for nonscientific use.

Commonly Used SI Units

	Unit	Symbol	Equals
Length	meter kilometer centimeter millimeter	m km cm mm	 1000 m 1/100 m 1/1000 m
Mass	gram kilogram centigram milligram	g kg cg mg	 1000 g 1/100 g 1/1000 g
Volume	liter milliliter cubic centimeters	L mL cm³	 1/1000 L 1 mL
Density	grams/cubic centimeter	g/cm³	
Temperature	degrees Celsius	°C	

SI Unit	English Unit Equivalent
1 km 1 m 1 cm	0.621 mile (mi) 39.37 inches (in) 0.394 inch
1 kg 1 g	2.2046 pounds (lb) 0.0353 ounce (oz)
1 cm³ 1 L 1 mL	0.0610 inch³ 1.06 quarts (qt) 0.034 fluid ounce (fl oz)
0°C 100°C	32 degrees Fahrenheit (°F) 212°F

The following approximations will give you an idea of the sizes of some SI measurements.

Unit	Approximation
1 km	total length of five average city blocks
1 m	length of a softball bat
1 cm	width of a pencil
1 mm	thickness of a dime
1 kg	mass of an average pineapple
1 g	mass of a dollar bill
1 mg	mass of a human hair
1 L	total volume of four single-serving milk cartons
1 mL	total volume of 20 drops of water

You may, at some point, need to convert temperatures from degrees Fahrenheit (°F) to degrees Celsius (°C) or from Celsius to Fahrenheit. In order to convert Fahrenheit temperatures into Celsius, you use the following formula:

$$°C = \frac{5}{9}(°F - 32)$$

For example, imagine hearing on the radio that the temperature is 68°F. How do you convert 68°F into °C?

*First, subtract 32 from 68°F. $68 - 32 = 36$

*Multiply your answer by 5/9. $36 \times \frac{5}{9} = \frac{180}{9}$

*Simplify the fraction by dividing. $\frac{180}{9} = 20°C$

In order to convert °C to °F, use this formula: $°F = \frac{9}{5}°C + 32$

Graphing Skills

You use a line graph when you are comparing two continuously changing values. For example, the table below shows data for two changing quantities: the mass of a sample of the mineral galena, and the volume of that same sample. Both values are changing, so a line graph is appropriate for graphing these data.

Mass and Volume of Galena	
Mass (g)	Volume (mL)
15.0	2.0
22.7	2.8
29.6	4.2

When making a line graph from a table of data, follow these general rules:

1. *Put a title on your graph.* The title tells your reader what the graph is about. Print the title at the top of your graph paper.

2. *Leave space for axis labels.* Leave some space between the edge of your paper and the horizontal and vertical axes.

3. *Decide which quantity to plot on the horizontal axis and which quantity to plot on the vertical axis.* Sometimes, one of the two quantities is being changed by you in a regular way. This would be called your controlled quantity and you would plot it along the horizontal axis. Label the vertical axis with the other quantity.

4. *Choose a scale for each axis.* The scales on the two axes do not have to be the same. Your scale should do two things. First, it must allow you to plot all the data. Therefore, the scale must have a range wide enough to include the highest and lowest data. Second, the scale should be easy to use. Make each square of your graph paper stand for a multiple of 1, 2, 5, or 10. Once you have chosen your scales, clearly mark them along the axes of your graph.

5. *Plot your data.* On a line graph, each data point is a combination of two values—one for each axis. To plot a data point, first find its horizontal axis value on the scale. For the mass given, the first horizontal axis value is 15.0 g. Follow that value up from the horizontal axis until you are across from the vertical axis value for that data point. In this case, the vertical axis value for 15.0 g is 2.0 mL. Where the horizontal and vertical axes meet, make a small dot or x. Plot all of the available data points in the same manner.

6. *Look at the data points to determine the pattern.* Often data points will appear to fall along a straight line. Other times the points will follow a smooth curve.

7. *Draw a line or curve to show the general trend of the data points.* Science data points are usually measured data. All measurements have some error. Therefore, measured data seldom fall exactly on a straight line, even if the points at first appear to fall on a straight line. Rather than connecting each data point, draw a straight line or a curve that best fits the data points. A good best-fit line often passes through some points, but also has some points above it and some below it.

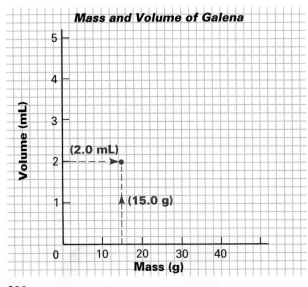

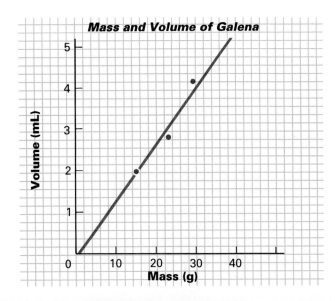

Care and Use of the Laboratory Balance

You use a laboratory balance to measure mass. Even though there is more than one type of lab balance, the different balances share several parts in common, as shown in the diagram.

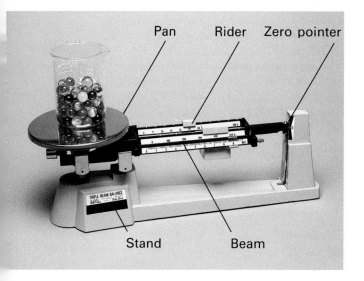

Pan   Rider   Zero pointer

Stand   Beam

Triple-Beam Balance

Many school laboratories have triple-beam balances. A triple-beam balance is a balance with a single pan. As the name implies, it also has three beams. The 500-g beam is divided into 5 marks of 100 g each. The 100-g beam is divided into 10 marks of 10 g each. The front beam is the 10-g beam. It is divided into 10 marks of 1 g each, and then each of these is divided into tenths of a gram.

To find the mass of an object using the triple-beam balance, follow these steps:

1. Be sure all the riders are set to zero.
2. Carefully place the object on the pan.
3. Move the 500-g beam rider, mark by mark, until the zero pointer drops. Move the rider back one mark.
4. Move the 100-g beam rider until the zero pointer drops. Move the rider back one mark.
5. Carefully move the 10-g rider until the pointer either points to zero, or is swinging the same number of marks on either side of zero.
6. Read the mass of the object by reading the numbers on the three beams and adding them together. Remember that the 10-g beam gives you both a number of grams between 0 and 10 in both whole grams and in tenths of a gram. You may even estimate the mass to hundredths of a gram by estimating the position of the arrow between the two 0.1-g marks.

Double-Pan Balance

The double-pan balance has two pans instead of only one. Typically, the double-pan balance has either one or two beams, and cannot measure large masses without the use of additional masses added to the second pan. These added masses are called *standard masses* because they come in standard, accurately measured units. A set of standard masses might include 500-, 200-, 100-, 50-, 20-, and 10-gram masses. These help balance the mass of the unknown object in the absence of masses on a second or third beam.

Finding the mass of an object using the double-pan balance is similar to using the triple-beam balance. Place the object on the left pan. First try to find the mass of the object, using only the riders on the beam(s). If the pointer does not move, you need to add one or more standard masses to the right pan. By adding masses to the right pan and by moving the rider(s) on the beam(s), you will eventually get the pointer to point to zero. The mass of the object is read by finding the sum of the standard masses on the right pan and the mass shown on the beam(s).

Proper Care and Use of the Lab Balance

Here are several rules to follow when using and handling any type of lab balance:

1. Always use two hands to carry the balance. Pick it up carefully by the stand and be certain to put it down gently.
2. Before using the balance, check that:
   a. the balance is on a level table;
   b. the pans are clean and the pointer swings freely;
   c. all riders are set at zero;
   d. the pointer lines up at zero.
3. Place objects carefully on the balance pans. Keep the pans clean and dry. Do not put chemicals or wet objects directly on the pans. Use a suitable container. This will prevent damage to the pan. (Remember to measure the mass of the container before measuring the mass of the substance and container combined. By subtracting the mass of the container alone from the combined mass, you can find the mass of the substance alone.)
4. Do not overload the balance. Your teacher will tell you the maximum mass that your balance can measure.
5. If your balance does not appear to be working as you would expect, ask your teacher for help.

APPENDIX E

Key to Topographic Map Symbols

Primary highway, hard surface ....
Secondary highway, hard surface ....
Light-duty road, hard or improved surface...
Unimproved road ....
Trail ....
Railroad: single track ....
Railroad: multiple track ....
Bridge ....
Drawbridge ....
Tunnel ....
Footbridge ....
Overpass—Underpass ....
Power transmission line with located tower ..
Landmark line (labeled as to type)...............

Dam with lock ....
Canal with lock ....
Large dam..
Small dam: masonry—earth..........................
Buildings (dwelling, place of employment, etc.)..
School—Church—Cemeteries........................
Buildings (barn, warehouse, etc.)...................
Tanks; oil, water, etc. (labeled only if water)...
Wells other than water (labeled as to type)....
U.S. mineral or location monument—Prospect...
Quarry—Gravel pit ....
Mine shaft—Tunnel or cave entrance...........
Campsite—Picnic area..................................
Located or landmark object—Windmill........
Exposed wreck...
Rock or coral reef..
Foreshore flat ....
Rock: bare or awash.....................................

Benchmarks..
Road fork—Section corner with elevation ...
Checked spot elevation ....
Unchecked spot elevation.............................

Boundary: national ....
State ....
county, parish, municipio..........................
civil township, precinct, town, barrio....
incorporated city, village, town, hamlet.
reservation, national or state ....
small park, cemetery, airport, etc. ....
land grant ....
Township or range line, U.S. land survey ..
Section line, U.S. land survey ....
Township line, not U.S. land survey ....
Section line, not U.S. land survey............
Fence line or field line ....
Section corner: found—indicated...............
Boundary monument: land grant—other...

Index contour   Intermediate contour
Supplementary cont   Depression contours
Cut—Fill........   Levee ....
Mine dump .....   Large wash......
Dune area........   Distorted surface
Sand area ....   Gravel beach ......

Glacier.............   Intermittent streams
Seasonal streams   Aqueduct tunnel
Water well—Spring   Falls................
Rapids...........   Intermittent lake
Channel ....   Small wash ...
Sounding—
Depth curve ..   Marsh (swamp)
                        Land subject to
Dry lake bed ...   controlled flooding

Woodland......   Mangrove........
Submerged marsh   Scrub ....
Orchard ....   Wooded marsh
Vineyard........   Many buildings ......
Areas revised since previous edition ....

624

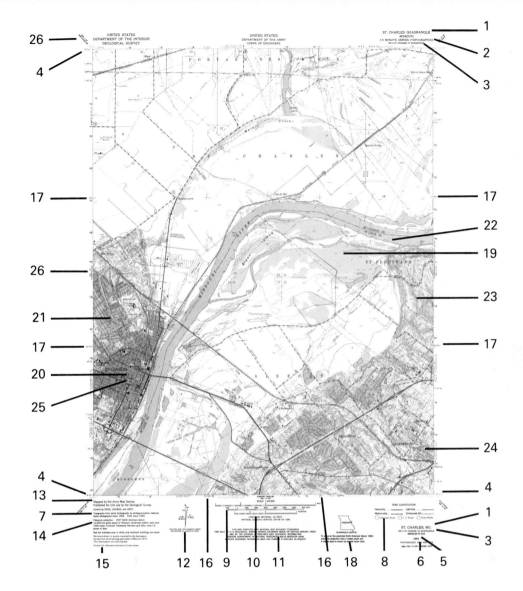

Key to Topographic Map Information

1. Name of this map sheet (*St. Charles, Missouri quadrangle*)
2. Name of this map series (*7.5 minute*)
3. Reference that tells you that this map is part of a different map series (*SW/4 St. Charles 15' Quadrangle*)
4. Latitude and longitude of map corners
5. Date this map was originally drawn
6. Dates this map has been revised
7. Notes on revision (*Revised from aerial photographs, 1968 and 1974.*)
8. Key to symbols used for roads
9. Map scales
10. Contour interval
11. Government office selling this map
12. Magnetic and geographic declination
13. Credits, sources, additional information on map preparation
14. Type of map projection
15. Additional notes on symbols used
16. Longitude tick marks
17. Latitude tick marks
18. Location of this map sheet in the state
19. Green tint indicates woodland.
20. Red tint indicates urban area.
21. Purple tint indicates areas that have been revised and have therefore changed since the previous edition of this same map.
22. Blue indicates water.
23. Contour lines are brown.
24. Human-made structures are shown in black.
25. Bench marks indicate places where the elevation has been measured precisely.
26. Name of adjacent map sheet

**Map of
the World**

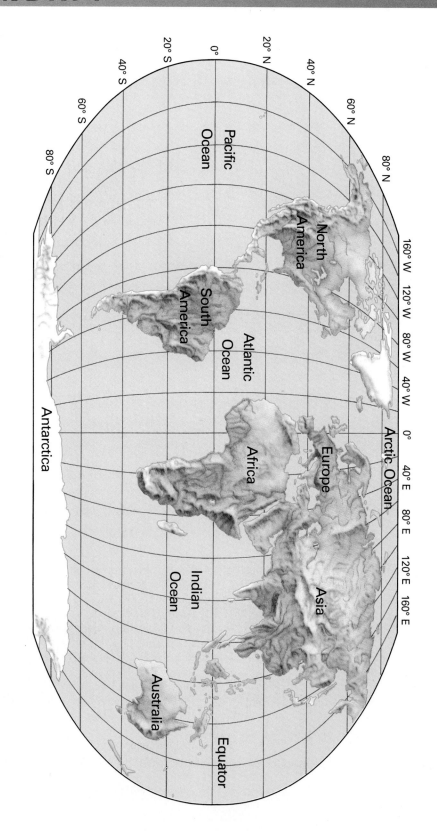

Map of the United States

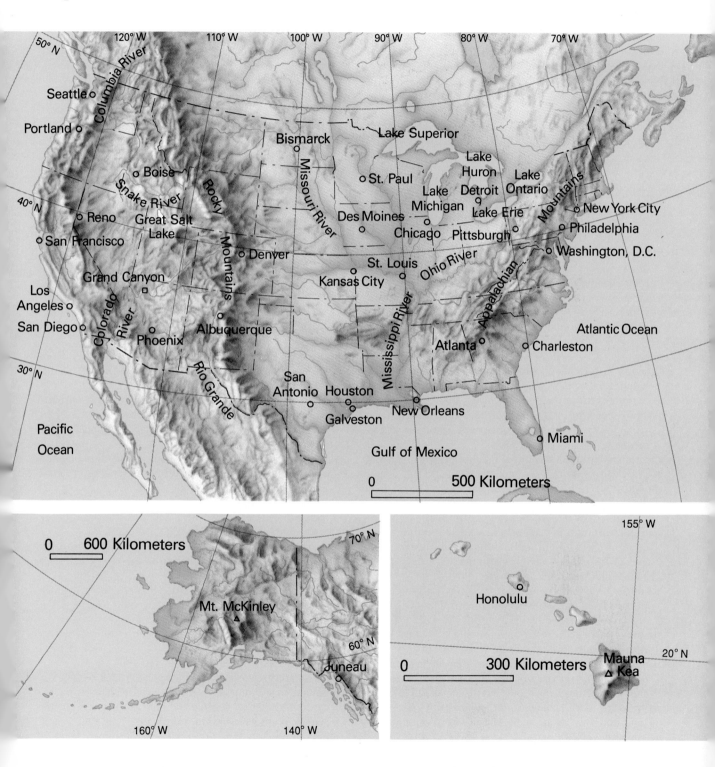

50° N
120° W
110° W
100° W
90° W
80° W
70° W

Columbia River

Seattle

Portland

Boise

Bismarck

Lake Superior

40° N

Snake River

Rocky

Missouri River

St. Paul

Lake Huron

Lake Michigan

Detroit

Lake Ontario

Mountains

Reno

Great Salt Lake

Mountains

Denver

Des Moines

Chicago

Lake Erie

Pittsburgh

New York City

Philadelphia

San Francisco

Washington, D.C.

St. Louis

Ohio River

Los Angeles

Grand Canyon

Kansas City

Colorado River

Appalachian

San Diego

Albuquerque

Phoenix

Atlantic Ocean

30° N

Atlanta

Charleston

Rio Grande

San Antonio

Houston

Mississippi River

New Orleans

Pacific Ocean

Galveston

Miami

Gulf of Mexico

0   500 Kilometers

0   600 Kilometers

70° N

155° W

Mt. McKinley

Honolulu

60° N

Juneau

20° N

0   300 Kilometers

Mauna Kea

160° W

140° W

GLOSSARY

NOTE: Some terms are indirectly derived from the Latin or Greek and have been coined by scientists for the International Science Vocabulary (ISV). They are usually, but not always, combinations of words, one of which is directly traceable to an ancient language, such as the word *radioactive*.

A

abrasion (ə brā' zhən): process of rocks grinding down when they rub against each other; from the Latin *abradere*, meaning "to wear away" (p. 313).

absolute age: the actual age of rocks, measured from when they were first formed; from the Latin *absolvere*, meaning "to set free" (p. 374).

absolute magnitude: amount of light a star gives off; from the Latin *magnus*, meaning "great" (p. 151).

abyssal plain (ə bis' əl plān): large flat area on the deep ocean floor; from the Greek *abyssos* and Latin *planus*, meaning "bottomless" and "flat" (p. 578).

acid precipitation (as' əd pri sip ə tā' shən): rain, sleet, or snow that is more acidic than pure rainwater; from the Latin *acidere* and *praecipitare*, meaning "to be sour" and "to throw down" (p. 487).

air mass: broad area with approximately the same temperature and humidity throughout; from the Greek *aer* and *massein*, meaning "air" and "to knead" (p. 496).

air pressure: weight of air on a unit area; from the Latin *pressare*, meaning "to press" (p. 454).

alluvial fan (ə lü' vē əl fan): a triangular shaped deposit of sediments on dry ground at a stream's end; from the Latin *alluere*, meaning "to wash against" (p. 343).

altitude (al' tə tüd): height of an object in the sky above the horizon; from the Latin *altitudo*, meaning "height" (p. 72).

alto- (al' to): prefix indicating a cloud at a middle height of two to seven kilometers; from the Latin *altus*, meaning "high" (p. 482).

anemometer (an ə mäm' ət ər): instrument used to measure the force or speed of wind (p. 460).

aneroid barometer (an' ə roid bə räm' ət ər): instrument used to measure air pressure, by the contraction or expansion of a metal can; from the Greek *a + neuron*, meaning "not water" and *baros*, meaning "weight" (p. 455).

anticline (an' tē klīn): upward fold of a rock layer; from the Greek *anti + klinein*, meaning "against + to incline" (p. 275).

apparent magnitude (ə par' ənt mag' nə tüd): the brightness of a star as observed from Earth; from the Latin *apparēre* and *magnus*, meaning "to appear" and "great" (p. 151).

aquifer (ak' wə fər): water-bearing zone of permeable rock; from the Latin *aqua* and *ferre*, meaning "water" and "to bear" (p. 555).

asteroid (as' tə roid): one of many bodies smaller than planets that revolve around the sun; from the Greek *asteroeidēs*, meaning "starlike" (p. 136).

asthenosphere (as then' ə sfiər): hot layer of Earth's upper mantle that acts like putty; from the Greek *asthenēs + sphaira*, meaning "weak + ball" (p. 267).

astronomical unit (as trə näm' i kəl yü' nət): average distance between Earth and sun, abbreviated A. U. (p. 119).

astronomy (ə strän' ə mē): scientific study of objects beyond Earth's atmosphere; from the Greek *astronoumia*, meaning "astronomy" (p. 10).

atoll (a' tȯl): ring-shaped coral reef (p. 581).

atom (at' əm): smallest unit of matter that cannot be broken down by ordinary chemical means; from the Greek *atomos*, meaning "indivisible" (p. 180).

atomic number (ə täm' ik): number of protons in an atom of that element (p. 181).

average slope: number that gives the elevation changes across a specified land distance (p. 56).

axis (ak′ səs): real or imaginary straight line that goes through the center of a rotating object; from the Greek *axōn*, meaning "axle" (p. 75).

B

barrier island: huge, offshore sandbar built up by action of waves and currents and found parallel to the shoreline (p. 609).

beach: deposit of sediment along a shoreline (p. 608).

big bang theory: theory that the entire universe began from a single, enormous explosion; from the Greek *thēorein*, meaning "to look at" (p. 165).

biomass (bī′ ō mas): term used to describe materials from living things that can be used as a fuel; from the Greek *bios* + *massein*, meaning "life + to knead" (p. 426).

black hole: star so massive that nothing can escape its gravity (p. 163).

breaker (brā′ kər): collapsing wave (p. 597).

C

carbonic acid (kär bän′ ik as′ əd): solution formed by water combined with carbon dioxide; from the Latin *carbo* and *acēre*, meaning "ember, charcoal" and "to be sour" (p. 315).

carbonized fossil (kär′ bon īzd fäs′ əl): carbon shape that remains on shale after an organism is chemically changed; from the Latin *carbo* and *fodere*, meaning "ember, charcoal" and "to dig" (p. 363).

cartographer (kär täg′ rə fər): mapmaker; from the Greek *chartēs* + *graphein*, meaning "leaf of paper + to write" (p. 42).

cast: object, such as a fossil, left when a substance fills a mold (p. 364).

Celsius degree (sel′ sē əs di grē′): unit of temperature measurement; named for Swedish astronomer Anders Celsius and the Latin *de* + *gradus*, meaning "down + step" (p. 17).

cementation (sē men tā′ shən): process by which sediment grains are glued together by minerals in water to form rock; from the Latin *caementum*, meaning "stone chips (used in mortar)" (p. 232).

chemical bond: a type of attractive force that holds together atoms in molecules; from the Latin *alchymia*, meaning "alchemy" (p. 188).

chemical change: change in the chemical identity of matter, producing matter with new properties (p. 186).

chemical formula: symbol that shows the composition of a compound; from the Latin *forma*, meaning "form" (p. 188).

chemical property: description of how a certain kind of matter reacts; from the Latin *propius*, meaning "one's own" (p. 186).

chemical rock: sedimentary rock formed from minerals dissolved in water (p. 231).

chemical weathering (kem′ i kəl we<u>th</u>′ riŋ): a process

whereby the minerals in a rock change into new minerals (p. 314).

chlorofluorocarbons (klor′ ō flür ō kär bənz): group of chemicals containing chlorine, fluorine, and carbon (p. 531).

chromosphere (krō′ mə sfiər): thin layer above the photosphere of the sun: from the Greek *chrōma* + *sphaira*, meaning "colored thing + ball" (p. 158).

cinder cone (sin′ dər cōn): volcanic mountain built of tephra; from the Latin *conus*, meaning "cone" (p. 302).

cirrus (sir′ əs): kind of thin and wispy cloud, found at high altitudes; from the Latin *cirrus*, meaning "fringe" (p. 482).

clastic rock (klas′ tik räk): sedimentary rock formed from smaller pieces of other rock; from the Greek *klastos*, meaning "broken" (p. 231).

cleavage (klē′ vij): the splitting of a mineral along smooth surfaces (p. 204).

climate (klī′ mət): typical weather patterns over a period of years in a given location; from the Greek *klima*, meaning "latitude, climate" (p. 520).

climate model (klī′ mət mäd′ əl): computer-generated imitation of one of Earth's climates; from the Greek *klima* and Latin *modulus*, meaning "latitude, climate" and "small measure" (p. 533).

coal (kōl): organic sedimentary rock and solid fossil fuel (p. 411).

cold front (kōld frənt): weather condition that results from cold, dense air pushing against warm, less dense air; from the Latin *frons*, meaning "forehead" (p. 497).

comet (käm′ ət): small body made of rock and ice with an elliptical orbit about the sun; from the Greek *komētēs*, meaning "long-haired" (p. 135).

compaction (kəm pak′ shən): squeezing together of sediment to form rock; from the Latin *compingere*, meaning "to put together" (p. 232).

composite cone (käm päz′ ət kōn): volcanic mountain made up of layers of lava and tephra; from the Latin *componere* and *conu*, meaning "to put together" and "cone" (p. 303).

compound (käm′ paùnd): matter that can be broken down by chemical means into more than one kind of element; from the Latin *componere*, meaning "to put together" (p. 187).

conclusion (kən klü′ zhən): opinion about an original hypothesis based on data collected; from the Latin *concludere*, meaning "to conclude" (p. 23).

condensation (kän den sā′ shən): physical change of a gas to a liquid; from the Latin *condensare*, meaning "to make dense" (p. 178).

condensation nuclei (kän den sā′ shən nü′ klē ī): extremely small particles that serve as condensation surfaces for cloud droplets; from the Latin *condensare* and *nux*, meaning "to make dense" and "nut" (p. 478).

constellation (kän stə lā′ shən): group of stars in a fixed pattern; from the Latin com + stella, meaning "with + star" (p. 144).

continental drift (känt ən ent′ əl drift): idea that continents move from one part of Earth to another; from the Latin continēre, meaning "to hold together" (p. 258).

continental shelf: gently sloping, submerged edge of the continent (p. 577).

continental slope: sloping boundary between the continental shelf and the ocean floor (p. 578).

contour interval (kän′ tür int′ ər vəl): vertical difference between two contour lines on topographic map; from the Latin intervallum, meaning "space between ramparts or walls" (p. 55).

contour line (kän′ tür līn): line on a topographic map that connects points on land having the same elevation (p. 54).

control: something kept the same during the test of a hypothesis; from the Latin contra and rotulus, meaning "against (a check on)" and "wheel" (p. 23).

convection (kən vek′ shən): movement of a fluid because of density differences; from the Latin convectus, meaning "brought together" (p. 270).

converging boundary (kən vərj′ iŋ baün′ də rē): place where two plates moving from different directions meet head-on; from the Latin con + vergere, meaning "with + to converge" (p. 273).

core (kōər): 1. sample taken by drilling into layers of sediment and rock (p. 576); 2. central part of Earth (see **inner core** and **outer core**).

Coriolis effect (kȯr ē ō′ ləs): curve seen by earthbound observers in the path of objects or substances, such as air, moving over Earth's surface; named for French civil engineer Gaspard G. Coriolis; from the Latin efficere, meaning "to cause" (p. 462).

corona (kə rō′ nə): main part of the sun's atmosphere; from the Latin corona, meaning "crown" (p. 158).

correlation (kȯr ə lā′ shən): process of matching rock layers from different locations; from the Latin com- + relatio, meaning "with- + relation" (p. 371).

crater (krāt′ ər): circular depression or hole on the surface of a moon or a planet; from the Latin crater, meaning "bowl" (p. 109).

craton (krā′ tän): stable area of Earth's crust that makes up the oldest part of a continent; from the Greek kratos, meaning "strength" (p. 276).

crest: highest point of a wave (p. 595).

crude oil: petroleum pumped directly from the ground; from the Latin crudus and oleum, meaning "raw" and "oil" (p. 414).

crust (krəst): top layer of Earth, including its surface; from the Latin crudus, meaning "raw" (p. 48).

crystal (kris′ təl): solid substance in which the atoms or ions are arranged in an orderly pattern that repeats over and over again; from the Greek krystallos, meaning "ice, crystal" (p. 197).

cubic centimeter [cm³] (kyü′ bik sent′ ə mēt ər): unit of measure equal to the volume of a cube with the length, width, and depth of one centimeter, equals 1 milliliter; from the Greek kybos and Latin centum + Greek metron, meaning "cube" and "hundred + measure" (p. 17).

cumulus (kyü′ myə ləs): kind of cloud, white and fluffy; from the Latin cumulus, meaning "heap" (p. 481).

D

data (dāt′ ə): plural term (sing. datum) used for the information gathered during an experiment; from the Latin datum, meaning "something given" (p. 22).

delta (del′ tə): deposit of sediments in a body of water at a stream's mouth; named after the Greek letter delta Δ from its shape (p. 343).

density (den′ sə tē): ratio between the mass and the volume of a substance, found by dividing an object's mass by its volume; from the Latin densus, meaning "dense" (p. 176).

deposition (dep ə zish′ ən): process in which water, wind, or ice drops sediments in new locations; from the Latin deponere, meaning "to put down" (p. 334).

desalination (dē sal ə nā′ shən): process of removing salt from seawater; from the Latin de- + sal, meaning "from + salt" (p. 585).

dew (dü): condensation that forms on surfaces when air is saturated with water (p. 478).

dew point (dü pȯint): temperature at which the air becomes saturated with water (p. 476).

dike (dīk): sheet of igneous rock that cuts through layers of older rock (p. 303).

direct measurement (də rekt′ mezh′ ər mənt): measurement comparing the quantity of an object to a standard unit; from the Latin directus and metiri, meaning "straight" and "to measure" (p. 18).

diverging boundary (də vərj′ iŋ baün′ də rē): place where two plates of lithosphere are moving apart and new lithosphere is formed; from the Latin de + vergere, meaning "away from + converge" (p. 271).

doldrums (dōl′ drəmz): area of calm and light, shifting air near the equator (p. 463).

downdraft: current of air caused by enormous numbers of falling raindrops (p. 489).

drainage basin (drā′ nij bās′ ən): area where surface water collects and from which it is carried by a drainage system such as a river (p. 340).

drizzle: fine misty rain; from the Greek driusan, meaning "to fall" (p. 486).

E

earthquake (ərth′ kwāk): trembling of the earth caused by the sudden release of stored energy (p. 284).

echo sounding: use of reflected sound to measure distance; from the Greek *echo*, meaning "to sound" (p. 262).

electromagnetic spectrum (i lek trō mag net' ik spek' trəm): total range of all electromagnetic waves; from the Greek *elektron* and the Latin *spectrum*, meaning "amber" and "appearance" (p. 152).

electron (i lek' trän): elementary particle with negative electric charge; from the Greek *elektron*, meaning "amber" (p. 180).

element (el' ə mənt): substance composed of a single type of atom (the building block of matter); from the Latin *elementum*, meaning "element" (p. 181).

ellipse (i lips'): oval shape that has two focal points, such as the orbit of Earth; from the Greek *elleipsis*, meaning "ellipse" (p. 78).

El Niño (el nē' nyō): warm surface current in the Pacific Ocean (p. 601).

energy (en' ər jē): that which is needed to move or change matter, also that which an object has because it is in motion; from the Greek *energeia*, meaning "activity" (p. 176).

energy balance (en' ər jē bal' ants): the balance between energy Earth receives from the sun and energy Earth gives off to space (p. 451).

epicenter (ep' i sent ər): point on Earth's surface directly above an earthquake's focus; from the Greek *epi-* and Latin *centrum*, meaning "at" and "center" (p. 287).

epoch (ep' ək): a division of a period on the geologic timetable; from the Greek *epochē*, meaning "ending" (p. 385).

equator (i kwāt' ər): imaginary east-west line that circles Earth halfway between geographic poles; from the Latin *aequus*, meaning "equal" (p. 42).

era (ir' ə): longest unit of time in the geologic timetable; from the Latin *aes*, meaning "copper, coin, counters" (p. 385).

erosion (i rō' zhən): process in which water, wind, and other agents carry away sediment; from the Latin *erodere*, meaning "to eat away" (p. 334).

escape velocity (is kāp' və läs' ə tē): minimum speed an object must have to escape the gravity of a planet or moon; from the Latin *velox*, meaning "quick" (p. 102).

esker (es' kər): long, narrow ridge of deposits from a stream flowing beneath a glacier (p. 349).

evaporation (i vap ə rā' shən): physical change of liquid to a vapor state (gas); from the Latin *evaporare*, meaning "to evaporate" (p. 178).

exfoliation dome (eks fō lē ā' shən dōm): round rock mass left after thin, curved sheets of granite break off from it; from the Latin *exfoliare*, meaning "to strip off leaves" (p. 313).

extrusive (ik strü' siv): igneous rock formed from lava forced out onto Earth's surface; from the Latin *extrudere*, meaning "to thrust" (p. 228).

F

fall equinox (fȯl ē' kwə näks): day about halfway between summer and winter solstices, when daylight and night are equal; from the Latin *aequi-* + *nox*, meaning "equal- + night" (p. 81).

fault (fȯlt): crack in Earth's crust along which some movement has occurred; from the Latin *fallere*, meaning "to deceive" (p. 272).

feedback process (fēd' bak präs' es): condition in which a change results in an effect that then causes more change; from the Latin *procedere*, meaning "to go on, proceed" (p. 525).

fission (fish' ən): splitting of an atomic nucleus; from the Latin *findere*, meaning "to split" (p. 418).

floodplain (fləd plān): wide level area containing small-grained sediments found on either side of a river; from the Latin *planus*, meaning "flat" (p. 343).

focus (fō' kəs): the true location of an earthquake and source of seismic waves; from the Latin *focus*, meaning "hearth" (p. 287).

fog: vapor of very fine droplets of water (p. 479).

foliation (fō lē ā' shən): in rock, the arrangement of minerals in parallel layers; from the Latin *folium*, meaning "leaf" (p. 240).

fossil fuel (fäs' əl fyü' əl): partly decayed remains of plants and animals that died long ago and are now burned to produce thermal energy; from the Latin *fodere* and *focus*, meaning "to dig" and "hearth" (p. 411).

fracture (frak' chər): breaking of a mineral along jagged or irregular surfaces; from the Latin *fractus*, meaning "irregular, weak" (p. 205).

frame of reference (frām, ref' ərnts): set of points or lines that acts as a guide, as on a map; from the Latin *referre*, meaning "to bring back, report" (p. 42).

frost: ice crystals formed when dew point is below freezing (p. 478).

fusion (fyü' zhən): combination of two atomic nuclei to form a single, heavier nucleus with the release of energy; from the Latin *fundere*, meaning "to spread out" (p. 420).

G

galaxy (gal' ək sē): a group of billions of stars held together by gravity; from the Greek *gala*, meaning "milk" (p. 164).

gas (gas): matter that has neither a definite shape nor volume (p. 177).

gaseous planet (gas' ē əs plan' ət): one of these four giant planets that lack solid surfaces—Jupiter, Saturn, Uranus, and Neptune; from the Latin *chaos* and Greek *planēs*, meaning "space" and "wanderer" (p. 130).

gasohol (gas' ə hol): mixture of alcohol (from grain) and gasoline (p. 426).

gem: a beautiful, rare, and valuable mineral used for

jewelry; from the Latin *gamma*, meaning "bud, gem" (p. 210).

geographic north (jē ə graf′ ik nȯərth): direction to the geographic North Pole; from the Greek *geographein*, meaning "to describe the earth's surface" (p.38).

geologic column (jē ə läj′ ik käl′ əm): complete stack of rock layers according to age; from the Greek *geo-* + *logos* and Latin *columna*, meaning "of the earth + word" and "column" (p. 372).

geologic timetable (jē ə läj′ ik tīm′ tā bəl): system used by geologists that attempts to place the major changes in Earth's surface and forms of life in the order in which they occurred (p. 385).

geology (jē äl′ ə jē): study of the materials of Earth, including its history; from the Greek *geo-* + *logos*, meaning "earth + word" (p. 11).

geosynchronous satellite (jē ō siŋ′ krə nəs sat′ əl īt): from the Greek *geo-* + *syn-* + *chronos* and Latin *satelles*, meaning "earth- + with- + time" and "attendant" (p. 104).

geothermal energy (jē ō thər′ məl en′ ər jē): energy from heat within Earth's interior; from the Greek *geo-* + *thermē* and *energeia*, meaning "of the earth + heat" and "activity" (p. 420).

glacier (glā′ shər): a large mass of slow-moving ice; from the Latin *glacies*, meaning "ice, ice field" (p. 346).

global warming (glō′ bəl wȯrm′ iŋ): predicted worldwide temperature increases due to an increase in greenhouse gases; from the Latin *globus*, meaning "ball, sphere" (p. 531).

gnomon (nō′ mən): instrument used to measure the sun's altitude; from the Greek *gnōmōn*, meaning "interpreter, pointer on a sundial" (p. 73).

gnomonic (nō män′ ik): map projection made as if a sheet of paper were laid on a point on Earth's surface, such as a geographic pole (p. 50).

Gondwanaland (gän dwän ə land): southern continent, landmass that included South America, Africa, Antarctica, and Australia (p. 396).

grain: small piece of rock or mineral crystal found in another rock or sediment; from the Latin *granum*, meaning "corn (grain of)" (p. 223).

gram [g]: unit of measurement of mass; from the Latin *granum*, meaning "grain" (p. 17).

greenhouse effect: effect of Earth's atmosphere trapping heat from the sun (p. 452).

greenhouse gas: gas that absorbs infrared radiation and thus helps heat the atmosphere (pp. 452, 531).

groundwater: water that has seeped below Earth's surface (p. 335).

guyot (gē′ ō): flat-topped seamount, named for American geographer Arnold H. Guyot (p. 579).

H

hail: pellets of ice formed in some thunderclouds (p. 488).

half-life: time required for half of a radioactive substance to decay (p. 376).

hardness: resistance of a mineral to being scratched (p. 203).

hard water: water in which there is a high concentration of dissolved minerals, such as calcium and magnesium salts (p. 560).

heft: to test the weight of a substance by lifting it (p. 205).

high-pressure area: area where isobars show higher readings toward the center of the pattern; from the Latin *pressus* and *area*, meaning "closed, supressed" and "open space" (p. 498).

hominids (häm′ ə nədz): humans and their most recent ancestors; from the Latin *homo*, meaning "man" (p. 403).

Homo sapiens (hō′ mō sap′ ē ənz): species that includes modern humans; from the Latin *homo* and *sapientia*, meaning "man" and "wisdom" (p. 403).

horse latitude (hȯərs lat′ ə tüd): either of two regions 30° N and 30° S latitude, characterized by high pressure, calms, and light winds; from the Latin *latus*, meaning "wide" (p. 463).

humus (hyü′ məs): dark-colored substance made of small bits of decaying plants and animals; from the Latin *humus*, meaning "earth" (p. 319).

hurricane (hər′ ə kān): large low-pressure storm with winds over 120 kilometers per hour (p. 513).

hydrocarbon (hī drə kär′ bən): burnable compound that contains the elements hydrogen and carbon; from the Greek *hydōr* and Latin *carbo*, meaning "water" and "ember, charcoal" (p. 411).

hydroelectric (hī drō i lek′ trik): type of electricity that is generated by the flow of water; from the Greek *hydor* and *elektron*, meaning "water" and "amber" (p. 425).

hypothesis (hī päth′ ə səs): possible explanation for an event or solution to a problem, which is based on information; from the Greek *hypotithenai*, meaning "to put under" (p. 22).

I

ice age: time (period) of widespread glaciation (p. 523).

ice wedging (īs wej′ iŋ): process whereby rock is broken down by freezing water (p. 313).

igneous (ig′ nē əs): kind of rock that has solidified from molten rock; from the Latin *ignis*, meaning "fire" (p. 222).

imprint (im′ print): shallow depression left by flat objects in soft sediment; from the Latin *imprimere*, meaning "to imprint" (p. 364).

index fossil (in′ deks fäs′ əl): remains of living thing that lived over a wide area, but existed for only a few million years; from the Latin *indicare* + *fodere*, meaning "to indicate + to dig" (p. 371).

indirect measurement (in′ də rekt mezh′ ər mənt): measurement that is made using direct measurements and calculations; from the Latin in + directus and metiri, meaning "not + straight" and "to measure" (p. 18).

inner core (in′ ər kȯ′ ər): central part of Earth's core, extending from a depth of 5100 km to Earth's true center (p. 48).

inner planet (in′ ər plan′ ət): one of the four planets closest to the sun; from the Greek planēs, meaning "wanderer" (p. 119).

insulation (in sə lā′ shən): substance that slows the flow of thermal energy; from the Latin insula, meaning "island" (p. 430).

international date line (int ər nash′ nəl dāt līn): imaginary north-south line in Pacific Ocean where the date changes when traveling west; from the Latin inter + natio, meaning "between + nation" (p. 85).

intrusive (in trü′ siv): igneous rock formed from magma cooling inside Earth; from the Latin intrudere, meaning "to thrust in" (p. 227).

invertebrate (in vərt′ ə brāt): animal that does not have a backbone; from the Latin in- + vertebratus, meaning "non- + jointed" (p. 390).

ion (ī ən): atom that has become electrically charged and that can form a chemical bond; from the Greek ienai, meaning "to go" (p. 188).

isobar (ī′ sə bär): line drawn through points of equal air pressure along a given surface; from the Greek baros, meaning "weight" (p. 498).

isostasy (ī säs′ tə sē): balance of plates floating on the asthenosphere; from the Greek isos + -stasia, meaning "equal + condition of standing" (p. 277).

isotope (ī′ sə tōp): atom of an element with the normal number of protons but a different number of neutrons; from the Greek isos and topos, meaning "equal" and "place" (p. 375).

J

jet stream: strong winds in the troposphere flowing in narrow bands from west to east; from the Latin jacere, meaning "to throw" (p. 464).

K

kelp: fast growing seaweed, harvested for food and chemicals (p. 584).

key bed: a widespread rock layer that is easy to recognize (p. 371).

krill: tiny, shrimplike creatures found in water off Antarctica (p. 584).

L

laboratory (lab′ ə rə tȯr ē): room used to conduct investigations, experiments; from the Latin laborare, meaning "to labor" (p. 24).

latitude (lat′ ə tüd): measurement of distance north or south of the equator; from the Latin latus, meaning "wide" (p. 42).

Laurasia (lȯr ā′ zhə): ancient landmass that included North America, Europe, and Asia (p. 396).

lava (läv′ ə): melted rock that reaches Earth's surface during volcanic eruption; from the Latin labi, meaning "to slip, slide" (p. 228).

leaching (lēch′ iŋ): process whereby water carries minerals to lower horizons of soil (p. 320).

leap year: every fourth year, in which there are 366 days rather than 365 (p. 88).

legend (lej′ ənd): list that explains the symbols on a map; from the Latin legere, meaning "to gather" (p. 38).

levee (lev′ ē): long ridge along each side of a river formed by large-grained sediments (p. 343).

lightning (līt′ niŋ): great electrical charge between a cloud and Earth that creates a giant spark (p. 489).

light-year: distance that light travels in one year, about 9.5 trillion kilometers (p. 150).

liquid (lik′ wəd): substance that flows and takes the shape of its container; from the Latin liquidus, meaning "fluid" (p. 177).

liter [L] (lē′ tər): unit of volume; from the Greek litrā, meaning "a weight" (p. 17).

lithosphere (lith′ ə sfiər): solid outer layer of Earth including both crust and upper mantle; from the Greek lithos and sphaira, meaning "stone" and "ball" (p. 266).

local wind: wind created by heating differences in land over small areas; from the Latin locus, meaning "place" (p. 459).

longitude (lŏn′ jə tüd): measurement of distance east or west of the prime meridian; from the Latin longus, meaning "length" (p. 43).

longshore current (lȯŋ′ shȯr kər′ ənt): current that moves along the shoreline; from the Latin currere, meaning "to flow quickly" (p. 604).

low-pressure area (lō presh′ ər ar′ ē ə): area where isobars show lower readings toward the center of the pattern; from the Latin pressus and area, meaning "closed, supressed" and "open space" (p. 498).

low-pressure system (lō presh′ ər sis′ təm): low-pressure area along with its fronts; from the Latin pressus and Greek synistanai, meaning "closed" and "to combine" (p. 503).

lunar eclipse (lü′ nər i klips′): dimming of the moon when the moon passes through Earth's shadow; from the Latin lucēre and Greek ekleipein, meaning "to shine" and "to omit" (p. 99).

luster (ləs′ tər): the way a mineral reflects light from its surface; from the Latin lustrare, meaning "to brighten" (p. 202).

M

magma (mag′ mə): melted rock beneath Earth's surface; from the Greek magma, meaning "thick" (p. 199).

magnetic declination (mag net′ ik dek lə nā′ shən): angle that measures the difference between geographic north and magnetic north; from the Greek *magnēs* and Latin *declinatio*, meaning "stone of Magnesia" and "turning aside" (p. 39).

magnetic north (mag net' ik nȯȯrth): direction from a given point to the magnetic pole in northern Canada (p. 39).

magnetosphere (mag net' ə sfiər): region surrounding Earth that is affected by Earth's magnetic field (p. 39).

main sequence (mān sē' kwəns): the distribution of ninety percent of all stars based on their colors and temperatures; from the Latin *sequi*, meaning "to follow" (p. 161).

mammal (mam' əl): warmblooded vertebrate that nourishes its young with milk secreted by mammary glands; from the Latin *mamma*, meaning "breast" (p. 400).

mantle (mant' əl): solid layer of Earth between the outer core and the crust; from the Latin *mantellum*, meaning "mantle, cloak" (p. 48).

map scale: line or number on map that shows relationship of distances on a map to distances on Earth; from the Latin *mappa* and *scala(ae)*, meaning "napkin, flag" and "rung(s)" (p. 52).

maria (mär' ē ə): smooth areas of dark rock caused by ancient lava flows on the surface of the moon; from the Latin *mare*, meaning "sea" (p. 111).

mass: measure of the quantity of material making up an object; from the Greek *massein*, meaning "to knead" (pp. 17, 176).

mass movement: result of gravity pulling loose, weathered materials downhill; from the Greek *massein* and Latin *movere*, meaning "to knead" and "to move" (p. 325).

matter: any substance having mass and volume; from the Latin *materia*, meaning "physical substance" (p. 176).

meander (mē an' dər): large curve in a river formed by sediment deposits on the inside of the curve; from the *Meanderes* river in Asia Minor (p. 344).

mechanical weathering (mi kan' i kəl weth̲' ə riŋ): breaking down of rocks into smaller pieces without changing their chemical composition; from the Greek *mechanē*, meaning "machine" (p. 312).

Mercator (mər kāt' ər): map projection made by drawing lines from the center of Earth to an imaginary cylinder of paper; named for Gerhardus Kremer (in Latin, *Mercator*), Flemish cartographer (p. 49).

mercury barometer (mər' kyə rē bə räm' ət ər): instrument used to measure air pressure from the rise or fall of mercury liquid in a tube; named for Mercurius, Roman god, and from the Greek *baros*, meaning "weight" (p. 455).

mesosphere (mez' ə sfiər): atmospheric layer between the stratosphere and the thermosphere; from the Greek *meso-* + *sphaira*, meaning "mid- + ball" (p. 444).

metamorphic (met ə mor' fik): rock that is changed into new rock by intense heat and pressure deep inside Earth; from the Greek *metamorphoun*, meaning "to transform" (p. 222).

meteor (mēt' ē ər): piece of an asteroid or comet that enters Earth's atmosphere; from the Greek *meteōron*, meaning "phenomenon in the sky" (p. 136).

meteorite (mēt' ē ə rīt): piece of debris that strikes the surface of a moon or planet (p. 109).

meteorology (mēt ē ə räl' ə jē): science that deals with changes in the atmosphere; from the Greek *meteōron* + *logos*, meaning "phenomenon in the sky + word" (p. 11).

meteor shower: yearly shower of meteors that occurs when Earth sweeps through rock fragments left behind by old comets; from the Greek *meteōron*, meaning "phenomenon in the sky" (p. 136).

meter [m] (mēt' ər): standard SI unit of length; from the Greek *metron*, meaning "measure" (p. 16).

microclimate (mī' krō klī mət): small area with distinct temperature and moisture pattern; from the Greek *mikros* + *klima*, meaning "small + latitude, climate" (p. 523).

mid-ocean ridge: long chain of underwater mountains (p. 264).

millibar (mil' ə bär): unit of pressure related to the weight of air pressing on 1 square centimeter; from the Latin *mille*, meaning "thousand" (p. 456).

mineral (min' ə rəl): naturally occurring, inorganic solid substance with a definite chemical composition and structure; from the Latin *mineralis*, meaning "ore" (p. 196).

mixture (miks' chər): physical combination of two or more kinds of matter; from the Latin *mixtura*, meaning "mixture" (p. 189).

mold: cavity in a rock formed when something dissolved, such as a shell; from the Latin *modulus*, meaning "small measure" (p. 364).

molecule (mäl' i kyü əl): smallest particle of a substance that retains all the properties of the substance and is composed of two or more atoms bonded by the sharing of electrons; from the Latin *moles*, meaning "mass" (p. 188).

moraine (mə rān'): accumulation of earth and stones carried and finally deposited by a glacier (p. 348).

mudflow: slide or flow of mud down a hillside as the result of precipitation (p. 326).

N

natural gas: gaseous hydrocarbon, formed from buried organisms or coal under great heat and pressure; from the Latin *natura*, meaning "nature" (p. 412).

natural resource (nach' ə rəl rē' sȯȯrs): material taken from Earth for human use; from the Latin *natura* and *resurgere*, meaning "nature" and "to appear again" (p. 410).

natural selection: the change in a species over time due to the ability of some individual organisms to adapt better to their environment than other individuals (p. 367).

nebula (neb′ yə lə): large body of gas and dust in space; from the Greek *nephelē*, meaning "cloud" (p. 162).

neutron (nü′ trän): particle with no charge in the nucleus of the atom; from the Latin *neuter*, meaning "neuter" (p. 180).

neutron star (nü′ trän stär): small hot star left after a supernova explosion (p. 163).

nimbus (nim′ bəs): a kind of cloud that produces rain or snow; from the Latin *nimbus*, meaning "rainstorm" (p. 481).

nodule (näj′ ül): small, rounded mass of minerals found on the ocean floor; from the Latin *nodus*, meaning "knob, knot" (p. 213).

normal fault (nor′ məl folt): a fault where the rocks above the fault move down; from the Latin *normalis* and *fallere*, meaning "normal" and "to fail" (p. 285).

nuclear energy (nü′ klē ər en′ ər jē): energy released when the nucleus of an atom is changed; from the Latin *nux* and Greek *energeia*, meaning "nut" and "activity" (p. 418).

nucleus (nü′ klē əs): small, positively charged center of the atom; from the Latin *nux*, meaning "kernel, nut" (p. 180).

O

occluded front (ə klud′ əd frənt): weather condition in which a warm air mass is trapped by two cold air masses above the ground; from the Latin *obcludere* and *frons*, meaning "to close in" and "forehead" (p. 497).

oceanography (ō shə näg′ rə fē): scientific study of the oceans and seas; from the Greek *Ōkeanos* + *graphein*, meaning "river that circles the earth + to write" (p. 12).

oil shale: sedimentary rock that contains trapped kerogen, a petroleumlike substance (p. 417).

orbit (or′ bət): path an object follows as it revolves around another object, as Earth's revolution around the sun; from the Latin *orbita*, meaning "path" (p. 78).

orbital period (or′ bət əl pir′ ē əd): time required for a satellite to complete one revolution around Earth; from the Latin *orbis* and Greek *periodos*, meaning "globe" and "circuit, period of time" (p. 103).

orbital speed (or′ bət əl spēd): speed of a satellite (p. 103).

ore (ōər): mineral or rock containing enough of a valuable material that mining it is profitable (p. 211).

organic rock (or gan′ ik räk): sedimentary rock type made from things that were once alive; from the Greek *organon*, meaning "tool, instrument" (p. 231).

outer core (aut′ ər koər): layer of Earth that surrounds the inner core and is beneath the mantle (p. 48).

outer planet: one of five planets farthest from the sun; from the Greek *planēs*, meaning "wanderer" (p. 119).

P

paleontologist (pā lē än täl′ ə jəst): scientist who studies the life and geology of the past; from the Greek *palai- + onta + logos*, meaning "ancient + existing things + word" (p. 364).

Pangaea (pan jē′ ə): name of the hypothetical great continent thought to have split into the landmasses known today; a word coined by meteorologist Alfred Wegener from the Greek *pan* and *gaiē*, meaning "all" and "land" (p. 257).

parallax (par′ ə laks): apparent shift in an object's position caused by the motion of the observer; from the Greek *parallassein*, meaning "to change" (p. 150).

parcel of air: small volume of air with the same temperature throughout; from the Latin *particula* and Greek *aer*, meaning "small part" and "air" (p. 454).

particulate (pər tik′ yə lət): solid particle or liquid droplet that is small enough to hang in the air; from the Latin *particula*, meaning "small part" (p. 527).

pattern (pat′ ərn): set of events that occurs repeatedly (p. 10).

penumbra (pə nəm′ brə): lighter part of the shadow cast by the sun; from the Latin *paene + umbra*, meaning "almost + shadow" (p. 98).

period (pir′ ē əd): division of the geologic time scale, smaller than an era; from the Greek *periodos*, meaning "period" (p. 385).

permeable (pər′ mē ə bəl): term for material into which water can seep; from the Latin *permeare*, meaning "to pass through" (p. 335).

petrochemical (pe trō kem′ i kəl): chemical compound derived from petroleum or natural gas; from the Greek *petros* and Latin *alchymia*, meaning "rock" and "alchemy" (p. 414).

petroleum (pə trō′ lē əm): liquid hydrocarbon, formed from dead organisms, buried and exposed to pressure and heat over a long period of time; from the Greek *petros* and Latin *oleum*, meaning "rock" and "oil" (p. 412).

phases (fāz′ ez): monthly change in appearance of the moon; from the Greek *phainein*, meaning "to show" (p. 96).

photosphere (fōt′ ə sfiər): visible surface of the sun; from the Greek *phōs + sphaira*, meaning "light + ball" (p. 158).

photovoltaic cell (fōt ō völ tā′ ik sel): device that changes light into electricity; from the Greek *phōs* and Latin *cella*, meaning "light" and "small room" (p. 424).

pH scale: method used to represent the concentration of hydrogen ions in a solution (p. 549).

physical change: change in the physical property but not the chemical identity of matter; from the Latin *physica,* meaning "physics" (p. 186).

physical property: characteristic of matter that can be observed without producing a new kind of matter; from the Latin *physica* and *proprius,* meaning "physics" and "one's own" (p. 186).

planet (plan' ət): large body that orbits the sun, such as Earth; from the Greek *planēs,* meaning "wanderer" (p. 118).

plate: large moving section of lithosphere that contains continents and seafloor; from the Greek *platys,* meaning "broad, flat" (p. 267).

plateau (pla tō'): flat, broad, raised area of land (p. 276).

plate tectonics (plāt tek tän' iks): theory that solid plates move on top of the puttylike asthenosphere; from the Greek *tektonikos,* meaning "of a builder" (p. 268).

polar (pō' lər): type of climate in which cold air masses are most common; from the Latin *polus,* meaning "pole" (p. 520).

polar easterlies (pō' lər ē' stər lēz): polar winds coming from the northeast (p. 464).

polar front (pō' lər frənt): meeting place of cool air moving south and warm air moving north, at about 60° N latitude (p. 464).

pollutant (pə lüt' ənt): contaminant in air or water that exists in enough quantity to be harmful to plants, animals, or property; from the Latin *polluere,* meaning "to defile, pollute" (p. 527).

polyconic (päl i kän' ik): map projection made as if a cone were wrapped around various parts of Earth's surface; from the Greek *polys* + *kōnos,* meaning "many + cone" (p. 50).

porous (pōr' əs): term for material that has spaces, or pores, between its grains; from the Greek *poros,* meaning "passage" (p. 335).

precipitation (pri sip ə tā' shən): any liquid or solid form of water that falls from the atmosphere to the earth; from the Latin *praecipitare,* meaning "to throw down" (p. 485).

prevailing westerlies (pri vā' liŋ wes' tər lēz): winds in the latitudes 40° N and 60° N; from the Latin *praevalēre,* meaning "to be strong" (p. 464).

primary wave (prī' mer ē wāv): seismic wave that causes matter to stretch and compress; from the Latin *primus,* meaning "first" (p. 288).

prime meridian (prīm mə rid' ē ən): imaginary line that passes from the geographic North Pole to the geographic South Pole, and used as a reference line for longitude; from the Latin *primus* and *medius* + *dies,* meaning "first" and "mid + day" (p. 43).

prominence (präm' ə nəns): a loop of solar material from the sun's corona that is falling back toward the sun; from the Latin *prominēre,* meaning "to jut forth" (p. 159).

property: quality special to a substance that aids in clas-

sifying it; from the Latin *proprius,* meaning "(one's) own" (p. 176).

proton (prō' tän): positively charged particle of the atom; from the Greek *prōtos,* meaning "first" (p. 180).

protoplanet (prōt' ō plan' ət): small lumps in the early solar system that eventually pulled together to form the planets; from the Greek *prōtos* and *planēs,* meaning "first" and "wanderer" (p. 134).

Q

quasar (kwā' zär): distant object that resembles a star and gives off great amounts of energy; from the Latin *quasi,* meaning "as if" (p. 164).

R

radioactive decay (rād ē ō ak' tiv di kā'): process in which one element changes into another element as the number of protons in its atoms changes; from the Latin *radius* + *agere* and *decadere,* meaning "ray, beam + to drive" and "to fall" (p. 375).

rain: large droplets of water falling on the earth (p. 486).

rain gauge (rān gāj): instrument used to measure precipitation (p. 486).

ray: on the moon, a streak that leads away from a crater; from the Latin *radius,* meaning "rod, ray" (p. 109).

recharge (rē chärj'): to refill, such as an aquifer by rain (p. 566).

red giant: large, bright, red star off the main sequence in the H-R Diagram (p. 163).

reflecting telescope (ri flekt' iŋ tel' ə skōp): instrument for viewing distant objects that uses a concave mirror to gather light; from the Latin *reflectere* and Greek *tēlescopus,* meaning "to bend back" and "far seeing" (p. 153).

refracting telescope (ri fract' iŋ tel' ə skōp): instrument for viewing distant objects that is made of a series of lenses that collect light; from the Latin *refringere* and Greek *tēlescopus,* meaning "to break open" and "far seeing" (p. 153).

relative age (rel' ət iv āj): age of rocks compared to each other; from the Latin *referre,* meaning "to carry back" (p. 368).

relative humidity (rel' ət iv hyü mid' ət ē): comparison of the amount of water vapor in the air to the largest amount possible in the air at that temperature; from the Latin *relatus* and *umidus,* meaning "carried back" and "damp" (p. 472).

relief (ri lēf'): term used for height and depth of land on a topographic map (p. 54).

reptile (rep' təl): cold-blooded vertebrate with dry, scaly skin; from the Latin *repere,* meaning "to creep" (p. 397).

residual soil (ri zij' ə wəl soiəl): soil that formed from bedrock (see **transported soil**); from the Latin *residuum,* meaning "residue" (p. 319).

reverse fault (ri vərs′ fȯlt): a fault where the rocks above the fault move up; from the Latin *revertere* and *fallere*, meaning "to turn back" and "to fail" (p. 285).

revolution (rev ə lü′ shən): movement of an object around another object as Earth's movement around the sun; from the Latin *revolvere*, meaning "to revolve" (p. 78).

Richter scale (rik′ tər skāl): numerical description of the size of seismic waves produced by an earthquake; named for American seismologist Charles F. Richter (p. 293).

rift: deep valley which runs down the middle of a mid-ocean ridge (p. 264).

rille (ril): long, narrow valley found mostly in the lunar maria (p. 111).

rip current: strong surface current that flows out from the shore; from the Latin *currere*, meaning "to move quickly" (p. 605).

rock: natural solid that is usually a mixture of different minerals derived from Earth (p. 222).

rock cycle: constant recycling (formation and destruction) of rock materials; from the Greek *kyklos*, meaning "circle" (p. 242).

rotation (rō tā′ shən): spinning of an object around an axis; from the Latin *rotare*, meaning "to rotate" (p. 75).

runoff (rən′ ȯf): rainwater that does not sink into the soil or evaporate (p. 339).

S

salinity (sə lin′ ət ē): measurement of dissolved salts in seawater; from the Latin *sal*, meaning "salt" (p. 571).

saturated (sach′ ə rāt əd): condition that exists when the number of molecules returning to the water equal the number leaving it; from the Latin *saturare*, meaning "to saturate" (p. 471).

scientific model (sī ən tif′ ik mäd′ əl): picture, object, or demonstration that tries to show or explain what is observed in nature; from the Latin *scire* and *modulus*, meaning "to know" and "small measure" (p. 23).

sea: large body of salt water usually considered part of a major ocean (p. 570).

sea cave: large hole in the sea cliff, formed by waves (p. 607).

sea cliff: steep portion of land or rock eroded by waves (p. 606).

seafloor spreading: theory that seafloor crust forms at mid-ocean ridges and then spreads in opposite directions (p. 265).

seamount: underwater mountain rising above the deep-seafloor (p. 579).

sea stack: column of rocks left seaward of a sea cliff and formed by wave erosion (p. 607).

second: standard SI unit of time; from the Latin *secundus*, meaning "second (time)" (p. 15).

secondary wave (sek′ ən der ē wāv): seismic wave that moves matter from side to side; from the Latin *secundus*, meaning "second" (p. 288).

sediment (sed′ ə ment): any material that settles to the bottom of a liquid; from the Latin *sedere*, meaning "to sit, sink down" (p. 231).

sedimentary (sed′ ə ment′ ə rē): rock formed by pieces of rocks, shells, or the remains of plants and animals squeezed and cemented together (p. 222).

seismic wave (sīz′ mik wāv): vibration produced by an earthquake; from the Greek *seismos*, meaning "shock" (p. 287).

seismograph (sīz′ mə graf): instrument that measures and records seismic waves; from the Greek *seismos* + *graphein*, meaning "shock + to write" (p. 288).

sewage (sü′ ij): human and other wastes mixed with used water (p. 561).

shadow zone: region on Earth where seismic waves are not received from a given earthquake; from the Greek *zone*, meaning "belt" (p. 289).

shield cone: volcanic mountain with a broad base and gently sloping sides, made from lava flows; from the Latin *conus*, meaning "cone" (p. 303).

sill: sheet of intrusive igneous rock that forms parallel to and between layers of older rock; from the Greek *selis*, meaning "crossbeam" (p. 303).

sleet: frozen or partly frozen rain (p. 486).

sliding boundary (slīd iŋ baùn də rē): place where two plates meet and slide past each other (p. 272).

slump: action wherein large chunks of rock or soil break off a slope or hillside and slide downhill (p. 326).

smelting (smelt′ iŋ): heating process used to separate metal from ore (p. 211).

smog (smäg): result of chemical reaction between nitrogen oxides and hydrocarbons from a mixture of fog and smoke (p. 529).

snow: falling ice crystals (p. 486).

soil creep: slowest type of mass movement (p. 326).

soil horizon (sȯiəl hə rīz′ ən): a layer of soil different from the layer(s) next to it (usually three horizons); from the Greek *horizein*, meaning "to bound."

solar eclipse (sō′ lər i klips′): total or partial blocking of the sun's light by the moon as seen from Earth; from the Latin *sol* and Greek *ekleipein*, meaning "sun" and "to omit" (p. 98).

solar energy (sō′ lər en′ ər jē): energy from the sun used for heating or lighting; from the Latin *sol* and Greek *energeia*, meaning "sun" and "activity" (p. 423).

solar flare (sō′ lər flaər): sudden outburst of energy from the sun's surface (p. 159).

solar wind (sō′ lər wind): flow of radiation and fast-moving gas particles from the sun (p. 135).

solid (säl′ əd): substance with a definite volume and shape that resists changes to its volume and shape; from the Latin *solidus*, meaning "solid or dense" (p. 177).

solution (sə lü′ shən): gas, liquid, or solid mixture in which ingredients are evenly mixed on a molecular level; from the Latin *solvere*, meaning "to loosen" (p. 189).

sounding (saùn′ diŋ): depth measurement that can be taken by lowering a line to the bottom of a body of water (p. 575).

space probe (spās prōb): spacecraft sent to explore planets and space and send data back to Earth; from the Latin *spatium* and *probare*, meaning "space" and "to examine" (p. 121).

specific gravity (spi sif′ ik grav′ ət ē): ratio of the mass of a material to the mass of an equal volume of water; from the Latin *species* and *gravitas*, meaning "outward appearance" and "weight" (p. 205).

spectroscope (spek′ trə skōp): instrument that separates electromagnetic waves into a spectrum; from the Latin *spectrum*, meaning "apparition" (p. 155).

spit: sandbar with one end attached to land (p. 608).

spring: place where groundwater flows out onto Earth's surface (p. 566).

spring equinox (spriŋ ē′ kwə näks): day about halfway between winter and summer solstices when the hours of daylight equal hours of nighttime; from the Latin *aequi-* + *nox*, meaning "equal- + night" (p. 82).

squall line (skwȯl līn): line of thunderstorms (p. 509).

standard time zone (stan′ dərd tīm zōn): area of Earth, determined by longitude, in which all clocks are set to the same time; from the Greek *zōnē*, meaning "belt" (p. 85).

stationary front (stā′ shə ner ē frənt): weather condition that results when neither a cold nor a warm air mass pushes against the other at the place they meet; from the Latin *status* and *frons*, meaning "position" and "forehead" (p. 497).

station model (stā′ shən mäd′ əl): pattern of meteorological symbols that represent the state of weather at a particular place (station); from the Latin *status* and *modulus*, meaning "position" and "small measure" (p. 500).

storm surge (stȯrm sərj): mounds of water piled against the shore by a hurricane; from the Latin *surgere*, meaning "to rise" (p. 514).

stratosphere (strat′ ə sfiər): atmospheric layer located between the troposphere and the mesosphere; from the Latin *stratum* + *sphaira*, meaning "blanket + ball" (p. 444).

stratus (strāt′ əs): kind of cloud characterized by gray layers, indicating cool surfaces; from the Latin *sternere*, meaning "to spread" (p. 481).

streak: color of the powdered mineral (p. 202).

strike-slip fault: fault where the rocks on either side of the fault break and slide past each other (p. 285).

strip mining: process of removing soil and rock to get at a buried layer of coal or ore (p. 416).

stromatolite (strō mat′ əl īt): laminated sedimentary fossil formed from layers of blue-green algae; from the Latin *stroma* and Greek *lithos*, meaning "bed covering" and "stone" (p. 390).

subduction (səb dək′ shən): pushing of the edge of one plate below the edge of another; from the Latin *subducere*, meaning "to withdraw" (p. 273).

submarine canyon (səb mə rēn′ kan′ yən): deep valley carved into the continental shelf or continental slope; from the Latin *sub* + *mare*, meaning "under + sea" (p. 578).

submersible (səb mər′ sə bəl): small submarine used for undersea research; from the Latin *submergere*, meaning "to submerge" (p. 577).

subsoil (səb′ soiəl): B horizon of soil that contains minerals and sticky clay; from the Latin *sub-*, meaning "under-" (p. 320).

summer solstice (səm′ ər säl stəs): day on which the sun's midday altitude is greatest; from the Latin *sol* + *status*, meaning "sun + stopping point" (p. 81).

sunspot: small dark spot on the sun's surface (p. 158).

supernova (sü pər nō′ və): explosion of a massive star that gives off millions of times more energy than the sun; from the Latin *super* + *nova*, meaning "above, over + new" (p. 163).

surface wave (sər′ fəs wāv): seismic wave that causes a rolling motion in the rock and soil (p. 288).

suspension (sə spen′ chən): condition in which grains of silt or clay hang in water that is moving; from the Latin *suspendere*, meaning "to suspend" (p. 341).

swells: equally spaced ocean waves of the same size formed by storms at sea (p. 596).

syncline (sin′ klīn): downward fold of a rock layer; from the Greek *syn-* + *klinein*, meaning "with + to incline" (p. 275).

T

tar sand: natural mixture of sand and tar that may be a future source of oil (p. 417).

technology (tek nâl′ ə jē): using science principles to solve practical problems; from the Greek *technologia*, meaning "the systematic treatment of an art" (p. 28).

temperate (tem′ pə rət): type of climate in which both warm and cold air masses affect temperatures; from the Latin *temperare*, meaning "to moderate" (p. 520).

temperature (tem′ pər chüər): measure of heat flow from a substance; as molecules or atoms of substance move faster, the temperature is higher; from the Latin *temperare*, meaning "to moderate" (p. 454).

tephra (tef′ rə): pieces of cooled lava that are sprayed in the air and fall back to the ground; from the Greek *tephros*, meaning "ash" (p. 299).

terrestrial planet (tə res′ trē əl plan′ ət): one of the four planets with a rocky surface—Mercury, Mars, Venus, and Earth; from the Latin *terra* and Greek *planēs*, meaning "earth" and "wanderer" (p. 128).

texture (teks′ chər): the visual pattern made by the size, shape, and arrangement of the crystals or grains in a rock; from the Latin *texere*, meaning "to weave" (p. 223).

theory (thiər′ ē): hypothesis supported by many experiments; from the Greek *thēorein*, meaning "to look at" (p. 23).

thermocline (thər′ mə klīn): ocean layer that separates warm, upper oxygen-rich water from colder, lower oxygen-poor water; layer of changing temperatures; from the Greek *thermē* and *klinein*, meaning "heat" and "sloping" (p. 572).

thermosphere (thər′ mə sfiər): atmospheric layer extending from the top of the mesosphere into outer space; from the Greek *thermē* + *sphira*, meaning "heat + ball" (p. 444).

thunder (thən′ dər): sound caused by explosion of intensely heated air during a lightning stroke (p. 489).

tide: daily rise or fall of sea level in oceans, seas, and other large bodies of water (p. 100).

topographic map (täp ə graf ik map): map illustrating height and depth of land, as well as natural and constructed features; from the Greek *topos* + *graphein*, meaning "place + to write" (p. 54).

topsoil (täp′ soiəl): soil that contains more humus than soil in other horizons (p. 320).

tornado (tor nād′ ō): violent, funnel-shaped storm descending from a cold front (p. 509).

toxic (täk′ sik): substance harmful to living things; from the Greek *toxikon*, meaning "poison" (p. 557).

trace fossil (trās fäs′ əl): record left by an animal while still alive, such as a footprint (p. 364).

trade wind (trād wind): steady winds between the equator and 30° N and 30° S latitude (p. 463).

transported soil (trans′ poərt əd soiəl): soil that came into an area from somewhere else or formed from parent material from somewhere else; from the Latin *transportare*, meaning "to carry across" (p. 319).

trench: deep, narrow ocean valley formed when one plate is subducted beneath another (p. 266).

tropical (träp′ i kəl): a type of climate affected most by warm air masses; from the Greek -*tropos*, meaning "turning" (p. 520).

troposphere (trōp′ ə sfiər): lowest portion of Earth's atmosphere; from the Greek *tropos* and *sphaira*, meaning "turn" and "ball" (p. 444).

trough (trof): lowest part of a wave (p. 595).

tsunami (sü näm′ ē): a giant ocean wave produced by underwater earth movement or volcanic eruption (p. 298).

turbidity current (tər bid′ ət ē kər′ ənt): underwater density current formed by fast-moving sediment-filled water; from the Latin *turbidus* and *currere*, meaning "confused" and "to move swiftly" (p. 578).

U

umbra (əm′ brə): darker part of the shadow cast by the sun; from the Latin *umbra*, meaning "shade" (p. 98).

unconformity (ən kən for′ mȧt ē): a break in the rock record; from the Latin *un-* + *conformare*, meaning "no, not + to conform" (p. 370).

uniformitarianism (yü nə for mə ter′ ē ə niz əm): doctrine stating that existing geological processes act in the same manner throughout time and are sufficient to account for all past geological changes; from the Latin *uniformis*, meaning "uniform" (p. 368).

universal law of gravitation: principle that states that each object in the universe has a gravitational attraction for every other object; from the Latin *universum* and *gravitas*, meaning "universe" and "weight" (p. 100).

updraft (əp′ draft): an upward moving hot current of air (p. 488).

upwelling (əp wel′ iŋ): current that brings cold water up from deeper water along the western coasts of continents (p. 601).

V

variable (ver′ ē ə bəl): something that is undetermined that may cause or change an event; from the Latin *variare*, meaning "to change, vary" (p. 22).

vertebrate (vərt′ ə brāt): animal with a backbone; from the Latin *vertebratus*, meaning "jointed" (p. 391).

volcano (väl kā′ nō): opening in Earth's crust where melted rock reaches Earth's surface; from the Latin *Vulcan*, the Roman god of fire (p. 299).

volume (väl′ yəm): measurement of the space an object occupies; from the Latin *volvere*, meaning "to roll" (pp. 17, 176).

W

warm front: weather condition that results from a warm air mass pushing against a cold air mass; from the Latin *frons*, meaning "forehead" (p. 497).

water cycle: continuous movement of water between Earth and the atmosphere; from the Greek *kyklos*, meaning "circle" (p. 547).

water table: top of the zone of saturation, below which rock pores are filled with water; from the Latin *tabula*, meaning "table, list" (p. 554).

wave-cut terrace: flat underwater area in front of a sea cliff, formed by erosion; from the Latin *terra*, meaning "earth, land" (p. 607).

wave height: the vertical distance between the bottom of a trough and the top of a crest (p. 595).

wavelength: distance between one point on a wave and the identical point on the next wave in a series (p. 152).

wetland: area of land covered with shallow water or that has wet soils, such as swamps, marshes, and bogs (p. 555).

white dwarf (hwīt dwȯərf): small, dim white star off the main sequence in the H-R Diagram (p. 162).

wind: air in motion (p. 458).

winter solstice (wint′ ər säl′ stəs): day on which the sun's midday altitude is smallest; from the Latin *sol* + *status*, meaning "sun + stopping point" (p. 82).

Z

zone of aeration (zōn, aər ā′ shən): layer of rock or soil between Earth's surface and the water table; from the Greek *zōnē* and *aēr*, meaning "belt" and "air" (p. 554).

zone of saturation (zōn, sach ə rā′ shən): layer of rock and soil where all pores and fractures are filled with groundwater; from the Greek *zōnē* and Latin *saturare*, meaning "belt" and "to satisfy" (p. 554).

ACKNOWLEDGMENTS

Photo research: Sue McDermott, Connie Komack
Cover design/photography: Martucci Studio

Illustration credits: Edmond Alexander/Alexander and Turner: pages 150, 157, 313, 317, 450, 452, 467. **Heath Art:** pages 52, 57, 190. **Gary Hinks:** pages 265, 266, 267, 268, 270 b, 271, 272, 273, 300, 302, 303, 580, 581. **Nancy Kaplan:** page 165 t. **Joe LeMonnier/Craven Graphics:** pages 11, 39, 43, 45, 47, 48, 49, 50, 54, 216, 276 b, 294, 340, 414, 496, 497, 514, 521, 522, 524 r, 570, 599, 601 t, 615. **Paul Metcalf:** pages 288 t, 289, 386, 387, 402, 419 b, 421, 424, 454, 455, 528, 531, 532. **Leonard Morgan:** page 197. **Network Graphics:** pages 59, 61, 63, 73, 83, 107, 115, 124, 138, 145, 146, 147, 149, 152, 153, 232, 247, 263, 372, 373, 427, 500, 517, 549, 558, 559, 571, 574, 595, 596, 597, 598, 603, 613. **Mathew Pippin:** pages 38, 40 b, 160, 472. **Bob Pratt:** pages 257, 258, 261, 275, 276 t, 277, 284, 285, 287, 288 b, 384, 385, 404, 577, 578, 579, 585. **Precision Graphics:** pages 16, 74, 110, 181, 309, 376, 378, 381, 432, 435, 446, 471, 524 l, 533, 572, 582. **Pat Rossi/Rossi and Associates:** pages 177, 180, 188, 337, 341, 343, 345, 349, 352, 369, 375, 410, 411, 412, 419 t, 428, 470, 473, 480, 481, 485, 486, 488, 489, 523, 547, 554, 555, 556, 557, 567, 601 b, 602, 604, 605. **Bruce Sanders:** pages 119, 120, 121, 123, 125, 126, 135, 136, 233, 243, 262, 270 t, 510, 513. **John Sanderson:** pages 40 t, 274, 292, 295, 296, 291, 394, 396, 407, 493, 498, 501, 504, 505, 550, 564. **Scientific Illustrators:** pages 76, 77, 79, 80, 81, 82, 84, 85, 86, 94, 95, 96, 98, 99, 100, 101, 103, 104, 105, 112, 448, 462, 463, 464, 499, 502, 503, 506. **Cynthia Turner/Alexander and Turner:** pages 162, 164, 165 b, 445, 447, 458, 459.

Photo Credits

Front Matter and Table of Contents: i: National Optical Astronomy Observatories/Phil Degginger. **iii:** l,r Nancy Sheehan/© D. C. Heath. **iv:** NASA. **v:** t NASA; b © Paul Silverman (Fundamental Photographs). **vi:** t Nancy Sheehan/© D. C. Heath; b © David Madison (Bruce Coleman, Inc.). **vii:** t Map of the World Ocean Floor by Bruce Heezen & Marie Tharp, © 1977 by Marie Tharp; m William E. Ferguson; b E. R. Degginger (Earth Scenes). **viii:** t © C. C. Lockwood (DRK Photo); m © Tom Bean (DRK Photo); b Tyrrell Museum of Palaeontology/Alberta Culture & Multiculturalism. **ix:** Richard Price (West Light); b Frans Lanting (Minden Pictures). **x:** t,r John D. Cunningham (Visuals Unlimited); bl,br Ralph Clevenger (West Light). **xi:** t Larry Ulrich (DRK Photo); m E. R. Degginger; b © C. C. Lockwood (DRK Photo). **xii:** t © Kathy Tyrrell/Oxford Scientific Films (Animals, Animals); b Nancy Sheehan/© D. C. Heath.

Unit One: 6: © Krafft-Explorer (Photo Researchers, Inc.). **6–7:** NASA (Photri). **8:** NASA. **10:** Ronald Royer (Photo Researchers, Inc.). **11:** Jeff Foot (Tom Stack & Associates). **12:** John Carnemolla (West Light). **13:** © David Muench. **14:** Nancy Sheehan/© D. C. Heath. **15:** Soames Summerhayes (Photo Researchers, Inc.). **17:** t Randall Hyman; b Nancy Sheehan/© D. C. Heath. **18:** Ken O'Donoghue/© D. C. Heath. **19:** l Keith Gunnar (Bruce Coleman, Inc.); r Nancy Sheehan/© D. C. Heath. **20–21:** Nancy Sheehan/© D. C. Heath. **22:** l Howard B. Bluestein; r Lawrence Migdale. **23, 25, 26:** Nancy Sheehan/© D. C. Heath. **28:** l TSW-Click/Chicago; r Nancy Sheehan/© D. C. Heath. **29:** Al Grillo (Picture Group). **30:** l Jane Faircloth (Transparencies); tr McKiernan (SIPA); br Herman J. Kokojan (Black Star). **32:** l WHOI; r Martin Marietta Corporation. **36:** Ken O'Donoghue/© D. C. Heath. **36:** Inset James Tallon (Outdoor Exposures). **39:** Frank Siteman (The Picture Cube). **41, 42, 44, 51:** Nancy Sheehan/© D. C. Heath. **52:** Science, v. 243, January 6, 1989, Cover, by Dr. V. Ramanathan/© By the AAAS. **55:** USGS. **56:** t David Madison; b Tim Davis (Photo Researchers, Inc.). **57:** t USGS; b Jerome Wycoff. **59:** Nancy Sheehan/© D. C. Heath. **60:** t Nancy Sheehan/© D. C. Heath; b Earth Satellite Corporation (Photo Researchers, Inc.). **64:** Michael Nichols (Magnum Photos, Inc.). **66:** Lanna Cheng. **67:** Carole Camillo.

Unit Two: 68: NASA. **68–69:** National Optical Astronomy Observatories/Phil Degginger. **70:** Myrleen Ferguson (PhotoEdit). **72:** Nancy Sheehan/© D. C. Heath. **73:** t Dennis di Cicco; b Nancy Sheehan/© D. C. Heath. **74:** Nancy Sheehan/© D. C. Heath. **75:** t Hansen Planetarium; b Robert Landau (West Light). **78:** Nancy Sheehan/© D. C. Heath. **80:** Ken O'Donoghue/© D. C. Heath. **81:** Stephen S. Myers (International Stock Photo). **82:** t © 1987 Hangarter (The Picture Cube); b Tom Pantages. **84:** l © S. Nelsen (DRK Photo); r Dennis di Cicco. **88:** © Tom Bean (DRK Photo). **91:** Tony Freeman (PhotoEdit). **92:** E. R. Degginger (Bruce Coleman, Inc.). **94:** Nancy Sheehan/© D. C. Heath. **95:** NASA. **97:** Ken O'Donoghue/© D. C. Heath. **98:** t © John Bova (Photo Researchers, Inc.; b National Optical Astronomy Observatories/Phil Degginger. **99:** t © Glenn Short (Bruce Coleman, Inc.); b Dennis di Cicco. **100:** Clyde H. Smith (Peter Arnold, Inc.). **102, 105, 106:** NASA. **107:** Ken O'Donoghue/© D. C. Heath. **108:** NASA. **109:** t The Observatories of the Carnegie Institution of Washington; b NASA. **111:** NASA. **112:** Jay Melosh and Marlan Kipp, Sandia National Laboratories (Dept. of Planetary Sciences, University of Arizona). **116:** NASA. **118:** Dennis di Cicco. **122:** NASA. **127:** John Urban. **128–131:** NASA. **132:** NASA (Photri). **133:** Nancy Sheehan/© D. C. Heath. **134:** © Hans Vehrenberg. **136:** Runk/Schoenberger (Grant Heilman). **137:** l © Tom Bean (DRK Photo); r James M. Baker (Dennis Milon). **142:** The Mendillo Collection of Astronomical Charts. **144:** l Dennis di Cicco; r Royce Bair (The Stock Solution). **148:** Ken O'Donoghue/© D. C. Heath. **150:** S. Nielsen (DRK Photo). **153:** Hale Observatories. **154:** California Association for Research in Astronomy. **155:** Commonwealth of Puerto Rico. **158:** Phil Degginger. **159:** t NASA; b Dennis di Cicco. **162:** Lick Observatory Photograph. **163:** t California Institute of Technology & Carnegie Institute of Washington; b M. Paternostro/SPL (Photo Researchers, Inc.). **164:** l,m Hale Observatories; r © by the Association for Research in Astronomy, Inc. The Cerm Tololo Inter-American Observatory. **165:** Jay Pasachoff (C. Pasachoff Educational Trust). **166:** Ken O'Donoghue/© D. C. Heath. **167:** © The Association of Universities for Research in Astronomy, Inc./Kitt Peak National Observatory. **170:** NASA.

Unit Three: 172: Breck P. Kent. **172–173:** © David Madison (Bruce Coleman, Inc.). **174:** Martha Swope. **177:** *l* Nancy Sheehan/© D. C. Heath; *m* Ken O'Donoghue/© D. C. Heath; *r* Lawrence Migdale. **178:** *t* Clive Russ; *b* Phil Degginger. **179:** Ken O'Donoghue/© D. C. Heath. **184:** *l* Ken O'Donoghue/© D. C. Heath; *l to r* E. R. Degginger, E. R. Degginger, E. R. Degginger, E. R. Degginger (Bruce Coleman, Inc.). **185:** Nancy Sheehan/© D. C. Heath. **186:** *l* Rod Planck (Tom Stack & Associates); *r* E. R. Degginger. **187:** *tl* E. R. Degginger; *tc* Breck P. Kent; *tr* Ken O'Donoghue/© D. C. Heath; *b* Dennis Brack (Black Star). **189:** *t* Ken O'Donoghue/© D. C. Heath; *b* Nancy Sheehan/© D. C. Heath. **190:** Nancy Sheehan/© D. C. Heath. **193:** Breck P. Kent. **194:** © Paul Silverman (Fundamental Photographs). **196:** Photo by Robert Weldon, Stones Courtesy of The G. I. A. Stone Collection. **197:** *t* Breck P. Kent; *b* Yoram Lehmann (Peter Arnold, Inc.). **198:** top, *l to r*: E. R. Degginger (Bruce Coleman, Inc.), Paul Silverman (Fundamental Photographs), Breck P. Kent, E. R. Degginger, E. R. Degginger, Breck P. Kent; *b* Paul Silverman (Fundamental Photographs). **199:** *t* E. R. Degginger; *b* Larry West (Bruce Coleman, Inc.). **200:** Nancy Sheehan/© D. C. Heath. **201:** *l* Breck P. Kent; *r* Paul Silverman (Fundamental Photographs). **202:** *tl* John Cancalosi (Tom Stack & Associates); *tr* Breck P. Kent; *b* Nancy Sheehan/© D. C. Heath. **203:** *t* Breck P. Kent; *m* Runk/Schoenberger (Grant Heilman); *b* E. R. Degginger. **204:** *t* Nancy Sheehan/© D. C. Heath; *bl* Thomas Ives (The Stock Market); *br* Breck P. Kent. **205:** *l* E. R. Degginger; *r* Runk/Schoenberger (Grant Heilman). **208:** *t* Nancy Sheehan/© D. C. Heath; *b* Paul Silverman (Fundamental Photographs). **211:** *t* Dr. Jeremy Burgess (Photo Researchers, Inc.); *bl* Grant Heilman (Grant Heilman Photography); *br* Dawson Jones (TSW-Click/Chicago). **212:** Martucci Studios. **213:** Robert Hessler (WHOI). **214:** *t* © Gianni Tortoli (Photo Researchers, Inc.); *b* Steve Elmore (Tom Stack & Associates). **215:** Nancy Sheehan/© D. C. Heath. **220, 222:** William E. Ferguson. **223:** Breck P. Kent. **224:** *tl* Breck P. Kent; *tm* William E. Ferguson; *tr* E. R. Degginger; *ml* E. R. Degginger; *mc* David Muench; *bl* Grant Heilman (Grant Heilman Photography); *br* Barry L. Runk (Grant Heilman Photography). **225:** Nancy Sheehan/© D. C. Heath. **227:** Grant Heilman (Grant Heilman Photography). **228:** *t* Jerome Wycoff; *bl* Tom & Pat Leeson; *br* Krafft-Explorer (Photo Researchers, Inc.). **229:** Breck P. Kent. **230:** Nancy Sheehan/© D. C. Heath. **231:** Grant Heilman (Grant Heilman Photography). **232:** *t* Ken O'Donoghue/© D. C. Heath; *c* William E. Ferguson; *b* William E. Ferguson. **233:** © Bill Stanton (Rainbow). **234:** William E. Ferguson. **235:** *tl,tr* Breck P. Kent; *b* Runk/Schoenberger (Grant Heilman Photography). **236:** *t* Spencer Swanger (Tom Stack & Associates); *bl,br* David Muench. **237:** *tl* Alan Pitcairn (Grant Heilman Photography); *bl* Breck P. Kent; *tm* Grant Heilman (Grant Heilman Photography); *bc* Breck P. Kent; *tr* Kunio Owaki (The Stock Market); *br* Breck P. Kent. **238:** Nancy Sheehan/© D. C. Heath. **239:** *l* William E. Ferguson; *r* Holt Confer (Grant Heilman Photography). **240:** *tl* Paul Silverman (Fundamental Photographs); *tc* Breck P. Kent; *tr* Breck P. Kent; *bl* William E. Ferguson; *bm* E. R. Degginger; *br* Breck P. Kent. **241:** E. R. Degginger. **242:** *t* © Peter Arnold (Peter Arnold, Inc.); *b* Breck P. Kent. **244:** Nancy Sheehan/© D. C. Heath. **248:** © Dennis Capolongo (Black Star). **250, 251:** Laurel Sherman.

Unit Four: 252: © Tom Bean (DRK Photo). **252–253:** © Stephen J. Krasemann (DRK Photo). **254:** © Lanny Johnson (Mountain Stock). **256:** Nancy Sheehan/© D. C. Heath. **259:** E. R. Degginger. **264:** Map of the World Ocean Floor by Bruce C. Heezen & Marie Tharp, © 1977 by Marie Tharp. **265:** Fred Grassle (WHOI). **269:** Ken O'Donoghue/© D. C. Heath. **271:** E. R. Degginger. **272:** John S. Shelton. **275:** *t* Nancy Sheehan/© D. C. Heath; *b* Breck P. Kent. **276:** Bill Ross (West Light). **278:** Nancy Sheehan/© D. C. Heath. **282:** S. Jonasson/Frank Lane (Bruce Coleman, Inc.). **285:** © Tom Bean (DRK Photo). **286:** Nancy Sheehan/© D. C. Heath. **290:** © Jeff Reinking (Picture Group). **293:** Doug Milner (DRK Photo). **295:** U.S. Geological Survey, Menlo Park, CA. **296:** Lewis Kemper (DRK Photo). **297:** Nancy Sheehan/© D. C. Heath. **298:** NOAA/National Geophysical Data Center, Boulder, CO. **299:** Frank Siteman (Stock Boston). **300:** E. R. Degginger (Earth Scenes). **301:** *t* David Weintraub (Photo Researchers, Inc.); *b* F. Gohier (Photo Researchers, Inc.). **303:** © Al Grillo (Picture Group). **304:** © Gary Braasch. **305:** USGS. **306:** *t* William E. Ferguson; *bl,br* Ralph Perry (Black Star). **310:** Alan Magayne-Roshak (Third Coast Stock Source). **312:** Dick Canby (DRK Photo). **313:** *t* Ken O'Donoghue/© D. C. Heath; *b* William Felger (Grant Heilman Photography). **314:** *tl* © David Muench; *tr* Grant Heilman (Grant Heilman Photography); *b* Ken O'Donoghue/© D. C. Heath. **315:** *t* JLM Visuals; *m* Jerome Wycoff; *b* © Tom Bean (DRK Photo). **316:** E. R. Degginger. **318:** Nancy Sheehan/© D. C. Heath. **319:** Chuck O'Rear (West Light). **320:** *l* William E. Ferguson; *r* Nancy Sheehan/© D. C. Heath. **322:** Steven C. Wilson (Entheos). **323:** *tl* © Jack Swanson (Tom Stack & Associates); *tr* Michael Nichols (Magnum Photos, Inc.); *b* Grant Heilman (Grant Heilman Photography). **324:** E. R. Degginger. **325:** Mark E. Gibson (The Stock Market). **326:** *tl* Lawrence Burr; *tr* William E. Ferguson; *b* E. R. Degginger. **327:** Nancy Sheehan/© D. C. Heath. **328:** *tl* George Gerster (Photo Researchers, Inc.); *tr* Spencer Swanger (Tom Stack & Associates); *b* Isaac Geib (Grant Heilman Photography). **331:** *l* Grant Heilman (Grant Heilman Photography); *m* The Bettman Archive; *r* Bruce Coleman (Bruce Coleman, Inc.). **332:** Breck P. Kent. **334:** John Gerlach (Earth Scenes). **335:** *tl,tr* Nancy Sheehan/© D. C. Heath; *b* Breck P. Kent (Earth Scenes). **337:** Breck P. Kent. **338:** *t* Breck P. Kent; *b* C. C. Lockwood (DRK Photo). **339:** Jeff Gnass (The Stock Market). **341:** D. Cavagnaro (DRK Photo). **342:** Nancy Sheehan/© D. C. Heath. **343:** *t* William E. Ferguson; *b* E. R. Degginger. **344:** *l* William E. Ferguson; *r* Stouffer Productions (Earth Scenes). **345:** Breck P. Kent (Earth Scenes). **346:** *l* © Tom Bean (DRK Photo); *r* © Holzman (Animals, Animals). **347:** *t* John S. Shelton; *bl,br* Breck P. Kent. **348:** Bill Ross (West Light). **349:** Stephanie S. Ferguson. **350:** © John Lemker (Earth Scenes). **351:** USGS. **352:** *t* © Tom Bean (DRK Photo); *b* E. R. Degginger. **355:** *l* William E. Ferguson; *r* U.S. Army Corps of Engineers, Vicksburg, MS. **356:** © Boyd Norton (Peter Arnold, Inc.).

Unit Five: 358: Breck P. Kent. **358–359:** Frank Jensen (The Stock Solution). **360:** William E. Ferguson. **362:** Jen & Des Bartlett (Bruce Coleman, Inc.). **363:** *t* Tass from Sovfoto; *b* © John Gerlach (Tom Stack & Associates). **364:** *tl* John Cancalosi (Tom Stack & Associates); *tr* Runk/Schoenberger (Grant Heilman Photography); *b* © Tom Bean (DRK Photo). **365:** Nancy Sheehan/© D. C. Heath. **366:** Breck P. Kent. **367:** Breck P. Kent (Animals, Animals). **368:** © Cindy Lewis. **369:** Breck P. Kent. **370:** *t* Jerome Wycoff; *b* William E. Ferguson. **372:** © Tom Bean. **374:** © David Muench. **377:** Joe Angeles, Washington University Photographic Services. **382:** John Dawson. **385:** © Tom Bean. **388:** Phil Degginger. **389:** Nancy Sheehan/© D. C. Heath. **390:** *t* S. M. Awramik (Dept. of Geological Sciences, U. of CA/BPS/Terraphotographics); *b* William E. Ferguson. **391:** *l* © American Museum of Natural History; *r* John Cancalosi (Tom Stack & Associates). **392:** *t* © William E. Ferguson; *b* © American Museum of Natural History. **395:** Nancy Sheehan/© D. C. Heath. **397:** *t* Tyrrell Museum of Palaeontology/Alberta Culture & Multiculturalism; *b* © American Museum of Natural History. **398:** *l* Vladimir Krb/Tyrrell Museum of Palaeontology; *r* Tyrrell Museum of Palaeontology/Alberta Culture & Multiculturalism. **399:** Nancy Sheehan/© D. C. Heath. **400:** © William E. Ferguson. **401:** © Gordon Wiltsie (Bruce Coleman, Inc.). **403:** *tl* Zdenek Burian; *tr* Royal British Columbia Museum, Victoria, British Columbia, Canada. **408:** Michael Tamborino (Leo de Wys, Inc.). **411:** E. R. Degginger. **413:** Nancy Sheehan/© D. C. Heath. **414:** *t* Jim McNee (Tom Stack & Associates); *b* Ken O'Donoghue/© D. C. Heath. **415:** *t* Richard Price (West Light); *b* William E. Ferguson. **416:** *tl* Bob Hahn (Taurus Photos); *c* Larry Ditto (Bruce Coleman, Inc.); *b* Steve Ogden (Tom Stack & Associates). **417:** Craig Aurness (West Light). **418:** E. R. Degginger. **419:** Pierre Kopp (West Light). **420:** Lewis Kemper (DRK Photo). **421:** E. R. Degginger. **422:** Ken O'Donoghue/© D. C. Heath. **423:** Roy Gumpel (Leo de Wys, Inc.). **424:** *t* T. J. Florian (Rainbow); *b* © Lowell Georgia (Photo Researchers, Inc.). **425:** *t* E. R. Degginger; *b* David Hiser (Photographers/Aspen). **426:** *t* © Holt Confer (DRK Photo); *b* Barry L. Runk (Grant Heilman Photography). **429:** *tl* Owen Franken (Stock, Boston); *tr* Lynn Pelham (Leo de Wys, Inc.); *b* Nancy Sheehan/© D. C. Heath. **430:** *t* NASA/Science Source (Photo Researchers, Inc.); *b* William Leatherman/© D. C. Heath. **436:** George V. Kelvin, *Scientific American*, Cover, September 1989. **438, 439:** Laurel Sherman.

Unit Six: 440: © Rod Planck (Tom Stack & Associates). **440–441:** Frans Lanting (Minden Pictures). **442:** Doug Lee (Peter Arnold, Inc.). **446:** NASA. **448:** Fridmar Damm (Leo de Wys, Inc.). **451:** Frans Lanting (Minden Pictures). **453:** Nancy Sheehan/© D. C. Heath. **455:** Maximum, Inc. **456, 457:** Nancy Sheehan/© D. C. Heath. **460:** E. R. Degginger. **461:** Ken O'Donoghue/© D. C. Heath. **463:** J. H. Peterson Marine Photographics. **464:** NASA. **468:** Keith Kent (Peter Arnold, Inc.) **471:** Ken O'Donoghue/© D. C. Heath. **473:** David Madison. **475:** Nancy Sheehan/© D. C. Heath. **476, 477:** Ken O'Donoghue/© D. C. Heath. **478:** *t* John Gerlach (Tom Stack & Associates); *b* Milton Rand (Tom Stack & Associates). **479:** Larry Lee (West Light). **481:** John D. Cunningham (Visuals Unlimited). **482:** *tl* Joyce Photographics (Photo Researchers, Inc.). *tm* Gregory K. Scott (Photo Researchers, Inc.); *tr* R&J Spurr (Bruce Coleman, Inc.); *bl* Chris Luneski (Photo Researchers, Inc.); *br* Keith Gunnar (Bruce Coleman, Inc.). **483:** *tl* John Colwell (Grant Heilman Photography); *tm* Grant Heilman (Grant Heilman Photography); *tr* Richard Weymouth Brooks (Photo Researchers, Inc.); *bl* Breck P. Kent; *br* Lincoln P. Nutting/National Audubon Society (Photo Researchers, Inc.). **484:** Ken O'Donoghue/© D. C. Heath. **486:** Runk/Schoenberger (Grant Heilman Photography). **487:** Tom Stack (Tom Stack & Associates). **488:** NCAR. **489:** Ralph Wetmore (Photo Researchers, Inc.). **490:** Nancy Sheehan/© D. C. Heath. **493:** E. R. Degginger. **494:** National Weather Service/NOAA. **507:** *l* WSI; *tr,mr* Breck P. Kent (Earth Scenes). **508:** Patricia Lanza (Bruce Coleman, Inc.). **509:** Phil Degginger (Bruce Coleman, Inc.). **510:** *t* National Weather Service (TSW-Click/Chicago); *b* NSSL/Phil Degginger. **511:** National Weather Service/Discover Magazine. **512:** Nancy Sheehan/© D. C. Heath. **513:** NOAA. **514:** © Jane Faircloth (Transparencies). **517:** © Steve Elmore (Tom Stack & Associates). **518:** © Tim Davis (Photo Researchers, Inc.). **520:** *l* © Brooks Dodge (Mountain Stock); *r* Allen Steele (Allsport USA). **522:** *t* David Madison; *b* Michael Fodgen (DRK Photo). **523:** Simon Fraser (Photo Researchers, Inc.). **525:** Roger Werths/Longview Daily News (West Light). **526:** Ken O'Donoghue/© D. C. Heath. **527:** Roger J. Cheng. **529:** Ralph Clevenger (West Light). **530:** Ken O'Donoghue/© D. C. Heath. **534:** *t* © David Muench; *b* R. J. Bowen (WHOI). **536:** © Joe Sohm/Chromosohm (The Stock Market). **540:** F. Damm (Leo De Wys, Inc.).

Unit Seven: 542: Nancy Sheehan/© D. C. Heath. **542–543:** Nicholas Devore III (Photographers Aspen). **544:** Warren & Genny Garst (Tom Stack & Associates). **546:** Nancy Sheehan/© D. C. Heath. **547:** E. R. Degginger. **548:** Larry Ulrich (DRK Photo). **551:** *tl,bl* Photos by K. H. Mills, from D. W. Schindler et al., *Science*, Vol. 228, pp. 1395–1401, 21 June 1985. (First Light, Toronto); *r* Breck P. Kent. **553:** James F. Quinlan. **555:** © Phil Degginger. **556:** Wide World Photo. **560:** *t* © Tom Bean (DRK Photo); *b* Gerard Photography. **561:** E. R. Degginger. **562:** *t* Larry Ulrich (DRK Photo); *b* © Marty Cordano (DRK Photo). **563:** © Doug Wechsler (Earth Scenes). **568:** Jeff Rotman. **572:** Richard Hoover. **573:** *l* Al Giddings (Ocean Images, Inc.); *r* Jerry Dean (WHOI). **575:** NASA/Photo Researchers, Inc. **576:** *l* Kenneth Garrett (Woodfin Camp & Associates); *r* William Haxby (Lamont-Doherty Geological Observatory). **577:** Rod Catanach (WHOI). **579:** *t* Dudley Foster (WHOI); *b* WHOI. **580:** *l* © Robert Frerck/Odyssey/Chicago; *r* William Haxby (Lamont-Doherty Geological Observatory). **582:** Ken O'Donoghue/© D. C. Heath. **583:** © David Madison. **584:** *t* Scott Blackman (Tom Stack & Associates); *bl* Ralph Clevenger (West Light); *br* Al Giddings (Ocean Images, Inc.). **585:** © C. C. Lockwood (DRK Photo). **586:** Frans Lanting (Photo Researchers, Inc.). **587:** Martin Rogers (Uniphoto Picture Agency). **588:** Nancy Sheehan/© D. C. Heath. **591:** © Charles Seaborn/Odyssey/Chicago. **592:** Vince Cavataio (Allsport USA). **594:** David Madison. **595:** TSW-Click/Chicago. **596:** Tony Arruza. **597:** Greg Vaughn (Tom Stack & Associates). **598:** Ken O'Donoghue/© D. C. Heath. **600:** O. Brown, R. Evans and M. Carle, University of Miami Rosensteil School of Marine and Atmospheric Science. **602:** © Kathy Tyrrell/Oxford Scientific Films (Animals, Animals). **604:** John S. Shelton. **606:** Larry Ulrich (DRK Photo). **607:** *t* John S. Shelton; *b* Scott Blackman (Tom Stack & Associates). **608:** *tl* E. R. Degginger; *tr* Greg Vaughn (Tom Stack & Associates), *b* John S. Shelton. **609:** © Ben Barnhart. **611:** USGS. **612:** *t* © Matt Bradley (Tom Stack & Associates); *b* E. R. Degginger. **614:** © John Serafin (Peter Arnold, Inc.). **616:** © Robert Winslow (Tom Stack & Associates). **618:** NOAA. **619:** © Charles Gupton (Uniphoto Picture Source).